THE SPIRITANS

A History of the Congregation of the Holy Ghost

DUQUESNE STUDIES

Spiritan Series

1

THE SPIRITANS

A HISTORY OF THE CONGREGATION OF
THE HOLY GHOST

by

HENRY J. KOREN, C.S.Sp., S.T.D.

DUQUESNE UNIVERSITY
Pittsburgh 19, Pa.

Editions E. Nauwelaerts,
Louvain.

Editions Spiritus Rhenen, U.,
Netherlands.

1958

IMPRIMI POTEST:

FRANCIS H. MCGLYNN, C.S.SP.

Provincial Superior

NIHIL OBSTAT:

JOSEPH A. NELSON, D.D.

Censor Deputatus

IMPRIMATUR:

FRANCIS CARDINAL SPELLMAN

Archbishop of New York

Feast of the Purification of the Blessed Virgin Mary, 1958.

Father Claude Francis Poullart des Places (1679-1709), Founder of the
Congregation of the Holy Ghost.

TO

CLAUDE FRANCIS POULLART DES PLACES,

Lawyer, Educator, Priest,

and

FOUNDER OF THE
CONGREGATION OF THE HOLY GHOST

in preparation for

the two hundred and fiftieth anniversary

of his death

this book is reverently dedicated

The *Spiritan Series* of Duquesne Studies is dedicated to the publication of documents and studies about the Congregation of the Holy Ghost and its works.

In preparation:

Adrian L. van Kaam, C.S.Sp., *Francis Libermann. A Psychological Study.*

Francis Libermann, C.S.Sp., *A Spiritual Commentary on the Gospel of Saint John,* translated by Leonard A. Bushinski, C.S.Sp.

Other projected titles:

The Life of Claude Francis Poullart des Places.

The Unpublished Writings of Claude Francis Poullart des Places.

Francis Libermann, *Spiritual Letters.*

Francis Libermann, *Spiritual Writings.*

Bibliography of the Congregation of the Holy Ghost.

Twenty percent discount on standing or continuation orders.

TABLE OF CONTENTS

———

PART ONE

GENERAL HISTORY

PART TWO

THE HOLY GHOST FATHERS THROUGHOUT THE WORLD

PAGE

CHAPTER FIFTEEN—The West Indies

CHAPTER SIXTEEN—South America

CHAPTER SEVENTEEN—Indian Ocean

APPENDICES

FOREWORD

The purpose of this work is to present in fully documented but nonetheless readable fashion the history of one of the Church's great clerical societies. Classified statistically among the ten largest, the Congregation of the Holy Ghost is also one of the oldest *congregations* (as opposed to orders) and ranks fourth among them in size. It began in 1703 and, after attaining a first period of bloom during which it served the Church nobly throughout the greater part of the eighteenth century, it came close to utter destruction in the French Revolution of 1792. Restored in 1804, but kept weak by recurrent persecution, criticized by all and vilified by many, it valiantly strove to continue its task in the first decades of the nineteenth century. This dark era ended and the tired society felt a burst of new life when the Venerable Francis Libermann and his confreres entered it in 1848. Since then the Congregation has enjoyed a period of steady growth and achievement.

Among its chief accomplishments in modern times, one may call attention to its introduction of a more human or, to use a currently fashionable term, a more existential form of spirituality; its powerful influence in eradicating the last traces of Gallicanism; and above all, its pioneering role in the systematic evangelization of Africa. While there were only a few stray Negro Catholics on the African continent when Bishop Edward Barron landed at Cape Palmas in 1841, there are now nearly twenty-four million, of whom some four million live in territories still served by Holy Ghost Fathers. In terms of human life, the price these missionaries paid was frightfully high, as one can readily see from the statistics and graph on page 282. The African landscape is dotted with more than a thousand graves in which Spiritans await the final resurrection among the peoples they have Christianized.

Although this book will be of particular interest to the seventy-five hundred members and aspirants of the Congregation and to their numerous friends, one ventures to hope that it may not be without appeal to the student of ecclesiastical history as well.

In preparing it for publication, the author decided to forego the more impressive but also more ponderous format of an extensive scholarly apparatus. He has attempted to find a happy mean between readability and over-documentation. To maintain full objectivity, however, he has employed marginal symbols which will

xix

provide the more curious reader with a complete system of reference to the sources that were drawn upon.

It should be noted that this book is not intended as a panegyric or as a work of propaganda—its mere publication under the aegis of a university will sufficiently indicate its character in this respect. Rather, it is set forth as an unbiased study of two hundred and fifty years of history. Glorious achievements are recorded, it is true, but mistakes and failures are also candidly admitted. Praise and blame are distributed with equanimity wherever circumstances warrant comment. However, in regard to more recent events, the text is limited to a simple recital of facts and trends because history which is still partly in the making and for which records are not yet fully available does not readily lend itself to critical analysis.

For the African reader, the author wishes to point out that the term "native" has been used in its original etymological sense. As a matter of fact, the text contains reference to natives of European and American countries as well. Moreover, allusions to certain aspects of savage practices previously prevailing in Africa should require no apology in a historical work. Barbaric customs were equally prevalent in Europe and America at one time. In fact, the modern African can derive no little measure of satisfaction from the fact that the peoples of his continent have advanced more rapidly than Europe did in the early stages of its civilization.

A history whose material spans several centuries and covers much of the globe cannot be recorded without some margin of human error. While every effort has been made to reduce inaccuracies to what is hoped may be an infinitesimal degree by checking and rechecking the data against all available sources, *lapsus linguae et calami* still remain a very real possibility. For that reason, the author wishes to assure his readers that their corrections and criticisms are actively solicited.

The geographical maps interspersed through the text have constituted a particularly difficult problem. Most mission districts and dioceses are developing so rapidly and population centers are so fluid in certain areas that current situations defy any attempt to indicate them fully.

There remains now only the pleasant duty of acknowledging a debt of gratitude to the many people who have aided in the preparation of this book. Although they are too numerous to be named individually, special mention must be made of the Very Reverend Vernon F. Gallagher, C.S.Sp., Ph.D., LL.D., J.U.D., President of Duquesne University who, despite his pressing occupations and cares, has devoted a great deal of time to recasting the material which I had set down in a language other than my native tongue; Brother Remigius Kney, C.S.Sp., who has skillfully drawn the numerous maps and graphs; Miss Mary Patricia Sheran, who for the past year has patiently typed and retyped the complex manuscript until it reached publishable form; and our friends of The Ad Press Ltd., whose careful artistry has been lavished on the work. May God bless them for their efforts.

HENRY J. KOREN, C.S.SP.

Duquesne University, Pittsburgh, Pa.

October 2, 1957, the 248th anniversary of Father des Places' death.

BIOGRAPHICAL SYMBOLS

For the complete bibliography see page 601.

A. A. S.	*Acta Apostolicae Sedis.*
A. C. H. S.	*Records of the American Catholic Historical Society.*
A. M. C.	*Annuaire des Missions Catholiques en Afrique Française,* 1955.
A. M. C. A.	*Annuaire des Missions Catholiques d'Afrique, 1957, D. A. Dakar.*
A. P. F.	*Annales de la Propagation de la Foi,* Lyons, 1822 ff.
Ap. H.	*Chronique des Missions confiées à la Congrégation du St.-Esprit. Aperçu Historique et Exercice 1930-1931.*
A. R.	*L'Ami de la Religion,* Paris, 1814 ff.
Arch.	Central Archives of the Holy Ghost Fathers.
Augouard	Chanoine Augouard, *Lettres de Mgr. Augouard* (4 vols.).
Beslier	G. G. Beslier, *L'Apôtre du Congo, Mgr. Augouard,* Paris, 1946.
B. G.	*Bulletin général (de la Congrégation du St.-Esprit).*
Bio.	*Biographies 1703-1803,* Paris, 1908.
B. M.	*Bibliotheca Missionum,* Muenster and Freiburg, 1916 ff.
Br.	Maurice Briault, C. S. Sp., *Le Vénérable Père F-M-P. Libermann,* Paris, 1946.
B. R. H.	*Bulletin des Recherches historiques.*
Brot.	Yves Pichon, C. S. Sp., *Le Père Brottier,* Paris, 1938.
C. A.	*Campagne Apostolique.* Statistical data about the Holy Ghost Missions.
Can. H. R.	*Canadian Historical Review.*

C. E.	*Circulaires du T. R. P. Emonet,* Paris, 1882 ff.
C. H. R.	*Catholic Historical Review.*
C. L.	*Lettres circulaires de Mgr. Le Roy,* Paris, 1896 ff.
Cl. C.	Joseph Janin, C. S. Sp., *Le Clergé colonial de 1815 à 1850,* Toulouse, 1935.
Comm.	Francis Libermann, *Commentaire du S. Évangile selon S. Jean,* Ngazobil, 1872.
Correia	Joaquim Alves Correia, C. S. Sp., *A Dilataçāo da Fé no Imperio Portuguēs,* Lisbon, 1936.
C. S.	*Lettres circulaires du T. R. P. Ignace Schwinden-hammer,* Paris, 1852 ff.
C. S. E.	*La Congrégation du St.-Esprit et ses Missions,* Paris, 1925.
C. S. Esp.	Georges Goyau, *La Congrégation du St. Esprit,* Paris, 1937.
C. S. L.	Martin J. Bane, S. M. A., *The Catholic Story of Liberia,* New York, 1950.
Daigre	P. Daigre, C. S. Sp., *Oubangui Chari,* Issoudun, 1950.
da Silva	A. da Silva Rego, *Curso de Missionologia,* Lisbon, 1956.
Dav.	Albert David, C. S. Sp., *Les Missionnaires du Sé-minaire du St.-Esprit à Québec et en Acadie au XVIIIe siècle,* Paris, 1926.
D. C.	Joseph Janin, C. S. Sp., *Les Diocèses coloniaux,* Paris, n. d.
Denz.	Henry Denziger, *Enchiridion Symbolorum,* Freiburg, 1937.
D. G. C.	*Decrees of the General Chapter,* Washington, 1950.
Döring	H. Döring, C. S. Sp., *Vom Juden zum Orden-stifter,* Knechtsteden, 1920.
D. S.	*Directoire spirituel ou Instructions du Vén. F. M. P. Libermann,* 2nd ed., Paris, n. d.
E. S.	Francis Libermann, *Écrits Spirituels,* Paris, 1891.
E. C.	Joseph Janin, C. S. Sp., *Les Églises Créoles Fran-çaises,* Paris, n. d.

Engel	Alois Engel, C. S. Sp., *Die Missionsmethode der Missionare vom heiligen Geist auf dem afrikanischen Festland,* Knechtsteden, 1932.
E. P.	*État du Personnel et des Oeuvres de la Congrégation du St.-Esprit,* Paris, 1885 ff. 31 vols.
Fl.	Henri Le Floch, C. S. Sp., *Claude François Poullart des Places,* 2nd ed., Paris, 1915.
Gay	Mgr. Jean Gay, C. S. Sp., *La doctrine missionaire du Vénérable Libermann,* Paris, n. d.
G. C. M. H.	Ralph M. Wiltgen, S. V. D., *Gold Coast Mission History, 1471-1880,* Techny, Ill., 1956.
Goyau	Georges Goyau, *La France Missionaire dans les cinq parties du Monde,* Paris, 1946.
Groves	C. P. Groves, *The Planting of Christianity in Africa,* London, 1948 ff.
Griz.	Joseph Janin, *Vie du R. P. Grizard,* Paris, 1941.
Guilloux	A. Cabon, *Mgr. Alexis-Jean-Marie Guilloux,* Port-au-Prince, 1929.
H. R. H.	A. Cabon, *Notes sur l'histoire religieuse d'Haiti,* Port-au-Prince, 1933.
K. K. A.	Johannes Beckmann, *Die katholische Kirche im neuen Africa,* Einsiedeln, 1947.
La.	F. Delaplace, C. S. Sp., *Le Père Jacques-Désiré Laval.* Revised edition by J. M. Pivault, C. S. Sp., Paris, 1932.
Lann.	Louis Lannurien, manuscript about the union of the Holy Ghost Fathers and Libermann's Congregation (*Lann.* preceded by *Arch.*).
Lann.	H. Le Floch, *Louis-Marie Brazar de Lannurien et la mission du Vénérable Libermann,* Rome, 1910.
Lav.	Mgr. A. Laveille, *Le Bienheureux L. M. Grignion de Montfort et ses familles religieuses,* Tours, 1916.
Lavig.	Mgr. Baunard, *Le Cardinal Lavigerie,* Paris, 1922, 2 vols.
L. B.	*Lettre à M. Berquet* [*sic*], Cologne, 1741, 2 vols.
L. H.	*Libermann Herdenking,* Gemert, 1952.
L. S.	Francis Libermann, *Lettres Spirituelles,* 2nd ed., Paris, n. d. 4 vols.

Martin.	*Nos Oeuvres et nos Victimes de la Martinique,* Paris, 1903.
M. C.	*Les Missions Catholiques* (periodical), Paris, 1868 ff.
Mgr. Augouard	Georges Goyau, *Monseigneur Augouard,* Paris, 1926.
M. M. A.	Antonio Brasio, C. S. Sp., *Monumenta Missionaria Africana,* Lisbon, 1952 ff.
M. M. C.	*Le Mouvement des Missions Catholiques au Congo* (periodical).
Moran	P. F. Moran, *History of the Catholic Church in Australasia,* Sidney, n. d.
MS Rath	German manuscript about the early Spiritan history.
N. B.	*Notices biographiques,* Paris, 1908 ff.
N. D.	*Notes et Documents relatifs à la vie et l'oeuvre du Vénérable F. M. P. Libermann,* Paris, 1929-1956. 13 vols., 2 appendixes, and 1 vol. of "compléments" (quoted as N. D. Comp.).
*N. D.	*Notes et Documents relatifs à l'histoire de la Congrégation du St.-Esprit,* Paris, 1917.
N. E.	*Nouvelles Ecclesiastiques,* Utrecht, 1730 ff. (Jansenist weekly).
N. F.	*Nova Francia* (periodical).
Not.	Rosalie Javouhey, *Notice sur les rapports de la Congrégation de St. Joseph de Cluny avec celle du St.-Esprit et de l'Immaculé Coeur de Marie,* Paris, 1867.
P. F. E.	M. C. Moreau, *Les Prêtres français émigrés aux Etats Unis,* Paris, 1856.
Piac.	R. Piacentini, C. S. Sp., *F. J. B. Delaplace,* Beauport-Montgeron, 1952.
Piolet	J. Piolet (ed.), *Les missions catholiques françaises au XIXe siècle.*
Pitra	Card. J. B. Pitra, O. S. B., *Vie du Vénérable Serviteur de Dieu, François-Marie-Paul Libermann,* 5th ed., Paris, 1913.
Pr. Exp.	Adolph Cabon, C. S. Sp., *La première expédition des missionaires du St.-Coeur de Marie en Guinée,* Paris, 1930.

Qu.	J. M. Quérard, *Vie du Bienheureux L. M. Grignion de Montfort,* Nantes, 1887.
Refl.	Claude Francis Poullart des Places, *Réflexions sur les Vérités de la Religion,* Paris, 1700 MS.
Rétif	Père Rétif, S. J., *Pauvreté spirituelle et Mission,* Paris, 1955.
R. H. C.	*Revue d'Histoire des Colonies.*
R. H. M.	*Revue d'Histoire des Missions.*
Roques	P. Roques, C. S. Sp., *Le pionnier du Gabon,* Paris, 1956.
Roy	Henri Goré, C. S. Sp., *Mgr. Alexandre Le Roy,* Paris, n. d.
R. U. O.	*Revue de l'Université d'Ottawa.*
R. V. C.	Pierre Blanchard, *Le renoncement dans la vie chrétienne selon St. Jean Eudes et ses disciples,* Paris, 1956.
Shanahan	John P. Jordan, C. S. Sp., *Bishop Shanahan of Southern Nigeria,* Dublin, 1949.
Storme	M. B. Storme, *Evangelisatiepogingen in de binnenlanden van Afrika,* Brussels, 1951.
Su.	Leonide Guiot, *La Mission du Su-Tchuen au XVIIIe Siècle—Vie et apostolat de Mgr. Pottier,* Paris, 1892.
Test.	Pierre Eyckeler, S. M. M., *Le Testament d'un Saint,* Maastricht, 1953.
Th.	Pierre Thomas, C. S. Sp., Manuscript about the life of Father Poullart des Places (Archives).
U. S. C. M.	*United States Catholic Magazine,* 1843 ff.
Va.	Alexandre Le Roy, C. S. Sp., *Le T. R. P. Fréderic Le Vavasseur,* Paris, n. d.
Vo.	Lambert Vogel, C. S. Sp., *Claude-François Poullart des Places,* Gemert, 1941.
Vogt	Roger Dussercle, C. S. Sp., *Du Kilema-Ndjaro au Cameroun. Mgr. F. X. Vogt,* Paris, 1954.
Walker	Reginald Walker, C. S. Sp., *The Holy Ghost Fathers in Africa,* Kimmage, 1933.
Witte	J. de Witte, *Mgr. Augouard,* Paris, 1924.

NOTE ON MAPS

Names in capital letters indicate the administrative centers of a Spiritan Province or of an ecclestiastical circumscription (diocese, vicariate, etc.).

Maps of the various provinces show the names of former residences between brackets but, as a rule, such residences are not noted on the maps of dioceses and other ecclesiastical circumscriptions.

Wherever the spiritual care of a territory is entrusted to the Congregation, all ecclesiastical residences have been included.

In areas not formally entrusted to the Congregation, only Spiritan establishments are shown.

PART ONE

GENERAL HISTORY

CHAPTER ONE

THE FOUNDER AND HIS WORK

1. *Biographical Sketch of Father Claude Poullart des Places*

Fl. 18 ff.

Claude Francis Poullart des Places was born in Rennes, Brittany, on February 26, 1679.[1] His father, one of the richest mer-

---

[1]The traditional date is February 21. However, the original baptismal record, dated February 27, clearly states that Claude was born on February 26. This document bears the signature of several persons of high standing in addition to that of the priest who performed the baptism. It is unlikely that such a solemn memorial would be mistaken about the date of Claude's birth. A photocopy of this document is reproduced opposite p. 4. We transcribe here the text and its translation:

Claude françois né du jour d'hiers fils de n(oble) h(omme) claude françois poullart, ad(vocat) en la cour et d(emoiselle) Jannes (Le) Meneust sa compagne s(ieur) et dame des Places a esté Baptizé en cette Eglize par n(oble) et d(iscret) M(essire) Julien Roussigneul R(ecteur) d'icelle et tenu sur les S(aint)s fonds baptismaux par haut et puissant Seig(neu)r Messire Claude de Marbeuf Chevallier Seig(neu)r de L'Aille, du gué et autres lieux, Con(seille)r du Roy en ses conseils et président de son parlement de Bretagne, parrain et demoiselle Françoise, Truillot dame de ferret marraine, lesquels ont signé ce Jour vingt et septiesme de feuvrier mil six cent soixante et dix neuf, avec plusieurs autres personnes de qualité.

Claude Francis, born yesterday, the son of nobleman Claude Francis Poullart, lawyer at the Court, and Madame Jeanne Le Meneust, his spouse, Lord and Lady des Places, has been baptized in this church by the noble and illustrious Sir Julian Roussigneul, its Rector. He was held over the holy baptismal font by the exalted and puissant Lord, Sir Claude de Marbeuf, Lord of Laille, Gué and other places, member of the King's Council, President of his Parliament in Britanny, Godfather; and Madame Francoise Truillot, Lady of Ferret, Godmother, who together with several other persons of quality have affixed their signatures this day, February the twenty-seventh, 1679.

(signed) Claude de Marbeuf (President of the Parliament)
    Françoise Truillot (Lady of Ferret)
    (Claude) de Marbeuf (Abbot of Langonnet)
    F. Thounenin, Marie Le Gouverneur, Francois Gouyon
    de Beaucorps, Gillette Lexot, Ferret, J. Roussigneul, Rector
      of St. George.

1

chants in the town[2] and a respected lawyer in the Sovereign Parliament of Brittany, stemmed from a family that proudly traced its patents of nobility back to the Middle Ages. His mother, also of noble lineage, was the daughter of a prosperous businessman.[3]

Fl. 29 ff.

Claude's earliest years were blessed by a careful and pious upbringing at home. At the age of eight he was enrolled as a day-student in the famous Jesuit Academy at Rennes. Aside from the remarkable intelligence which he displayed from the very inception of his schooling, this bright little boy revealed a phenomenal degree of religious zeal by quietly organizing some of his fellow-pupils into a society whose members devoted their free time to prayer, penance, and devotional exercises.

Fl. 44 ff.

At the amazingly early age of twelve he had already finished the classical course, but since everyone felt that he was too young to start studying philosophy, his parents sent him to the College of Caen to take an advanced course in oratory, a discipline for which he appeared to be especially gifted. As at Rennes, Claude distinguished himself among the two thousand students of this college also by his piety as well as by his success in the strenuous studies to which his young mind was subjected. At the conclusion of this interlude, he returned to Rennes for a two-year course in philosophy.

Fl. 66 ff.

It was during this time that he became the intimate friend of a boy, six years older than he, who was destined to make history in the Church under the name of St. Louis Mary Grignion de Montfort, the apostle of Mary and the founder of at least two religious orders: the Society of Mary and the Daughters of Wisdom. The two boys had been classmates all through their classical studies, but at that time they knew each other only superficially as close competitors for first place in examinations. Now that Claude had reached the age of thirteen and was giving evidence of a maturity that would have done credit to a much older boy, it did not take the two very long to realize how much they had in common. As

Fl. 539 f.

[2]The size of his fortune may be gaged from the fact that at his daughter's marriage in 1705 he gave her a dowry of one hundred thousand livres plus ten thousand livres worth of silverware and furniture. For purposes of comparison at present day values, two thousand livres were considered adequate compensation for maintaining a noble family with their coachmen and servants for a period of six months.

[3]Claude had two younger sisters, one of whom died in infancy.

they joined in prayer and pious works, the future apostle of Mary kindled in the heart of his young companion that flame of great devotion to the Blessed Virgin which was to remain burning forever in his soul and which prompted him later to add her Immaculate Conception to the title of his Congregation.

This pious association with the future saint should not lead us to believe that Claude was a shy and withdrawn youngster who loved to be alone with his thoughts or to share them only with a favored few. Although he practised penance to the extent of giving up wine altogether—which in a Frenchman would be comparable to an American boy's forsaking ice cream and soft drinks—he liked company and pleasure. In fact, he looked forward with enthusiasm to the long vacations away from school, for it was during those months of leisure that his parents did their best to endow him with every social refinement one would expect of a member of the city's leading family. Travel, marksmanship, riding, hunting, and dancing constituted his favorite recreational activities during these carefree days.

Fl. 74 ff.

He especially loved play-acting and had a real talent for dramatic activities. On one occasion this penchant for drama nearly resulted in very real tragedy. While he was earnestly trying to study an assigned role, his little sister kept teasing him with childish interruptions. At length, he threatened her with what he thought was an empty gun and pulled the trigger. The household was terrified when a bullet passed between his sister and his mother, missing their heads by a few inches! The careless use of firearms appears not to have been unusual in those days for, on another occasion while Claude was hunting with a few friends, he was felled by a shot in the abdomen from a distance of ten feet. Divine Providence evidently wanted to save him for his future work, for when his frightened comrades rushed to the prostrate body, they found that he had sustained only a superficial wound.

Arch. Th. 3
Fl. 79

Arch. Th. 4
Fl. 80

Aside from vacation periods, however, Claude studied seriously and with great success. Although he was the youngest of all, he placed first among the hundreds of students who took the final examination at Rennes. For that reason he was chosen to be the defendant in the customary philosophical debate at the end of the academic year in 1694. At the time, such disputes were held with much more solemnity than obtains nowadays in

Arch. Th. 6
Fl. 81

seminaries where the custom still survives. Weeks beforehand the theses were advertised in detail on bill-boards throughout the city, invitations were sent to learned societies, and no expense was spared to make the assembly as solemn as possible. The pageantry of these sessions surpassed by far the color and solemnity that attends commencement exercises in modern American universities. Along with the full faculty and student-body, kings and nobles, members of Parliament, bishops and canons, and cultured society in general came to these affairs and took an active part in the argument.

Fl. 84 ff.

On Claude's big day everything took place with the customary pomp and ceremony. Dedicating his defense to the King's son, Louis de Bourbon, the fifteen year old boy thrilled and charmed his audience by the clarity and simplicity of his replies, the breadth and depth of his knowledge, the charm of his youth and the grace of his eloquence. With little or no help from his professor, he deftly disposed of his opponents by a shattering display of logic. Then, as the thunderous applause died down around him, this stage of Claude's career came to a brilliant and memorable end.

Fl. 110 ff.

Exceptionally intelligent, charming in manner, handsome, richly endowed with material goods, universally beloved, he had the world at his feet. Now it was time for him, his parents thought, to enter society, relax from the drudgery of seven years' intensive study, and become an "accomplished gentleman." In a city which feverishly tried to emulate the social amenities of Paris, invitation followed invitation: a party here, a banquet there, the chase, the concert, the ball, the theater—every host and hostess clamored for his company.

It would be dishonest to pretend that Claude did not feel deeply gratified by all this adulation and that he spurned the pleasures held out to him on all sides. In fact, his earlier thoughts about becoming a priest seemed at this point to have faded completely from his mind. Highly pleased with himself and his achievements, he began to look around for a career that would offer him a chance to fulfill his ambitions for more honor and glory. To this end, friends of the family suggested that it might

Fl. 114 ff.

be advantageous to attach the young man to the Versailles Court in the service of the Duke of Burgundy, grandson of King Louis XIV. The marvellous defense of his theses had already attracted the Court's attention.[4] There was nothing left but to arrange for Claude's marriage to one of the Princess's ladies-in-waiting in order to assure such a position for this promising scion of an ancient and noble line.

Fl. 117 ff.

Claude travelled by coach to Paris where he took up residence with friends of the family. As soon as he arrived, the best drawing-rooms of the capital quickly opened their doors to him and before long he was presented to the Duke of Burgundy at the Court of Versailles. The splendor of the court made a deep impression on him and he would have been glad to plunge into its endless round of glittering events but for the fact that the proposed marriage was

Arch. Th. 7
Fl. 121

not to his liking. As his first biographer expresses it: "He passionately desired glory and renown. But becoming involved with a woman in marriage was an obstacle rather than a means to the attainment of such a goal." Moreover, his lordly old father did not relish the idea of Claude's "spending his life in antechambers, courtyards and staircases." He wanted something better for this son of whom he was immensely proud. As a result, it was decided that Claude should leave the Court, at least for a while.

The sacrifice was a painful one because he realized that, with his talents and charm, success would not have been slow in coming.

Fl. 123

Somewhat reluctantly he returned to the less glamorous surroundings of provincial Rennes to start once more on the old routine of parties and social affairs. After all, he was the son of the richest man in town, and what else could be expected? Although his parents provided him with a generous allowance for his social life, Claude wanted only the best of the best, and the best costs a great

Arch. Th. 8
Fl. 123

deal of money. Soon he had to resort to borrowing to keep abreast of the mounting bills, meanwhile engaging in all kinds of camouflage to hide his insolvency from his father who, he was well aware, would have strongly disapproved of such prodigality.

Arch. Th. 8
Fl. 128

Qualms of conscience began to follow these financial worries. Although the piety of his early youth had safeguarded him thus far from the dangerous pitfalls so common in a life of this sort, Claude felt ill at ease. He realized that he was no longer as intimately united with God as before. With a feeling of longing his thoughts returned to the days when all his young heart had desired

Fl. 84

---

[4]This may seem unlikely in our days. Yet in those times intense interest was displayed in these tourneys of the mind. One of the reasons why Emperor Charles IV founded the University of Prague was his desire to have similar intellectual duels in that city.

was God and God alone. He who had thought of becoming a priest was now rapidly drifting closer to the raging torrent of pride and worldly concupiscence, and this uneasiness induced him to make a retreat to examine his conscience and decide what to do with his life.[5]

Arch. Th. 9
Fl. 129

During those days of recollection he saw how unfaithful he had been to grace and how much he had exposed himself to the danger of sin. He again felt the call to God's service. Now he was going to become a great preacher for God. In his imagination he saw his pulpit surrounded by thousands of entranced listeners, swayed by his powerful eloquence and eager to return to their Heavenly Father. He would study theology at the Sorbonne, renew there his academic triumphs, and then begin the conversion of France. Sincere as his desire was for the priesthood, he did not realize how much his ambition for personal glory played a part in these dreams. Nonetheless, he at last decided to confide the plan to his doting father.

It was a rude shock for the man who had pinned on this only son all his worldly dreams of glory and renown for the des Places family, but he was too good a Christian to oppose the idea openly. Instead of antagonizing Claude and thus strengthening his resolve, the father thought it would be best to postpone a decision. Accordingly, he quietly suggested that such a step should be taken only after long and careful deliberation. Furthermore, he said, to become a good preacher one did not have to study at the Sorbonne. "I have heard quite a few doctors preaching sermons," the old man observed, "and none of them was any better because he had a degree." While testing his vocation, Claude could study law. That would be useful for him either as a priest or as a man of the world. If he still insisted on being a priest after

Fl. 130 ff.

that, parental consent would not be withheld. Claude saw the reasonableness of his father's proposal. Besides, the effects of the retreat were beginning to wear off anyway, and he welcomed a chance to have more freedom than he could enjoy at Rennes under the eyes of his parents. Accordingly, he accepted the offer and

---

[5]The first retreat houses had been established in the seventeenth century throughout Britanny by the efforts of Father Kerlivio, Father Huby, and Mother de Francheville, who founded the still vigorous Congregation of the Daughters of Our Lady of the Retreat. Probably Claude made this retreat in their local retreat house in Rennes.

went off in October 1697 to the School of Law at the University of Nantes.

Arch. Th. 10 ff. Fl. 139 ff.

It was not long before his high ideals and noble aspirations began to fade from his mind. Human respect and the sarcastic remarks of fellow students did the rest. Claude began to set aside his religious practices so that he might indulge in the frivolous pastimes of his friends. He tried desperately to be one of the crowd, but in the midst of it all, his conscience gave him no peace. Remorse so completely spoiled whatever pleasure he engaged in that, as he himself said later in describing this dark period of his life,

Arch. Refl. 10 Fl. 142

"it cost me considerable trouble to sin." "How often did I not find grace surrounding me like a wall of steel and setting up an obstacle which a thousand times in succession crushed my criminal efforts and turned me away from my irregularities." The thought of the priesthood began to haunt him again and its insistent gnawing increased his uneasiness. He longed to break away from his present surroundings and to be alone with God.

Fl. 143 f.

Fortunately, Divine Providence soon provided an opportunity. His father wanted him to transfer to Paris and there receive the best legal training France had to offer. Paris! That was the place where Father Descartes[6] was presently stationed. The good Jesuit priest had directed him in his early years at school in Rennes and could be counted on now to provide the spiritual guidance that he needed so much. Claude readily obeyed his father's command and set out for Paris at once.

Fl. 144 ff.

The sincerity of his desire to be really faithful to God this time is demonstrated by the fact that he refused to have his own apartment in Paris. Experience had taught him to fear the freedom of bachelor quarters and for that reason he humbly asked the Jesuits of the College of Louis the Great[7] to allow him to board with them while he pursued his legal studies at the Sorbonne.

Fl. 153 ff.

Under the saintly guidance of Father Descartes, his spiritual life now began to flourish once again. By the time he had received the licentiate in law (1700), he was ready for another retreat.

---

[6]A nephew of the famous philosopher and mathematician.

[7]The College of Louis the Great was one of the most important colleges of France. More than one hundred Jesuit Fathers were attached to the teaching staff of this institution. Its student body numbered more than 3,500. About 600 students boarded there, each with his own valet or governor. Voltaire became a student there while Claude was following its theological curriculum.

During the course of this one he would really probe his soul and
do his best to emerge with a definite vocational objective. The
decision could not be postponed any longer.

After all, he had fulfilled all the requirements necessary for the
position to which his father had destined him and would be expected
to make his grand entrance into the world of law very soon. On the
other hand, his old desire for the priesthood had grown extremely
Fl. 167 ff.   keen again with the renewal of his spiritual life. Carefully and
methodically examining himself in the light of God and eternity,
Claude finally excluded a worldly career for once and for all. With
characteristic honesty he decided to abandon himself unreservedly
to God's grace in order to prepare himself for the divine call. Rosy
visions of personal fame and accomplishment were at last resolutely set aside.

Fl. 187 ff.   Only one obstacle remained to be overcome—his parents. Since
they were totally unaware of their son's decision, they had been
busily arranging for him to take his place as a lawyer in Parliament. His mother had even bought an official barrister's gown for
him and had it hung out ready to wear. To please her, Claude put
on the garment, took a long look at himself in the mirror, then
quietly turned and told his parents the shocking news. Although
it broke his heart to be the cause of disappointment and sorrow to
his mother and father, his decision remained irrevocable. Des
Places *père* did everything he could to make Claude change his
mind, but realizing at last the uselessness of his opposition, he
Fl. 192   finally gave in. He even generously consented to his son's apparently quixotic idea of setting aside all hope of ecclesiastical preferment so that he might devote himself entirely to God's service as
a simple priest.

Fl. 201 ff.   To break more definitely with the past and with family ties,
Claude resolved to study theology in Paris, far away from his
father's home. Since the theological faculty of the Sorbonne was
then tainted with Gallicanism, and since Claude was seeking moral
and spiritual training as well as theological erudition, he gave the
University a wide berth and returned instead to the College of
Louis the Great. In this institution, the Jesuits conducted a theological school for the best students of their own society and a limited
number of outsiders. By studying here, Claude automatically excluded himself from obtaining a recognized degree in theology, for
the Sorbonne jealously monopolized the granting of doctorates.

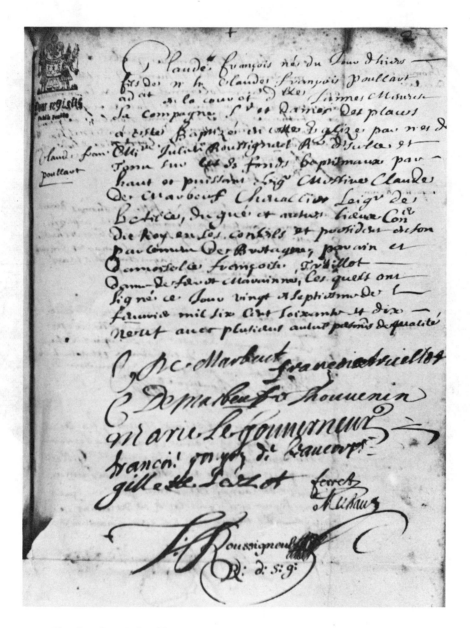

The Baptismal Certificate of Claude Francis Poullart des Places.
(Courtesy *Institut de Recherches Historiques, Faculté des Lettres,* Rennes, and Father Coudray.)

ESCUTCHEON OF THE DES PLACES FAMILY

Arch. Th. 22
Fl. 223

Since a Sorbonne degree was the open sesame for ecclesiastical advancement, his entrance into this seminary in 1701 caused much excited wagging of tongues and shaking of heads in the fashionable salons of Paris. Claude, who had at last definitely broken with the world, took no notice of the gossip. Only God mattered for him now, and every day found him drawing closer to his Creator in prayerful union. Filled with sorrow for his past aberrations, he tried to make up for them by severe penance and thus become ever more like the suffering Christ whom he felt he had offended so much.

2. *The Foundation of the Seminary and Congregation of the Holy Ghost*

A Humble Beginning. With the growth of Claude's severity in his own regard, his goodness and charity towards others developed apace, thereby constituting an unmistakable sign of his virtue's

Arch. Th. 19
Fl. 249

supernatural character. Soon his attention began to be drawn to the poor little Savoyards who worked in Paris as chimney-sweeps and tried to earn a few sous for their destitute families at home. Lonely, abandoned, and homesick, they desperately needed a friend who would preserve their faith and morals. Claude induced a few friends to help him teach them reading, writing, and the elements of religion. Little by little he began providing for their material needs as well.

Fl. 264 ff.

After he was formally inducted into the clerical state by the reception of tonsure in August, 1702, he seems to have become increasingly aware that some of his fellow-students were almost as needy as the little chimney-sweeps. Seminaries as we know them now were not yet the general rule in France at that time. Students attended lectures at the university or at other theological institutes but they were free to live wherever they wished. For many of the poorer ones, this often involved a precarious state of affairs whereby they snatched a few courses when they were free from the menial jobs that enabled them to eke out a living. It will readily be seen that this procedure was not only detrimental to their health and studies, but also, especially in such a licentious city as Paris, it seriously jeopardized their morals.

While it is true that charitable persons had already founded a few houses to take care of these unfortunates, there were not nearly enough to accommodate their increasing numbers. Claude had only to look around him to see scores of these pale and exhausted young men. With the approval of his director, therefore, he began by secretly helping some with the savings he managed to squeeze from his father's modest allowance. Soon he went farther and gave them the food that was served to him at the College, satisfying his own wants with a few leftovers from the Jesuits' table. There was not yet any thought in his mind about setting up a new foundation. As he himself wrote later: "There was question only of quietly providing the necessary food for four of five poor students." Soon, however, other people began to share his interest and offered their help. It was a big step forward, for instance, when Father Peter Megret told him that he might have whatever remained after the meals of the six hundred boarders.

With a growing number of dependents on his hands, Claude felt the need of feeding their souls as well as their bodies, for many of them gave evidence of a woeful lack of spiritual training. After he had rented a house in the *Rue des Cordiers,* he selected a dozen of them and on Pentecost Sunday, May 27th, 1703:

> Mr. Claude Francis Poullart des Places . . ., then only an aspirant to the ecclesiastical state, began the establishment of the said community of the seminary consecrated to the Holy Ghost under the invocation of the Blessed Virgin conceived without sin.[8]

A short time before, he had preached a retreat to the little group, applying to them the Gospel text: "He hath sent me to preach the Gospel to the poor." At its conclusion, they observed the feast of Pentecost by going to the Church of St. Etienne des-Grès and there, in the chapel of Our Lady, these ardent young souls consecrated themselves to bring the Glad Tidings to the poor. Back at their modest home, a quiet but happy celebration closed the first day of a foundation that was destined to write brilliant and glorious chapters in the history of the Church.

Because Claude could not bring himself to refuse anyone who fulfilled his stipulated conditions, their little establishment in the

Fl. 281 ff.

Arch. Refl. 7
Fl. 280

*N. D. 1

B. G. 34, 137

[8]The traditional date is May 20th. However, in 1703 Pentecost fell on May 27th.

According to Father John Letourneur, C.S.Sp., who is preparing a special study on the early history of the Congregation, the expression "Seminary of the Holy Ghost" indicates the official title of the Congregation.

N. D. 2 *Rue des Cordiers* was soon outgrown. Just then a few generous friends came forward, and the young seminary found itself installed by 1706 in much better accommodations on the *Rue Neuve Sainte Geneviève,* now *Rue Tournefort.* Henceforth, the Congregation of the Holy Ghost would move forward on its own initiative.

Poullart des Places and St. Louis de Montfort. Shortly after Claude began his theological course, his friendship with St. Louis

Qu. II, 260 f. de Montfort took on new life. In 1702 the Saint returned to Paris and visited his friend. Just at that time he was seriously thinking of organizing missions and retreats all over France so that the rural population might be saved from immorality and degradation. For this work he obviously needed collaborators and Claude, with his splendid oratorical gifts, would have been just the man to help him

Fl. 287 ff. start it. They discussed their views, took counsel, and prayed for divine guidance. But in the end, Claude had to tell his friend that he did not personally feel called for the preaching of missions. All his time had to be spent in providing future priests with a decent home and an adequate training for their sublime task. However, he made this promise:

Test. 7 If God gives me the grace to succeed in this, you can count on missionaries. I will train them for you, and you will put them to work. In this way both you and I will be satisfied.

St. Louis went back to Poitiers and in 1703 laid there the first foundation of the Sisters' Congregation of the Daughters of Wisdom. After Easter, however, he returned to Paris for at least a year to aid Claude in the foundation and organization of his Seminary. In fact, it was under his impulse that Claude decided to expand his charitable activities in behalf of theological students by renting the house in the *Rue des Cordiers.* St. Louis' influence can be seen also in the dedication of the new foundation to the Holy Ghost and Mary's Immaculate Conception. Because of this close association, therefore, and because the Saint had come to Paris for the sole purpose of assisting his friend in establishing the new foundation, there can be little doubt that he was present at the

Test. 8 official opening of the institute on the day of Pentecost, 1703. Moreover, since he was the only priest in the group, it is more than likely that he said Mass for them at the Church of St. Etienne-des-Grès before they dedicated themselves to the apostolate.

Ordination to the Priesthood and Death. Despite his preoccupation with the new seminary, Claude continued to prepare himself for his ordination, for he was still a simple cleric. Then suddenly God withdrew from him those consolations which He uses in the beginning to attract fervent souls to Himself. It was in the purifying loneliness of aridity that Claude had to prepare himself. Qualms of conscience about the past rose up to plague him and he reproached himself bitterly for having started his seminary without being sufficiently prepared for such a great responsibility. Convinced of his own unworthiness, he kept postponing his ordination to the priesthood for three years. In the end, however, his director was able to calm his fears and restore peace to his troubled soul. On December 17th, 1707, he became a priest forever, together with the charter members of his foundation who were now aiding him in the task of organizing the new work.

Fl. 308

Fl. 358

Less than two years after his ordination, God called him to his heavenly reward. Exhausted by the cares and worries of the growing foundation (at his death there were already seventy students) and weakened still more by his severe and incessant penances, he had driven himself to a premature death. At the end of September 1709, pleurisy and an abdominal disease attacked his emaciated body. He suffered terrible pain, but in the midst of all his suffering he repeated over and over again: *"Quam dilecta tabernacula tua, Domine Virtutum. Concupiscit et deficit anima mea in atria Domini"* (How lovely are thy tabernacles, O Lord of Hosts! My soul longeth and fainteth for the courts of the Lord. Ps. 83, 1.) Four short days of illness sufficed to snuff out the spark of life in his enfeebled body. On October second, at five o'clock in the afternoon, his soul quietly went forth to the lovely dwellings of the Lord.

Father Poullart des Places has never been formally proposed for canonization although there appears to be substantial evidence that his brief span of years encompassed a record of heroic virtue. Up to the present, historical developments have been inimical to the introduction of his cause. The orphaned seminary which he left behind in a still precarious financial condition was scarcely able to undertake such a process. Then, just as it had achieved a measure of security and stability, the social upheavals of the late eighteenth and early nineteenth centuries consigned to oblivion many of the documents that would have been invaluable to the biographer. Lastly, the advent of Father Libermann and his confreres of the Holy Heart of Mary caused the Founder to be almost forgotten in the flood of veneration shown to the saintly Restorer. It is only since the beginning of this century that the original Founder is being accorded the attention which he so richly deserves.

In 1959 the spiritual children of Father des Places will celebrate the two hundred and fiftieth anniversary of his death. Perhaps this observance will initiate the long-postponed intro-duction of his cause. The late Cardinal Vivès was very much in favor of it and insistently urged the Holy Ghost Fathers to pro-ceed energetically toward that much-desired end. May Divine Providence look kindly upon it when the proposal becomes a reality.

B. G. 23, 612

3. *Purpose and Organization of Father des Places' Foundation*

*N. D. 3 ff.

A candidate for admission to the Holy Ghost Seminary had to fulfill two conditions over and above the usual requirements: he had to be poor, and he had to be willing to consecrate himself to the most difficult and most abandoned works in God's vineyard. The requirement of poverty echoed a decree of the Council of Trent which, in ordering the erection of seminaries, specified:

> In general, the Council recommends that the sons of the poor be selected, although it does not exclude those of richer families, provided that they pay their board and give evidence of true zeal for the service of God and the Church.

Fl. 269 ff.

It is not hard to understand the reason for this directive. Through the right of primogeniture, the eldest sons of noble and wealthy families inherited nearly everything and, as a result, it was common practice for such families to destine their younger sons for the army and the Church. Ambitious to achieve honor and riches, these young men had little or no interest in the care of souls and thought only of becoming beneficiaries, abbots and bishops.

Fully acquainted with the social fabric in which he lived, Claude intended to bar the way to those who were more interested in a career than in souls by requiring poverty as a condition for admis-

Fl. 324 f.
N. E. 1743,
p. 158

sion.[9] Moreover, his concept of poverty did not involve, as the Jansenists later charged, recruiting priests from the lowest strata of society. He always thoroughly investigated the background of an applicant's family and admitted only those aspirants who came from decent, if humble, surroundings. As long as their families could not pay the board required in other institutions, such candidates were welcome in his seminary. Because families were usually quite large and because, as we have seen, the inheritance laws assigned nearly everything to the oldest son, even many children of noble birth might be regarded as poor in this sense.

Thus "poor" did not necessarily mean "destitute." In fact, it was applicable to that great segment of the population which earned its bread by any sort of toil: teachers, shopkeepers, craftsmen, farmers, etc. Briefly, it applied to what we would now call the middle class. Even in our own day, few middle class families with numerous children are able to send their sons to a private boarding school. It was for vocations from just such people that Father des Places started his seminary. He wanted to train and educate them in a house that would maintain the modest standards of living to which they were accustomed, for experience had shown that once they were used to a richer and more abundant way of life in an institution for the wealthy, they refused to accept the humbler clerical assignments that carried too small an income for their expensive tastes.

Fl. 329

It is scarcely necessary to point out that for Claude "poor" was not to be identified with "dirty" or "rude." His rules stressed personal cleanliness and prescribed napkins for the students and clean white cloths for the tables. True to his early training, he always remained an "accomplished gentleman" and insisted that his students conduct themselves in genteel fashion at all times.

Fl. 319 ff.

Father des Places' second requirement for admission aimed at providing a remedy for the frightful lack of pastoral care from which much of France was then suffering. As has been pointed out, the younger sons of noble families used the Church to advance their own position and cared little about souls. Despite the fact that there were large numbers of these priests actively pursuing

MS. Rath, 62 f.

[9]Father des Places' original plan made provision for the admission of wealthy students: he would welcome them if they were willing to help support their poor fellow students and share the way of life followed in the seminary. However, this provision had to be eliminated by his successor. Otherwise, the seminary's legal recognition would have been jeopardized.

careers in all the large cities of France, the daily round of spiritual activity in the parishes received scant attention. Conditions were even worse in rural areas. Like absentee landlords, the appointed pastors lived in the city and sent ill-fed and poorly-prepared substitutes, scarcely able to read a missal, to take their place. As a result, in many areas ignorance of the faith was appalling and morals had sunk to frightful depths of depravity. The founder wanted his priests to be priests in the true sense of the term—good shepherds of the flock, not hirelings. This was the reason behind his specification that they should be willing "to accept and even prefer the most humble and difficult functions in the Church, for. which it is difficult to find laborers."

Dav. 25 ff.

The foundation of such an institute was very timely from the missionary point of view also. The great Seminary of the Foreign Missions of Paris had just then entered into a period of profound crisis. In 1695 only two Directors remained and its aspirants had dwindled to a mere handful. Shortly after Father des Places' death, three of its Directors had to be expelled for Jansenistic teachings; the number of its seminarians was often no more than five or six; sometimes there were none at all. Its situation remained most precarious throughout the eighteenth century. Fortunately, the flourishing condition of Holy Ghost Seminary was able to offset this weakness to some extent by recruiting vocations for the Foreign Missions from among its students.

Fl. 309 ff.

From the beginning, the senior seminarians helped Father des Places with the administration of the new house. They assisted him especially as bursars and as tutors in philosophy and theology. From among these seminarians, in 1705, Claude chose Vincent Barbier and James Garnier as his first official associates and after a two-year period of trial they were formally admitted as members of the Congregation of the Holy Ghost. In Father des Places' mind, this was to be a society which would assure the survival, the proper functioning, and the expansion of the work he had founded. Thus there are two distinct though inseparable aspects to his foundation: the Seminary of the Holy Ghost and the Congregation of the Holy Ghost. By its very nature and purpose, the Congregation was to remain limited in number, at least as long as the original organization was preserved. It was an association of professors and directors chosen because of their particular ability and talents to teach, train and direct future priests.

Although its members were secular priests who did not bind themselves by the three vows of religion, they lived in common, promised obedience to their superiors, and surrendered the income from their ministry to a common fund. The congregation thus formed was a teaching society, and its educational activities were to be directed for the most part toward training priests for the domestic and foreign missions. To this day, both the Seminary and the Congregation still exist, but it was the Congregation that later developed, through the vivifying influence of the Venerable Francis Libermann, into the present world-wide organization known as the Holy Ghost Fathers or, more briefly, Spiritans.

Fl. 330
*N.D. 4

Another feature of Father des Places' foundation merits our attention at this point, *viz:* his curious prohibition against taking degrees in theology. At first sight one would be inclined to regard this as a strange type of obscurantism, but as a matter of fact there were good reasons for the regulation. First of all, the Sorbonne, which at the time held a virtual monopoly on the doctorate in theology, had aroused suspicions as to its orthodoxy. With Gallicanism, Jansenism, and Quietism rampant in France, Claude preferred to see his students take their theology at the Jesuit College, whose loyalty to the Pope and whose purity of doctrine were beyond question. Then too, a cleric who could boast of a theological degree was eligible for one of the many benefices which were reserved for Sorbonne graduates. Those on whom degrees had been conferred usually became ambitious for ever higher and better paid positions and, since this would have destroyed the spirit of Claude's foundation, he wisely obviated the difficulty at its very source.

Fl. 344

From all this it is clear that he was not opposed to degrees in principle. As a matter of fact, he allowed his students to take a degree in Canon Law, a field of study in which the above-mentioned objectionable features did not exist. Still less should his prohibition be seen as a manifestation of an anti-intellectual attitude which tries to be satisfied with the bare minimum. Aside from the fact that Father des Place's own intellectual brilliance would scarcely justify such an interpretation, the regulations he drew up for his seminary put great stress on experimental science[10] and even added two years of special studies to the customary cycle

Fl. 434

[10]As a rule, no one was allowed to begin his theology without having studied mathematics and experimental physics.

of philosophy and theology which other seminaries regarded as adequate. Intellectual minimalism would never have given rise to the excellent reputation for ecclesiastical erudition which his society enjoyed throughout the eighteenth century and which induced several bishops to offer the direction of their seminaries to the Holy Ghost Fathers and prompted others to take on des Places' graduates as professors of philosophy and theology in their own seminaries. This academic renown soon gained such wide currency that graduation from Holy Ghost Seminary was held equivalent to a degree from the Sorbonne.

Fl. 430

All this clearly demonstrates, therefore, that the early prohibition against theological degrees must be regarded as a prudent safeguard against certain heretical tendencies of the age. Under no circumstances should it be interpreted as an example of that miserable obscurantism which sometimes dons the trappings of humility to maintain that knowledge endangers holiness. In fact, Father des Places is frequently quoted as having said:

Fl. 571

> A priest who is full of ardor for God's cause but who lacks learning is blind in his zeal, and a learned priest who lacks piety is close to falling into heresy and rebellion against the Church.

One might also ask why Father des Places, who gave his foundation the full practice of religious life, did not formalize it by directing the members to take vows of poverty, chastity, and obedience, and thus make it a religious institute in the technical sense of the term. There is a ready answer for this. In the first place, with few exceptions the old religious orders in France had entered into a state of regrettable decadence during the late seventeenth and early eighteenth centuries. We need not examine here the reason for this sad state of affairs. It is fully recorded by contemporary historical documents such as the ones which tell how an ecclesiastical committee of the period was busily engaged in abolishing all monasteries that did not have at least fifteen occupants. By reason of numbers alone, therefore, it would have been practically impossible for Claude to start his foundation as a religious order. Secondly, the establishment of new religious communities in France was expressly forbidden. Finally, the modern type of religious community known as a "Congregation" (in contradistinction to an "Order") hardly existed at that time. All the great religious foundations of seventeenth century France, such as the

B. G. 31, 640

Oratorians (1601), the Vincentians (1625), the Sulpicians (1642) and the Foreign Missions (1660), were secular institutes with an intense religious life but without official religious vows. Any deviation from this pattern would have meant needless trouble for the nascent community of Father des Places. Suffice it to say, therefore, that while there was no question of public religious vows, the routine of religious life was fully observed.

CHAPTER TWO

FROM THE DEATH OF THE FOUNDER TO THE FRENCH REVOLUTION, 1709-1802

1. *The Immediate Successors*

Bio. 17

After the death of Father des Places, his associates chose as their Superior a young man of twenty-three, Father James Garnier. Unfortunately, the burdens of his office, coupled with the rigors of the severe winter of 1709, proved too much for him. He died in March 1710, leaving the nascent Society orphaned for the second time within six months. Providence then came forward with a priest who was destined to rule the Congregation and its works for the next fifty-three years.

Bio. 20 ff.

Father Louis Bouic (1684-1763) must have been a remarkable young man. He had entered the seminary as a deacon only four months before the assembled members of the Congregation elected him to the superiorship. In their triennial inquiry whether a new Superior ought to be elected, his confreres no less than seventeen times declared themselves satisfied with his rule. Such talents for government and so long an incumbency gave him an opportunity to consolidate the young society firmly and to build up its defenses against a variety of hostile forces that soon began to threaten its very existence.

2. *Continuing Relations with St. Louis de Montfort*

Once the Seminary of the Holy Ghost was formally established on Pentecost Sunday, 1703, St. Louis left Paris and plunged into his own apostolic activities. His first idea of organizing retreats and missions had evolved into the more durable plan of founding

Test. 29

a congregation for this specific purpose. Therefore, in June 1713, he wrote a Rule for his new religious society, which he called the Society of Mary. This institute was not to engage in any teaching activities; instead, he insisted that it devote itself exclusively to mission-work and preaching. Since the recruitment of vocations was to be taken care of by his agreement with Father des Places, he inserted the following provision into the Rule:

Test. 26

> This society accepts only priests who have been trained in seminaries. Therefore, clerics in the lower orders are excluded until they are ordained. However, there is a seminary in Paris [that of the Holy Ghost] in which young clerics who have a vocation for the missions are prepared for admission by study and virtue.

Although the exact nature of the Saint's agreement with Father des Places is not known, it is interesting to see that de Montfort considered the Seminary of the Holy Ghost as a house of his own society. He explicitly refers to it in his Rule as one of the two houses the Society may have as its own:

Test. 27

> The Society may not possess more than two houses in the Kingdom [of France]: the first in Paris, to train clerics in the apostolic spirit; the other outside Paris in a province, where those who are unable to work can go for a rest.[1]

Lav. 173

Shortly after writing his Rule, St. Louis went to Paris "to remind his friend's successors about the agreement and to make certain that this training school for priests . . . would really function as the seminary of his Society of Mary." There was ample reason for this reminder. Ten years had elapsed since he had made his agreement with Father des Places and the Saint had

Qu. III, 544

not yet received any of the promised recruits for his work. Now that his own plans had assumed definite form, he wanted "to enter into a serious, carefully planned, and definite convention with the growing community of the Holy Ghost" regarding the recruitment of members for his Society of Mary.

Test. 35

As soon as he arrived in Paris, de Montfort must have realized at once that the Holy Ghost Seminary was now leading a life of its own. Although it was one of the few places where they received him with a sincere display of respect and friendship, he saw that he could no longer consider this institution as a house of his own Society. However, there was still no reason why the Seminary should not play the role he had assigned to it in his Rule—*viz.,* the education of aspirant priests who would join him after their ordina-

Test. 37

tion. Father Bouic and the other directors were quite willing "to

---

[1]In 1713 St. Louis had at his disposal a house in the country which he wanted to use as a rest home for the old and sick members of his new society. Historians agree that the house in Paris can be no other than the Seminary of the Holy Ghost.

1.º on ne recoit en cette compagnie
que des prestres desia formez dans
les seminaires, ainsi les ecclesiastiqs
des ordres inferieurs en sont exclus
jusqu'à ce qu'ils aient receu le sacerdoce
il y a cependant a Paris un seminaire
ou les jeunes ecclesiastiques qui ont vocation
aux missions de la compagnie se dispo-
sent par la science et la vertu a y
entrer.

3. la compagnie n'a et ne peut avoir en
propre que deux maisons dans le
roiaume; la premiere a Paris pour
former des ecclesiastiques a l'esprit appliqué
la seconde hors de paris en une province
du Roiaume pour s'y aller reposer lorsqu'on
est hors du combat pour y finir ses jours
dans la retraitte et sa solitude apres en

Sections of the Rule written by St. Louis de Montfort which show the
close relationship between his Society and the Holy Ghost Fathers.
(Archives of the Society of Mary.)

Father James H. Garnier, second Superior
General of the Congregation of the Holy
Ghost (1709-1710).

Father Louis Bouic, third Superior General
of the Congregation of the Holy Ghost
(1710-1763).

aid him efficiently by training aspirants capable of supporting and
continuing the good work" of the Society of Mary.　Accordingly,
Test. 36　a new agreement was drawn up between the Saint and the
Spiritans: they were to operate independently, but would train,
free of charge, candidates who desired to enter his Society, thereby
eliminating the need of special Montfortist seminaries.　To make
his community more attractive to such aspirants and to permanently
seal the covenant, St. Louis went so far as to change the name of
his Society to that of the Holy Ghost.[2]　Accordingly, after his
return from Paris, he began to refer to his Society in this fashion
Test. 39　and signed official papers as "Louis-Mary de Montfort Grignion,
priest-missionary of the Society of the Holy Ghost."[3]

This new agreement was considerably more productive.　The
Saint's first associate, Father Vatel, came to him from Holy Ghost
Seminary, and others, such as Fathers Thomas, Heydan, Le
Vo. 230　Vallois and Besnard followed later.　Father Thomas was one of
the directors of the Seminary and therefore a Holy Ghost Father
in the strict sense of the term.　It looks as though he was about
to assume an important role among the Montfortists, for in 1723
he officially dedicated the Motherhouse of St. Louis' Society to the
Holy Ghost.　Shortly after, however, he was called back to Paris.
Father Bouic could not carry on without him.　It was Father
Besnard who later became the successor of St. Louis as Superior
General of the Society.　Then even the saintly Father Caris, bursar
of Holy Ghost Seminary, very nearly joined St. Louis.　Father
Bouic found it necessary to detain him at the very moment when
he was bidding his Seminary confreres farewell just prior to his
departure.

During the course of the nineteenth century, however, the Holy
Ghost Fathers began to direct all the aspirants in their Seminary

---

[2]Devotion to the Holy Ghost was very popular in those days among the
faithful of Brittany.　Three religious foundations of the time were dedicated
to Him: Poullart des Places' Congregation, St. Louis de Montfort's Society,
and the Sisters of the Holy Ghost founded by Father John Leudeger (1649-
1722).　In addition, there was in Brittany a Holy Ghost Missionary Band
led at that time by Father Francis Le Grand, S.J. Cf. W. M. Stadelman,
C.S.Sp., *Glories of the Holy Ghost,* Techny, Ill., 1919 pp. 241 ff.

MS. Rath, 37　　[3]This close association between the two societies explains why historians
occasionally are deceived by the similarity of titles and erroneously present
ibid. 76 f.　St. Louis de Montfort as the founder of the Holy Ghost Fathers.　On the
other hand, the Jansenists inveighed against the Company of Mary which,
they said, had "gone underground" in the Holy Ghost Society because it
could not obtain separate legal recognition.

Vo. 247

to the missions. The Society of St. Louis, therefore, had to modify its Founder's text of the Rule in order to assure the recruitment of members. As amended in 1872 it now reads:

> This society accepts not only priests who have been trained in seminaries, but also young men who have finished only the classes preparatory to theology. As a source of vocations, this scholasticate replaces the Seminary of the Holy Ghost.

It was also during the nineteenth century that the Society of St. Louis began to call itself again the Society of Mary, as the Saint had called it before his visit to the Holy Ghost Fathers in 1713.

Although relations between the Holy Ghost Fathers and the Society of Mary are no longer as intimate as they were in the eighteenth century, the two congregations have always continued to regard each other as close relatives, united by the bonds of common origin, lengthy association, and cordial affection.

3. *The Struggle for Legal Recognition*

Fl. 330 ff.

Like most other religious institutes in the Church, the Holy Ghost Society began its existence as a diocesan foundation under the sole authority of the local bishop. In this case it was the Archbishop of Paris, Cardinal de Noailles, who gave Father des Places permission to start his work. Soon, however, opposition began to arise. The powerful Sorbonne felt slighted by the fact that, despite all its pressure, Claude's students avoided its courses as a matter of principle. The Gallicanists were irked by the Seminary's inviolable attachment to the prerogatives of the Holy See. The Jansenists were furious because they could not lay hold on the minds of these future priests who carefully avoided every contaminated source of doctrine. These enemies soon succeeded in turning even Cardinal de Noailles against the work he had previously blessed. To make matters worse, it was not long before the Parliament of France joined the ranks of these formidable opponents.

Bio. 24 ff.

A legacy left to the Seminary provided them with a welcome opportunity for an all-out attack. In 1723, a pious priest, Father Charles Le Baigue, bequeathed 44,000 livres to the young foundation on condition that the Spiritans build their own seminary in the parish of St. Medard. As often happens in such cases, Father LeBaigue's nephews and nieces were chagrined to see so much money going to charity. Claiming that the Fathers "had circumvented the holy piety of their deceased relative by their clever machinations," they appealed to the courts to obtain an annulment of the legacy. The Sorbonne joined forces with them and contended that Holy Ghost Seminary, by refusing to take its degrees, was violating the University's established rights. Even the pastor of St. Medard entered the fray to voice his fears that soon all benefices within his parish would be taken over by the Seminary.

Legal grounds for the annulment of the legacy were soon found: a royal edict of 1666 prohibited the foundation of any college, monastery, or community without previous royal permission. Any contravention of this edict deprived such a college, monastery, or community of all legal rights and even of the hope of ever being legally recognized. It was argued, therefore, that the Holy Ghost Society should not only be deprived of the legacy; it did not even have the right to exist.

Luckily, the royal edict had made an exception for seminaries, which, under episcopal authority, could be founded without previous permission from the King, and it looked as though this might save Father des Places' foundation. Meanwhile, however, Cardinal de Noailles, the Archbishop of Paris, had fallen under the evil influence of his Jansenistic surroundings and was induced to object to the recognition of Holy Ghost Seminary on the pretext that his Archdiocese was well provided with seminaries and had no need of this new one dedicated to the Holy Ghost.

N. D. 3 ff.

Fortunately, the Society had powerful protectors also, and they succeeded in obtaining from the King not only the necessary papers for local recognition, but even an annual royal grant of six hundred livres and the validation of any possible irregularities in the legacy of Father Le Baigue. In spite of all this, the Jansenists prevailed on Parliament to voice strong opposition to the King's decision. Repeatedly, government lawyers found new legal obstacles to bar the registration of the royal document and thus render it ineffective. No less than four times the King had to issue new papers before all avenues of escape were blocked. He even went so far as to revoke the edict of 1666 to the extent that such a move was necessary to save the Holy Ghost Fathers and their seminary. The struggle lasted eleven years, but in the end the Congregation emerged victoriously, thanks especially to the protection of Cardinal de Fleury, the King's Minister of State. In 1734, legal recognition was finally granted, although the legacy which had occasioned all the trouble was lost somewhere along the way.

*N. D. 15 f.   The protracted battle had a beneficial side-effect inasmuch as it compelled the Spiritans to complete the Rule which had been left unfinished by Father des Places. After the death of Cardinal de Noailles, this Rule was presented to the new Archbishop of Paris, Charles de Vintimille, and it was he who granted *in writing* the first official ecclesiastical approbation of the Society (1734). In the finished version of the Rule, Father Bouic made one significant addition to the text. Among the specific aims of the Society, he listed the preparation of students for foreign missionary work and in this brief item we find the first clear indication of that strong apostolic trend which was to assume such an ever-increasing importance in the history of des Places' foundation.

4. *Growth of the Society*

Although Kings and Cardinals, Bishops and nobles made frequent gifts to the seminary, most of the support for its hundred seminarians came from the voluntary contributions of the ordinary faithful. It was not always easy to find the necessary funds,

Bio. 45 ff.   especially at the beginning. The first procurator or bursar, saintly Father Peter Caris (1684-1757), who was known throughout Paris as "the poor priest," often had anxious moments trying to make ends meet.[4] In general, however, he must have been an excellent provider, for under his stewardship the financial situation

*N. D. 14   of the young Spiritan community improved sufficiently to make it possible for him to acquire the necessary land and to build on it a permanent home for his seminarians. Construction began in 1732 on a sizable plot facing on what is now the *Rue Lhomond*. Two years later the new seminary was dedicated. It was a simple but beautiful building, one of the best in Paris at that time. To this

---

Bio. 46 f.   [4]The annals of the Congregation relate that on one occasion he returned home empty-handed when there was neither food in the house nor further credit at the butcher's and the baker's. Undaunted, the community went to the refectory, recited prayers before and after meals, and then repaired to the chapel for the customary adoration of the Blessed Sacrament. They were still there when an unknown source delivered such an abundance of food at the door that the meal which followed was the best they ever had. That same day enough money was received to pay outstanding meat and grocery bills.

An interesting anecdote about Father Caris tells us that one day, as he was making his rounds in Paris, he was drenched by the foul contents of a pail emptied from a second-story window. As the frightened householder offered his abject apologies, he was so struck by the saintly humility of this priest who had taken no offense whatsoever that he made a large contribution to the Seminary.

Bio. 33   day it still serves as the Motherhouse of the Congregation. Most likely, it was at this time also that the students began to take courses at home and ceased to go to the Jesuits for all their classes.

*N. D. 13   A few years earlier, in 1729, a small property had been acquired at Gentilly and this served as a combined farm and summer retreat. In 1752 Bishop Peter Dosquet of Quebec gave the

*N. D. 18   Society another property near Paris at Sarcelles, in gratitude for the services the Seminary had rendered to the Church in Canada.

*N. D. 20   A third property, called *la Chyperie,* near Orleans, was donated to the Society in 1777. It soon became the favorite retreat of the Directors of the Seminary.

Fl. 404   Far more important than these material acquisitions, however, was the fact that in 1736 the bishop of Meaux, Cardinal de Bissy, confided his diocesan senior seminary and seminary-college to the Society. Under the capable direction of Father James Lars (1705-1782) the previously debt-ridden institutions saw their dilapidated structures replaced by beautiful buildings, their obligations paid, and their students increasing in numbers and quality. The future priests trained in them were imbued by the new directors with that same love for humble and neglected positions in the diocese which had become the hallmark of Holy Ghost Seminary in Paris. The senior seminary remained under the direction of the Spiritans till 1807, when their Congregation, dispersed by the French Revolution, was no longer able to provide personnel for it. The example of Cardinal de Bissy was followed in 1737 by the Bishop of Verdun, who offered his seminary to the Congregation in an effort to purify it of Jansenism.[5] The acceptance of this offer once more brought the Holy Ghost Fathers into conflict with the adherents of that heresy.

5. *Renewed Struggle Against the Jansenists*

Fl. 434 ff.   As we have seen before, from the very beginning the Holy
N. E. 1735,   Ghost Society had been the object of the Jansenists' hatred. From
p. 211 ; 1741,   crude jokes and deprecating remarks about its graduates they had
p. 52 ; 1743,   proceeded to an all-out attack in their efforts to crush the Society
pp. 158 ff. ;   and prevent its Seminary from gaining legal recognition. One can
1746, pp. 33 f.   easily imagine how infuriated they must have been in 1737 when,

---

*N. D. 18   [5]In 1777 another seminary was accepted in Corsica, but extant records do not show that personnel was actually sent to this institution.

at the end of that long drawn-out litigation, the seminary of Verdun,
then a stronghold of Jansenism,[6] was confided to the Society they

Fl. 423 ff.

so thoroughly detested. Not a single one of the priests trained in
Holy Ghost Seminary had ever gone over to the Jansenists, and
now these people were invited to take over one of the bulwarks of
Jansenism! Father Bouic entrusted this delicate mission to a capable Director, Father Peter Thomas, who was accompanied by
several professors, notably Father Francis Becquet, one of his
best theologians.

The Jansenists had prepared a hot reception for them. Insinuations, insults, and accusations rained down on them from all sides.
Soon the whole diocese became involved in a controversy whose
climax was reached in 1741 when two anonymous pamphlets were
published under the title *Lettres à M. Becquet* (*Letters to Father
Becquet*). They were Jansenist replies to a number of theological
theses that Father Becquet had published in defense of the Catholic
view. To give the reader an idea of the venomous tone of these
pamphlets, let us quote a few sentences that illustrate the acrimony
of the controversy:

L. B. I, 3

Whoever mentions the name of Placist [i.e., Spiritan] refers
to something even worse than a Jesuit, at least if that is possible.

ibid. 20

If the cheeks of a Placist could blush, yours should be red
with shame . . .

ibid. 78

You deserve to have the Bishop shut you up forever and
send you back to wallow in the gutters of Clermont College
whence you have come forth to breathe over us all the pestiferous
and horrid odors that exude from this source.

The Bishop of Verdun sharply condemned the pamphlets in a
pastoral letter of 1744, and ordered all the priests of his diocese to
send him in writing statements that they agreed with this condemnation. Then, since Father Jolly was known to have had a hand
in the publication, he was promptly relieved of his parish.

MS. Rath,
81 ff.
N. E. 1746,
pp. 33 f.; 117 ff.

If the Bishop thought that his action would settle the affair, he
was much mistaken. In short order the whole of Lorraine was in
an uproar, some siding with Father Becquet and the Bishop, others
supporting the Jansenists. Soon the Royal Courts of Paris and

MS. Rath, 74 f.

---

[6]Bishop de Bethune of Verdun (+1720) and Father Habert, Vicar General under Bishop de Bethune, were among the leaders of the Jansenistic
movement in France. Their evil example had corrupted many of the secular
and regular clergy. For example, the Canons Regular, who directed the
seminary, had made it a hot-bed of Jensenism.

Nancy were drawn into the controversy. From his residence at Nancy, Stanislaus, King of Poland and Lorraine, appointed a parliamentary commission to find out who had dared to print these *Letters* without legal permission. Before long, the police began to make wholesale arrests of suspects, print shops were closed, and a number of pastors were turned out of their parishes. In Pont-à-Mousson alone, where the *Letters* had been secretly printed, approximately thirty persons were condemned to heavy fines and imprisonment. Then, when influential Jansenists succeeded in having these convictions declared illegal, the parliamentary commission established a special court of justice from which there was no further appeal. In 1746 this court sentenced Father Jolly to a sharp reprimand, three years in prison, and a fine. Another pastor lost his parish. The printer was fined, publicly reprimanded "with his head uncovered and on his knees," and deprived of his licence. King Stanislaus then closed this particular episode with a royal edict whereby anyone found with the *Letters* in his possession was to be punished by a fine of five hundred livres. Shortly after, Rome placed the *Letters* on the *Index of Forbidden Books* (1746), where they have remained till this day.

Fl. 441 ff.
Although these decisions of the supreme authorities of Church and State terminated the struggle to the advantage of the Spiritans, the influence of the Jansenists remained strong in Verdun—too strong for a peaceful and effective administration of the seminary. For this reason the Congregation regretfully informed the Bishop of its decision to withdraw its personnel to Paris in 1747.

Fl. 410 ff.
Back in Paris, in the more academic milieu of the Sorbonne, Father Becquet continued his battle against the Jansenists for fifteen more years until at last, in 1763, he was elected to assume the leadership of the Congregation. Since he was better trained in theological controversy than in business matters, he soon encountered financial difficulties when he undertook to complete the seminary by the addition of a large chapel and some new wings.

Fl. 660 ff.
In fact, things became so serious that there was even danger of a forced sale. Finally, he was rescued by the Archbishop of Paris, who persuaded the authorities to assign to the Seminary part of the income derived from certain defunct monasteries of the Celestines.

Father Becquet's superiorship is important for two reasons: for the first time in the history of the Congregation territories were officially entrusted to its spiritual care and, for the first time also, members of the Congregation itself departed for the foreign missions.

6. *First Missions Entrusted to the Congregation*

Dav. 51 ff.

In 1763, King Louis XV of France decided to replace all religious orders in the American French colonies by secular priests. This sweeping resolution caused Father Peter de la Rue, the Chaplain General of the Colonies, to send a long memorandum to the Court advising the King to entrust these missions to the Spiritans. In support of his recommendation, he said:

ibid. 52 f.

> Only the Holy Ghost Seminary is capable of furnishing as many subjects as will be necessary, both in number and quality, because of the kind of training that is given in their house.

*N. D. 19

Acting in accord with this advice, therefore, the Propaganda confided to the Congregation its first territory: the tiny islands of St. Pierre et Miquelon, off the coast of Newfoundland.

By the treaty of Paris in 1763, France had been forced to cede Canada to the British and these little islands were all that remained of its former vast possessions in North America. At the request of the King of France, Rome withdrew them from the jurisdiction of the Bishop of Quebec and in 1766 erected them into an Apostolic Prefecture, which it entrusted to the Congrega-

*N. D. 19

tion—an arrangement which has continued to this day. At about the same time, the suppression of the Jesuits in France had deprived French Guiana in South America of its missionaries. After several attempts to obtain good priests had failed, this territory also was entrusted to the Spiritans, who sent their first mis-

Bio. 56

sionaries into this distant French possession in 1775. A few years later, African Senegal likewise came under the spiritual care of the Congregation.

*N. D. 19

Slowly its Superior General—a title assumed by Father Becquet in 1766—took over the function, formerly exercised by the Chaplain General of France, of being the intermediary between the French Government and the Propaganda in religious matters pertaining to French colonies.

B. G. 32, 428

It was the new responsibility for Guiana in particular that made Father Becquet examine more closely the way in which Spiritans were henceforth to handle missions entrusted to their care. Although extant records do not treat the matter very clearly, this much appears certain: it was decided that from then on membership in the Congregation would no longer be limited to the professors of its seminaries and colleges; it would now be open to missionaries as well. Moreover, with the aid of the Government, a special retirement fund was created to take care of these men when sickness or old age would force them to return to France.

Bio. 97 ff.

The first departure under this new *modus agendi* took place in 1778, when a member of the Congregation, Father Dominic de Glicourt was sent to French Guiana to become its Prefect Apostolic. He was accompanied by Father James Bertout, the future restorer of the Congregation after the French Revolution. When their vessel was shipwrecked off the coast of Africa, both priests were among the seventeen survivors of the disaster. Captured subsequently by Moorish bandits, they were dragged on a two-month journey through the desert to the settlement of St. Louis in Senegal.

Their Moorish captors hoped to get a sizable ransom for the two priests, but the colony had been captured by the English twenty years before and the British governor was less than enthusiastic about the prospect of spending huge sums of money to rescue dangerous Frenchmen. However, under the pressure of European residents in the town, he finally agreed to buy their freedom after the pirates had considerably lowered their demands. Great was the rejoicing among the numerous Catholics of St. Louis who, since the capture of Senegal by the British, had been deprived of the services of a priest and were living their faith as best as they could under the direction of a layman.

But the governor felt differently about the situation. Fearing a return of French influence, he refused the priests permission to exercise any pastoral functions and finally went so far as to forbid them to celebrate Mass. Within six days of their arrival, he had them shipped to Gorée on a British vessel. Short as their stay in Senegal had been, however, the Fathers had seen and heard enough to analyze the situation: the colonists wanted desperately to oust the British; they earnestly desired freedom to exercise their religion; and there was only a small garrison of sixty men to maintain British rule.

Bio. 101 f.   In Gorée the two priests were transferred to an English vessel
sailing for London. Buffeted by storms, the ship twice came near
to being wrecked. It took nine weeks to reach the Channel. Then,
just before entering the Thames, it was overtaken and captured
by a daring French privateer, who took all the passengers and
crew to Le Havre as prisoners of war. Freed at last when their
identity was established, the two Spiritans returned to Paris where
they related their adventures to the Minister of the Navy, who
was then in charge of the colonies. The Minister displayed more
than usually keen interest in their description of the situation at
St. Louis. He recommended that they hold themselves in readiness
for a new departure—so he said—to Guiana.

Bio. 103 ff.   A month later sailing orders arrived. By that time, however,
Father Bertout was ill and had to be replaced by another member
of the Congregation, Father Seveno. Arriving at Lorient, their
port of embarcation, they saw that a squadron of sixteen warships
was being readied to accompany them. Evidently, their voyage
was not going to be a simple crossing of the Atlantic to South
America as they had assumed when they set out. It was not till
they were off the coast of Africa that the commander revealed
the intentions of the Government: the fleet was to capture Senegal,
as well as all other British establishments on the West Coast of
Africa. Father de Glicourt was presented with written orders
from the King to stay in Senegal after the conquest and look after
the spiritual needs of the population. Father Seveno, as far as we
know, continued on to Guiana.

After the British Governor recognized the futility of resistance
and ran up the white flag of unconditional surrender, the Catholics
of St. Louis received Father de Glicourt with delirious demonstrations of joy. Shortly afterward, the Propaganda named Father
de Glicourt Prefect Apostolic of Senegal and everything pointed
Ap. H., 79 f.   to a peaceful beginning. Then France sent out a new Governor
who was radically anticlerical. When Father de Glicourt saw
his Vicar General jailed and learned that he himself was to share
the same fate, he secretly embarked for Paris in 1782 and promptly
obtained the recall of the obnoxious Governor.

Father de Glicourt himself did not return to Africa. His post
was filled by Father Costes who with Father Chevalier established
missions at Albreda and Joal. Although both of these efforts were
blessed with much success, Father Costes succumbed to the ravages

of the climate in 1784 and his companion followed him to the grave shortly thereafter. It was not till the middle of the nineteenth century that a member of the Congregation would return to these regions which subsequently were to assume such a central position in the work of the Holy Ghost Fathers.

This first excursion of members into the foreign missionary field was soon followed by similar apostolic endeavors. Available records do not indicate with any degree of accuracy how many members of the Congregation left France to engage in apostolic work, but we do know that between 1778 and 1792 Guiana alone was blessed by the labors of Fathers Seveno, Lanoe, Legrand, Duhamel, Moranvillé, Hérard and Hochard.

B. G. 32, 428

7. *The French Revolution*

Fl. 450 ff.

In 1788, on the eve of the Revolution, Father John Duflos (1726-1805) became Superior General. He was the son of a wealthy family and thus could not normally have entered Holy Ghost Seminary. But the young man found an ingenious solution: by abandoning his income in favor of the Seminary, he made himself unable to pay for his board and room and thereby found a justifiable title to admission. He was accepted as a member of the Congregation in 1750. Soon after, he became professor of moral theology, a function which he fulfilled quite ably for the next thirty years.

Bio. 79 ff.

Father Duflos barely had time to pay the last debts contracted by Father Becquet when, in 1789, the National Assembly put all ecclesiastical goods at the disposal of the nation and compelled him to submit a detailed inventory of all the Congregation's assets. Outright suppression followed on August 10, 1792, and the possessions of the Congregation were put up for sale. Nine days later a mob of several thousand armed revolutionaries descended on the peaceful neighborhood of the seminary. Thirty-two priests of the Eudists, who lived close by, were arrested and faced the firing-squad and guillotine shortly thereafter. Part of the mob that captured them next turned its attention to the Seminary and invaded it by scaling the walls. Apparently the strenuous climb had made them thirsty, for once inside they immediately headed for the wine cellar. Quickly decapitating the bottles and dispatching their contents, these wild insurgents celebrated the great Revolution with gleeful savagery. Meanwhile, the community and the few remaining seminarians had gathered upstairs expecting the worst. They sorrowfully bade each other farewell with "Till we meet again in eternity," and then proceeded to ready their souls for the last moment.

Providentially, however, the wine was strong and heady. It made the mob forget the objects of its vengeance. One by one these poor besotted maniacs directed their uncertain steps to the front door and sought to recover their wits in the fresh air outside. The escape had been close. It was repeated two weeks later when the wholesale murder of priests all over Paris again left the Spiritans untouched. However, because no one could reasonably hope for a continuation of such good fortune, the members of the Society decided to disperse in civilian clothes and seek shelter individually. Some fled to Switzerland, others to Italy and England, and still others courageously went into hiding in the neighborhood.

Bio. 85 ff. In 1793 the Government first leased out and then sold the seminary. Part of it saw service as a wall-paper factory and the remainder was sublet as "rooms for rent." Before long these quarters were occupied by disguised nuns from confiscated convents. Even a number of Holy Ghost Fathers quietly rented back their old rooms and stayed there unknown throughout the Terror. However, in 1797, when the tide of persecution rose to new heights of severity, they thought it more prudent to seek refuge elsewhere. Only one priest was left behind, and he concealed himself in the spacious library. This lonely figure out of the past never left his hiding place except to hold services in the seminary chapel, which somehow had escaped destruction and which now was used again, first in secret and then more and more openly, for religious worship.

Bio. 104 f. In Meaux, the Government had appointed a "constitutional" bishop, who bitterly complained to the civil authorities that the Holy Ghost Fathers in the seminary there refused to recognize his authority. Immediately things began to happen. Plundered by revolutionary mobs, the Spiritan College and Seminary of Meaux had already been closed in 1792. Of the seven Holy Ghost Fathers assigned to it, four returned to Paris, while the others stayed behind to exercise their sacred ministry. One of them, Father de Glicourt, the former Prefect Apostolic of Senegal, was arrested in 1795. Although subsequently released, he suffered imprisonment again in 1799 and was later condemned to deportation. The fall of the Directory, which occurred later that same year, found him in the fortress of Oléron, and he was then promptly released. A similar fate befell Father Thomas Rupalet (1718-1799), the superior of the Seminary-College. He was arrested in 1797 after his return from Paris and only released from prison to die in a nearby hospital. His post remained unfilled until, after the signing of the Concordat in 1802, Father de Glicourt was appointed Superior and charged with the task of re-establishing the seminary.

Fl. 459 f.
cf. pp. 388 f.

Throughout these harrowing years of revolution and persecution, the Society was buoyed up by one great consolation. Although its possessions had been confiscated, its students were dispersed, most of its members suffered exile or imprisonment, and its very existence before the law had vanished, not a single Holy Ghost Father had followed the easy path of compromise which led other priests to take the schismatic oath imposed on the clergy by the Revolutionary Government.

From its foundation in 1703 until the Revolution drew a bloody veil over its activities, the Congregation had educated and trained about 1600 priests in its Parisian seminary alone. Throughout France and far beyond its borders, Spiritans were known for their unshakable adherence to the Holy See, their purity of doctrine, and the careful way in which they trained students in the duties and virtues of the priestly life. It should not come as a surprise, therefore, when the documents of history show that, although in principle its students were prepared for the humblest functions in the Church, many of them were entrusted with highly responsible positions in the dioceses and missions where they served. A number of them were raised to the episcopal dignity, while countless others became professors at various seminaries where they further propagated the ideals which the Congregation had instilled in them.

Although the priests issuing from Holy Ghost Seminary were not *ipso facto* members of the Congregation itself, they were known throughout the world as *"Spiritans,"* which is the familiar equivalent of "Holy Ghost Fathers." They were proud of this title, and the Congregation has every reason to be proud of them. To omit their work entirely from the history of the Holy Ghost Fathers would be almost as unreasonable as to limit the history of the Foreign Mission Society of Paris to the local events of its Parisian Seminary and ignore entirely the labors of its priests in the Far East.

CHAPTER THREE

A GLANCE AT THE MISSIONARY LABORS
OF THE HOLY GHOST FATHERS IN THE
EIGHTEENTH CENTURY

1. *Fields of Labor*

At the end of their studies, priests trained in the Holy Ghost Seminary were perfectly free to choose the diocese or mission in which they wished to work or, if they preferred, to join a religious order. At the beginning especially, many placed themselves at the disposal of bishops in France and thus became members of the diocesan clergy. In fact, the French bishops soon came to regard Holy Ghost Seminary as an interdiocesan institution to which all of them could appeal for men.

Of those who entered religious orders, a notable proportion went to the Society of St. Louis de Montfort. A great number also felt the call of the orient and set off for the Far East as missionaries under the auspices of the Foreign Missions of Paris. This additional source of personnel was a particularly welcome blessing for the Foreign Missions Society because that organization was just then experiencing a severe shortage of priests.

cf. p. 15

Far East. The number of Spiritans[1] who went to China and other Far Eastern countries must have been considerable if we

MS. Rath,
83 f.

---

[1]Before 1848, the following meanings of the term "Spiritan" or Holy Ghost Father may be distinguished:

1. Any priest trained in Holy Ghost Seminary.

2. Any foreign missionary trained in Holy Ghost Seminary, whether directly presented by the Seminary to his Ecclesiastical Superior or through the Foreign Missions of Paris.

cf. p. 36

3. A foreign missionary trained in Holy Ghost Seminary and directly presented by it to his Ecclesiastical Superior.

cf. p. 29 and p. 397

4. Foreign missionaries associated as members of the Congregation.

5. Directors of Holy Ghost Seminary.

p. 64

6. Members of the Second Order (cf. Chapter IV).

7. Members of the First Order (cf. *ibid.*)

cf. p. 58

In addition, the term was sometimes usurped without right by priests working in missions entrusted to the Congregation but having no special connection with Holy Ghost Seminary. In 1848 the term became reserved exclusively for members of the Congregation. In this chapter we use it in its broad eighteenth century sense as applicable to categories two, three and four.

34

may judge by the statistics on those who were appointed Vicars Apostolic. In Cambodia, Cochin China, the Spiritan Bishop William Piguel succeeded his confrere Bishop Edmund Bennetat. Both became confessors of the Faith for, after suffering prison and persecution, they died in exile. In 1746, Father Louis Devaux became Coadjutor with the right of succession of the Bishop of West Tonkin. He too went through life victimized by bitter persecution. Father John Maigrot, who had gone to China in 1740, was appointed Vicar Apostolic of Szechwan thirteen years later. The documents arrived too late, however, for by then the intrepid priest had already died. In 1764 the Holy See named Father Peter Kerhervé Vicar Apostolic of the same mission, but this Spiritan returned the papal bulls saying that Father Andrew Lee, a Chinese priest, would be more suitable. He died two years later. Father Urban Lefebvre, who also became a Vicar Apostolic in China, returned to France after thirteen years of untold sufferings and died a martyr's death in September 1789, a victim of the French Revolution. The most important of all Spiritan bishops in the Far East, however, was undoubtedly Bishop Francis Pottier, who for thirty years labored in the immense Vicariate of Szechwan. His story will be told later.

Goyau, I,
411 f.

Other Holy Ghost Fathers of the period became outstanding missionaries in the Far East without being raised to the episcopal rank. Cochin China benefitted by the apostolate of Father Rivoal who, after thirty years of unremitting toil in the Orient, returned in 1763 to end his days in France. The Christians of Siam were strengthened during the cruel persecution of Emperor Phaia-Tacs by the fearless ministration of Father James Corre. Father John Perrin spent twenty years in India and is known not only for his missionary work but also for his scholarly publications dealing with the Far East.

The West. It is known also that many of these eighteenth century Spiritans came to the Western Hemisphere to labor in French Guiana, the West Indies, and the immense diocese of Quebec.[2] In fact, as early as 1732, we find one of them, Father Frison de la Mothe, on the faculty of the Quebec seminary. Other outstanding characters of this group will be treated more fully in the course of this chapter.

B. R. H.,
1929, 315

---

[2] The history of many of these early Spiritans in Canada has been traced by Father Albert David, C.S.Sp. Cf. Bibliography, pp. 603 f.

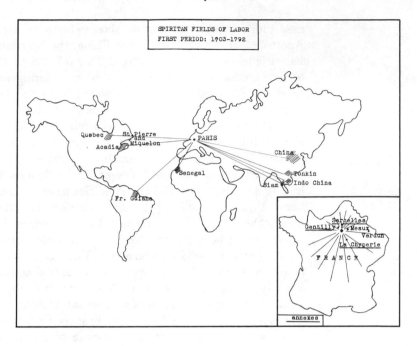

SPIRITAN FIELDS OF LABOR
FIRST PERIOD: 1703-1792

R. H. M. 13,
567 ff.

At first, the priests sent to Canada applied to the Foreign Missions of Paris to obtain their ecclesiastical and civil appointments, but the scarcity of other priests in the Foreign Missions Seminary and a variety of other reasons soon forced the Bishop of Quebec to deal immediately with the Holy Ghost Fathers. From 1752 on, his Vicar General in Paris selected his own Spiritans and sent them directly to the Bishop for their appointments. A number of these were used as professors at the Seminary of Quebec or as pastors in the environs of the diocesan see, while others took care of the French settlers and the Indians in Acadia.

The number of Spiritans who went to Canada during the eighteenth-century is difficult to determine since complete lists are not available. Father Peter de la Rue, Abbot of Isle Dieu, who was Chaplain General of the colonies, in charge of the religious interests of French overseas territories, wrote to the Propaganda in 1771 as follows:

Bio. 56

> During the thirty-eight years that, as Vicar General, I have been in charge of all French and Indian Missions in the vast and extended Diocese of Quebec in North America, I have sent only subjects trained and educated at the Seminary of the Holy Ghost. All have always surpassed our hopes, and not a single one has betrayed our confidence.

Dav. 21

Dav. 21

R. U. O.,
V, 60

B. R. H. 1929,
444

Dav. 47

R. H. C. 37,
173 ff.

About twenty years earlier, in 1753, he had written that "the majority of the staff in the Seminary of Quebec" had been furnished by Holy Ghost Seminary.[3] Although it is true that Father de la Rue was very fond of the Holy Ghost Fathers and therefore may have exaggerated somewhat, nevertheless there is every reason to believe that his reports are substantially correct. Moreover, as we have seen, Bishop Dosquet of Quebec gave the Spiritans a substantial property at Sarcelles in gratitude for their services. He would scarcely have done this if their contributions to his diocese had not been quite significant. Again, Father Becquet, the Superior General, wrote in 1768 that his Congregation "for the past thirty years had trained all the missionaries employed in Acadia and among the savages of that peninsula." The Chaplain General of the Colonies was so impressed by the work done by these priests that he wanted them to replace the Recollects, whose missions in Canada had fallen on evil days. He began by placing the Recollects under the control of a Holy Ghost Father, Peter Maillard, Vicar General of the Bishop of Quebec. At the same time he advised the Bishop to staff his seminary with Spiritans.

Unfortunately, the cession of Canada to the British in 1763 put an end to these plans and doomed the successful efforts of the Canadian Holy Ghost Fathers to complete frustration. Fearing their influence on the people, the British conquerors had denied further admission to any French priests. Only two more Spiritans succeeded, during 1772, in gaining entrance on the ground that they were of Canadian extraction. Others tried again in 1784, including the Bishop's own nephew, but they were stopped in London and sent back to France. However, during the French Revolution, in 1792, two Spiritans from St. Pierre and Miquelon, who had refused to take the schismatic oath imposed by the Government, were allowed to take refuge in Canada. The last survivor of these early Holy Ghost Fathers died in Canada in 1835.

It is interesting to note at this juncture that the Congregation's first representatives in the United States arrived in 1795. They came as refugees from Guiana, which was then experiencing the blessings of Liberty, Equality and Fraternity. There were three of them: Fathers Moranvillé, Duhamel, and Hérard, and they were Holy Ghost Fathers in the strict sense of the term for they were actual members of the Congregation.

---

[3]The French text has the term *sujets* which obviously does not refer to seminarians.

It would lead us too far afield to describe the labors of all these priests in detail. An exception, however, must be made in the case of Peter Maillard, the Apostle of the Micmac Indians; John Le Loutre, the Father of the Acadians; and Bishop Francis Pottier, the Founder of the Missions of Szechwan in China.

2. *Peter Maillard, the Apostle of the Micmacs, and John Le Loutre, the Father of the Acadians*

B. R. H. 1929,
365 ff.

Acadia, long a bone of contention between the French and the British, was finally ceded to England by the Treaty of Utrecht in 1713. It was promptly renamed Nova Scotia. Provisionally, the conquerors had to spare the proud national feelings of the French settlers of Acadia, for a mass emigration to neighboring Cape Breton Island, still in French hands, would have utterly ruined the economy of Nova Scotia and considerably strengthened the French forces nearby. On the other hand, their loyalty to France and their unshakeable profession of the Catholic Faith were considered so dangerous that as early as 1720 there was some question of forcibly deporting the entire French population. A kind of uneasy truce was reached in 1730 when the Acadians swore loyalty to the British Crown on condition that they would be allowed to remain neutral in case of conflict between France and England.

The territory was inhabited also by nomadic Micmac Indians, who had been converted to Catholicism and wanted very much to remain loyal to the King of France. The situation was further complicated by the fact that the conquerors hoped to make Protestants out of these Micmacs who were so fiercely attached to their religion and their priests. Thus national and religious aspects became inextricably interwoven. French and Catholic came to be the alternative of British and Protestant. It is in this politico-religious context that the activity of Father Le Loutre must be interpreted.

R. U. O., V, 55
Can. H. R. 11,
105 ff.
B. R. H., 1929,
365

When he arrived in Acadia in 1737, Le Loutre was received by another Spiritan who had arrived there two years earlier: Father Peter Maillard, the Apostle of the Micmac Indians. Father Maillard had been the first to acquire a complete mastery of their difficult language, for which he created a hieroglyphic alphabet, a

R. H. M. 13,
481 ff.

grammar and a dictionary, in addition to a book of prayers, hymns and sermons.[4] After studying the formidable language under his direction, Father Le Loutre received his appointment for the mission of Chigabenakady, a settlement of Acadians and Indians that had not seen a priest for a period of twelve years.

B. R. H., 1929,
367
Can. H. R. 11,
112 f.

Loyal to his promise to keep the Acadians subject to England, he spent five years there exercising his ministry and building churches and chapels throughout the area. However, in 1744, war broke out again between the French and British. With the aid of the Micmacs, accompanied by Father Maillard as their military chaplain, Marquis Duquesne, the French Governor, tried to capture the British fortress of Annapolis. Instead, the English turned the tables and captured the French stronghold of Louisbourg. They immediately insisted on seeing both Father Maillard and Father Le Loutre. Upon their sworn promise that he need have no fears for his liberty, the former presented himself and was promptly arrested and deported to Boston. Father Le Loutre distrusted the British assurances, however, and escaped to Quebec, together with a deputation of Micmacs.

Now that Father Maillard was gone, the Quebec Government considered Father Le Loutre as the man in charge of Indian Missions. After supplying the Micmacs with copious ammunition, the Governor confidentially told the priest that a French naval squadron was expected within the year and that it would expel the English. For that reason it was important to keep the Indians in readiness so that they might aid the French operation by cutting British communication lines. Apparently, the British commander heard of this development, for he ordered the immediate arrest of Father Le Loutre. The priest and his Indians, however, were too deeply ensconced in the forest to be much troubled by the threat of arrest.[5]

Goyau, I,
162 ff.
Can. H. R. 11,

Late in 1746 the French squadron arrived, but in a state of complete disorganization. Its commander had just died and a contagious disease was rapidly killing its complement of men. Under

---

[4]A printed edition of his Micmac grammar appeared in New York in 1864, while his manual of prayers, hymns and sermons was printed in 1866 in Vienna, and again in 1921 in Restigouche, Quebec.

[5]The Indians had sworn allegiance to France and thus were bound to help the French forces. Father Le Loutre was their chaplain and leader, and it is in this capacity that he took part in their expeditions. On the other hand, he carefully abstained from appealing for help to the Acadian French settlers, who had sworn to observe neutrality in any conflict between France and England.

114 ff.

the circumstances, there was little the fleet could do but return to France. Shortly thereafter, Father Le Loutre followed them to Paris to plead the cause of his people. Urged to return as soon as possible to Acadia, he sailed in the spring of 1747 but was captured on the high seas by the British. After spending three months in jail at Winchester, he was released and sent back to France. Undaunted, he embarked again only to meet the same fate once more. Meanwhile, in 1748 the diplomats at Aachen had again declared that France and England were at peace and had returned Cape Breton Island to the French. The following spring Father Le Loutre was back in Acadia once more ministering to his beloved Indians and Acadians.

Goyau, I,
164 ff.

ibid. 165

He soon noticed that the pious phrases of the diplomats had changed nothing in the state of tension existing in the country. The new British Governor, Cornwallis, declared war on the Micmacs, offering a bounty of ten pounds for every scalp. With respect to the Acadians, Governor Shirley of Massachusetts had proposed "to chase the Catholic Priests from Nova Scotia and substitute French Protestant ministers for them, open Scottish schools, and favor those inhabitants who become Protestants and see to it that their children learn English." Cornwallis made it clear that they had to choose between deportation and confiscation of all their possessions or unconditional allegiance to England with military service under the British flag. As their shepherd and leader, Father Le Loutre could not find it in his heart to stand idly by. He resolved to defend both Indians and Acadians against these cruel and unjust measures.

Can. H. R. 11,
118 ff.

While arranging the resettlement of a number of Acadians on islands that were still in French hands, he spent the winter of 1749 with the Micmacs, baptizing and instructing his new converts. At the same time, he directed the Indians to patrol the peninsula and intercept all British messengers. With a bounty on the head of everyone of his Indian flock, one can hardly blame the priest for taking so active a part in political and military affairs. At the same time, however, he took care that no harm befell their English prisoners. When the Micmacs brought in their captives, Father Le Loutre was on the spot to purchase their lives with money borrowed from the Acadians. While the English Governor had put a price of 500 livres on his head (and soon raised it to a thousand), the priest spent as much as twenty-five thousand livres in redeeming English prisoners from his

Indians.[6] The Micmacs grew bolder with their success. In a daring raid in 1751, they went so far as to penetrate into an English fortress to liberate a priest who had been held prisoner there for six months.

The following year, leaving his Indians in the care of a fellow priest, Father Le Loutre again crossed the Atlantic to plead more urgently at Paris the cause of his Acadians. New hope came to these unfortunate people when he returned in the spring of 1752 with a fairly large amount of money and supplies to aid in their resettlement on land still held by France. One can readily see why, when he built a beautiful church and fortress at Beauséjour, many Acadians flocked to him from English-held territories. The enraged British Governor now raised the price on his head to six thousand livres, but to no avail. Not a single hand, whether Acadian or Indian, could be induced to earn such blood-money by murdering this beloved priest who fearlessly continued his daily rounds among his flock. The Governor then tried to buy the priest's loyalty for a hundred thousand livres and a promise of freedom of religion. Freedom of religion might have induced him to waver for a moment, but in view of past experiences, what value could anyone attach to such assurances? As to his loyalty, it was not for sale.

Goyau, I, 169 ff.

In 1754 Father Le Loutre made certain proposals to the British in behalf of the Micmac Indians. They were scornfully rejected by Governor Lawrence, who had other plans in mind. Soon after, he sent three thousand soldiers from Boston to besiege the fortress of Beauséjour. On June 16, 1755, the fort crumbled and resistance ceased. With a heavy heart, shortly before the surrender, Father Le Loutre set fire to the beautiful church he had just finished. He preferred to see it go up in flames rather than let it fall into Protestant hands.

Can. H. R. 11, 123 f.

While the French commander of the fort fraternized with his conquerors at a lavish meal, the priest quietly slipped away through a secret exit and after trudging through three hundred leagues of dense forest he finally reached Quebec. By the middle of August he was again skimming over the waves to seek help in France. Captured once more on the high seas, this valiant defender of the Acadians was thrown into prison in Jersey, where this time he languished for eight years. Meanwhile his Acadians were deprived of their priests, hunted down and stripped of all their possessions. Six thousand of them died of starvation; others went into exile;

Goyau, I, 171 ff.

Can. H. R. 11, 125 f.

---

[6]The British subsequently reimbursed him for these expenses.

the remainder were loaded on ships and scattered all along the
East coast of America. As all of us know, the tragic story of these
Acadians wanderers has been immortalized by Longfellow in his
Evangeline, but the worst fate of all befell those who were deported
to New England. Puritans, full of hatred for anything Catholic,
deprived them of every religious comfort and even went so far as
to separate them from their children.

After the peace treaty of 1763, Father Le Loutre once more
regained his freedom. Without delay he went to work on a program
to resettle twenty-five hundred Acadians who had sought refuge in
France. Every ounce of his customary energy was poured into the
project, but even his powerful influence had little effect on a people
whose homesickness for the New World made them highly reluctant to take up permanent residence in France. In the midst of
this melancholy work of resettlement, Father Le Loutre died at
Poitou in 1772.

B. R. H.,1929,
444

After their beloved champion had passed to his eternal reward,
most of the Acadian exiles in France set sail for Louisiana. There
they joined a large group of their displaced compatriots who had
drifted down to the New Orleans region from various points along
the eastern coast of America. While a great number of them established permanent domicile here, during the ensuing decades many
quietly slipped back into Canada and settled once more in the land
where they had been born. Moreover, a large group of Acadian
families that had previously been dispersed throughout New England were now gathered together by Father John Brault and guided
back to peaceful homesteads on Montreal Island. It seems particularly fitting that Father Brault, himself an Acadian and a Holy
Ghost Father like Le Loutre, should have been the one to bring
this tragic saga to a close.

As for Father Maillard, whom we left deported in Boston in
1745, no power on earth was able to keep him away from the
flock entrusted to his care. From Boston he was shipped to England and from there to France, but in the fall of the next year he
was back again in Acadia, just in time to replace Father Le Loutre,
who wanted to leave for Paris to plead the cause of his Acadians.

B. R. H.,
1929, 368

As chaplain of the Micmacs who were officially at war with the
English, he lived with them in the woods and accompanied them
on their military expeditions. As a result, on several occasions he
was able, like Father Le Loutre, to save their captives from torture
and death.

R. U. O.,
V, 73 ff.

In 1758, when the fall of Louisbourg definitely sealed the fate of Acadia, Henry Schomberg, commander of the British troops, gave Father Maillard an ultimatum: allegiance to the King of England with a promise of freedom of religion and guaranteed property rights or death to all his Indians. Though at first sight the offer may seem to have been rather generous, in reality it was all to the advantage of the British. The woods of Nova Scotia were swarming with roaming bands of Micmacs, all of them firmly resolved to perish rather than surrender. Without hesitation they scalped any British colonist who fell into their hands. The situation was so bad that the colonists of Halifax did not dare to leave the protection of their palisades. Belatedly, therefore, the English learned that only Catholic priests would be able to induce the Indians to make peace. Father Maillard, on the other hand, was wise enough to see that there was no longer any hope of a French coup in Nova Scotia. He therefore agreed to use his influence in bringing about peace between the Micmacs and the English.

B. R. H.,
1929, 371

Sir Charles Lawrence, the Governor of Nova Scotia, called him to Halifax, where he gave him a pension of one hundred pounds and the use of a building for Catholic religious services. Till his death, Father Maillard was the only Catholic priest tolerated in Nova Scotia.

B. R. H.,
1929, 372

At once he courageously began to take care of his flock, which consisted not only of the few score Catholics who lived in Halifax, but of all the Acadians and Indians scattered throughout the Province. His position was a very delicate one, for he faced the hostility of the Protestant ministers and the special bitterness of a French apostate priest who had been called to Nova Scotia for the avowed purpose of proselytizing the remaining Acadians. Nevertheless, his genteel manners, his learning, and his diplomacy secured him general good will. He used it to organize his Acadians and Indians for the preservation of their Faith despite the lack of priests. Everywhere, lay volunteers were put in charge of scattered groups to instruct the faithful, lead them in Sunday prayers, baptize their children, and witness their marriages. The Indian tribes were induced to bury the hatchet. Copies of his manuscripts containing prayers, hymns and sermons were placed in the hands of every chieftain. In the absence of a priest, the chief was to hold Sunday services as described in the book, and to use its formulas for baptisms, marriages, and funerals. Thanks to these books, the Micmacs continued to resist every effort of the Protestant missionaries to proselytize them.

B. R. H., 1929, 373 R. U. O., V., 427

In 1762, when he was about to meet a group of Indians who were opposing the government, he fell seriously ill. Medical care was provided by Dr. Thomas Wood, a former army surgeon, who had become an Anglican minister. Soon it became apparent that death was not far away. Since there was no Catholic priest available, Dr. Wood offered him the religious assistance of the Anglican Church. Father Maillard politely declined, saying: "I have served God all my life. Every day I have prepared myself for death by offering the holy sacrifice of the Mass." He died on August 12, 1762, and the size of his funeral testified to the high esteem in which he was held. Over and above his beloved Indians and Acadians, nearly all persons of rank were in attendance, and the President of the Council as well as the Speaker of the House

B. R. H., 1929, 373

acted as pall-bearers. The funeral was held at St. Paul's Episcopal Church by Dr. Wood, who read the Anglican funeral service and tried to convince the Acadians and Indians that Father Maillard had appointed him as his spiritual successor.

R. U. O., V., 429 ff. N. F. 99 ff.

He succeeded only in revealing himself as an impostor, however, for even after his death Father Maillard's carefully organized program continued his apostolate among the Indians. Thanks especially to Maillard's prayerbook, the Micmacs soon dicovered the ruse when Dr. Wood began to masquerade among them as the successor of their apostle. They demanded a Catholic priest. When at first their demand was rejected, their attitude became so threatening that upon the advice of the military commanders of Nova Scotia the government finally gave in in 1768 and provided a priest

B. R. H., 1929, 446

for them. In 1774, Father Joseph Bourg, another eighteenth century Spiritan, took over the spiritual care of Nova Scotia and New Brunswick. He earned the gratitude of the Government by pacifying the Indians during the American War of Independence. In fact, it was largely through his influence that Catholics subsequently obtained freedom of religion in Nova Scotia.[7]

The mortal remains of Father Maillard were buried in the common cemetery of Halifax, without any monument to blazon forth his praise. He did not need any. The Faith preserved among his Micmacs to this day constitutes a living monument to the work of their great apostle.

---

[7] A statue in his honor has since been erected in Carleton, Nova Scotia.

John Le Loutre, the Father of the Acadians.
(Courtesy Public Archives of Canada).

Bishop Francis Pottier, the Founder of the
Szechwan Missions.
(Portrait by a contemporary Chinese artist).

The Spiritan Motherhouse at Paris. Construction was started in 1732. The main wing visible on this photo was designed by Chalgrin, the architect of the Arc de Triomphe.

3. *Bishop Francis Pottier, 1726-1792, the Founder of the Szechwan Missions*

Su. 51 ff.

Francis Pottier was born in 1726 at Chapelle-Saint-Hippolyte in the present Province of Indre-et-Loire, France. Orphaned at the age of eight, he entered the home of a wealthy maternal uncle. Later he was sent to the local college of Loches for his classical and philosophical studies.

Su. 63 ff.

In 1748 the young man entered Holy Ghost Seminary in Paris, specifically because his uncle hoped that by taking a degree at the Sorbonne Francis would be able to enter upon a distinguished ecclesiastical career. Apparently the old man did not realize that students in this seminary neither studied at the Sorbonne nor prepared themselves for careers in the Church. Francis himself, however, immediately caught the spirit of the house, for during the opening retreat of his first year he grew conscious of a burning desire to consecrate himself to the Missions.

In another respect, the new seminary proved somewhat disappointing to him: Father Bouic, the Superior, told him that, like most of the other newcomers, he would have to begin his philosophy all over again. According to the standards of Holy Ghost Seminary, the course he had finished at the small country college of Loches was judged to be deficient in several respects. The next year he was still in doubt as to whether he would be permitted to start

Su. 72

theology for, he wrote, "the Superior usually does not grant this privilege to those who have not studied physical science."[8] Then

cf. p. 16

too, as we have seen above, the course of studies at Holy Ghost Seminary lasted two years longer than was customary in most other seminaries.

Accordingly, his ordination was to take place much later than his relatives had at first expected. They found this delay most annoying for they were impatient to see him return to his native town and begin his quest for a rich benefice. Francis himself, however, was completely disinterested in becoming the possessor of a substantial income. The missionary idea which had seized him at the very inception of his seminary career continued to gain ground in his mind. He began to prepare his family for a grave disappointment of their fond hopes by telling them that he had no desire to

---

[8]Twice weekly, the Holy Ghost seminarians went to a Jesuit College for experimental physics.

take any degrees and by alleging that, if necessary, such a degree could even be bought later for a few francs.

Su. 88 ff.

In fear that a visit home might expose him to the danger of betraying his intentions, he refrained from joining his family for the long vacation and spent his holidays instead at the summer villa of the Seminary. He realized, of course, that he could not conceal his plans forever. When the end of his studies approached in 1753, he began to prepare his relatives for the bad news. After a few more or less distinct hints, he finally opened his mind and told them that, with the consent of his director, he had decided to become a missionary. As he expected, his family fumed and fretted, but Francis stood firm. After Easter of that year, he followed the example of some of his fellow-students and joined the Foreign Missions Society, under whose auspices alone he could be sent out to the Far East.

Su. 103 ff.

Six months later he was on his way to China. Passing through Gorée, off the west coast of Africa, and sailing around the Cape and across the Indian Ocean, he arrived in September 1754 at Macao, the Portugese enclave in China. Fifteen months later, he started his perilous journey through the Celestial Empire toward his destination in the Province of Szechwan.

Su. 177 ff.

Szechwan, "The Four Rivers," is a populous and fertile territory of about 200,000 square miles, lying east of Tibet. At the time Father Pottier made his journey, a recent papal condemnation of the idolatry implicit in the exaggerated honor paid to Confucius and to ancestors in general had resulted in a Chinese decree against Christian missionaries. Consequently, he had to be smuggled into the country in disguise, oft-times concealed under a pile of merchandise carried by the riverboats. The strange food, the total lack of exercise, the absence of companionship, and everlasting inspections by Chinese police, all conspired to work on his nerves. When sickness struck the lonely priest, his courage was at the breaking-point. Homesick, he thought with immense longing of the green rolling hills of his native land and the kind sweet friends in faraway France, the France he was destined never to see again. Grace, however, promptly gained control. Slowly he began again to look forward with enthusiasm to his apostolate among the Chinese and by the time he reached Szechwan three months later, his self-confidence had fully revived.

Su. 127 ff.   Two Chinese priests were all that was left of the once flourishing mission. All Europeans had been expelled and persecution
was still rife. As a matter of fact, it was never to stop completely
during the more than thirty years that Father Pottier was to spend
in this remote mission. Fortunately, the Faith had been kept alive
by the magnificent work of a number of native catechists. Father
Pottier began at once to recruit more of them and to train them
better for their task. He then undertook long and weary marches
to visit personally the scattered survivors of persecution throughout his immense territory.

Su. 147 ff.   In August, 1760, the edicts of prohibition were intensified.
Many of his Christians were thrown into jail. The next month,
in order not to expose more of them to this fate, he allowed himself to be captured. After spending two and a half months in a
dungeon and being questioned several times under torture, he was
condemned to exile and a military escort led him away with a
heavy chain around his neck. However, by means of a clever bribe
he succeeded in having the exile rescinded and then quietly returned to his mission.

Su. 159 ff.   Two years later his secret correspondence was intercepted
when the mission's private mail-carrier was arrested. It should
be mentioned here that all supplies, books, correspondence, and
money had to be secretly imported. For this purpose, the missions had set up a large smuggling system with headquarters in
Macao. Even the smallest non-Chinese article, such as a ritual
or a stole, was bound to arouse the suspicion of customs officials.
Customs existed not only at the borders of the country but everywhere throughout China where different provinces met. Nevertheless, these smugglers for the Lord were rarely caught during
the thirty-two years Father Pottier spent in China. In the investigation that followed upon interception of his mail, the authorities tried to discover Father Pottier's whereabouts, and he was
forced to go into complete hiding again. A Chinese fellow-priest
was caught, tortured, and exiled, but despite this new wave of
persecution, the mission work continued to make astonishing
progress.

Goyau, I, 411 f.   During all these years the mission had been without a Vicar
Apostolic. In 1762, the Holy See had appointed another Spiritan,
Father Kerhervé, to this position but he declined the honor and
returned the papal Bulls with a letter advising Rome that Father

Su. 171 ff.
Andrew Lee, a Chinese priest, would be the better choice. Five years later, Father Pottier, who had also tried to have someone else named, was made Vicar Apostolic of Szechwan and Titular Bishop of Agathopolis. The news of this appointment reached him only in 1769. It coincided with a fresh outbreak of persecution which made it necessary for him to avoid arrest by hiding for some time in a lonely cave. Then, when things quieted down he marched two hundred and fifty leagues over mountains and valleys to a neighboring province where, in deepest secrecy, he received his episcopal consecration from the hands of a fellow bishop. In the interim, troubles had abated somewhat in Szechwan, so he quietly returned to his post.

Su. 203 ff.
Although new local persecutions continued to break out with monotonous regularity, the apostolate was carried on successfully despite this opposition or perhaps even because of it. The striking change of life evident in many of the new converts and their steadfast loyalty to Christ did not fail to make a profound impression on the neighboring Chinese who witnessed their trials. As a result, many more sought admission to the Chuch even though it could offer them no immediate worldly prospects other than prison and torture.

Su. 293 ff.
Because European priests were much more exposed to the danger of discovery and exile than were the Chinese, Bishop Pottier made determined efforts to increase his native clergy. For this purpose he sent a number of suitable boys to the College of Pondicherry in India, where they could study Latin. When this measure did not have the desired result, he approached the Propaganda in 1779 and obtained permission to ordain Chinese priests locally without teaching them any Latin whatsoever. He then founded a small college in a remote part of the Province, where he hoped it would function quietly without drawing the unwelcome attention of civil authorities. In two years' time Bishop Pottier had the great consolation of ordaining the first three priests who completed its course of studies. His Christians proved to be too indiscreet, however, and all hope of peaceful operation had to be abandoned. In 1782 the institution was transferred to a still more remote part of the country. There, despite wars and oppression, it performed nobly for more than three decades before a disastrous fire levelled it to the ground. Though its career was regrettably brief, it had rendered invaluable service to the Church in the Orient.

Su. 321 ff.

While thus providing for a future clergy, Bishop Pottier had his hands full in moderating the excesses of some of his French missionaries. Under the pretext of aiming high, they had introduced all kinds of extraordinary "obligations" for the faithful: compulsory vigils throughout the night before all major feasts and Communion days; on Fridays, fast and abstinence from wine, tobacco, and heating, in addition to one hundred strokes of the discipline; two hours of prayer every day and hundreds of prayers on Sundays; the list was endless. Moreover, they had modified the rules of the Institute of Virgins, founded in 1745 by Bishop de Martillat. Girls down to the age of eleven were now permitted to take the public vow of chastity, roam around from house to house teaching catechism, and even preach in the absence of a priest. After consulting the Propaganda, Bishop Pottier vigorously condemned these practices. He did not, however, succeed in restoring unity among his missionaries until the principal author of these innovations decided to leave China.

Su. 347 ff.

In 1784 the aging prelate received news from Rome that one of his priests had been appointed his coadjutor and had been formally ordered not to refuse the position. It was a great relief for the old Bishop, who feared that sooner or later he himself would fall into the hands of the authorities and thereby leave the mission without any center of jurisdiction. His joy, however, was shortlived. In the same year another persecution broke out. The government had learned that more European priests were trying to steal into the country. During the wholesale investigation that ensued, his coadjutor was captured. The arrest caused great excitement, for the chief officers of the Province had proudly reported to the Imperial Court that there were no Europeans left in their territory and now, to save their flock from torture, a number of missionaries had surrendered to the governor. All were transported to Peking and sentenced to life imprisonment. However, shortly after, when two of them had already died in their dungeon, the others were released and exiled.

Su. 363 ff.

Bishop Pottier and the priests who had not surrendered were left undisturbed, undoubtedly because the local authorities feared that the arrest of more Europeans would unfavorably reflect on their vigilance in the past and thus more surely expose them to the Emperor's ire. These missionaries felt so secure that on two occasions they even dared to hold public processions in a town whose mandarin had secretly become a Catholic. In this manner, active missionary work continued more or less openly wherever there was a local lull in persecution.

Su. 368 ff.

To the great joy of the Bishop, his intrepid coadjutor and another priest were smuggled back into China and soon joined him. Now, worn out by thirty years of unremitting toil—he had never left his mission to return to Europe or even to take a rest elsewhere—the prelate realized that his days were numbered. He therefore left the care of the Vicariate to his coadjutor and reserved to himself only a small district where he might work till death would claim him.

Su. 408 ff.

Three years later, on September 28, 1792, the valiant old missionary went to his reward. Though it was important to avoid attracting the attention of the authorities, a large number of his Christians insisted on accompanying the body to the grave. Despite efforts of the priests to avoid anything spectacular, even the beggars of the city contributed money to make his funeral as solemn as possible.

Su. X ff.

Bishop Pottier is venerated as the Founder of the Catholic Missions in the immense Province of Szechwan. Although others had labored there before him, it was only under his leadership that the mission really developed. Where there had been only 3,000 Christians on his arrival, there were more than 25,000 at the time of his death. During the twenty-three years of his episcopate, nearly a 100,000 souls had been regenerated for Christ in the redeeming waters of Baptism.

Throughout his long life Bishop Pottier remained attached to the Holy Ghost Seminary in which he had found his vocation.

Su. 434

Nearly every year he managed to smuggle out of China a letter addressed to Father Bouic or to his successor Father Becquet. Their answers, however, only rarely reached him in the hiding places of Szechwan. Nevertheless, he continued writing. As he expressed it in one of his letters:

> Gratitude dictates this duty to me, and death alone will be able to prevent me from fulfilling it. God forbid that I ever forget the inestimable benefits I have received in the Seminary.

CHAPTER FOUR

FROM THE RESTORATION TO THE ENTRANCE OF THE VENERABLE FRANCIS LIBERMANN, 1802-1848

1. *The First Restoration*

N. B. 243 ff.

cf. p. 29

One of the Holy Ghost Fathers who had gone into exile during the French Revolution was Father James Bertout (1753-1832), a nephew of Father Duflos, the Superior General. As we have seen in Chapter II, he had accompanied Father de Glicourt on the voyage to Guiana which had ended in shipwreck off the coast of Africa and indirectly brought about the recapture of Senegal by France. Back in Paris, he had been appointed professor of theology first at Paris and then at Meaux. In 1787 he was elected Assistant to the General and in that capacity he had witnessed the horrors of the Revolution. While secretly administering the sacraments in his native diocese of Boulogne, he had suffered betrayal and fled to England just in time to avoid arrest.

N. B. 245

In 1802 peace between Church and State was finally declared in France. Eager to resume his duties, Father Bertout returned at once to Paris, where everything had to be started all over again. Close by the Seminary he found his seventy-six-year-old uncle, sick, blind, his mind no longer lucid, and wholly incapable of exercising his function as Superior General. The other members of the Congregation were all scattered and had assumed positions in various dioceses which, because of the scarcity of priests, they could not easily abandon. Moreover, they showed little interest in the restora- of the Congregation. With no money, no house, no students, no personnel, and a Superior General in his dotage, they felt it was hopeless even to think of it. Father Bertout, however, was not the man to give up so easily. Courageously and almost singlehandedly he undertook the task and finally succeeded in spite of almost insuperable odds.

Fl. 472 f.

The first step was to get permission from the Government for the Restoration. For this purpose a joint memorandum was addressed to Napoleon by the Vincentians, the Foreign Missions of Paris, and Father Bertout for the Spiritans. In reply, Napoleon

51

issued a decree enjoining these three societies to fuse into one centralized missionary institute. None of the three societies, however, reacted favorably toward this forced union. They fully realized it could not be carried out.[1] Consequently, the affair remained unsettled till 1804 when Pope Pius VII came to Paris to crown Napoleon. On that occasion the Pontiff presented the Emperor with a memorandum containing twelve articles regarding the Church in France. Father Bertout had previously appealed to the Pope and personally saw to it that one of these articles demanded the restoration of his congregation and seminary. The following year, in compliance with the Pope's wishes, Napoleon legally restored the Congregation and gave back the old Spiritan property of "La Chyperie," near Orleans. (All the others had been sold.) Strengthened by this initial success, Father Bertout determined to do his utmost to regain possession of the Congregation's former seminary buildings in Paris, for the remote location of "La Chyperie" made it quite unsuitable for his purposes. While biding his time in this respect, he did not remain idle. He rented a building in the *Rue du Cherche-Midi,* and opened a college and junior seminary whose student body soon numbered a hundred and thirty, of which twenty-five were seminarians. In 1824 this work was transferred to a building adjoining the old Motherhouse in the *Rue Lhomond.*

*N. D. 25 f.

2. *New Suppression and Restoration*

N. B. 248 f.

Soon, however, Napoleon was once more in conflict with the Pope and his troops were marching off to occupy the Eternal City. Realizing where the traditional sympathies of the Holy Ghost Fathers lay, he impulsively decreed the Society's suppression in 1809. Undeterred by this outburst of imperial ire, Father Bertout simply continued to run his college and seminary, for he knew well that time always has its way with tyrants. Meanwhile he devoted his attention to the sadly neglected state of the Faith in the colonies, and did what he could to remedy it.

*N. D. 27

N. B. 251 ff.

After the fall of Napoleon, in 1814, when the restored monarchy immediately demanded a large number of missionaries for these colonies, Father Bertout pointed out that he could not do anything until the Congregation was legally restored and reestablished

N. B. 250

[1]For the same reason this proposed fusion was rejected again in 1806 when Cardinal Joseph Fresch, the Chaplain General of France, urged a similar idea.

in the possession of its former properties. His persistent pressure finally produced the desired result: a royal decree of February 3, 1816 proclaimed the reestablishment of the Congregation and officially charged it with providing clergy for all French colonies; its properties were returned to it, and an annual subsidy of 5,000 francs was granted. Unfortunately, the restitution of the properties was found to be against the Concordat and the documents had to be rescinded. Nothing daunted, Father Bertout reopened his senior seminary in a rented building in 1817 and continued his battle to repossess the former seminary properties.

The struggle seemed hopeless, for the Department of Education had rented the buildings from their new owners. It turned them over to the State Superior Normal School, and this institution had no intention to leave its roomy quarters. Quietly Father Bertout entered into negotiations with the owners and privately arranged to have the property sold to the Congregation. Just to make sure, the contract specified that if such a sale would be vetoed by the Government, the priest himself would buy it in his own name. In either case he would become the Normal School's landlord, and thus be in a position to refuse renewal of the lease in a few years' time. After much haggling, the Government was induced to let the Congregation buy back its former property. In the end it agreed and, surprisingly enough, even paid the bill of sale. By a stroke of luck, the recalcitrant Normal School incurred the displeasure of King Louis XVIII and was temporarily suppressed in 1822. Thus after twenty years of continuous strife, Father Bertout's efforts were finally crowned with success and the Congregation was once more established in its ancient Motherhouse.

3. *Approval by the Holy See*

The Holy See itself was impressed by the energy, perseverance and businesslike way in which Father Bertout had handled all these negotiations, as well as by his zeal for a religious revival in the colonies. When the Propaganda expressed a desire to see the Rules of the Congregation, Father Bertout promptly dispatched a copy, making known at the same time his wish to see them approved by the Holy See. A few years later—Rome always moves slowly in such affairs—formal approval was given to the Rule. The only change that had to be made was the explicit recognition of

Margin notes: *N. D. 28 f. N. B. 254 ff. *N. D. 31 ff. A. R. 34, 200 f. N. B. 271 ff.

the Propaganda's authority with respect to anything pertaining to the missions. By this approval, dated February 7, 1824, the Congregation changed its status from that of a purely diocesan institute to one that was immediately dependent on the Holy See. However, the right to confirm the Superior General still remained in the hands of the Archbishop of Paris. With all other details out of the way, Father Bertout was now able to re-open his junior seminary in the fall of that same year.

*N. D. 37 ff.

N. B. 269 f.

4. New Dangers and Trials

Fl. 491

The restoration of the Monarchy after the fall of Napoleon was accompanied by a revival of Gallicanism. In 1816 the French Government went so far as to impose the teaching of Gallican principles on the seminaries of France. True to its proud traditions, the Congregation turned a deaf ear to this order. As a result, its relations with the Government became more and more strained, although, as mentioned above, Father Bertout still succeeded in obtaining the restoration of the Seminary and even several grants for maintenance and repairs.

N. B. 278

A new danger arose in 1825 when a committee of French Bishops decided that they must have the buildings in the *Rue Lhomond* for their proposed Institute of Higher Ecclesiastical Studies. Apparently, the intention was to do away with the Holy Ghost Seminary and let each diocese of France supply two priests for the colonial missions. It was only with considerable manoeuvering that Father Bertout succeeded in side-stepping this threat.

N. B. 279 f.

Religious persecution flared out more openly again in 1828. The Jesuits saw their colleges closed, and the following year Parliament once more debated the suppression of the Spiritans. Fortunately, the final vote was favorable to the Congregation. Shortly after, the 1830 revolution overthrew the Monarchy of the Bourbons. In the ensuing riots, Father Bertout had to stand by and watch powerlessly while surging mobs invaded his houses and pillaged everything he had built up at the cost of so much labor.

Fl. 492 ff.

Still worse trials lay ahead for him. The new government of King Philip disliked the Congregation and wanted very much to exclude its priests from the colonies. After first forcing the closure of its junior seminary in 1830, the Ministry cut off all subsidies, leaving Father Bertout no alternative but to send home his senior seminarians. Politically speaking, this government action was sheer folly, for, as the former Colonial Minister pointed out to his new successor:

Fl. 493

> The colonies have been deliberately deprived of the only institution that is able to render less dangerous the now inevitable changes in the situation of the slaves and the rights of the colored people.

With the aid of the Propaganda, Father Bertout reopened his seminary again in 1831, although necessarily on a reduced scale because of lack of funds. Meanwhile however, most of his associates had lost heart and withdrew in despair.

N. B. 282 ff.

The following year struck a last cruel blow at the intrepid old man. Cholera had broken out among the French troops and assumed such proportions that military hospitals were unable to care for all the sick and dying. Moved by their plight, Father Bertout allowed the seminary buildings to be requisitioned as an emergency hospital, after exacting from the Government a precautionary written guarantee that the house would be immediately evacuated after the disease had subsided. But when the danger was over, the ungrateful Government refused to return the seminary to its owners. This was the last straw. After thirty years of intense struggle, dashed hopes, and ceaseless harassments, the eighty year old Superior General found himself almost in the same position as when he had so hopefully started the work of restoration: most of his students had left, his funds were cut off, nearly all his confreres had abandoned him, and the government had seized his buildings once more. The shock was too much. He died before the end of the year 1832. Had he lived in happier times, his achievements undoubtedly would have rivalled the magnificent record of Father Bouic in the eighteenth century. As it is, his indomitable energy, perseverance, and diplomacy in the service of God saved the Congregation from what would otherwise have been inevitable extinction.

Br. 172

Goyau, I, 361 f.

Despite the multiple tragedies he had to sustain, Father Bertout succeeded in sending out to the colonies ninety-seven priests in the fifteen years preceding his death. For the sake of comparison, we may give here the figures of the Foreign Mission Seminary of Paris which, like all orders and congregations, had to make a fresh start after the French Revolution. Between 1804 and 1815 it was able to send only two priests to the Far East. In 1822 the number of its seminarians did not amount to more than seven, and 1831 the total number of its missionaries was only fifty-three. Thus we see that, in comparison to this sister institution, the Spiritans could boast of consoling success even during these years of profound crisis.

5. *Father Amable Fourdinier*

Fl. 496 ff.
N. B. 290 ff.

At the death of Father Bertout there were only three Holy Ghost Fathers left in the seminary: his nephew, Father Amable Fourdinier (1788-1845), who had formerly been a professor at the seminary of Boulogne; Father Hardy, a rich young man, somewhat

pp. 113 f.

mentally unbalanced and emotionally abnormal, who later had to be expelled for persistently fomenting revolt in the seminary; and Father Carandiou, a recent recruit, who did not persevere. With a special dispensation, however, Father Carandiou was allowed to vote in the election of the new Superior. If this had not been the case, Father Hardy might have aspired to the position, for it was unlikely that Father Fourdinier would have voted for himself. As it is, Father Fourdinier was elected to assume the unenviable task. He had been Father Bertout's assistant since 1817 and was all too well informed about the mighty problems facing him. It required almost heroic courage to accept the burden that was laid on his frail shoulders. Humanly speaking, it would have been so much more attractive to return to his professorship at Boulogne or accept an honorable and less heartbreaking function in the diocese of Paris and let the Congregation die a natural death.

Attacking the most urgent problems immediately, Father Fourdinier succeeded in obtaining several excellent new associates, such

N. B. 292 f.

as Father Warnet and Father Gaultier who, after their probation, became members of the Congregation. He then resumed negotiations with the Government to have the armed forces evacuate his seminary buildings. Forcefully pointing out the illegality of the whole affair, he succeeded in getting the support of the powerful Ministers of the Navy, the Treasury, and Ecclesiastical Affairs, who finally persuaded their recalcitrant colleague of the Army to surrender the property he was arbitrarily occupying. In 1835 the soldiers left, and the Congregation at last had full use of the whole complex of buildings belonging to it.

Father Francis Becquet, fourth Superior General of the Congregation of the Holy Ghost (1763-1788).

Father James M. Duflos, fifth Superior General of the Congregation of the Holy Ghost (1788-1805).

Father James M. Bertout, sixth Superior
General of the Congregation of the Holy
Ghost (1805-1832).

Father Amable Fourdinier, seventh Superior
General of the Congregation of the Holy
Ghost (1832-1845).

N. B. 293 f.
Fl. 509 ff.

There remained one hurdle to be overcome before the Seminary could efficiently fulfill its function. In the past, Government subsidies had provided most of the funds necessary for the training of the colonial clergy. Now the income of the Seminary consisted almost entirely of gifts sent to it by former students working in the colonies. Although substantial when compared to a missionary's income, these benefactions were far from adequate to maintain a good-sized seminary. The only solution seemed to lie in a renewed battle for subsidies.

At this juncture, political events came to the rescue. The abolition of slavery in the colonies was in the air and, since the Government anticipated serious trouble, it wanted to prepare the slaves for their emancipation by instructing them in religious and moral principles. Accordingly, a plan was set up to multiply churches and schools which would be staffed by priests, Brothers and Sisters. A special budget was set aside for this purpose and 50,000 francs a year, enough to maintain about sixty seminarians, was allocated to the Congregation. The Government suddenly realized that it had been acting against its own interests in harassing the Spiritans and now humbly wrote to their Superior:

N. B. 294

The Seminary of the Holy Ghost is now the only Congregation which, by the very purpose of its institution, is capable of training and supplying the colonies with priests who are thoroughly reliable, not only because of their good studies and purity of conduct, but also because of a special vocation, a zeal that is directed toward the very special situation at hand, and the unity of teaching which they all must follow. Accordingly, it is exclusively to you, Father, that we entrust the education, choice, and general direction of the priests called to work at the laborious and difficult task of morally training the colored in the colonies.

As far as the seminary was concerned, then, the situation had considerably improved since the death of Father Bertout.

6. *Attempted Incorporation of the Colonial Clergy into the Congregation*

Cl. C. 218 ff.

In the colonies entrusted to the Congregation, however, the situation was much different. Ever since the end of the Revolution the Government had been clamoring for priests and more priests, while at the same time all efforts to train them carefully were continually wrecked by official interference at home. In the colonies themselves Government officials often arbitrarily intervened in the appointments of priests, dismissing those who displeased them and accepting others at their own discretion. Sometimes those going to overseas territories were priests of doubtful character who were in trouble with their bishops and had gone to the colonies on their own initiative. To acquire some respectability, they usurped the title of "Holy Ghost Father," although they were neither members of the Congregation nor trained in its seminary.[2] Soon the colonial clergy was greatly discredited, precisely at a time when all eyes were turned on these colonies to watch the impending abolition of slavery. The Congregation was blamed for everything because it was officially in charge of the colonies. No one seemed to remember that it had no control whatsoever over the priests after they were sent out to these missions.

Fl. 523

Father Fourdinier's appeal for real authority over the priests in the colonies fell on deaf ears in Rome. The Propaganda feared that its authority would slowly be taken over by the Archbishop of Paris, who at that time still had the right to confirm the Superior General of the Congregation. To strengthen his position somewhat, Father Fourdinier was made a Prothonotary Apostolic (1839), but at that time this did not even involve a purple robe and a Monsignor's title. In any case, they would have been poor substitutes for real authority. It would have been relatively easy for the Propaganda to strengthen his position without sacrificing or endangering its own authority. If the Superior General had been appointed Prefect Apostolic of all the colonies with the right to delegate his powers to Vice Prefects in each of them, he would have obtained effective control. As a matter of fact, this system was adopted in the second half of the nineteenth century with respect to the Zanguebar and Congo missions entrusted to the Congregation.

N. B. 302

B. G. 5, 3 ; 9, 55

N. D. 11, 245
and 594

---

[2]The point may be illustrated with the story of Fathers Albertini, Paoli and Marchese. These three Corsican priests had no relation whatsoever to the Spiritans and had been refused permission to go to the colonies. They decided to go anyhow. In passing through the port of Le Havre they presented themselves as Holy Ghost Fathers and shocked everyone by their behavior. When shortly after them two genuine well-behaved Spiritans passed through the same port, no one wanted to believe that they were Holy Ghost Fathers.

N. D. 9 App.,
1 ff.
ibid. 12 ff.

ibid. 16 ff.

Cl. C. 252 ff.

B. G. 32, 428 f.

In an effort to remedy the situation, Father Fourdinier, in 1836, conceived a plan whereby he would absorb all colonial priests into his Congregation. The Propaganda regarded this utopian project as "very useful" but doubted that it could be put into practice. While allowing him to use persuasion, it definitely warned him not to force anyone to enter against his will. Father Fourdinier's first efforts at persuasion met with almost no results, but he did not give up hope and continued striving toward his goal for the next few years.

In reality, his plan was not as revolutionary as some people seem to have thought. In fact, it was rooted in a tradition that goes back to pre-revolutionary times for, as early as 1778, members of the Congregation had begun to go to the missions. At the outbreak of the Revolution in 1789, there were at least five members working in Guiana. They had joined the Spiritans with the

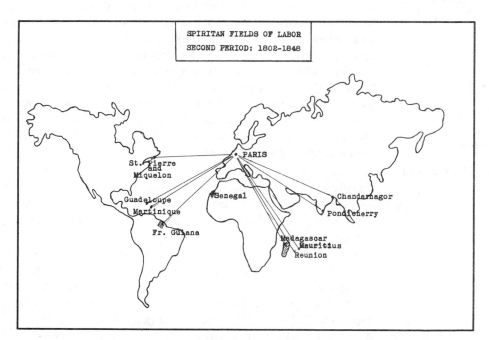

specific intention of doing missionary work. Extant records do not cover the matter with great clarity, but most likely the whole question of missionary members had been thoroughly discussed in 1778 when the first large territory was confided to the Congregation. In 1807, shortly after the restoration of the society, a plan similar to that of Fourdinier appeared in a memorandum of Father Perrin, the man whom Father Bertout had proposed as Prefect of the French West Indian Islands. Other proposals along the same line were made later by Bertout himself. For various reasons, however, all these plans had been shelved to await more auspicious times. As we will see in Chapter VI, it was only in 1848 under Father Libermann that this particular thread of eighteenth century Spiritan tradition came to full pattern.

N. D. 2, 10 ff.

Meanwhile a little group of future missionaries made an effort to join the Congregation for the very purpose Father Fourdinier and his predecessors had in mind. In 1840 he was approached by a seminarian, Frederick Le Vavasseur, who had been born and raised on the island of Reunion. The young man was introduced to him by Father Warnet, one of the directors of Holy Ghost Seminary. The two had met during Father Warnet's missionary years in the colonies. Le Vavasseur told him that, together with some other seminarians, they were going to start a new religious congregation dedicated to the christianization of the slaves in the colonies. They would like to associate themselves with the Holy Ghost Fathers to secure canonical and legal recognition. The idea pleased Fourdinier, but when it became clear that he wanted these priests to be wholly assimilated into the colonial clergy, the condition proved entirely unacceptable to them. They desired to live as religious and not as secular priests.

N. D. 2, 88 ff.

Approached again about the same matter somewhat later, Fourdinier expressed his willingness to entrust to them the complete service of Guiana. This offer too was rejected by their leader, Francis Libermann, because it would have meant limiting the scope of their congregation to one territory and engaging most of its members in ordinary parish work. Libermann desired to work in all the colonies alongside the Holy Ghost Fathers, but to devote his attention to the abandoned slaves and not to parish routine. The announcement of this intention made Father Fourdinier highly suspicious of the newly-projected Congregation. It meant competition, he thought, and all things considered, a dangerous competition. These men would have a number of well-trained and exceptionally fervent priests, who would contrast sharply with many members of the clergy then serving the colonies. Making inquiries about them, he found nothing reassuring. Their leader, Francis

Libermann, was known in ecclesiastical circles as an ambitious Jewish convert, who wanted to trick a bishop into ordaining him and was ruthlessly pursuing dreams of greatness. Sooner or later such a man was bound to try to replace the Holy Ghost Fathers with his own creation. Fourdinier decided to have nothing to do with the newcomers and resolved to oppose them wherever he could. Nonetheless, under governmental pressure and orders from the Propaganda he was forced to admit a few of them into the colonies.

N. D. 9 App., 64 ff.

Returning to his plans to incorporate the colonial clergy into the Congregation, he thought that perhaps a relaxation of the rules might produce the desired result. Accordingly, in 1843, he circulated an excerpt of the rule, adding to it a personal note in which he considerably toned down the practice of poverty. For his personal expenses each member was to receive a fixed sum along with the Mass stipends which he would be allowed to retain. Again, however, the response from the colonies was not sufficient to permit execution of the plan. Forced to postpone his project, Father Fourdinier planned to open a novitiate and start the integration by admitting the best of his seminarians into the Congregation. His death in 1845 put an end to all these schemes.

N. B. 302

Strict disciplinarian as he was, he had succeeded in giving back to the Seminary something of its former reputation for ecclesiastical learning and sound training of future priests.[3] This gain, however, was offset by his failure to solve the religious crisis in the colonies. He can hardly be blamed for a failure that stemmed ultimately from his lack of authority to solve the problem, but the resultant disorganization considerably weakened the Congregation's position and soon threatened its very existence.

7. *The Reform of Father Leguay*

N. B. 306 ff.

At the death of Fourdinier none of the four Holy Ghost Fathers in Paris felt equal to the formidable task facing them in

---

[3]An indication of the spirit of its teaching may be seen in the fact that years later Alexander Le Roy, the future Archbishop and Superior General, was at first refused permission to enter the Congregation by his Ecclesiastical Superior, Bishop Bravard of Coutances. This Gallicanistically inclined prelate repeatedly rejected Le Roy's plea on the ground that Father Gaultier, C.S.Sp., professor of theology at Holy Ghost Seminary, was too staunch a defender of the prerogatives of the Pope. Cf. Henri Goré, C.S.Sp., *Msgr. Alexandre Le Roy,* Paris, 1952, pp. 32 f.

the colonies. Father Nicolas Warnet (1795-1863), reluctantly agreed to act as Superior General while efforts were being made to have an outsider come in and assume charge. Negotiations were in progress with Father Alexander Leguay, the vicar general of the Bishop of Perpignan. He was a good friend of the Congregation, but there were already plans for him to succeed his bishop in Perpignan. After four months of deliberation, he generously made the sacrifice of ecclesiastical preferment and came to Paris to direct the Holy Ghost Congregation and Seminary. It was the first and only time in history that an outsider had to be called in to assume the superiorship.

Meanwhile, Father Warnet had limited himself to expediting current affairs which could not be delayed. Among the unfinished business he left for his successor was a new suggestion to unite

N. D. 5, 101 f.   with the Congregation of the Holy Heart of Mary. The Propaganda had spoken about it in a letter to Father Libermann in 1845 and suggested that he contact Father Warnet. The latter was very much in favor of it, but having accepted his position only to give Father Leguay time to make up his mind, he could not very well change the entire organization by taking such an important step.

N. D. 7, 478 ff.   Father Leguay (1794-1865), promptly decided to turn his back on Libermann's Congregation. Having lived at Holy Ghost Seminary in Fourdinier's time, he had heard scores of rumors about this "hypocritical schemer" and the trouble he had caused. His predecessor had been far too weak in his resistance, he thought. Now that he was in charge, he would show no mercy. Let the Government and the Propaganda insist as much as they liked, it would be only over his dead body that one of Libermann's men would be admitted to the colonies. Taking care of the neglected Negroes was part of the ordinary duties of pastors and did not require the services of a new congregation.

N. D. 9 App., 108 ff.   Energetically he went to work on the most pressing problem— the reorganization and reform of the colonial clergy. Taking up the plans of Father Fourdinier, he laid down the following rules:

1. Henceforth only aspirants to the Congregation would be admitted to the Seminary.

2. A novitiate of two years and a junior seminary were to be opened at once.

3. In the colonies, community life would be maintained as a rule.

4. Ecclesiastical Superiors in the Missions were to be chosen from among the members of the Congregation and were to remain subject to its Superior General.

5. Troublesome priests were to be recalled at once; the others were free to join the Congregation if they wished.

6. Each member might retain his salary and other income for his own expenses, without having to render an account to the Motherhouse, but once a year the surplus was to be put into a general fund.

His invitation to the colonial clergy to join under this easy rule of poverty had some results: about thirty were admitted to the novitiate before the end of 1848, including his own successor, the future Vicar Apostolic of Reunion, Father Alexander Monnet. Moreover, his threat of recalling troublesome priests was not idle: quite a few were forced to return to France.

Bio. 316   Turning his attention to the Seminary, he proceeded to eliminate rigorously anyone whose vocation appeared to him subject to doubt. At the same time he added three new priests to the seminary faculty. In addition, he made recruiting trips through several dioceses and succeeded in gaining several excellent vocations to swell the student body.

Bio. 314 f.   Meanwhile the Government was formulating its own program for religious service in the colonies and reportedly was planning to proceed again without Holy Ghost Seminary. Father Leguay moved in quickly. He argued forcefully on the basis of the Spiritans' past record of service and before long he had won his point. The Government hastened to assure him that they did not intend to eliminate Holy Ghost Seminary from their new plan of colonial administration.

Bio. 318 ff.   In introducing the above-mentioned changes in the rule, Father Leguay had overlooked the fact that he had no power to modify the rules of a pontifically approved Congregation. As a result, the canonical status of all newly-admitted members was irregular. In N. D. 9, App., rectifying this situation, the Propaganda granted the necessary dis-
186   pensation, but only for one year, thereby indicating that Leguay

had to conduct himself henceforth in accord with ecclesiastical law and the rules of the Society that he was governing.

N. D. 9 App., 210 f.

Strict canonical procedure was followed, therefore, in 1847 when Father Loewenbruck, who later was to play an important role in bringing about the entrance of Libermann and his Congregation, went to Rome with a new set of changes that had been agreed on by the Council of the Congregation. The salient points of these changes are listed here:

N. D. 9 App., 198 f.

1. The purpose of the Congregation is to educate *its members*[4] for the most abandoned works in the Church.

2. The Congregation depends only on the Holy See, but its members are under the jurisdiction of the ordinary of the place where they reside.

3. There are two orders of members; those of the first order who put their annual surplus into a common fund; those of the second order who have only spiritual bonds with the Congregation.

8. *New Threat of Suppression*

N. D. 10, 414

While Father Loewenbruck was in Rome, the February Revolution of 1848 broke out in Paris, the monarchy was abolished, and the Republic was proclaimed. The new Director of the Colonies, Mr. Victor Schoelcher, was violently opposed to slavery and somehow conceived the notion that Father Leguay was equally violent in his support of it. Seeing their chance, some priests who had been forced by Father Leguay to return to France presented themselves as victims of his anti-negro attitude. In short order, Mr. Schoelcher recalled the priests sent out by Father Leguay and restored the others to their former positions. Moreover, he openly threatened to finish off the Spiritans once and for all. Under the circumstances, Father Leguay realized that there was only one way to save the Congregation from this new danger: to resign immediately and have as his successor someone who was more acceptable to the new rulers of France. On March 2, 1848 the Congregation accepted his resignation. Shortly after, Father Leguay withdrew entirely from any association with it.

---

[4]The original text, with considerably more logic, used the word "clerics". See below p. 123, footnote 12.

In Rome meanwhile, the Propaganda, which was unaware of developments in Paris, had approved his unfortunate revision of the Rule on March 11, 1848. His changes had wrecked the community life of the Congregation by the practical abolition of poverty and burdened it with a second order for which it would be responsible in the public eye but over which it would have no control. In his eagerness to attract the necessary personnel, he had disregarded the existing rules of the Congregation and had liberally dispensed from them as the occasion seemed to demand. Many of the newly admitted priests were more or less members, but exactly to what extent they had bound themselves was difficult to determine. Through the many reform projects, the rule itself had grown quite confused. In the colonies, constant dismissals and appointments of ecclesiastical Superiors and parish priests arising out of the incessant conflicts between the Government and the Church had now reached a climax. It was doubtful whether anything could still be salvaged from the chaos that seemed to reign on all sides.

N. D. 9, App., 209 ff.

9. *Father Alexander Monnet*

Bio. 331 ff.

The most pressing problem facing the Congregation after Father Leguay's resignation was Mr. Schoelcher's threat to annihilate it. There was one man who could effectively neutralize this danger—Father Alexander Monnet (1812-1849). In 1840 Father Monnet had become a missionary in Reunion, where his excellent work among the slaves had made him known as "the Father of the Negroes" and a "second Peter Claver." In recognition of his merits, the Government had made him a Knight of the Legion of Honor. Returning to France in 1846, he had joined the Congregation. The next year he was sent back to Reunion. Shortly before his boat, the *Calcutta,* was due to arrive, French newspapers had reached the island reporting a demand of Mr. Schoelcher (then a member of Parliament) that the slaves be freed at once and without compensation to their owners.

N. D. 9 App., 184
Bio. 331 ff.

The whole island was in turmoil. Many falsely blamed Father Monnet for having had a hand in the plan. Therefore, when the arrival of the *Calcutta* was signalled to the island, an angry mob of slave-owners gathered on the docks. As soon as the priest descended into the little boat that was to row him ashore, he was greeted with threats and shouts: "Down with Monnet! Drown him! Kill him!" Somehow he reached the safety of a rectory, but for days angry mobs milled around it, hurling stones and demanding his death. Several times the police charged into the noisy rioters, leaving casualties but not restoring peace. Finally the Governor of the island capitulated to the crowd: he interned the priest in a hospital and sent him back to France on the first available boat. Dissatisfied with the Governor's cowardly behavior, Paris decided to withdraw him.

Meanwhile Mr. Schoelcher had become Director of the Colonies and Father Monnet was now something of a hero in the eyes of the new Director, for he had faced death and expulsion because of Schoelcher's plans. With Father Monnet as Superior General, Mr. Schoelcher could hardly execute his threat to suppress the Congregation. As a matter of fact, he expressed his pleasure at the election, though it did not prevent him from acting as a genuine cesaropapist in the matter of ecclesiastical appointments. He forced Father Monnet to accept his own candidates as Prefects Apostolic and to recall the priests who were currently occupying these posts. Moreover, he coldly announced his intention to immediately cut the Seminary's subsidy by fifty percent.

Bio. 342

One of the last acts of Father Monnet was to accept three new priests into the Congregation in August, 1848. It was a provisional admission, for by then the definite and final reorganization of the Holy Ghost Fathers was in an advanced stage of preparation. Fourdinier's nightmare was on the point of becoming a reality. Father Libermann was about to take over. If only he could have known it, the admission of the convert Jew and his confreres into the Congregation was destined to revitalize the old Society of the Holy Ghost, renovate its antiquated structure, flood it with a fervor it had not experienced for decades, and thus turn it into one of the greatest forces in the whole history of missionary activity.

CHAPTER FIVE

FRANCIS LIBERMANN AND HIS CONGREGATION OF THE HOLY HEART OF MARY

1. *His Early Life*

N. D. I, 4

Jacob, as he was called before his conversion, was born April 12, 1802,[1] the son of Rabbi Libermann of Saverne, Alsace. Destined by his father to become a Rabbi also, he was introduced at an early age to the Hebrew Scriptures and to other sacred Jewish texts such as the Mishna and the Talmud. Even the German he learned to read had to be in Hebrew characters. Neither he nor his brothers were ever permitted to study anything else, for in the eyes of his ultra-conservative father, sacred Scripture and other books of Hebrew learning contained all that it was necessary to know. With an intelligence matched only by his docility, Jacob acquired a profound knowledge of Jewish lore and seemed to justify his father's fondest dreams of a son who would become a great light in Israel.

N. D. I, 23 ff.

One can easily imagine the bitterness and grief of the old Rabbi when, after carefully training each of his nine children, he watched five of his sons turn away one by one from the Synagogue and become Catholics. The conversion of his beloved Jacob inflicted

N. D. I, 60 ff.

an especially deep wound. He had allowed this son to go to Metz for advanced rabbinical studies, but Jacob had used his time to become acquainted with European culture, studying French and Latin and avidly reading such contemporary best-sellers as Jean Jacques Rousseau's *Emile*. Soon he had given up the faith of his fathers and proudly described himself as a free-thinker. Introduced to Christianity by the reading of the New Testament in Hebrew and struck by the inner peace and happiness that seemed to radiate from his eldest brother who was converted in 1825, he let himself be persuaded to examine the credentials of the Catholic

---

N. D. 1, 4
N. D. 13 App.
89 ff.

[1]The year 1804, often given by biographers, is not exact. Jacob had eight brothers and sisters. Two of these, David (also called Christopher) and Nathanael (also called Alphons) migrated to the United States. Other immigrants from his immediate family were Lazarus Libman, the widower of Jacob's sister Esther, and their children.

N. D. I, 73   Church during a quiet retreat in Paris. After an agonizing inner struggle, he finally capitulated to grace and was baptized on Christmas eve, 1826, taking the names of Francis, Mary, and Paul.

L. S. 4, 327

N. D. I, 157

N. D. I, 351

N. D. I, 664

From the very first moment of his conversion, God granted extraordinary favors to this young man, whose moral life had remained unsullied even during the days of his agnosticism. Shortly after his conversion he was raised to the state of passive prayer, a supernatural privilege which lasted for about five years. Having manifested a desire to become a priest, he was admitted in 1827 to the seminary of St. Stanislas, and later that same year he transferred to St. Sulpice. Struck down by epilepsy shortly before he was scheduled to receive the subdiaconate, he was allowed to stay on in the Sulpician seminary of Issy because he exerted such an extraordinarily wholesome influence over his fellow students. In 1837, although only in minor orders, he was offered the position of Novice Master by the Eudist Fathers who were then slowly recovering from their suppression by the French Revolution. He remained in that difficult position directing priest-novices until 1839. It was then he became convinced that God wanted him to take charge of a project launched by some of his former associates at St. Sulpice in behalf of the neglected slaves in the French colonies.[2]

2. *The Foundation of the Congregation of the Holy Heart of Mary*

N. D. I, 589 ff. ; 599 ff.

First Origins. The first idea of seriously undertaking the Christianization of slaves in the French colonies and other West Indian islands had come from two seminarians—Frederick Le Vavasseur (1811-1882), and Eugene Tisserant (1814-1846) Frederic had been born in Reunion, the son of one of the island's most prominent families. Received in St. Sulpice, he began to think about the sad state of neglect and ignorance in which the slaves on his father's estate and on neighboring plantations dragged out their existence. He foresaw terrible consequences to the impending emancipation unless the slaves were morally prepared for

---

[2]It is hoped that the reader will not find this sketch of Father Libermann's early life too brief. His story is sufficiently well known to justify the succinct character of its presentation here. Moreover, a penetrating study of his life and personality by Father Adrian L. van Kaam, C.S.Sp., will follow in the *Spiritan Series* of DUQUESNE STUDIES.

N. D. I, 628 f.   freedom. From time to time he spoke about his preoccupations with his fellow seminarian and friend, Francis Libermann.

N. D. I, 647 ff.   At about the same time, Libermann was being consulted on similar matters by Eugene Tisserant, the son of a Haitian mother. Tisserant also traced the shocking conditions of Haiti's recently liberated slaves to a lack of Christian instruction and guidance.

N. D. I, 633 f.   Hardly acquainted with each other, the two young men went on the same day, February 2, 1839, to the shrine of Our Lady of Victories in Paris to recommend their intentions to Father Desgenettes, the Director of the Shrine and of its Archconfraternity. The pious priest introduced them to each other and enjoined them to pray for divine guidance. Shortly thereafter, a courageous director at the Sulpician seminary, Father Pinault, allowed them to plan the establishment of a community which would devote itself to the evangelization of abandoned slaves.

Consulted again by both separately, Libermann gave his blessing to the project, but advised them to go slowly. Frederic was

N. D. I, 636   all fire and had already chosen a name for the new society: the Congregation of the Holy Cross. He wanted all seminarians who were interested in the plan to go to Rennes, where, he assumed, they could easily make their novitate under Francis Libermann, the expert spiritual director and Novice Master. This arrange-

N. D. I, 659 ff.   ment, however, was broached at a most inopportune moment. Just at that time Francis was experiencing great difficulties in his position and saw the day approaching when it would be morally impossible for him to continue his task, no matter how much the Eudist Fathers wanted him to stay.

Sensing this uncertainty, Mr. de la Brunière, a rich young man and former fellow seminarian, came to consult Francis about the venture and tried his best to persuade him to join them. Despite the fact that the idea intrigued him, Francis hesitated. The only thing that mattered for him was God's will, and at that moment he was groping for guidance. He preferred therefore to wait for

N. D. I, 660   a surer sign from heaven. On two successive occasions about a month later, God granted him an extraordinary insight into the future and a preview of his role in the new work. When the voice of his spiritual director added itself to these graces, all hesitation was gone. Ridiculous as it may sound, he, a poor uncured epileptic, permanently barred from ordination, lacking influence and wealth, assumed leadership of the project.

N. D. I, 670 ff.

N. D. 2, 88

Voyage to Rome. The first thing on the agenda, he felt, was to obtain from Rome a word of approval or permission. He started off for Marseilles, where de la Brunière was to join him, and stopped at Lyons to seek out the Superior of the Jesuits in order to get his reaction to the plan. Looking at the emaciated and poorly-clad ex-seminarian, whose facial contortions and poorly controlled voice marked him as the victim of some sort of neurosis, this worthy Superior listened for a short time in polite silence. The convert Jew was propounding fantastic plans. When he could no longer contain himself, he burst out laughing and without a word left the room. Others rebuffed Libermann in similar ways. Only Father Pinault, his Sulpician director, supported him. Because of this encouragement and the conviction that he was doing God's will, Francis was not much perturbed by what people said or did. Unless and until the Church itself turned him down, he would persevere in his efforts to the end.

Early in January 1840, he arrived in Rome with his companion, de la Brunière, who had covered the cost of the trip. The time was not very propitious for the presentation of such plans in the center of the Church. Just then Rome was suspicious of anything coming out of France. Planners were literally arriving in droves. As Cardinal Sala, the Prefect of the Congregation of Bishops and

N. D. 2, 3

Religious, dryly told Dom Guéranger in 1837, "Not a day passes without some request coming in from beyond those mountains for the approval of rules and new congregations. In France there are only founders."

Looking for special support, Francis took into his confidence a former friend and fellow seminarian, Monsignor de Conny, then residing in Rome. The Monsignor listened and frowned. By what devious ways this little fellow was trying to get himself ordained despite his illness! Immediately he warned other ecclesiastics who

N. D. 2, 1,ff.

might be approached by Francis, such as Father Vaures and the two influential French Jesuits, John de Rozaven and Philip de Villefort. Soon Libermann was depicted as a dangerous and irresponsible psychotic who had already succeeded in turning the heads of some seminarians and was now trying to fool the Pope himself. Together with Monsignor de Conny, Father de Villefort did his best to talk some sense into de la Brunière. Making use of confidential information received from Libermann in the course of spiritual direction (Francis had chosen him as director and confessor during his stay in Rome) de Villefort succeeded in persuading the young man to return to France and give up his dreams of founding a new society.[3] Afterwards, Francis alluded to this painful experience when he wrote to a friend:

N. D. 2, 146

> For two days I was sorely tempted against charity with respect to these persons and what they had done. Then I went to see my confessor [de Villefort] and told him everything that was going on in me. The effect was perfect, for I was entirely freed from my temptation.

Only one man was willing to help him in Rome—Dr. Drach, another convert Jew, famous for his learning, who was then librarian of the Propaganda. Years before, Dr. Drach had been influential in bringing Francis into the Church. Now the two went to an audience with Pope Gregory XVI, who put his hand in blessing on Libermann's head. When Francis had withdrawn, the saintly old Pontiff asked Dr. Drach about his companion. At the end of

N. D. 2, 55

the pathetic story, Gregory concluded the audience with these words: *"Sarà un santo!"* "He will be a saint."

N. D. 2, 4 ff.;
69 ff.

Encouragement by the Propaganda. On Dr. Drach's advice Libermann presented the Propaganda with a memorandum describing his plan. He did not ask for formal recognition, but only whether in conscience he would be allowed to proceed. With complete objectivity, he added that he felt it would be possible to find recruits but that he himself suffered from the canonical impediment of epilepsy, which, however, was decreasing in violence. The answer was slow in coming. A visit he made to the Propaganda was quite discouraging. The Secretary coldly told him that he would have to be a priest before anything could be discussed, for "one does not treat about a future society of priests with a simple cleric." It was not a formal refusal but it seemed to leave little hope.

There was, however, a definite purpose behind the somewhat chilly reply. The Propaganda always acts with the utmost prudence. It wanted time to investigate him. In the interim, there was no point in raising hopes which, considering the information locally

---

N. D. 2, 61 f.

[3]Libermann and de la Brunière always remained on friendly terms. De la Brunière joined the Foreign Mission of Paris, was sent to China and appointed Vicar Apostolic and Bishop of Tremita. He disappeared in 1846. Four years later it was learned that in July 1846 he had been murdered by marauding tribesmen.

N. D. 2, 77 ff.

N. D. 2, 14 f.

obtainable, had little chance of being realized. After the arrival of a highly favorable report from the Papal Nuncio at Paris, however, the Propaganda debated the whole affair in council and, once the Pope's approval had been obtained, decided to do even more than Libermann had asked. On June 6, 1840, it encouraged him and his companions to persevere in their plan and expressed the hope that his health would improve sufficiently to permit his ordination to the priesthood. As usual, a formal approval would be forthcoming only when the new society had demonstrated its vitality by several years of successful operation. This was more than anyone had dared to hope for.

With some difficulty the messenger from the Propaganda discovered the whereabouts of the humble acolyte, who apparently had not even left an address. He was found sharing an attic with a flock of pigeons in the *Vicolo del Pinacolo,*[4] one of Rome's numerous back alleys. When Libermann came to thank the Cardinal Prefect of the Propaganda, His Eminence urged Francis not to hesitate about being ordained, and Bishop Caladini, the Cardinal's secretary, made it clear that if he could not find a bishop willing to ordain him, the Propaganda itself would assume the responsibility.[5]

N. D. 2, 6 ff.

While waiting for a decision on his ordination, Francis used his time to compose a provisional rule for the new society, which he dedicated to the Holy Heart of Mary. Later, in September 1840, he began to write his spiritual commentary on the Gospel of St. John. Toward the end of the year, when there was still no news

N. D. 2, 31

about his ordination, he set out on foot to make a pilgrimage to the Holy House of Loretto. Once there, he longed to hide himself in the numerous grottoes of the mountains to spend the rest of his life with God and God alone, far from the hustle and bustle of man! But at Loretto God favored him again with extraordinary graces

---

[4]Although this alley was demolished in Mussolini's removal of Roman slums, the attic occupied by Father Libermann was rebuilt from the original materials on one of the loggias of the French Seminary in Rome.

N. D. 2, 28; 33

[5]Shortly after, however, both Father de Villefort and Bishop Caladini suddenly changed their mind about taking this step. Undoubtedly, they were influenced by new unfavorable rumors about the convert Jew, who continued to be plagued by defamation until his very death. A year later, Father de Villefort regretted his attitude so much that he wrote Libermann a letter beseeching him in the name of God and the Blessed Virgin to persevere in his plans, and become ordained, because, as he now recognized, it was in accord with God's will.

N. D. 2, 228 and showed clearly that for him the divine will lay in an active life consecrated to the service of souls. Since God's will was all that mattered for him, he hurried back to Rome shortly before Christmas, stopping only to make a brief visit to Assisi and become a member of the Third Order of St. Francis.

N. D. 2, 374 ff. *Ordained a Priest.* Back in his attic, a letter from Strassburg was waiting for him. His brother, Dr. Samson Libermann, wrote that Bishop Raess, the Coadjutor of the Diocese of Strassburg, was willing to accept him in the seminary and prepare him for ordina-
N. D. 2, 400 tion. It was imperative that he come to Strassburg as soon as possible. Exactly one year after his arrival in the Eternal City, Francis left, travelling by coach to Alsace. In February 1841, after an interruption of ten years, he re-entered the seminary.[6] Seven months later, on September 18, he was ordained a priest forever by Bishop Mioland of Amiens.

N. D. 2, 427 Profoundly moved by the supernatural happiness radiating from the man upon whom he had just imposed hands, the Bishop spoke
N. D. 2, 423 about him later the same day to some Jesuits of St. Acheul who had come to a meeting in his palace with the Vicar Generals of the
Br. 94 diocese. "Libermann!" they exclaimed. "Sorry to say so, Your Excellency, but your good nature has been imposed on. The man you have ordained cannot persevere anywhere. He causes trouble wherever he goes. You have made yourself responsible for something which you are going to regret." Poor Francis surely was out of favor with the Society of Jesus, although he always had the greatest respect for it.[7] Fortunately, one of his former directors at St. Sulpice, Father Mollevaut, happened to visit the Bishop late the same evening and was able to restore peace to the Prelate's troubled mind by telling him the truth about Francis. He con-

---

N. D. 2, 408 ff.
[6]Although Libermann kept himself in the background during the short time he spent there, he made a profound impression on all he met. Several of the most distinguished early members of the congregation followed him from this seminary: Ignatius Schwindenhammer, his succesor as Superior General; Aloysius Kobès, the future Bishop of the Two Guineas; Melchior Freyd, theologian and Superior of the French Seminary in Rome; John, Burg and John Bangratz, professors at the seminary of Strassburg. Bangratz, then a seminarian, was the one whose impersonation of a Rabbi on the day of Libermann's arrival had injected a painful note into an otherwise happy day.

[7]Cf. his kindly judgment of the Jesuits in *N. D.* 1,468. In later years, when they became better acquainted with him, the Jesuits of France learned to esteem the holiness and diplomacy of the Venerable Francis Libermann.

N. D. 2, 424   cluded his commendation by saying: "Your Excellency, what you
have done today is the most magnificent deed of your life."

N. D. 3, 1   *Opening of the Novitiate.* Only nine days after his ordination,
Francis opened the first novitiate of the new society at la Neuville,
Amiens, close to the Jesuit College of St. Acheul. Almost im-
N. D. 3, 373   mediately an incident arose. The Jesuit Superior, Father Sellier,
feared that the newcomers would soon take over all ministry
in the surroundings. He was much annoyed to see them settle in
the neighborhood and went to warn the Bishop that he had admitted a troop of schemers into his diocese. However, when he
noticed that Francis and his companions did not try to supplant
the Jesuits, he changed his mind and told the Bishop that these men
were true saints whose prayers did a lot of good for the diocese.
Through it all, Francis was indifferent to what people, even good
and holy people, said about him. He quietly went about his tasks
directing the nascent foundation.

N. D. 3, 366 ff.   Two novices had arrived with him—Father Le Vavasseur and
Mr. Marcellin Collin, still a seminarian. Others were momentarily
delayed, but followed soon. A house had graciously been put at
their disposal by the diocese—thanks to Father de Brandt, the
Bishop's secretary.[8] The kind Sisters of a nearby convent had
furnished it soberly but sufficiently. Materially speaking, the new
community was better off than many others at their first begin-
N. D. 3, 424 ff.;   nings. Trouble, however, arose from an unexpected angle. Both
4, 187 ff.   Le Vavasseur and Tisserant, who arrived later, felt that they ought
to have more to say over the young congregation and its rules.
Le Vavasseur was especially vehement in trying to make his own
extravagant ideas prevail.[9] He developed such an antagonism that,
no matter what Libermann said or did about anything at all, he at
once took the opposite stand. It was an attitude which some of his
biographers have been able to explain only as the result of a dia-
bolical temptation.

---

[8]Father de Brandt was a former novice of the Eudists, who had caused
untold troubles to Father Libermann during his period as Novice Master in
Rennes. De Brandt finally left and became a secular priest. Throughout
his life he remained very devoted to the Venerable and to his work. On
at least two occasions he exercised considerable influence on its early
orientation.

[9]To give a few examples: he wanted to allow only one meal a day, no
beds, no private rooms, and only one common room to serve all purposes.

At length, things got so bad that Father Libermann thought it best to give him a chance to acquire some experience and maturity

N. D. 3, 134
of judgment. Accordingly, four months after his arrival, Father Le Vavasseur made his consecration to the apostolate and left

N. D. 3, 402
for the island of Reunion in the Indian Ocean. The same solution was found for Father Tisserant. Three months after entering the novitiate he was on his way to Martinique, where he awaited his

N. D. 2, 438;
cf. p. 137
chance to enter strife-torn Haiti. These two departures had been preceded by that of Father James Laval, who, without benefit of a novitiate, set sail for Mauritius in June, 1841.[10] Scarcely a year after the opening of its first house, therefore, some of the most prominent members of the Congregation of the Holy Heart of Mary had already gone out to labor in abandoned regions of the Lord's vineyard.

3. *The Resumption of the African Missions*

Africa in the Sixteenth and Seventeenth Century. As late as the middle of the nineteenth century most of Africa was still *terra incognita,* a land of mystery. Contemporary maps sketched out its coastline and its trading posts, leaving the rest blank or filling it with fanciful pictures of dangerous animals. From the standpoint of religion, the situation was hardly any better. The island dioceses of Cape Verde (1532) and San Tomé (1534) exercised jurisdic-

M. M. A. 2, 26
tion over the mainland from Cape Palmas to the Cape of Good Hope.

M. M. A. 1,
86 ff. ; 2, 209 ff.
da Silva, 259 ff.
R. H. M. 8,
481 ff.
M. M. A. 3, 553
da Silva, 281 ff.
M. M. A. 1,
Back in 1490, Portuguese missionaries had arrived in the Congo, and the Jesuits began to work there in 1548. They were followed by Capuchin priests and other missionaries. Success quickly attended their efforts, and soon the whole royal court of the Congo was baptized. In 1596 Pope Clement VIII established a special diocese in Angola and the Congo. As early as 1512, and again in 1608, the native kings sent an embassy to the Pope to acknowledge their submission to his authority. By the middle of

---

Br. 101 f.
[10]The ease with which Father Libermann dispensed in whole or in part from the novitiate must not be seen in the light of modern canonical requirements, which date only from 1894. Strange as it may sound, in Libermann's time Rome regarded the novitiate as something proper to the old religious orders and did not favor it for mere congregations. Thus it was rather common practice to shorten it if need arose or even to allow priests to make it privately as best as they could.

270; 5, 393

the seventeenth century there was a large number of Christians, although for the most of them it was merely a question of Christian baptism and not of Christian life.

Groves I,
132 ff.
da Silva, 323 ff.

da Silva, 225 ff.
G. C. M. H. 6

On the east coast, the Jesuits had established the first missions in Mozambique in 1560. Seventy years later they and the Dominicans served a total of twenty-one stations there, and the Augustinians had made a foundation at Mombasa in Kenya. Abyssinia admitted Jesuit missionaries in 1557 and again in 1622, but it expelled them eight years later.

ibid., 14

In the northern part of West Africa, Mass had been offered as early as 1482 in the Gold Coast region. In fact, the church developed to a point where natives of this area had been sent to Lisbon to study for the priesthood. In 1495 they returned to their country and began to preach in the territory around the Gulf of Guinea.

ibid., 20 ff.

In 1572 Portuguese Augustinians undertook missionary work there, but a few years later the natives plundered their mission stations and their efforts came to nought. The Capuchins took over in 1637. Despite a frightful mortality rate, they established flourishing missions in Guinea, but their work came to an end about twenty-five years later when the Dutch captured this territory.

ibid., 32 ff.

ibid., 67 ff.
Goyau, I,
288 ff.

The Dominicans tried again in 1687, but failed and withdrew in 1703 or 1704. The seventeenth century saw other Capuchin missions established in Sierre Leone, but these too were of brief duration. With Pombal's suppression of religious orders in Portugal, all Portuguese missions slowly disappeared for lack of personnel. A few lazy and ignorant native priests were all that was left of the once-flourishing mission of Angola, which at an earlier date had even boasted a native African bishop.[11]

The only other ecclesiastical jurisdiction in Negro Africa was the prefecture of Senegal, entrusted since 1779 to the Holy Ghost Fathers.[12] However, the activity of its few priests was largely limited to the town of St. Louis and the little island of Gorée. It was not that the priests sent there by the Congregation were disinterested in the natives and preferred to lead an easy life in more

M. M. A. 1,
417 ff.

cf. pp. 442 f.
N. D. 5, 142

[11]Prince Henry, the twenty-four-year-old son of the native king, named by Pope Leo X, May 8, 1518.

[12]We prescind here from the Vincentian missions in Ethiopia (1839) and Egypt (1844) and the Vicariate of Cape of Good Hope (1837), which occupy a special position. The 1844 statistics show a total of fifteen priests for Ethiopia, Cape of Good Hope and Mauritius.

civilized surroundings.[13] Rather, they were contractually bound to serve as chaplains to the French military forces, and therefore could not move far from their assigned residences. Moreover, their tour of duty generally did not last long enough to enable them to learn a native language. Lastly, utter ignorance of tropical medicine and hygiene would have made any effort to penetrate inland almost equivalent to an attempt at suicide.

True, the Superior General of the Spiritans, Father Fourdinier, was thinking about the evangelization of all Africa at a time when the Venerable Francis Libermann was still Novice Master for the Eudists. With the cooperation of Mother Javouhey[14] he brought three African students to his seminary, and then wrote to the Propaganda in 1839:

Fl. 525 f.

> If these Africans reach the priesthood, as I hope they will, they can be used in an attempt to bring the Faith to the interior of Africa by travelling up the Senegal river to lands which white people can hardly enter because of the heat. Whatever comes of it, it is always a great advantage to have learned from experience that, just like white people, negroes can acquire a knowledge of theology and reach the priesthood. If these experiences could only be multiplied, they would perhaps serve as the means by which the Faith can be made to penetrate into regions of Africa that are totally abandoned.[15]

Va. 154 f.

[13]The type of conditions under which they lived and worked may be seen from a complaint of Father Giudicelli, a Prefect Apostolic of Senegal:

> My house consists of one room, which is a vestibule to the one in which I say Mass. . . . I have a mattress and a hospital blanket. My trunk serves as the only seat. For more than eight months I have been unable to learn whether anyone in Senegal is supposed to pay my salary. A very dirty and unsuitable room does service as my church, a wretched bar table, which the poorest worker would not even tolerate in his kitchen, acts as my altar; a broomstick supports my crucifix.

The only effect of this complaint was a threat to have him thrown into jail for insubordination.

cf. p. 576

[14]Blessed Ann Mary Javouhey (1779-1851) founded the Congregation of St. Joseph of Cluny (1807). Originally destined only for educational works, the Sisters began to undertake colonial hospitals in 1817. From 1819 on they were established in Senegal. Mother Javouhey was a particularly strong woman. King Louis Philip called her a "great man." Her Congregation has always been closely associated with the Holy Ghost Fathers.

Cl. C. 236 ff

[15]All three reached the priesthood. In 1842 and 1843 they returned to Senegal. In France, where they had been under close supervision and

However, Fourdinier was kept so busy with the muddled affairs of the colonies that he could do nothing further in this direction.

N. D. 5, 13 ff.
Storme, 65 ff.
A. C. H. S. 40,
249 ff.
Pr. Exp. 4 ff.

American Efforts. The first successful effort to resume Catholic missionary activity in Africa had its origin in the United States. After the War of Independence, England had settled a number of liberated slaves in Sierra Leone, and American philanthropists now planned to open a similar refuge in the territory that has since come to be known as Liberia. Feeling responsible before God for these former slaves, the missionary-minded American Bishop John England, of Charleston, addressed a memorandum to the Propaganda in 1833 urging that priests be sent to them. The Propaganda

N. D. 5, 12

referred the matter to the Second Council of Baltimore, which was being held that same year. There it was decided to appeal to the Jesuits, who, the Propaganda thought, would be willing to undertake this mission. However, the Society of Jesus declined and its example was followed by the Dominicans and several other religious orders that were approached for the purpose. Finally the Propaganda had to leave the matter in the hands of Bishop England and his episcopal colleagues of New York and Philadelphia. An

N. D. 5, 145 ff.
A. P. F. 15,
314 ff.

appeal for secular priests produced only two volunteers—Father Edward Barron, Vicar General of Philadelphia, and Father John Kelly,[16] the brother of a prominent New York banker. Joined by a layman, Denis Pindar, they sailed from New York for Liberia on December 21, 1841.

N. D. 5, 14 ff.

Arriving at Monrovia, the capital of Liberia, they found only a few Catholics among its five thousand immigrants from the States. An inspection of another settlement of five hundred at Cape Palmas revealed only eighteen Catholics. The priests therefore decided to turn their attention to a nearby native village of about three thou-

---

guidance, they had made an excellent impression. In Senegal, where Ecclesiastical Superiors had little effective control and were changed quite frequently, they did less well. Around 1851 all three were recalled to France. One of them, Father Boilat, remained in France and became pastor of Nantouillet. He enjoyed the esteem of all his parishioners and wrote several books. In 1901 he died at the age of eighty-eight. The second, Father Fridoil, returned to Senegal and did good work under the firm direction of Father Guyard. He died in shipwreck on the way back to France. The third, Father Moussa, was a failure. Left alone in Gorée, he

H. R. H. 453

slowly returned to the life of a savage. After his recall to France, he went to Haiti, which at that time was the last refuge of troublesome priests.

[16]Father Barron was born in Ireland, the son of a rich family. His eldest brother was a baronet and member of the British Parliament.

sand souls. The reception was very cordial, to the great surprise of the American immigrant Negroes, who shortly before had witnessed the same village badly treating a delegation of Protestant pastors. As they learned later, the reason for this change of heart lay in the fact that the new missionaries were celibates and were not interested in trading. Soon requests for priests arrived from other villages and it seemed that there might be some reason to hope for success.

After observing local conditions and possibilities for about three months, Father Barron went to Rome to report to the Propaganda. As a result, on September 28, 1842, Rome created the immense Vicariate of the Two Guineas and Sierra Leone. Father Barron was consecrated bishop and placed in charge of the vast new mission that stretched between Senegal and the Orange River in South Africa—a distance of five thousand miles—and extended without limits into the interior.[17]

N. D. 5, 82 ff.

Libermann and the New Mission. The first task of the new bishop was to find personnel for his Vicariate, the scope of which went far beyond anything intended by the Council of Baltimore. Before his departure from New York, he had been told by Bishop

A. C. H. S. 43, 65 ff.

Pr. Exp. 8

---

[17]It is not our intention to solve here the problem of the exact southern boundary of the Vicariate of the Two Guineas. We are concerned solely with the mission as it *de facto* appears in the history of Africa. The official document of the Holy See speaks of "Upper and Lower Guinea [Congo] and the whole region which is called Sierra Leone." Bishop Barron interpreted these vague indications to mean the entire territory between the Senegal River to the North and the Orange River to the South, except for the few isolated towns over which the Senegal Prefecture and the old Portuguese dioceses effectively exercised jurisdiction. Because he was not a prelate who wanted to usurp as much territory as possible (he asked the Holy See to relieve him of Sierra Leone), his interpretation must have been based on an oral explanation furnished by the Propaganda, for in 1845 that Congregation replied to Libermann's inquiry about the exact boundaries by referring him to Bishop Barron for information. The next year Libermann wrote that the Bishop's successor had power over the same regions—"the interior as well as the coast; moreover, we are authorized to exercise our ministry in all surrounding countries where no jurisdiction has yet been established." As late as 1864, Cardinal Barnabo, then Prefect of the Propaganda, declared that the Vicariate still extended to all areas "not comprised within the limits of other missions," i. e. those of the Senegal Prefecture, the Diocese of Angola and the newly created missions of Sierra Leone and Dahomey. On the basis of this declaration Libermann's successor in the generalate considered himself responsible for all this territory as far south as the Orange River and in 1878 sent Father Duparquet to organize missions in Cimbebasia, i.e. Southern Angola and South West Africa.

N. D. 5, 84

B. G. 11, 507
cf. M. C. 10, 93

N. D. 5, 63

N. D. 5, 108;
Compl. 73

N. D. 8, 77

B. G. 4, 5
cf. M. C. 11, 477
R. H. M. 9, 61 f.
A. P. F. 36, 113

cf. pp. 194 ff.

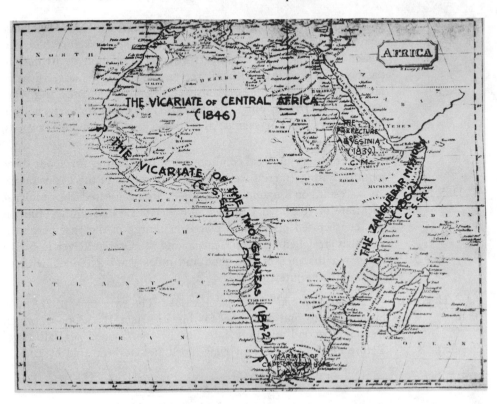

Rosati[18] of St. Louis, Missouri, that a new congregation had just been started by a convert Jew at Amiens. It was suggested that

N. D. 3, 4　　he might seek help there. The Propaganda, however, had dissuaded him from doing so, observing that the new society was still too weak to render any effective assistance. Accordingly, Bishop Barron tried elsewhere. All his efforts met with failure,

N. D. 5, 118 ff.　　even though the Capuchins did promise to send a few Spaniards whom persecution had exiled from their homeland.[19]

Distressed by this failure, the Bishop went to say Mass at the Shrine of Our Lady of Victories in Paris and told its director, Father Desgenettes, how he was burdened with an immense and promising mission, but had no personnel with which to staff it.

N. D. 4, 24 ; 184　　[18]Bishop Rosati knew Father Libermann, whom he had met personally in Paris.

[19]Bishop Barron was anxious to obtain some Capuchin Priests in an effort to revive the ancient Capuchin missions of the Congo.

Shortly before, Father Libermann had called on the same good priest to discuss his difficulties. His novititate was full of young priests eager to go off and work in the Lord's vineyard, but all of a sudden political circumstances had closed Haiti, Reunion, and Mauritius,—all fields to which his first missionaries had gone. "I do not know where to send them," said Libermann.

N. D. 5, 133

The kind old man did not immediately remember Libermann's problem when Bishop Barron came to see him, but it struck him quite suddenly the next day during his Mass at the Shrine. He could hardly wait till the Bishop had finished his, before telling him about Father Libermann's predicament. Soon the two made each other's acquaintance and Libermann gladdened the prelate's heart with an immediate offer of five missionaries for his Vicariate. Later, he added two others when the promised Spanish Capuchins failed to materialize.[20] Instructed by the Bishop to prepare everything needed for the expedition, Father Libermann

N. D. 5, 208

assembled no less than twenty-four tons of luggage, to the great surprise and profound disgust of the departing missionaries, whose apostolic dreams left room for only a crucifix and a breviary.[21]

Pr. Exp. 19
N. D. 5, 181 ff.

Departure of the Expedition. After considerable delays, the party finally set sail from Bordeaux on the vessel *Deux Clémentines.* All were fervent and courageous priests[22] who fully realized that they might be in for a very trying time. The same cannot be said of three laymen who at the last minute were added to the expedition because the Bishop wanted some Brothers. To the great concern of Father Libermann, they had been picked up at a foundling home and were being taken along without preparation of any kind. Father Bessieux called them Brothers, although only one

N. D. 5, 122

[20]The Superior General of the Capuchins had selected five of his subjects, one of whom was officially appointed Prefect Apostolic of the Two Guineas. These five travelled as far as Marseilles. At that point, two of them refused to continue their journey, alleging that they had requested permission to stay at home. When no replacements came, the other three gave up and returned to Italy.

[21]If the amount of luggage seems large, it should be kept in mind that literally nothing would be available locally. Everything, except some few provisions, had to be imported.

[22]The names of these pioneers are: John Bessieux, the future successor of Bishop Barron; Louis Roussel and Francis Bouchet, destined for Guinea; Leopold de Regnier, a former lawyer; Paul Laval, the convert son of a Protestant pastor (this last had succeeded Libermann as novice master for the Eudists and now joined his missionaries); Louis Maurice and Louis Audebert, destined for Senegal.

of them, Gregory Sey, was destined ever to become a Brother. None of the party had any experience of the country in which they were going to work. Bishop Barron himself had spent only a few months there, and he was planning to follow the expedition at a later date. The priests had read whatever they could about the territory and Father Libermann himself had gone to great lengths of research in gathering information. Really useful data, however, seemed unavailable.

Pr. Exp. 20

After an uneventful passage, they arrived at Gorée, off Senegal, where they were received by Father Arsenius Fridoil, a native priest who had been ordained at the Holy Ghost seminary of Paris and was now pastor of the local church. When one of the priests contracted fever after visiting the mainland, Father Bessieux insisted that all stay in their crowded and stifling cabin aboard the two hundred and fifty ton sailing vessel, even though the ship was to remain two weeks at Gorée. Dressed as they were in heavy black cassocks, this confinement must have been sheer torture. The same may be said of the month-long voyage through tropical seas to the port of Cape Palmas, where they arrived weak and emaciated on November 29, 1842. Father Kelly, the priest who had been left behind by Bishop Barron, received the newcomers with open arms. Conversation, however, at first proved difficult. The Frenchmen knew almost no English, and Father Kelly did not understand French. Recourse to Latin appeared hopeless, for Latin with an American accent differs considerably from its French version. They had to resort to gestures, at least till Father Kelly attuned his ear to the heavily accented and broken English spoken by Father de Regnier.

Pr. Exp. 21 f.

N. D. 5, 208

Inauguration of the Mission. On the feast of St. Francis Xavier, Sunday, December 3, the new missionaries inaugurated their ministry. With a number of hastily recruited boys dressed in soutanes and surplices, a solemn procession, preceded by a crucifix, slowly wended its way to a native village, while the priests sang the *Exsurgat Deus* and the *Magnificat*. Great was the enthusiasm among the natives at this colorful and unusual spectacle. However, they tired quickly when Father Bessieux opened a big bible and began to preach a sermon in Latin, translated into English by Father Kelly, and then into the native Grebo language by an interpreter. We may smile at this naive procedure, but this first effort contained two elements then almost neglected in missionary work: 1) the priests presented themselves purely as men of God and not as representatives of any European government and 2) they tried to approach the natives through the medium of their own language. With all their energy they devoted themselves during the following days to the study of Grebo. Moreover, they were eager to adapt themselves to the natives as much as possible—

N. D. 5, 212; 7, 292

perhaps too much. They refused to wear a helmet in the sun and adopted what they supposed to be an African diet: boiled rice, yams, and a little piece of meat or fish once a day. All around them were stacked the abundant and strengthening provisions Father Libermann had shipped out for them, but these remained untouched.

Pr. Exp. 22

Disasters. The results of this folly and the penalties of inexperience soon became evident. Fever began to strike ten days after that famous first sermon. Within two weeks seven of the

N. D. 5, 263

eleven were ill. On December 30, Father de Regnier died after writing with a feverish hand: "I am happy to have left everything for Our Lord. If I had the choice, I would do it again, a thousand times over." Three days later Denis Pindar suffered a sunstroke and expired almost immediately. Brokenhearted,

Pr. Exp. 25

without news of his bishop, and unable to converse with anyone, Father Kelly could not resist the lure of a passing American vessel and suddenly embarked on January 18, leaving Father Bessieux to disentangle his confused business affairs.[23] Five days later a third victim, Father Roussel, had to be carried to his grave. Only then did the fever begin to diminish.

Pr. Exp. 29 f.
N. D. 5, 221 ff.

Slowly the survivors went back to their study of the Grebo language. March brought the long-awaited arrival of Bishop Barron and two new helpers. Mr. James Keily, a seminarian, and John Egan, a layman. The Bishop had heard the bad news from Father Kelly when their paths crossed in Sierra Leone and now he proposed a new change of plans—to abandon Cape Palmas and to establish three new bases at Assinia, Bassam and Gabon. Though loath to leave the graves of their confreres and everything they had built up at the cost of so much sacrifice, the missionaries readily obeyed. Only Father Bessieux and one of the "Brothers"

C. S. L. 70 ff.

[23]Father Kelly died in 1866 in Jersey City where he ended his days as a resident pastor.

stayed behind to guard the possessions which could not be shipped at once. The others sailed away with the Bishop on the *Eglantine*.

Four weeks later their ship arrived at Bassam. Bad news awaited them there. An epidemic had broken out and a landing was far too risky. In short order, messages began to arrive from Assinia and Gabon bringing word that neither place was ready to receive them. In the face of this impasse, they took counsel and decided to land the whole party at Assinia in spite of the discouraging reports. From there they planned to send some men overland to Bassam. As they were landing at Assinia, the ill-tempered crew out-did their captain in showing the missionaries every possible discourtesy, and nearly all their supplies were dropped into the sea during the process of debarkation. While some of the men sought temporary shelter in a military post, Father Audebert, Father Laval and "Brother" Gregory set out for Bassam through swamps and forests, without supplies, money, or even spare clothing. The scant luggage they had managed to retrieve was supposed to follow, but it fell into the hands of thieving tribesmen and only a small part of it was rescued by a military expedition.

Pr. Exp. 33 ff.
N. D. 5, 230 ff.

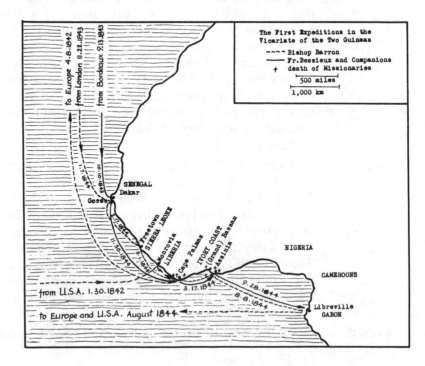

The First Expeditions in the Vicariate of the Two Guineas

---- Bishop Barron
—— Fr. Bessieux and Companions
+ death of Missionaries

500 miles
1,000 km

Pr. Exp. 37 ff.   Soon it became apparent that both Assinia and Bassam offered no possibilities for successful missionary labors. Bishop Barron therefore decided to fall back on Senegal and gradually to transfer all his personnel there. He set out from Assinia with Father Bouchet, but that unfortunate companion died of a stroke soon after they boarded the *Eglantine*. The captain refused the customary honors of burial at sea with a cannon ball or a bag of sand He refused even to allow any prayers to be said. Instead, he simply had the body dumped overboard, telling the Bishop: "Just watch and see what a lovely foot-bath that fellow is going to take."[24]

Stopping over at Bassam, Bishop Barron found the whole community sick with fever and dysentery and deprived of the most elementary necessities. In spite of everything, they were valiantly trying to make contact with the natives. Withdrawal to Assinia seemed inevitable, but because only one additional man could find even a temporary shelter there, Father Laval alone went back with the Bishop. At Assinia, death claimed one more victim, Mr. Keily, before a doctor finally arrived from Senegal. He immediately ordered the evacuation of all the sick to Gorée but Father Laval was too far gone even to be taken aboard. He died soon afterwards. Only Father Maurice, John Egan, and "Brother" Andrew were able to go. All three later returned from there to Europe, where Egan died shortly after, and the other two definitely abandoned every thought of further work in the African mission.[25]

Pr. Exp. 41   Meanwhile in Bassam, death had put an end to the sufferings of Father Audebert. There had been no one to give him the last sacraments, for his sole companion was the sick "Brother" Gregory, to whom he had administered Extreme Unction just a short time before. Until rescue came, the poor Brother was destined to spend six months alone in a wretched hut without adequate care or food.

Pr. Exp. 42 ff.   *Departure of Bishop Barron.* Discouraged by all these disasters, Bishop Barron gave up and sailed on a passing vessel to Senegal. From there he made his way to Rome to report to the Propa-

---

N. D. 5, 249   [24]For this and other atrocities the Captain was to face a court martial on the complaint of his fellow officers. Realizing that he would be stripped of his command, he blew out his brains.

A. C. H. S., 1950, 155 ff.   [25]Father Maurice left the Congregation and in 1846 came to the States as a Jesuit novice. Later he left the Jesuits and became pastor of St. Ambrose Church in Greece, near Buffalo, where he died in 1895.

ganda and resign.[26] Three men were left behind: Father Bessieux, his companion at Cape Palmas, and "Brother" Gregory. Before his departure, the Bishop asked the French authorities to transport these men to Gabon if they were still alive. Picked up by the *Zèbre,* the three invalids finally arrived in Gabon on September 28, 1844. The French navy, which had just established a base there, received them most cordially.[27]

Father Bessieux's lay companion had to be shipped back to Europe immediately. Probably struck by the sun, he was completely insane and a merciful death overtook him while the ship was still at sea. The other two stayed in Africa. Through the care of a doctor and the generosity of the French commander, they slowly recovered from their ordeals. Father Bessieux courageously applied himself to the study of the local Pongue language, preparing feverishly for his future missionary work. To the amazement of the French officers, there was no thought in his or his companion's mind of giving up and returning to France. Missionaries they were and missionaries they would always remain.

N. D. 5, 286 ff.   Ever since their first departure for Africa, the one great cross that weighed them down was the complete absence of news from Father Libermann, although Bessieux had written nine times. The poor man blamed himself for the situation, thinking that his faults and mistakes had rendered him odious to everyone. At times it even crossed his mind that the new society might have been disbanded, leaving the two of them alone and forgotten in the confusion. At last, one year after their arrival in Gabon, a pack of letters came from Gorée, sent by Father Briot. In forward-

---

G. C. M. H. 119   [26]Although Bishop Barron erroneously thought that Father Libermann ultimately was to blame for the disaster of the expedition, there were no recriminations on either side. Both men had suffered intensely under their common disaster, but they continued to hold each other in high esteem.

C. S. L., 65 ff.   Bishop Barron returned to the United States in 1845 and turned down several offers of an episcopal see, preferring to do more humble work. While caring for yellow fever victims in Savannah, Georgia, he himself contracted the disease. A hurricane blew the roof off the house in which he was dying.

N. D. 5, 124 ff.   He was buried in the local cemetery. In the Cathedral of Waterford, Ireland, a monument was erected in his honor, bearing the inaccurate statement that he and one other were the sole survivors of the twenty-one man expedition to Africa.

Beslier, 30   [27]The *Notes et Documents* show not the slightest evidence in support of G. Beslier's fantastic story that Father Bessieux "had been captured by the Methodists who for two years tortured him with the evident intention of getting rid of him, but [that] he had managed to survive this long ordeal and to take refuge near the estuary of the Gabon River."

ing the letters, Father Briot announced his impending departure for Gabon to reinforce the community. With tears in their eyes the two men hungrily read the news and then went over to chant a *Magnificat* in their humble chapel.

N. D. 6, 351   *The News Reaches Libermann.* The Venerable himself, on the other hand, had received no news of his priests, although he himself had written every time a ship sailed for Africa. Rumors took the place of definite information: the priests had been ship-wrecked, burned at the stake, or killed by the natives. His enemies took advantage of the situation to spread further distrust of a madman who appeared to be sacrificing young lives for his personal glory. Finally, a full account of the disaster reached la Neuville

N. D. 5, 64 ff.   by way of a letter from Bishop Barron on October 8, 1844. Calling his spiritual children together, the Venerable announced the bitter news in a saddened but calm voice.

N. D. 6, 511;
N. D. Compl.,
54   The reaction was just the opposite of what, humanly speaking, he might have expected—one by one all came forward begging to be sent out to the Two Guineas. His volunteers were so insistent that he had to issue a formal order forbidding them even to broach the subject. While Libermann had no intention to abandon Dark Africa, which the Propaganda officially entrusted to his Congregation shortly after (January 1845), he had no desire to send his priests away to die like flies in the

N. D. 6, 391 ff.   tropics. Before long he too began to formulate a plan for saving Africa by means of a native clergy. Thus he unwittingly took over the idea proposed by Father Fourdinier and mentioned above. We will speak of this plan later when we discuss the missionary ideas of the Venerable Francis Libermann.

Br. 195 ff.   *Reinforcements Sent.* As has been mentioned, Father Briot was sent to the rescue of the two lonely men making a last stand in Gabon. In virtue of faculties granted him by the Propaganda, Father Libermann had appointed Father Eugene Tisserant Prefect Apostolic of Guinea. However, the new Prefect was detained by illness and Father Briot, together with Father Arragon and Brother Peter, had gone on before him. All these men had been forced to withdraw from Haiti because of political difficulties on that much-disturbed island. They now received definite and prudent orders to stay at Gorée and become acclimatized before un-

dertaking any long trips.[28] Libermann issued these orders despite
the fact that Father Leguay, then Superior General of the Holy
Ghost Fathers, had bluntly refused to recommend the new-comers
to his priests there. Leguay feared these upstarts, on whom "he had

N. D. 7, 478 ff. declared war, with no holds barred." He went so far as to send
instructions to this effect to Father Boilat, a native Vice-Prefect
of Senegal who was then stationed at Gorée.[29] However, once
Father Libermann's men had arrived in port, personal contact
gradually smoothed away most of the difficulties with the local
clergy.

Canonically speaking, the situation was dangerously complicated. The old Spiritan Prefecture extended over "Senegal and
all its dependencies," while the Guinea mission included all non-
occupied territories on the West Coast. Obviously, the vagueness
of the terms "dependencies" and "non-occupied" could easily lead
to conflict. The biggest source of surprise and indignation on the
part of the old-timers, however, proved to be the fact that Father
Arragon began immediately to study the local languages, Wolof
and Arabic, for the avowed purpose of preaching the Gospel to
the Negroes in their own tongue. Not even the native priests were
willing to condescend that far. They preferred to have their French
sermons only half understood or not at all. Meanwhile, Father
Briot and his confrere left Arragon to his language studies and
went off in search of a permanent base on the mainland.

N. D. 7, 467 ff. Father Tisserant, the Prefect Apostolic, sailed on a steamer in
November 1845. Caught in a violent storm off the coast of Africa,
the vessel was wrecked and the new Prefect was one of those who

N. D. 8, 38 failed to survive. He was replaced by Father Jerome Gravière
who sailed shortly after with two companions, and was later
followed by four others. This contingent was sent to build up the
base of action at Dakar, the place selected by Father Arragon as
most suitable. Within a year after Father Briot's arrival at Gorée,
it was at last possible to send reinforcements to the two lonely
men holding the vanguard in Gabon, about twelve hundred miles
southeast of Dakar.

Pr. Exp. 17   [28]Half of the first expedition should have done the same, but they had
misunderstood Libermann's orders. Gorée, off the coast of Senegal, was an
old Spiritan mission established in the eighteenth century. It had, in addition
to a church, schools staffed by Brothers and Sisters, a decent hospital and
competent doctors.

N. D. 7, 441   [29]When his conduct became known, Father Leguay had to swallow a
severe reprimand from the Papal Nuncio.

N. D. 8, 186 ff.

N. D. 8, 222 ff.
G. C. M. H.
119 ff.

N. D. 9, 36

Bishop Truffet Appointed. Meanwhile, Father Libermann had gone to Rome to discuss the affairs of the African Missions with the Propaganda. In a long memorandum he pressed for the appointment of a Vicar Apostolic who would reside in Dakar and canonical erection in the foreseeable future of other Vicariates in Sierra Leone, the Ashanti kingdom (near the Gold Coast), Dahomey, and Gabon. The Propaganda concurred with his views and on his recommendation they named Father Stephen Truffet Vicar Apostolic of the Two Guineas. The new bishop was still an unsuspecting novice when informed of his inpending episcopal consecration. Albeit a novice, he had had twelve years' experience as a priest, teacher and author. In April, 1846, therefore, he sailed for Dakar, accompanied by seven members of the Congregation. The African missions, which only a year before had seemed to be doomed to failure now appeared well on their way to success.

Br. 216 ff.

Libermann's Congregation Expands. Father Libermann found it possible to provide the personnel necessary for this vast enterprise because, despite all efforts to defame and oppose him, and despite the disasters reported from Africa, his novitiate abounded

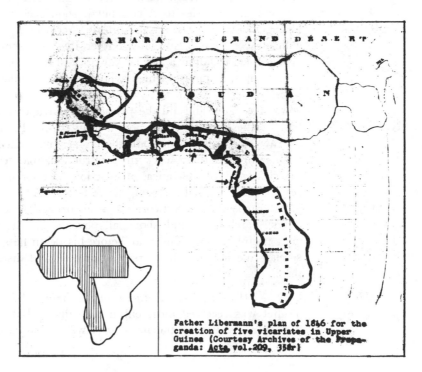

Father Libermann's plan of 1846 for the creation of five vicariates in Upper Guinea (Courtesy Archives of the Propaganda: *Acta* vol. 209, 358r)

in recruits who had been attracted by the holiness of its founder. Although he had enlarged the house at La Neuville twice already, it was still too small for all who came to join him. They decided, therefore, to take over a former orphanage in Noyon, a suburb of Amiens, and in addition, to buy the medieval abbey of Gard, which the Trappists had abandoned when a new railroad line cut its acreage in two. In 1846, then, Noyon became the site of the novitiate and the abbey began to serve as the senior scholasticate of the Congregation. A convent bought the house at La Neuville which was the birthplace of Libermann's society, and the money realized from this sale was used to pay for the abbey.

At the outset, Father Libermann had thought only of a congregation of priests. However, he soon realized that too much time would be taken up with material cares if his priests had to do everything themselves. He first tried to work with simple laymen whom everyone charitably addressed as "Brother," even though they had no intention of becoming religious Brothers. The

N. D. 3, 375   most famous of these was one called Brother "Sadsack," whose constant comment on everything was: *"C'est triste."* ("It is sad.") Three such "Brothers," as we have already seen, had accompanied

N. D. 6, 119 ff.; 9, 184   the first missionaries to Africa but it soon became clear that this arrangement was most unsatisfactory. Accordingly, in consultation with his confreres (especially Father Le Vavasseur), the Venerable decided to admit a second category of members into the Congregation, viz., pious laymen who had no intention of becoming priests but who wanted to consecrate their lives to God by the vows of religion and aid the priests in their apostolic work. The

N. D. 3, 403   first of these entered the novitiate in 1843. Father Libermann foresaw that these men would be of inestimable assistance to his priests through their work in construction, maintenance, care of the sick, and the technical instruction of apprentices. For this reason, he expressed a strong desire to attract to this second cate-

N. D. 9, 81   gory "carpenters, woodworkers, ironworkers, weavers, . . . mechanics, architects, and above all physicians, who would be the most useful of all." The year before his death he saw to it that a

N. D. 11, 487 ff.   special rule for the Brothers was printed and distributed among them.

Br. 227 ff.   *The African Mission Again on the Brink of Disaster.* Bishop Truffet was received most enthusiastically at Dakar, not only by his confreres, but by the natives as well. The enthusiasm of his

N. D. 9, 439 f.

African friends was not entirely disinterested for they were plotting a war against a neighboring tribe and the Bishop's support would be immensely helpful. Since their enemies had just imprisoned two missionaries, they felt confident that a plausible case could be built up. However, the Bishop wisely declined to enter into local village politics, especially when the two prisoners returned unharmed after a few weeks' absence and expressed surprise at all the commotion in their behalf.

N. D. 10, 67 ff.;
Compl. 221 ff.

To prevent any repetition of such incidents, the prelate forbade his priests to take any trips away from the compound unless he was with them. It was an effective measure to stop all trouble, but it also stopped all missionary work. The small school had just opened, and its seven pupils could not keep everybody busy. The priests began to fret about their inactivity. When their frustration reached dangerous proportions, Bishop Truffet organized the community on the lines of the novitiate he had just left. Action was replaced by meditation; he himself gave them three conferences a week; no letters were to be written about the mission to anyone but himself; and, because the community was in Africa, everyone had to speak the local Wolof language, although only Father Arragon possessed a fairly adequate knowledge of it. Worst of all, he ordered the immediate adoption of the native diet: canary seed, rice and fish—no wine, no bread, no meat, save on Sundays and Thursdays. As Father Warlop later remarked, it was not long before the younger priests were literally shaking with hunger and secretly devoured anything edible they could lay their hands on.

Br. 230 ff.
N. D. 10, 42 ff.

The inevitable happened: within six months everybody was ill, including the Bishop himself. He refused to let a doctor come from nearby Gorée. Only supernatural means were to be used. He prescribed his own remedy: a diet of sugar water. When he finally consented to treatment, it was too late. Less than seven months after his arrival in Africa, he died, the victim of his own imprudence. The others responded to treatment and medical care at the hospital of Gorée and then returned to the simple but sane diet adopted before Bishop Truffet's arrival.

N. D. 10, 79 ff.

Administratively also, the attitudes assumed by Bishop Truffet and Father Arragon brought the mission to the brink of disaster. In 1843, with the full approval of the Propaganda and Bishop Barron, Father Libermann had concluded an agreement with the French Government in virtue of which his missionaries were to notify the naval authorities whenever they went off on exploratory trips. They were to report on the local population in the area visited, but otherwise they retained full freedom of apostolic activity. In return, the Navy provided free transportation, hospital care, rations, and an annual subsidy—in all about $25,000 worth. For a new mission without resources of any kind in an unknown and sometimes hostile territory, this agreement was highly advantageous. Nonetheless, Bishop Truffet wanted to break entirely with the Government because he had an exaggerated fear of civil interference in the missionary work which he himself had so radically restricted.

During his few weeks as Acting Superior after the death of the Bishop, Father Arragon decided to make a complete break. In a blunt and insulting letter he told the Navy that as free and independent citizens of Savoy the Fathers did not want any French help.[30] As an immediate result of this folly, the French government took him literally and cut off all support from the Mission. Fortunately, Father Libermann's diplomacy succeeded in restoring the good will of the government at home, while Father Bessieux, who was highly respected by the French naval authorities in Gorée, rushed over from Gabon to appease their anger. In the end, Father Arragon had to swallow his words and pledge observance of the covenant. Had Libermann and Bessieux failed, the whole African enterprise might have been ruined for, unlike Bishop Barron who could use his personal fortune, Liberman and his missionaries had no funds with which to support the mission.

N. D. 10, 367

Br. 310 f.
Va. 199 ff.
Storme,
107 ff.

Bishop Bessieux and Bishop Kobès. With the appointment, in 1848, of Father Bessieux as Vicar Apostolic of the Two Guineas[31] and of Father Aloysius Kobès as his coadjutor, one could say that the African missions were at last in good hands. Too good, perhaps, for Bishop Kobès especially was so full of Africa that he could see no sense in using any member of the Congregation elsewhere. This question of manpower soon became very acute. Father Libermann had other projects in mind and, in further com-

---

[30]Several of the Fathers in Dakar had come from Savoy, a country which at that time was not yet part of France and was proud of its independence.

[31]Father Bessieux had always been the logical man to take charge of the mission. His extreme reluctance to accept any post of authority had caused Father Libermann to present Father Truffet's name to the Propaganda in 1847. This time the Venerable overrode Bessieux' objections.

plication of the problem, it was just at this time that the Congregation of the Holy Heart of Mary was disbanded and its members
entered the Society of the Holy Ghost, thereby assuming respon-
cf. pp. 119 ff.   sibility for the old French colonies as well.   We will return to
this point later when we discuss the acceptance of works in Europe
and treat of the history of the Congregation under Libermann's
successors.

4. *The Australian Venture*

N. D. 7, 249   In July 1843, Father Libermann was visited at La Neuville by
Bishop John Brady, an Irishman who had studied at Holy Ghost
Seminary and had later gone out to Australia.   After exploring
the regions around Perth, he had been consecrated bishop of the
territory and was now charged with the task of establishing mis-
N. D. 7, 501;   sions there.   He was looking for personnel to staff one of the two
Compl. 93 f.   Vicariates which he intended to open for the two million inhabitants he mistakenly supposed to be there.   It appeared to Father
Libermann as if he had come in answer to unspoken prayers.   At
the moment, all French colonies were closed to his missionaries
by the opposition of Fourdinier, the political turmoil in Haiti
precluded any pastoral activity, the plans for Madagascar might
have to be abandoned, and the first mission of the Two Guineas
in Africa had just suffered appalling disasters.   Somewhat hastily
N. D. 7, 294   he agreed to supply personnel for one of the Vicariates to be
founded near Perth.   "Don't worry about a thing," the Bishop
said, "I will supply everything necessary.   Just send all the men you
can spare to London."

N. D. 7, 317 f.   The next month, Father Francis Thévaux, the newly appointed
Superior of the mission, departed with two Fathers and two
Moran, II,   Brothers for London.   It was going to be a great expedition.
558   Bishop Brady had assembled seven priests, two Brothers, six
Sisters, three seminarians, and eight lay catechists to accompany
him to Perth.   Innocently trusting the Bishop's promise regarding
ample supplies, the poor Fathers had not even taken any spare
clothing with them.   Nothing, however, was forthcoming.   On
reaching the Cape of Good Hope they had to cut up bed sheets to
serve as substitutes for their bedraggled shirts.   When fever broke
out, there was not even a medicine chest on board.   As they
approached Freemantle, in southwestern Australia, Father Maurice

Bouchet had to be carried off the ship and given Extreme Unction. He died soon afterwards.

Br. 184 f.   At Perth new trials awaited them. Instead of a large town, Perth proved to be a miserable settlement consisting of a few bungalows. The white settlers were nearly all Protestant and the innumerable native population existed only in the imagination of Bishop Brady. The newcomers found a Dutch priest, Father Joosten, already working there and, after some discussion, Father Thévaux and his confreres were assigned to the future Vicariate of Albany in King George Sound, two hundred and fifty miles away through tangled forest. With his blessings and but little else, the Bishop sent them on their way in company with one of the Irish priests, Father Powell. When they opened a letter of

N. D. Compl. 93

instructions from the Bishop, they discovered that the agreement he had made with Father Libermann was broken: their jurisdiction was limited to the natives and they were to remain dependent on Father Joosten, who had been appointed Vicar General by the Bishop. Moreover, Father Powell claimed that he was their superior, for the Bishop had told him that he was to be the Vicar Apostolic of Albany. In spite of all this, they decided to go on.

Br. 185   Searching for the 50,000 natives who, according to the Bishop's estimate, lived around Albany, they travelled through a region of a hundred miles and found less than a score. Yet the Bishop persisted in his illusions of large populations. Soon he began to reproach the Fathers for their lack of zeal and ordered them to disperse and start two or three communities in the interior. Obediently they set out in the midst of the rainy season, sick with fever, without adequate supplies, fruitlessly searching everywhere for native settlements. Father Powell, the Irish secular priest, had enough of it. Giving up the prospective Vicariate and his episcopal dreams, he left, never to return. The seminarian as well as one of the two Brothers had to be sent away. Appeals to Bishop Brady for help and at least some limited food supplies were answered with new orders to go farther into the interior

N. D. 11, 93   and set up stations in the forest. Moved by pity at the sight of their extreme need, the captain of a passing sailing vessel gave them some food and a small loan of money. Then the emaciated priests and the Brother once more trekked three days deeper into the woods and began to build a house which they called Santa Maria. Food being unavailable locally, they had to rely on the produce of a little garden they had started at their first place of residence, marching three days every time they wanted to reach it. Soon they were reduced to eating chopped grass and frogs.

Br. 188

Meanwhile, at Perth, Bishop Brady continued making all kinds of fantastic plans—including the opening of a college for his non-existent population. Not having the slightest notion of financial matters, he was over his head in debt. When it finally came to his rescue, the Propaganda specified that three thousand gold francs of its subsidy were to be given to Father Thévaux and his companions. "Give us at least half of that sum," the distraught priest pleaded in vain, when the payment of his share was slow in coming. But even this plaintive request fell on deaf ears.

Br. 188

Early in 1847 a reply finally came from the Bishop. His Excellency was most indignant over a letter Father Thévaux had written to an Italian layman who had been assigned to the future college of Perth. In it a slight allusion had been made to the Bishop's impending bankruptcy and the prelate demanded an apology under pain of suspension. Father Thévaux marched all the way to Perth to explain the situation, but to no avail. "As a punishment," the Bishop said, "I am taking away from you the mission of King George Sound. The Passionists will soon arrive to take it over. You and your confreres are henceforth confined to Perth." Since this restriction was definitely against the agreement with Father Libermann, Father Thévaux refused to accept the Bishop's decision and asked money to leave Australia for Reunion or Mauritius. "That you can have" was the reply, "Here are fifteen pounds, and in addition you are hereby suspended for disobedience, false testimony, and offensive language to your Superior."

Br. 189

With a heavy heart, the poor priest wearily tramped two hundred fifty miles back through the woods—to convey the bad news to Father Thiersé, his sick companion. There was nothing for it but to make their annual retreat and watch for a boat. Meanwhile, the Bishop sent a message appointing Father Thiersé Superior and giving him faculties to absolve his confrere from the suspension. Father Thiersé, however, thought that he could not accept this appointment because it had not come through his religious Superiors. Thus he did not see how he could make use of the faculty to absolve Father Thévaux from the suspension. As he

N. D. 10, 365

discussed it with the victim of the Bishop's wrath, they came upon an ingenious solution. Father Thiersé had faculties to receive members into the Third Order of St. Francis and vaguely remembered something to the effect that entrance into this Order automatically lifted ecclesiastical penalties. Accordingly, he absolved his confrere by making him a member of the Third Order, thus enabling Father Thévaux to start saying Mass again two months after he had incurred the Bishop's displeasure. Since these two men could not avail themselves of canonical consultation and had no reference books whatsoever, one may excuse them for an action which made Father Thévaux irregular. The affair was closed only in 1848 when Father Libermann obtained an absolution from the Propaganda.

Br. 190

It was July 1847 before they had an opportunity to sail for Mauritius. For forty-eight days the ship kept trying to leave this inhospitable shore, but every time it put off, heavy seas drove it back. Father Thiersé was so sick that he had to be landed again. He had hardly reached the land in company with the Brother when the wind changed and the vessel sailed off to Mau-

N. D. 11, 93

ritius with Father Thévaux aboard. The two unfortunates who were left behind spent another year of misery in the forest until at last a ship came along and took them to join their community in Mauritius.

As for Bishop Brady, Rome grew increasingly disturbed over reports of his maladministration and soon demanded his resignation. The Bishop retired to his native diocese of Kilmore and a sad chapter of missionary history thus came to a close.

Moran, II, 558, 565

In the foregoing pages we have been forced to reveal Bishop Brady's administrative ineptness, but it would be wrong to leave the reader under the impression that nothing good can be said about him. Before his appointment to Australia, he had spent twelve laborious years as a missionary in Mauritius. He sold his personal property to help the mission, lived in a miserable hovel, subsisted on the coarsest kinds of food and gave every evidence that personal comfort meant nothing for him when the Church's welfare was at stake.

CHAPTER SIX

FATHER LIBERMANN AS SUPERIOR GENERAL OF THE HOLY GHOST FATHERS, 1848-1852

1. *The Entrance of Father Libermann and His Confreres into the Congregation of the Holy Ghost*

From the very beginning of the Congregation of the Holy Heart of Mary there had been some discussion about incorporating its membership in the Congregation of the Holy Ghost. Rome itself had proposed the idea rather bluntly in 1840, when Francis Libermann presented his plan for a new congregation. "You want to raise altar against altar," he was told. "The Society of the Holy Ghost takes care of this work. You are not needed." For this reason, as we have seen above, contact was sought with Father Fourdinier, but without success. The time was not yet ripe for such an association. Nevertheless, Father Libermann did not give up hope and continued working toward it. As he wrote in 1848:

N. D. 10, 339

cf. pp. 60 f.

N. D. 7, 67, 227; 370

N. D. 10, 339

> The union of our two societies has always appeared to me as being in line with God's will. The societies have the same purpose and work along the same lines. It is not in the order of Divine Providence to raise up two societies for a special work if one can suffice.

N. D. 5, 101 f.

In 1845 the Propaganda itself again suggested that the two combine their efforts, but the temporary status of Father Warnet as Superior of the Holy Ghost Congregation prevented him from taking action just then. As we have seen, Father Leguay, his successor, refused to have anything to do with Libermann. After his resignation, Father Monnet took the helm. He knew the priests of the Holy Heart of Mary from personal experience, for he had worked with them in Reunion. His relations with Father Le Vavasseur were particularly cordial. As a matter of fact, Monnet originally wanted to join Libermann's congregation because it was dedicated to work among abandoned slaves and Libermann had even considered admitting him without requiring him to return to France for the novitiate. Nothing had come of this plan because Father Le Vavasseur recommended Monnet as an excellent mis-

N. D. 3, 301; 510; 519; 527

97

sionary but a poor candidate for life in a religious community. Despite the break-down in negotiations, however, relations continued to be friendly on both sides. It is not surprising, therefore, that Father Monnet was not troubled by that dark prejudice against Libermann which nearly all the older Holy Ghost Fathers, except Father Warnet, shared. The same might be said of Father John Loewenbruck, who had joined the Congregation only in 1847 and who was destined to play a decisive role in the impending incorporation of Father Libermann and his priests.

In general, the atmosphere was more favorable toward a union than it had ever been before. Therefore, when Mr. Schoelcher

N. D. 10, 396

wanted to nominate two unsuitable priests as Prefects Apostolic in Martinique and Guadeloupe, one can understand why Father Monnet sought contact with Libermann to prevent the nominations.

N. D. 10, 218

In his reply, Father Libermann pointed out that he not only wished to live in harmony with the Holy Ghost Fathers, but sincerely desired to see the two congregations united into one. His letter arrived at a moment when Warnet, Loewenbruck and Monnet themselves were thinking of seeking a way to reach a decision on this same question. Father Monnet jumped at the offer, for Mr. Schoelcher once more was threatening to by-pass the Holy Ghost Fathers, and this practically amounted to a threat of suppression.

He set out at once for Notre Dame du Gard to open negotiations, but the affair developed into a protracted process. Several

N. D. 10, 416

Holy Ghost Fathers, notably Father Gaultier,[1] were still vehemently opposed to any idea of union. In view of all the stories that had been circulated in Paris about the ambitious plotting of the convert Jew, one cannot blame them for the aversion they experienced. Moreover, Father Monnet's desire for the union was inspired for the most part by the difficulties he met in his relations with the temperamental Mr. Schoelcher. As Schoelcher's animosity against the Spiritans rose or fell, so did Father Monnet's enthusiasm for the union. Then too, a newly appointed official Com-

N. D. 10, 395

mission for the Clergy unexpectedly turned out to be quite favorable to the Holy Ghost Fathers. Lastly, a governmental reorganization was in the air, and it was hoped that this would remove most of the problems.

---

[1]He remained opposed to the very end. However, once the decision was taken, he was loyal and did his utmost to secure its success. Libermann made him his first assistant.

N. D. 10, 356   When this Commission began to operate late in 1848, it transferred responsibility for religious service to the colonies from the Navy to the Ministry of Ecclesiastical Affairs, then headed by a pious Catholic, who sincerely desired to give the Church all possible freedom to organize itself overseas. With this new development, most of the difficulties experienced by the Spiritans were on the point of disappearing—at least temporarily, for the only permanent feature of the French government was its instability. This explains why Father Monnet was no longer in a hurry to achieve a union.

N. D. 10, 397   Fortunately, he had already appointed Father Loewenbruck to negotiate an agreement with Libermann and his priests. Loewenbruck was quick to realize Father Libermann's exceptional abilities. Having considerable experience himself in handling men and

N. D. 10, 416   affairs, he clearly saw that Father Monnet lacked the diplomacy and abilities needed to administer and lead a congregation, despite his unquestionable talents for missionary work. He feared the worst unless someone of Libermann's caliber assumed the helm. For this reason he applied himself successfully to overcoming Father Monnet's hesitancy.

N. D. 10, 214   On the Feast of Pentecost, June 10, 1848, both parties gathered in formal session at Holy Ghost Seminary and unanimously accepted the union in principle, leaving the settlement of details for a later date. The most important issue was the

N. D. 10, 215   identity of the new Superior General. Nearly all agreed that it should be Libermann and not Monnet. However, a simple resignation was not the answer. Apart from making it look as if Father Monnet had been coldly pushed aside, it would have caused serious trouble with Archbishop Affre of Paris, whose dislike of Libermann was a matter of common knowledge. To make matters worse, the Archbishop had just made Father Monnet

N. D. 10, 245   his Vicar General. Thus, if Monnet was to be replaced, it had to be by way of promotion. Father Libermann knew a possibility: the Propaganda was looking for a suitable candidate to be promoted to the episcopacy and sent to Madagascar as its Vicar Apostolic. If Rome could be persuaded to accept mission-minded Father Monnet for this post, the problem would be solved to everyone's satisfaction. At least, it was worth trying. They all decided, therefore, that Libermann and Monnet should both go to Rome to consult the Propaganda.

Before this decision could be executed, new political events caused a change of plans. The year 1848 was a year of revolutions all over Europe. France had opened the series by its February Revolution, but a single one in such a monumental year apparently was not enough. Before the end of June another broke out. Much of the fighting was concentrated in the area around Holy Ghost Seminary, which was completely surrounded by barricades. Though the bloody struggle lasted only a few days, the situation during the following weeks was so uneasy that neither Monnet nor Libermann could leave their congregations unprotected. Therefore, they resolved to make use of Father Loewenbruck's diplomatic abilities. He was sent N. D. 10, 370 to Rome with two letters—one from Father Monnet, explaining and 244 the desirability of the union, the other from Father Libermann, recommending Monnet for the Vicariate of Madagascar.

In Rome, too, revolution was in the air. In a fever of anticipation, the pontifical offices were operating with abnormal rapidity, doing their best to expedite unfinished business before political events could stop the affairs of the Church from running their course. Thus, Father Loewenbruck was able to achieve quick results: the Propaganda was fully in favor of the plans and quite willing to consider Father Monnet as a candidate for the Vicariate N. D. 10, 407 of Madagascar. The official answer, they said, would be dispatched to Paris immediately after a decision had been taken by the Council of the Propaganda in its meeting of September 14 and its approval by the Pope. Happy to have succeeded and anxious to escape another revolution, Father Loewenbruck returned to Paris with the good news.

N. D. 10, 417 To his surprise and pain, his reception was far from enthusiastic. Under the influence of Father Gaultier, Monnet had changed his mind again. He no longer wanted a union. Only after considerable effort on Loewenbruck's part could he be induced to look kindly on it again. Ultimate success was due in large measure to the fact that Loewenbruck could repeatedly point to the episcopal nomination which was expected at any moment. August 24, 1848, both parties signed an agreement which stipu-N. D. 10, 411 lated the conditions of the fusion. These were the salient items: 1) that the title and rules of the Holy Ghost Congregation were to be retained, 2) the practice of poverty was to be re-established, and 3) the second order was to be suspended till a decision respecting it could be obtained from the Propaganda. On this occasion also, the negotiators unanimously accepted Monnet's proposal that Libermann be the new Superior General. A month later, on September 26, 1848, the Propaganda sent the promised official approval, and on October 3, Father Monnet was named Vicar Apostolic of Madagascar. The document read in part:

N. D. 10, 375 f.

It is your task to bring this union of your two congregations to a conclusion in such a way that from now on the Congregation of the Immaculate Heart of Mary ceases to exist and its associates and members are aggregated to the Congregation of the Holy Ghost, thereby becoming its associates and members, sharing the same rights and privileges and being subject to the same disciplinary rules.

Both congregations gained great benefits from this aggregation. The case has sometimes been represented as if the Holy Ghost Fathers were the only ones to benefit, while the others came away with only additional burdens. For this reason it may be useful to point out the strengths and weaknesses of both bodies.

At the time when Libermann and his confreres entered, the Congregation of the Holy Ghost had thirteen members,[2] while about thirty others were making their novitiate in the colonies prior to being accepted under the modified rule introduced by Father Leguay. The Seminary contained sixty aspirants to the priesthood, who, according to the rule revised by Father Leguay

N. D. 9, App.,
191; 198
N. D. 11, 582 f.

and approved by the Holy See, were to be considered as aspirants to the Congregation.[3] Most but not all of these novices withdrew under the reform introduced by Father Libermann. According to Father Le Vavasseur, none of the novices in Reunion were good enough to join the Congregation; yet one of them, whom he would "never consent to admit," was accepted by the Trappists.

---

[2]Because it is often said that there were only four or five, we give here the list of their names: Father Monnet, Father Warnet, Father Gaultier, Father Hardy, Father Loewenbruck, Father Vidal, Father Weber, Father Hervé, Father Hersent, Father Cheroutre, Father Orinel, Father Lucienne, and Father Richard. Cf. *N.D.* 10, 352 ff. and 11, 92 and 582.

[3]*"Pro fine habet . . . SODALES educare,"* as the rule of the Congregation still reads.

Among the thirteen old Holy Ghost Fathers there were men of outstanding ability, such as Father Gaultier, a close collaborator of Migne, who was renowned for his theological learning; Father Loewenbruck, a famous preacher of popular missions in France, whose diplomatic abilities so impressed the Propaganda that he was charged with a delicate mission to Corfu and even designated to become Archbishop of the place; Father Monnet himself, whose real talent lay in missionary work; Father Vidal, who became Prefect Apostolic of Senegal. What they lacked was a man who could solve the ever-recurring crises resulting from government interference in the ecclesiastical affairs of the colonies and exercise strong leadership within the walls of the Seminary itself.

In the current situation, any serious conflict of views between the Government and the Spiritans immediately became a threat to the very existence of the Congregation. Their independence was far too limited by the single aim of training colonial clergy. In fact, the turbulent first half of the nineteenth century emphasized this serious defect in the organization of the Congregation. Membership was largely restricted to the minimum required for the proper functioning of the colonial seminary and the small number of members offered only a small chance of finding one of outstanding ability, capable of assuming the leadership.

Moreover, while other congregations and orders had been able to concentrate on rebuilding their ranks after the Revolution before they resumed their apostolic labors, the Holy Ghost Fathers were not given a chance to do likewise. The reason lies in the anomalous position in which they found themselves at that time: they had to supply priests for the old French colonies where the Revolution had decimated the clergy, and yet the government interfered at every step. Paris insisted on having priests and more priests for the colonies because, since the abolition of slavery was imminent, all eyes were fixed on these territories and everyone feared the revolts that might occur if there were no priests to prepare the slaves for their freedom. At the same time, as we have seen, interference continued to make a normal development of the seminary impossible. The Spiritans had to send every available priest to the missions and never had a chance to resume their eighteenth century custom of retaining the best products of their seminary to strengthen their own ranks. Finally, out-

Father Nicolas Warnet, Eighth Superior General of the Congregation of the Holy Ghost (1845).

Father Alexander Leguay, Ninth Superior General of the Congregation of the Holy Ghost (1845-1848).

Bishop Alexander Monnet, Tenth Superior General of the Congregation of the Holy Ghost (1848).

Venerable Father Francis Libermann, Founder of the Congregation of the Holy Heart of Mary, Restorer of the Congregation of the Holy Ghost and its Eleventh Superior General (1848-1852).

siders who were foreign to the traditions of the Congregation had to be called in to help operate it, with such disastrous consequences as we have related in the case of Father Leguay.

N. D. 10, 345   The entrance of Father Libermann and his confreres brought remedy to these evils. It strengthened the ranks of the Holy Ghost Fathers with thirty-four priests and ten novices. In addition, Libermann had thirty-four aspirants in his senior seminary (twenty-one in theology and thirteen in philosophy), along with twenty-eight brothers. Father Libermann himself possessed abundantly all the qualities necessary for leadership; he enjoyed the esteem and confidence of many high government officials; and he was beyond all dispute one of the ablest directors a seminary could desire.

Materially and financially speaking, the Holy Ghost Congregation was neither rich nor poor. Its seminary was well-equipped,
N. D. 10, 219   free of debt, and enjoyed an independent income of about 8,000 gold francs a year. The Government paid its professors a small salary and provided for the maintenance of sixty seminarians. This income, however, was too dependent on the vagaries of governmental decisions to provide any permanent security for
N. D. 10, 394   the functioning of the seminary. As a matter of fact, in January 1849, the government allocation was arbitrarily reduced by fifty percent. One could hardly say then that Father Libermann was
N. D. 10, 291;   attracted by the riches of the Holy Ghost Seminary. Neverthe-
295; 323; 326   less, he had to deny repeatedly the widely circulated story that, being on the verge of bancruptcy, he was trying in this way to recoup his finances. It must be admitted that the Congregation of the Holy Heart of Mary possessed little or no fixed income and had to manage quite economically to make ends meet. The bottom of the money box was continually visible, even though its income nearly always stayed a few francs ahead of expenses. Despite this record of solvency, the official report of the Prop-
Fl. 605   aganda states that without the union Libermann's congregation "would necessarily have to be disbanded for lack of economic
N. D. 10, 340   resources." Libermann himself merely admits that "through the union we will secure for ourselves to some extent the resources [we need] for the maintenance of the novitiate and the support of missionaries who are no longer able to work." As we have seen, the only independent income that could be diverted to such a

purpose amounted to only 8,000 francs a year, just enough to maintain sixteen persons.

The really priceless possession enjoyed by the Holy Ghost Congregation was its legal recognition by the French Government, dating back to the times of King Louis XV. The value of this recognition was demonstrated very clearly in 1901 when the anticlerical government of Combes could find no legal way to expel the Congregation and confiscate its properties. In fact, the Supreme Council of State, by an act unique in its history, had to reverse itself and rescind its own decree of suppression. Libermann lacked such a recognition and realized that it could no longer be obtained.[4] Yet, in the words of the Propaganda, his congregation needed it, "in order not to be subject to dissolution in the near future." The Venerable himself appeared to allude to this when he wrote:

cf. pp. 238 ff.

N. D. 10, 220

N. D. 10, 340

> If we had remained separate, the Society of the Holy Heart of Mary would have been exposed, if not to shipwreck, at least to a lingering existence for a considerable time and to experience perhaps some years hence such difficulty and opposition that all its efforts would have been thwarted.

Thus we see that the legal status of the Holy Ghost Fathers was one of the major considerations that inspired Libermann to seek the union.

A second impelling reason was the fact that the Holy Ghost Congregation was officially in charge of the old French colonies, where Libermann's priests had begun their work. Serious jurisdictional conflicts were bound to arise and had, in fact, already occurred in Reunion and Senegambia. Libermann was very much disturbed by them and realized that he was at a disadvantage because the Spiritans had the official recognition of both Church and State, while his congregation had neither. In one stroke the union removed forever any possible source of further conflict of this sort.

N. D. 10, 371

N. D. 10, 340

---

[4]Apart from the Holy Ghost Fathers, only three clerical societies enjoy legal recognition in France. They are the Vincentians, the Sulpicians and the Foreign Missions Society of Paris. Like the Spiritans, all three obtained it before the French Revolution of 1792. During the Second World War the Vichy Government extended it to the Carthusians.

Tabulating the position of both congregations in the summer of 1848, before Libermann became Superior General of the Holy Ghost Fathers, we arrive at the following:

		Holy Ghost Fathers	Fathers of the Holy Heart of Mary
Total personnel		13 priest-members 30 priest-novices 60 aspirants	34 priest-members 10 priest-novices 34 aspirants 28 Brothers
Missions	territories	1. St. Pierre et Miquelon 2. Martinique 3. Reunion 4. Guadeloupe 5. Senegal 6. Guiana 7. Pondicherry 8. Madagascar 9. Malgaches Islands*	The Vicariate of the Two Guineas One foundation in Mauritius and another in Reunion
	personnel	about 180 secular priests; 7 members	26 priests 10 Brothers
Europe	houses	Seminary in Paris one country house	Notre Dame du Gard residence in Bordeaux
	personnel	6 priest-members 2 others	8 priests 18 Brothers

*After the death of Bishop Monnet in 1849, Madagascar and the Malgaches Islands were handed over to the Jesuits. Later, the Holy Ghost Fathers were to take charge again of about one-third of Madagascar.

2. *Reorganization*

A young and vigorous branch had been grafted onto an aging tree. Would it flourish or would the two organisms show so much incompatibility that the branch would wither away and the old stump itself would be bereft of life? Everything depended on the adaptability of the men who had formerly belonged to two separate groups and on Libermann's ability to cope with difficulties as they arose. His election as Superior General—the eleventh in a line started by Father Poullart des Places—and the incorporation of his associates into the Holy Ghost Congregation placed on Libermann's shoulders these three additional burdens:

1. overcoming internal and external opposition to the new state of affairs;

2. giving proper direction to the colonial seminary;

3. solving the religious crises of the old colonies.

a. INTERNAL OPPOSITION

With respect to the first item, much depended on how the members would react to unification. The old Holy Ghost Fathers in Paris caused no great concern. Libermann himself was able to report soon after his election as Superior General:

N. D. 11, 87

We no longer have to fear any difficulty on the part of the old members of the Holy Ghost. They are no longer attached to the former state of affairs. Our moderation, kindness, and confidence in them has won them over completely.

As we will see, only one of them, Father Hardy, was going to cause any trouble in the future. Three of them became Vicar or Prefects Apostolic shortly after Libermann's accession—namely, Father Monnet in Madagascar, Father Weber in the Malgaches Islands, and Father Vidal in Senegal, while Father Loewenbruck was constantly occupied in Corfu by a special mission for the Propaganda. Of those in the colonies, some accepted the new arrangement and remained members, others gradually dropped out. All of them were isolated in colonial parishes and would not have been able to cause trouble even if that had been their intention.

N. D. Compl., 140

Surprisingly, the greatest opposition came from Father Libermann's own confreres of the Holy Heart of Mary. Mail service at that time was rather slow, and he had been forced to proceed without consulting those who were scattered through Mauritius, Reunion, and Africa. He had tried to keep them informed by letters, but off in the distance, with wild rumors reaching them from everyside, it was difficult for them to get a clear picture of the whole affair. Some, including Father Laval in Mauritius, apparently learned of the union through the newspapers before word

N. D. 11, 587 f.

reached them from Father Libermann. Father Duteil, a Benedictine, poured fuel on the discontent by stories about quarrels between the two congregations. Father Thiersé declared that he would be anything rather than a Holy Ghost Father. However, when it became clear that, apart from the name, nothing much had been changed in their status and that they would "continue to live in the missions as they had done before," they soon regained their composure and accepted the new order of things.

N. D. 11, 62

In Notre Dame du Gard, however, there was at first an angry outburst. Father Kobès, then assistant novice master, happened to be near the door when a postman delivered the document from the Propaganda addressed to Libermann. Impulsively he tore open the letter, read it, and stormed into the community room where Father Libermann was giving a conference to the novices. "Treason!" he shouted, "We have been betrayed!" He, as well as the others, had expected a substitution of their own congregation for that of the Holy Ghost or at least an *ex aequo* union of the two. Instead, the Propaganda had simply suppressed the Congregation of the Holy Heart of Mary and directed its members to enter the Congregation of the Holy Ghost. The document did not even recommend retention of the rule or the combination of names.[5] Even Father Lannurien, Libermann's intimate friend, called the decree a betrayal of the whole past.

Döring, 278

Francis Libermann's personal reaction, unlike that of his confreres, was the acquiescence of a saint. As Father Le Vavasseur testified in the apostolic process dealing with the heroic nature of the Venerable's virtues:

N. D. Compl.
141

> "In order that the Congregation of the Holy Ghost might not be considered as a new Congregation, Father Libermann eagerly accepted the decree of the Holy See by which his own Congregation was totally dissolved before its members entered that of the Holy Ghost."

---

[5]Father Loewenbruck had not dared to mention these two points in his negotiations at Rome because he feared that it would jeopardize the whole union. Only a few months before, the Propaganda had approved Leguay's revision of the rule. He was afraid that they would object to another radical change coming so soon after that one. At least, it would have delayed the whole affair and, with a revolution hovering over Rome, there was no time for delays.

In his article "Le Bienheureux Père Eymard," *Études*, July 1925, p. 136, Paul Dudon claims that some of Libermann's confreres refused to follow him into the Congregation of the Holy Ghost and organized a short-lived independent community at the *Rue d'Enfer*, Paris. The records of Libermann's suppressed society published in *Notes et Documents*, vol. 13, App., pp. 44 ff., clearly show that the author's assertion is utterly without any foundation: not a single member of the Congregation of the Holy Heart of Mary left at the time of the "fusion."

After all, Libermann was not too worried over the omissions. He was convinced that Rome would allow him to make the necessary changes. As a matter of fact, a few weeks later he travelled to Rome and obtained without difficulty the suspension of the second order, the restoration of poverty, and the insertion of the Immaculate Heart in the title of the Congregation. The full title, which is used only in certain official ecclesiastical documents, used to be "The Congregation of the Holy Ghost under the Protection of the Immaculate Virgin." This now became "The Congregation of the Holy Ghost under the Protection of the Immaculate Heart of Mary."[6]

Fortunately, Libermann's tact and patience eventually succeeded in overcoming the opposition of his own confreres. Slowly they came to accept the union as it had been ordered by the Propaganda. Many, however, objected for a long time to being called Holy Ghost Fathers and in their writing and thinking continued to oppose the Congregation of the Holy Heart of Mary to that of the Holy Ghost. They could not bear to think that Libermann's congregation had simply been disbanded and suppressed by Rome. Even his successor, Father Schwindenhammer, continued to speak about the "former" Congregation of the Holy Ghost, and he referred to Libermann as the *Founder* of the Congregation of the Holy Ghost and the Immaculate Heart of Mary and its *First* Superior General. Traces of this resistance can be found even in our times. Some, for example, out of habit still say that Libermann was the *first* Superior General and others still call him the Founder. In later years, as we shall see, this reluctance to face facts and submit to the decision of Rome gave rise to a severe crisis for the Congregation in France.

Now, with peace more or less restored among his own spiritual children, Libermann set himself to the task of supplementing the brief rule of the Holy Ghost Congregation by a set of additional regulations covering the many points in which the old rule was insufficient for the new state of affairs. Being careful to consult the old Holy Ghost Fathers on the matter, he was happy to report that

D. C. 184 ff.

Va. 240

cf. pp. 238 ff.

---

[6]The second part of the new title not only resembled the old one in meaning but did not even alter the aspect under which the Congregation honored the Mother of God. In 1828, long before Libermann's congregation came into existence, the Spiritans erected in their Motherhouse the Confraternity of the Most Pure Heart of Mary.

*N. D. 39; cf. N. D. 9, App. 195

N. D. 11, 57

"they were delighted" with his additions. The necessity of adding these new regulations, which constitute the basis of the present Constitutions of the Congregation, gave him a welcome opportunity to revise his own provisional rule by discarding impractical points and incorporating the experiences of the previous eight years.

b. CONFLICT WITH THE ARCHBISHOP OF PARIS

While internal difficulties were being solved in this way, a major problem arose from an unexpected angle: Archbishop Dominic Sibour of Paris, the successor of Archbishop Affre, who had been killed on a barricade during the June revolution of 1848. Following the example of Father Monnet, Libermann had abstained from asking the Archbishop of Paris to confirm his election as Superior General. According to the rules approved by the Propaganda, the right of confirmation now belonged to Rome. This was too much for the Gallican tendencies of the new Archbishop,

N. D. 4, 265
N. D. 11, 458

whose chancery was full of Libermann's enemies. In a bitter and injurious letter he accused the priests of the Congregation of misleading the Propaganda, of celebrating Mass, preaching, and hearing confessions without his permission, and even perpetrating open acts of hostility. Moreover, he warned them that their withdrawal

N. D. 11, 16;
462

from his control had made them lose their legal recognition. Father Libermann's reply failed to sooth his ire. He demanded a return to the ancient rule of 1734, which had been approved by his predecessor.

Realizing that Rome would never allow a Congregation with works on four continents to return to diocesan status, Libermann told the Archbishop that such a decision could be taken only by the Propaganda and suggested that the Archbishop apply for it. His Excellency, however, was not attracted by the prospect of altercations with Rome. He ordered Libermann to request the

N. D. 11, 463

change as if the idea was initiated by the Congregation itself. All the while he kept insisting that a return to his control was necessary for legal recognition.

N. D. 11, 464;
465; 466; 468

When none of Father Libermann's proposed drafts of a letter to the Propaganda proved satisfactory, the Archbishop ordered him to sign a letter composed by the archiepiscopal secretary. Mean-

N. D. 11,
143 f.; 470 f.

while, Libermann was having a legal expert examine the Archbishop's claims regarding recognition. The lawyer concluded that a change in rule approved by Rome had no influence whatsoever on the legal status of the Society. It was obvious that the question had been raised only as a pretext to regain control over the Congregation. To avoid sharpening the conflict, therefore, Libermann signed the letter. But the Archbishop had forgotten that more than one letter can be written. Father Libermann had no scruples about sending a confidential note to the Secretary of the Propaganda explaining the background of the whole affair and asking him to tell the whole story to the Cardinal Prefect.

N. D. 11, 329

N. D. 11, 332

The papers reached Rome just when the long-expected revolution had broken out in Italy. With the Pope in exile at Gaeta, the central offices of the Church were so disorganized that they could expedite only the most urgent questions. The little quarrel of the Archbishop was not important enough to fall into this category and no answer whatsoever was given to the request. As Libermann himself had advised, it was better to delay a decision and give time a chance to solve the problem.

N. D. 13, 191

Meanwhile the Archbishop continued to raise difficulties. Efforts were made in all secrecy by members of his chancery to have Libermann and his priests removed from the Seminary and to place the institution under the direction of a diocesan Vicar General. When Sibour's signature was needed to legalize a bequest in favor of the Congregation, he refused to give it and thereby caused the loss of the legacy. In 1851 the Venerable began to fear that his priests would be refused faculties in the Archdiocese. Then the Vicar General of Paris, Father Lequeux, offered his mediation. Knowing the extreme Gallican tendencies of this priest (who was soon to be condemned by Rome), Libermann feared the worst and decided to reject his offer. He did this, knowing full well how angry the Chancery would be. "I have become hardened," he said, "against all these angers both official and unofficial. Let the good God do with us what He will. We cannot give way to thunder."

N. D. 12, 142

N. D. 13, 189

N. D. 13, 254
N. D. Compl.,
172

N. D. 13, 279

With no reply from Rome and no concessions from Libermann who, incidentally, was supported by other French bishops, Archbishop Sibour's campaign made very little progress. The affair was still unsettled in 1857 when a murderer's hand put an end to the Archbishop's life. Libermann himself had died five years before. Their respective successors, Cardinal Morbot and Father Schwindenhammer solved the problem without too much difficulty.

C. S. 11, 56

N. D. 13, 739

The settlement left the Congregation under the authority of Rome, except for the normal jurisdiction exercised by any bishop over non-exempt religious in his diocese.[7] Underlying the whole dispute had been the outspoken pro-Roman tendencies of the Congregation, whose Parisian Seminary traditionally had been a stalwart proponent of papal supremacy. In fact, just at the time of the union, Father Gaultier had made many enemies among the French clergy by his staunch defense of the Pope's prerogatives. Now Libermann's influence had given further impetus to this anti-Gallican trend. Thus it is not surprising that prelates who were still imbued with ideas of French independence in Church affairs tried to regain control over this stronghold of opposition to Gallicanism.

With respect to the outside world, including even ecclesiastical circles, it was important to achieve full realization of the changes brought about by the new organization. From now on there had to be a clear distinction between members of the Congregation and the secular priests who had studied at the colonial seminary. Until the union, both members of the Congregation and the secular priests trained by them had been known everywhere as Holy Ghost Fathers. Henceforth this title, or its popular form "Spiritan," was to be reserved exclusively for members of the Congregation. Although it was some time before the distinction was generally recognized, it is from this moment on that we must cease to pay special attention to the secular clergy of the old French colonies. Its history is no longer a history of the Holy Ghost Fathers.

c. REFORM OF THE SEMINARY

The venerable Holy Ghost Seminary was showing unmistakable signs of the critical times it had weathered since the death of Father Fourdinier, three years before. Far too often and too long its Superior had been absent on recruiting journeys through France without being replaced by someone who was capable of adequately directing the seminarians. As a result, these young men were often left to their own devices and discipline suffered greatly. The house was always full of priests on their way to or from the colonies, and

---

Va. 236
C. S. 44 bis, 7 ff.

[7]However, Archbishop Darboy, his successor, who was in conflict with Rome because of his Gallicanism, reopened the battle. It ended definitely only when Father Schwindenhammer saved the life of his Vicar General during the brief communist rule of 1871. The Archbishop himself was murdered. Since then relations between the Congregation and the Archdiocese have always been excellent.

these visitors would harangue any audience they could muster about their views on the emancipation of slaves, the iniquities of the colonial Government, the unreasonableness of their ecclesiastical superiors, and their fears of what might result if Libermann were to take over. In addition, the Seminary had been in the midst of the two bloody revolutions of February and June 1848, just before Libermann assumed charge. Barricades around the house and the crackle of gun-fire are not exactly conducive to the recollected atmosphere that a seminary demands. Finally, although a large majority of the seminarians were suitable candidates for the priesthood, certain members of the student body simply did not belong there.

Strictly speaking, the presence of a few unsuitable candidates is nothing special in a seminary, for one of its very functions is to probe the character and motives of aspirants to the priesthood. Obviously, there will always be some who fail to pass the test. Holy Ghost Seminary usually had a relatively high number of these misfits because it received aspirants from all over France and some foreign countries as well. Contrary to the usual procedure in other seminaries, its directors were unable to interview candidates before their admission. They often had to rely on information supplied by distant pastors who were personally unknown to them, and misplaced pity sometimes induced these priests to give unsuitable candidates another chance in different surroundings. Without a capable director at the Seminary, the presence of these misfits gave rise to dangerous consequences.

At first, Father Libermann did not encounter any great difficulty. The Government had just reduced its support of the seminary by fifty percent, and this justified his dismissing fifteen

N. D. 12, 142

of the more doubtful characters. Those who were left received his fullest attention and in general responded fairly well to the guidance of this expert director. Unfortunately, in April 1849, Father Libermann fell seriously ill when the cholera swept Paris[8] and it was six months before he could return to the seminary.

During his absence, agitation started. At first it began with the usual trivial complaints about the quality of the food, the parsimony of the bursar, and the restrictions of daily life. The

---

[8]Although the Seminary was in one of the most infected areas of the city and his priests fearlessly visited the sick, the dread disease struck only one of those living in the Seminary.

unusual feature of these customary complaints, heard in any seminary, was that they were circulated all over France and communicated even to the Government. Soon the affair became more

N. D. 12, 662

serious: the Congregation was accused of wanting to close the colonies to the secular clergy and of using the Government subsidy for its own interests. The first climax was reached when,

Br. 281

after Libermann's return, five newly-ordained priests decided to hold a demonstration and collectively refused to accept their appointments for Guiana. Libermann's quiet reaction succeeded in bringing them back to reason, but in the excitement of the moment these demonstrators revealed who was behind the wave of discontent—Father Hardy.

As we have mentioned before, Father Hardy suffered from a mental and emotional imbalance which was shrouded in a deceptively pious exterior. In 1844 he had been expelled by Father Fourdinier, but Father Leguay took him back later. At first he

N. D. 11, 207

graciously accepted Father Libermann, but when a new General Council was chosen and he did not receive a single vote, he flew into a rage and sought to avenge himself.

The easiest way to achieve his end seemed to lie in causing as much trouble as possible in the Seminary. He had ample time to foment dissension for, under the pretense of illness, he had never accepted any work. Joining forces with certain persons at

N. D. 12, 661

the diocesan Chancery, he plotted the expulsion of the "Libermannists" and their replacement by a Vicar General of the diocese,

N. D. 12, 478

a function to which he himself aspired. At night he went to the rooms of the seminarians to announce the impending expulsion of Father Libermann and his priests and to feed the fires of revolu-

N. D. 12, 662

tion. Feigning innocence and submission to the Superior, he devised a secret code of communication by which he could keep the

N. D. 12, 661

ringleaders informed and the resistance active. The whole affair was plotted and executed with the utmost secrecy. Seminarians who were involved in it took great care not to commit any overt act that could cause their expulsion. They obeyed all rules scrupulously until they had received major orders. Then they threw off the mask, in the belief that now it was safe for them to act openly.

N. D. 12, 666

Complaints were sent to politicians and to the Ministry of Ecclesiastical Affairs about Libermann's embezzlement of funds; Father Warnet and Father Gaultier were brought to court for allegedly having falsified, to the detriment of Father Hardy, the

N. D. 12, 663

last will of Father Fourdinier; the Government was petitioned to expel the "Libermannists" from the seminary. Even an accusation of simony was drawn up to be sent to Rome. It claimed that Father Libermann had sold a bishopric to gain control of the Holy Ghost Congregation.

The Venerable Father found it difficult to take any action against Father Hardy, because too many of his opponents in the Chancery were watching for a chance to openly attack the new regime at the Seminary and institute expulsion proceedings against Libermann. Of course, there was little hope of success in such efforts, but the resulting publicity would certainly have had an adverse effect on the Congregation and the Seminary.

N. D. 13, 545

The situation soon became intolerable. A solution had to be found, no matter what the consequences. Father Hardy was told to move from the Seminary to Notre Dame du Gard or, if he preferred, to the colonies. When he refused to obey, he received his canonical warnings and was excluded. However, he merely took lodgings nearby and continued his nefarious work until the end came suddenly for him in January, 1851. On his way to secure the support of a visiting colonial bishop, he slipped before the entrance of the seminary and fell in front of a heavy water cart.

N. D. 12, 669

Its wheels crushed his abdomen. Carried inside the house, he was given the last sacraments and died the following day among his former confreres whom he had so furiously and so bitterly fought.

N. D. 12, 203

With his death, the agitation and discontent at the Seminary came to an end. Deciding to clean up once and for all, Father Libermann expelled all those who had taken part in Father Hardy's various plots. However, he recommended to other seminaries those whom he still considered capable of becoming good priests. As one of the ringleaders wrote to him after his dismissal:

N. D. 12, 668

> I dare say this: in everything that happened we were only little wheels and blindly obeyed a director whom we falsely believed worthy of our respect. Yes, it was Father Hardy alone, who through his gestures and suggestions maintained a violent hatred of the Directors of the Holy Ghost Seminary in the minds of all without exception. He told us a thousand times: "I guarantee that you will not be expelled. Go on acting as you have done till now and I will take full responsibility."

d. The Solution of the Religious Crisis in the Old Colonies

It may be useful to point out here that this crisis was not caused by the corruption of the clergy trained at Holy Ghost Seminary. Although the opposite view was generally accepted in France, it was based, not on facts, but on unwarranted generalizations drawn from a few isolated scandals and on a host of unproved rumors. Not a single one of the colonial priests who had been educated in the junior and senior seminary of the Holy Ghost became a bad priest in the colonies. Those who had spent at least a few years in this seminary were nearly all beyond reproach. This is a record that is rare even in the best seminaries of the Church.

Cl. C. 306 ff.

However, these priests constituted only about half the colonial clergy. The rest consisted of volunteers from various dioceses and a small number of drifters who had gone to the colonies without any authorization. Because of the chronic shortage of priests, these wanderers often managed to get themselves accepted after their arrival. Nearly every scandal that occurred in the colonies had its source in them. Because priests occupied an official position in the French possessions, these scandals received great publicity, not only in the colony itself, but also in the homeland. As usual, a few cases were sufficient to lead most people to the conclusion that the whole clergy was corrupt.

Even a man like Father Libermann was far from flattering in his appreciation of the colonial clergy, at least before he became Superior General of the Holy Ghost Fathers and was able to know the whole situation from first-hand information. Then he did not hesitate to change his mind. Thus, for instance, in 1850, he wrote confidentially to Father Schwindenhammer:

N. D. 13, 322 f.

> The majority of the colonial clergy is just as good as the majority of the French clergy. The clergy of Britanny are generally held in high esteem. Nevertheless, most of these priests, if they had been transferred to the colonies, would not have done better than those who are there.

Cl. C. 354 ff.

If the clergy of the colonies had been as bad as has often been suggested, they would never have succeeded in raising the Church from Revolutionary ruins to an established hierarchy in a few short years. The most serious fault of this clergy was its lack of subordination to the local Ecclesiastical Superiors.

N. D. 12, 265

Undoubtedly, there was a religious crisis in the colonies, but its cause did not lie in the corruption of the clergy. Its main factors were to be sought in the insufficiency and lack of homogeneity of the colonial clergy, the weakness of the authority of the Prefects Apostolic and their utter dependence on the civil administration. A few words must be said about each of these points before we can consider how the Venerable Francis Libermann succeeded in arriving at a solution.

Insufficient Clergy. In 1849 there was one priest for every 761 souls in France; in the old colonies there was only one for three times that number. Yet the colonies should have had more priests than France because of the absence of good roads and means of communication, the greater frequency of illness, and above all the urgent necessity of caring for the former slaves whose religious and moral training had so long been neglected. Libermann calculated that more than three hundred additional priests would be needed at once to obtain an average of one for every eight hundred souls.

. N. D. 11, 199

Lack of Homogeneity of the Clergy. The constantly changing attitude of the Government regarding Holy Ghost Seminary had resulted in the necessity of recruiting priests elsewhere throughout France. According to Libermann's calculation, merely to maintain the existing proportion of one priest per 2,250 souls there should always be at least sixty seminarians in training for the colonial clergy. Since the Government grant did not provide for that many, about half the priests had to be taken from among those offering themselves for this work. Far too often these volunteers were wholly unprepared for church work in tropical lands. Even at best, they were set in their habits and wanted to work in the manner they were accustomed to at home, although conditions overseas did not remotely resemble conditions in France. Then, when they died or were transferred, another priest would arrive from a different part of France and begin to run everything just as he used to do it in his old parish at home.

N. D. 11, 201

Weakness of the Ecclesiastical Authority. Each of the old colonies was governed by a Prefect Apostolic. This ecclesiastical superior did not possess the episcopal dignity; he was not even entitled to the purple robes of a Monsignor, because at that time

Cl. C. 142

it was not yet customary to give Prefects this honor. He was just another priest among many and the precise nature and extent of his powers had not yet been determined by canon law. The priests within his jurisdiction received their faculties directly from the Propaganda, not from him. Thus the Prefect's authority and moral ascendancy depended to a large extent on his personal qualities and understanding of the numerous factors entering into the government of human beings.

Cl. C. 409

N. D. 11, 228;
231
Cl. C. 183

Cf. p. 420

Moreover, it often happened that new ecclesiastical superiors followed each other in quick succession. For instance, Senegal alone had eleven Prefects and Vice-Prefects between 1817 and 1849, and Guadeloupe had four between 1844 and 1849. It is obvious that these men simply did not have the time to achieve effective control over their clergy. This weakness of ecclesiastical authority was rendered still more acute by the Prefects' utter dependence on the Government. In fact, when the Governor of Reunion was in conflict with the Prefect he arrogantly said, "I am the Bishop here." For the most part, Prefects were considered as just another type of state official who had to act in accord with the wishes of the civil command. When they refused to do so, they were often unceremoniously shipped back to France.

As one would expect, conflicts between the government and a Prefect usually resulted in a divided clergy, some siding with the Prefect and others with the Governor. This was especially true when civil authorities assigned priests to their posts and transferred them without too much concern for the opinion of the Ecclesiastical Superior. The constant insubordination of the clergy that is characteristic of this period, therefore, is understandable when viewed in this unfortunate political and canonical context.

R. H. M. 5,
225 ff.
N. D. 11, 199;
226
N. D. 11, 185;
13, 513

N. D. 11, 186

Libermann's Plan. To remedy these evils, Father Libermann developed a project which struck at the very roots of the problem. His plan, which he outlined in long memoranda to the Minister of Ecclesiastical Affairs and to the Propaganda, aimed at homogeneity in the clergy by insisting that only alumni of Holy Ghost Seminary be admitted to the colonies. This forced priests from elsewhere to spend at least a year of training in his Seminary. The ecclesiastical authorities of the colonies were to be given proper control over their clergy and adequate independence from civil authority by being raised to the episcopal dignity, at least in the

N. D. 11, 186

N. D. 11, 188

N. D. 11, 188

more important colonies of Guadeloupe, Martinique, and Reunion.[9] The scarcity of priests was to be alleviated by governmental support of the seminary sufficient to maintain at least sixty clerical aspirants. Finally, a native clergy was to be built up in the old colonies so that their missionary status would not be permanent. For this purpose, Libermann advocated the erection of junior seminaries in the principal colonies. Finally, religious communities of priests should be founded to take care of extra-parochial works.

While both the government and the Propaganda ultimately gave him nearly everything he had asked, it was not simply a matter of presenting his suggestions. First, the departmental ministers themselves had to be won over to his plan. This in itself was not an easy task, for the government had always insisted on retaining as much control as possible over the colonial clergy and their ecclesiastical superiors.

N. D. 11, 219;
472

Fortunately, Libermann presented his plan at an auspicious moment, for just then a sincere Catholic held the Ministry of Ecclesiastical Affairs. The powerful Minister of the Navy and the Colonies was also persuaded to support these recommendations, and much of the credit for this was due to his wife, whose aid Libermann had previously enlisted. Though the government fell before the affair was concluded, the successors of these two Ministers were also brought into line. Next, Parliament had to be lined up to vote the necessary funds. To this end, Libermann managed to win influential politicians over to his proposal and

N. D. 11, 189 ff.

even to convince that fanatical enemy of Holy Ghost Seminary— Mr. Schoelcher—that the plan had merit.

Because of the delicacy with which these multiple negotiations were carried off, Libermann gained quite a reputation for diplomacy.

N. D. 12, 214

The Minister of Ecclesiastical Affairs held him in such high esteem that he readily struck from the slate of episcopal candidates anyone to whom Libermann objected. This tremendously advantageous arrangement assured the elimination of schemers who

N. D. 12, 312

might have sought one of the new bishoprics for themselves or for their friends. With a strong colonial hierarchy thus virtually

N. D. 11, 351

ally guaranteed, the Holy See caused Libermann's cup of joy to

N. D. 12, 433;
13, 427

[9]Libermann tried to have Guiana erected as a Vicariate. However, death took him before his negotiations with the Government had been completed. It was only in 1934 that his wish was realized. The other colonies (St. Pierre et Miquelon, Pondicherry and Senegal) remained simple Prefectures.

overflow by instructing its new bishops to accept no priest who had not spent at least a year in Holy Ghost Seminary.

Cl. C. 212 ff.

Due to the government's liberal support, Holy Ghost Seminary entered into a new period of bloom after 1850. Applications were numerous. Screening was rigid. Only rarely were transfers from another seminary accepted and then only when their record was unblemished. The student body increased so rapidly that by 1857 the ordination class numbered forty-five. Usually there were about eighty seminarians, though at one time the total reached as high as a hundred and five.[10] Between 1850 and 1878 the Seminary was able to send over 360 well-trained priests to the colonies. A decline in numbers, but not in quality, set in after 1890 when a resurgence of anticlericalism in France once again cut the resources of the Seminary. Then, with the separation of Church and State in 1905, the numbers began to drop sharply. The nadir was reached shortly before the First World War when only eight students occupied the Seminary.

Br. 283

However, after the war a slow rise began and the total levelled off at between thirty and forty. It has remained there ever since. More recently, in 1954, the Seminary was transferred from the noise of Paris to a quiet spot at Croix-Valmer (Var), in Southern France. Most of its students nowadays come from the colonies themselves and thus constitute a genuine native clergy.

B. G. 43, 473

Libermann's final recommendation, viz., that religious orders take responsibility for non-parochial works in the colonies, came to function more slowly. He led the way by sending his own men to Guiana where they served leprosaria, prisons, and other houses of correction. As time went on, moreover, large numbers of Spiritans fanned out through all the old French colonies. But of this, more anon.

N. D. 13, 94

3. *Works in the Homeland*

Thus far most of our attention has been devoted to the eighteenth and nineteenth century missionary activity of the Congregation and its revitalization by the entrance of Father Libermann and his priests. This kind of work was and still is the main apostolate engaged in by the Spiritans. However, there is another

cf. p. 364

---

[10]This all-time high resulted from the entrance of Haitian candidates for the priesthood. Later Haiti opened an independent seminary near Guiclan in Finistère.

large field of activity in which Libermann's sons had already begun to function during his life and which under the rule of his immediate successors acquired an ever-increasing importance, viz., educational and social works. To understand that these phases of the apostolate did not constitute a deviation from Father Libermann's intent, we may find it helpful to examine certain aspects of the Venerable's plans which hitherto have been almost completely neglected.

a. The Origin of Educational Institutions

When Father Libermann wrote his provisional rule in Rome, prior to the foundation of his Congregation of the Holy Heart of Mary, he had fixed as its general purpose the evangelization of the most abandoned souls. He had further specified this purpose by saying that "missions in foreign and distant lands" were to be the aim of his priests. His intention was to keep in the homeland only such personnel as would be strictly necessary for the maintenance of the Congregation. He had even explicitly formulated a rule that his priests should never teach anything except theology.

N. D. 2, 240

N. D. 2, 254

Strange as it may seem, as soon as he had entered the seminary of Strassburg to prepare himself for the priesthood and for his role as the Superior of a new society, he felt himself again supernaturally attracted toward the training of priests. The word "again" is used advisedly, for prior to becoming involved in the missionary project of Father Le Vavasseur, his whole Christian life had been dedicated to this work. In the houses of St. Sulpice he had been the heart and soul of little groups of seminarians who earnestly aspired to intimate union with God. He had continued in this role even when his epilepsy seemed to bar him forever from the priesthood. As Novice Master of the Eudists, he had devoted all his time to training priests in the religious life.

In the light of past events, therefore, it is hardly surprising to see Father Libermann's desire to educate priests revive as soon as he re-entered a seminary to prepare himself for ordination. There is, however, one noteworthy aspect to this desire as it returned to flood his soul in 1841. He now wanted to give it fulfillment through the foundation of his own Congregation. He had heard about the sad condition of the clergy in Germany and aspired at making himself "useful to this country by aiding in the education of holy priests." For this reason he intended to establish the new con-

N. D. 2, 376

N. D. 2, 377

gregation in Strassburg, close to Germany. In a long letter to Father Le Vavasseur he explained that his priests could perform this task without betraying the purpose of the new society. It would be extremely interesting to see how the Venerable managed to reconcile this work with "missions in foreign and distant lands," but this letter has not been preserved.[11]

He had already rented a house in Strassburg to serve as the cradle of his Congregation and was earnestly negotiating with German priests when he was brought up short by a painful surprise. His shock and disappointment are expressed in a letter to his friend Dr. Drach:

N. D. 3, 64

> Without my knowledge, several priests who are interested in our little work for the Negroes have taken steps to get our foundation established in "the interior" of France.

Most prominent among these priests was Father de Brandt, formerly his most troublesome novice in the Eudists' house at Rennes, who had left that Congregation and was now Secretary to the Bishop of Amiens.

Humanly speaking, Father de Brandt's appearance at this juncture should have impressed the Venerable as another effort to thwart his plans. However, Libermann was accustomed to take the supernatural rather than the human view. Father de Brandt was able to offer him not only an assurance of ordination by the Bishop of Amiens, but also a house in the diocese to receive the first members of his nascent foundation. The offer possessed too many advantages to be rejected and Libermann accepted it because

N. D. 3, 65

"he thought to see in it a sufficiently clear indication of God's will." Nevertheless, he added, the decision was a painful one, for he wanted to make himself useful to the German clergy and attract German vocations to the Congregation. To his future successor, Father Schwindenhammer, he confessed:

N. D. 3, 192

> As far as Germany is concerned, I am forced to give up the idea. It causes me great pain, but what can I do about it? Our Lord has not judged me worthy of such great work.

---

[11]At least, it is not included in the 13 volumes of *Notes et Documents*, unless the passage alludes to *N.D.* 9, 282 ff., which, however, does not speak of the training of priests and is also of much later date.

Nonetheless, the idea continued to haunt him. He must have spoken about it frequently to his confreres for, a year after his death, Father Lannurien, his confidential secretary, mentions once again the direction of "seminaries, whether in Germany or in other lands," as proper to the Congregation. Ignorant of the future, Libermann did not see why God kept inspiring him with a desire to work at the training of priests, while at the same time arranging things in such a way that this desire could not be satisfied. It was only later in his life that the ways of Providence became clear.

For the moment, we merely wish to point out that even at the very time when he was founding his missionary congregation he was already thinking and making plans for this type of educational work in the homeland. It is irrelevant to point out that the project of his earliest collaborators was purely missionary and that he himself had written a rule specifying work in "missions in distant and foreign lands." We have to take into account not only what was concretely the starting point of his work but also how it developed under the direction of this man who did not make any move unless he clearly saw it was God's will. In a letter to Father Le Vavasseur he does not hesitate to say that if this rule has to be interpreted in such a way that everyone must go to the missions and that "we may not have several houses in Europe, it is important that the constitution of the Congregation be changed." Despite his explicit order not to engage in any teaching except that of theology, he wrote as early as 1844: "The Rule says that we must not undertake the instruction of youth. However, conditions show that probably we will be obliged to take charge of it."

The whole question of assuming educational work outside the missions became acute again in 1848 when his own society was dissolved and its members entered the Congregation of the Holy Ghost. As we have pointed out before, the Holy Ghost Fathers were primarily and traditionally a society of educators and professors, although a minority of their members had gone to the missions.[12] When Rome demanded that Libermann and his con-

Arch. Lann. 74

N. D. 9, 293

N. D. 6, 121

---

[12]It may be useful to remind the reader that before the French Revolution they conducted not only the seminary of Paris but also the senior seminary and the seminary-college at Meaux and a seminary at Verdun, and that after the Revolution their first work again was a seminary-college.

freres accept the rules of the old Holy Ghost Congregation, it meant that they had to share in the task of training seminarians.[13]

More concretely speaking, it implied a broadening of the aims which Libermann and his associates originally had in mind. His God-given desire to make himself and his priests useful in the training of clerical aspirants suddenly found ready release when the fusion with the Holy Ghost Fathers became a fact. In addition to missionary work, in the proper sense of the term, they had to undertake the education of future priests as well. The difficulty was that practically all his confreres wanted to be missionaries and

Arch. Lann. 73 nothing else. Thus it should not surprise us to hear that "nearly all or perhaps even all" of them were against their incorporation into the Holy Ghost Congregation, and that Father Lannurien called it a "betrayal of the whole past." Only gradually and through repeated conversations with the Venerable did he come to the conclusion that he and his confreres had been too one-sided and too much inspired by their own personal preferences.

Father Lannurien's conversion to Libermann's view is important, for all recognized that, as the confidential secretary, he had been Libermann's closest associate during the last years of his life. It was for this reason that after the Venerable's death in 1852 the others asked him to explain exactly what their Superior had in mind during the last decisive years of his life. In a long memorandum, Father Lannurien stated *inter alia*:

Lann. 24 ff.;
cf. N. D. Compl.,
214

[Libermann] either betrayed his mission, trespassed the commission God had entrusted to him, and gave a mortal blow to his work and the Congregation . . . [or acted in accord with] God's plans. . . . If God had called Father Libermann only to found a Congregation of missionaries for Negroes and other abandoned souls, it would be difficult to see for what special reason He had given him such extraordinary talents for

cf. N. D. 12, 529   [13]Let no one say that this responsibility was limited to the training of priests who are members of the Congregation because the Latin rule reads: "Sodalitii finis est . . . *sodales* educare." The term *"sodales"* or *"members"* was substituted for *"clericos"* by Father Leguay in his ill-advised attempt to incorporate the clergy. It has been maintained in an effort to retain as much as possible of the rule as it was when Libermann entered. However, the ineptness of the expression is striking. No religious society has as its purpose the education of its own members. What would the educated members do? Educate other members and so on to infinity? To make any sense, there would have to exist a kind of an inner circle, to which alone this rule would apply. However, such a circle does not exist and never has existed in the Congregation.

spiritual guidance and training for the interior life. . . . Therefore, both the fusion with the Congregation of the Holy Ghost, which was so dangerous for us, and the nature of the special gifts of grace possessed by Father Libermann appear to me as signs of the second purpose of his foundation and vocation—namely, that God had also destined his spiritual sons for the training of holy and zealous priests. Accordingly, I do not at all consider it a coincidence that the first new foundation of the Congregation after the death of our beloved Father was the foundation of a seminary and this in the most important city of the world, the very center of the Church.[14]

Arch. Lann. 74

For this reason Father Lannurien concluded that, to remain faithful to Libermann's idea, the Congregation had to expand in Europe by accepting "seminaries, whether in Germany or in other lands." An echo of the same idea could be heard in 1927 when the French Seminary in Rome, founded by Father Lannurien, celebrated its diamond jubilee. On this occasion, the *Bulletin* of the Congregation spoke of the work of training future priests:

B. G. 33, 633

This work corresponds in two ways with the Congregation's aim as it was when the fusion of 1848 called forth a second founder to further define its organization.

B. G. 9, 313 ff.

Father Libermann did not merely theorize about the question. In 1850, Archbishop Purcell of Cincinnati came to Paris and offered him the direction of his senior seminary. The Archbishop wanted this seminary to become a central interdiocesan institution serving the whole ecclesiastical province. "Despite the pressing needs of the missions and the colonies," therefore, Libermann accepted the offer and chose Father Ignatius Schwindenhammer as Superior of this work. Three others were to follow later. In July 1851, the new rector booked passage on an American steamer, but for some unknown reason Archbishop Purcell had to leave suddenly and the plan came to nought. Nonetheless, although the project fell short of realization, it clearly demonstrates Father Libermann's position regarding the scope of his society's work.

No doubt, more than one modern Spiritan will ask how all this can be reconciled with the general purpose of caring for the most

cf. pp. 337 ff.

[14]The Seminary in question is the Pontifical French Seminary in Rome in which, since 1853, the Holy Ghost Fathers have trained the elite of French aspirants to the priesthood.

abandoned souls. As far as we know, Father Libermann himself has not offered any explanation. Nevertheless, it is easy to see the thought behind it. As Father Lannurien explained to his confreres,

Arch. Lann. 74

> With this union [with the Holy Ghost Fathers] God had another and permanent aim in mind. This aim, I think, is that Father Libermann's Congregation, in addition to the apostolate exercised by its own members, should be charged with the training of secular priests, filled with a similar spirit of zeal and dedication, suitable for the apostolic care of souls and especially the preaching of the Gospel to the lower classes of society, the poor, who long enough have been abandoned to their fate and who now are destined to play such an important role in society.

In other words, just as the old Spiritans had aimed indirectly at the apostolate among the poor by way of priests trained under their care, so now Libermann's spiritual sons, their successors, were to undertake this indirect apostolate along with their direct ministry among the abandoned and neglected of the earth. This thought of an indirect apostolate was explicitly mentioned by Libermann's successor, Father Schwindenhammer, when he justified the acceptance of a college and junior seminary in Martinique:

B. G. 1, 552

> This establishment is destined to produce great benefits not only among the students themselves, but also through them among the poor colored class of the colony, on which the higher white class has always exercised a considerable influence for either good or evil.[15]

As experience has proved over and over again, junior seminaries often function best when they are an integral part of a college destined for all students who desire a thoroughly Catholic education. In this way the aspirants to the priesthood are more likely to obtain a better education because the college is forced to maintain standards which stand up under outside scrutiny and, at the same time, additional vocations may be fostered among the non-seminarians. Moreover, the arrangement is advantageous in

---

cf. p. 416

[15]Another typical example of this indirect apostolate among the poor was the College of Lima, Peru (1892). Through the education of Peru's leading classes, it tried to imbue the future leaders of this nation with sound Catholic principles.

establishing more widespread interest in the works of the Congregation. For these reasons there is nothing abnormal in the fact that soon after Libermann's death the Holy Ghost Fathers began to run large educational institutions, most of which were combined seminaries and colleges. Undoubtedly, not many of their lay students will ever be able to give the lay apostolate such a world-

cf. pp. 495 ff.

wide impetus as did Frank Duff, the founder of the Legion of Mary, who received his secular and religious training from the Holy Ghost Fathers at Blackrock College, but there are legions of Spiritan alumni who, thanks to the initiative of Father Libermann, were prepared to take part in the apostolate in less spectacular ways.

It should be noted here that Father Libermann made no recommendations regarding the extent to which his Congregation should devote itself to such educational endeavors. As usual, he wanted to be guided by Divine Providence and its various manifestations in the evolution of history. For that reason, he preferred to leave the decision to his successors in the Generalate. As we shall see, they did not betray his trust. According to the exigencies of time and place they have always kept faith with Spiritan traditions by forwarding the apostolate through whatever channels the known Will of God directed them and their men.

b. The Origin of Social Works

We have noted above how Father Libermann had pointed the general purpose of the Congregation toward the care of abandoned souls. In his travels through France it did not take him long to realize that many of the poor in Europe were almost as much

N. D. 9, 288

abandoned as were the people in mission territories. Specifying what he means by "the poor," he indicates "the working classes in general," to which he adds "seamen, soldiers, . . . forced laborers, prisoners and beggars." All of these groups lived beyond the reach of ordinary parish agencies, for even at that time the laborers of France had already lost much of their contact with the Church. The parish meant little or nothing to them. In that sense they were abandoned souls and Father Libermann wanted his priests to work among them. In a letter to Father Le Vavasseur he explains his position:

N. D. 9, 288

These works are not against the purpose or the spirit expressed in the Rule. True, in the beginning we did not think of them, but this does not prove that God did not want them. Here is my plan: The work which we will undertake in Europe will be concerned mainly with the salvation of the working class, sailors, [and] soldiers. . . . We will begin our establishments in the principal ports serving our missions, such as Bordeaux, Marseille, Toulon, Brest, Nantes and Lorient.

N. D. 10, 314

N. D. 9, 275

Work among the laboring classes was not to be limited to catechetics. It was to include also "their instruction in profane science, . . and the improvement of their material condition." He was not satisfied with merely undertaking it in an amateurish way. Instead, he regarded this kind of work as "one of the most important" tasks of the Congregation and desired "to give it the greatest possible extension according to the resources in personnel and funds that Divine Providence might supply." He wanted his Congregation to become a veritable center for this work:

N. D. 9, 290

Many priests and zealous laymen are actively engaged in this kind of apostolate, but there does not exist a single work that is formally dedicated to the purpose. The old religious orders do not undertake it because, at the time of their foundation, there was no need for it and they did not engage in it then.

N. D. 10, 313

N. D. 9, 274

N. D. 9, 246;
11, 48, and 95
N. D. 12, 182 f.
Griz. 91

Sensing that results were poor because a systematic approach was lacking, Libermann tried to start an organization which would cover all kinds of social work and act as a clearing-house for ideas and methods in this new form of ministry. Even though the revolutions of 1848, the added burdens resulting from union with the Holy Ghost Fathers, and his premature death in 1852, prevented him from executing all these plans, he saw to it that the Congregation began social and religious work among the laborers and servicemen of Amiens, Bordeaux, and Paris.[16] He was even on the point of accepting the chaplaincies of the French navy, a commitment which would have required about thirty priests at a time when the whole potential of the Congregation did not amount to more than fifty Fathers. However, political events prevented the execution of this plan.

N. D. 11, 100

[16]Better than many contemporary priests, the Socialists realized what would have been the result if Father Libermann's social program had become a reality. They began a violent newspaper campaign against him and his companions. Anonymous threats were made, one of which ended with: "You rabble! Your heads are going to roll soon. Swine, your grease will come in handy for the illumination."

N. D. 10, 177;
13, 171

In addition to these educational and social works, he planned a "house of diocesan missionaries" in Brittany, whose personnel would engage in the preaching of parochial missions and closed retreats.

From all this we may infer that Father Libermann definitely did not consider the Congregation as a purely missionary institution which was engaged only by accident in works outside the foreign mission field. The establishment of seminaries was inspired by his whole-hearted acceptance of the indirect apostolate of the old Holy Ghost Congregation, and by his desire to strengthen the Society at home. As for social works, he was fully convinced that they fell within the scope of caring for abandoned souls.

However, there was still another reason why he seemed so anxious to give the Congregation a broader base in Europe. The decay of the old Holy Ghost Society showed him what a sad fate can befall a religious organization which systematically sends every available man to the missions and resigns itself to being

N. D. 9, 292
ibid.

ibid.
ibid.
N. D. 9, 293

"purely and simply a mission seminary." Its authority over the personnel sent to the missions is soon reduced to "zero or almost zero," because of the power of the bishops to whom these missions are entrusted. Yet, it is "of the greatest importance" that "the balance between these two powers be preserved," for otherwise the Congregation cannot "maintain the spirit of its Rules and the bond resulting from its constitution." Moreover—and here again the old Holy Ghost Society could serve as an example—with the personnel at home reduced to a skeleton staff, inevitably the time will come when the Congregation will not have enough qualified men at home. When this happens, it will be useless to appeal for help to the missions, for "we would never get the most capable men." The reason is clear:

N. D. 9, 292 f.

The bishops would not be obliged to allow those we want to return to Europe. Moreover, capable candidates who are doing good work would themselves be loath to return. If any difficulty were to arise between the Bishop and the Mother-house—and this is bound to happen—the Motherhouse would have to give in, even if it saw the spirit of the Rule in danger. The bishops will always have the fate of the Motherhouse entirely in their hands, for they only have to send back to it men of mediocre talents in order to ruin its influence and authority completely.

If, however, works are established in the homeland, the Congregation "could always be certain to have at its disposal a number of wise, serious, capable, learned and experienced men." The same idea again is expressed in a letter which Libermann's secretary wrote on his behalf to Father Schwindenhammer about the excessive demands made by the African missions:

Va. 205 f.

Our beloved Father reproaches you for having believed that Guinea is gaining the upperhand. He says that you should lay down the following principles:

1. When Guinea asks something reasonable, it should be examined and, if it can be granted, it should be given. If not, then not. Therefore, do not feel disturbed.

2. The course which we have hitherto taken must necessarily lead to our total ruin. Therefore we have to change it. This modification will consist in a delay in sending missionaries— a delay that has to be accepted—in order to strengthen the life of the Congregation by undertaking works which can help it to expand and consolidate itself now. During this delay we will do what we can.

3. It is the task of the Superior General and of him alone to determine what can or cannot be done for the mission.

4. He cannot agree to consider the mission as the only work of the Congregation. Therefore, if the Vicars Apostolic find that the Congregation is unable to fill their wants, it is up to them to try something else—such as addressing themselves to other congregations. All we can do is promise to help them always to the best of our ability, without however doing harm to the life and development of our own congregation.

5. One cannot reject this view without going against the intentions of Rome, which certainly wants the Congregation to secure its existence and development, on which the missions of the Guineas depend perhaps exclusively. It is not enough *to do* and *die*, but we must *do* and *keep alive* to do again and keep doing.

c. THE QUESTION OF PERSONNEL FOR THE NON-MISSIONARY WORKS

What about the problem of supplying personnel to operate all these domestic works? Were the missions to be deprived of priests who had entered the Congregation with the intention of becoming foreign missionaries? On several occasions Father Libermann considered this question and his answers show clearly that he did not conceive of the Congregation as a purely missionary society. He admitted two kinds of members: those destined for the missions, and others intended for the homeland. With due regard for aptitude and character, the choice between these two categories was left to the individual in question. He even allowed a further distinction to be made between missionary work in uncivilized regions and missionary work in the more civilized old colonies. His thoughts on this subject are appended herewith:

N. D. 6, 115   1. If we succeed in founding a seminary for Guinea, we will establish it in France. In that case it will be staffed only by men who have no vocation for the missions.

N. D. 7, 281   2. Our rule is to send to the missions in uncivilized countries those who show a pronounced inclination for them, and to the missions in the colonies those who desire it or do not show too much interest in savages. Of course, we could not accept anyone who makes it a condition of his entrance that he be sent to this land rather than that. The acceptance of members making conditions would result in grave inconveniences for any congregation.

N. D. 7, 305   3. I have not hesitated to accept your young deacon. However I have formally declared to him that I am not taking him for the missions, but for Europe.

N. D. 9, 52 f.   4. It is our policy not to run counter to a given calling.
cf. 9, 114   Those who are really anxious to go to the missions must be sent. I cannot keep them home. . . . Why don't you look for some good priests who would like to join our Congregation? They could make their novitiate and then be sent to help you staff your [proposed social] works.

N. D. 9, 290   5. It will be an absolute rule with us that any cleric who comes to our novitiate with the formal intention and the positive desire to go to the missions cannot be used in Europe in this kind of establishment [social works]. . . . The houses in Europe will be staffed only by missionaries who are unable to stand the African climate and secondly, by those who will offer themselves to us with little definite attraction for the missions in foreign lands or even with sufficiently pronounced desires for ministry in Europe. We will never, or hardly ever, accept anyone on the explicit condition that he be kept in Europe. However, in actual practice, we would keep him there if he came to us with this preference. If it is God's will that we undertake this work in Europe, I think that such candidates will present themselves.

N. D. 10, 201   6. It would not be permissible to retain missionaries when only the interest of the European work itself is at stake. . . . In the beginning we could make use of a few of those destined for the foreign missions to give diocesan missions. When the work becomes more extensive, the vacancies should be filled only with new arrivals who from the very beginning have no definite vocation for the Negro missions. In a few years' time I think, there would be a sufficient number in Brittanny to join us for this purpose [diocesan missions].

N. D. 10, 451   7. The priests of the Congregation whose vocation appears to be definitely for the missions must not be used in the works [of Europe].

N. D. 11, 323   8. I should not want those who have a positive calling for the missions to be used in this work [chaplaincies of the Navy]. . . . If I find enough vocations to fill the staff of thirty [Navy chaplains], it will be of a twofold advantage to us. The most weighty point is that we will be putting an important work back on its feet and thereby do a real good; the second is that it would be a substantial source of income for the maintainance of our novitiate.

N. D. 13, 172   9. If there are clerics who are suitable for the exercise of their sacred functions in France and want to enter the Congregation, we would be willing to accept them and use them in France. It would not be prudent or fitting that they make it a condition of their entrance to stay in France. We could not accept them on such a condition. However, if we see in them the desire, vocation and aptitude for the works in France, we would be happy to use them there and certainly we would not send them to the missions.

From these many texts we may gather that Libermann did not want anyone with a missionary vocation (i.e., aptitude and desire) to be held back indefinitely in the mother country. On the other hand, he positively refused to make it a rule that everyone had to go to the missions. Moreover, he allowed certain preferences to be voiced regarding the two kinds of missions and the various works of Europe, for he distinguishes, on the one hand, work in uncivilized countries from work in the old established colonies, and on the other, candidates for naval chaplaincies from prospective diocesan missionaries.

That his distinction between foreign missions and domestic assignments was not purely theoretical appears from Libermann's letters. For instance, writing to Father Lannurien, he said:

N. D. 8, 201   Tell Mr. Levavasseur not to be afraid: we will arrange
cf. N. D. 8, 174   everything in accord with his desires; he is and will remain destined for the missions, unless his attraction changes and we find him more useful for Europe. Those two factors have to concur.

Moreover, another one of the early novices, Father Delaplace, wrote to his mother:

Piac. 62   Father Libermann has promised me that I will exercise the ministry in Europe, inasmuch as everyone is free to go to the missions or not.

People unacquainted with the internal workings of societies engaged in missionary work may find it strange that Father Libermann should have adopted this position. Many of them labor under the misconception that all candidates for such organizations *must* go off to foreign lands. Others assume that the requisite number of missionaries would never be met if individual preference and aptitudes were taken into account. As a matter of fact, the great problem that has always plagued Father Libermann and his successors is the difficulty they have encountered in recruiting enough priests and Brothers who do not positively *want* to labor in distant fields. They have consistently found it difficult to staff the less romantic works at home.

We have stressed this question of Libermann's attitude toward the foreign and domestic apostolate in order to avoid any misapprehension about Spiritan aims and purposes. A religious society can expect the blessings of God only when it knows and follows the intentions of its founder and its place in the Church can be understood only in the light of those objectives. Like all orders and congregations, the Holy Ghost Fathers trace their development through a series of historical complications, accretions, and adjustments, but despite the accommodations to time and place which wisdom dictates, it is important that there be no basic departure from the ultimate goal. When this happens, any group becomes disorganized from within and anomalous from without. A clear statement of policy constitutes the best safeguard against such a debacle. Fortunately, Father Libermann left us one in unequivocal terms.

4. Libermann's Death

The multitude of activities described in the foregoing pages are not nearly a complete enumeration of Father Libermann's endeavors. Nothing at all has been said as yet regarding his work in Europe itself. We have thus far limited our attention to the importance of his position as renovator of the African missions, restorer of the old Congregation of the Holy Ghost, and diplomatic saviour of the old colonies. While his multiple activities in other fields will have to be passed over in silence because they have no direct bearing on the history of the Congregation as such, we must reserve for later treatment his development of a new asceticism and his contributions to modern missiology.

In 1851 the Venerable began to feel very tired. "The care of all the churches" was wearing him down. The Two Guineas, Reunion, Mauritius, Guiana, Australia, French India, Guadeloupe, Martinique, Senegal, St. Pierre and Miquelon, Madagascar—all clamored for his attention. Nonetheless, his Congregation could look into the future with confidence. In Africa, several bases had been firmly established and the work of Christianization was seriously under way. True, his men on the West Coast would have to wait fifteen years before another order of priests, the Society of African Missions, would come to share in the vast undertaking; and his spiritual children would work alone on the East Coast from 1862 until the White Fathers came in 1878 to organize their caravans at a Spiritan base for their daring push to Uganda. Nevertheless, the work in Africa went ahead purposefully aiming at the establishment of native churches, and in Mauritius and Reunion Spiritans were working wonders among the liberated slaves.

In 1842 Libermann had said that he needed ten years to bring his task to a successful conclusion and felt God would grant him that much time. The allotted decade had now elapsed. While much remained to be done and no one could have done it better than himself, it was time for him to pass the torch to his successors. A moment comes when every organization has to be separated from the physical presence of its founder or restorer and begin to function independently through the spiritual impulses he has communicated to it.

Br. 417 ff.

In October 1851 Libermann began to complain of extreme fatigue. His health, always dangerously fragile, now deteriorated rapidly. Intestinal troubles developed and a kind of stupor sometimes seized him after his frugal meals. Nevertheless, he continued to work to the utmost of his ability. Sick as he was, he travelled to Notre Dame du Gard in the beginning of December, when the proclamation of the Second Empire caused fear of a new revolution. Most of his stay there was spent in the infirmary. When a new nervous attack seized him, his confreres decided to send him back to Paris where more competent medical care would be available. Soon he was unable to retain any food. By the end of January it was evident that he had only a few more days to live. It was at this time that he indicated Father Ignatius Schwindenhammer as the one best suited to be his immediate successor. A few days later, on February 2, 1852, at 3:15 P. M. his soul went forth to see the God to whom his life had been wholly dedicated. In the adjoining chapel, the choir was chanting the Vespers of our Lady's Purification. It had just reached the words of the Magnificat, *et exaltavit humiles* (He hath exalted the humble), when Libermann expired.

The first official steps in the long process of his beatification were taken in 1868. At first the difficulties seemed insurmountable.

Br. 440

Roman circles were rather sceptical about a candidate who was formerly a free-thinking Jew, a psychologically disturbed epileptic with strong suicidal inclinations, whose enterprises had often encountered disaster and whose spirituality deviated so sharply from the well-trodden traditional paths of holiness. Even the saintly Pope Pius IX felt little enthusiasm for the introduction of this cause. Nevertheless, in 1876 he signed the official decree that started it on its way.[17] In 1886, after careful scrutiny, Libermann's

[17]Libermann's letter about Pius IX (N. D. 9, 276) seems to have changed the Pope's attitude toward him.

cf. p. 162
Br. 446

numerous writings were found to be free of any errors. The heroic character of his virtues was officially recognized by the Church in 1910. Again the incumbent Pontiff, Saint Pius X, had at first been reluctant to issue the decree of heroicity because of the nervous disorders from which the Servant of God had suffered. For this reason, the Congregation of Rites had instituted a more than usually rigorous examination of Libermann's life. In the end, there could be no doubt at all about the heroic nature of his virtue.

Since the founding of the Congregation of Rites in the Middle Ages, Libermann's process was the first one ever introduced in favor of a Jew. It has progressed to a point where only one major step remains to be taken before his beatification: the approval of miracles obtained through his intercession. In this respect, the cause has not gone forward. Not that there has been any lack of

Br. 447

extraordinary cures. No less than thirty-four of them were presented at the apostolic process of 1881. However, they did not possess the strict juridical form required by the Congregation of Rites and were therefore disqualified as evidence toward beatification. No doubt in his own time and at the moment when God wills it, the Venerable will satisfy the desire of his spiritual sons and of the many souls all over the world who are devoted to him.

5. *Profiles of Some of His Early Collaborators*

a. FATHER JAMES LAVAL, 1803-1864

La. 7 ff.

James Laval was born in Croth, Normandy, on September 18, 1803. His father was a wealthy landowner who had been forced, when the grandfather died, to give up a legal career and return home to manage the family estate. On these ancestral acres, the six Laval children spent a happy childhood that was saddened only by the memory of James's twin brother Michael, who died soon after birth. James himself enjoyed excellent health, however, and when people asked him what he planned to be when he grew up, he invariably answered: "Either a priest or a doctor." Little did he or they suspect that both ambitions would ultimately be fulfilled.

La. 11 ff.

At the age of fourteen, he went to live with his uncle, a priest. Formerly a teacher in a junior seminary, this country pastor used his spare time preparing half a dozen boys for college or the seminary by private tutoring. After three years under the direction of this kindly old man, James was sent to the Seminary-College of

Evreux. He withdrew twice because of homesickness and returned to his father's house, but Laval *père* was not the man to stand such nonsense. Realizing that firmness was necessary, he listened to his son's complaints about the difficulties of academic life, and then quietly replied: "So, Latin makes your head spin? All right, I'll give you something that will make your arms spin in their sockets." Whereupon he assigned him a full share of the heavy farm labor. The ruse must have worked, for James soon asked permission to resume his studies. Just to make sure that he would not be coming home again with another spell of homesickness, Mr. Laval decided to send him to St. Stanislaus College in Paris. But James had learned his lesson and now applied himself earnestly to his work. In 1825 he graduated from St. Stanislaus with a bachelor's degree.

La. 16 ff.

Now he was faced with a decision about his future. For a while he thought he might enter the seminary or else go off to America, but in the end he resolved to study medicine at the Sorbonne. Five years later he took the Hippocratic oath and obtained his doctor's degree with a dissertation on articular rheumatism. Then he returned to Normandy and set up practice in the little town of St. André, where he soon became very popular. The poor especially liked him because he was not in the least concerned about payment for his services. Instead, he preferred to live on the income of the legacy his deceased parents had left him.

La. 22 ff.

Although James had remained a sincere and practising Catholic despite the ridicule of his fellow students and professors in Paris, a change came over him in the little town where he now lived. Gradually he became ashamed of the fact that he was the only educated man in the place who was still going to church. Little by little he gave up the practice of his Faith. For several years he did not even fulfill his Easter duty. Instead, he became interested in flashy uniforms (he was commander of the National Guard), horses, dancing, and parties. However, his conscience gave him no peace. He had to struggle bitterly to keep up a false front that did not conform to his own inner convictions. Instinctively he struck up a friendship with a neighboring priest, who gradually induced him to make his peace with God. In 1835, five years after his graduation from medical school, he made a sorrowful confession and returned to the practice of his Faith.

La. 30 ff.   The young doctor had been converted as only a Frenchman can be converted—radically. Gone were the beautiful uniforms, the costly furniture, the elaborate dinners, the thoroughbreds, and the dances. Savings thus realized were lavished on the poor. Instead of going to parties, he now spent long hours before the Blessed Sacrament. As a fee for his medical services to the poor he invariably requested a decade of the rosary. It was not long before his thoughts returned again to the priesthood. After much prayer and consultation with his confessor, he came to a decision: in the fall of 1835 he entered the seminary of St. Sulpice.

La. 36 ff.   It was not easy for the thirty-two year old doctor to adapt himself to the restrictions of seminary life. Nevertheless he set himself resolutely to the task and succeeded in becoming a model seminarian. Among his best friends were Frederic Le Vavasseur, Eugene Tisserant and Francis Libermann. James himself wanted to become a missionary and had been thinking of joining the Vincentians. However, he was advised against this step and told to wait till there would be an opportunity to become a missionary in some French-speaking territory.

La. 60 ff.   Obedient to the decision of his director, Father Laval returned to Normandy in 1839, there to await a call to the missions. The Bishop assigned him to the small country parish of Pinterville, a spot where he worked and prayed for two years among indifferent parishioners. In the summer of 1840 he heard about the plan of his seminary friends to start a new congregation for the care of abandoned souls in the colonies. Seeing in this new venture the long-awaited opportunity, Father Laval immediately expressed his willingness to join them.

La. 92 ff   The call came in the spring of 1841 when he was told to hold himself in readiness to accompany Bishop Collier, the newly appointed Vicar Apostolic of Mauritius. In May he was on his way to this distant island lost in the Indian Ocean. Before leaving

N. D. 2, 42 f. France, he had generously given Father Libermann his own personal fortune to aid the new congregation.

La. 109 ff.   Two years earlier, in 1839, the British Government of Mauritius had granted complete liberty to about sixty thousand slaves in this former French colony. At first, for nearly all of these new freedmen, liberty consisted in doing no work. Soon, however, those who had been born in slavery realized that one had to work to live. They quickly returned to their jobs as craftsmen or house-boys. The large majority, however, were natives from Africa or Madagascar who been forced into slavery. These rebelled against any kind of work, for they were unable to do anything but the heavy plantation labor which they so detested. Instead of working, they preferred to beg or steal. Crimes of every kind were rampant among these unfortunate victims of the slave trade. Yet it was among these people that Father Laval was destined to work miracles of grace.

La. 111 ff.   On September 14, his ship entered the harbor. No crowds or delegations were waiting to welcome the Bishop and his priests. The newspapers limited themselves to a line listing their names among the new arrivals. Readers would not care about the arrival of a few priests anyhow, for religious ignorance on the island—even among the educated classes—was appalling.[18]

Early in 1842 Father Laval was able to begin his apostolate among the liberated slaves. His first concern was to adapt him-self as fully as possible by learning their creole language and sharing their abject poverty. The beginning was not easy. After three months of hard labor he had succeeded only in converting five persons.

La. 134 ff.   The situation quickly improved when he learned the correct method. Instead of travelling around from one estate to another, he decided to concentrate on Port Louis, the capital. Day after day he spent most of his time instructing little groups in the rudiments of the Faith. At night he held larger gatherings which were open to all who wished to come. At these meetings he instructed his listeners and replied to their questions. Because at that time a color bar in the only church in Port Louis relegated the Negroes to a few pews in the back, he introduced a special Mass for them at noon. His kindness, perseverance and radiant holiness did not fail to make a profound impression on these former slaves. They felt that here at last was a man who was their friend. Gradually the numbers of those willing to be in-structed increased to an encouraging degree.

La. 159 ff.   As could be expected, opposition developed in proportion to his success. The British Government feared the influence of this

---

[18]Shortly after his arrival, Father Laval was called to the sickbed of a rich merchant for a blessing "to put an end to his sufferings." On leaving he was asked: "Father, should we need you again and you happen to be absent, who can we inform? Can your wife take the message?"

Father Eugene Tisserant, one of Francis Libermann's first collaborators.

Father James Laval, the Apostle of Mauritius, who converted 60,000 former slaves. His process of beatification recently took an important forward step.

La Neuville, near Amiens, France, where Father Libermann started his
Congregation of the Holy Heart of Mary.

Shrine on Father Libermann's grave in
Chevilly, France.

French priest and for six years refused to allow any others to come and share his labors. Protestant ministers campaigned against him. People who felt themselves personally attacked by the conversion of their partners in sin looked for vengeance. Ribald songs about the poor missionary began to circulate and even became the customary tune for a "Laval dance." Others tried to ambush him and give him a severe beating. Once they went so far as to slink into the church looking for women while his instructions were going on. He chased them indignantly, and when they threatened to kill him, he calmly replied: "I am not afraid of your threats or of death." Pointing to the cross, he added: "Here is my Master. He is the only one I fear. If you want to kill me, know that I will presently be walking back to the rectory." On another occasion a furious and frustrated Negro gave him an unmerciful thrashing. When it was over, the culprit was so struck by the priest's patience and forgiveness that he became a convert and led many others into the Church.

La. 168 ff.;
276 ff.

La. 224 ff.

The increasing number of converts forced Father Laval to avail himself of catechists who were specially trained to give religious instruction. He soon had dozens of them working all over the island. Each one set up a little chapel and many of these subsequently developed into full-fledged parish churches. Thanks to this system of catechists, in a few years' time he was able to number his converts in the thousands. He himself took care of all final instructions. They literally enjoyed going to confession to Father Laval. Whatever time he could spare from his instructions was spent in the confessional. It became, as it were, a private pulpit from which he preached to each of his penitents.

La. 211 ff.

Throughout all these years there was one thing that seriously troubled the holy priest: who was going to take over the work when he would no longer be there? Hitherto all of Bishop Collier's and Father Libermann's efforts to arrange for the admission of other French priests had been in vain. Fortunately, in 1847 the British Government relented sufficiently to give one other priest a renewable permit for three months. Shortly after, two other confreres arrived in Mauritius from Perth, the survivors of the ill-fated Australian venture. They also secured permission to stay. From then on, of course, the work went ahead in giant strides. The confidence of the former slaves, old and young alike, in Father Laval knew no bounds. For instance, it was a customary thing for girls to visit him and say: "Father, I am now fifteen years old. I would like to get married. I have no special choice. I will marry whoever you suggest." Father Laval would then counsel them to begin a novena while he looked around for a suitable partner. After that, a second novena would be held in preparation for the wedding with the candidate he had chosen. Strangely enough, countless happy marriages were arranged in this way.

La. 267 ff.

The transformation brought about by Father Laval in the former slaves slowly made its influence felt also among the white population. The ladies especially were the first to see what a profound change religion had made in their servants. Admiration was followed by esteem and in many cases by a return to the half-forgotten practice of their Faith. In this way family life all over the island gradually became Christian once again.

La. 318 ff.

Fifteen years of this incessant labor, coupled with severe penitential practices, sufficed to exhaust the strength of the missionary. In 1856, and again in 1857, he suffered a stroke while hearing confessions. The next year he had another attack in the pulpit. When two more seized him shortly afterward in the confessional and during a sermon, Father Laval realized that his active work had practically come to an end. From now on he could only suffer and pray for his beloved converts. When he felt well enough, he still managed to give religious instructions to the little children and even to adults from time to time. In addition, he continued giving spiritual advice to those who came from all over the island to visit him at his rectory. Most of the time, however, he could be found in a little corner near the altar, silently adoring the divine Master to whom he had dedicated his life. In 1859 he had the consolation of pronouncing his perpetual vows in the

La. 361 ff.

Congregation, which he loved with all his heart. Death came to him in 1864 on September 9, the feast of St. Peter Claver, that other great apostle of the slaves.

About sixty thousand souls had been converted by him during the fifteen years of his active life. Ten thousand of these had preceded him into eternal life, struck down by the various epidemic diseases which afflicted the island during those years. Where there had been no one to welcome him on his arrival in Mauritius, more than forty thousand people accompanied their beloved apostle to the grave. Nor did his spiritual children cease to have confidence in him after his death. The little monument erected over his grave has become a shrine at which great graces and miraculous cures have been obtained through his intercession. It is a center of devotion not only for the Catholic population but for many others—even Mohammedans—who come to pray at his grave. Each year, on the anniversary of his death the number of pilgrims exceeds thirty thousand.

In 1893 the first steps were taken in the process of his beatification. It was officially introduced in Rome after the first World War. Since then it has slowly continued to make progress.

b. FATHER FREDERICK LE VAVASSEUR, 1811-1882

Va. 19 ff.
N. D. 1, 599 ff.
Frederick was born in Reunion on February 25, 1811, of a Creole family that owned large estates on the island. After a thoroughly irreligious upbringing by his non-practicing parents, the boy came under the influence of Father Warnet, a Holy Ghost Father who had recently arrived in the colony and had taken over the direction of the local college. Naturally inclined to be generous and kind, and easily driven to extremes, Frederick gave himself as wholeheartedly to God as he had formerly dedicated himself to
N. D. 1, 603 f.
pleasure, to the great disgust of his father who did not want to have anything to do with what he called piosity.

Va. 23 ff.
N. D. 1, 606 ff.
N. D. 1, 612
At the age of eighteen, Frederick went to France to develop his great intellectual gifts by further study there. Before he left, his father told him: "Become whatever you want, even a gangster if necessary, but do not become a priest. Otherwise I shall no longer recognize you as my son." "Don't worry," he answered, "I have no intention to study for the priesthood." In Paris the boy threw himself so ardently into the study of mathematics that he soon had a nervous breakdown and failed his examination. In addition, he was becoming scrupulous. It took him several hours, for example, to prepare himself for confession because he felt that he must shed tears to be sure of his sorrow. Giving up his idea of becoming an engineer, he transferred to law in order to help his father, whose business affairs had just suffered severe reverses. Meanwhile, however, the thought of becoming a priest had entered his mind and it annoyed him constantly. At last, after consulting the Bishop of Versailles, he announced his
N. D. 1, 620
decision to his parents. Unexpectedly, he succeeded in obtaining the consent of even his father, although the old man cried when

his son came home for a short visit and he saw him for the first time in a cassock.[19]

Va. 33 ff.
N. D. 1, 620 ff.
In the fall of 1836 Frederick entered the Sulpician seminary of Issy. Once there, he was given over to the care of Francis Libermann, the "guardian angel" of all newcomers. Two more opposite spiritual temperaments were hardly conceivable: the fiery Creole, inclined to exaggeration in everything he did, plagued by scruples, given to extraordinary penances, bent on making himself holy by sledge-hammer blows; and the apostle of childlike and total surrender to God through peace of heart, averse to positive mortification, quietly willing to let only God act on his soul. Nevertheless, the two saw in each other an equal sincerity in their desires for God and immediately felt attracted to each other. Thus it is not surprising that Frederick kept in touch with Libermann, even when the latter had to leave the seminary to become novice master for the Eudists. During these years, it was Le Vavasseur who interested Francis Libermann in the apostolate among the neglected slaves. We have related above how this interest gradually led to the foundation of a new Congregation, the resumption of the African missions, and Father Le Vavasseur's appointment to Reunion to inaugurate there the missionary work which he had so ardently promoted.

Va. 77 ff.
On February 16, 1842, he sailed from Brest, via Rio de Janeiro, to Reunion in the Indian Ocean, where the vessel arrived on the evening of June 10. Since he was not expected, no one was waiting for him at the port. As he walked up to the local rectory, however, he saw himself suddenly surrounded by about two hundred Negroes dressed in white, who greeted him most respectfully and happily. They were first communicants, and they cf. pp. 65 f. had been prepared by their pastor, Father Alexander Monnet, whose story we have told above. Under such favorable auspices he set to work in his homeland.

Va. 79 ff.
He soon realized that not everything was as rosy as this first encounter. Part of the clergy looked askance at this newcomer who was going to work outside the traditional framework of parochial activity; most of the white population saw him as a kind of a revolutionary who was bent on causing trouble among the slaves; and the Government distrusted this priest who refused to be inscribed on the list of Government-paid and controlled

---

[19]Later Frederick had the satisfaction of seeing his father converted.

clergymen. Contrary to the practice of Father Laval in Mauritius, Le Vavasseur decided to work by erecting small chapels on the large plantations and visiting them in turn to instruct the slaves. Despite the opposition, he had success, and when reinforcements arrived in the persons of several confreres, there was already enough to do to keep all of them very busy.

Va. 91 ff.

One of these confreres, though a good and pious priest, did not show all the energy and initiative required by the standards Father Le Vavasseur had set for himself. Impetuously, as always, Frederick jumped to the conclusion that Father Libermann was becoming too lax and therefore the Congregation was doomed to failure. Sending the priest back to France, he hurled dire reproaches at the Founder and forthwith announced his intention to leave the sinking ship and become a Jesuit, if Libermann would

N. D. 8, 28 ff.

give him permission. The Venerable's calm reply that "with principles as severe as yours, you would have to expel at least half the members of the Society of Jesus" failed to make the slighest impression on him. Again, he insisted on permission to join them. Pointing out that by agreeing to the request, he would fail in his duty to God, Libermann added:

N. D. 8, 365

Do not think that I am trying to retain you . . . I do not ask you to stay, but I do not give you the permission. . . . Make your decision and let me know.

As suddenly as it had arisen, Father Le Vavasseur's "great temptation," as he himself later called it, vanished. In his next letter he had reached the opposite extreme:

Va. 95

At the moment I would endure anything rather than leave you. . . . If you send me away, I will act like a dog and lie down at the door.

Va. 101 ff.

After this episode, Father Le Vavasseur continued his work with his accustomed zeal and impetuosity. When the Prefect Apostolic wanted him and his confreres to take regular parishes, he threatened to leave; when he was forbidden to ring the bells at 4:30 A. M. for the Mass of the slaves, he again threatened to shake the dust from his feet; when a French petty officer refused to leave the church during his instruction of the slaves, he took

N. D. 10, 53

him by the arm and put him out. On the other hand, when the shouts of "Drown Monnet!" penetrated into the church where he was gathered with hundreds of the slaves, he managed not only to restrain himself but also to prevent his audience from joining the fracas and seeking bloody vengeance for the insults showered on their apostle.

Va. 105 ff.
N. D. 10, 441 f.
Meanwhile, the long-expected liberation of the slaves was about to take place. There were between sixty and eighty thousand of them on the island, as against about forty thousand free people. Everyone feared the riots and bloodshed that might follow. Violence had already occurred in Mauritius in 1835, a few years before Father Laval's arrival, and by way or repercussion, there had been a plot in Reunion to set fire to all "white" property and kill the "bad white people." Fortunately, the plot had leaked out in time to prevent its execution. What would happen now when the government commissioner was coming to announce the liberation in Reunion itself? The commissioner was wise enough to realize the extent of Father Le Vavasseur's influence and to seek his advice about the best way to proceed. The priest urged him to give the whole affair a strongly religious character and to go about personally explaining to the little groups of slaves under his direction exactly how freedom would be given them. Accordingly, on the appointed day, December 20, 1848, a solemn High Mass was celebrated in every town, then trumpets sounded and guns saluted the new free men. There followed a sermon explaining the rights and duties of both white and colored, and then the official declaration of freedom was read. In the evening an open air Benediction and a freedom torchlight procession took place. Thanks to this religious approach, there were no riots, no fires, and no murders, despite the fact that it was necessary to announce a two-thirds cut in wages to prevent general bank-

N. D. 10,
427 ff.
ruptcy on the island. A totally different scene occurred in Martinique, where our old friend Mr. Schoelcher noisily presided over the liberation.

Va. 113 ff.
Now that the slaves were free, it became more important than ever to teach them to work. For this reason, the tireless missionary was induced to found a number of trade schools. Right on the island of Reunion he opened a novitiate for Spiritan Brothers in order to supply trained personnel for these technical schools. Then, when religious vocations for the Sisterhood made their appearance, Father Le Vavasseur became the founder of a new congregation of Sisters, the Daughters of Mary (1849).

Their success was so great that they later spread to Mauritius, Madagascar and East Africa.

Va. 143 ff.

At about this time, there was much discussion regarding the question of establishing a hierarchy in the colonies. Bishop Monnet, who knew the capacities of Le Vavasseur, made efforts to have him appointed as the first Bishop of the island. Although Libermann did not want to interfere, he wrote to him:

N. D. 11, 133 f.

> My conduct in this affair has been to remain perfectly neutral. I was and I am still convinced that you will do more good by remaining in the Congregation than by being at the head of a colony. God has inspired you first with the idea of the foundation of our work. It seems evident to me that he destines you to be its support. . . . Returning to France will be a great sacrifice for you, but I know that this will not stop you.

Totally disinterested in the prospect of an episcopate, Father Le Vavasseur at once returned to France, leaving Father Collin in charge of the Sisters' congregation he had just founded. It was now his task to help the Venerable in the problems raised by the fusion with the Holy Ghost Fathers. His first assignment was to make a trip throughout France recruiting personnel for both the colonies and the Congregation. The unfavorable public opinion about the Holy Ghost Fathers in France, caused when the name was usurped by those who had no right to it, shocked him horribly. Forthwith he wrote Father Libermann a letter, demanding that he close Holy Ghost Seminary, return to Notre Dame du Gard, and abandon the colonies. Once more, the Venerable had to calm down his impetuosity by a letter that said in part: "I am convinced that this would be one of the gravest faults and one of the most serious injustices our Congregation could make itself guilty of before God." Once more he warned Le Vavasseur against his exaggerated quest for perfection in frail humanity:

cf. p. 58

N. D. 10, 199

N. D. 10, 319

> Beware of that imagination which drives you to want absolute perfection in human beings, institutions, and things in general. We must have the desire to see everything perfect and quietly do our best, with moderation and wisdom, to lead men and things to perfection. However, we should be absolutely convinced that wherever there are human beings

we will find imperfection. We should try to obtain what is possible without breaking everything; otherwise the loss will be twenty times as great as the gain.

Letters like this and, to an even greater degree, the continuous presence of Father Libermann gradually succeeded in subduing the impetuosity and extremism of the fiery Creole.

Va. 161 ff.

N. D. 12, 669

During the next few years Father Le Vavasseur expended all his energies on Holy Ghost Seminary at Paris and on the various religious and social works attached to it. Libermann made him Provincial Superior of France. When the Venerable lay on his death-bed in 1852, Le Vavasseur, reminded the dying man of his impetuosity and thereby succeeded in eliciting an expression of preference for Father Schwindenhammer as Superior General. In deference to this last wish, the latter was elected, and Le Vavasseur became his assistant.

Va. 184 ff.

Despite the temperamental gulf that separated the precise, methodical and somewhat distant Alsatian who was inclined to excessive regimentation, and the impressionable, sympathetic, and exuberant Creole, the two got along very well. With complete freedom, Father Le Vavasseur would remind Schwindenhammer of the faults he detected in him: too much interference in the details of the work of others and too great concern with affairs foreign to the Congregation. In this way, for nearly thirty years they worked together most effectively to consolidate and develop it.

B. G. 34, 712 ff.

Va. 222 ff.

Le Vavasseur took an active part in the foundation of the Archconfraternity of the Holy Ghost[20] and in 1854 he arranged for the Congregation's acquisition of the famous twelfth century Cistercian abbey of Langonnet. He converted it into a combined college and junior seminary. The next year he was entrusted with a particularly delicate mission. A huge institute for orphans at Saint-Ilan was threatened with disaster, because the association of "Leonist" Brothers who conducted the orphanage had shown themselves unable to give a firm direction to the work. In his distress, the layman-founder, Achilles du Clésieux, searched for a substitute congregation. He was referred to the Holy Ghost Fathers, who confided the task to Father Le Vavasseur. After a quick visit, the priest transfered the Brothers'

---

[20]Originally started in 1861 by Miss Emma Boulargey as the Association of the Holy Ghost to work and pray for the missions.

novitiate of the Congregation to Saint-Ilan and then took charge of the place. The Leonists did not relish the arrival of these "strangers" and complained bitterly to the Bishop. His unexpected reply was: "Thank God. Allow yourselves to be directed by the Holy Ghost Fathers, for you are unable to direct yourselves." Almost immediately, Father Le Vavasseur brought both the Leonists and the Spiritan Brothers together for a common retreat. The eloquence of the preacher and the fervor of the retreat so impressed the Leonists that they asked to be incorporated into the Congregation as Holy Ghost Brothers. Only one of the thirty dissented and left.

Va. 229 ff.
The next year Father Le Vavasseur took over an orphanage at Cellule, and to this he soon added the newly restored junior seminary for the colonies which Father Bertout had originally started in 1808. Through it all, the old French colonies remained his work of predilection: he was officially in charge of everything concerning them and became the guiding spirit behind their development in the latter half of the nineteenth century.

Va. 253 ff.
In 1868, when the Superior General became gravely ill, he replaced him temporarily. From that time on he had to assume a great deal of responsibility for the central administration, for the General's health remained seriously impaired. When Schwindenhammer died a dozen years later, Father le Vavasseur, despite his objections, was elected as his successor. By this time, his character had considerably mellowed. He had gained in wisdom what he had lost in impetuosity and extremism. He was not called, however, to remain long at the head of the Congregation. Soon after his election in August 1881, a serious illness struck him down. On January 16, 1882, he ended his holy life with a peaceful death. His body was buried alongside that of Father Libermann in the little shrine at Chevilly, the Senior Scholasticate of the French Province.

c. FATHER EUGENE TISSERANT, 1814-1845

N. D. 1, 623 ff.
Eugene was born in Paris of a French father and a Haitian mother who was the daughter of General Louis Bauvais. When the colored people of Haiti took up arms to gain their freedom in 1791, they chose Louis Bauvais as their chief. He soon forged the motley crowds into a well-disciplined army and succeeded in vindicating the rights of the non-whites. Two years later, slavery

was abolished in Haiti. Freedom, however, was followed by civil war between opposing factions. General Bauvais refused to take sides in the internecine struggle and resolved to take his family to France. When their vessel was wrecked by a storm and there was not enough room in the single lifeboat, he gave up the place assigned to him in favor of his wife, convinced that their children would have more need of a mother than of a father. Later, one of these children married a French pharmacist and became the mother of Eugene.

In his young manhood, Tisserant entered the seminary of St. Sulpice with the idea of going to Haiti as a missionary. However, the Archbishop of Paris was reluctant to release him for this island, N. D. 1, 626 since its clergy had an unsavory reputation. Very emphatically he stated his position: "Do you think perhaps that we take so much trouble to educate good priests and then send them to their perdition in Haiti? As long as I live, I will never give you this permission."

N. D. 1, 654 ff. The Archbishop's opposition will perhaps be better understood if we devote a brief word to the religious situation in this island. When the French Revolution broke out, most of the Dominican and Capuchin priests working in Haiti were dispersed. The few who had remained left in 1804, when Haiti declared itself independent of France. Only one or two stayed behind to set up a kind of schismatic Church. From 1820 on, the island became a haven for all sorts of clerical characters who had been expelled from their dioceses or their orders. They had no contact with Rome and were N. D. 5, 388 simply appointed by the President of the Republic. One can easily ff.; 416; 423 ff. imagine, therefore, how corrupt such a clergy must have been and how sadly the religious interests of the people were neglected. The leading classes, both white and colored, were imbued with the ideas of Voltaire and Freemasonry, while the lower classes, though baptized, lived in complete paganism. In 1821 Rome had vainly tried to remedy the situation by sending a Vicar Apostolic. As soon as he arrived, he was forcibly driven from the island. In 1834 Bishop England, of Charleston, was appointed its Apostolic Delegate. He resigned four years later, convinced that the Government would never cooperate in reforming the clergy and establishing the hierarchy.

As early as 1838, Father Tisserant had entered into relations with the Haitian Government to obtain permission to enter the

island. Though he could appeal to his Haitian origin, even he did
not succeed. Moreover, as we have said, his Archbishop refused

N. D. 3, 3 ff. him permission to go. Shortly after, however, in 1841, the Holy
H. R. H. 287 ff. See appointed a new Apostolic Delegate, Bishop Joseph **Rosati** of
St. Louis, and the Propaganda recommended that he get in touch
with Father Libermann. In Paris, Bishop Rosati met Father
Tisserant, then an assistant director of the Archconfraternity of

N. D. 3, 361 Our Lady of Victories. The end result of this meeting was that
H. R. H. 295 ff. the Propaganda asked Libermann to send priests to Haiti.

N. D. 3, 23 ff. Before this request could be acted upon, a violent earthquake
H. R. H. 308 ff. shook the island. In the ensuing chaos, negotiations between the
Holy See and Haiti were broken off, so that the priests assigned
to Haiti had to be sent elsewhere. Nonetheless, Father Tisserant
himself was sent to the West Indies to study the situation in
Haiti and enter it at the earliest opportunity. When he tried at
first to stay in Martinique, he was taken for a "spy" by the local

N. D. 4, 29 Vice Prefect Apostolic and was refused permission to exercise his
N. D. 4, 371 ff. priestly functions. He therefore went to the more hospitable island
of St. Lucia, in the Vicariate of Trinidad. After a few months in
St. Lucia, the Bishop was about to send him to the island of
Tobago, which had been without a priest for thirty years, but in
August 1843, he at last had a chance to enter Haiti.

H. R. H. 384 ff. Father Tisserant arrived just when a new revolution had over-
N. D. 5, 392; thrown the government. After obtaining permission to preach and
400 ff. administer the sacraments, he entered into negotiations with the
provisional government in order to arrive at a solution for the

N. D. 5, 92 religious crisis. When these negotiations seemed to be successful,
Rome, in January 1844, appointed him Prefect Apostolic of Haiti.

N. D. 5, 471 f. However, the situation was so delicate that he did not dare to
make his appointment publicly known. In a short time, Libermann

N. D. 5, 480 was able to send him two priests and one Brother, but when they
landed, a new revolution had broken out; the Spanish-speaking
East was bent on separation from the French-speaking West, and
in the West itself rival parties were battling for control. Despite

N. D. 5, 480 this political chaos, Father Tisserant managed to obtain the creation of a government committee to examine the religious problem.
He was even officially recognized as the "Head of the Catholic

N. D. 5, 492 Church of Haiti." The situation began to look a little more hopeful.

Meanwhile, the unfortunate island was plagued by a yellow
fever epidemic which swept through the population. Both Father

N. D. 5, 504
N. D. 5, 476 ff. ;
532 ff. ; 637 ff. ;
Compl., 274
N. D. 13, 396
H. R. H. 339
f., 375 ff.

Tisserant and his confreres contracted the disease while ministering to the sick. In August 1844, he went to Europe in search of a cure for his shattered health and an answer to his personnel difficulties. During his absence, one of the priests in Haiti, Father Cessens, ambitious to become "Head of the Church," began to act more openly against the Prefect Apostolic and succeeded in creating a strong opposition. The newspapers supported the plot and began a violent campaign against Father Tisserant and his confreres.

N. D. 6, 604 ff.

In February 1845, when Tisserant returned to the island with four Spiritan recruits to aid him in his work, new political disorders had broken out. Again there was a new government, and this one was unfavorable to him. The ecclesiastical control it demanded as the price for recognizing him was completely inadmissible. When, despite his protests, the President of the Republic began once more personally to appoint priests of his own choice as pastors, Father Tisserant displayed a deplorable lack of diplomatic abilities to deal intelligently with the new situation. At least he might have kept open some line of communication with the Holy See by appointing one of his confreres as Vice-Prefect, but he chose instead to withdraw all his priests and return to France. Eighteen years were to pass before the perennial religious crises of Haiti could be solved through the creation of the Hierarchy.

N. D. 8, 171 f.
H. R. H. 351
cf. pp. 361 ff.
N. D. 7, 385
N. D. 7, 467 ff.

Meanwhile, a new appointment was waiting for him. Libermann had him made Prefect Apostolic of Guinea and he sailed to his new post in November, 1845. On December 6, the ship was caught by a violent storm and thrown on a sandbank. While wave after wave battered the stricken vessel, Father Tisserant prepared the crew and passengers for death and baptized a Jew, who at this supreme moment wanted to become a Christian. During the early morning hours the few survivors of the sinking ship were still clinging to the mast. In a desperate effort to obtain help from the land nearby, the intrepid priest jumped into the raging waves, hoping to be carried ashore. Instead, a treacherous current seized him and hammered him to death against the hull of the boat. Thus ended the short but eventful life of this co-founder of Libermann's Congregation of the Holy Heart of Mary.

d. FATHER STANISLAUS ARRAGON, 1819-1855

The informed reader undoubtedly will ask what Father Arragon has done to be singled out for inclusion among Libermann's early collaborators. The reason lies in our concern for historical objectivity. By speaking only about those who excelled through holy lives or great deeds, we might create the impression that Libermann was surrounded only by near-saints and shining heroes in his congregation. As a matter of fact, the situation was quite different. Most of his associates were thoroughly average, hard-working priests. Then there were others who did not measure up to what might have been expected. Thus we find, e.g., a Father Louis Acker, who was so anxious to stay another year in the novitiate that he refused his appointment to the Australian mission and had to be expelled. There was Father Stephen Clair, who under Libermann was successively Novice Master of the Brothers, Director of the Senior Seminarians in philosophy, and Professor of theology. Nonetheless, a year after Libermann's death he left the Congregation, brought several lawsuits against it, and ended sadly as an apostate. Finally, there was Father Stanislaus Arragon. He never left, but he proved that even very imperfect men can be useful members of a religious congregation if they are carefully handled.

Stanislaus Arragon was born near Grenoble, the son of a moderately wealthy family. At the age of twenty-four he entered the novitiate. Ordained shortly thereafter, he made his consecration to the apostolate and in 1844 was appointed to Haiti. As we have related above, the Haitian mission failed and Libermann's men had to return almost immediately after their arrival. In May 1845, therefore, Father Arragon was back in France. The next month he was appointed to the Two Guineas, where he spent the ten remaining years of his life. Thus, the main external facts of his life have nothing very exciting to offer except a fairly substantial amount of travel. What is interesting about him is the fact that, despite Father Arragon's extremely difficult character, Libermann managed to mold him into a useful member of the Society. He provided a living illustration of two principles which Libermann regarded as essential to the good administration of his Congregation.

The first of these principles demanded that each superior treat his men as human beings and not as puppets. In this vein he wrote to one of his superiors:

N. D. 7, 349

N. D. 13,
App. 50

N. D. 13,
App. 44

N. D. 8, 34

The norm you propose is so severe that it is completely impractical. You would like all members of a Community to be so perfect and so given to self-renunciation that they can be handled as puppets in a Punch and Judy show. That would be very nice, but such a thing has never existed and never will exist in the Church.

Or again:

N. D. 8, 113

The most important means I use to direct confreres is to tolerate those defects which I feel I cannot correct. I occasionally put up with the most improper and crude behavior, and above all I leave everyone to his own way of being and try to perfect him along the lines in which he is naturally constituted.

Libermann's second principle was concerned with the minimum conditions required before one could become a member of the Congregation. We have it expressed in his own words as follows:

N. D. 11, 270
cf. N. D. 8, 35

Regarding admission to the Congregation, there is no difficulty in making a decision with respect to candidates who are all-perfect. Likewise, there is none if they are all-bad. The difficulty arises only when they combine both good and bad features. Then we must examine whether the imperfections are such that they can do harm to the confreres in the community by introducing laxity, bad spirit, grave disorder, etc. For these dangers, compensation is not possible. Such a candidate is unsuitable and must not be admitted. On the other hand, the imperfections of the candidate in question may inconvenience only himself or be disagreeable to his Superior or his confreres—to the Superior, because he is not easy to handle and is likely to be whimsical in his functions, etc.; to his confreres, because he is gruff and touchy. In such a case one must see how deeply these faults are ingrained in the candidate. If they go so far as to give rise to fear of disorder in the community, he falls into the preceding category and cannot be admitted. If they do not go so far, but one forsees nasty disagreements and difficulties, then one must take into consideration the needs of the Society and of its missions and the service such a candidate can render. If his usefulness is greater than the inconveniences, he must be admitted. If, however, the inconvenience surpasses the usefulness, he must be refused admission.

Father Arragon was not exactly a man to be handled like a puppet. He had a most violent temper, little self-control, and a penchant for extreme measures. Libermann described him as a "real savage" and sent this advice to a confrere who lived with Arragon:

N. D. 8, 157

N. D. 8, 113

> Trying to make Father Arragon a man of moderation, polished and amiable in his manners, would be like trying to build castles on the clouds. It would be easier to stop the sun in its course.

N. D. 11, 64 and 70

When Arragon's mother sent money for a new soutane and complained that her son's clothing looked dirty and worn, Libermann replied: "Madame, we will have a new one made for him, but I can guarantee its newness only for the first day. Two days' wear by your son is enough to make any soutane look quite 'venerable'."

Br. 232

The temper and impetuosity of this man may be judged from a few examples. In 1846, a native tribe captured both him and a Brother in the course of an exploratory trip they were making. The naval commandant at Gorée, who was responsible for the safety of the missionaries, sent an armed vessel to the rescue. Later, he made a few polite remarks about the dangers of going on such explorations and asked that henceforth the authorities be notified of their general direction. Furious about this "interference in ecclesiastical affairs," Arragon wrote him an insulting letter and declared that all relations between the mission and the Navy were severed.

The next year, he heard that Father Gravière was coming to take charge of the mission and that a new effort had been undertaken in Australia. His rage knew no bounds. In a biting letter, the twenty-seven-year-old hothead told the Venerable Francis Libermann that he was not going to accept Father Gravière as Prefect:

Arch. Arragon, 3/24-25/1846 cf. N. D. 8, 143 and 147

> The appointment of Father Gravière is evident proof that you have no trust in your missionaries or confidence in their courage. . . . I am so mad about it that I would like to invite the other missionaries to a meeting to elect a Superior and

refuse the one you are sending. . . . The possible reaction of your missionaries carries no weight with you. The African missionaries are only children and idiots: they need a mature man to direct them. Beware lest these missionaries, so despised and disgraced in your eyes and the eyes of your grave councillors, despise you in turn. . . . You want to send your missionaries again to certain death, but this time they will not go.

N. D. 10, 153   In 1848, when he needed some money for his mission, he simply wrote a bank-draft in the amount of 10,000 francs against the non-existent funds of the Congregation without even notifying Father Libermann. It was only with the greatest difficulty that Libermann succeeded in honoring the draft and preventing either the mission or the Congregation from going into bankruptcy.

Improbable as it may appear, this "savage" was ferociously— that is the proper word for it in his case—attached to the Rule wherever any concrete situation had been definitely regulated. His impulsive refusal to recognize Father Gravière was motivated by the fact that this priest "had not been long enough in the

N. D. 8, 143   novitiate" and "did not know the Rule well enough." Libermann

ibid.   countered this by a formal command—the only one that seems to exist in his extensive correspondence: "In the name of our Lord Jesus Christ, I order you to receive Father Gravière kindly, charitably, and with the dispositions one should have towards his Superior." The command immediately produced the desired effect.

Br. 232   After the death of Bishop Truffet, when Arragon was temporarily acting as Superior, he did not dare change the starvation diet previously prescribed by the prelate. He even imposed the same regime on Father Briot who was merely passing through Dakar on his way to France. When Briot became so ill that there was serious question about his ability to reach the ship, Arragon told him that it was more perfect to die at his post. Being reasonable, Father Briot thought it better to stay alive and work. He finally succeeded in obtaining the necessary food and recovered almost immediately. Only then did Father Arragon dare to discontinue the diet that the Bishop had imposed on the community.

N. D. 9, 46   Having heard by chance that Father Schwindenhammer kept a chalice in his room, he jumped to the conclusion that private property was being countenanced. The usual formal protest was immediately sent off to Libermann and the Venerable had to pacify this recalcitrant son by pointing out that he personally had put that chalice there for temporary safekeeping. Arragon was so

N. D. **8, 132**

much concerned over uniformity in the community that he addressed a reproach to Father Libermann for having more furniture in his room than the novices had. Again, Libermann had to justify himself by showing that as Superior General he needed at least a desk that could be locked.

Despite all these annoyances, Libermann loved and trusted Father Arragon. He knew how to handle him, in friendly but

N. D. **8, 157**

firm fashion as one would handle "a boy or a child," without "allowing him to meddle in things that do not concern him." By means of numerous letters he kept close watch over him and his work. Guided in this way, Father Arragon did excellent work in the mission. He prepared useful studies of the Wolof language, learned Arabic, and became the founder of several missions. The

Ap. H. **81 f.**

most important of these was established near a wretched native village, called Ndakarou. Struck by the potentialities of the location, Father Arragon concluded a treaty of friendship with the local king and secured his protection. With the aid of his confreres he manufactured bricks and put up a substantial building that measured a hundred and ten by forty-six feet. He had judged the site very well. Ten years later France claimed the area as a colony and Ndakarou became Dakar, one of the largest cities of Africa. In addition, he founded the Missions of Ngazobil, Joal, and St. Mary's in Gambia, which is still the chief residence of the Bathurst diocese. In 1855 he set out for Europe to restore his broken health. However, he was not to see his native country again. Shortly before the boat was due to enter the harbor, Father Arragon died off the coast of France.

CHAPTER SEVEN

THE DRIVING FORCE OF THE CONGREGATION: FATHER LIBERMANN'S SPIRITUAL AND APOSTOLIC DOCTRINE

The history of a religious order is not the proper place for a full presentation of the spiritual and apostolic doctrine it regards as its own. On the other hand, one would hardly be justified in omitting entirely the driving force which, since the middle of the nineteenth century, has animated the Congregation of the Holy Ghost and influenced the accomplishments of its members. History is not merely a collection of facts and dates. Above all it strives to achieve an insight into the motives which have guided men and their actions. For this reason, we have added here two short studies: one concerning Father Libermann's spiritual doctrine insofar as it applies to men engaged in the active life, and another regarding his missionary theory.

It is particularly important that his teaching on those two points should be considered here because they differed significantly from the commonly accepted views of his contemporaries and because they still exercise a profound influence far beyond the relatively narrow confines of his Congregation. In these, as in many other spheres, he proved himself a pioneer. He introduced a concept of spirituality whose essential features were later popularized by the Little Flower, St. Therese of Lisieux, as the way of "spiritual childhood." We are glad to note that Libermann's role in this renewal of spiritual thought and practice is becoming ever more widely recognized. As Pierre Blanchard, Professor at the Catholic University of Lyons and a well-known authority on ascetical theology, recently wrote:

R. V. C. 106   The claim is often made that it was St. Therese of Lisieux who caused a real revolution in the history of spirituality and the realm of mortification by substituting an asceticism of the little for the asceticism of the great and the search for crucifying deeds. . . . But from 1835 to 1850 in France the Venerable Father Libermann had already started this revolution in the

156

direction he gave to the innumerable souls who entrusted themselves to him.

His missionary theory was likewise strikingly ahead of the times and has since found official confirmation in many of the more recent pronouncements of the Holy See.

1. *Father Libermann's Spiritual Doctrine*

Although Father Libermann never wrote a complete treatise of spirituality, specialists in ascetical theology do not hesitate to follow Pope Pius XII and call him "an outstanding master of the spiritual life."[1] His spiritual teaching is to be found in his voluminous correspondence with seminarians, priests, sisters and pious persons in the world, in a number of conferences and instructions published after his death, and in his commentary on the Gospel of St. John.

B. G. 40, 418

It may not be amiss to point out here that Libermann's spirituality contains nothing which restricts its usefulness to a single nation, to a certain period of time, or to the members of his own congregation. Ascetical writers and spiritual directors often permit national characteristics to color their thought so extensively that their work loses much of its value outside the confines of their own country; others become outmoded with the passage of time because they have relied too heavily on contemporary trends of thought; still others associate their teachings so closely with the mentality proper to their own religious order that their spiritual legacy has little importance for outsiders.

Rétif, 26

Father Libermann's science of holiness escapes the confines of his native France, rises above the romanticism and self-conscious mortification of the nineteenth century, and exercises its appeal far beyond the personnel of his own congregation. The universality of his spiritual doctrine flows from his emphasis on the Holy Spirit's operation in the individual soul. Paradoxically, it transcends the limitations of time and space by its very concreteness, for Libermann is concerned with the soul—any soul—in the exact situation where Divine Providence has placed it. This concrete

---

[1] For instance, Msgr. Saudreau, who quotes him at least fifty times in his classical work *Les degrés de la vie spirituelle*, Paris, 1935; de Guibert, S. J., and de la Taille, S. J., (cf. *Revue d'ascetique et mystique*, 1938, p. 141). Cf. also Rétif, S. J., *Pauvreté spirituelle et mission*, Paris, 1955, p. 12; Pierre Blanchard, *Spiritual Guide for Our Times*, Washington, 1956, p. 11.

wholesomeness in Libermann's approach gives his spirituality a kind of timelessness and occasionally seems to confer on it a modern touch. One might even characterize it by the currently fashionable term "existential."[2]

Contemplation and Practical Union. Father Libermann soon realized that *contemplation* is a form of perfection rarely attained by men who are engaged in the active life. A supernatural
E. S. 526 f.   state of soul in which man is so lost in God that he forgets the world around him presupposes as a natural condition certain favorable circumstances which are not easily fulfilled by people whose lives are enmeshed in mundane things. For this reason Libermann devoted much of his attention to *practical union with God.* In such a union the soul is faithful to God's grace in all the
L. S. I, 275   big and little circumstances of everyday life and sees everything in its relationship to God and God alone.

L. S. II, 451   *Total Surrender to God.* The only way to reach this union lies in what he calls *"abandon,"* which perhaps may be best translated by the phrase "willing and total surrender to God." By
L. S. I, 74 ; 76 ;   this term he understands the submission of all our powers and
L. S. II, 517   activities to the will of God, no matter in what way this will manifests itself, whether it be through the special illumination of the Holy Ghost, the commands of superiors, the accepted rule of life, or in the external historical setting in which divine Providence
L. S. I, 296 ff.   has placed our lives. Thus *"abandon"* means a total and uncon
L. S. I, 278 ;   ditional surrender of ourselves to God.[3]
285 ; 296   A soul which has surrendered itself to God in this way allows Him to do to it and in it whatever He wants; it places itself at
N. D. 4, 104 f.   God's disposal without any reservation regarding its own aspirations, impressions and comforts. It is as a plaything in the hands of the Divine Child, allowing Him to do as He likes. It is con-

---

[2]The term "existential" may shock the reader whose only contact with it has been the sorry and farcical excesses to which Sartre's atheism has led many of his followers. The sane existential approach, however, is a plea for concreteness in place of excessive abstraction and systematization. It exercises a profound and generally wholesome influence on philosophy, psychology, and the social sciences insofar as its students now try to see their issues in the concreteness of man's situation in the world.

One is struck by the fact that Libermann's reaction against exaggerated systematism in spirituality and asceticism occurred just when Sören Kierkegaard's (1813-1855) revolt against Hegel's rationalism laid the foundation-stone for an existential approach to philosophy and religion.

[3]Others have characterized his spirituality as one of self-denial, passivity, or spiritual poverty. Cf. Rétif, *op. cit.,* p. 10; Blanchard, *op. cit.,* p. 20.

L. S. I, 295

N. D. 3, 259

cerned with only one thing: to please God in all it does. Such a soul acts only under the influence of grace. The Holy Ghost himself, as it were, has become the only source of its life.

This doctrine avoids two opposite extremes—the one which tends to leave everything to God and remain purely passive (for Libermann insists that the soul must *act* according as it is directed by the Holy Ghost); the other, which strives to take the initiative in everything (for Libermann wants the soul to act only under the influence of God's grace). Libermann's total surrender must not be confused with the total passivity of Molinos, for it is not merely the attitude of a mind desirous of perfection. His total surrender implies considerable personal effort on the part of man to control his impulses, master his impatience, and overcome self-set patterns of judgment and activity.

N. D. 3, 265
Comm. 231 f.

N. D. 4, 105
and 315

The total surrender to God's grace does not fit into any predetermined system of spirituality, for the simple reason that systems are something abstract and artificial, while all souls are concretely different and therefore influenced by God in different ways. It is not surprising, therefore, that Father Libermann disliked spiritual systems and abstract patterns of spiritual life, because these nearly always constitute an obstacle to the free action of God's grace on the individual soul.[4] His dislike was shared by that great Saint of our times, St. Therese of the Child Jesus, whose spiritual message so strikingly resembles Libermann's surrender to God, not only in doctrine but even in expression.[5]

D. S. 331 ff.

Total Surrender and Self-Renunciation. By self-renunciation Libermann does not mean that we should inflict all kinds of positive mortifications on ourselves. In fact, he was definitely averse to such practices.[6] Instead, he recommends that we remove from

---

[4]*L. S.* 3, 349: "You must not follow any system of the spiritual life; otherwise you will do harm to souls. . . . I consider it a cardinal point of direction that grace be permitted a great freedom of action."

[5]Cf. Louis Liagre, C.S.Sp., *Ste Thérèse de l'Enfant Jésus et le Vénérable François Libermann,* Paris 1937; N. D. 4, 105; 315.

[6]Cf. *N. D.* 4, 315: "All your mortifications are nothing; your prayers unimportant; your good works valueless . . . . I laugh at your good works and am really not interested in your mortifications. I ask you only one thing: your heart . . . for the divine Jesus Himself."

N. D. 9, 195: "The greatest temptation I had to fight against in him was his desire for mortification. I finally took away his discipline and forbade him all kinds of mortification."

D. S. 338: "Mortifications are very good and very useful for our sanctification, but only if God calls us to do them and inspires us with an attraction for them."

ourselves all attachment to our own views, our own comforts
and our own inclinations, for it is these that hamper grace. This
attachment finds its source in self-love and sensuality, which are

L. S. I, 347;
II, 180; E. S.
298 ff.

the twofold root of all our spiritual evils. By self-love man allows
himself to be guided by considerations which center in him instead of in God. He replaces God by himself. Through sensuality

L. S. II, 275

man yields to created goods instead of surrendering himself to
God. These two roots of self-love and sensuality should constitute

E. S. 477; L. S.
I, 419

the object of our efforts at renunciation. Here, again, Libermann
rejects the artificiality of any spiritual system which advises us
to attack our defects one by one until none are left and holiness

L. S. I, 315

is reached. Instead, he wants us to strike down the evil in its
very roots and thus remove all defects by depriving them of their
ultimate source of life and growth.

E. S. 475

In the ordinary process, perfect self-renunciation is not something to be reached or even approximated by a single act of will,
even though such an effort may be prompted by grace. Normally
the process advances by stages. First the soul striving for God
tends to avoid seeking its own self and such pleasures as would
involve a complete break with God through mortal sin. The
second stage is reached when man tries to become detached from
himself wherever attachment would imply even the slightest deviation from God's law. Finally, he becomes so detached that he
wants only what is most agreeable to God. These are the three
stages traditionally described as the purgative, the illuminative
and the unitive way.

L. S. III, 321

Total Surrender and Mental Prayer. For a soul that sincerely
endeavors to surrender itself to God, mental prayer does not mean
an interruption of its ordinary life to consider something which
normally receives only occasional attention. It means leaving
aside for some time the everyday cares and relations with other
men and creatures to devote itself *consciously and fully* to the
God who always dominates its every action. Thus again there is

L. S. II, 354;
462

no need to follow any special method of mental prayer, whether
it be Sulpician or Ignatian, except perhaps at the beginning of
one's spiritual life when the soul has not yet become sufficiently
engaged in God. As soon as possible these artificial methods of
prayer have to be given up in favor of a simple contact with God.

L. S. II, 355

The prerequisite of mental prayer is *recollection,* which means
the renunciation of our own self during the time of prayer. Such

recollection is possible only if we endeavor to live with God during the day. For one whose life moves on a purely natural level and tends to stay there, mental prayer will always be nothing but a dreary exercise, an unpleasant way of wasting time, a burden to be dropped as soon as possible.

Persons who lead an active life, beset with all kinds of cares and occupations, may experience great difficulties in recollection, even though they sincerely try to practice surrender to God throughout their work. To such people Father Libermann offers this advice:

L. S. III,
462 f.
N. D. 7, 37 f.

Make your method of mental prayer as simple as possible. Do not make too many considerations. Do not seek to follow slavishly the method of St. Sulpice; this would not benefit you at all. In what, then, ought your mental prayer to consist? It should consist in remaining restfully, peacefully and truthfully in the presence of Our Lord. That is all. Do not aim at making numerous reflections or eliciting many affections. Force nothing; abide in Christ's presence as a wretched little child before his father; that is enough. Do not seek to express to Him the sentiments you have or wish to have; do not violently expose your wants. Keep your soul at his feet in all its poverty and weakness. Put yourself at His disposal that He may do with you what He pleases. Regard yourself as a thing belonging to Him, which is in His presence that He may use it to the full extent of His will. Do this without effort and avoid a multiplicity of interior or exterior words. The soul must be accustomed to live in God's presence, and then, during prayer, be interiorly separated from all things, in order to lay itself open before the Divine Lord. . . . Remain in His presence, willing to be at His disposal. Let it be enough for you to direct your soul's gaze on Him from time to time with this intention. When distractions come, try now and again to put them gently and quietly aside, and be content with looking peacefully at Him to whom you belong.

Surrender and Sin. Surrender must be practiced even with respect to our sins and our desire for holiness. Constant self-analysis puts the soul in considerable danger of self-love, self-complacency and presumption. Impatience with ourselves is a sign

L. S. I, 331
and 361 ; N. D.
4, 135 f. ;
L. S. I, 115

of natural activity—we are trying to make ourselves holy, whereas God alone can sanctify us. As to sin, he advises us "to seek less to know in what things we fail in regard to God than to strive peacefully to please Him in all the acts of our souls."

L. S. I, 23 ; 54 ;
E. S. 49

The main fruit of such a total surrender to God during our life is a profound peace of soul whose inner depth no trials, no temptation and no discouragement can disturb. Having no desires of its own, the soul rests in the embrace of God, it has obtained "the peace of God which passeth all understanding."

Such in brief outline is the basis of Father Libermann's spiritual doctrine insofar as it concerns people who are engaged in an active life. As Bishop Gay summed it up in a few words:

Gay, 79

> Never act with violence. Combat your defects without tenseness or impatience. Learn to be patient with yourself. Put yourself simply at God's disposal. Abandon yourself to grace without endeavoring to exceed it or go beyond it.

B. G. 14, 6

Father Libermann's spiritual writings were submitted to the Sacred Congregation of Rites in the course of his process of beatification. After a searching and detailed analysis from the dogmatic and ascetic viewpoint, which lasted from 1883 to 1886, the Sacred Congregation delivered its "*Nihil obstat.*" On this occasion, Cardinal Oreglia remarked: "It is rare that in a cause of beatification the examiners arrive at so favorable a verdict." In the fifteen volumes submitted to their critique they had been able to find only a single text which did not quite meet their approval, and this text was concerned with something of relatively minor importance.

2. *Libermann's Missionary Doctrine*

Father Libermann's importance in the history of modern missiology is rapidly gaining widespread recognition. Thus for example, Father Rétif, S.J., writes: "In the history of missionary thought time will assign a special place to him as one who was strikingly ahead of his age." John Dindinger, O.M.I., gives a detailed analysis of all his writings "because of his extraordinary importance," and declares that his work was "of decisive importance for the Negro mission." The best tribute of all, however, lies in the fact that, as was pointed out by Bishop Chappoulie, he was a "precursor whose ideas will be found in the Pontifical documents of the twentieth century."

Rétif, 12

B. M. 17, 423

ibid. p. X

B. G. 42, 273

In the following pages we will present a brief survey of Libermann's missionary doctrine and show how they have found an authoritative and official affirmation in the pronouncements of the Holy See.

a. PERSONAL HOLINESS AS THE BASIS OF THE APOSTOLATE

In the preceding pages we have seen the spiritual principles which in Libermann's view constitute the basis of all apostolic labors. As he expressed it,

D. S. 191

> The mission is the purpose, but religious life is its necessary condition.

D. S. 183

> The people of Africa will not be converted by the work of clever and capable missionaries, but through the holiness and sacrifices of their priests.

His position is diametrically opposed to that of certain modern minds who, neglecting the supernatural aspects of missionary activity, concern themselves solely with the missionaries' natural talents for management and organization. Thus they reduce the expansion of the Mystical Body of Christ to the level of a purely human society, as if it were a business enterprise or a political colonization.

In his apostolic letter *Maximum Illud* of November 30, 1919, Pope Benedict XV stressed the idea which Father Libermann

A. A. S. 11, 449

shared with many other founders of religious societies: "The missionary who wants to be fully equipped for the apostolate must first of all acquire the indispensable and most important factor of all— holiness." Previously, Pope Leo XIII had sounded the same

Denz. 1971

warning when he condemned the errors of Americanism: "It is difficult to understand that those who are imbued with Christian wisdom can exalt the natural virtues above the supernatural ones and attribute to them a greater efficacy and fruitfulness."

The fundamental reason for this viewpoint is rather obvious. As the Mystical Body of Christ, the Church is a supernatural organization in which God, and God alone, constitutes the source of all life and growth. The role of men in the Church is the humble

N. D. 9, 63

role of being "instruments in His hands." The most man can do is endeavor to be a perfect instrument which offers no resistance but operates at all times under the influence of and in accord with the will of the craftsman. In other words, the more man abandons his own views and follows God's guidance, the better his missionary activity will be.

Apart from this reason, which applies not only to missionary work but to any kind of labor in God's service, Libermann indicates two others that are specifically proper to the missions. The first is that missionaries labor among pagan or newly converted peoples who are not yet fully transformed into branches of God's Church. Lacking the traditions of long-established centers of Christianity, this neo-Christian environment depends almost entirely on the missionaries' example for its edification and imitation. Thus, as he expresses it, their "sins would be original sins" transmitted to the newborn Christian community, just as their virtues would impress a lasting stamp on it. One is reminded here of St. Peter's definition of the missionary bishop's tasks in Apostolic times: he was to be the *forma gregis,* the model of his flock.

N. D. 9, 325

A second special reason is that the missionary meets with many difficult situations which demand a much higher degree of virtue than would be required of him in a traditionally Christian society. patience and perseverance in the face of seemingly endless failures and extraordinary willingness to take up the cross daily.

N. D. 9, 43;
154; 329

L. S. IV, 75

Natural Talents. The emphasis which Libermann placed on the supernatural basis of the apostolate should not give rise to the impression that he scorned the missionary's natural talents as a powerful asset in the work of Christianization. After all, an instrument must be suitable for the purpose assigned to it. A sledge hammer would be of little use in adjusting the delicate mechanism of a watch, and a saintly missionary who is woefully lacking in natural talents is just as unfit for apostolic endeavors. It is hardly necessary to point out that Libermann nurtured no false concepts of the grace of state, such as are sometimes found among religious superiors who presumptuously call upon it to make up for a lack of ability in their subjects.[7] In fact, he was so convinced of the usefulness of natural talents and training that he always directed his missionaries to prepare themselves for their task and carefully plan their work. For the same reason he stressed natural gifts whenever he presented the names of priests as candidates for the

Gay, 99

---

[7]Thus, for example, when religious point out that they are completely unprepared to teach a certain subject, or assume an administrative post, or undertake specialized professional duties, their superiors sometimes answer this very real objection with: "But God will give you the grace of state!"

N. D. 8, 277;
Compl. 69

cf. p. 131

episcopacy, always characterizing them as "well-educated," "capable," "conciliatory," "used to dealing with men of the world." For the same reason again, he wanted his priests to take such worldly business precautions as insuring their luggage and packing adequate supplies instead of leaving everything to divine Providence. For the same reason finally, he insisted that *aptitude* and *desires* be taken into account in giving appointments to the members of his congregation.

b. PURPOSE OF MISSIONS

Establishment of a Native Church. The collapse of so many flourishing missions established in former ages had made a profound impression on Libermann.

N. D. 8, 241

> Everywhere our Holy Church wants to conquer souls by her prayers and sighs, by labor, sweat, privations, and even blood, to produce something solid, stable and secure. Nevertheless, as we see with sorrow, for many of these missions it seems that any ill wind is enough to destroy everything. Several, even of the most brilliant conquests, have collapsed at different times, at the very moment when they were at the height of their bloom.

da Silva, 280

Africa itself presented just such a sad spectacle in the ruined missions of Angola and the Congo, where in former centuries the Capuchins alone had maintained four hundred missionaries. Undoubtedly, in these territories,

N. D. 8, 235

> The [early] missionaries . . . must have made manifold conquests for Jesus Christ and his Holy Church . . . and produced numerous Christian communities, [but] perhaps without using sufficient means to consolidate the fruits of their labors by giving to these communities the stable force of a Church.

In an effort to avoid repeating this mistake, Francis Libermann saw the necessity of clearly impressing on his missionaries the exact purpose of their work and the general plan of action to be followed. In a memorandum addressed to the Propaganda in 1846, as well as in numerous letters, he boldly and unhesitatingly outlined his thoughts, which deviated considerably from general contemporary practice.

N. D. 8, 242
N. D. 8, 275

The purpose of the missions, he wrote, is "permanently to implant our holy religion" by "beginning the construction of the stable edifice of a canonically established Church." Pope Pius XI later stressed this same idea in his encyclical *Rerum Ecclesiae:*

A. A. S. 18, 74

What is the purpose of the missions if not to found and implant the Church of Christ permanently in these immense regions?

cf. N. D.
Compl. 62 f.

Of course, this idea was not exactly new in the history of the Faith. The Apostles themselves had propagated the Church by founding local branches wherever they went. However, in the course of time, their *modus agendi* had been largely forgotten. Missions had come to be established more and more as "foreign religious colonies,"[8] and even though natives were allowed to join them, the whole mentality of the operation remained proper to the colonizing power. All too frequently, also, missionary efforts were directed to the immediate conversion of the greatest possible number of individuals rather than to the planting of a new branch destined to take root and thus safeguard the future of a whole people. Against this shortsighted view Libermann argued:

N. D. 11, 193 f.

I perfectly understand your grief to see so many souls on the road to perdition and your desire to go to their aid. . . . [However], do not forget that you are there not only for the present, but to build for the future. . . . The ten souls you save by a hurried and ill-conceived step, by a measure which produces an immediate good result, may perhaps mean the loss of more than a hundred thousand. . . . [The loss of souls] certainly is a great misfortune, but it would be incomparably more unfortunate if in your hurry to save a few of these souls you allow a whole people to perish.

D. S. 211

As to the desire for martyrdom which in the past often seemed to dominate missionaries, Father Libermann soberly remarked that his priests should "not go to seek death in the missions, but to work for the salvation of souls." He added that ordinarily he "would not want to accept a vocation based on such a desire." Because their lives were consecrated to the service of God, he told his missionaries to take care of their health:

---

[8]Term used by Bishop Constantini, the Secretary of the Propaganda, in describing the method formerly used in missionary work. This method produced only "miserable results." Cf. *Missiewerk,* 1940, pp. 86 ff.

L. S. IV, 223 f.   To sacrifice one's life for the salvation of a single soul is undoubtedly something excellent, but it is still better to preserve one's life for the salvation of a hundred others. To fear neither death nor disease is the mark of a zealous missionary dedicated to God alone, but to take precautions for the safeguarding of one's life in order to save a greater number of souls marks the missionary who unites perfect prudence with perfect zeal and perfect dedication.

Native Clergy. Libermann's campaign for native Churches necessarily implied as a *sine qua non* the formation of "a natural

N. D. 8, 235   clergy," a "native clergy, rooted in the country, a native hierarchy."

N. D. 8, 242   To arrive [at permanent success], only one way seems practical to us—namely, to base ourselves from the very beginning on a stable organization inherent in the soil which we want to cultivate.

D. S. 537   The formation of a native clergy . . . supplies the only means whereby the light of the Gospel can be widely diffused and the Church solidly established in the countries which we are called to reclaim.

N. D. 8, 235   The newly established bishop should not be satisfied with having a "flying column" of missionaries, but should form a native clergy rooted in the country, a native hierarchy. Undoubtedly, in the beginning he would need white priests, but if the preservation of an exclusively white clergy would be a policy adopted permanently or at least for too considerable a time, decay [of the new Christian community] would be inevitable.

Here again his words find an echo in the Apostolic Letter *Maximum Illud* of Pope Benedict XV:

A. A. S. 11, 445   Wherever, therefore, there is a well-trained native clergy, worthy of its vocation, in adequate numbers, there one may rightfully say that the work of the missionary has been brought to a happy conclusion and that the Church has been excellently established.

The insistence of Father Libermann on this aspect of missionary work explains why his priests, within a few years of their arrival, opened seminaries wherever they were sent.[9]

N. D. 6, 611   [9]It was not always easy to get the idea of native priests accepted. Father Le Vavasseur, for instance, wrote from Reunion: "If they knew that we were even thinking of sending a negro to France to become a priest, they would literally hack us to pieces."

He likewise encouraged native religious foundations of Brothers and Sisters and urged that they be fully adapted to the condition of the land of their origin. Thus it was wholly in accord with his views when his missionaries founded religious congregations of native Brothers and Sisters within a few years of their arrival in Reunion and in the Two Guineas.

N. D. 11, 114 ff.

c. Means for Accomplishing this Purpose

Religious Life. As a safeguard for the personal holiness of his missionaries, Libermann insisted that they carefully observe the practices of the religious life. "Although the apostolate is the purpose," he warned, "the religious life is its necessary condition." It was his firm conviction that

D. S. 191

> If we maintain ourselves in fervor and piety, we will work with more zeal and have better results than if we become lax, as is bound to happen without fail to most of us living in isolation.

N. D. 2, 71

> The regulation of our time, our main activities, and our contacts with others bars the entrance of our soul to a host of bad habits and dangers. The practice of poverty protects us against the desire to seek our ease. . . . Obedience makes us practice the most intimate of all self-denial, that of our intellect, and thus cuts down the very root of egoism. . . . Having all the time before our eyes the edifying example of our confreres, obliged to perform every day several religious exercises, we are ceaselessly filled with the desire to sanctify ourselves.

E. S. 436 ff.

Evidently, what Libermann means here by religious life is not just taking public vows of religion—they were introduced only in 1856, after his death—but the practice of community life according to the rules of the Congregation.

cf. p. 214

Representatives of the Church. To make sure that the natives could recognize his missionaries as sent by the Church and not by a political power, he warned them:

N. D. 7, 162

> Take care never to go beyond the sphere proper to a minister of the Gospel. The people must never consider you as a political agent of the French Government, but should see in you only the priest of the Almighty.

Pope Benedict XV in *Maximum Illud* wrote:

A. A. S. 11, 447

> The Catholic missionary worthy of the name must always remember that he represents the interests of Christ and not at all those of his country. His conduct should be such that everyone unhesitatingly recognizes in him the minister of a religion which extends to all men who adore God in spirit and and truth and therefore is not foreign to any nation.

This motive was one of the reasons why as his first bishop in Africa Libermann chose Father Benedict Truffet, a native of Savoy, which then was still independent of France. Bishop Truffet echoed the doctrine in his well-known words:

Pitra, 448

> We do not go to Africa to establish there Italy, France or any other European country, but only the Holy Church of Rome, without regard to nationality. With God's grace we will divest ourselves of everything that is exclusively European and retain in us only the thoughts of the Church.

To protect his priests against any narrow-minded preference of their own congregation to the detriment of their function as missionaries, Libermann wrote:

N. D. 12, 464

> Before everything else the missionaries must be men of God and of the Church, and only in the next place members of the Congregation.

N. D. 10, 512

> They will never aim at their own interests or even those of the Congregation or any other human object, but only at the interests of God and His glory.

Pope Pius XII says much the same thing in his encyclical *Evangelii Praecones*:

A. A. S. 33, 506

> The missionary certainly should dearly love his fatherland and his order, but the Church should be loved with a still more ardent devotion. And let him remember that nothing will be to the advantage of his own order which is detrimental to the good of the Church.

Extending the Frontiers of the Church. Even the purest intention of acting only on behalf of the Church, however, leaves room for considerable variation in policy. Is it better, for instance, to concentrate on a small number or to occupy in short order as much territory as possible and postpone until a later time the intensification of the Christian spirit? Here, again, Father Libermann's answer is quite definite. Replying to Father Le Vavasseur, who wanted all available resources concentrated on his little island of Reunion, he wrote:

N. D. 6, 112

> I think that the apostolic spirit consists rather in extending the frontiers of the Church than in perfecting a small part. If we can achieve an extension of these frontiers and prevent Protestantism from establishing itself in all these vast territories, then, I think, we will have done something stable which will last even through the coming centuries.

The great missionary Pope Pius XI approved Libermann, for in *Rerum Ecclesiae,* he recommended:

A. A. S. 18,
79 f.

> Take care to disperse the sacred preachers in such a way that no part of the territory is deprived of the preaching of the Gospel and reserved for later.

In contrast to the narrow vision of his first followers, Libermann was not afraid of thinking and planning in a big way. Instead of limiting himself to Reunion, he gradually extended his cares to Africa, Australia, South-America, the West Indies, Madagascar and even India. "If we could only expand and embrace everything," he said.

N. D. 7, 269

He maintained that the practical way to occupy a large territory with relatively little man-power was to found central residences from which his priests could fan out over large areas where simple stations would be erected:

N. D. 2, 247

> Stations consist in stopping for a sufficient time in a definite section to instruct the poor people in our holy religion by means of formal catechism lessons for the children and a series of instructions for the adults.

Then the missionaries were to leave the station and perform the same ministry elsewhere, returning in a regular cycle to each post. Between these visits, the stations were to be taken care of by catechists. Once every two months at least, the priests were to return to the central residence "to be together for a few days and refresh the fervor of their interior life." Pope Pius XI confirmed this idea in his oft-quoted encyclical *Rerum Ecclesiae*:

N. D. 2, 274

A. A. S. 18, 80   Advance your residences as far as possible by establishing your missionaries in a central place, surrounded on all sides by smaller stations, which are entrusted at least to a catechist and provided with a chapel. From this central residence the missionaries should go and visit these stations from time to time at fixed dates to carry out their ministry.

Libermann wanted these catechists to be recruited from students in the central schools "who show talent and ability and reveal signs of sincere piety, without being able to advance to the priesthood. . . . They are to be given a solid course of instruction and taught the chant and the ceremonies of the Church." Going back to the practice of Apostolic times, as he so often did in his plans, Libermann even suggested that they be given tonsure and minor orders and allowed to wear a cassock in the church, because in this way

N. D. 8, 246

N. D. 8, 246 f.   They will be gently encouraged in their zeal for the spiritual welfare of their fellow countrymen; they will be obliged to lead an exemplary life in their families and among their fellow citizens; they will be more respected and thus able to do more good. Finally . . . being minor clerics, they will be able to replace the priests to some extent by presiding at the meetings of the faithful, leading in public morning and evening prayers, singing the offices on feastdays, and giving suitable instructions to the people.

Father Libermann could have appealed here to the Council of Trent which in its 23rd Session had declared:

In case there should not be at hand unmarried clerics to exercise the functions of the four minor orders, this place may be supplied by married clerics of approved life.

Though Rome did not dare to accept his suggestion of conferring the minor orders on the catechists,[10] Pope Pius XI gave the official seal of approval to the other ideas expressed by Libermann with respect to the catechists (*Rerum Ecclesiae*):

The Assisi   [10]In the liturgical congress held at Assisi in 1956, Bishop William van
Papers,   Bekkum, S.V.D., and other prelates went even further than Libermann and
p. 110   suggested that married laymen be raised to the diaconate and allowed to
                  assist the priest at High Mass.

A. A. S. 18, 78   It is hardly necessary to point out to you what the catechists must be and how they ought to gain pagans for Christ
less by their words than by the example of their life. Take it
as your inflexible rule, Venerable Brethren and Beloved Sons,
to train them with the greatest care. They must have a thorough knowledge of Catholic doctrine, and when they explain
or comment on it, they should be able to adjust themselves to
the mentality and intelligence of their listeners.

Libermann suggested also the formation of lay associations of
N. D. 10, 142   men and women, whereby he hoped to inculcate "industriousness,
Christian life or at least good moral conduct and the proper educa-
N. D. 11, 114   tion of children." In addition, he made efforts to have laymen
N. D. 6, 7 and   participate in the planting of the Church. For this reason he was
330   happy to accept a young physician, Dr. Brunet, as an *agrégé* of
the Congregation. Later Pope Pius XII was to write (*Evangelii
Praecones*) :

A. A. S. 33,   We desire that everywhere, insofar as it is possible, there
514   be constituted associations of Catholic men and women, of students, workmen, and craftsmen, of those who are interested in
sports and gymnastics, of other societies and pious sodalities
which can be called the auxiliary forces of the missionaries. . . .

As to medicine and surgery, it will certainly be advisable to
enlist the services of laymen also.

Mission and Civilization. According to Libermann, one must
do more than simply preach the Gospel to establish native
Churches; civilization must be brought to the people.

N. D. 8, 248 ;   We think that our Faith will never be able to acquire a stable
cf. N. D. 10,   form among these peoples nor will the nascent Churches ever
452   have a secure future without the aid of a civilization that attains
a certain degree of perfection. . . . By such a civilization we
mean one that is based on science and work in addition to
religion. . . . It is not sufficient to show these new men the
practice of work. Rather, they must be taught slowly how
things operate so that they may gradually reach a point of
understanding that will enable them to continue working without the aid of missionaries. Otherwise, these people will never
progress beyond a sort of childhood from which they will fall
back into their barbarous condition as soon as the missionaries
begin to withdraw.

The missionaries themselves must perform this work of civilization. As Libermann pointed out:

N. D. 8, 248 f.

> Civilization is impossible without Faith. Hence it is the task—nay, the duty of the missionary to work at it, not only insofar as morality is concerned, but also in its intellectual and physical aspects, i.e. in education, agriculture and technology. By virtue of his supernatural authority as an emissary of God, by his charity and priestly zeal, he alone is capable of producing a complete effect; therefore, it is on him alone that the task rests. Moreover, if the missionary takes charge only of the moral aspect of civilization, without worrying about the rest, others will take over, and he will often see them destroy in a short time what he has tried to build at the cost of so much trouble and labor.

In Libermann's opinion both civilization and the establishment of a native Church were to be reached by means of *schools and education*. Nonetheless, it was hard for him to convince his priests of the necessity of founding schools and colleges for the natives. He did not want them to leave this most important educational work to other orders or congregations as if it were something

N. D. 9, 50

that exceeded the scope of their own task, for "otherwise disorders and misunderstandings are bound to arise." When they objected that "the missionary is not a school-master," he replied:

N. D. 9, 50

> I understand that it would cost the missionaries very much to act as teachers. Nevertheless, it is urgent to take this step in order to consolidate their efforts and aim at the formation of a colored clergy, of teachers and of catechists.

N. D. 9, 44

> In my opinion, to abandon the schools is to destroy the future of the missions. Your reply that you will start them again at a later time is a joke. Once badly started, a mission is difficult to bring to a successful conclusion. Just because the work of schools is time-consuming and full of trouble, it is important to undertake it from the very beginning.

Pius XII urged the same ideas in *Evangelii Praecones*:

A. A. S. 33, 514 f.

> Since young men, and especially those who have had the advantage of a classical and liberal education, will direct the course of the future, no one can be blind to the supreme importance of devoting the best of care to elementary schools,

high schools and colleges. Therefore, with paternal solicitude We exhort Superiors of missions to spare neither labor nor expense in proportion to their means in vigorously promoting this phase of missionary activity.

His Masterplan of Education. Libermann was not satisfied with vague suggestions about starting schools, but proposed a complete masterplan of education. Everywhere elementary schools were to be established which would be open "to all who present themselves." The most promising of the children in these schools were to be kept at the mission in a kind of native boarding school where their aptitude for higher education would be tested. The best of them were to be sent to centrally located schools of tripartite character, offering classical studies for those who revealed themselves suitable for the priesthood; pedagogical instruction for others who were capable of becoming teachers and catechists; and training in agriculture, crafts and trades for the rest. For all, however, this advanced education in secular knowledge was to be accompanied by equally progressive religious and moral training. In this respect, he made some very astute observations:

N. D. 8, 244 ff.

N. D. 6, 66 f.;
cf. N. D. 10,
453

The science of the lay scholar must be based on the same foundations as that of the cleric. Moreover, the influence of these sciences must tend to the same purpose—namely, to enlighten the peoples and to confirm them in virtue and religion. . . . In addition, the men destined to spread civilization among the Africans must tend to the same goal and live according to the same principles as those who are charged with their moral and intellectual training. Otherwise, what one builds another will immediately tear down.

We see here clearly how Libermann insists on the formation of an elite whose leadership, example and labor will gradually penetrate the masses.

What will be the result of such a program? The Venerable indicates it in these words:

N. D. 6, 66; cf.
N. D. 10, 452

The execution of this plan will result in the perfect education of our African negroes. Religion will influence their intelligence and the moral order generally; it will render them more perfect and give them a spiritual and superhuman happiness. The trades and skills of civilization will rule the social and civil order and teach them how to secure for themselves an honest well-being on the natural level.

Adaptation. If missionary activity is to lead to the implantation of the Church in a new region as a self-sustaining Christian community, it will have to be rooted in the mentality, customs and culture of the people and not in the civilization proper to the missionary's home country. Father Libermann vigorously insisted on this point, long before the question was agitated among missiological theorists under the name of "acculturation." With a deep sense of urgency, he wrote:

N. D. 9, 330   Do not judge according to what you have seen or have been accustomed to in Europe. Divest yourselves of Europe, its customs and mentality. Become negroes with the negroes, and you will judge them as they ought to be judged. Become negroes with the negroes, to train them as they should be trained, not in the European fashion but retaining what is proper to them. Adapt yourselves to them as servants have to adapt themselves to their masters, their customs, taste, and manners, in order to perfect and sanctify them, to raise them from their low level and transform them slowly and gradually into a people of God.

N. D. 10, 452   [The missionaries] must pay particular attention to which customs and habits [of a people] are characteristic of the people and the nature of the land. They must carefully avoid disturbing these customs (unless they are against God's law) and modifying them in a European fashion. They will simply try to make [the natives] more perfect in their own way of life and in accord with their own customs.

Pope Pius XII stressed the same idea in *Summi Pontificatus* and *Evangelii Praecones*:

A. A. S. 31, 429   When the Gospel is being introduced into any new land, let it not destroy or extinguish whatever its people possess of the naturally good, just or beautiful. . . .

Whatever there is in native customs that is not inseparably bound up with superstition and error, will always receive kindly consideration and, when possible, will be preserved intact.

A. A. S. 33, 523   The office of an apostle does not demand that he transplant an exclusively European civilization and culture to foreign soil, there to take root and propagate itself. His task in dealing with these peoples . . . is to teach and form them so that they are ready to accept willingly and in a practical manner the principles of Christian life and morality—principles, I may add, that fit into any culture, provided it be good and sound, and which give to that culture greater force in safeguarding human dignity and in gaining human happiness. Catholic inhabitants of missionary countries, although they are first of all citizens of the Kingdom of God and members of His great family, do not for all that cease to be citizens of their earthly fatherland.

Libermann energetically and repeatedly protested against any attempt to describe the Africans as an inferior race, destined to remain forever on a low level of civilization and incapable of intel-

N. D. 8, 226

lectual achievements. "The negroes are not less intelligent than other peoples," he maintained, and he went on citing numerous examples to prove his point. If so many of them seem inferior, the reason is that they have been forced to live in extremely harsh conditions and have been deprived of any semblence of instruction. Pius XI in *Rerum Ecclesiae* states:

A. A. S. 18, 77

It is wrong to consider the natives as dull-minded inferior beings. Long experience has shown that people living in the distant regions of the East and South do not have to yield place to those of our regions and that their brilliance of mind allows them to compete with the latter. If one finds among people coming out of a barbarous condition an almost extreme intellectual slowness, it is a necessary consequence of the fact that their exercise of mind has been limited to the bare necessities of life.

Adaptation presupposes exact knowledge of native mentality, customs and language. Hence it is not surprising to hear Libermann demand that his missionaries

D. S. 537

Study the tastes, inclinations and likings of the natives. In this way they will be able to use the correct means to acquire authority over their minds, admission to their hearts, their good will and their confidence.

This demand did not fall on deaf ears. As early as 1854, Spiritan studies on ten different African languages had already appeared or were in preparation. So much emphasis was placed on the necessity of learning native languages that Libermann's successor, in indicating the purpose of residences in Africa, always

C. S. **3, 19 ; 21,** used the formula : "the conversion of the pagans and therefore the

37 ff. study of native languages." As early as 1847, the first native print-

ing press began to function in Dakar, thus anticipating by a hundred

A. A. S. **33, 515** years Pope Pius XII's exhortation about "the usefulness of print-

ing and publishing suitable works." The Holy See has also repeat-

edly stressed the necessity of studying the native languages.

Maximum Illud for example, emphasizes that one of the primary

A. A. S. **11, 448** duties of a missionary is to study "the language of the people to

whose salvation he will devote himself."

d. Ecclesiastical and Religious Superiors

In mission territories, as a rule, the Ecclesiastical Superior
(Bishop, Vicar or Prefect Apostolic) belongs to the same society
as the priests working under his direction. Nonetheless, the relationship between the Ecclesiastical Superior and the Religious
Superior of the missionaries has always constituted a thorny problem. It was still more so in the nineteenth century when the Holy
See had not yet laid down any firm directives in this regard.

D. S. 443   At first, Father Libermann thought that complications would
be avoided by uniting the two distinct powers in the one person
of the Ecclesiastical Superior. However, in 1846, after careful study
of the situation, he definitely changed his mind and urged that the
two jurisdictions be vested in distinct persons. Here are his
reasons :

N. D. 8, 208   No matter how regular a missionary bishop is and how
much he loves the Congregation to which he belongs, once he
is the head of the mission, he wants to be just that. . . . It is
in the nature of things that once a man is placed in charge of
a mission he gradually becomes detached from the rule. . . .[11]

N. D. 8, 210   It is sufficient that the Bishop have enough respect for regularity and the spirit of the community to realize their necessity for
maintaining the missionaries in their fervor. I say that this is
enough, because the Bishop must not be Superior of the community and represent the Superior General. We need a separate

---

[11]If he had been able to foresee the future, Father Libermann probably
would have been very pleased with the way most Spiritan bishops continued
to observe the rules of their society and with the fraternal attachment they
displayed in its regard.

Superior for this purpose . . . The difficulties are the same with respect to a Prefect Apostolic, and perhaps even greater. . . . It should be noted too that in Rome the Superior of the Congregation will always be wrong when there is a disagreement

N. D. 8, 212

with a Prefect as well as with a Bishop. . . . In Rome they are wholly in favor of the head of the mission, who is always right when he pleads his cause, even when he is wrong . . . If an Apostolic Constitution had given positive rules, one would know what to do, but there is nothing.

Fully aware of the evil consequences which were likely to follow if, in the mind of his priests, the Bishop's authority seemed to be in opposition to the Religious Superior's authority, he continually stressed the importance of unity and harmony:

N. D. 12, 468

Unity is the only view that must be suggested to the missionaries. They should see this unity in the Congregation to which they belong. Let there never be question of a distinction between the Bishops and the Congregation. The Bishops are one with the Congregation to which they belong. They are the head of the mission which is entrusted to the Congregation.

After describing the practice followed by other Superiors, who tried to retain full control over the members of their societies, he continues:

N. D. 8, 213

I do not like to go against the intentions of the Holy See nor do I like those continual struggles. God's spirit is not in them. Therefore, I am going to try another way, which could be successful without resulting in new inconveniences.

We can see from this that Father Libermann was fully aware that he was proposing a new way of handling the relations between religious and ecclesiastical superiors. It is remarkable how closely the well-known Instruction of the Propaganda of December 8, 1929,

N. D. Compl. 86

parallels his rules and practices in many points.[12] As Libermann himself had summarized them, they meant "absolute power for the

N. D. Compl. 314

[12]When the Propaganda received Libermann's proposed regulations, it praised the wisdom of his rules and considered the feasibility of adopting them for general use. However, in 1857, after careful examination, it decided to maintain the *status quo.* It was not until 1929 that this supreme governing body of all Catholic missions finally attached its stamp of approval to Father Libermann's proposals.

Bishop in his mission, and a perfect safeguard of religious life for the Congregation." For the sake of comparison we will place the Instruction of the Propaganda side by side with the rules which Libermann had written over eighty years before. According to Libermann:

N. D. 8, 249 f.
A source of the trouble lies in the two interests existing in the missions. These two interests are represented by two authorities: that of the Bishop, who is the head of the missionaries as missionaries, and that of the religious Superiors, who are heads of the missionaries as members of the community. If harmony exists between these two representatives of authority, the two interests will aid each other powerfully; if not, then they tend to destroy each other, and great evils may result. Therefore, rules must be fixed to reconcile the two interests, maintaining to its full extent the power of the Bishop in his mission, yet at the same time giving the community sufficient guarantees for the maintenance of its rules and spirit.

The Propaganda confirms this view, saying:

A. A. S. 22, 114
Although each of the two has a sphere of action that is proper to him and wholly distinct, one being in command of the missionaries, the other ruling the religious as religious, nevertheless anyone can see how important it is that they act in harmony, because their actions concern the same persons . . . Therefore, to avoid as much as possible a conflict of the Superiors' authorities and to make both powers tend in perfect harmony to the good of the missions and of souls which they so ardently desire, it will be useful to say something more about their mutual relationship.

We now give some of the rules formulated by Father Libermann:

N. D. 9, 91
The Superior of the Congregation does not claim any right over the administration of the Vicariate and the action of the missionaries in anything pertaining to ecclesiastical ministry, appointments, or canonical and liturgical discipline.

The Superior General of the Congregation retains his full authority over all the members of the said Congregation in everything concerning the internal direction of the communities, the perseverance and spiritual progress of the individuals, and their relations with their local superiors. The special superiors named by the Superior General for the direction of the various communities will have the same power in the district of which they are in charge.

N. D. 10, 456   A certain number of communities established in the same region shall constitute together a Province. Every Province shall have its special Superior, aided by two assistants.

In a similar vein, the Propaganda writes:

A. A. S. 22, 112   The only true Superior of the Mission is the one named by the Holy See. . . . Accordingly, in the [mission] territory he is charged with and controls all activity which aims at making converts to the Faith . . . Without him, no one, no matter what may be his authority, can start, change or suppress any work in the missions. . . .

A. A. S. 22, 113   It is excellent that the Institutes [religious congregations and orders] to which the Holy See entrusts these missions appoint regional Superiors. However, their task, as defined by the statutes of their order, is wholly limited to the religious life of the missionaries. They are in charge of these missionaries as members of a religious society to provide for both their spiritual and their temporal needs and conveniences.

A. A. S. 22, 114   It is the task of the Superior of the Mission to appoint the Superiors of the mission stations, to transfer them, as well as the missionaries, to another place, to use them for the various positions and offices according as it is necessary or useful for the missions.

Libermann:

N. D. 8, 252   When the Bishop wants to assign a post to a missionary or change him, it will be advisable that he give his orders, as a rule, through the religious Superior of the mission to which the missionary belongs. At least, he must notify him of these orders. In this way, the Bishop will often obtain information about the value of the missionary (whom he cannot know as well as does the [Religious] Superior) with respect to the position he wants to give him or the location to which he wants to assign him.

The Propaganda:

A. A. S. 22, 114   In appointing or transferring the superiors of stations or in choosing missionaries for the various functions and offices, [the Ecclesiastical Superior of the mission] should make use of all the assistance the Religious Superior can offer. Because of his position, this [religious] superior usually knows his subordinates more fully and has a better understanding of their temperament, capacities, mental abilities and aptitudes for the various offices. Therefore, the Religious Superior should propose suitable men as superiors for the different stations or for the various offices, but the Superior of the Mission appoints them.

Regarding the foundation of religious establishments whose purpose is not limited to one mission territory, Liberman wrote:

N. D. 8, 252   The Bishop of the place will have no right to use these missionaries outside the house or to regulate their occupations in it. If he needs their help, he will have to ask the Superior of the house, who alone is charged with the direction of these young priests.

Or again:

N. D. 9, 93   The Superior [of this house] will be appointed in accord-
N. D. 9, 92   ance with article eight [which states that] the Superior General has the right to appoint and depose local Superiors in accord with the Rules [of the Congregation].

The Propaganda recognized the usefulness of such foundations:

A. A. S. 22, 113   With due observance of the laws, it is not forbidden to establish in the missions religious—even exempt—houses or even religious provinces. The Sacred Congregation is very much in favor of such foundations, not only because they are wholly in agreement with the desires expressed by His Holiness Pope Pius XI in his encyclical *"Rerum Ecclesiae"* but also because they are highly useful, especially when there is question of a mission to be entrusted to the native clergy.

Finally, Father Libermann entered into a special convention with Bishop Truffet, the Ecclesiastical Superior of the Two Guineas. Concerning such conventions, the Propaganda declared:

A. A. S. 22, 113 . . . All this does not prevent the Ecclesiastical Superior from making special conventions with the Institutes of both men or women to arrive at an equitable agreement concerning their mutual rights. To give these conventions a greater force and stability, it is customary to submit them to the Sacred Congregation of the Propagation of the Faith [i.e., the Propaganda].

e. RELATIONS WITH CIVIL AUTHORITIES

From the very beginning, Father Libermann laid down certain rules to be followed with respect to the civil authorities governing the countries in which his priests were to work. These rules aim at preventing conflicts and securing good-will, while at the same time safeguarding the essential freedom of the priests in their special sphere. We have already pointed out above that he warned them not to do anything which in the eyes of the people would reduce them to the status of political agents. On the other hand he insisted:

N. D. 7, 162
cf. N. D. 4, 435

Be on good terms with the authorities, for this is God's will and is demanded by the good of souls. Endorse their plans and help them as long as these plans remain within the limits of justice and truth and are not opposed to the propagation of the Faith and the moral order.

Even if the government officials' conduct is far from edifying, it is important to retain their benevolence.

N. D. 7, 161

Should you become angry with them, he asked, when you see them commit grave sins? That would not be advisable. Imitate our good Master, who was so kind to sinners. Always adapt yourself to everyone and have patience with the faults of all without bitterness or rigidity. You know that this is a general rule which all our missionaries must observe.

The reason for this insistence on good relations with the government is plainly set forth as Libermann continues:

N. D. 4, 436

Although government officials have no spiritual powers, they can cause you trouble and frustrate you in many ways. On the other hand, if they think well of you, they can be useful in advancing the work of the salvation of souls.

To prevent troubles, he suggests that the following rules of prudence and diplomacy be observed:

N. D. 9, 241 f.

1. As much as possible avoid giving the impression that you have any doubt regarding their good will toward you. Such an attitude would be enough to turn them against you. If you appear to have confidence in them, and act as if you suspected nothing, they will often lack the courage to show their ill-will.

2. Do not speak and act in an authoritative way, i.e., with an assumed air of authority. The haughtiness which they reveal in the exercise of their powers in civil and military matters must not show up in your conduct of ecclesiastical administration. Be firm in everything that belongs to your duties of state, but be firm in a kind and humble way. . . .

3. Take care to avoid clashes. These men are never accustomed to being worsted by their subordinates. . . . Therefore, once they have taken a position, they do not withdraw, and if by steps that they cannot prevent you succeed in getting the best of them, they will make you pay for it on other occasions. . . .

4. If a conflict is inevitable, and your conscience obliges you to hold out against the will of the French Government agent . . . and you get the best of him, do not take on an air of triumph and make him feel that it is you who have won. Be nice about it and avoid discussing anything that could bring up the question again. Be humble and charitable and do not humiliate others under any pretext whatsoever.

5. Finally, avoid as much as possible any exchange of letters and official requests. . . . Go and see them, and gradually bring the conversation around to the point. Prepare the ground and make your request orally. . . . Even if you make a decision which is within your competence alone and you want to notify the commander, it is often better to speak to him about it [first].

Above all, there should be no systematic opposition:

N. D. 9, 233

Once war is declared, they will not give in. Therefore, take your precautions lest there ever be any declaration of war, even when government agents ask you something which you cannot do in conscience. Briefly, kindness and charity will always be of great help, while rigidity and inflexible ways of acting will always be interpreted as intolerance. And you know that once you are considered as intolerant, you will be good for nothing.

That Libermann practiced what he preached appears from the fact that he nearly always succeeded in obtaining what he wanted from the Government, whether the officials he had to deal with were fervent Catholics or full of Voltairian ideas. As an example we may refer to the foundation of the dioceses of Guadeloupe, Martinique and Reunion. The French Government had always been opposed to bishops in these colonies, fearing that their influence would diminish that of the local Governors. Yet in spite of all opposition, Libermann succeeded in bringing the Government around to his view.

CHAPTER EIGHT

THE GENERALATE OF FATHER IGNATIUS SCHWINDENHAMMER, 1852-1881

1. *Introduction*

Va. 169 f.   Ignatius Schwindenhammer was born in Ingersheim, Alsace, the eldest son of a pious and respected family. Following his example, his five brothers and sisters all joined religious orders: one brother as a Spiritan priest and another as an *agrégé* of the Holy Ghost Fathers, the third as a Redemptorist, and his two sisters as nuns in a convent at Amiens. Ignatius himself first met his future superior when Francis Libermann enrolled in the Seminary of Strassburg. In 1843, soon after the founding of the Congregation of the Holy Heart of Mary, he submitted his application for admission. Father Libermann had a very high opinion of this compatriot, for the following year we find him writing to Father Le Vavasseur in Reunion:

N. D. 6, 115   Father Schwindenhammer has just asked me permission to make his promises and his consecration. He is an excellent fellow, highly pious and very capable, a wise adviser and a born administrator. He is destined to remain here and not to go to the missions.

N. D. 10, 105   In 1847, after the death of Bishop Truffet, there was question of sending him to Africa as Vicar Apostolic. However, Libermann made it clear to the Propaganda that he needed Schwindenhammer, so that in the end Father Kobès was appointed in his cf. p. 191 ff.   stead. In the light of the sharp difference of opinion between these two men five years later, it would be interesting to speculate on what might have happened if their roles had been reversed: Schwindenhammer Vicar Apostolic of the Two Guineas, and Father Kobès Superior General.

cf. p. 146   In deference to the Venerable's wishes, as we have already seen, Father Schwindenhammer was elected Superior General after Libermann's death. Since 1844, the thirty-four year old Superior had been closely associated with the general administration of the Congregation. He possessed an intimate knowledge not only of all current affairs affecting it, but of Libermann's intentions and plans as well. Moreover, Le Vavasseur, Libermann's trusted friend and co-founder of the Holy Heart of Mary Congregation, now became Schwindenhammer's first assistant. Lastly, as a further precaution against any tendency to deviate from Libermann's ideas in the future conduct of the Congregation's business, he asked Father Lannurien, the Venerable's secretary and the recipient of many intimate confidences during his last years, to indicate exactly how Libermann had felt about the union with the Holy Ghost Fathers and how this union affected the aims and purposes of the Congregation.

cf. pp. 120 ff.   We have already presented the answers Father Libermann and his secretary gave to this question. Hence it is not necessary for us to repeat them here. We may simply summarize them in this way:

1. So-called social works in the homeland fall directly within the scope of the Congregation's purpose.

2. The Congregation must consolidate itself in the homeland against excessive demands from the missions.

3. Although the Congregation wants to retain Africa as its main mission territory, it remains fully responsible for the religious service of the Holy Ghost missions in the old French colonies.

4. Educational works are indirectly in line with the purpose of the Congregation and serve to consolidate its position in the homeland.

2. *New Foundations and Their Reasons*

After this reminder, let us have a look at what happened under the generalate of Father Schwindenhammer. The tables on pp. 187 ff. tell a graphic story. Of seventy-nine new foundations, thirty-three were in Europe and the United States. Among these, there are nineteen colleges and seminaries, only two of which served exclusively for training aspirants to the Congregation, and in addition there were five social works such as orphanages and industrial schools for juvenile delinquents. Of the forty-five foundations in mission territories, twenty were in Africa, and twenty-five in the West Indies and the old French colonies. Of these overseas foundations, eleven were seminaries and colleges.

New Foundations established during the generalate of Father Schwindenhammer in Europe and the United States (1852-1881)

Year	Colleges and Seminaries	Social Works	Others
1853	1. French Seminary, Rome 2. College, Ploermel, France; and ⟶		1. Chaplaincy Our Lady of Victories, Paris ⟶ Chaplaincy Brothers
1854	3. Seminary-College, Gourin, France	1. Orphanage, industrial and agricultural schools, Saint-Ilan, France	
1855		2. Industrial and agricultural schools, Carlan, France	
1856	4. Seminary-College, Cellule, France; and ⟶	⟶ Orphanage	
1858	5. Seminary-College, Langonnet, France; and ⟶	⟶ Industrial and agricultural schools	
1859		3. Industrial and agricultural schools, St. Michel, France	
1860	6. College, Blackrock, Ireland		
1862		4. Orphanage, Glasnevin, Ireland	
1863	7. Senior Seminary, Chevilly, France *(for Congregation only)*; and ⟶	⟶ Orphanage	2. Retreat House for clergy, Kaiserswerth, Germany
1864	8. Seminary-College, Rockwell, Ireland 9. Seminary-College, Marienstadt, Germany; and ⟶	⟶ Orphanage; and ⟶	⟶ Retreat House 3. Parish and Shrine, Retreat House, Marienthal, Germany
1866		5. Holy Family Institute, Toulon, France (youth organizations)	
1867	10. Junior Seminary, Santarem, Portugal *(for Congregation only)*		
1870	11. College, Gibraltar		

(Continued on Succeeding Page)

Year	Colleges and Seminaries	Social Works	Others
1872	12. Seminary-College, Braga, Portugal		4. Parish, Russia, Ohio
1873			5. Parish, Piqua, Ohio
			6. Parish, Berlin, Ohio
1874	13. Seminary-College, Beauvais, France		7. Parish, Sharpsburg, Pa.
1875	14. College, Langogne, France		
1876	15. College, Gravelines, France		
	16. Seminary-College, Merville, France		
1878	17. Seminary-College, Mesnières, France; and ⟶ Orphanage		8. Colony, Arkansas
	18. Seminary-College, Pittsburgh, Pa.		
1880	19. College, Rambervillers, France		9. Mission Band, Gourin, France

In all, therefore, thirty colleges and seminaries—an average of one a year—were established under Father Schwindenhammer. Although some of these were of brief duration and others were subsequently combined with existing institutions, quite a number of them have carried on their excellent work down to the present day.

In analyzing the Superior General's motivation in founding so many non-African works, we learn that:

C. S. 4, 5

1. With respect to the old Holy Ghost Missions, he felt "a kind of obligation in justice." Moreover, he regarded seminaries in these missions as "directly within the scope of the Congregation."

2. With respect to seminaries in the homeland, after indicating that they achieve the ends of the Congregation only indirectly, he echoes the words of Father Lannurien:

cf. p. 123

C. S. 4, 18 f.

It is to be noted that seminaries do not appear to be excluded from the list of works the Congregation may assume. The old Congregation of the Holy Ghost itself had taken charge of seminaries and directed, in addition to that of the Holy Ghost,

New Foundations established during the generalate of Father Schwindenhammer
in mission territories (1852-1881)

| Year | Outside Africa | | In Africa |
	Colleges and Seminaries	Other Works	
1853	1. Senior Seminary, Martinique 2. Seminary, Guadeloupe		
1854		1. Parish, Morne Rouge, Guadeloupe 2. Agricultural School, Guadeloupe	
1858		3. Orphanage, Trade and Agricultural School, Providence, Reunion 4. Parish, Neuville Reunion	
1859	3. Seminary-College, Martinique	5. Parish, Chaplaincy of leper colony, Mana, Guiana	
1860		6. Parish, Port-au-Prince, Haiti	1. Station, Rufisque, Senegambia
1861		7. Trade School, Chandernagor, India	
1862	4. Seminary-College, Port of Spain, Trinidad	8. Agricultural and Trade School, Mondelice, Guiana	2. Mission, Zanzibar 3. Station, St. Joseph, Senegambia
1863	5. College, Fort de France, Martinique	9. Parish, Petionville, Haiti 10. Agricultural School, Ilette à Guillaume, Reunion	4. Mission, Freetown, Sierra Leone
1864			5. Trade and Agricultural School, Ngazobil, Senegambia
1865			6. Mossamedes Mission, Angola 7. Ambriz Mission, Angola
1866			8. Loanda Mission, Angola
1867	6. College of St. Louis, Mauritius		
1868	7. Seminary-College, Guadeloupe	11. Parish, St. Croix, Mauritius	9. Bagamoyo Mission, East Africa
1872	8. Seminary-College, Haiti	12. Parish, St. Ann, Haiti	

(Continued on Succeeding Page)

| Year | Outside Africa | | In Africa |
	Colleges and Seminaries	Other Works	
1873	9. College, Miquelon	13. Parish, Cassis, Mauritius	10. Landana Mission, Congo 11. Station Sedhiu, Senegambia
1874	10. Junior Seminary, Reunion	14. Chaplaincy Prisons, Maroni, Guiana	
1875			12. Rio Pungo Station, Sierra Leone
1877			13. Mhonda Mission, East Africa
1878			14. Omarara Mission, South West Africa
1879	11. College, Pondicherry, India	15. Mission, Pondicherry, India	15. Fadiut Station, Senegambia 16. Cimbebasia Mission, South West Africa 17. Central Cape, South Africa
1880			18. Boma Mission, Belgian Congo 19. Carabana Station, Senegambia
1881			20. Mandera Mission, East Africa

the senior seminaries of Meaux and Verdun. Moreover, our Holy Founder, who so fully possessed the true spirit of Christ's priesthood, would seem to have left in his society the seeds of this priestly life so that it might be developed in the Church at a time indicated by divine Providence.

C. S. 4, 20
C. S. 10, 10

3. As to the colleges, he repeatedly emphasized that they serve "to consolidate and develop the Congregation and its work" and "bring in recruits."

4. Regarding the foundation of colleges and other works in Ireland, Germany, the United States, and Portugal, he cited not only the personal desire of Father Libermann to see the Holy Ghost Fathers spread to these countries, but also the necessity of having non-French personnel to staff missions in foreign colo-

B. G. 3, 7 ff.   nies. Moreover, he pointed out the dangers of being at the mercy of
the French government and this would be almost a certainty if
the Spiritans remained restricted to France.

3. *The Two Guineas*

a. THE CONFLICT WITH BISHOP KOBÈS

The table on p. 189 shows another striking phenomenon.
Between 1852 and 1862 only one small station was opened in
Africa. Schwindenhammer preferred to go slow in Africa. We
learn the reason for this caution from his circular letters of 1853:

C. S. 3, 14   1. The enormous loss of personnel in Africa: of the seventy-
four missionaries sent out since 1842, twenty had died and fifteen
others had to be permanently withdrawn. These losses were so
heavy that a continuation of them would have prevented the Congregation from developing and thus would have ultimately tended
to destroy the mission itself.

C. S. 3, 15   2. The heavy financial burden of these missions, a liability
which the Congregation could ill afford to increase. By sending
nearly every available man to Africa, the Congregation sacrificed
income for support of the central administration and thereby found
it impossible to consolidate its position.

C. S. 3, 15   3. The instability of the missions. Death, sickness and plunder
had caused the closure of seven out of thirteen stations. A careful
reappraisal of the situation was in order.

C. S. 4, 7   4. The discredit which the loss of so many young lives brought
on the Congregation. Under conditions prevailing at the time, only
the most heroic souls would seek entrance, and such heroic souls
were few and far between.

cf. p. 128 ff.   Father Libermann himself had advised a slow-down on the
African enterprise for fear of destroying the Congregation. Nevertheless, as was natural, the reaction of the men in Africa was
most unfavorable toward retrenchment. Even while Father Libermann himself was still alive, the African missionaries registered
cf. p. 153   strong protests against a diversification of works. In 1845, for instance, when he embarked on the Australian venture, there had
been a particularly violent outburst of anger, for which Father

Va. 210
N. D. Compl.
191 ff.

D. C. 150

Va. 207

Va. 215 f.

Ap. H. 83

Va. 206 ff.

Arragon had bluntly assumed the position of spokesman. Similarly Bishop Kobès argued vehemently that the Congregation should be nothing more than a source of personnel for the African missions. To his way of thinking, only a skeleton staff was to be retained at the Motherhouse; anyone else not in Africa was a walking demonstration that the Spiritans had deviated from their original purpose. The African missionaries insisted on the abandonment of the old Holy Ghost missions, the closure of Holy Ghost Seminary, the return to Notre Dame du Gard, and the withdrawal from all other establishments of the Congregation except those in Africa! This obstinacy in putting Africa first made Father Collin, one of Libermann's first two novices, compare Bishop Kobès to "a savage who, in order to get at the fruits of a tree, cuts it down by the very root."

It must be admitted, of course, that Bishop Kobès had ambitious plans for Africa and therefore wanted a good deal of manpower. He had projected missions at a distance of five leagues all over his immense territory: a dozen between Dakar and Senegal, another dozen between Dakar and Albreda, and a whole string along the Senegal river. His colleague, Father Boulanger, the Prefect Apostolic of Senegal, demanded six men for St. Louis alone. However, in Bishop Kobès' projects there was not enough systematic planning. He was particularly unfortunate in his choice of centers wherein new stations were to be established. When he died in 1872, only four of the stations in his territory had survived the continuous disasters and misfortunes which kept harassing him in everything he undertook.

In his argument with Father Schwindenhammer, despite long letters of explanation to and fro, little progress was made toward a solution. In the hope that a personal interview would be more productive, therefore, the Bishop accepted an invitation to come to Paris and discuss the affair. Long conferences followed in which both men appealed to Libermann's intentions to justify their respective positions. Still there was no agreement. If anything, the misunderstanding was intensified by a sharp difference of opinion regarding the Ecclesiastical Superior's position and the Motherhouse's responsibility in matters pertaining to the missions and the missionaries. Later, however, Bishop Kobès had long conversations with several prominent confreres for whom he had great esteem, such as Fathers Le Vavasseur, Lannurien and Collin.

At last he began to realize that the Superior General was not alone in his position and that the missionaries' fears for Africa were entirely groundless. In a letter of March, 1854, Father Collin happily records the return of peace:

Va. 211

I have restricted myself to pointing out that the general meeting, held after the retreat, had taken place in the best of spirits and in perfect harmony; that the resolutions taken there must be regarded as the expression of the whole Congregation; that the new works undertaken are indispensable because of our circumstances; and finally that the African mission is not the Congregation, but only one of its works. We were in perfect agreement on all this.

Shortly after, Bishop Kobès returned to Dakar, reassured and confident. Although Father Schwindenhammer's circular letters, in which we find numerous echoes of this conflict, continued to annoy him somewhat, and although he never did obtain all the personnel he wanted, he was now much better adjusted to the situation. Without entirely changing his viewpoint, he appears to have resigned himself to let the Superior General make the final decision as to which works would be undertaken and who should staff them. There was no longer any reason to fear that Africa would be left to its fate. This is evident from his own report to the Propaganda:

B. G. 3, 104

between 1853 and 1862 the Two Guineas received twenty-three priests and thirteen Brothers. Their mortality, however, was still frightful: of the hundred and eight men sent out between 1843 and 1862, no less than forty-two had died, while thirty-four others had left because of sickness or discouragement. Although at the end of Father Schwindenhammer's generalate only seventy-five Fathers (23%) were working in Africa, at least an equal number of others had been sent to this mission and died there at an early age.

b. WELCOME AID

L. H. 85 ff.
C. S. L. 76 ff.
Storme, 120 ff.
A. P. F. 31,
246 ff.; 479;
33, 393 ff.

In 1859, one of the most ardent desires of the Holy Ghost Fathers became a reality; another congregation of priests tried to come to their aid in the immense mission of the Two Guineas. Neither Libermann nor his successor nor the Vicars Apostolic in the missions had any desire to reserve for themselves alone a territory stretching over a coastline of five thousand miles without limits to the interior. They were delighted, then, when Bishop Melchior de Brésillac, the Founder of the Society of African Missions (1856), offered to take over part of their territory. On the advice of Father Schwindenhammer, who was convinced that Sierra Leone offered the best chance of success, Bishop Brésillac abandoned his plan to start in Dahomey. In March 1859, he and his companions sailed for the place recommended by the Spiritans. As events turned out, the advice was so unfortunate that it nearly wrecked the new society. In the absence of any other information, however, it was the best available, for the Spiritan missions were relatively close to Sierra Leone, and it was natural to assume that conditions in the two regions would be similar.

After spending seven weeks as the guests of the Holy Ghost Fathers in Gorée and Dakar, and receiving from Bishop Kobès faculties for the whole Vicariate of the Two Guineas, the new missionaries sailed for Sierra Leone. When they reached their destination by the end of May, the terrible tragedy of Cape Palmas repeated itself for these newcomers: on June 2, the first priest died, and he was followed in ten days by a Brother. Before the month was over, the Bishop-Founder himself succumbed, and so did the one remaining priest. Only a Protestant minister was left to officiate at their grave. One lone survivor, a Brother, had escaped death and made his way back to Europe. In Rome, the Propaganda thought that the new group itself could not survive this tragedy and sadly assigned Sierra Leone again to the Holy Ghost Fathers, who established the mission of Freetown there in 1864. However, within two years the Society valiantly returned to Africa, this time to Dahomey. In 1868 the territory was separated from the Vicariate of the Two Guineas and erected into an independent mission. In this way the Society of African Missions became the first Congregation to come to the aid of the Spiritans in their assault on the treacherous and stubborn territory of West Africa.

A. P. F. 38, 247 ff.

c. First Efforts South of the Equator

In the southern part of the Two Guineas, the old diocese of Angola was still functioning. It was first visited by a Holy Ghost Father in 1852. He found a resident bishop assisted by five priests. The exercise of his jurisdiction was confined to the two coastal towns of Loanda (four priests) and Benguela (one priest). In these two settlements there was a numerous white population of soldiers, traders and Portuguese government officials, but the

B. G. 4, 643 ff.
A. P. F. 38, 233

rest of the country was abandoned as far as religious ministration was concerned. As early as 1851, Bishop Bessieux had wanted to resume missionary work in this part of his Vicariate, but it was not before 1866 that the first Holy Ghost Fathers, Father Charles Duparquet and Father Victor Poussot settled in Angola. These two were followed by others and, four years later, after having tried three different locations and lost three priests, they had to leave the country because at that time Portgugal was still suspicious about the possible political intentions of "foreign" missionaries.

Nevertheless, in 1873 Father Duparquet returned and founded the mission of Landana in what is now called the Portuguese Congo. From this central location he and his fellow priests roamed far and wide among the tribes of northern Angola. In their wanderings they came across populations which had retained some Catholic practices from the days of the extinct Portuguese missions. For example, in San Antonio the natives still sang the *Salve Regina,* the local king sprinkled water, preached, and gave his blessings with a crucifix; in San Salvador a royal "secretary" said "Mass" every Sunday, which seemed to consist mainly in switching a book back and forth on an improvised alter. All these people were haunted by a desire to see Catholic priests established among them and they staunchly resisted all efforts of Protestant missionaries to convert them.

In 1878 the tireless Father Duparquet went on an exploratory trip from Capetown to the southernmost end of the Two Guineas. On this trip he acquired his famous "prairie schooner," the "Raphael." It was a kind of combined chapel and bed-room mounted on axles and drawn by eight pairs of oxen, and it required a crew of three men to manage it. After travelling four hundred miles to the north of Walvis Bay without finding a single Catholic missionary anywhere, he stopped at the Bay and founded the mission of Omarara (1878), laying claim to the territory as part of the Vicariate of the Two Guineas. The next year, the Prefect of the Propaganda confirmed his view that the Spiritans had charge of the area and erected it into the Prefecture of Cimbebasia. Father Duparquet became its Vice Prefect. More than one million square miles were confided to his care and for good measure the Prefecture of Central Cape of Good Hope was added. It was a territory that belonged to the Society of African Missions, but they were anxious to exchange it for the Spiritan territories on the Gold and Ivory Coasts.

Margin notes:
B. G. 14, 753 ff.
Storme, 510 ff.
M. C. 1, 14 ff.; 23 ff.; 31 ff.; 210 ff.
M. C. 5, 259
Ap. H. 245 f.
M. C. 10, 496 ff.; 524 ff.
A. P. F. 49, 377 ff.
B. G. 11, 532 ff.
M. C. 12, 367 ff.; 379 ff.; 404 ff.; 416 ff.; 432 ff.
B. G. 11, 507 ff.; 33, 167
Cf. p. 104
G. C. M. H. 140

4. *The Opening Phase of the Evangelization of East Africa*

A. P. F. 35,
124 ff.
B. G. 3, 4 ff.
Storme, 378 ff.
R. H. M. 10,
107 ff.; 13,
44 ff.

While these Holy Ghost Fathers were establishing their bases of operations in the West, others launched an attack on the East. The first initiative came from the island of Reunion. In 1858, its Bishop, Armand Maupoint, sent his Vicar General, Father Armand Fava,[1] to Zanzibar on a preliminary exploration. The next year he appealed to the Holy Ghost Fathers to undertake the mission. Meanwhile he had founded a first base on the island of Zanzibar, off the east coast of Africa (1860). We say "base" advisedly, for the construction undertaken was so enormous that it aroused the suspicions of the British. Their consul reported to his government that the buildings could "easily accommodate 1,200 men, and probably as many as 2,000." Fearful of possible political implications, England could be pacified only by a joint Anglo-French declaration to respect the territorial integrity of Zanzibar's sultan. There was really no reason for concern, however, for the construction had been undertaken to accommodate the schools, hospitals, and huge workshops to be established there by the Spiritans. In 1862, the Congregation took charge of the Prefecture of Zanguebar or Zanzibar ("the Land of the Infidels"), which stretched from Cape Guardafui, near Arabia, to Cape Delgado in Mozambique, a distance of nearly two thousand miles, again without limits to the interior. In 1863, this mission, which is justly called "the Mother of all Churches in East Africa," received its first pioneers: Father Anthony Horner and Father Edward Baur, accompanied by Brothers Celestine and Felician. In addition to the base on Zanzibar, they established a similar one on the mainland at Bagamoyo (1868). Within two years after the foundation of the Bagamoyo mission, a junior seminary began to function, and three native youths went to France to enter the Brothers' novitiate.

Groves, II,
285 f.

B. G. 9, 115 ff.

B. G. 3, 431 ff.

B. G. 6, 415
M. C. 1, 65 ff.
Ap. H. 332 ff.
B. G. 7, 265

Zanzibar is infamous in history as the greatest slave market in the world: every year fifty to sixty thousand slaves were sold on its markets. Despite the general degradation, however, the Moslem world was soon agape with admiration for the work of the pioneer Spiritans. Camps for liberated slave children, schools

---

B. M. 17, no.
7197

[1]Father Fava had studied at Holy Ghost Seminary in Paris. In 1851 he went to Reunion. Twenty years later he became Bishop of Martinique. In 1875 he was transferred to the See of Grenoble, where he died in 1899.

and workshops, hospitals and plantations, a college, a seminary, and a novitiate arose in the mission centers of Zanzibar and Bagamoyo. The workshops especially drew the admiration of the Sultan. He became a steady visitor of the Brothers, one of whom was the only European allowed to enter the palace at his own discretion to confer with His Majesty about the royal enterprises. By 1872 the Bagamoyo mission alone comprised over fifty buildings. Although a fierce hurricane destroyed nearly everything but four wretched shelters, the Fathers and Brothers immediately began the task of reconstruction and succeeded so well that the next year Sir Bartle Frere recommended the mission "as a model to be followed in any attempt to civilize or evangelize Africa." This same Bagamoyo mission became world-famous as the starting point for Livingstone, Stanley, Cameron and other explorers when they set out on their expeditions to the interior. While these men returned to the civilized world singing the praises of the humble Catholic missionaries they had met, tomtoms were carrying the news into the bush. Soon messages came from the interior begging for "the white men who teach good religion."

By way of response to these requests, a new center of operations was established at Mhonda in 1877. Before long it was followed by others, for increasingly large numbers of priests and brothers began to flow in through Zanzibar and Bagamoyo. When the first children had grown up in their missions, the Fathers set out to establish Christian "freedom villages," from which the Faith, they hoped, would radiate over the surrounding tribes and prepare them for the Glad Tidings. In 1878, eighteen years after the founding of the Zanzibar mission, the Holy Ghost Fathers rejoiced to learn that another society of missionaries was coming to take part in the common task. Organized in the Spiritan mission at Bagamoyo, three successive caravans of White Fathers set out in a daring push to the lands of Nyassa and Uganda, deep in the interior of Africa, whence the messengers had come to beg for the "white men who teach good religion."

5. *Educational Works*

a. IN EUROPE AND THE UNITED STATES

While the missionary work went blazing ahead in Africa, Father Schwindenhammer applied himself seriously to the con-

M. C. 12, 314

B. G. 7, 707

Groves, II, 268

M. C. 4, 370 f.

A. P. F. 44, 416 f.

M. C. 5, 417

Ap. H. 333 ff.

M. C. 4, 69; 5, 267; 327 ff.; 10, 304; 11, 440

M. C. 10, 177 ff.; 189 ff.; 202 ff.

B. G. 11, 125; 730

B. G. 11, 712 ff.

L. H. 99 ff.

cf. pp. 337 ff.

cf. p. 124

solidation of the Congregation at home by means of educational works. The first of these was the foundation of a seminary for the French clergy in Rome. It was the personal desire of Pope Pius IX that the Spiritans undertake this work and Father Schwindenhammer who had himself come close to being a seminary rector in Cincinnati just two years before was delighted to accept the invitation. This Roman seminary was destined to render great service to the Church by stamping out the remaining traces of Gallicanism among the French clergy, for during the first century of its existence more than 3,000 priests and one hundred bishops were to receive their spiritual training in it.

B. G. 43, 77

cf. pp. 187 ff.

This foundation was followed by a long list of colleges and seminaries both in France and abroad. Although some of these were short-lived or only of a provisional character, others quickly acquired a solid reputation and showed that the nineteenth century Holy Ghost Fathers were rightful heirs of their eighteenth century predecessors in the field of academic achievement. The most important of these colleges were those of Beauvais and Mesnières in France, Blackrock and Rockwell in Ireland, Braga in Portugal, and Holy Ghost College (Duquesne University) in Pittsburgh, Pennsylvania. Most of them were combined with other works—nearly always a junior seminary of the Congregation, but occasionally also there were orphanages, trade-schools and novitiates for Brothers.

These various foundations adequately fulfilled the purpose for which they had been established. Despite the high death rate in the missions, Father Schwindenhammer's generalate was blessed with a six-fold increase of priests and a ten-fold increase in Brothers.[2] The charge has often been made that he and his successor, Father Emonet, undertook so many works in Europe and North America that the missions were neglected. This charge is utterly without foundation as the reader can see from the statistical tables on page 200. At the end of his generalate, no less than 57% of the Fathers were working in the missions and the figure went down only four percent under Father Emonet. On the other hand, at a later time under Archbishop Le Roy, when all the colleges in France and Portugal were closed, the percentage of Fathers in the missions kept its current level of 53% and the

---

[2]From 56 priests and 33 Brothers to 329 priests and 305 Brothers. The figures for 1852 are based on the lists of *N. D.* 13, App., pp. 44-84.

Brothers even dropped from 33% to 32%. Father Schwinden-hammer's rate of 57% has never been surpassed and it has been equalled only in very recent times.

cf. p. 200

It is true, of course, that the percentage of personnel *in Africa* was lowest (23%) at the end of his generalate, but, we have already pointed out why he had to proceed more deliberately there. Subsequently, when Father Emonet and Archbishop Le Roy began to send larger contingents of Fathers and Brothers to Africa, the average age of Spiritans who died there began to drop

cf. p. 231

alarmingly. In 1895 it reached the low of twenty-nine years and eight months. Between 1890 and 1910, one hundred and fourteen of them failed to reach the age of thirty, while eighty-one others died between thirty and thirty-five years of age. It is quite apparent from this that Father Schwindenhammer had good reasons for caution in the days when the Congregation was still too weak to sustain such heavy losses.[3]

b. IN THE MISSIONS

Outside Africa. The missions themselves were not forgotten

cf. pp. 189 f.

in this educational movement. In mission territories other than Africa, eleven seminaries and colleges were founded during Father Schwindenhammer's generalate. With respect to them, there was no question of seeking to consolidate the Congregation itself. Their purpose was directly in line with that of all missionary work: to establish a local church with a local clergy and a local elite of Catholic laymen, capable of imbuing society with Catholic princi-ples. Some of these colleges and seminaries did not survive be-

cf. pp. 389 ff.
cf. pp. 364 ff.

cause their establishment had been premature. Others, however, such as St. Mary's College in Trinidad and St. Martial's College in Haiti, made amazing progress and still fulfill at present the role for which they were created.

In Africa. As Father Libermann had demanded, the African missions did not fail to work toward educating a Christian elite. Native colleges and seminaries began to function as early as 1845

Ap. H. 84

in the Two Guineas and from 1870 on in Bagamoyo. Although Bishop Kobès was able to ordain his first native priest in 1852

---

[3]The statistics and graph on p. 231 deviate from the one compiled by Brother Novatus Ebbers, C.S.Sp., and published in *B. G.* 25, p. 467. Although frequently referred to as applying to missionaries, Brother Novatus' statistics are based on all members of the Congregation.

TERRITORIAL DISTRIBUTION OF PERSONNEL AT THE END OF EACH GENERALATE

Year		Total		Europe and N. America		All Missions		Continental Africa		Elsewhere	
		No.	%	No.	%	No.	%	No.	%	No.	%
Libermann 1852	Priests	56	100	23	41	33	59	24	43	9	16
	Brothers	33	100	11	33	22	67	17	50	5	17
Schwindenhammer—Le Vavasseur 1883	Priests	329	100	143	43	186	57	75	23	111	34
	Brothers	305	100	221	72	84	28	52	17	32	11
Emonet 1896	Priests	599	100	279	47	320	53	209	35	111	18
	Brothers	531	100	356	67	175	33	140	26	35	7
Le Roy 1926	Priests	1,042	100	488	47	554	53	370	35	185	18
	Brothers	621	100	421	68	200	32	164	26	35	6
Le Hunsec 1950	Priests	2,457	100	1,054	43	1,403	57	988	40	415	17
	Brothers	777	100	565	72	212	28	176	23	36	5
Griffin till 1955	Priests	2,994	100	1,273	43	1,721	57	1,297	43	424	14
	Brothers	799	100	567	71	232	29	189	24	43	5

The personnel figures for Europe and North America include also the aged, the sick, and young Brothers in their technical training period. *Elsewhere* refers to West Indies, South America, St. Pierre et Miquelon, Cape Verde, Madagascar, Reunion, Mauritius, and Pondicherry.

Territorial Distribution of Personnel at the End of Each Generalate

Priests

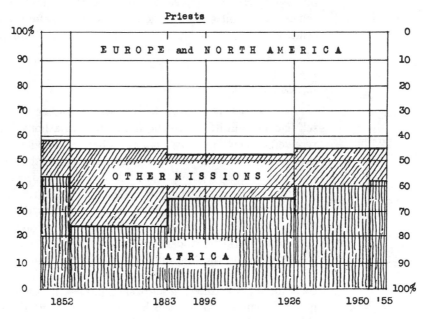

Brothers

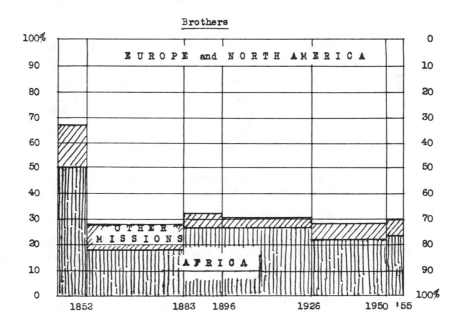

and five more during the remaining years of his episcopacy, this phase of academic endeavor did not share the success of the schools and colleges. In fact, it was not before the twentieth century that appreciably larger numbers of African priests were to issue from the African seminaries.

cf. pp. 498 ff.

6. *The Development of Social Works*

In Europe. The social works, which Father Libermann himself had inaugurated with the foundation of a house in Bordeaux, received a new impetus under Father Schwindenhammer. The most important of these were the large establishments of Saint-Ilan, Saint Michel, and Carlan in France. They served as juvenile detention homes, orphanages, industrial and agricultural schools. The Government was delighted to see the Spiritans take charge of these abandoned and wayward youths and elevate them morally and socially to a high level. It was more delighted still when the bill came in and the cost appeared to have gone down to less than one franc a day per boy, despite the fact that these schools were soon among the finest and best equipped in the country. The guiding genius of this work was Father Le Vavasseur. His ability in this respect procured for the Congregation a tremendous reputation for competence in the handling of problem children. Soon there was a flood of invitations to take up similar works throughout France. If these had not been declined, the Spiritans would in short order have found themselves devoted exclusively to the abandoned youth of France. Nevertheless, one more orphanage was accepted in Ireland to aid in establishing the Congregation in this country. Even in their colleges the Fathers did not forget the orphans, for several, such as those of Cellule and Mesnières, had an orphanage attached to them. In 1874 the Holy Ghost Brothers, who had assumed a large share of responsibility for these institutions, were officially certified as teachers by the French Government and this recognition exempted them from compulsory military service.

Va. 224 ff.

cf. p. 204

B. G. 10, 1 ff.

In the Missions. Similar works were undertaken in the missions of the Congregation. The best known of these was Providence Institute in the island of Reunion. It was a huge establishment, comprising a hospital, an orphanage, a technical school, a school of agriculture, and a juvenile detention home, all of which the

Va. 228
Ap. H. 425 ff.

local government had obliged itself by contract to support for twenty-five years. Under the Spiritan Brothers' capable direction, the schools of this institution were very successful—too successful in fact, for local industries began to complain about unfair competition. Then the newspapers took up the complaint and began a campaign against the institution. Popular resentment smouldered. On the occasion of a local riot, the frenzied mob sacked a nearby Jesuit College and then laid siege to Providence, demanding that it be closed. Meanwhile, a weak colonial Governor stood by and did not dare to oppose the demand. Although the Congregation later entered a breach of contract suit against the colony before the National Superior Court and won the case, nevertheless the institution could not be reopened. As the island's Senator, Mr. Drouet, sadly remarked, "We have managed to destroy Providence Institute, but we have not been able to replace it."

B. G. 11, 454

In faraway Chandernagor, India, other Holy Ghost Brothers dedicated themselves with equal success to another school of trades and agriculture (1860), while still more operated similar schools in Senegambia, Zanzibar and Bagamoyo. In addition, there were other schools in Guadeloupe and Martinique, but these two did not live up to expectations, for the Congregation found it impossible to supply these institutions with technically qualified instructors.

D. C. 154

7. *International Expansion*

We have already referred several times to Father Libermann's desire to see the Congregation expand beyond the borders of France. He personally made efforts to establish his society in Ireland, England, Spain, Portugal, Belgium, and the United States, and his thoughts constantly turned in a special way toward Germany. Although he did not live to see this desire fulfilled, his successor was able to introduce the Holy Ghost Fathers into Ireland, Germany, Portugal and the United States.

a. FOUNDATIONS IN IRELAND

N. B. 278

First Contacts. The first Irishman to join the Holy Ghost Fathers was Father Henry Power of the diocese of Cork. Following the example of several of his countrymen, he had entered Holy

Ghost Seminary in 1820. Two years later he became a member of the Congregation. However, when the French Government forced the closure of its junior and senior seminaries in 1830, Father Power thought that it was only a matter of time until the Congregation would become extinct. He withdrew and returned to Ireland.

N. D. 3, 434
N. D. 3, 206

N. D. 9, 483

In 1842 Father Libermann seriously considered the project of founding a branch of his Society in Ireland, but when he heard that Father John Hand was just then establishing the missionary college of All Hallows, he modestly postponed his plan on the assumption that two simultaneous foundations of the same type would hamper each other's efforts. He did have the satisfaction, however, of receiving the first Irish Brother in 1849. He was William Farrel of Dublin.

B. G. 1, 555;
2, 118

First Foundations. In 1859, seven years after Libermann's death, the Spiritan Fathers at last opened a junior seminary at Blanchardstown. Father Jules Leman, the founder of this first Irish house, reported that he was quite pleased with his charges. "These young Irishmen are charming and very intelligent, but somewhat mischievous," he wrote to the Motherhouse. The work gave such promise of success that the next year it was decided to transfer the community to Blackrock and add a college to the seminary. For the next eighty-four years they leased a large estate, the main house of which was formerly occupied by a Protestant boarding school and was now supposed to be haunted. During the first few nights everyone was awakened several times by the violent clanging of bells, but the old records report that this phenomenon ceased after the house had been blessed.

B. G. 4, 673

B. G. 3, 417

From its very beginning the new institution was successful. It immediately began to show those characteristics which were later to make it Ireland's leading college. In 1864, the Bishop of Longford, who had personally known Father Libermann, was so impressed by Blackrock's rapid advances that he offered the direction of his own seminary to the Congregation. Only lack of personnel prevented acceptance of the offer. Two years earlier, the Spiritans had accepted an orphanage at Glasnevin, near Dublin, but this work was shortlived because the St. Vincent de Paul Society failed to keep its agreement with the Congregation and insisted on retaining internal control of the institute.

B. G. 4, 217
B. G. 4, 286 ff.

B. G. 9, 98

B. G. 4, 777

B. G. 9, 93 ff.

The Scottish Lawsuit. The year 1864 saw the opening of another Seminary-College at Rockwell, Tipperary. The foundation of this college involved the Spiritans in a long lawsuit with the Hierarchy of Scotland—a complication into which both parties stepped quite innocently. Mr. Thiébault, a rich French businessman, was anxious to provide priests for Scotland and on this basis he gave the Congregation his three hundred and eighty acre estate. At the same time, he promised an annual endowment of 10,000 francs on condition that the Congregation train twelve seminarians for the dioceses of Scotland. Beyond that, the Spiritans were given full liberty to start any additional works of their choice on the Rockwell property. Although the Bishop of Cashel, in whose diocese Rockwell was situated, at first showed some reserve toward the Fathers, they soon gained his entire confidence to such an extent that he wanted to confide his own seminary and college to their direction.

Unfortunately, the enthusiasm of Mr. Thiébault, who was a pious but rather irascible gentleman, soon began to diminish. In 1867, things became really serious when the Bishops of Scotland, who were ignorant of the exact situation, claimed full control over the institution. Four years later the climax was reached. The Archbishop of Glasgow sent a curt note announcing that, with the approval of Mr. Thiébault, the Bishops of Scotland had decided to suppress the seminary and sell the Rockwell property.[4] Not a word was said about the acquired rights of the Congregation or compensation for buildings constructed and services rendered. The next year the Motherhouse was formally notified that the property had been put up for sale by the Scotch party!

Soon the dispute reached the Court of Justice in Dublin. In his verdict, the presiding judge severely reprimanded the legal representatives of the Scotch party for falsifying evidence presented to the Court. He unhesitatingly gave his decision in favor of the Congregation and required Mr. Thiébault and the other plaintiffs to pay costs. Great was the rejoicing in Tipperary County, where the Fathers had come to be much beloved. The people lit bonfires all over the hills in celebration of the victory. In Rockwell itself, however, where Mr. Thiébault still lived beside the lake on the property, everyone spared his feelings by refrain-

---

[4]Legally, Rockwell College was owned by a board of trustees, the majority of whom were always to be Holy Ghost Fathers.

ing from any open celebration. From then until his death in June
1873, he continued to agitate through the Protestant newspaper of
Cashel[5] against the very work he himself had founded, but Rockwell College forged ahead undisturbed.

B. G. 9, 692   When the Scotch Bishops registered their dissatisfaction with
the Dublin decision by appealing to Rome, their representative
made no mention of the fact that their solicitors had been reprimanded in the Irish Court. As can well be imagined, the Congregation's procurator at the Holy See was not so reticent and thereby considerably strengthened the Spiritan case. Nonetheless, the
Superior General offered to settle the whole matter amicably by
submitting it to arbitration by the Cardinal Archbishop of Dublin.
It appears that this was regarded as a sign of weakness, for the
opposing party tried immediately, though in vain, to have the
Congregation declared responsible for the cost of the Dublin law-
B. G. 10, 74   suit. At last, in 1874, an agreement was reached. Because the
Bishops of Scotland categorically refused to have their seminarians
remain in Rockwell, it was agreed that the property should be
ceded to the Congregation at a reduced price in compensation for
services rendered and that the Scotch students should return to their
native country. Throughout this whole period of trial, these
seminarians were not ignorant of the litigation yet their behavior
remained exemplary and full of respect. It was with great sadness
that the Spiritans watched them depart, for from the very beginning
those young Scots had stolen the hearts of the Fathers by their
B. G. 4, 288   seriousness and piety. A Spiritan report to the Motherhouse had
this to say about them: "These boys are really good. It is said
that young Scots generally are better than Irishmen. Be that as
it may, without prejudice to the Irish [we must say that] the
Scots we have here seem to be excellently disposed." These were
the fine young men who had to leave. After they had gone, Rockwell continued as a combined college and seminary of the Congre-
tion, and soon took its place among the outstanding colleges of
the land.

B. G. 14, 187 ff.   *Development of Blackrock.* As we have mentioned, Blackrock
College caught on magnificently almost from the first day of its

---

B. G. 11, 242   [5]His last will distributed all his possessions to various charities. The
Congregation succeeded through Cardinal Manning in obtaining from his
legal heirs one half payment of the endowment he had promised to the
Rockwell foundation.

foundation. It soon surpassed all other colleges, including the heavily endowed Protestant colleges of Cork and Galway. Before long, a university college was added to the existing secondary divisions and at once established itself as top-ranking in its field. As might be expected, these constant successes were bound to excite a measure of envy. The chancellor of the University deliberately refrained from even mentioning Blackrock in the opening session of the Royal University in 1885 and reserved all his praise to the Jesuit College of Stephen's Green. When the London *Tablet* did the same, Archbishop Walsh of Dublin could stand it no longer. In a letter, published in the *Tablet,* he severely took to task the paper's Dublin correspondent, who called Stephen's Green "the only great successful college in the country." From the official statistics of examinations and prizes gained, he showed how Blackrock had constantly far surpassed all rival institutions despite the fact that its students were handicapped by having to take their examinations before a board composed exclusively of teachers from the other institutions. The Archbishop's defense was indeed a grand tribute to the academic excellence of this great institution.

b. HOUSES IN GERMANY AND EXPULSION

cf. p. 120 f.

In Chapter VI we have seen how Father Libermann's thoughts had turned toward Germany from the very beginning of his Congregation. He wanted very much to start his work close to the German frontier and thereby attract German aspirants who might be trained for the German diocesan clergy. Although external pressures caused him to modify this plan, he never abandoned his project to establish the Congregation in Germany. In fact, shortly before his death he made a quick trip through the Rhineland. By then he had already personally admitted at least seven aspirants of German extraction from such distant areas as Westphalia, Bavaria and Württemberg. Among these was the first German priest of the Congregation, Father Francis Düllmann (1825-1892).

N. D. 9, 768

N. D. 9, 465 ff.

The First Foundations. By 1855, the General Council had decided "in principle" to undertake a foundation in Germany at the first suitable opportunity. However, it was 1863 before the plan could be executed. Appropriately, the first foundation was a retreat house for the clergy at Kaiserswerth in the Rhineland. The next year the ancient Cistercian abbey of Marienstadt in the Duchy

B. G. 4, 9

B. G. 4, 215 f.

of Nassau was acquired to serve as a college, junior seminary and novitiate. Moreover, in the same year the shrine of Marienthal[6] in the diocese of Cologne was entrusted to the Congregation. Various local works were attached to these houses: parishes, an orphanage, retreat-centers and the ministry at two shrines. As a result of this quick development, a Vice-Province was erected in Germany before the end of 1864.

B. G. 9, 71 ff.   *Expulsion by Bismarck.* This promising development was cut short by a religious persecution originated by Bismarck, the so-called "Iron Chancellor." Once the Jesuits were expelled, the Spiritans saw the handwriting on the wall and decided to transfer the older aspirants of the Congregation to France and Ireland and then temporarily suspend the Marienstadt seminary, vainly hoping to save at least the buildings. This precautionary move was com-

B. G. 9, 422 ff.   pletely useless. For some mysterious reason Bismarck was convinced that the Spiritans were just another form of Jesuits in

B. G. 9, 568 ff.   disguise. An imperial decree of 1873 expelled the Congregation from Germany under the pretext of its affiliation with the Jesuits. The vigorous protests of Father Joseph Strub, then Vice-Provincial of Germany, as well as those of the German Catholic newspapers—

B. G. 9, 778 ff.   and German papers can be very vigorous—were to no avail. For the time being at least, the Congregation had to leave Germany. Relinquishment of these German houses was all the more serious because vocation-rich Alsace had become part of the German Reich as a result of the Franco-Prussian War of 1870.

c. The Congregation Established in Portugal

B. G. 6, 74 f.   Shortly before his death, the Venerable Francis Libermann had
N. D. Compl.   considered opening a house in Portugal and was planning to send
171 f.   Father Lannurien to explore the possibilities. The same plan came up again in 1857 and in 1860, but political difficulties prevented its execution till 1867. By that time the Holy Ghost Fathers had spread into African territories over which Portugal claimed control and it was imperative that provisions be made to attract Portuguese candidates. Father Charles Duparquet, one of the well-known pioneers in the African missions of Angola and the Congo,

B. G. 6, 74   was selected to found the new province of Portugal. In 1867 he
B. G. 8, 2   opened the first junior seminary of the Congregation at Santarem,

---

[6]Father Libermann himself had made a pilgrimage to this shrine in May 1846. Cf. *N. D.* 7, 106 and 8, 454.

but three years later the government's anticlericalism necessitated
its closure. The personnel was transferred to Gibraltar, where the
Spiritans took over St. Bernard's College while they waited for a
more favorable time to go back to Portugal.

Although the situation had hardly improved by 1872, they decided to try again, this time in Braga, the "Rome of Portugal."
They opened a college there and immediate success attended their
efforts. From the very start of the College, which was dedicated
to the Holy Ghost, God's special blessings were upon it. Within
a few years it established itself as the finest college in the country.
Although it did not survive the onslaught of the Portuguese revolution of 1910, people speak about it to this day with respect and
admiration. Subsequently, then, other works were founded throughout the land.

d. First Beginnings in the United States

Earliest Contacts. The first contact of the Holy Ghost Fathers
with the territory that was later to become the United States seems
to have taken place in a Boston jail. As we have related above,
Father Maillard, the Apostle of the Micmac Indians in Acadia, was
captured by the British through a breach of promise and was deported to Boston in 1745. Later they shipped him to England and
the next contact occurred after the Acadians had been deported
from Nova Scotia. It was then in the latter part of the eighteenth
century that Father John Brault quietly went to work in New
England and gathered up a large group of Acadians to resettle
them on Montreal Island.

In 1794, the extension of the French Revolution to Guiana
forced all priests of that territory to take the schismatic oath of
the clergy. Just then, five Spiritan Fathers, in the strict sense of
the term, were working in this colony. When they refused to become schismatics, they were forced into exile. Three of these
refugees, Fathers Moranvillé, Hérard and Duhamel, sought shelter
in the United States. Father Moranvillé became pastor of St. Patrick's in Baltimore and in 1806 replaced the old church by a large
and beautiful edifice, then one of the most imposing Catholic
churches in the States. As a result of the killing pace he kept up
while ministering to the yellow fever victims in 1819 and 1821, he
fell dangerously ill. When a quiet holiday at the country estate of
Charles Carroll failed to improve his health, he finally agreed to

B. G. 8, 730

B. G. 9, 58

cf. p. 39

B. R. H. 1929,
444

B. R. H. 1929,
281
B. G. 32, 428 ff.
R. H. C. 37,
137 ff.

A. R. 40, 86 ff.
P. F. E. 200 ff.
U. S. M. A. 1,
433 ff.

A. R. 103,
229 ff.
P. F. E. 175

take a short vacation in France. It was too late, however. He died in Amiens on May 16, 1824. Father Duhamel accepted a pastorate near Enimitsburg, Maryland, and it was there that he died in 1818. Both were survived by the third refugee, Father Matthew Hérard, who spent some time at St. Croix as Vice-Prefect of the Virgin Islands and then became Vicar General of the Archdiocese of Baltimore (1816). After another tour of duty in the West Indies, he returned to the United States, became chaplain of the Poor Clares in Pittsburgh and then pastor in Newark, New Jersey. In 1838 he travelled to Paris to celebrate his golden jubilee among his confreres, but died the next year before he could carry out his intention to go back to his parish in Newark.

B. G. 9, 313

N. D. 9 App.
197 f.

Contact was resumed again in 1847 when Archbishop Purcell of Cincinnati, Ohio, urged the Congregation to supply priests for his diocese. Father Leguay, then Superior General, consulted the Prefect of the Propaganda, who replied that he would be delighted if the Congregation could undertake to help relieve the shortage of priests in the United States. Anticipating a favorable reply, Father Leguay had already sent Father Loewenbruck to Cincinnati to arrange matters and to negotiate with other bishops who had made similar requests. However, a violent storm drove the sailing vessel back to the shores of France. Apparently, Father Loewenbruck was not a good sailor, for he did not repeat the attempt.

B. G. 10, 274 f.

Father Libermann, meanwhile, had been directing his attention to the United States even before his ordination. While still a seminarian, he had wanted to go to America to be ordained there and consecrate himself to abandoned works. However, because of his epileptic condition, his directors had dissuaded him from

N. D. 6, 472

taking such a perilous step. After he had founded his little congregation of missionaries, he began as early as 1844 to think about works among the slaves in the States, and the thought grew more insistent when Father Fourdinier tried to exclude the "Liber-

N. D. 9, 374 ff.

mannists" from the old French colonies. Three years later, just when Father Loewenbruck was undertaking his voyage to America, Libermann again investigated the possibility of working among the slaves, even though he realized that "for a long time to come he would not be able to start" such a work. Shortly after, Providence brought the Venerable Francis and Father Loewenbruck together in the preparation of the "fusion" of Libermann's society with the Holy Ghost Fathers.

Once he and his priests had entered the Congregation of the Holy Ghost and the whole had become a smoothly functioning unit, Libermann again directed his attention to the United States. In 1851, as we noted in Chapter VII, Archbishop Purcell wanted the Congregation to establish an interdiocesan seminary in the archdiocese of Cincinnati. Libermann accepted the offer and appointed Father Schwindenhammer director of the new work. However, we have already learned that that project fell short of realization.

cf. p. 124

B. G. 9, 375

After Libermann's death in 1852, a steady flow of invitations came to the Venerable's successor from various dioceses in the States: in 1852 from Savannah, Georgia; in 1859 and again in 1865 from Bishop Verot, the Vicar Apostolic of Florida; in 1867 from Bishop Wood of Philadelphia, the Bishop of Buffalo, the Bishop of Wheeling, and Bishop Elder of Natchez, Mississippi; and in 1870 from the Bishop of Charleston, South Carolina. Despite his interest in these offers, Father Schwindenhammer was forced to refuse them for lack of personnel.

B. G. 4, 675

B. G. 5, 638;
6, 105; 5, 640

B. G. 9, 316 f.

First Foundations. The manpower problem was abruptly solved in 1872 and 1873 when Bismarck expelled the Spiritans from Germany. The Congregation decided to accept the first favorable offer that would reach them from the United States. This offer came in 1872 from Bishop Tobbe of Covington, Kentucky. His Excellency wrote that he was willing to entrust a mission to the Holy Ghost Fathers and place at their disposal a large property at White Sulphur which was already improved with a church and buildings that could be used as a college. The Propaganda approved and Father Schwindenhammer accepted the offer. He dispatched four Fathers to Kentucky, but when they arrived in Covington they found that the proposed college and mission were not yet available.

B. G. 9, 597 ff.;
849 ff.; 868 ff.

This situation left them at least temporarily unemployed, but just then Cincinnati's Archbishop Purcell offered them parishes in Piqua, Berlin, and Russia, Ohio. Moreover, a local priest, Father Meyer, promised to give most of the money for the purchase of an estate at Pontiac that could be used very nicely as a training school for American aspirants. These offers were gratefully accepted. Soon reinforcements, including a dozen Brothers, arrived to take care of the new works. On March 1, 1874, Father Schwindenhammer officially erected the Vice-Province of the United States.

B. G. 10, 270 ff.   In a very short time the Fathers realized that they had concentrated their houses in too small an area. For this reason Father Joseph Strub, the Provincial Superior, began to look about for other possible sites. He passed through Wheeling, West Virginia, where the Bishop invited him to open a college and take over his seminary, but it appears that he preferred to turn northward and visit Bishop Domenec in Pittsburgh. This saintly prelate received him with open arms. As the chronicler reported, it all seemed very providential. As Father Strub sat before the Bishop's desk, he looked up and saw that the episcopal coat of arms bore the device: "Come Holy Ghost." Right then and there, Father Strub felt at home.

The most urgent need of the diocese was a Catholic boys' school. There had been a number of unsuccessful attempts to get one going, and now Bishop Domenec did his best to persuade the Fathers to try again. He pledged his full support for the College and promised that at the first available opportunity he would give the Spiritans one of the largest parishes in the diocese to provide financial help for the school. Shortly after, in April 1874, the Bishop offered the parish of St. Mary in Sharpsburg, and Father Strub decided to leave Berlin, Ohio and accept it. Very prudently, he decided to wait a little and see how the situation would develop before starting the boys' school.

B. G. 10, 912 f.   Meanwhile, difficulties had arisen regarding the remaining houses in the Cincinnati Archdiocese. Archbishop Purcell began to impose conditions that made community life almost impossible. For this reason the Spiritans decided to withdraw entirely from the Archdiocese and concentrate provisionally on the Pittsburgh area. Temporarily a small seminary was set up for the few American aspirants at Perrysville, Pa., in the now extinct Diocese of Allegheny (1876).

B. G. 11, 187 f.   The question of a Catholic academy in Pittsburgh was solved in 1878. Bishop Tuigg, who had succeeded Bishop Domenec, promised to use all his influence on the clergy and the people to make the work a success. Fully conscious of the risks involved, the Spiritans let themselves be persuaded to open a school in the

B. G. 30, 888   center of town despite the fact that four previous attempts to establish a Catholic College in Pittsburgh had failed miserably. No one was anxious to run the chance of another defeat. The prospects of success were particularly poor because the Catholic population itself had little confidence in any new effort. Father Joseph Strub demonstrated more than usual courage, then, when he undertook the new venture. Two years later, however, Pittsburgh's College of the Holy Ghost was able to report that the number of its students had risen to more than a hundred and fifty. It was then that the construction of a permanent building was undertaken on a low hill in the center of the town. The cornerstone-laying appears to have been a major event in the history of the city: twenty-five thousand people are reported to have come to attend the ceremony.[7] This was the college that was destined to develop later into the institution of higher learning now known as Duquesne University.

Meanwhile other Holy Ghost Fathers undertook an ambitious project in Arkansas, where a railroad company had granted Father Strub a tract of 200,000 acres of land near Morrilton. It was to be used for the settlement of German immigrants, who at that time were flocking to the United States by the thousands. Many of them were Catholics, eager to find across the Atlantic that security and freedom which was denied them in their homeland. Very soon, the German Government became alarmed at this mass emigration and blamed the Spiritans for depopulating the Reich. It honored them by publishing an official warning against their colony in Arkansas. As a result, this colony became even more widely known in Germany. Moreover, it gave the Central Party a chance to attack the Iron Chancellor in the *Reichstag* (Parliament) and point out the folly of his religious policies. As one Deputy expressed it:

> It is not the Holy Ghost Fathers but the Prussian policy and its wretched Kulturkampf that are depopulating the country and causing our best people to migrate to the United States, where these religious men offer them the comforts of religion which they cannot have in the homeland.

Near Morrilton, Arkansas, the Spiritans reserved for their own use about one thousand acres of their immense concession.

B. G. 13, 314 ff.

B. G. 13, 320 f.

B. G. 11, 1085 ff.

B. G. 11, 1091

B. G. 11, 1094 ff.

B. G. 13, 1305 f.

---

[7]Pittsburghers may be interested in a sidelight on smoke control reported by the Fathers in 1886: "The introduction of natural gas has not only caused a revolution in industry, but has also produced a great change in the atmosphere of the city. Only with great difficulty and on rare occasions could the sun pierce through the dense layer of smoke which constantly shrouded the city. Today the situation is no longer the same. Slowly this dirty and dark town is transforming itself into a magnificent city."

It was to serve as a central community of the Province. Nostalgically they called it Marienstadt, after their ancient abbey in Nassau. A novitiate for Brothers was established there, and the Fathers fanned out from this house to build churches and schools throughout the concession. At first, the colony was quite successful, but in 1881, tornadoes and severe droughts during the next few years thoroughly discouraged the settlers. One after another, the German immigrants began to leave, seeking a more benign climate elsewhere. Pernicious fevers now began to take their toll of the Spiritan commmunity, and the novitiate had to be transferred to another place. In 1892 another tornado wrecked the beautiful gothic church of Marienstadt which had just been finished. Nowadays, only ruins remain of this original foundation in Arkansas, but there are many flourishing parishes in the State which owe their origin to the labors of these immigrant Holy Ghost Fathers.

B. G. 13, 322 ff.; 327 ff.; 1325 ff.

B. G. 15, 1019 ff.

8. *Internal Consolidation*

The Congregation's internal organization was the object of Father Schwindenhammer's constant care. Although some of the features he introduced have not survived and others have been considerably modified, many of them are still in force.

C. S. 11, 36 ff.

In 1855 the old Rule of the Spiritans and the "Constitutive and Organic Regulations," added by Father Libermann after the fusion, were revised and more systematically arranged. The old Rule remained as the fundamental law of the society, while the preceptive part of Libermann's Regulations became what are presently known as the Constitutions. We list here the most important modifications contained in the revised Rules and Constitutions which were approved by Rome in 1855:

1. Instead of the private vows hitherto taken by most members, public simple vows were to be pronounced by all members of the Congregation. This official religious status, which Father Libermann had always wanted, met with unanimous approval in the general meeting of 1853.

N. D. 6, 439

2. The practice of community life was to be maintained. Superiors were forbidden to assign any member to a post where he would be deprived of the company of a fellow member, unless very urgent and exceptional reasons dictated it.

3. The Congregation was to be divided into autonomous Provinces which would be directly dependent on the Superior General.

4. Periodically General Chapters were to be held to discuss the more important affairs of the Congregation.

C. S. 13, 19 ff.

C. S. 22, 18 ff.

The proposed division into provinces was implemented in 1856, when Father Schwindenhammer erected the Provinces of France, West Africa, the Indian Ocean, and America. In 1862, the rapid growth of the Congregation caused these provinces to be subdivided into vice-provinces which soon numbered nearly twenty.[8]

C. S. 15, 14 ff.

In 1875, Father Schwindenhammer submitted to Rome a second revision of the Rules and Constitutions which contained only three slight modifications and certain reworded passages. This would not be worth mentioning, were it not for an incident that arose in Rome regarding the ancient Rule of the Holy Ghost Fathers. Despite the fact that the Roman consultants, Fathers Ballerini and Massaratti, S. J., had nothing but praise for the revision, the Cardinal in charge submitted the text to still a third consultant.

This last disagreed completely with the two Jesuits. Although the Rule had been approved several times by the Holy See, the new consultant advised its total abolition, alleging that there are only four religious Rules in the Church—namely, those of St. Basil, St. Augustine, St. Benedict, and St. Francis. Furthermore, when it came to the Constitutions, he recommended changes of such sweeping nature that they would have modified the very nature of the Congregation. Finally, even if all these conditions were met, he advised that only a provisional approval should be granted if the society could find any bishops to recommend it. Obviously, he did not realize that he was reading the charter of a society whose history of service to the Church at that time stretched back 172 years! At any rate, the very radicalism of his proposals defeated their purpose, for the Rules and Constitutions were approved without

---

[8]For those interested in details: the Province of France was composed of the independent vice-provinces of Paris, Vannes, St. Brieuc, Clermont, Bordeaux, Rome and Dublin. The next year the Vice-Province of Germany was added, and the Province of France became "the Province of Europe." The Province of West Africa contained the vice provinces of Senegal, Senegambia, and Gabon. That of the Indian Ocean was composed of the independent vice-provinces of Mauritius, Reunion, Zanzibar, and Chandernagor (India). The Province of America included the independent vice-provinces of Martinique, Haiti, Trinidad, and Guiana.

any modification, just as Father Ballerini had recommended. Thus it happened that, although modern congregations usually have only Constitutions, the Spiritans were allowed to keep their ancient Rule that dates from 1734 and to consider their Constitutions as the official commentary and interpretation of that Rule.

In 1857 Father Schwindenhammer founded the *Bulletin Général* to serve as a vehicle of general communication within the Congregation as well as a record of its achievements. At the present time it comprises forty-five volumes of up to 1400 pages each, covering a century of historical development and constituting a rich mine of information not only about the society but also about Africa and the other lands where Spiritans have labored. Wars, persecution, and the ravages of time have made the nineteenth century volumes of the *Bulletin* extremely rare. They are the prized possession of some of the older houses of the Congregation and of a few important libraries.

9. *Political Dangers in France*

Father Schwindenhammer's last years were saddened by the increasing threat of political dangers in France. During the first few years of the Second Empire (1850 ff.), the political climate was favorable to the Catholic Church in general and to the Congregation in particular, but as early as 1860, less propitious events began to cast their shadows before them. Napoleon III supported the aspirations of Piedmont regarding the Papal States and thus found himself in direct opposition to the Pope. Shortly after, the B. G. 4, 471 ff.　Holy Ghost Fathers at the Pontifical French Seminary were violently attacked in the Senate as French ultramontanists in Rome.[9] B. G. 5, 632 f.　During the course of the next year, the Colonial Minister refused to pay the Congregation a salary that was still due to a deceased member, alleging that since the fusion the Spiritans were no longer the congregation that the Government had originally approved.

The amount involved was comparatively insignificant, but the Minister's refusal served to point the direction in which future attacks would move. A few years later, the Holy See rejected a Va. 238　Government candidate for the bishopric of Martinique. Although the Congregation had nothing to do with this rejection, the Government assumed it had and seized the opportunity to portray the

---

[9] This term characterized Frenchmen who supported the prerogatives of the Holy See.

Spiritans as unpatriotic citizens who fraudulently used public funds to support their ultramontanist seminary in Rome. The ensuing investigation could not uncover the slightest evidence in favor of this accusation, but the government again renewed its threat to suppress the Congregation on the ground that it was no longer identical with the eighteenth century Holy Ghost Congregation approved by the State. Only after much trouble and effort did Father Schwindenhammer succeed in convincing the Government that its allegation was totally false.

B. G. 8, 29 ff.;
51 ff.
cf. pp. 306 f.

In 1870 and 1871, the Franco-Prussian War and the succeeding Revolution in Paris forced the Motherhouse to disperse once more. The senior seminary at Chevilly was gravely damaged, the Motherhouse itself plundered, and recruitment temporarily brought to a standstill. The Second Empire went down in this military and political chaos and was succeeded by a Republic whose

Roy, 118

government reeked with anticlericalism. In 1880, just before Father Schwindenhammer's death, the new Government decreed the expulsion of all religious orders that were not officially recognized. While their official status saved the Spiritans from exile, they soon felt the weight of the State's powerful weapon of taxation. The first of the antireligious tax laws was passed in 1880. It levied an income tax on the revenues of all authorized religious societies.

One year later, the Superior General died. His health had been weak for many years and now, after governing the Congregation for nearly three decades, he could drive himself no longer. He had been cold and distant, much too formal in his relations and sometimes bombastic[10] in his administration. He did not inspire affection in the hearts of his associates, but he did win everyone's respect for the magnificent way in which he engineered the Congregation's firm foundation and promoted its solid growth.

B. G. 1, 322

[10]Here is an example: "We, Ignatius Schwindenhammer, Superior General of the Congregation of the Holy Ghost and the Immaculate Heart of Mary,

Whereas *primo*. . . .;
Whereas *secundo*. . . .;
Whereas *tertio*. . . .;

Having invoked the Holy Ghost, and in agreement with our Council, have decided and do decide as follows:

One and Only Article . . . The Brothers must take care of the rooms of the Fathers . . .

Given in Paris, at the Motherhouse, September 8, 1857."

CHAPTER NINE

THE GENERALATE OF FATHER AMBROSE EMONET, 1882-1895

1. *Introduction*

cf. p. 147
As we have previously indicated, the General Chapter elected Father Frederic Le Vavasseur as Father Schwindenhammer's successor. It was more a gesture of homage for the past than a mandate for the future, for the health of the seventy year old co-founder of Libermann's Congregation was so seriously impaired that no one expected him to live much longer. As a matter of fact, after only one month in office he fell gravely ill and died in January 1882.

N. D. 13,
App. 53

The next Superior General, Father Ambrose Emonet (1828-1898), was born in the Duchy of Savoy, which at that time was still independent of France. In 1846 he entered Libermann's Congregation. After teaching for two years at Notre Dame du Gard, he became Religious Superior of Martinique in 1853. Three

D. C. 157

years later, there was question of appointing him Bishop of the island even though he was only twenty-eight at the time. The Ordinary of the diocese was to be transferred and he wanted no one but Father Emonet as his successor. However, the Congregation was not anxious to have more bishops than was absolutely necessary, so Father Emonet kept his post as Religious Superior. He spent almost twenty years on the island, most of them in the College of St. Pierre.

In 1872 he was sent as official visitor to Guiana and became

D. C. 158

its Prefect Apostolic. Five years later, the Government of Haiti nominated him for a bishopric on that island. The nomination had already been officially published and Rome had been asked to pre-conize it, when an unexpected obstacle arose. No one in Haiti had thought about inquiring first how the Holy Ghost Fathers would react to the proposal. When Rome notified the Superior General of Emonet's nomination and its intention to grant the preconiza-tion, Father Schwindenhammer replied that it was his firm policy not to accept any dioceses. As a result, Msgr. Emonet stayed on as Prefect in Guiana. Seven years later he was recalled to

B. G. 12, 509 Europe and made Assistant of the Superior General. This was the man who became Father Le Vavasseur's successor.

In the main, Father Emonet continued the policies of his predecessors. He added a number of new colleges and seminaries to those already operated by the Congregation: at Epinal, Seyssinet and Castelnaudery in France; at Rathmines in Ireland; at Porto in Portugal and Ponta Delgada in the Azores; at Ballerat in Australia; at Para in Brazil and at Lima in Peru. The social works of the Congregation were increased by new institutions for abandoned or wayward youths at Grand Quevilly, St. Mauront, Douvaine, St. Joseph du Lac and Orgeville in France; at Drognens in Switzerland; and in Philadelphia, Pennsylvania. Over and above these, the Portuguese Province expanded by adding an orphanage at Cintra and an old people's home at Campo Maior. The internationalization of the society continued apace by the restoration of the German province and by the above-mentioned educational establishments in Australia, Brazil and Peru.

2. *The Restoration of the German Province*

B. G. 13, 888 Fathers Ignatius Stoffel and Daniel Weik were the first to take active steps toward restoring the German Province in 1885. Father Stoffel had just returned from an exploratory trip in the Cameroons, where he had made a very favorable impression on the German officials who were then arriving to lay claim to that colonial territory. Father Weik came from Haiti, where he had become acquainted with Prince Henry, the Emperor's grandson. The two priests travelled to Berlin and tried to get permission for Catholic missions in the Cameroons and Spiritan seminaries in Germany. They had the powerful support of the Empress and other members of the imperial family, and the advantage of a sustained campaign in certain important newspapers that had taken up the cause of missionary work in Africa. They were reassured that the Government would no longer endeavor to exclude Catholic missionaries from the Cameroons, but no amount of effort could enable them to have the Congregation declassified as Jesuit-affiliated and therefore unwelcome in Germany.

B. G. 15, 665 In 1890, after the German bishops had been invited by Rome to open a national missionary seminary, they asked the Spiritans to undertake it. Once more they appealed to Berlin for permission to enter, but in spite of the Center Party's vigorous assistance and the favorable disposition of many highly-placed Government officials, these efforts again ended in failure.

B. G. 18, 196 ff.   Meanwhile the Congregation's man-power problems were mounting. Catholic Alsace, the source of so many vocations to the priesthood and the religious life, had become part of Germany after the Franco-Prussian War.[1] It was imperative that houses be opened somewhere near Germany—perhaps in Luxemburg—to secure German aspirants. Providence, however, had other plans. Father Amand Acker, a French Alsatian, had worked as a missionary in German East Africa. While there, he came to know the celebrated German explorer Eugene Wolff and found him to be a most enthusiastic admirer of the achievements brought about by Spiritan zeal and industry. Mr. Wolff pointed out to Father Acker that the German government owed so much to the Congregation in its colonies that it could hardly refuse them the necessary seminaries in Germany itself. He offered to accompany him on a trip to Berlin and lend his assistance in convincing the Reich that its policy was short-sighted and foolish. Travelling in cassock, as he always did, Father Acker was a startling sight in this predominantly Protestant city.[2] Undaunted by the glares and stares, he visited Princes and Ministers to plead his case.

Members of the Catholic Central Party held out little hope of
B. G. 18, 198   success. As one of them ruefully observed: "For twenty years we have fought in vain to get these laws of expulsion changed, and here comes a poor little missionary, fresh from the bush, who thinks
B. G. 18, 200   that he can succeed where we have failed." The Prime Minister looked disdainfully at the sorry black figure before him and coldly stated: "The law is the law. If we let you in, the Redemptorists will want to return, and then the others. There will be no end to it. No, it is impossible." But little did His Excellency dream that he had just given the Redemptorists an idea! They immediately set about having a Bavarian Deputy attach a rider in their favor to any motion that might be made in behalf of the Holy Ghost Fathers. This situation did not make things easier for Father Acker, but he was not a man to be easily discouraged. Circulating

---

[1] In the second half of the nineteenth century Alsace supplied no less than 538 members to the Congregation. Cf. Th. Hück, *P. Ludwig Karl Gommenginger*, Rixheim, 1900, App., pp. 1-21.

[2] On one occasion he had to remove his shoes before he could obtain lodgings in a hotel, because the owner was convinced that Catholic priests were in league with the devil and therefore had goat hooves in place of feet.

Father Ignatius Schwindenhammer, twelfth
Superior General of the Congregation of the
Holy Ghost (1852-1881).

Father Frederic Le Vavasseur, thirteenth
Superior General of the Congregation of the
Holy Ghost (1881-1882).

Father Ambrosius Emonet, fourteenth Superior General of the Congregation of the Holy
Ghost (1882-1896).

Archbishop Alexander Le Roy, fifteenth Superior General of the Congregation of the
Holy Ghost (1896-1926).

freely among politicians, he succeeded in winning over even the most fanatically opposed leaders of the National Liberal Party. Wherever new opponents arose, Father Acker or one of his friends managed in the most unpredictable ways to overcome their opposition and even to change them into advocates of the cause. Before too long, a unanimous vote declared that the Spiritan Fathers were not affiliated with the Jesuits. This, in principle, enabled them to return to Germany. The victory was so complete that even the rider in favor of the Redemptorists squeezed through with a slim majority.

If the Center Party had reason to be amazed at Father Acker's success, there was still another surprise in store for it. After his victory, the priest had quietly slipped away to preach a nuns' retreat when he was hurriedly summoned back to Berlin. In the course of an audience, the Colonial Minister pointed out to him that neither Cardinals and Bishops nor the Motherhouse would have any success in obtaining permission for the Congregation to settle anywhere in Germany. Only a German Provincial, appointed by the Vatican, could expect any cooperation. Then he added: "You are the man we want." Father Acker's objections that he was a Frenchman, not a German, and that the Vatican does not appoint Provincial Superiors, failed to make any impression on the Minister's Teutonic mind. Since the Motherhouse did not object, the Vatican took the unusual step of appointing Father Acker Superior of the new German Province, a function he held for the next quarter of a century.

B. G. 18, 203 ff. He immediately began the work of reorganization by acquiring the famous medieval Premonstratensian abbey of Knechtsteden (1895), near Cologne. It is a shrine of the Mother of Sorrows, whose church is the most beautiful Norman-style edifice along the Rhine. The Carthusians were about to take it over twenty years before, but a devastating fire broke out and partly destroyed the great complex of buildings. It had stood empty ever since and that is why Father Acker got it so cheaply. With the practical eye of a missionary, he estimated its vast potentialities and saw that the half-ruins would offer plenty of opportunity for training future brothers in the trades which are so indispensable in the missions.[3] Accordingly, in February 1896, the first junior seminary

---

[3]It is interesting to note that in the thirteenth century a Jew called Libermann (an ancestor of Father Libermann?) several times lent money to the abbey of Knechtsteden. Cf. Ehlen, *Die Premonstratenser Abtei Knechtsteden,* Köln, 1904, pp. 81 ff.

of the restored Province began to function in that great and venerable cloister.

3. *Africa*

a. THE PUSH TO THE INTERIOR

cf. pp. 445 ff.
Engel, pp. 15 ff.

On the African continent, the early necessity to cling to the coast was now definitely overcome and nearly everywhere people began a drive toward the interior. In 1885 the Holy Ghost Fathers penetrated Southern Nigeria and founded the mission of Onitsha, and then that of Aguleri (1891). In Gabon they established inland missions in Lambarene (1881), Lastourville (1883), Franceville (1887), Ndjole (1887), etc. In Angola the inland thrust began in 1892 with the foundation of Murindi and Kimbenza. Between 1883 and 1894, under the energetic direction of Bishop Prosper Augouard, the "Cannibal Bishop," a whole string of central missions arose in the Congo from Linzolo (250 miles inland) to Bessu (1250 miles inland).

In East Africa, too, the Spiritans were able to penetrate more deeply. Under the able leadership of Bishop Raoul de Courmont, central residences were established at Tununguo (1884), Kondoa (1885), Ilonga (1886), Kilema (1890) and Kibosho (1893). It should be remembered, however, that all these fearless advances, often far ahead of the colonizing powers, did not come about without exacting a cruel toll in human lives. During the generalate cf. p. 231 of Father Emonet the average life-expectancy of Spiritan missionaries in Africa sank from a previous low of thirty-eight years and one month to a mere thirty-four during the years 1893 to 1895. Out of this silent martyrdom the African missions slowly took root and bore fruit a hundred-fold.

b. CONFLICT WITH CARDINAL LAVIGERIE

B. G. 14, 180 ff.
Lavig. II, 368-373

Since 1865, Spiritans had been working in the Prefecture of the Congo and by 1886 this vast jurisdiction could boast of eight flourishing central residences, a senior seminary, and scores of small stations. The exact limits to the interior had not yet been fixed for the simple reason that the interior was still unknown. cf. p. 197 f. Cardinal Lavigerie, whose first missionaries had left for the interior of Africa from the Bagamoyo mission in 1878, induced the Lavig. II, 314
Storme, 449 ff.; Propaganda to establish the two Pro-vicariates of Nyanza and Tanganyika. This realignment of territorial jurisdiction left the

577 ff.; 640 ff.
M. C. 12, 584

old Spiritan mission of Zanguebar largely cut off from the interior. The Cardinal, moreover, asked for two other Vicariates in the Upper Congo and recommended that they extend as far West as Stanley Pool. Because he did not yet have any missionaries in the Congo, the Propaganda did not grant his request. It did allow him, however, to establish two mission centers there.

Meanwhile, Father Emonet began to fear that the influential Cardinal would gradually succeed in obtaining everything he desired. Had this happened, it would have meant that the Holy Ghost Fathers would have been entirely cut off from the interior and thrown back upon the coast. In order to avoid a conflict, Bishop Le Berre, C.S.Sp. and Father Duparquet, C.S.Sp. met with His Eminence and discussed the limits of the missions confided to the two congregations. The session ended in full

B. G. 14, 183 f.

agreement. The Spiritans were to penetrate as far inland as they wished, as long as they remained twenty leagues away from the White Fathers' missions. Moreover, the Cardinal recognized in writing that Holy Ghost missions would be "wholly and entirely independent." No one had reason to be apprehensive about fulfilling the agreement for the White Fathers had not yet engaged in anything beyond an exploratory trip in the Congo during which one of their priests had drowned. They had no residences whatever in the territory.

cf. pp. 269 ff.

After the 1885 Berlin Conference, which settled the territorial claims of Portugal, Belgium, and France, and set fixed boundaries to their respective areas of the Congo, the Spiritans had to relinquish all their stations in the Belgian Congo and assign them to others. King Leopold insisted on admitting only Belgian missionaries and at that time there were only a few Belgian nationals in the Congregation. The readjustment had its compensations, however, for now that boundary conflicts were settled, Rome could finally be petitioned to create a Vicariate in the French Congo. Father Duparquet went to Rome to negotiate the affair and showed himself an accomplished diplomat as well as a famous African pioneer. Six weeks after his arrival, the Propaganda issued a decree erecting the Vicariate. It was said that the Roman officials had never worked so fast on such an important affair. The Vicariate, whose boundaries were to coincide with those of the French Congo itself, was entrusted to the Holy Ghost Fathers.

Delighted with the success of his negotiations, Father Duparquet took the train back to Paris to report to the Superior General. As he rode, the telegraph spread the news and one of those who heard the report was Cardinal Lavigerie. Deeply shocked at this blow to his own Congo plans, he immediately wired a strong protest to the Propaganda. Letters followed in which he demanded the annulment of the decree since it was "against the prior delegation he had received from the Holy See over a land bathed in the blood of his missionaries." Similar protests went to the Papal Nuncio in Paris and to the French Government, both of whom had supported the Spiritans in their request for the Vicariate. When these protests proved ineffective, the Cardinal personally travelled to Rome.

At that point things began to look rather bad for the Spiritans. The famous Cardinal was highly influential in the Propaganda. In fact, he himself was a member of this supreme council on missionary matters. Moreover, the French Ministry of Foreign Affairs now pledged him its support. With good reason, then, Father Duparquet was dispatched to Rome to explain the situation on behalf of the Spiritans. His defense lay in facts rather than in powerful influence and he appealed with telling effect to the history of the Holy Ghost missions in the Congo and to the 1881 agreement between the Cardinal and the Congregation. In the last analysis, he argued, the Holy Ghost Fathers could really derive their jurisdiction by tracing it back to the Vicariate of the Two Guineas, which dated from 1842. Their Spiritan Prefecture of the Congo was already fifteen years old when the Cardinal appeared on the scene, and the agreement of 1881 had been made precisely to guarantee these ancient rights.

Lavigerie soon began to realize that his claim had little objective support. He now declared that, once "the question of right and honor" was settled, he would be willing to negotiate the whole matter. Accordingly, Pope Leo XIII, who had reserved the final decision to himself, told both parties concerned to make a common proposal. Because of the Cardinal's high rank, the Propaganda advised the Holy Ghost Fathers to take the first step and ask him to agree to the limits assigned by the decree.

Now that his honor had been saved, Lavigerie made no difficulties. October 6, 1886, he explicitly renounced all his jurisdictional claims on the French Congo. By way of compensation, the

B. G. 14, 185

B. G. 14, 185 ff.

Propaganda gave him two other Vicariates in Africa. On December 21, of the same year, a papal decree erected the Vicariate of the French Congo and, to prevent any further trouble, warned that its content "was and would remain . . . valid . . . and that all . . . are to judge it as such . . . be they Nuncios of the Holy See, or Cardinals of the Holy Roman Church . . . whatever be their power or eminence."

4. *Other Missions*

Outside Africa, the Spiritans contined their work in the island dioceses of Haiti, Trinidad, Martinique, Guadeloupe, Reunion and Mauritius. Most of them were concentrated in the large colleges the Congregation maintained in these islands. In addition, they served in the Prefectures of French Guiana, Pondicherry, and St. Pierre et Miquelon. All these Prefectures were abandoned during the generalate of Father Emonet, although not all for the same reason as we shall see.

a. THE WITHDRAWAL FROM PONDICHERRY

D. C. 102 ff.

After the French Revolution, when religious care of all the old French colonies was entrusted to the Congregation, its solicitude had to be extended to the French enclaves of Pondicherry and Chandernagor in India. Both of these enclaves constituted a Prefecture whose jurisdiction was limited to the Creoles, while the rest of the population belonged to the Apostolic Vicariate of Pondicherry. The distinction between the two jurisdictions, oddly enough, was based on dress: anyone wearing a hat and coat belonged to the Prefecture; all the others fell under the powers of the Vicariate. Obviously, conflicts were bound to arise, especially when the French Government decided to abolish the distinction between Creoles and natives, and the latter took to dressing themselves in European fashion. The only sane solution would have been to abolish either the Prefecture or the Vicariate. Both Paris and Rome agreed on this, but while Paris insisted that the Prefecture absorb the Vicariate, Rome insisted with equal vigor on the reverse. At bottom, the controversy stemmed from a question of control: the Parisian Government had been given the right to nominate the Prefect but not the Vicar Apostolic, and whenever a new Prefect had to be appointed, the quarrel broke out afresh.

Caught between the two competing authorities, both of which expected the Congregation to take its side, the Superior General could do nothing but wait for them to come to an agreement and declare himself willing to abide by whatever decision would be taken. However, it was not till 1886 that a final agreement was reached: Pondicherry was to become an Archdiocese. Through this solution Father Francis Corbet, C.S.Sp., then Prefect Apostolic, was deprived of his jurisdiction. Although he himself had favored this step, the Creoles were very much disturbed when they learned of the Spiritans' impending departure. Their appeals to Rome resulted in an offer from the Holy See to create a new Holy Ghost Prefecture in Chandernagor, extending over a large part of Bengal. However, already overburdened with its heavy commitments in Africa, the Congregation showed no interest in adding territory in India. Despite the insistence of the Apostolic Delegate, all offers in this direction were politely declined. The same fate befell numerous petitions urging the continuation of Pondicherry College and the flourishing school at Chandernagor which was staffed by Brothers of the Congregation. On January 29, 1888, the last Holy Ghost Father left this mission, where members of the Society had been working since 1861.

b. The Expulsion from French Guiana

cf. p. 28
B. G. 13,
225 ff.

While the withdrawal from Pondicherry was quite voluntary, the same cannot be said of the departure from Guiana, one of the Congregation's oldest fields of labor. In 1881, after Msgr. Emonet relinquished his post as the local Prefect Apostolic, French anti-clericalism raised its ugly head in this colony. Despite the protests and determined resistance of the people, the Government progressively secularized all of its schools. Everywhere it created new and expensive schools with high-salaried teachers, even though most people stubbornly refused to use them for their children. Even pastors had to stand by while their rectories were invaded by strangers who had leased them from the civil authorities.

B. G. 13,
1273 ff.

Through it all, the local Governor kept up his campaign to have the Holy Ghost Fathers exiled from Guiana. After shouting publicly at the commencement exercises of a secular college that "it is those Fathers who are our enemies." he finally induced the Colonial Minister to request their withdrawal. The request was illegal, but to pacify them the Superior General recalled two

B. G. 16,
928 ff.

priests. As might have been expected, this move failed to satisfy the radicals. By 1891, government interference had gone so far that priests needed official permission from the civil authorities—to be obtained through seven administrative steps!—before they visited the sick or went to confession to a neighboring pastor.

The next year, the Government arbitrarily dismissed Father Guyodo, C.S.Sp., acting Prefect Apostolic, and just as arbitrarily thrust a secular priest in his place. When it became known that Father Guyodo, a veteran of forty years' service and much-beloved by all, had been recalled to Europe, a violent storm of protest rumbled through the colony. Although the priest was planning to leave secretly in order to avoid further intensification of the conflict, the Governor grew so apprehensive that, as the appointed hour approached, he called out the garrison, the constabulary and the local police-force to maintain order. The next year, 1893, all the other Spiritans were forced to leave and the Governor's jubilation was keen but brief. He was deposed that same year and had to leave the colony in disgrace under a protective guard, while the people whistled and hooted their derision. For the Holy Ghost Fathers his departure came a few months too late. Though urged to return immediately, they were not to see Guiana again for thirty years.

D. C. 164

c. The Departure from Saint Pierre et Miquelon

B. G. 16,
1035 ff.

Since 1874 members of the Congregation had been operating a small college in these tiny islands off the coast of Newfoundland. They had gone there at the pressing invitation of the Prefect Apostolic, whose intention it was to have Spiritan Fathers assume complete charge of all religious service after his death. However, in 1892, when he reached the end of his career, the French Government nominated another secular priest, Father Tiberi, without previously consulting the Congregation. When the Propaganda accepted this nomination and appointed him Prefect Apostolic, there could no longer be question of the Holy Ghost Fathers serving the whole Prefecture with their own men. Moreover, this Prefecture, which is the smallest in the whole world, did not provide sufficient scope for both a secular and a religious clergy. Accordingly, the Congregation decided to withdraw and leave the field free for diocesan priests. Just then the new Prefect moved in to accelerate the departure.

D. C. 99 f.

Disappointed by the small size of his spiritual domain, Father Tiberi, a former navy chaplain, appears to have compensated for its lack of extension by an intensive use of his powers. Since his biggest power was that of suspension and interdict, he exercised it liberally. Soon Father Frécenon, C.S.Sp., the Superior of the College, was struck by a personal interdict. Subsequently, the other Spiritans shared the same fate. The secular clergy followed, with such rapidity and thoroughness that, by 1899 when the Prefect left, all priests in the islands had been either suspended or interdicted. By this time, however, the Holy Ghost Fathers had already shaken the dust from their feet. Before the end of 1892, all men had been recalled and the college was closed.

B. G. 16, 1640 f.

To replace it, a new college was created and lay men were hired to staff it. To the dismay of the population, it offered a sharp contrast to the old Spiritan institution. Shortly after his arrival, its director had to be arrested for drunkenness and shipped back to France. Then one of the teachers became involved in an affair with a girl in a waterfront cafe. Before the year was over, the staff was on a partial strike protesting against the low wages. This melancholy situation dragged on for some time. In fact, fifteen years were to pass before the Congregation once again returned to these islands, which are the oldest of all missions entrusted to the Holy Ghost Fathers.

cf. p. 28

d. Work Among the Colored in the United States

cf. p. 210

As we indicated in Chapter VIII, Father Libermann showed great concern for the Negro slaves of America and Father Schwindenhammmer, his successor, was deeply interested in a colored mission that was being planned for Florida. Nothing developed along these lines, however, until the Spiritans were rather well established in the United States. Then, almost simultaneously, they took on Negro Missions in Pittsburgh and in Arkansas.

B. G. 15, 898

The Pittsburgh effort was begun by opening a chapel with a basement school. It subsequently became the present-day parish of

B. G. 13, 326 and 345 f.

St. Benedict the Moor. In Arkansas, the Fathers at Marienstadt and at Conway tried desperately to get something going, but the

B. G. 19, 154 f.

Bishop advised them to wait for better times. The field was far from ripe for the harvest: there was only one conversion in ten years.

B. G. 15, 912

In 1889, Archbishop Ryan asked the Spiritans to undertake a special work for the colored in Philadelphia. The Belgian Sisters of Notre Dame had opened a school for colored girls there ten years earlier, and now Brother Celsus was placed in charge of a boys' school. Father Patrick McDermott opened a special chapel

B. G. 16, 1012 ff.

for Negroes, which he dedicated to St. Peter Claver. Thanks to the tireless work of these two men and the powerful support of Mother Katherine Drexel,[4] the work prospered so well by 1891 that the pastor was able to take over a large Presbyterian church in the neighborhood. To this day it still serves as the church of St. Peter Claver on the corner of Twelfth and Lombard Streets.

cf. p. 348

In later years, as we shall see, the colored missions within the States assumed greater and greater importance in the apostolate of the Holy Ghost Fathers.

5. *Shadows of Persecution in France*

It will be remembered that shortly before Father Schwindenhammer's death the French Government had instituted an indirect persecution of the recognized congregations by means of a new tax

Roy, 118 ff.

program. The first law (1880) merely imposed a tax on the income of these societies. Four years later, however, a special inheritance law was passed. It assumed that each member of a religious society was part-owner of its total possessions and therefore the congregation "inherited" his share when he died. The new law, a most rickety statute, required that this "inheritance" be taxed in every place where the congregation was established. Moreover, religious congregations were to pay regular taxes just like other legal corporations.

Convinced that the "inheritance" law was unconstitutional, the Holy Ghost Fathers and the other recognized congregations

B. G. 15, 919

refused to pay. They seemed to enjoy some public sympathy as is evident from contemporary comment. A newspaper, for example, reported how Father Allaire had narrowly escaped the cooking pots

---

[4]Mother Katherine was the heiress of the fabulous Drexel fortune. She made her novitiate with the Mercy Sisters in Pittsburgh and then returned to Philadelphia to found the Sisters of the Blessed Sacrament, a congregation of women devoted to Indian and Negro Missions. Every cent of her income from the legacy (in 1890 it was estimated to be $1000 a day) went to further the apostolic work among Negroes and Indians.

of cannibalistic tribesmen in the African jungle and then sarcastically remarked that if they had made a stew of him, the Spiritans would have had to pick up the check. Nonetheless, since it refused to pay these taxes, the Congregation was soon engaged in numerous lawsuits against the Office of Internal Revenue. Determined resistance achieved some success, for in 1892 the Supreme Council of State declared the inheritance law unconstitutional, but three years later a new and iron-clad law was passed. Instead of being based on a fictitious inheritance, it was a straight annual levy calculated on the assets of the congregations and the annual mortality rate of their members. The avowed aim of the law, if applied in all rigor, was to tax the recognized congregations to death.

B. G. 15, 919   Although strongly pressed to continue their ten year old passive resistance, the Spiritans and the other authorized congregations thought it more prudent to submit. They could then work toward the abolition or diminution of such punitive measures instead of exasperating Parliament and goading it into a program of outright suppression.

D. C. 188 f.
Griz. 49-61

This act of submission resulted in fierce attacks from the rightist press, which considered the act a break in the resistance front to which the non-recognized religious orders were still adhering. The Holy Ghost Fathers were blamed most of all, because they were supposed to have been the guiding spirits behind this new conciliatory attitude. No one seemed to recall that the Spiritans had ample reason for their action: no matter how unjust the law was, they could not expose their enormous missions in French territories to the danger of carrying on deprived of priests and bereft of every form of religious service. Fortunately, the rightist campaign did no lasting harm to the Congregation and in the end the tax proved less burdensome than had been anticipated. After all, the bureaucrats of Paris soon realized that it would be politically inexpedient to hamper a French organization so much that "foreign" missionaries would gain control of the French colonies. As they astutely observed: "anticlericalism is not an export article." For this reason they did their best to keep the tax to a minimum.

In the midst of all these troubles, Father Emonet suffered a stroke that left him severely paralyzed. In 1895 he delegated all his powers to his first assistant, Father John Grizard, and three years later he died.

During his generalate, despite appalling losses in Africa, the number of Fathers in the Congregation increased by 79%, Brothers by 62%, and aspirants by 40%. Although the expansion of colleges, seminaries and social works was greater than ever, the personnel distribution for 1896 shows that 53% of the Fathers were stationed in the missions (35% in Africa, and 18% elsewhere), while Europe and North America had only 47% of the total. For the Brothers these figures are 33% in the missions (26% in Africa, 7% elsewhere), and 67% in Europe and North America.

cf. p. 200

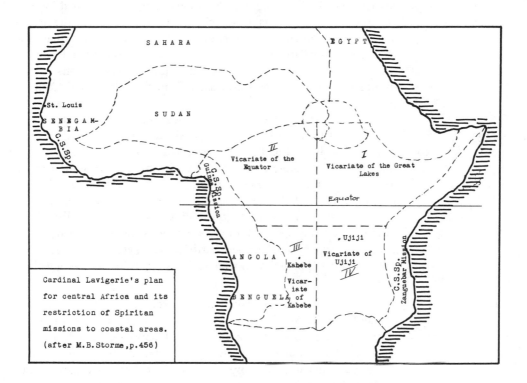

Cardinal Lavigerie's plan for central Africa and its restriction of Spiritan missions to coastal areas. (after M.B.Storme,p.456)

CHAPTER TEN

THE GENERALATE OF ARCHBISHOP LE ROY,
1896-1926

1. *Introduction*

B. G. 17, 865
Griz. 64-73

The Vicar General. After Father Emonet resigned on October 20, 1895, his First Assistant and Delegate, Father John Grizard, was elected Vicar General in charge of current affairs until the General Chapter could be convoked. It was far from being an enviable position at the moment. The whole of France was in turmoil over the antireligious tax laws and the declaration of submission, which the recognized religious congregations had signed, was considered a betrayal of the common cause. Most of the odium created by it fell on the unfortunate Vicar General, who had appended his signature and was generally thought to have induced the other congregations to sign also. Insults and insinuations rained on him from all sides and especially from the overheated Catholic press.

Roy, 121 ff.

In the midst of the confusion, a voice from the depths of Africa came to add to his trouble. Bishop Alexander Le Roy, C. S. Sp., Vicar Apostolic of the Two Guineas, had been opposed to the submission and had advocated continuing the struggle in some way or other. Now that the recognized congregations, including his own, had given up the fight, he wrote a letter to the Catholic newspaper *La Croix,* the leading protagonist of the resistance and a sharp critic of the Holy Ghost Fathers for their submission. Congratulating the paper "on the good battle it was keeping up," Le Roy sarcastically explained why the tax laws would not trouble him in Africa:

Roy, 126

> Won't we too be asked to give something to the Government? Perhaps. If there is question of a special tax for us, as there is for you, we would hardly, I suppose, be able to consider it as an honor. However, we are rather used to these things. In China it happens very often. In that happy land they frequently confiscate even our very heads. While we allow them to decapitate us, we generally do not go to the trouble of cutting off our own heads and handing them over Perhaps that is what we will do here.

232

As could be expected, *La Croix* and the other papers advocating passive resistance interpreted the letter as an approval of their position and as a sign that Father Grizard did not have the support of his own men. After all, there were other signs pointing in the same direction. Father Leo Lejeune, Prefect Apostolic of the Niger, gave an interview to the press and openly joined the opposition. Other missionaries sent individual or collective protests. All these observers far away in the jungle failed to understand what serious consequences would have flowed from the course of action they advocated. They seem to have derived their information solely from inflammatory articles in the rightist newspapers that had been mailed to their jungle stations. As a result, they completely misjudged the situation. While one cannot blame them for their ignorance of the facts, it is hard to excuse them for their hasty judgment. It constituted a painful shock for Father Grizard, especially since *La Croix* had previously insinuated that he took advantage of Father Emonet's illness to submit to the tax laws against the Superior General's wishes.

In addition to this conflict and the ever-present threat of persecution, Father Grizard was faced with a most critical financial situation. The Congregation had not built up any reserves for emergencies and had plunged deep in debt to support its missions and other works. Unable to cope with the perplexing difficulties facing him on all sides, the poor Vicar General more and more withdrew within himself and sighed for the day when a Superior General would be elected so that he could resign his function.

Election of Bishop Le Roy as Superior General. In May 1896, the General Chapter convened at Orly, near Paris. Two strong personalities were seriously considered as candidates for the vacancy: Bishop Prosper Augouard and Bishop Alexander Le Roy. Bishop Augouard was famous as the "Cannibal Bishop," who had established a 1300 mile chain of missions along the Congo and Ubangui rivers. The other candidate was equally famous for his exploratory trips in East Africa and his brilliant writings about the Dark Continent. Both men had undeniably great qualities of heart and mind and both would have made splendid Superior Generals. However, Bishop Augouard's intense nationalism detracted somewhat from his magnificent missionary record, and this contradicted the principles which the Venerable Father Libermann had so vigorously stressed. In addition, he had a reputation

Griz. 67 ff.

B. G. 17, 870

C. L. 10, 8 ff.

'Roy, 130

cf. pp. 504 ff.

for being rather blunt and abrupt in his dealings with others. Bishop Le Roy, on the other hand, had cultivated a conciliatory attitude and had not made the mistake of identifying religion and politics. As could be expected, the delegates regarded him as the preferable candidate. Dispite his reluctance and his efforts to declare himself ineligible, Bishop Le Roy was chosen.

Roy, 16

Alexander Le Roy, a farmer's son, was born in 1854 at La Gralemois in Normandy. After studying at the "White Abbey,"[1] the junior seminary of Mortain, he began his theolgical studies at the diocesan seminary of Coutances. In 1874, Father Horner, one of the pioneer missionaries of Zanguebar, found that this young man wanted to consecrate himself to the missions and promptly kindled his interest in the Holy Ghost Fathers. With great difficulty, Le Roy secured the necessary episcopal permission to leave his diocese. Ordained in 1876, he received his first appointment shortly after his profession in 1877.

cf. p. 61

This first assignment was a great disappointment for the young priest. Instead of being sent to Africa, he was called to teach at the flourishing College of St. Denis, Reunion. The Spiritans had opened it three years before at the urgent request of the Bishop. Then, only a few months after Le Roy's arrival, the college had to be closed, because the Bishop died and his successor saw no use in spending money on higher education. In March 1878, Father Le Roy was back in Paris, confident that this time he would surely be sent to Africa. Instead, he ruefully accepted an assignment to the College of Cellule, France. Two years later, he was appointed to the missions—this time to Pondicherry (India), but again in a teaching capacity. He was to be Director of the local college, which had just been entrusted to the Congregation. Meanwhile Father Schwindenhammer died, and Father Le Vavasseur, his successor, decided to fulfill Le Roy's long-thwarted desire to be appointed to Africa. In December 1881, the young man landed in Bagamoyo on Africa's east coast. He travelled far and wide throughout the immense Vicariate to replace sick fellow priests and made exploratory trips to determine the best locations for new missions. A gifted writer— his bibliography covers ten pages—he used his spare time to publish a series of interesting

Roy, 49
D. C. 323

cf. p. 425

Roy, 54 ff.

M. C. 14, 342 ff; 16, 17 ff.; 22, 435 ff.; 24, 369 ff.

B. G. 31, 306 f.

[1]In 1923 this twelfth century abbey, which had been confiscated by the French Government in 1906, was bought by the Spiritan Fathers to serve as a senior seminary of the Congregation.

B. M. 18,
98 ff.

Roy, 76 ff.

M. C. 21, 319

B. G. 16, 379

Roy, 99 ff.

B. G. 30, 137

cf. pp. 29 ff.

and widely read books and articles about his encounters and adventures, and these soon made his name a by-word with all who were interested in Africa.

While he was there, England and Germany agreed on a partition of East Africa, and in 1886 Germany laid claim to Tanganyika, the region in which Father Le Roy was working. The Germans looked askance at the activities of this zealous French Missionary and deeply resented his open criticism of the colonizing powers. In 1892, they asked him to leave the Territory. Arriving in Paris in the spring of 1892, he read to his great surprise in the *Bulletin Général* that he was being proposed as the new Vicar Apostolic of the Two Guineas. Despite his pleas to the contrary, the appointment was made.

Bishop Le Roy spent the next three years reorganizing his vicariate and its personnel in order to build up a smooth and efficient adminstrative unit. Then, as we have seen, he was called to assume responsibility for the whole Congregation in 1896. He was destined to govern the Congregation for thirty years. On the twenty-fifth anniversary of his election as Superior General the Holy See made him titular Archbishop of Caria.

The election of Bishop Le Roy as Superior General was marked by several "firsts." He was the first African missionary to be chosen for this position. His two immediate predecessors, Fathers Le Vavasseur and Emonet, had been missionaries in the old Holy Ghost Missions of Reunion, Martinique and Guiana, but not in Africa.[2] He was also the first bishop who became Superior General of the Congregation. All his predecessors had been simple priests. Le Roy was the first successor of Libermann who, as the Venerable would have expressed it, came "from the interior of France." Libermann and Schwindenhammer were Alsatians, Le Vavasseur came from the French colony of Reunion, and Emonet had been born in a free and independent Savoy. Finally, Archbishop Le Roy was the first successor of Libermann who had not personally known and been trained by the Venerable restorer of the Holy Ghost Congregation.

The generalate of the Archbishop covers a period of severe storms and stresses for the Congregation and its works: progressive

---

[2] Of all the Superiors General before Libermann, only Father Bertout had been in Africa proper. In Chapter II we related the circumstances of his brief sojourn in Senegal. Father Monnet, of course, had been a missionary in Reunion.

persecution in France, expulsion from Portugal, and the miseries of World War I. However, despite persecution and war, or as Le Roy himself sometimes said, because of them, the Congregation grew and expanded to keep up with the enormous task in Africa. It was there that he directed most of its potential. When he resigned in 1926, six new Provinces had been started, the number of members had grown from 1130 to 2096; and in the Spiritan missions of Africa the number of Christians had increased by 830%.

A Program. In addition to electing a new Superior General, the Chapter of 1896 drew up a program of recommendations and decisions. The following points are of interest for the history of the Congregation:

1. Great caution must be exercised with respect to the acceptance or continuation of educational and social works especially in France. As has been mentioned, several of those accepted by Father Emonet proved very onerous and offered no proportionate compensation in recruitment or resources. Thus they were judged to be often more of a hindrance than an aid in the apostolate of the Congregation. Hence the Chapter laid down this rule:

Educational institutions which, after payment of their staff and expenses, supply the Congregation with resources or vocations fall within the means foreseen for the attainment of our purpose. For this reason it is important to secure the prosperity of these houses by supplying them with a stable personnel that is devoted to this sort or work. This personnel must possess the required aptitudes and offer guarantees of the necessary competence, certified, when required, by degrees.

2. To remedy the critical financial situation, the Chapter unanimously recommended the levying of a personnel tax to be paid for each of its members, except for those who engaged in the training of aspirants. Similar rules exist in other congregations and orders.

3. As we have seen above, Father Schwindenhammer had loosely organized all communities and residences into a number of Provinces and Vice-Provinces. However, most of the houses wherein the Congregation's aspirants and junior members had their training were still centralized in France. With the expansion of the Society in so many different lands and the progressive colonization

B. G. 38, 526

C. L. 2, 20

C. L. 2, 21

cf. p. 215

C. L. 2, 4 f.

of its missions by different European powers, the Chapter considered it necessary to create in Europe and America national centers of education for its own members. Those countries which supplied their own personnel were to become Provinces: the others could not be Provinces and would be called Districts. A Province would be composed of the necessary "houses of training for the clerical and lay aspirants [and] a certain number of communities and works." They would be directed by a Provincial Superior and have a representative at the Motherhouse. The Chapter correctly thought that this decentralization would result in more local initiative and a greater development of the Congregation.

C. L. 2, 9 ff.

4. Hitherto it had been customary for clerics to make their novitiate after ordination and immediately prior to their first appointment. However, a pontifical decree of 1892 prohibited the ordination of unprofessed religious on the canonical title of "common table" or "mission." For this reason, it was decided that the novitiate must take place immediately after the termination of the classical course and before the inception of ecclesiastical studies.

2. *Reorganization in France. Religious Persecution*

a. REORGANIZATION

Roy, 131
C. L. 10, 9 ff.

When Le Roy was elected, there were still a number of lawsuits pending for non-payment of the anti-religious taxes. After disposing of these, the new Superior General addressed himself to the delicate task of withdrawing his men from those establishments in France which now proved quite burdensome. Before this could be achieved, he had to see that their debts were settled and that others were ready to assume responsibility for the relinquished works. Despite numerous difficulties, he succeeded in bringing about the voluntary withdrawal from five foundations that embodied colleges, technical schools and similar works in France.[3] The rest had to be retained at least temporarily till someone could be found to take them over. Archbishop Le Roy then accepted several carefully selected works of considerable magnitude, as, for example, the asylum for 500 Parisian orphans at St. Michael,

B. G. 19, 346
B. G. 21, 346

Brittanny (1898), the orphanage and agricultural school at Misser-

---

[3]Outside of France also, a number of colleges, trade schools and other works were gradually given up.

B. G. 31, 423   ghin in Algeria, (1901) and the Boys' Home and trade schools of
Auteuil (1923). Under the direction of the saintly Father Daniel
cf. pp. 288 ff.   Brottier, this last was to develop into a magnificent chain of institutions stretching across France. It presently cares for nearly
four thousand orphans and homeless boys.

b. Danger of Suppression

Roy. 151 ff.   At the turn of the century, France's government became more
*N. D. 94 ff.   and more dominated by a virulent form of Freemasonry. In 1901
a new law required all religious associations and congregations to
submit a list of their houses and establishments. Though harmless
in itself, the law prepared the way for confiscation. Prime Minister
Waldeck-Rousseau then asked the Supreme Council of State for
a legal opinion regarding the position of the recognized congregations, i. e. the Vincentians, the Sulpicians, the Foreign Missions
Society and the Holy Ghost Fathers. On the basis of a report
for which Mr. Dislère, a divisional President of the Council, had
C. L. 10, 4.ff.   supplied the documentation, the Supreme Council advised the
Prime Minister that one of the recognized congregations, that of
the Holy Ghost Fathers, had ceased to exist in 1848. At that time,
they maintained, it had been surreptitiously replaced by the un-
recognized Congregation of the Holy Heart of Mary. As for the
other three congregations, their status was legally unassailable.
The decision against the Spiritans was based *inter alia* on the way
these priests spoke about their own congregation in the *Bulletin
Général* and their other publications: they referred to the *former*
Congregation of the Holy Ghost, they called Libermann their
founder and *first* Superior General, they spoke about a *fusion* of
two congregations, as if a new Congregation had arisen out of the
two, etc., etc.

This legal conclusion of the Supreme Council of State came as
the proverbial thunder clap in a blue sky. While other congregations were being persecuted, the Holy Ghost Fathers had been confident that they, together with the Vincentians, Sulpicians and
Foreign Missions could rest secure in virtue of the legal recognition which had been granted them in 1726 and again in 1816. Now
they were suddenly faced with complete disaster in France. The
decision would inevitably lead to the dissolution of the Congregation at home, the secularization or exile of all its members, the

confiscation of the Motherhouse, the closing of the colonial seminary, the loss of all other establishments and their sale at public
auction for the profit of the State, the immediate call to military
service of all members who were of the required age, and ultimately
the ruin of most of the missions.

Roy, 154   In his anxiety, Archbishop Le Roy went to see Mr. Dislère,
who had prepared the documents on which the decision had been
based, and asked him what could be done. "That is easy," said he,
"all you have to do is disband and return to your respective dioceses. Don't worry about your buildings. The State will take care
of them." To make matters worse, the decision in question had now
been pronounced by the Supreme Council in plenary session. As
such, it was comparable to a decision handed down by the United
States Supreme Court. No further appeal was possible. The only
hope, if hope it could be called, lay in a reversal of the decision
by the Council itself, but that august body prided itself in the fact
that in all the years of its existence it had never yet reversed any
decision taken in plenary session. How then could it be expected
to break precedent almost immediately after taking this fateful
step? Nonetheless, this is exactly what had to be done if the
Congregation was to be saved in France.

Roy, 154 f.   The Archbishop's anxiety was compounded by the fact that
he had never been a member of the general administration of the
Congregation before he became its Superior General. As he read
the government's menacing report he actually believed it was completely in accord with the facts. This is particularly significant
because it demonstrates how completely the Spiritans of that age
had failed to adjust to the fact that the Holy Heart of Mary Society
was suppressed when Rome directed Libermann and his fellow
Va. 142   priests to enter the Congregation of the Holy Ghost. While the
Venerable himself had wholeheartedly and unreservedly accepted
Rome's decision, the others had considered it as a mere formality
of no serious consequence. Strange as it may seem, these old-
timers had remained so deeply attached to the suppressed congregation that they hardly ever mentioned the ancient congregation
of which they were now a part. As a result, those who were not
intimately familiar with the official documents of the general administration knew nothing about the exact canonical and legal position
cf. p. 247 ff.   of their Congregation. In fact, one of the accidental benefits of
the suppression threat at this time was the clearer conception of

their historical development and their canonical status which the modern Spiritans derived from it. They were at last forced to discard their sentimental attachment to an irrevocable and suppressed past.

But let us return to the problem at hand. Father Désiré Barillec, the Archivist of the Congregation, "was not convinced that we dated [only] from 1841 or 1848." He and Archbishop Le Roy made a profound study of the exact legal situation of the Holy Ghost Fathers in France. Their study showed beyond the shadow of any doubt that, in his hurry to finish off the Congregation, Mr. Dislère had supplied the Supreme Council with a very incomplete set of documents. In fact, his report had made no mention of the most essential papers. Moreover, legal advice gave assurance that, although the Supreme Council had never reversed its decision, there was nothing in the code to prevent it from doing so, even if the likelihood of such an eventuality was not great. Hoping against hope and ordering a series of prayers for success in his endeavors, the Superior General drew up a memorandum in which he pointed out the mistakes on which the Supreme Council's decision was based and appealed from an ill-informed to a well-informed Council. He sent copies of this memorandum to all members of the Supreme Council and multiplied his appeals to politicians, high government officials, and colonial Governors to exercise political pressure. He pointed out the disastrous consequences in the French colonies if the Spiritans were forced to disband.

Most members of the Supreme Council still opposed recognition, but Waldeck-Rousseau, the Prime Minister, was wise enough to see all the implications. He personally informed the Supreme Council that "legal recognition of the Holy Ghost Fathers was a political necessity." Despite its reluctance to reverse itself, therefore, the Council finally issued a new legal opinion on August 1, 1901, which stated that new documents submitted by the Superior General proved that the Congregation of the Holy Ghost had never ceased to exist and that consequently it should be considered as a legally recognized religious association. One can well imagine Le Roy's relief. Throughout the controversy, he had kept the impending disaster hidden from his confreres and even the General Council had not known how desperate the situation really was. Now he could breathe a fervent *"Deo Gratias."*

Roy, 164

*N. D. 97 ff.

Roy, 165

*N. D. 100 f.

Roy, 164

c. COMBES' RELIGIOUS PERSECUTION

Although victory was theirs, the Holy Ghost Fathers still had good reason to be uneasy. After all, a perverse legal mind could easily distinguish between the Congregation and its establishments, declaring the Congregation recognized, but refusing to extend that recognition to its institutions. Waldeck-Rousseau himself was rather moderate and not likely to resort to such a subterfuge, but the others were not above it. Indeed, the situation once again grew serious when Waldeck-Rousseau resigned his post and was succeeded by Emile Combes, an ex-seminarian who was now bitterly opposed to the Church. Combes personally took control of the Ministry of Ecclesiastical Affairs and forthwith launched an open persecution. He closed Catholic schools and colleges, even those that were operated by authorized religious congregations. In March 1903, he declared illegal fifty-four orders and congregations because they engaged in teaching, preaching or even, as in the case of the Carthusians, simply in praying. They were given from eight days to three months to leave their houses and disband. Next, the numerous "unauthorized" establishments of the "authorized" congregations came in for the attack. In 1902, Archbishop Le Roy had requested approval for twelve educational and charitable establishments staffed by the Spiritans in France. In November, 1903, Combes replied:

Roy, 171 ff.

*N. D., 102

> I have decided that there is no reason why the papers should be transmitted to the Council of State for the requested authorization. Accordingly, I have the honor of notifying you that your request has been rejected with respect to the above-mentioned establishments of your Congregation.

After drawing attention to the penalities of fine and imprisonment for failure to comply with the order to withdraw from these institutions, the Minister ended cynically: "Allow me, dear Sir, to assure you of my greatest respect."

*N. D. 104

A few days later, a Presidential decree revoked the Congregation's approval as a teaching society. Only the Motherhouse in Paris was considered formally recognized and protected by the decision of the Supreme Council. Subsequently, Archbishop Le Roy was able to induce the government to tolerate also the Spiritan seminary at Chevilly, two procures in the ports of Marseille and

Bordeaux, and two rest houses for old and sick missionaries in Langonnet (Britanny) and Misserghin (Algiers). Fourteen other "unauthorized" houses had to be abandoned, but because of the legal standing of the Holy Ghost Fathers, they were not confiscated. The Congregation was able to place most of them in good hands under the authority of the local bishops. Nevertheless, a large number of boys and young men from various educational and social works had to be sent back to their homes or to the misery of the city slums from which they had been rescued and the Superior General looked on hopelessly while nearly three hundred of his priests and Brothers were expelled from the institutions to which they had devoted a large part of their lives. In spite of it all, the Spiritans suffered less than most other religious groups. As Archbishop Le Roy pointed out at the General Chapter of 1906 in Chevilly: "We are the only religious[4] who are actually able to live in communities on the soil of France, and we are now more numerous and more vigorous than at any other period of our history."

In 1905, the French Government decreed the separation of Church and State. When the Pope refused to accept this unilateral action, and declined to establish legal associations which would function as owners of Church property, the Government issued a military draft call for all seminarians less than twenty-six years old, and seized all churches, rectories, seminaries and episcopal residences. Since the decree covered the old French colonies as well, it entailed the suppression of the institute which served as the combined seminary of the colonial dioceses, i.e. the old Holy Ghost Seminary in Paris. Indirectly, the Motherhouse itself was again in danger. In 1819, when Father Bertout had bought back the buildings in which both the Motherhouse and the Holy Ghost Seminary were established, the Government had paid the bill under the explicit condition that "if for any reason whatsoever the seminary should cease to exist . . . the State would immediately enter into the possession of the buildings as their sole owner." After suppressing the seminary of the colonial dioceses, therefore, the Government laid claim to the buildings which since 1734 had been the seat of the Congregation and of the Holy Ghost Seminary.

B. G. 24, 692

C. L. 10, 6

C. L. 10, 7

B. G. 23, 424 ff. and 815 ff.

*N. D. 34

B. G. 26, 461 ff.

---

[4]None of the other recognized clerical societies were religious in the strict sense of the term.

Fortunately, Archbishop Le Roy succeeded in convincing the Government that legal suppression of Holy Ghost Seminary *as a colonial seminary* did not entail its total suppression but merely reduced it to the legal status it enjoyed before the Concordat of 1851. Even then, however, the Government refused to list its newly-ordained priests with the colonial clergy, despite the fact that local colonial administrators expressed grave fear of an invasion of American Protestant missionaries. The Congregation was forced to send these young priests elsewhere, to the United States, to Mexico and to Puerto Rico, wherever suitable positions might be found for them. As could be expected, recruitment for Holy Ghost Seminary suffered severely under these conditions, and the situation was further aggravated by the military draft of seminarians. At one point there were only eight seminarians left, but after the first world war their numbers rose again. Through it all, by some strange anomalous policy, the Government continued to pay for the seminary's maintenance till 1911.

Partial Exile. Evidently, the few houses left in France were insufficient to assure the adequate recruitment of future Spiritans in that country. Consequently, the Congregation found it necessary to establish junior seminaries for French candidates across the border in Belgium and in Italy. These houses functioned until after World War I, when persecution in France began to diminish. At that time the Government was planning to exile the surviving priests and Brothers who had fought in its armies and risked their lives for their country, but it suddenly met with concerted opposition. The survivors joined forces, defied the government, and refused to go. Their act of defiance won support and applause from the thousands of ex-soldiers who Father Daniel Brottier, C.S.Sp., had organized into a League of War Veterans. Through the intimate contact of trenches and field hospitals the soldiers of France had learned to admire and appreciate the heroism and charity of these mobilized priests and Brothers. Combat experiences were far removed from the newspaper pictures of fat, lazy, and self-indulgent monks. When, therefore, the Government saw it was confronted by a popular revolt against the proposed exile, it abandoned the program of expulsion. Little by little the religious orders and congregations began once more to establish themselves on French soil.

D. C. 331 ; 342

*N. D. 107 ;
113

cf. p. 326 and
p. 340
C. H. R. 18,
222

Brot. 104 f.

3. *The 1910 Revolution in Portugal*

After founding its splendid Holy Ghost College in Braga (1872), the Congregation opened several other flourishing institutions in Portugal.

B. G. 13, 1299

St. Mary's College, begun at Porto in 1886, soon rivaled the school of Braga in importance and renown. It continued to grow in size and reputation even though the Jesuits opened a rival college almost across the street. These foundations were followed by an orphanage and a novitiate at Cintra (1887), a procure at Lisbon (1892), St. John Fisher College at Ponta Delgada in the Azores (1892),[5] a junior seminary at Formiga (1894), a home for the aged at Campo Maior (1894), and a senior seminary at Carnide (1907). The Province of Portugal was indeed in full bloom when disaster struck.

B. G. 14, 321; 16, 319; 17, 375; 18, 289; 20, 400

B. G. 24, 334

B. G. 21, 76

The Gathering Storm. A long time before, powerful secret societies had been agitating against religious institutions, stirring up popular resentment and endeavoring to restore the law of 1834 which had expelled all religious orders from the land. In 1901 the Government closed several monasteries and convents, but the Holy Ghost Congregation escaped with a mere inspection. In 1903, however, leftist newspapers began a violent campaign which at first centered on the person of Father Christopher Rooney but was soon directed against the Congregation and its works in general.

B. G. 23, 40 f.

Father Rooney was the Congregation's procurator at Lisbon and confessor to the Countess Camerido. Journalistic attacks on him began when the Countess donated a property which the Spiritans planned to use for a Procure to help the African Missions. Since her family fortune had been derived from the slave trade, it was only natural that the pious Countess would want to make some kind of restitution by devoting part of her possessions to a work dedicated to the Negro race. The leftist papers, however, spoke of the whole affair as an intrigue of fortune-hunting Jesuits.[6] The campaign grew so violent that the timorous Papal Nuncio became alarmed and appealed to the Holy See, asking that the Congregation be forced to return the property and that Father Rooney be removed as the countess's confessor and even exiled

---

[5]This college was endowed by collateral descendants of St. John Fisher who had settled in the Azores. It was abandoned in 1907.

[6]In the leftist press the term "Jesuit" had become a term of opprobrium applied to all religious orders of men.

from Portugal. In accord with its traditions, the Motherhouse agreed to the first demand for the sake of peace, but strenuously objected to the second point, arguing that Father Rooney's removal would constitute an implicit avowal of guilt. Moreover, it would be a grave injustice to exile an innocent man simply because a few radical newspapers had unjustly slandered him. Archbishop Le Roy succeeded in making this view prevail in Rome and Father Rooney was allowed to remain a confessor to the countess, particularly since she wanted him and him alone to prepare her for her death.[7] When she finally died in 1905, her last will left the disputed property to the Holy See, and her possessions in Campo Maior and Cintra to three unsuspecting Holy Ghost Fathers, who learned about it only through a renewed campaign of defamation in the radical press.

B. G. 23, 598

Meanwhile the political situation in Portugal deteriorated rapidly. After the murder of Don Carlos in 1908, the situation became especially precarious. Everyone expected a revolution, although in some quarters there was a forlorn hope that the forces of law and order would prevail.

B. G. 25, 694
ff.; 729 ff.

The Revolution. This hope proved completely idle. At 1:00 A. M. October 4, 1910 the community at Lisbon was aroused by gunfire. Fearing the worst, Fathers and Brothers ran up to the turret of the house to watch developments. One priest ventured out to gather news and returned in great alarm; everywhere parents were taking their children out of schools and institutions, for an immediate attack on convents and monasteries was expected. The community quickly dispersed, leaving three Brothers, later joined by Father Riedlinger, to guard the house. The next morning, around 4:00 A. M. a band of armed soldiers and revolutionists demanded to be let in, shouting: "Give us the Jesuits. The Jesuits or you die!" Father Riedlinger argued with the mob, brought them into the house to search for weapons and Jesuits, and ultimately persuaded them to depart without doing much harm.

Elsewhere things did not go nearly so well: several Vincentian Fathers were killed when their house was invaded, and in Carnide twenty-two Spiritans were thrown into jail, some barely escaping immediate execution. Meanwhile in Lisbon itself, Brother

B. G. 24, 522

[7]Later Father Rooney went to the United States, where he became the founder of the Portuguese parishes operated by the Spiritans in Rhode Island.

Xavier—an American citizen who used to operate a barbershop in the U. S. A.—hoisted the Stars and Stripes over the Procure in the vain hope of scaring off the roving mobs.

At Cintra, four hundred armed sailors and riflemen advanced on the Novitiate and trained their artillery on the house. Actual bombardment was prevented when the revolutionists were invited to engage in a fruitless search for arms, but many of the Brothers were sent to jail nonetheless. Later, when these poor unfortunates were trying to snatch a few hours' sleep on the bare floor of their prison, they were suddenly roused by the announcement that they were to be executed at once because the Jesuits had thrown bombs among the people. Fortunately the threat proved to be just as groundless as the motivating cause behind it.

While this was going on, the Carnide prisoners were incarcerated in the fortress of Caxias, together with eighty-two Jesuits and several hundred other victims. A number of Spiritans had disguised themselves in lay clothes to escape the rioters, but they were soon recognized and severely beaten. In Porto and Braga there was less violence, but it soon became apparent that there was no hope of saving the famous colleges there when the revolutionary government revived Pombal's notorious laws against religious orders, dispersed all communities, and confiscated their possessions.[8] Only the Procure in Lisbon succeeded in remaining open till 1911.

On the eve of the Portuguese revolution, the province could proudly point to its forty-seven novices, the brilliant record of its educational institutions, and the vigor of its foreign missions. Within a few short days this tragic political upheaval left it a broken and pathetic shadow of its former glory.

The Restoration. While waiting for a chance to restore the Province, the Congregation opened a junior seminary for Portuguese subjects in the Spanish town of Zamora just across the frontier. Then in 1915 the Spiritans ventured to re-open their Lisbon mission procure which, as even the masonic government realized, was indispensable for the maintainance of missions in

B. G. 29, 764

[8]Because the houses of the Congregation in Portugal legally belonged to individual Spiritans of French, German and English nationality, the governments of these countries brought suit against Portugal in the International Court of Justice at the Hague. This suit ended by mutual agreement in 1920 when Portugal agreed to pay limited indemnities to the Congregation.

Angola and the Congo. Despite its political and religious philosophy, the Government knew that the missions had to carry on their noble task if public order was to be preserved.

In 1918, a counter revolution took place and hopes for a quick restoration of the Province rose immediately. The next year, Father Moses Pinho, the future Archbishop of Loanda, quietly opened a junior seminary in Braga and the students of Zamora were transferred there in 1920. At the same time, a house for Brothers and a special retreat center for the reform of the clergy were opened in the same city. In 1921 another seminary was established in Godim, near Regua, and in 1922 a third in Vianna do Castello. The next year the Government granted an annual subsidy to the Portuguese Province to help it train future missionaries for Angola,—a subsidy, be it noted, which is in addition to the considerable grants by which Portugal supports the missions themselves. Once more, then, the province began to retrace the path of greatness. It differs from the old organization, however, in one important aspect: it has not reopened any colleges. Rather, it has limited itself almost solely to the task of evangelizing and civilizing Portugal's enormous possessions in Africa.

4. *An Internal Controversy Over the "Fusion"*

In a previous section of this chapter we learned how the French Government's threat of suppression caused Archbishop Le Roy to discover to his surprise and delight that the Holy Ghost Fathers dated from 1703 and not from 1841 or 1848. Moreover, it was pointed out that Father Libermann's humble submission to the decision of Rome was in marked contrast to the sentimental attachment that caused nearly all his confreres to cling to a suppressed past and close their eyes to the fact that the Congregation of the Holy Heart of Mary no longer existed. As soon as Le Roy had studied the documents and gleaned a true picture of the situation, he courageously devoted himself to setting the record straight. It was not an easy task, for he had to act against the strong opposition of those who for brevity's sake we may label "the Libermannists." The most prominent spokesman of this group was Father John Grizard, the first Assistant of the Superior General.

Under Le Roy's leadership a new school of thought sprang up. For convenient reference, we will call its adherents "the Placists."

Marginal references:

B. G. 29, 760

B. G. 30, 376; 888
B. G. 31, 226

cf. pp. 239 f.

Griz. 99-116

They devoted themselves to gaining recognition for Poullart des Places as the founder of the Congregation and acquainting the Spiritans with their own long-neglected history in the period be-

B. G. 41, 366

tween 1703 and 1841. Le Roy found a potent ally in Father Henry Le Floch, then Director of the Senior Seminary at Chevilly. Le

B. G. 27, 700

Floch, whose historical research on the origin of the Congregation and the life of its founder was later to gain the coveted distinction of being crowned by the *"Académie Française,"* opened the controversy in 1902 by means of the traditional February 2 confer-

B. G. 41, 367

ence which he gave in honor of Father Libermann. The speaker showed that it was historically unjustifiable to call Libermann the founder or even a co-founder of the Congregation. At most he could be called its restorer and the guiding spirit of its missionary activity. One can easily imagine the emotion of Le Floch's older confreres when they were thus for the first time put face to face

B. G. 41, 367 ff.

with the facts. This conference and even more Le Floch's publication of a 556 page book on Father Poullart des Places, the Founder of the Congregation of the Holy Ghost, provoked a series of lively discussions and memoranda in which the Libermannists tried to defend their position. It did not particularly help matters when Cardinal Merry del Val, writing on behalf of Pope Pius IX, called

B. G. 23, 511

des Places "one of the great personalities of the Church in France [and] the Founder of the Congregation of the Holy Ghost." Moreover, Archbishop Le Roy and his adherents were basing their position on a most telling argument: to know exactly what happened at the so-called fusion, they maintained, the important thing was not to argue about the original intentions of the two parties concerned, but to see what action Rome itself had taken. In this respect, the documents left room for only one view—that of the Placists.

B. G. 41, 371 f.

Just then another controversy arose to further electrify the atmosphere. It centered around the basic purpose of the Congregation. In 1910, when the Holy See declared Father Libermann Venerable by affirming the heroic nature of his virtues, Father Le Floch, then Superior of the Pontifical French Seminary, published a booklet about Louis Lannurien. Libermann's private secretary and the founder of the Pontifical French Seminary. In this booklet Le Floch quoted with evident approval Lannurien's state-

cf. pp. 123 f.

ment that the work of seminaries falls within the aim of the Congregation as Libermann viewed it after the "fusion." Obviously, so forceful an expression of this particular idea was greeted by something less than enthusiasm by those whose zeal for Africa rendered them oblivious to any other work. They characterized Le Floch as a man of subversive ideas and even accused him of having falsified Lannurien's memorandum. As we have seen in Chapter VI, however, Le Floch's thesis reflected Libermann's position most accurately.

cf. pp. 120 ff.

B. G. 27, 542 f.

Meanwhile, the periodic report on the French Seminary, which was published in the 1914 *Bulletin Général,* emphasized once more that the work of seminaries was perfectly in accord with the pur-

B. G. 28, 365 ff.

pose of the Congregation. Shortly thereafter, Father Le Floch made public a letter which Cardinal Gasparri had written on behalf of Benedict XV. The Pope had read his life of Poullart des Places and congratulated its author on the successful application of des Places' principles and methods which were evident in the training that the Seminary was giving the elite of the French clergy. No mention whatsoever was made of Father Libermann, an omission that may appear innocent enough to the modern reader, but to that generation of Spiritans it constituted a cruel blow to their most cherished ideas.

B. G. 41, 373

And so, the controversy went its stormy way. In 1915, when a second edition of his *Life of Father des Places* became necessary, Le Floch prepared a special chapter on the historical facts. The type had already been set when he decided to omit the chapter and distribute it privately as a fifty page booklet entitled *The Act of Union.* Hewing rigorously to the facts and appealing throughout to official documents, the booklet demonstrated that there had been no fusion of two congregations. Instead, Libermann's Congregation had simply been dissolved by the Holy See, Libermann and his confreres had entered the Congregation of the Holy Ghost, and subsequently Libermann had been elected to succeed Bishop Monnet as the eleventh Superior General of the Holy Ghost Fathers. Many Libermannists were completely unmoved. With magnificent obduracy, they refused to budge from their position. Before long, a second booklet followed: *A Note on the New Edition of the Life of Claude Francis Poullart des Places.* The opposition promptly countered with a *Memorandum on the Fusion.* At this juncture the dispute assumed a medieval flavor. Amusing exergues were added to the titles: *Gaudium de Veritate* and *Cor Unum et Anima Una.* A rejoinder to the *Memorandum* later followed under the title: *Supplement to the Act of Union: A Footnote to the Memorandum on the Fusion.* With this rejoinder the controversy reached dead center.[9] It was difficult and useless to argue against people who based their arguments on sentiment rather than on reason.

Nonetheless, Archbishop Le Roy saw to it that a collection containing all the pertinent documents at last saw the light of day. Through a direct reference to the sources, he hoped, everyone would be able to see the facts of the case for himself and thus form his own opinion. In the Preface to this publication, he listed the conclusions of the long debate but we shall not repeat them here, for they coincide with the position we have taken in this book. Although they did not allow Father Libermann to be called the Founder of the Congregation, they sanctioned the use of the term "Second Founder." While the old-timers were not likely to change their mind for, as the French saying goes: the heart has reasons which reason does not understand,[10] Le Roy knew that time would solve the problem. He directed that copies of this collection be placed at the disposal of all novices and senior seminarians throughout the Congregation and thereby prepared a new generation of Spiritans for whom the whole controversy would have importance only as an interesting bit of history. In 1922 it was officially decided that thereafter the annual commemoration of Father des Places' death should be celebrated with a special conference on the Founder and his work, Benediction of the Blessed Sacrament, and a festive dinner. In 1950 the General Chapter specified that his feast "should be celebrated with the same solemnity" as that of Father Libermann. At the same time it directed that the biography and writings of Father des Places be made available to all members of the Congregation. The heat of debate had given way to the light of unity.

N. D. pp. V. ff.

B. G. 28, 590

B. G. 30, 751

B. G. 41, 375

---

[9]The above-mentioned memoranda and brochures are only some of the many that appeared between 1900 and 1924.

Griz. 112

[10]As a matter of fact, Father Grizard never abandoned his position till his death in 1929. By then the saintly old man had become the lonely and somewhat pathetic survivor of an old school. Apart from his profound veneration for Father Libermann, there seems to have been another reason for his stubborn adherence to the old view—viz., his fear of a return to the antiquated organization which nearly wrecked the Congregation in the first half of the nineteenth century.

5. *The Start of New Provinces*

The religious persecutions in France and Portugal forcefully impressed the Holy Ghost Fathers with the danger of being too dependent on a few countries when recruiting new members. To keep abreast of the demands made on the Congregation by its world-wide apostolate, it was now imperative that new provinces be established in other countries. No less than six of them were inaugurated during the generalate of Archbishop Le Roy: in Belgium, the Netherlands, England, Canada, Switzerland and Poland.

a. BELGIUM

Libermann's Efforts. From the very beginning of his foundation, Father Libermann had turned his attention to Belgium. In 1843 he received his first Belgian candidate, Henry Warlop, who later became a hard-working missionary priest in Senegal. This first acquisition whetted his appetite for more, for in the Spring of the following year he wrote: "We will need all available space, especially if Bishop Collier sends people. I hope that they will be Belgians." Later in the same year he redoubled his efforts in that direction but without success. In January, 1845, he announced: "I hope to establish a house of studies in Belgium." He dispatched Father Tisserant to Belgium to recruit aspirants and later went there himself to investigate the possibilities personally. When serious difficulties arose, the Prefect of the Propaganda took the unusual step of urging him not to give up: "I will be greatly pleased if you endeavor to pursue this project and bring it to realization." Libermann then submitted to Canon Beckers of Liege a long memorandum for the Belgian Hierarchy in which he explained his ideas about making their country mission-minded. Because Belgium now ranks very high on the list of countries which play a significant part in the expansion of the Church, and because Libermann's memorandum is said to have exercised a powerful influence on the inauguration of the Belgian missionary movement, we will quote here certain passages from this document.

N. D. 6, 241;
cf. 7, 188

N. D. 7, 12

N. D. 7, 374

N. D. 8, 90

B. G. 26, 446
M. M. C. 1911,
101 ff.; 149 ff.
*Africa
Christo,* 1952
No. 4, pp. 9 ff.

N. D. 9, 91

> It is quite certain that as long as Belgium does not have a house destined exclusively for the missions, it will have only a few missionaries. However, it is more than probable that a foundation for this purpose will give the necessary impetus and

that sooner or later Belgium will be the rival of the countries which are most fruitful in missionaries. . . .

N. D. 9, 93

It may be objected that others have already tried and failed. However, they have not tried to start a Belgian work; they have not undertaken it in the form and according to the plan which I am about to propose and which eliminates the principal causes of their failure.

This plan is very simple. It is a question of establishing a seminary whose sole objective would be the missions, a seminary with wholly Belgian missions. An institution conceived in this way would naturally attract the majority of Belgian vocations; it would stimulate missionary thinking in a large number of young men who would otherwise be unconcerned; it would maintain and develop nascent vocations; its first successes in pagan lands would make a profound impression and give impetus in a wholly natural way to Belgian clerics, just as the French missions give it to Frenchmen. . . .

N. D. 9, 94

From what I have seen in travelling through your excellent country, all the Bishops and all the directors of the senior and junior seminaries are inclined to favor such a work. This favorable disposition will increase when they see a foundation which is in conformity with the ideas and tastes of the Belgian clergy. . . .

To make the seminary conform to the tastes and ideas of the country and secure its success, it will have to be Belgian and only Belgian. . . . It would therefore have to be directed by Belgian priests. . . .

To follow these plans there are, I think, two ways. The first would be to found an entirely independent congregation. The second would be to connect the work with an existing congregation which is solely occupied with missions. . . . The first method would give rise to a few additional difficulties. Nevertheless, I am convinced that it would meet with success if a wise, zealous and stable man is placed at the head of the work.

If the second method is followed, it would be easier and there would be more encouragement. However, I think that in this case it should be a connection rather than a fusion. In a fusion, the house in Belgium would be a subsidiary entirely dependent on a Motherhouse and obliged to follow its prescriptions in every respect. This could give rise to inconveniences. It would no longer be a Belgian work; in the course of time its fundamental plan would run the risk of being changed; moreover, the administration would not proceed too smoothly because the Belgian way of doing things would not be sufficiently known and understood by foreigners. If, however, the method of connection is adopted, the new work will be a Belgian work, and as it were, a sister of the already existing work; it will be an integral part of it and will have the same spirit, follow the same Rules, be directed by the same general administration. Just as the French branch, it will have a share in this administration and be represented in it by a fixed number of members. But in addition it will have its own special administration, with a Superior and a Council charged with the general administration. The French branch will be similarly organized. . . .

N. D. 9, 95

If divine Providence wants to make use of us to help in the foundation of this establishment, we will be very happy to be of service. Our Rules are still in the provisional stage; hence we would be more amenable to a modification in our organization, as would be demanded by the arrangement I propose. . . . With respect to the missions, the same system would be followed. The communities established there will be staffed exclusively from the house in Belgium; they will report directly to a Belgian member representing these houses in the General Council of the Congregation. He will be in charge of their immediate direction and report about them to the Council and to the Superior General. The same system will be followed in the French Missions.

Unfortunately, Father Libermann's efforts did not produce the effect he had hoped for. He sadly concluded after his first trial that Belgium, which had only recently been liberated from the yoke of its Protestant Dutch rulers, "was not yet sufficiently ripe for the missions."

N. D. 7, 374

B. G. 21, 98
L. H. 100 ff.

The Foundation. Half a century later, his successor, Archbishop Le Roy, was visited in Paris by Mr. Wegimont, a rich merchant of Antwerp and owner of vast concessions in the French and Belgian Congo. This pious merchant-prince wanted missionaries for his holdings, but the Superior General had to decline his request. By way of explanation, Le Roy told him: "Unlike commercial institutions, a missonary congregation has reserves neither of personnel nor of funds, for the demand always exceeds the supply." This answer would have checkmated anyone else, but not Mr. Wegimont. Knitting his brows, he threw down his challenge: "I understand. Well, come and get them in Belgium. I will give you a house."

Under these propitious auspices, the Congregation opened its first junior seminary in 1900 at Lier. Its first superior, Father Albert Sébire, was destined to preside for many years over the activities of the Spiritans in Belgium as well as in neighboring Holland. In the course of the thirty-six years which remained to him, he was to be the founder of ten houses and two Provinces. His first task, of course, was to publicize the Congregation and its work. Without sparing himself, he began to travel all over the country, giving more than two hundred illustrated lectures in less than three years. As a result of this, Cardinal Mercier, then still President of Louvain's Higher Institute of Philosophy, stated that Father Sébire contributed powerfully to the awakening of Belgium's interest in the missions. Although this enthusiasm was later to attain prodigious proportions, the Congregation was to share in its fruits only in a very modest way.

Belgium is a country inhabited by French-speaking Walloons and Dutch-speaking Flemish. The difference in language and the cultural opposition between these two groups made it impossible to train aspirants from both in the same junior seminary. Since Lier lay in Flemish territory, another junior seminary was necessary to take care of the French-speaking part of Belgium. This problem was solved when exiled French communities found a refuge in Gentinnes and gave a much-needed stimulus to the budding Belgian Province (1903). Four years later a novitiate for Brothers was opened in Donck, but lack of space and other reasons forced the abandonment of this house in 1913, when it was exchanged for a new location straddling the Belgian-Dutch border at Baarle-Nassau and Weelde. Two years earlier a foundation had been made at Louvain, where French confreres had been in residence since 1902 to attend the lectures at the philosophical institute. The new foundation was perfectly timed to receive Portuguese aspirants who had been exiled from their country by the terrible revolution we have already described. After the First World War this house became the senior seminary of the Province.

B. G. 23, 512

B. G. 24, 241

B. G. 28, 123

B. G. 23, 512

B. G. 26, 450

b. THE NETHERLANDS

B. G. 6, 107

First Efforts. In 1867, Bishop Elder of Natchez, Mississippi, had entered into negotiations with the Holy Ghost Fathers regarding the admission of Dutch priests into the Congregation. In search of priests for his diocese, he had approached the Dutch Hierarchy and found that they were willing to let him have some priests, if these priests would join a religious order or congregation. This proviso was based on their fear of the dangers which face any missionary who remains alone. The Congregation accepted Bishop Elder's offer quite readily because it provided a good opportunity to establish the Spiritans in the Netherlands. Unfortunately, His Excellency was disappointed in the great expectations from Holland and the whole project came to nought.

B. G. 34, 472 ff.

cf. p. 208
B. G. 9, 849

B. G. 37, 782

The next year, 1868, Brother Pius Orbons became the first Dutchman to join the Congregation. He entered in Marienstadt, Germany, just before Bismarck expelled the Holy Ghost Fathers from the Reich. Shortly thereafter some of the German exiles considered taking refuge in Holland and laying the foundations of a new Province there, but it was ultimately decided that they should cross the Atlantic and begin the Province of the United States. Brother Pius accompanied Father Strub to America, but sickness soon forced him to return to Europe. He was sent to France, where another Dutch Brother, Augustine Jansen, joined him in 1886. Later on, Brother Pius was destined to spend the last twenty-five years of his life helping to build a province in his native land.

L. H. 99-110

B. G. 22, 679
and 745

B. G. 23, 519

The Foundation. In 1900, as soon as the Holy Ghost Fathers had opened a Belgian junior seminary in Flemish-speaking Lier, several young Dutchmen asked permission to enter. Their candidacy prompted the Motherhouse to consider the feasibility of establishing a house in the Netherlands themselves. Somewhat hesitant about the chances of success in such a Protestant country, the Spiritans opened a junior seminary in Weert, just "to give it a trial." In the beginning, a little hastily-converted restaurant was rented for this purpose, but in two years' time the number of students increased to such a degree that much more room was needed. Providence helped, for just then Father Albert Sébire, the founder of the Belgian-Dutch Province, chanced to meet a philatelist on the train and gave him a few interesting stamps.

In return, his grateful fellow-passenger eventually presented him with a donation sufficient to build a junior seminary!

The rapid progress of the work was unexpectedly gratifying to the French Fathers who continued to marvel over the fact that everyone in Holland, even in the cities, carefully fulfilled his religious obligations. Nonetheless, they were much concerned over their aspirants' apparent lack of interest in the missions. Being Frenchmen, they looked in vain for the flying sparks and wildly leaping flames which enthusiasm generates in the youths of their country. They could not see the quietly burning fire of apostolic zeal which is more proper to northern climes. Because of this psychological gap between directors and directed, the initial development was rather slow. As years passed, however, and as more Dutchmen were given responsibility for the training and direction of local recruits, the situation improved and Weert became one of the most important junior seminaries of the Congregation. A large share of the credit for the flourishing condition of this house should go to Father Lambert Vogel who, undeterred by the depression, expanded the buildings into one of the most efficient and practical seminary plants in the country.

B. G. 28, 241   In 1913 a special training school for Brothers was built on the Belgian-Dutch border at Baarle-Nassau. It provides a very special atmosphere in which postulant Brothers, novices and newly-professed spend about five years training for the religious life and becoming expert at the various useful trades for which they show particular aptitude. Because of these splendid facilities, the Dutch Province has always been blessed with a relatively large number of vocations to the Brotherhood.

B. G. 30, 239   In 1914, when the First World War closed the doors of his Senior Seminary at Louvain, Father Sébire went in search of a temporary house for his Dutch seminarians. Through the accident of missing a bus, he found himself stranded in a small village, called Gemert, where some French Jesuits exiled by Combes had taken refuge. He told them why he was travelling through Holland, and they very generously offered to teach his senior seminarians. Makeshift lodgings were found in the neighborhood and a temporary community (so they thought) was organized under the direction of Father Charles Luttenbacher. Little by little the Jesuits were recalled from exile to defend with their lives the country that had no use for them in time of peace. As their numbers decreased, more and more room became available in the medieval castle of the Teutonic Knights which they had occupied. As a result, the Spiritans were generously invited to move in and they have stayed there ever since, for they subsequently purchased the property. The old castle and its modern additions, its various out-buildings, and its magnificent park have caused visitors to regard it as the Congregation's most beautiful establishment.

c. ENGLAND

N. B. 244 f.

Preliminaries. As early as 1792 a Holy Ghost Father took up residence in England. He was Father James Bertout, the future restorer of the Congregation after the French Revolution. Till 1802 he lived in the county of York, exercising his priestly functions and waiting for peace to return to France so that he might undertake the work of restoration.

Father Libermann, as early as 1842, had been thinking about establishing a branch of his society in England to train English and Irish missionaries in their home country. At that time, in a letter to Father Tisserant, he said:

N. D. 3, 117

It would be good to propagate our work in England and to form either English or Irishmen with a view to the same purpose and in the same spirit as our own, so that the English could go to their colonies and the French to theirs. . . . It does not matter how the project is put into practice: whether English and Irish would enter into our Society under one Superior, or form a Society apart with their own Superior. The important thing is to get something done: the need [of the British colonies] is more pressing than that of the French. . . .

N. D. 3, 124 f.

There is no question of mixing the Englishmen with the Frenchmen; each nation will remain separate unless subsequently it would be considered advisable to unite them. Perhaps it will even be possible to establish a colonial seminary for Englishmen in which those who are destined for parish work

N. D. 3, 135

would be trained. . . . For I think that if Irishmen are educated in England or Ireland, their ecclesiastical training will be much better than the one they get in France. They would be made much more capable of serving the Church and would be safeguarded against so many vices which, to the scandal of the poor faithful and the heathens, cause so many of them to be lost in the missions.

N. D. 3, 153 ff.　He sought to interest Cardinal Wiseman in his plan and was even on the point of visiting England for this purpose. The more he thought about the plan, the more enthusiastic he grew. He considered his impending visit to England even more important than

cf. p. 572　a serious proposal to merge his society with the Congregation of Holy Cross. Unfortunately, under pressure from Father de

N. D. 3, 437　Brandt he had to give up his planned visit to England and his friends advised him to wait at least a year in order to consolidate

N. D. 3, 206　his society in France. Meanwhile a Father John Hand visited Libermann and outlined his plan to start a missionary college in Ireland. Realizing that his own foundation would in some degree compete with this new institution during its most difficult initial period, Father Libermann decided to postpone his own plans indefinitely. He did accept Father Hand's advice, however, and retained the religious service of the British colony of Mauritius as a stepping-stone toward a future foundation in England.

B. G. 4, 672　　　After Libermann's death, an opportunity seemed to present itself in 1863 when the Spiritans were asked to take charge of St. Mary's College and St. Joseph's Orphanage in London, but the death of Cardinal Wiseman prevented the execution of these plans.

B. G. 4, 672　That same year the Archbishop of Birmingham offered the Con-
B. G. 4, 674　gregation a parish, and in 1865 another request came to undertake a mission at Kupar in Scotland. Because the scope of these two works was too limited, both were regretfully declined.

B. G. 22, 711　　　*Foundation.* It was not till sixty-four years after Libermann's efforts that the Spiritans established themselves in England. In 1904, when it began to look as though all French houses would be confiscated, the Congregation rented a large property in Prior Park, Somerset County, to serve as a reception center for the

B. G. 23, 560　exiles. When the danger of exile had passed, this house came to
B. G. 25, 5　be used as a Brothers' novitiate for the Irish Province. Three years later, an exorbitant increase in rental rates caused the Irishmen to abandon Prior Park and settle in Castlehead, Lancastershire. Since a junior seminary for English subjects was opened in the same house, Castlehead became the first foundation intended for local aspirants and the starting point of a new province. Within

B. G. 26, 296　three years the house was too small for the Irish novices and the British seminarians. Consequently, the novices were transferred to Ireland and the whole house was left free for the growing junior

B. G. 26, 854   seminary. Some years later, another foundation of the Irish Province in England, the residence at Peasley Cross near Liverpool (1912), was taken over by the English Province.

B. G. 30, 270   World War I wrought its havoc in the English Province also. The Alsatian Fathers and Brothers stationed there had to be removed and all seminarians of military age were mobilized. This draft of seminarians seriously hampered the Province's growth, for only a small proportion of the aspirants returned when hostilities ended. Immediately after the war, however, their numbers began to increase once again and Castlehead had to be expanded. In 1924 the upper years were transferred to Bebington, near

B. G. 31, 705   Birkenhead, where the Congregation had been offered a property
B. G. 34, 241   free of charge for five years. During that period of grace, the Spiritans enlarged Castlehead to a point where all junior seminarians could be housed there. When they completed the new wing, Bebington was closed and Castlehead functioned thereafter as the junior seminary of the Province of England.

d. CANADA

cf. pp. 28 ff. ;   Chapters II and III of this book were devoted to the eighteenth
pp. 35 ff.   century history of the Holy Ghost Fathers in Canada. The last survivor of these early Spiritans, a refugee from St. Pierre et Miquelon who had refused to take the schismatic oath imposed by the French Revolutionary Government, died in Canada in 1835.

N. D. 3, 407   As early as 1846, a Canadian by the name of MacHarron had entered Father Libermann's novitiate, but it was not until after the foundation of the French Seminary in Rome (1853) that contact between Canada and the Congregation was renewed. Several Canadian Bishops knew Father Libermann from their seminary days in St. Sulpice and were happy to entrust to his spiritual children at the Pontifical Seminary the ecclesiastical training of their most promising candidates for the priesthood. A number of these aspirants later rose to very prominent positions in Canada. For example, Cardinal Taschereau and Cardinal Begin, both of Quebec, Archbishop Bruchesi of Montreal, and Bishops Labrecque, La Rocque, Emard and Archambault were all former students of the French Seminary. It is not surprising, therefore, that the Congregation soon began to receive invitations to establish itself in

B. G. 3, 26   Canada. As early as 1862 it was offered the mission of Sandwich,

B. G. 4, 674
B. G. 9, 375

B. G. 23, 630
Piac. 231

B. G. 23,
630 ff.

B. G. 29, 334

Piac. 231

in West Canada, but lack of personnel prevented acceptance of this offer. In 1865, and again in 1870, the same fate befell a proposed College-Seminary in Kingston. Cardinal Taschereau in particular made several tempting offers to induce the Spiritans to settle in Canada. He went so far as to offer them the famous shrine of St. Ann de Beaupré, but to the surprise and pain of His Eminence even this was turned down by the Superior General, Father Emonet, who obviously did not realize the extent of the Cardinal's generosity.[11]

It was not till the beginning of the present century, under the pressure of threatening persecution in France, that serious thought was given to establishing the Congregation in Canada. At first, the plan involved founding a Canadian national institute of foreign missions, similar to the Foreign Missions of Paris, but some Canadian Bishops considered this project still too far advanced for their country. In 1905, Father Amet Limbour, who had taken up Archbishop Le Roy's search for a suitable work in Canada, bought a property of 1600 acres about five miles from Ottawa. The place has since come to be known as St. Alexander le Gatineau. When the owners realized that they had sold to a Catholic institution, they and the local Orangemen were furious—so furious in fact that they vainly offered to buy back the property at twice the price! The forest alone contained a million maple trees from which the famous Canadian maple syrup is produced.[12] Hydraulic energy up to 2000 H. P. was available in the Gatineau river; phosphate and mica deposits lay beneath the surface, and large expanses of arable land stretched out on all sides. Staffed by capable Brothers, the whole establishment could soon be self-supporting, and was admirably suited for the agricultural training school for French immigrants which the Fathers originally intended to begin there. However, very few Frenchmen could be induced to migrate to Canada, and fewer still considered themselves in need of long agricultural preparation. From 1912 on, therefore, St. Alexander became a junior seminary open to all aspirants to the priesthood, both diocesan or religious. Later, lay students also were admitted

---

[11]His successor, Cardinal Begin, was so distressed over this refusal that he still complained about it twenty years later.

[12]In early spring, when the trees are tapped, the community is host to thousands of people who come to sample this delicacy. Its guests have included dukes, governors and, during the second world war, the Dutch royal family.

and the whole became a regular college. From the start, its students were prepared to take official university examinations in classics and philosophy, and the college was affiliated with Laval University.

B. G. 31, 717 ff.; 33, 602 ff.

Until 1924, French and English divisions existed at St. Alexander and a surprising degree of harmony was maintained in spite of the antagonism between these national groups which Pope Benedict XV so greatly deplored. With an increasing enrollment, however, serious conflicts were bound to arise and, after some hesitation, the college administration decided to discontinue the English division, even though this meant the loss of eighty students. At that time, other colleges and seminaries in Canada were doing the same thing for similar reasons. Although St. Alexander's took only a few years to make up the loss and even to increase the number of students to the maximum its facilities would allow, one regrets that the Spiritans did not use these eighty English-speaking students as a nucleus for a new foundation.

At the end of their course of studies, aspirants to the priesthood trained in St. Alexander were, and still are, free to join any diocese or order of their choice. A rather large proportion of them have always preferred to enter the Congregation. Despite this steady flow of candidates, however, the Holy Ghost Fathers did not emulate other orders in expanding mightily after World War I when Canada awoke to its great potential in the apostolic

B. G. 33, 610

activities of the Church. *"Right now* there are immense apostolic possibilities here," the Superior of St. Alexander wrote to the Motherhouse, "but it is certain that our efforts will be destined to have very limited success as long as we have in Canada only the one house of St. Alexander, situated as it is at the extreme limit of the Quebec Province." Despite his pleas, however, nothing could be done immediately to improve the stiuation.

e. Switzerland

B. G. 13, 765

In 1885 the Spiritans assumed charge of two orphanages at Douvaine, near Geneva and close to the Swiss border. They

B. G. 16, 221

established a recruiting center there and then accepted an invitation in 1891 to take over St. Nicolas Industrial School for delinquent boys at Siviriez. This step was taken because political conditions were uncertain in France and the Congregation wanted

B. G. 17, 898

to attract Swiss candidates. Unfortunately, a number of circumstances kept the work from fulfilling expectations and the school was abandoned five years later. The time was not ripe for a Spiritan foundation in Switzerland.

B. G. 22, 645   When Combes' religious persecution began, however, the Congregation decided to build a senior seminary in Fribourg (1904) where younger members of the Congregation could reside while studying at the local university. This had to be accomplished with considerable legal ingenuity, for at that time Swiss laws did not allow new Congregations to establish themselves in the Alpine State. The foundation finally merited approval on the plea that its objective was to house university students. This seminary still exists and serves its original purpose as an interprovincial house of studies, to which all provinces send selected members to pursue higher studies.

In the same year (1904) another residence was opened in Fribourg. It is across the street from the seminary and it serves as an administrative annex of the Motherhouse. Then, too, shortly before the first world war (1913), the Spiritans rented a villa in Montana where tubercular members might recuperate in the B. G. 29, 600   pure mountain air. At the war's end, a sizeable gift enabled the Motherhouse to build a special sanatorium there. It still functions and serves not only the Congregation, but other priests and seminarians as well.

None of these establishments, however, aimed specifically at attracting Swiss aspirants. Rather, they served the needs of the B. G. 29, 284   Congregation in general. It was not before 1919 that increasing personnel needs induced the Spiritans to open a junior seminary at Bois-Noir, Valais. It was a pitifully small establishment that was constantly exposed to the threat of floods from a nearby torrent. Moreover, the local bishop opposed any enlargement of the seminary and thereby effectively prevented the Swiss Province from developing for many years.

f. Poland

B. G. 22, 688   In 1904, Princess Oginska invited Archbishop Le Roy and Father Acker, the Provincial of Germany to come to Poland and discuss the establishment of the Congregation in Bobrek, near the border of Hungary. As a start, she offered a large orphanage to which a junior seminary could be attached later. Father Acker also made some efforts on his own to open a house in

B. G. 32, 198

the diocese of Chelmno, but for some reason nothing came of these plans. After World War I, however, the memory of these visits still lingered on. Father Sigismond Rydlewski, a member of the American Province who served as chaplain to the Polish forces of Canada, France and Poland, proposed founding an orphanage at Welczak for the children of Polish war heros and learned to his surprise that the people there still spoke of the Holy Ghost Fathers. Permission was quickly granted, and the orphanage was opened in 1921. In the same year Father Kolipinski and Father Baranski found a bargain property at Bydgoszcz and the orphanage was transferred there during the

B. G. 34, 264

course of the next year. Because the house was too small to accommodate an orphanage, a junior seminary and a novitiate for clerics and Brothers, the Spiritans soon opened a novitiate at Dembowalonka where an old castle was available for immediate

B. G. 36, 350

occupancy and probably could be bought cheaply later on. However, this expectation was somehow thwarted, and at the end of 1925 the community was transferred to another recently purchased house in Bydgoszcz. Through the generous aid of American Spiritans and their friends, a new wing was added and the house became a full-fledged junior seminary. It looked very much as though a new province of the Congregation was now solidly launched.

6. *The First World War, 1914-1918*

C. L. 19, 4 ff.

This monstrous conflict, in which thirty-five million souls were locked in deadly combat, dealt cruel blows at the various European Provinces of the Congregation. In France, Belgium, and Germany, 600 Fathers, Brothers and seminarians of military age were called up for armed service or for war-time duties. In the enemy nations recruitment almost came to a standstill.

B. G. 29, 624

France alone had one hundred and ninety aspirants in military service[13] and saw no way of replacing them.

B. G. 30, 415

---

[13]During the war, 320 French members of the Congregation were mobilized; 81 of them killed in battle; 108 received a total of 169 citations or decorations for bravery. A survey of twenty-four orders and congregations show that 7,873 of their members saw military service: they earned a total of 3,578 citations and decorations for bravery; 1,278 of them were killed in action. It is to be noted that all but four recognized congregations had been exiled, yet all of them responded immediately to the call for military duty in defense of a country that did not even permit them to live on its soil!

The effects of the conflict made themselves acutely felt in the African Missions as well. Many missionaries were drafted and others joined the war as military chaplains. Although the fighting on African soil was rather limited, half a dozen Spiritan missions in Tanganyika were wrecked by advancing Boer armies from South Africa. Their German personnel were taken prisoners and sent to internment camps in India and Egypt.

C. L. 19, 4 f.

When peace finally came, the Congregation counted its losses in one hundred and twenty-four of its men killed outright on the battlefield or fatally wounded; scores of others returned maimed for life or broken in health; and the general membership was reduced from 1,804 in 1914 to 1,665 in 1919.

Despite these losses, Spiritans rallied to the call when the Holy See asked the Congregation to replace those German missionaries who had worked in the former German colony of the Cameroons. Obviously, it was more important than ever to intensify the campaign for vocations. Under the energetic direction of Archbishop Le Roy, strenuous efforts were made in this direction and dramatic results crowned the endeavor. By 1920 there were again 145 novices and 940 aspirants preparing to join the Congregation.

7. *The Missions*

a. THE INAUGURATION OF MISSIONS IN THE INTERIOR OF BRAZIL

B. G. 19, 531

In 1893, Father Xavier Libermann, a nephew of the Venerable Francis, had been appointed official visitor of the Holy Ghost Missions and communities in the West Indies and South America. From Peru, he travelled over the Andes to Buenos Aires and in the course of his trip he met the newly-appointed Bishop of Manaos. The Bishop appealed to him for priests and emphasized the need by reporting that there were parts of his immense diocese which had not seen a priest for over a hundred years. When the Holy See reinforced the bishop's plea in 1897, Archbishop Le Roy sent Father Libermann with three Fathers and two Brothers to the bishop's rescue. Just then someone providentially contributed enough money to buy a small steamer, a most essential item of equipment since all traffic in the interior of Brazil goes by water. A Brother purchased the boat in Philadelphia and delivered it to Manaos.

At once two missions were started: one in Manaos itself and the other deep in the jungle at Tefe, several weeks away by boat. These regions are so wild that, as someone said, God has not yet finished creating them. They are sometimes more realistically called the Green Hell. Nonetheless, the Fathers and Brothers set to with axes and machetes to reclaim a part of the jungle at Boca de Tefe. Laboriously cutting boards from tree-trunks by hand, they constructed a small residence for themselves and a large building in which Spiritan Brothers soon began to teach agriculture and various trades that would be useful in these remote regions.

B. G. 22, 8 ff.; 23, 821 ff.

Meanwhile the Fathers busied themselves with the spiritual care of the people confided to them by the Bishop of Manaos. Their zeal and charity contrasted sharply with the indolence of the few native priests, who looked on enviously while people flocked to the Spiritans from every direction. Soon their work suffered from numerous restrictions: their jurisdiction was limited, their subsidies were cut off, their church was "closed for repairs", and a newspaper campaign was launched against the intruders. There seemed to be no alternative to withdrawal.

Ap. H. 66 ff.

However, the Holy See definitely opposed leaving the whole territory of the Manaos diocese—three times the size of Texas —in the hands of the half dozen secular priests who constituted the entire diocesan clergy. It urged the Spiritans to stay on and make the best of it until part of the diocese could be erected into a separate ecclesiastical territory. This occurred in 1910 when the bishop died and a Spiritan-trained priest, Father Frederic Costa[14] became his successor. Realizing the impossibility of manning his immense diocese with his own priests, the new prelate allowed five new circumscriptions to be carved from his domain: the Prelatures of Upper Purus and Rio Branco, and the Prefectures of Tefe, Upper Solimoes and Rio Negro. The Holy See entrusted Tefe, the largest of the new circumscriptions, to the Congregation. Two years later, the upper Jurua regions in the Territory of Acre were added to this and the Spiritans

B. G. 24, 140; 306 ff.

---

[14]He had studied at the College which the Congregation had opened at Belem (Para) in 1885.

now found themselves charged with a river basin stretching over two thousand miles.

B. G. 23, 827

Meanwhile the Government was much impressed by the amazing success which the Spiritan Brothers had achieved in their agricultural and technical school at Boca de Tefe, and in 1905 it asked them to take over a similar State-owned institute at Paracatuba, near Manaos, the famous jungle capital of the Amazones. They accepted the offer, but the school lasted only three years. By then another Governor had come to power and his hostility to the Church forced the Brothers to withdraw from their new school. Falling back on Boca de Tefe, they continued their educational work. Since then, it has operated regularly down to the present, interrupted only for a brief time during the Second World War, when a critical personnel shortage caused a suspension of its activities.

B. G. 24, 695; 25, 195

b. The Congregation and the Old French Colonies

D. C. 333 ff.

All things considered, the separation of Church and State did more good than harm to the Catholics of France by giving the Church a new freedom along with its enforced poverty. The same cannot be said, however, at least not immediately, with respect to the old French colonies of Martinique and Guadeloupe in the West Indies, and of Reunion in the Indian Ocean. Frightened by the prospect of threatened riots, the local government officials did not dare to confiscate the churches. The local bishops warned them that, if they touched the rectories, all priests would be withdrawn. Consequently, they abstained from seizing the priests' residences although they did liquidate all other church properties, including all Mass endowments, and they stopped the payment of salaries to the clergy, except those few who were official chaplains in State institutions. Because people had been accustomed for generations to see the State take care of all expenses for the maintainance of churches and the clergy, they paid little heed at first when their Bishops appealed for support. As a result, the Church was rapidly approaching a state of financial crisis.

In addition, the secular clergy itself was slowly disappearing. Since 1890, various pressures from the Government had reduced the number of priests to a bare minimum. After 1905 the French Government systematically refused to inscribe any new priests on the list of colonial clergy. In the interim, death, disease, old age, and departures further decimated the ranks of the survivors. Many formerly flourishing parishes were now without priests, and in Martinique the entire northern half of the island had no resident pastor.[15] In 1909 the situation had grown so desperate that the Holy See once more put the old French colonies under the Propaganda.

D. C. 337 ff.

Before very long the Propaganda saw that it would have to confide these territories to a religious organization capable of assuming responsibility for them. As one might expect, its choice fell on the Holy Ghost Fathers whose entire past history made them logical candidates for the task. Moreover, they were the only religious congregation that already had establishments in these colonies. No wonder, then, that it came as something of a surprise to the Propaganda when the Spiritans reacted unfavorably to the proposal. In fact, they did their very best to have the honors and the burdens of insular administration transferred elsewhere. While they were quite willing to prepare a secular clergy for the colonies and to undertake auxiliary works such as colleges, social works and mission bands, the Holy Ghost Fathers had no desire to staff parishes, chanceries, and episcopal sees. Once again, as they did when Father Schwindenhammer decided to send more men to these colonies, the missionaries in Africa raised their voices in vigorous protest. They feared that these "new" missions would absorb too much of the total potential available for the apostolate. Archbishop Le Roy, himself a veteran African missionary, was inclined to be sympathetic to their view.

The Propaganda, however, was not to be dissuaded since no other organization offered the remotest chance of success. Moreover, the French Government, anticlerical as it was, now grew more and more alarmed over the results of its folly in disorganizing the religious services of the old colonies and it concurred fully with the Propaganda's proposed solution. Nonetheless, the Congregation still turned a deaf ear. New objections were raised until at last the Roman Procurator of the Congregation told Archbishop Le Roy that "the Cardinal Prefect of the Propaganda and his secretary had had enough of his evasive action." Pope Pius X

D. C. 46
Roy, 183

[15]The volcanic eruption of Mount Pelé in 1902 had killed twenty-six priests, seventy-one Sisters, and 30,000 people. Seven parishes were wiped out, as was also the College of the Holy Ghost. When the danger of new eruptions had passed, the survivors returned to their farms and villages, but there were no priests available to restore religious services.

was on the point of giving a personal and formal order. It was high time to submit to the wishes of the Holy See.

C. L. 13, 2

ibid., 3

D. C. 341

B. G. 26, 571; 669

B. G. 28, 347

The official document entrusting the three dioceses, as well as the Prefectures of Guiana and St. Pierre et Miquelon to the Congregation bears a trace of the long resistance: it does not say that the Spiritans have consented to accept them. Instead, the text states that "We have considered it opportune that [the Holy Ghost Fathers] consent to assume them again." In accepting the decision "with respectful submission" because he was "unable to escape from the imposed task," Archbishop Le Roy tried to follow the practice of not proposing any Holy Ghost Fathers as residential bishops, but when the Propaganda first refused his proposed diocesan priests because they were not members of a religious congregation and then a religious because he was not a Spiritan, the Superior General finally realized that he had no alternative. Again, the Roman documents appointing the first Spiritan Fathers to the bishoprics of these islands give evidence of their reluctance to become residential bishops: "Considering the present circumstances, we have decided to entrust the Diocese of . . . . to the care of the Holy Ghost Fathers." From then on, the Congregation had to resign itself to having a number of residential bishoprics reserved for its members. In 1916 this same arrangement was extended to the British island of Mauritius in the Indian Ocean.

D. C. 221 ff.
C. L. 13, 15

E. C. 33 ff.

One of the immediate benefits flowing from this new state of affairs was the seriousness with which priestly vocations were now promoted in these territories. Previously, the secular bishops had in general been quite conservative in this respect. The Spiritans followed a different policy. They decided to foster vocations prudently but nonetheless diligently and the policy eventually produced gratifying results. In the future, most of the students at Holy Ghost Seminary were recruited from these territories rather than from France.

c. Progress in Africa

cf. pp. 440 ff.

In Chapters XIX and XX the reader will find a fuller discussion of developments in Africa, but for the present a few facts and figures may be found helpful in assessing the extent of missionary advancement under Archbishop Le Roy's generalate.

E. P. 7, 69
C. A. 1925

In 1895, just before Le Roy became Superior General, the Holy Ghost Fathers were responsible for the ten ecclesiastical circum-

C. S. E.
69 ff.
scriptions of Senegambia, Sierra Leone, Southern Nigeria, the Two Guineas (Gabon), the French Congo, Ubangi, the Lower Congo, Cunene, Cimbebasia, and Zanguebar. Three hundred and twenty-six Fathers and Brothers dispersed over seventy-four residences supervised two hundred and ninety-one native schools, took care of 14,239 Christians, and prepared 11,420 pagans for baptism in that year alone. By 1926, at the end of his generalate, the number of ecclesiastical circumscriptions manned by Spiritans in continental Africa had grown from ten to eighteen through the addition of the Cameroons, Northern Katanga in the Belgian Congo, Kroonstad in South Africa, and by the division of other missions into autonomous Vicariates or Prefectures. In addition, the Congregation was charged with eleven ecclesiastical areas outside the African continent. The number of Fathers and Brothers in Africa had risen to five hundred and thirty-four, and the statistics of 1925 showed a total of one hundred and fifty-seven residences, with two thousand five hundred and forty-three schools in Africa alone. The Fathers cared for 385,563 Christians and instructed 232,200 pagans for baptism. The number of native priests, Brothers and Sisters had risen from twenty-four in 1895 to one hundred and fourteen by 1925. Without question, the Church was making giant strides throughout these parts of the Dark Continent.

d. The Return to the Belgian Congo

Ap. H. 300 ff.
B. G. 12, 711 ff.
Storme, 536 ff.
Aequatoria,
1950, 67 ff.; 93
ff.; 1951, 41 ff.
Early Work in the Congo. Since 1865 the Holy See had entrusted the Prefecture of the Congo[16] to the Congregation. From this Prefecture, Spiritan Fathers travelled inland and became the first Catholic missionaries to penetrate the regions which now constitute the Belgian Congo. As early as 1876, Father Carrie, later Bishop Carrie, Vicar Apostolic of Loango, went from Landana in what is now the Portuguese Congo up the Congo River to Boma. There a local king sold him a hill which seemed to provide an eminently suitable site for his mission.[17] After the necessary building materials were prepared in the workshops of the Landana Mission and two exploratory trips had been made up
M. C. 13, 1 ff.
the river, the first priest went to live in Boma in March 1880. Per-

---

[16]This Prefecture was erected in 1766, but had been without an occupant for many years.

[17]For the contract of purchase see *B. G. 12, 714*.

manent buildings were immediately constructed and, although the mission was dedicated to Our Lady of Victories, the hill which dominates the river has ever since been known as Mount Holy Ghost.

Another piece of land was donated to the mission by a local Portuguese commercial agent, but political problems arose when this man was replaced by another agent who refused to recognize the gift and appealed to the commander of a Portuguese gun boat to back up his position. At this juncture, Father Carrie announced that he had already appealed to the Admiral of a French naval force at the mouth of the Congo. The implied threat effectively forestalled any further difficulty.

It should be remembered that the colonial powers were dividing Africa among themselves during the eighties. With the exception of the Dutch, other colonial-minded European nations were busily engaged in expanding their coastal factories and blockhouses into full-sized colonies. Willy-nilly, but sometimes quite intentionally, the missionaries themselves became involved in these political enterprises. To carry on their missionary work among savage tribes, they needed support and protection. Usually, the only source of such protection was the local colonizing power. Where two or more nations had designs on the same territory, any missionary who did not collaborate in the plans of his own nation exposed his confreres in Africa to the danger of incurring the displeasure of the home government and the resentment of its

cf. pp. 504 ff.   local representatives. On the other hand, it must be admitted that a few of these apostolic figures experienced great difficulty in distinguishing between religion and politics. In their eyes, France was equated with Catholicism while England (or Germany) was identified with Protestantism. Where this opposition did not play a role, as in conflicts of interest between France and Portugal or France and Belgium, nationalistic motives were likely to exercise too much influence on their actions.

B. G. 12, 723 ff.   The next year, 1881, the future "Cannibal Bishop," Father
M. C. 13, 447   Prosper Augouard, set out with a caravan of thirty-two carriers
f.; 517 ff.; 14,   on a twenty-seven-day march along the Congo River to Stanley
100 f.; 113 f.;   Pool. After a cordial reception by the local king who had re-
125 ff.; 140 f.   cently been visited by the French explorer Brazza, Father
Augouard selected a site for his future mission near the present city of Leopoldville, the Capital of the Belgian Congo. Stanley

was then in the employ of the King of the Belgians and had reached the place five days before him, but the natives were most unfriendly to him when he came. On Brazza's suggestion, therefore, the French Government sent a subsidy of 11,000 francs for the mission which Augouard planned to establish near Stanley Pool. Brazza's desire to work hand in hand with this valiant Spiritan is evident from the following excerpt from one of his letters:

B. G. 12, 727

> Father, you are working for your God, who is also mine. I am working for my country, which is also yours. We shall succeed in making civilization penetrate these regions and, as you say, in making the name of our France known and loved in them.

B. G. 13, 921

Situated above the waterfalls of the Congo at the beginning of nearly one thousand miles of navigable water, the mission occupied an extremely important strategic position. As a matter of fact, in the near future it was to become the site of the Congo Capital and the starting point of nearly all other Congo missions. It is not surprising, therefore, that the French Government gave Brazza 1,270,000 francs in 1882 to colonize the area for France. With high hopes, then, Father Augouard set out from Landana with a hundred and twenty carriers and great quantities of building supplies for the new mission, but when he arrived at the designated area, he found the natives' disposition so much changed that he decided to withdraw to the other side of the Congo River and construct his new mission at Linzolo.

B. G. 13,
945 ff.
M. C. 18,
10 ff.; 17 ff.;
28 f.; 56 f.;
69 ff.; 80 ff.;
92 ff.; 103 ff.
B. G. 14, 516

In 1885 this intrepid priest travelled over the Congo River right up to the equator and reached the spot now occupied by Coquilhatville, where he bought a huge piece of land for another mission. At the same time he established another center at Kuamouth, a station of the International Congo Association[18], five days' march from Brazzaville. The next year, in 1886, he founded his last mission in Belgian Congo territory at Nemlao on the northern bank of the river. The project came into being under particularly trying circumstances, for local tribesmen repeatedly invaded the compound to destroy and plunder under the pretext of removing the curse

---

[18] The International Congo Association was the forerunner of the Independent State of the Congo, established in 1885 by the Berlin Conference. In 1908 the Independent State become a colony of Belgium.

emanating from one or other piece of furniture which, they said, was responsible for the current drought. On one occasion the missionaries had to be rescued by the combined military forces of a neighboring Belgian army post and a French factory.

Storme, 644 ff.

The Departure. Father Augouard's close collaboration with Brazza, the promoter of a French protectorate, soon aroused the suspicions of Stanley and his patron, King Leopold of Belgium. It should not be surprising, therefore, that when the Conference of Berlin (1885) recognized the Independent State of the Congo under the sovereignty of King Leopold, there was little if any inclination to leave these Congo missions of the Congregation in the hands of French priests. Since, politically speaking, Leopold felt that Frenchmen were not to be trusted, he requested and obtained from Pope Leo XIII an assurance that only Belgian missionaries would be assigned to the Independent Congo. Unfortunately, the Holy Ghost Fathers had very few Belgian nationals in the Congregation in 1886. Father Emile Callewaert was the only Belgian Spiritan in the Congo and the Province of Belgium had not yet been founded. When a mission seminary for the Congo was founded in 1886 at Louvain and failed to generate sufficient interest, the Holy See asked the young Belgian Scheut Congregation to take charge of evangelizing the Independent Congo. The Holy Ghost Fathers, after transferring the residence of Kuamouth to Brazzaville on the French bank of the Congo, stayed a few more years in the stations of Nemlao and Boma until the Scheut Fathers were able to relieve them.

K. K. A. 79
B. G. 14, 498

B. G. 14, 601 f.

Storme, 684 ff.
B. G. 15,
619 ff.

B. G. 24, 41 f.

The Return. Obviously, the young Congregation of Scheut was not able to cover the nearly one million square miles of Congo territory alone. In the extreme east, the White Fathers, who already had started a Province in Belgium, retained control of their missions and a few years later the Jesuits, the Trappists, the Redemptorists and many other orders came to the Scheut Fathers' aid. As soon as the Spiritans had established their first foundations in Belgium (1900) and the Netherlands (1904), they indicated that they were ready to resume missionary activity in the Belgian Congo. The Scheut Fathers were quite willing to assign the Katanga section to them, but first it was necessary to obtain the permission of the Congo authorities in Brussels.

cf. pp. 251 ff.

Difficulties arose immediately, for official archives contained a full account of the political activities in which Father Augouard had engaged.   Although some of these activities had been grossly misinterpreted, the Congo authorities refused to allow French Holy Ghost Fathers into the territory and frankly showed their displeasure that the Scheut Fathers were willing to cede Katanga to such *personae non gratae*.   After extensive negotiations and discussions, Father Callewaert and Archbishop Le Roy managed to convince Brussels that the proposed mission was politically harmless.   In Katanga the Spiritans would be more than a thousand miles away from the scene of the old Franco-Belgian rivalries. There would be no danger of political infiltration and the mission would provisionally remain under the control of the Scheut Fathers until it was staffed by Belgian and Dutch members of the Congregation.   Moreover, the mission would be under the direction of Father Callewaert, a Belgian citizen and a veteran of the Congo.

On the basis of these guarantees, Brussels finally acquiesced to the proposition and recognized the Spiritans as official missionaries, with all the rights and privileges thereunto attached. B. G. 24,361   In what appears to be an endeavor to show that there were no hard feelings over the past, they even added a few special favors, such as free transportation from Belgium to the mission, payment of installation costs, and an annual subsidy.   By 1907, everything was settled.   Father Callewaert and three confreres set out on B. G. 26, 250   their ten-week voyage from Antwerp to Katanga.   Four years later, the Holy See erected there a special Prefecture for the Holy Ghost Fathers and named Father Callewaert its ecclesiastical superior.

e. Repercussions of the Portuguese Revolution in Angola

B. G. 25, 600   The suppression of religious orders by the revolutionary government in Portugal could easily have resulted in persecution of the missionaries who were working in Angola and Portuguese Congo, and their expulsion would have destroyed all missionary work in these territories.   To prevent such a disaster, Archbishop Le Roy ordered the Fathers and Brothers in Angola and the Congo to appeal to the Berlin Conference of 1885, the Anglo-Portuguese Treaty of 1891, and the Brussels Conference of the same year, all of which guaranteed the freedom and protection of religious missions.   They were directed to stay at their posts, no matter what happened.   "If the missions are confiscated, withdraw into native huts," he commanded.

(marginal notes)
B. G. 24,361

B. G. 26, 250

B. G. 25, 600
Correia, II,
67 ff.

B. G. 26, 43 ff. ;
146 ff. ; 176 ff. ;
189 ff. ; 243 ff.

In general, however, the colonial officials were well disposed and tried to minimize the effect of political upheavals at home. Arguing that the decree of suppression was not applicable to the colonies, they resisted the efforts of local Portuguese settlers—many of whom were deported criminals bent on plunder—to drive the missionaries from their residences. Occasionally, it is true, subordinate local officials temporarily closed a mission, arrested a priest, or submitted the Fathers to vexatious treatment. Thus, for instance, in Cabinda, when a few semi-intoxicated officers caused a riot during the Christmas Midnight Mass in 1911, the resulting inquiry charged the celebrant and his assistant with attempted murder. Although the ridiculous charge had to be dropped, it supplied fuel to the anti-religious campaign.

The occasional closing of a mission, however, did not deter the missionaries. Following instructions faithfully, the Spiritans refused to depart. They appealed to the international treaties, and sought support for their appeal by calling on foreign consuls. For the most part, therefore, things did not go beyond recriminations, threats, and ridicule. The higher colonial officials realized all too well how much public law and order depended on the work of the Holy Ghost Fathers and they hesitated to play into the covetous hands of other colonial powers by giving them a pretext for moving in on Portuguese territories. Moreover, a famine and a number of native revolts occupied the government so fully that it had neither the time nor the energy to persecute missionaries. As a result, the Spiritan effort in Angola and Portuguese Congo did not suffer too severely from the Revolution at home. Even Government subsidies to the missions were maintained, although on something of a reduced scale.

f. The Return to the Cameroons

B. G. 30, 723
Vogt 72 ff.

Early Efforts. As early as 1883, the Holy Ghost Fathers traversed their immense Vicariate of the Two Guineas to explore the possibility of establishing missions in the section known as the Cameroons.[19] They had been invited to come by two Polish explorers who had settled there and acquired vast tracts of land. One of the two Poles ceded his properties to the Congregation as

---

[19]The region derives its name from the Portuguese explorer Fernando Po, who discovered the mouth of the Wuri River in 1472 and called it Rio dos Cameroes, i.e. Shrimp River.

a contribution toward the new mission. Meanwhile, however, the German explorer Dr. Nachtigal had entered the picture and proclaimed the protectorate of Germany over that same territory. He was well-disposed toward the Spiritans and encouraged them to begin their missionary work at once. Similar encouragement came from the German Admiral Knorr, who commanded the German navy stationed in the area, and from Baron von Soden, the first German colonial governor. As a matter of fact, the German authorities went to visit the Fathers in Gabon, were delighted with what they saw, and urged them to come to the Cameroons and establish similar works there. Since Alsace had become part of Germany in 1871, the Alsatian Father Stoffel was sent to select a suitable site. The native population welcomed him and he was able to obtain the tract he considered ideal for the purpose.

B. G. 13, 812

Before any mission could be inaugurated, however, it was necessary to obtain authorization from Bismarck, the German Chancellor. Despite the pleas of Dr. Nachtigal, Admiral Knorr, and Governor von Soden, and despite the pressure exercised by German politicians, Bismarck obstinately refused to admit the Congregation to the Cameroons. He stubbornly maintained that he wanted no Jesuits in German-controlled territory. As the reader will recall, for some mysterious reason we have not been able to fathom, the "Iron Chancellor" persisted in seeing a disguised Jesuit in every Holy Ghost Father. Father Stoffel could achieve nothing beyond a promise that Catholic missionaries would not be excluded from the Cameroons. As a result of Bismarck's obstinacy, Rome had to separate the Cameroons from the Two Guineas in 1890. It then erected a special Prefecture for the territory which it entrusted to the German Province of the Pallotine Fathers. These priests did magnificent work in the colony and quickly transformed it into a very flourishing mission. In twenty-four years, starting from nothing, they established fifteen central residences and reported 30,000 Christians by the beginning of World War I.

B. G. 15, 633

Vogt 73 f.

The Return. This isolated German colony was unable to resist the superior forces of the Allied armies which converged upon it from British Nigeria, French Guinea and the Belgian Congo, and by February 1916 all resistance had ceased. Despite the preventive efforts of Catholic chaplains in the Allied armies, the military authorities decided to exile all German missionaries from the territory. Since the Allies were reluctant to leave the missions unoccupied, the Commander of the French army then released five Spiritan chaplains from his forces to take care of abandoned missions. This small group was a scant substitute for the thirty-five German priests, thirty-nine Brothers and thirty-three Sisters who had been banished, and the army was subsequently induced to release seven other Holy Ghost Fathers who were on the point of being called up for military service.

This pitiful number was all that could be spared under the circumstances, and it should be emphasized that the circumstances were particularly difficult. All possessions of the missions had been temporarily sequestered by the occupying powers, the country was ravaged by war, and the whole organization of the Church had been wrecked by the exile of German clerics just at the moment when a mass movement of the population toward the Church had gotten under way. Moreover, it was impossible to regulate the religious status of the Cameroons in any definite fashion till long after the war. The uncertainty of the political situation made it difficult to undertake anything of a definitive nature. Finally, in 1923, although the Spiritans were not especially anxious to add another 166,000 square miles to their African responsibilities, the Holy See entrusted the French-controlled section of the Cameroons to the Congregation. The smaller British-controlled part of the territory was given over to the Mill Hill Fathers. Bishop Francis Xavier Vogt, who had been Administrator of the Cameroons since 1922, became Vicar Apostolic of this mission. Under his direction it was destined to develop into one of the finest in all Africa.

g. THE RETURN TO SOUTH AFRICA

B. G. 33, 154 ff.   *Early Work.* In Chapter VIII it was noted that Father Duparquet took over the Prefecture of Cimbebasia in 1879. It was a vast area covering a large part of Angola, South-West Africa, and Bechuanaland. By 1886 this tireless pioneer had penetrated as far as Mafeking, on the border of Transvaal, and established there a Holy Ghost Mission. Father Thomas Fogarty was appointed Vice-Prefect Apostolic of this new missionary enterprise, which itself covered a territory twice the size of Texas.

B. G. 13, 1386

B. G. 14, 595 ff.

Because there was little prospect of success among the already Methodist natives in the neighboring villages, the Fathers decided to direct their efforts toward the gold mining district of Malmani B. G. 15, 70 ff. in Transvaal. However, by 1889, the constant opposition of Protestant missionaries and the difficulty of communication between this mission and its headquarters on the West Coast—about a thousand miles away as the crow flies—caused the Spiritans to B. G. 16, 605 ff. withdraw from Mafeking. Three years later, at the request of the Congregation, the Holy See entrusted the whole of South West Africa, then a German colony, to the Oblates and Bechuanaland became an integral part of the Vicariate of the Orange Free State (Kimberley).

B. G. 31, 421   *Return.* It was not until after the First World War that the Spiritans returned to South Africa. In 1923 the Prefecture of Kroonstad in the Orange Free State was separated from the Oblate mission of Kimberley and confided to the German Province of the B. G. 31, 745 Congregation. Hampered by lack of personnel, the Oblate Fathers had established only two posts in the territory and these had a combined Catholic population of 350. Since most of these were whites, the native population had received scant attention. Under B. G. 31, 557 the energetic direction of the new Prefect, Monsignor Klerlein, the German Fathers and Brothers went to work. Their efforts were so successful that in 1951 the Holy See created the two Dioceses of Kroonstad and Bethlehem to serve what was once the old Prefecture.

h. A CONFLICT IN KENYA

Although the time has not yet come to present a full picture of the conflict which caused considerable trouble in Kenya Colony, British East Africa, we cannot pass over it in complete silence. B. G. 21, 499 ff.   In 1901 the Congregation was approached by a priest who had just founded a new missionary institute. He requested permission to send some of his priests and Brothers to the Zanzibar Vicariate of the Holy Ghost Fathers. They intended to stay only a short while to acquire some experience in missionary work before undertaking the evangelization of the Gallas tribes in Southern Ethiopia. *ibid.*   "Desirous of favoring as much as possible the development of new apostolic societies," the Congregation and Bishop Emile Allgeyer, the Vicar Apostolic of the Zanzibar mission, readily consented to admit them as auxiliaries on condition that they take care of their own expenses, limit themselves to the district assigned to their activity, remain under the jurisdiction of the Vicar Apostolic of Zanzibar, and not request the Propaganda that part of the Vicariate be ceded to them without previous authorization of the Vicar Apostolic and the Superior General of the Holy Ghost Fathers. Upon their written guarantee to observe these conditions faithfully, Bishop Allgeyer welcomed them to his jurisdiction and personally conducted them to one of the most promising sections of his Vicariate.

B. G. 21, 715

M. C. 38, 481 ff.

B. G. 23, 739 ff.   Trouble began soon after their arrival. The newcomers sent for reinforcements and began to disregard the limits assigned to their activity. When the Bishop complained about this, they appealed to Rome and obtained the erection of a separate mission extending over all of Kenya Province and had it assigned to their care. As a result, the Spiritans had to evacuate their residences in the area and fall back on what was left of their territory. Moreover, within the Zanzibar mission of the Holy Ghost Fathers itself, the new society obtained a residence and surrounding territory at Limuru where, they said, they had to have a procure.

B. G. 28, 360 f.   To make up for the lost stations, the Congregation founded new residences in Kikuyu land at Manga (1906) and Gatanga (1913), but in 1916 the newcomers produced a modified map showing that Gatanga was situated in their domain and therefore should be surrendered to them. Although for some strange reason the boundaries of their Vicariate on this map differed from the one indicated in the original document erecting the Kenya Mission, the Spiritans were willing to sacrifice Gatanga for the sake of peace, provided that the Limuru Station inside the Holy Ghost mission be returned to the Spiritan jurisdiction. The Propaganda tried to find a middle way by deciding that Limuru was indeed part of the Zanzibar Vicariate but that the procure in question should be transferred elsewhere "in the way and at the time" judged

B. G. 30, 527 f.   proper by the Propaganda itself. However, by 1922 the newcomers' Kenya Vicariate had added the Limuru district also to its domain and at the same time managed to secure permission to establish its priests in Nairobi itself, the very residential city of the Vicar Apostolic of Zanzibar. These men soon acquired a procure, a public church and a "Rest House" for Christians of their missions who desired to visit Nairobi!

B. G. 35, 119 f.   In 1931 these continual encroachments were partially redressed when a report of the Apostolic Delegate, Archbishop Hinsley, and of a special Apostolic Visitor, prompted Pope Pius XI personally to order the Limuru region restored to the Zanzibar Vicariate "without compensation of any kind," and to declare that this decision would "be and remain valid and effective forever." At the same time the Holy Ghost Fathers were directed "to cede voluntarily" the Laikipia region to the Nyeri Vicariate, which was one of the two missions into which the former Kenya Vicariate had been divided.

i. The Withdrawal from Spanish Guinea

B. G. 13, 805 ff.   In many regions of Africa the Spiritans had established missions long before these territories were effectively claimed by European colonial powers. One of these regions was the domain which is presently known as Spanish Guinea and which was then the object of political claims and counterclaims between France and Spain. As early as 1884, French Spiritans acceded to the request of the local populace and founded a residence at Bonito.

B. G. 15, 508 ff.; 16, 462 ff.   Although they were cordially received by most of the natives, it appears more than likely that one of the Fathers fell victim to poisoning. In addition, communications with their headquarters in Gabon proved difficult to maintain. However, when they decided to transfer the center of their activities to Bata in 1889 and abandon Bonito altogether, the natives appealed to the Spanish authorities at a nearby post and asked for priests from that quarter. Seizing the opportunity, the Spaniards promptly dispatched a steamer with a few Spanish priests and a copious supply of Spanish flags. Whereupon the French Governor of Gabon urged the Holy Ghost Fathers to re-occupy the post.

B. G. 20, 684   The political situation was not clarified until 1900 when France and Spain finally settled their claims on the disputed territory. A treaty of that date gave Spain control over about one hundred miles of coast-line and a depth of nearly one hundred and twenty

B. G. 21, 560   miles inland thereby bringing both Bata and Bonito into Spanish territory. Since the Spiritans were reluctant to give up the flourishing missions which they had established at the cost of such great

B. G. 22, 166   sacrifice, they decided to continue their work under the jurisdiction of the Spanish Vicar Apostolic of Fernando Po. As a matter of fact, the change in civilian administration was pleasant: instead

B. G. 24, 620

B. G. 26, 907

B. G. 22, 133

B. G. 22, 503
and 679

B. G. 29, 145
and 278

of dealing with troublesome anticlerical civil officials, the Fathers enjoyed cordial relations with a Spanish Governor who was in full sympathy with thier work. In 1908 Spain granted an annual subsidy of 18,500 pesetas for the support of the mission, and Father Fcrrc, the Religious Superior, was named municipal treasurer of Bata. With such encouragement, the Fathers did not hesitate to open another mission in Embula.

Meanwhile, the Congregation was seriously weighing the question of founding a Province in Spain so that it might have Spanish confreres for its works. For this purpose, a residence was established in Cogullada, near Saragossa (1903) but the next year a new Spanish law made the legal position of the Congregation too tenuous and the project was abandoned. The failure of this attempt, coupled with the pressing demands for personnel elsewhere, resulted in a regretful decision to withdraw from Spanish Guinea. While the First World War delayed the execution of this plan, the Spiritans ultimately surrendered their stations in the territory to Spanish missionaries in 1919.

8. *Revisions of the Rules and Constitutions*

C. L. 12, 7 ff.

Various Pontifical decrees regarding religious institutes of simple vows made it necessary to revise the Rules and Constitutions twice during Le Roy's generalate. On the occasion of the first revision, 1906-1909, there was question again of abolishing the Rules because Rome had decided that only religious orders founded before the Fourth General Council of the Lateran (1215) were permitted to have Rules as well as Constitutions. Although the Spiritans fell short of this date by nearly five centuries, the Holy See once again authorized retention of the Rules and looked on the Constitutions as an official commentary thereof.

We list here the most important modifications introduced in the 1909 revision:

1. As a religious institute, the Congregation was henceforth to be dependent on the Holy See through the Sacred Congregation of Religious which had just been established by the Pope.

2. The practice of remaining indefinitely in the Congregation without pronouncing perpetual vows was abolished. Hence-

forth after a period of temporary vows a member had to engage himself for life.

3. The Superior General was to be elected for a period of twelve years. His term of office could be renewed if he were to obtain at least two thirds of the votes.

Later, in 1917, the Holy See introduced its new Code of Canon Law. All religious orders and congregations were obliged to revise their rules or constitutions anew and bring them into consonance with the new general ecclesiastical law governing all religious institutes. The resulting modifications gave rise to the actual text of the Rules and Constitutions as it was published in 1922. Since then, no substantial changes have been made.

9. *The Missionary Sisters of the Holy Ghost and the Missionary Sisters of Killeshandra*

B. G. 30, 452 ff.
Roy, 234 ff.

Although the Spiritans had always been efficaciously assisted in their missionary work by several Congregations of Sisters, notably the Sisters of St. Joseph of Cluny, the extensive development of their missions at the beginning of the century caused a pressing demand for more Sisters capable of assuming charge of hospitals, dispensaries, schools for girls and the training of women for Christian motherhood. This situation led to the foundation of two new religious congregations of Sisters especially dedicated to assisting the Holy Ghost Fathers in their apostolic labors: the Missionary Sisters of the Holy Ghost in France and the Missionary Sisters of Our Lady of the Holy Rosary in Ireland. The first of these congregations was founded in 1921 by Archbishop Le Roy and three years later the first twenty-five of its members made their Consecration to the Apostolate. Since then the Sisters of the Holy Ghost have attained provincial organization in Portugal, the Netherlands, Canada and, of course, France. They aid the Fathers in many missions throughout Africa and the West Indies.

Shanahan,
288 ff.

At about the same time another Spiritan Bishop, Joseph Shanahan, of Nigeria, experienced great difficulty in securing enough nuns to teach the young girls in his territory. Like Archbishop Le Roy, he was encouraged by the Pope to start a new missionary institute for this specific purpose, but when he also wanted to call his projected congregation "The Missionary Sisters of the Holy

Ghost," Rome told him to choose another title lest it give rise to confusion. Accordingly, he selected the name "Missionary Sisters of Our Lady of the Holy Rosary" and placed the society under the special protection of the Holy Ghost. Their Motherhouse and novitiate were established at Killeshandra, Diocese of Kilmore, Ireland. This Congregation also has enjoyed the blessing of phenomenal growth. It renders splendid assistance to the Holy Ghost Fathers in their Nigerian missionary endeavors.

*   *   *   *   *

B. G. 32, 345 ;
387 ; 674

By 1925 the seventy-one year old Superior General's health began to deteriorate to such a degree that he received the last sacraments in October. Realizing that the Congregation should be led by a strong and vigorous man, Archishop Le Roy convoked a General Chapter and tendered his resignation. Oddly enough, once he was relieved of the burdens of office, the Archbishop's health improved sufficiently to accord him twelve additional years of life.

B. G. 37, 670
B. G. 38, 481

In 1938, two years after celebrating the sixtieth anniversary of his ordination, he closed a glorious career at the age of eighty-four years.

AVERAGE AGE AT DEATH OF HOLY GHOST FATHERS AND BROTHERS

IN CONTINENTAL AFRICA, 1843-1955

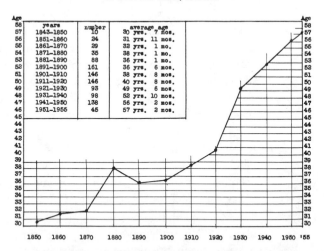

years	number	average age
1843-1850	10	30 yrs. 7 mos.
1851-1860	24	31 yrs. 11 mos.
1861-1870	29	32 yrs. 1 mo.
1871-1880	35	38 yrs. 1 mo.
1881-1890	88	36 yrs. 1 mo.
1891-1900	161	36 yrs. 6 mos.
1901-1910	146	38 yrs. 8 mos.
1911-1920	146	40 yrs. 8 mos.
1921-1930	93	49 yrs. 6 mos.
1931-1940	98	52 yrs. 10 mos.
1941-1950	138	56 yrs. 2 mos.
1951-1955	45	57 yrs. 2 mos.

These statistics are based on the district of death mentioned in the necrology of the Congregation. Between 1890 and 1910 one hundred and fourteen missionaries in Africa did not reach the age of thirty, and eighty-one others died between thirty and thirty-five years of age.
The worst years were: 1895 with an average age of 29 yrs. and 8 mos.
1896 with an average age of 32 yrs. and 1 mo.
1897 with an average age of 30 yrs. and 2 mos.
1898 with an average age of 33 yrs. and 2 mos.
1901 with an average age of 30 yrs. and 9 mos.

CHAPTER ELEVEN

THE GENERALATE OF ARCHBISHOP LOUIS LE HUNSEC, 1926-1950

1. *Introduction*

After the resignation of Archbishop Le Roy, an extraordinary session of the General Chapter was convened to elect a new superior general. On the second ballot nearly all votes went to Bishop Louis Le Hunsec, the Vicar Apostolic of Senegambia, who had come to the Chapter as Religious Superior of that District. It was the second time that the Chapter had elected a bishop, and, to prevent the system from becoming customary, the Holy See significantly added to its confirmation of the election that it did so "by way of a special favor . . . for this time" but it warned that "in the future those who have been raised to the episcopal dignity must not be elected to the office of Superior General of the Institute."

B. G. 32, 728 f.

Bishop Le Hunsec was born in 1878 in Britanny. At the age of twenty-one he joined the Congregation and was sent to Rome for doctoral studies in theology. After his ordination to the priesthood he taught philosophy for one year at Chevilly before he was granted permission to become a missonary in Senegal (1903). At the end of World War I he was elected a member of the General Council of the Congregation but he had hardly time to assume this function when an event took place which temporarily altered the course of his life.

B. G. 44, 35 ff.

On January 9, 1920, Bishop Jalabert of Senegambia and eighteen Spiritan Fathers and Brothers embarked on the SS *Afrique* on their way to Africa. Two days later the vessel was wrecked in a violent storm. All nineteen members of the Congregation were among the five hundred and sixty-three victims of the disaster who perished in the waves. Rome then appointed Father Le Hunsec to replace the deceased bishop as Vicar Apostolic of Senegambia. Only six years later, at the age of forty-eight, he became Superior General, a position he was destined to hold for two full terms of twelve years each until his advanced age caused him to beg his confreres not to re-elect him again in 1950. In 1945, on the occasion of the silver jubilee of his episcopal consecration, the Holy See

C. L. 20, 1 ff.

conferred on him the titular Archbishopric of Marcianopolis. He died on Christmas day, 1954, at the age of seventy-six.

With the generalate of Archbishop Le Hunsec we have reached the contemporary period of the Congregation's history, a period that has not yet passed through the crucible of time. We will therefore limit our story to a few salient points and reserve a more detailed report for the second part of this book wherein we will survey the work of the Holy Ghost Fathers throughout the world.

2. *The Affair of the "Action Française"*

Archbishop Le Hunsec had just laid his hand to the helm when his ship ran into the turbulence of the *Action Française*. Obviously the time has not yet come to present a definitive appraisal of the events conjured up by this name, but they have caused such widespread public comment that their complete omission from this book could not be justified.

The Action Française. The movement thus referred to was founded at the beginning of the twentieth century by Charles Maurras, a brilliant writer but a confessed atheist who had no regard for moral principles.[1] Oddly enough, Maurras somehow conceived a strange respect for the strong central authority and social consciousness of the Catholic Church. He edited a newspaper and a bimonthly review, both called *"l'Action Française,"* which for many years remained strictly orthodox—liberally quoting the Pope and Thomas Aquinas, campaigning against the errors of modernism,[2] and even defending the victims of French religious persecution. The paper went so far as to advise its Catholic subscribers not to read certain works of Maurras, the editor. It is not surprising, therefore, that many priests and prelates of the Church gave their enthusiastic support to the *Action Française*. The "integrists"[3] and the royalists were especially sanguine about the new movement. It had many defenders in Rome itself, and

---

[1] In 1939 Maurras was reconciled with Rome.

[2] Modernism is a system which endeavors to reduce all supernatural events to natural phenomena by means of "scientific" explanations. In the realm of politics it made the Church subordinate to the State.

[3] The "integrists" were militant antimodernists who in their zeal often went too far and denounced men for modernism when there was no ground for such an accusation. According to Sforza, when Cardinal della Chiesa become Pope Benedict XV in 1914, he found among the papers left on the desk of his predecessor a memorandum in which he himself was accused of modernism.

C. H. R. 18, 217

C. H. R. 18,
223

even Saint Pius X is said to have called Maurras *"un bel difensore della fede."*

A few prominent French bishops, however, grew alarmed at the growing influence of Maurras and Leo Daudet, his principal assistant. They strongly urged that certain of his works be condemned. Accordingly, in January 1914, a document proscribing these books was drawn up, but St. Pius X decided to postpone publication of the condemnation because he felt that the time was inopportune. The First World War and its aftermath prevented his successor Pope Benedict XV from carrying out the project and putting the works on the Index. Consequently, it was not before 1926, during the reign of Pius XI, that any action was taken against the *Action Française*. At that time, the Archbishop of Bordeaux publicly issued a condemnation. His words were published with a congratulatory message from Pius XI on the front page of the *Osservatore Romano*. The following year the Pope finally published the long-delayed condemnation of many of Maurras' books and of the *Action Française* itself. (The original document was dated January 29, 1914).

C. H. R. 18,
225 f.

While most bishops of France at once promulgated the papal decree in their dioceses, the names of one Archbishop and two Bishops were conspicuously absent from a document in which the French Hierarchy signified its submission to the Pope in this matter. A number of theologians, both secular and religious, continued to support the movement, alleging that submission to the Pope's decision in this instance was not necessary. Others externally submitted, but showed in their private conversations where their sympathies lay. Pope Pius XI decided to take stern measures in three notorious cases and make examples of three clerics who held very prominent positions: the famous Jesuit Cardinal Billot; the renowned Dominican theologian Father Pégues, Regent of St. Maximin Friary; and Father Le Floch, the Spiritan Superior of the Pontifical French Seminary in Rome.

Cardinal Billot had sent a letter to Leo Daudet, congratulating the leaders of the *Action Française* on their reply to their condemnation by the Archbishop of Bordeaux, although the Pope had already praised the Archbishop for his action. Shortly thereafter, Pius XI condemned Maurras, and the Cardinal offered to resign. His offer was accepted and the Superior General of the Jesuits personally conducted Billot to Gallero where he was to end his life in absolute retirement. Father Pégues' mistake had been to give a scandalous reply when he was consulted about reading the *Action Française*. Although he recanted six weeks later, he was nonetheless relieved of his office. Because Father Le Floch was a Holy Ghost Father, we shall have to analyse his case somewhat more in detail, especially since efforts were made to place the whole Congregation in jeopardy because of one member's imprudence.

B. G. 41, 69 f.   *Father Henry Le Floch.* Undoubtedly Le Floch was one of the most discussed figures in the *Action Française* affair. After joining the Congregation, he had been sent to Belgium and Italy for advanced studies. He held doctorates from the University of Louvain and from the Gregorian University in Rome. His appointment as Rector of Holy Ghost College in Beauvais was followed by his assignment to the directorship of the Senior Seminary of the Congregation at Chevilly. In 1904 Pope Pius X made him

B. G. 41, 371   Superior of the Pontifical French Seminary in Rome. In 1910 and again in 1912 there was question of making him a titular bishop to add dignity to his position in the Seminary and it was not without considerable trouble that the Superior General succeeded in preventing this ecclesiastical promotion on the grounds that it would have been contrary to the tradition of the Spiritans, who prefer to have no more church dignitaries among their members than is absolutely necessary.

B. G. 41, 377 f.   During the war years of 1914 to 1918, Father Le Floch spared neither time nor effort defending Benedict XV against certain French papers which alleged that the Pope was pro-German. By 1922, after the coronation of Pius XI, he had reached a position of exceptional influence in the Eternal City. He was a Consultor of the Holy Office, the Propaganda, the Consistory, the Congregation for Seminaries and Universities, and the Congregation for the Oriental Church, as well as an intimate friend of many Cardinals. He was highly regarded by the French episcopate—not less than

B. G. 41, 387   sixty of his students became bishops—and was the idol of many of his former seminarians. Moreover, success appeared to bless whatever he undertook. Inevitably, a man in such a favored position was bound to have enemies watching his every move in order to discredit him.

B. G. 41, 378   His downfall came about with dramatic swiftness. On May 25, 1927, Pius XI received the students of the French Seminary in a special audience. Father Le Floch pronounced the customary address. It contained an allusion which, as Pius XI later declared, he found shocking. Although Le Floch protested that he had spoken completely without malice, his words were quickly exploited by his enemies. At all events, when the Pope replied, he made no special reference to what had shocked him but he did speak sharply against the *Action Française* and went on to declare that to be in harmony with the Church it is not enough to come to Rome and study there. He cited the life and post-Roman works of de Lamennais to underscore his point.

B. G. 33, 148 f.
B. G. 41, 378 f.

A few days later, Archbishop Le Hunsec made his annual visit to Rome and was twice called into audience with the Pope. Ignorant of what had happened at the special audience, he was astonished to hear Pius XI complain that Father Le Floch was no longer a man to be trusted in his position and that an Apostolic Visitor had been appointed for the French Seminary. This Visitor was Dom Schuster, the Benedictine Abbot of St. Paul-Outside-the-Walls and the future Cardinal Archbishop of Milan. In his report to the Pope after the visit, Abbot Schuster stated that there was nothing worthy of blame in the Seminary as far as discipline, piety, and studies were concerned. While this statement was true, it would have been difficult to deny that the attitude of several students was free from reproach in matters political. Nevertheless, the Abbot's report did not supply any basis for proceedings against Father Le Floch. The trouble stemmed from a counter-report made by Cardinal Bisleti. According to the regulations governing apostolic visits, Le Floch should have abstained from all administrative activities while the Visitor was at the Seminary. Since this prescription had not been perfectly observed, someone reported the delinquency to the Cardinal Prefect of the Congregation of Seminaries and Universities, who in turn carried the whole matter to the Pope.

In July 1927, Archbishop Le Hunsec was called back to Rome. Pius XI demanded the immediate departure of Father Le Floch on the ground that he was an adherent of the *Action Française*. Although Le Hunsec tried to make a distinction between a royalist and an adherent of the *Action Française*, the Pope was adamant. He did, however, consent to the Superior General's request that the Superior of the French Seminary be permitted to resign. Father Le Floch complied at once and left Rome for Paris three days later. His brilliant twenty-three year term as seminary rector thus ended with tragic abruptness. The remaining twenty-three years of his long life—he died at the age of eighty-eight—were spent in retirement at the Novitiate of Orly and later in a chateau in southern France.

In spite of the unfortunate controversy, Father Le Floch's former students continued to hold him in high esteem. At the golden jubilee of his ordination in 1937, they composed a three hundred and fifty page book in his honor. Two years later, after the election of Pius XII, he travelled to Rome and was accorded a long and cordial audience by the present Pope. Nothing more is heard of him until 1950, when death closed his brilliant but sad career. One ventures to hope that some future historian will succeed in unveiling much that still remains obscure in this melancholy affair.

3. *The Expansion of Social Works: Father Daniel Brottier*

cf. p. 242

In Chapter X we have seen how development of many Spiritan social works was brought to a standstill by various persecutions. In France, the existing institutions had been able to maintain themselves under a "secularized" personnel. Outside France this type of activity had been engaged in to some extent in the United States and after World War I in Poland, but only on a small scale. As soon as conditions in France permitted its redevelopment there, Providence offered the Congregation an opportunity to engage in social endeavors to a degree that surpassed anything that had been done in the nineteenth century.

cf. pp. 347 f. ; 263

B. G. 37, 22

In 1923 Cardinal Dubois, the Archbishop of Paris, asked the Spiritans to take over the Orphans' Institute of Auteuil. Investigation showed, however, that the proffered work was not too attractive: the number of boys was relatively small, the buildings were dilapidated, the staff was underpaid and dissatisfied, and the deficit mounted with the years. Despite this bleak outlook, it was a work such as both Poullart des Places and Francis Libermann would have loved. The Motherhouse accepted.

Brot. 115 ff.

Auteuil Institute had its birth in 1865 when Father Roussel, a priest of the Archdiocese, saw an urchin groping through a heap of garbage on a cold winter day. Asked what he was looking for, the boy replied: "Something to eat." The priest promptly took him to the rectory, gave him a warm meal, and lodged him for the night. Eight days later he had six similar cases on his hands and the Institute was under way. Although Father Roussel had the satisfaction of seeing the work prosper during the thirty years he remained in charge of it, his successors helplessly watched its fortunes decline in the years of economic crisis immediately following World War I. By the time Cardinal Dubois appealed to the Spiritans, things had come to a desperate pass.

B. G. 37, 23   It was not the first time that the Congregation had been asked to take charge of the work. In 1876 Father Roussel himself had wanted to give it to the Spiritans. At that time the Institute was very prosperous and free from any debts and Father Schwindenhammer, then Superior General, favored acceptance of the proposal which "harmonized perfectly with the purpose of the Congregation." For some unknown reason, however, the affair came to nought when it was close to being accomplished. Forty-seven years later, when the Cardinal renewed the founder's request, the proposal was accepted.

Brot. 115   "Make sure that you choose capable personnel, for we must succeed," was the warning given by the Cardinal, when Le Roy notified him of his decision to accept. His words must have been taken to heart, for the man appointed to direct the new venture was Father Daniel Brottier. As subsequent events were to show, no better choice could have been made.

Brot. 11 ff.   Daniel Brottier was born in 1876 at Ferte-Saint-Cyr. Ordained a priest in 1899, he entered the Congregation three years later.
Brot. 23 ff.   In 1903 he was sent to Senegal as a missionary and it was not long before the young man began to reveal his organizational talents in the various tasks that were assigned to him in Dakar.
Brot. 41 ff.   In 1911, when Bishop Jalabert, the Ordinary of the place, needed a man capable of realizing an ambitious plan, no one was surprised that his choice fell on Father Brottier. The project in question was called the "African Memorial."

The originator of the plan had been Mr. Merlaud-Ponty, the Governor-General of French West Africa. One day, the Bishop spoke to Merlaud-Ponty about the need of a Cathedral in that fast growing city, and the Governor told him quite frankly that no help could be expected from the Government. On the other hand, he said, the idea of a Memorial honoring all Frenchmen whose bodies lie buried in unnamed graves throughout Africa would certainly have a strong national appeal. He himself would be willing to put his own name at the head of a list of supporters. The idea had possibilities. To exploit them, the Bishop placed Father Brottier in charge of an African Memorial Fund. Under the priest's enthusiastic direction, the Fund was making rapid progress when the First World War broke out and all plans had to be shelved until the armistice.

Brot. 67 ff.

The war gave a new turn to Father Brottier's career. He immediately enlisted as a military chaplain and before long acquired an almost legendary fame. Without the slightest regard for personal comfort or danger, he spent all his time where his help was most needed—in the front lines. Officers and soldiers alike admired and listened to the Padre whose heroic deeds earned him many citations and decorations.

When the fighting ended, Father Brottier set about to preserve the national unity which is so often shattered in France by political divisions. The best way, he decided, was to unite his former comrades-in-arms into one central organization: a League of War Veterans. To assure the necessary funds and support, he did not hesitate to pay a visit to Clemenceau, the "Tiger," who at that time was Prime Minister of France. Despite his bitter anticlericalism, the "Tiger" gave not only his wholehearted support but a personal gift of a hundred thousand francs as well. Encouraged in this way, Brottier launched his League of War Veterans under the slogan, "United as at the Front." The organization soon became a powerful factor in post-war France, but once it was established, the priest modestly withdrew and returned to his job as organizer of the African Memorial Fund.

Brot. 56 ff.

Despite the fact that he became Director of the Orphans' Institute of Auteuil in 1923, Brottier continued to devote himself to the raising of funds for the Memorial Cathedral. The foundation stone had been laid in 1922, but fourteen more years were to pass before the magnificent structure was finished and solemnly consecrated by Cardinal Verdier as the official Legate of Pope Pius XI. Built on the site of Dakar's old cemetery, where Libermann's first spiritual sons were buried, the massive monument dominates the harbor and stands as a silent witness to the Divine Majesty which is adored within its sacred walls.

Brot. 171 ff.

But the man whose untiring zeal gave Africa this glorious monument never saw it himself. With characteristic energy, he plunged into the problems of Auteuil and drew up a four-point program

Father Daniel Brottier, C.S.Sp., Founder of the French League of War Veterans, Organizer of the African Memorial, and Father of the Orphans of France, whose process of beatification has been begun.

The Auteuil Institute as it was when Father Brottier took over in 1923.

A view of the campus of the Auteuil Institute at the death of Father Brottier in 1936.

The Saint Philip Annex of Meudon, near Versailles, one of twenty branches of the Auteuil Institute.

for the work as soon as he was appointed its Director. Like a modern Don Bosco, he pledged himself:

1. To save as many homeless boys as possible by expanding the work at Auteuil itself.

2. To build a beautiful chapel in honor of Saint Therese of Lisieux, whom he had chosen as the heavenly Patron of the Institute, and to make this chapel a shrine for the Catholic population of Paris.

3. To generate interest in his work among the pilgrims flocking to the shrine and thus secure a necessary income for the realization of his plans.

4. To establish branches of the Institute in the country and thus save not just a few hundred boys but thousands of them. "The Orphans of Paris" were to become "the Orphans of France."

The Chapel was ready at the end of 1925 and immediately became the shrine its creator had envisioned. Every year on Saint Therese's feast day, fifty thousand Parisians flock to this place of pilgrimage.

Once the shrine was built, the number of boys began to increase rapidly. Soon Auteuil was as well known throughout France as Boys Town is in the States. Homeless youngsters began to arrive from all over the country. Although millions were spent on more dormitories, more workshops and other facilities, it was impossible to accommodate all deserving applicants. Up to two thousand times a year the poor Director had to repeat his heart-rending: "No, we have no room" to teen-age boys who hopefully looked to him as their last refuge. Intensifying his efforts to create space, Father Brottier began to open annexes throughout France. In five years' time no less than fourteen of them were founded. Only an insider can guess the amount of worry and care such an expansion added to the burden carried by this sickly priest who literally did not pass a single day of his life without enduring violent headaches. Even the tremendous expansion of facilities he had achieved did not suffice to take care of all applicants.

Brot. 213 ff.   Looking around for new ideas, Brottier was struck by the depopulation of rural France. Everywhere villagers were flocking to the big cities, while the farmers cast about anxiously for enough hands to gather in the harvest. Why not kill two birds with one stone, the priest thought, by placing suitable boys with farmers who would teach them to love the land and at the same time give them an opportunity to acquire their own homes in the country? In 1933 Father Brottier started the French equivalent of a Catholic Rural Life Conference. Within two years, close to five hundred boys had been placed with decent Catholic families and saved from the physical and moral miseries of city slums. Under the careful supervision of Brottier and other Spiritans, these youngsters were soon on their way to a happy Christian life in the peaceful French countryside.

Brot. 197 ff.

Despite all his efforts, however, there were still far too many for whom the priest could find no place. Unwilling to abandon them entirely, he expanded the existing First Communion Program. Four times a year a large group of boys from twelve to twenty years of age who could not be admitted permanently were allowed to come to Auteuil for a period of ten weeks. The time was used to give them an intensive preparation for their first Holy Communion. Father Brottier exercised such a marvellous influence over these boys that many of them returned totally transformed to their squalid surroundings in the city slums and became excellent promoters of a living Catholic Faith.

Brot. 391

When the saintly priest died in 1936, his Institute and its annexes sheltered fourteen hundred homeless boys. "The Orphans of Paris" had really become "the Orphans of France." Since then, the work has continued to prosper and grow. It now extends over a network of twenty establishments, directed by nearly sixty Spiritans and it takes care of close to four thousand boys. In this way the Congregation has once more emphasized the social role which Father Libermann had assigned to it on the European scene.

B. G. 44, 421

As a final note to this section on Auteuil, we are happy to report that in 1956, after the preliminary hearings in the Archdiocese of Paris, the process of Father Brottier's beatification was introduced in Rome.

4. *Nazi Persecution in Germany*

cf. p. 219 ff.

In Chapter IX the reader has seen how the German Province was restored when the Holy Ghost Fathers finally managed to

B. G. 21, 122
ff.; 22, 616;
24, 752 f.; 29,
544.
B. G. 27,
166 f.

B. G. 29, 276

B. G. 30, 39
and 107
B. G. 31, 853;
33, 771
B. G. 37, 117 ff.

B. G. 40. 397 ff.

convince the Government that they were not affiliated with the Jesuits. Under Father Acker's capable direction, new houses in addition to the Abbey of Knechtsteden were founded at Sabern (1900), at Neuscheuren (1904), at Broich (1908) and at Heimbach (1914). The German Government continued to favor him. It even invited him in 1913 to the imperial reception in honor of the Kaiser's jubilee, a celebration to which only the highest ranking personalities in the Reich were welcomed.

After the First World War, when Alsace was returned to France and the houses in this area became part of the French Province, it became necessary to restore the losses by new foundations in other parts of Germany. Meanwhile the Province had a new Superior, Father Leo Klerlein, the future Vicar Apostolic of Kroonstad in South Africa. He founded new junior seminaries in Donau-Eschingen, near the Swiss frontier, (1921) and in Speyer, the ancient Capital of the Holy Roman Empire (1922). In 1924 he was succeeded by Father John Hoffmann, who added a Provincialate in Cologne (1925) and another junior seminary in Menden, Westphalia (1927). In 1936 the Province had reached a total membership of 471 professed and 455 aspirants. No one then foresaw to what extent Father Hoffmann and his hardworking confreres were going to feel the full fury of religious persecution by the Nazis.

Later that same year, serious trouble began when Father Hoffmann and Father Pohlen, the Provincial Procurator, were sent to jail on unproved charges of having violated the complex foreign currency regulations of the Reich. Their imprisonment was followed by governmental attempts to uncover moral scandals in the junior seminaries of the Congregation. Nazi police officers subjected the boys to a brutal series of interrogations, but no trace of the alleged offenses could be discovered.[4] Once these trials were concluded, all seminarians and Brothers were forced to enroll in labor-camps, there to be indoctrinated in Nazi philosophy. It is a flattering testimony to the solidity of the scientific and religious training previously received by these young men that

---

[4]On one of the stairway walls at Broich there remains to this day a flamboyantly Gothic-lettered sign which the Nazis had painted there in the days of their pride: "The priests and their religion will never save Germany. Only the Fuehrer and his legions can do that." It has been preserved so that future generations of seminarians may ponder its tragic message as they pass by on their daily rounds.

not a single one of them embraced Nazism. On the contrary, political instructors in the labor-camps found their searching questions so troublesome that they became reluctant to give any more lectures to such a critical audience and finally dispensed them from attendance.

Now that the seminaries were almost empty, the Nazis began to "requisition" them for other purposes. Matters went so far that at the beginning of the Second World War not a single house remained at the free disposal of the Congregation. Then, toward the end of hostilities, the Government decided to sell the Abbey of Knechtsteden for the benefit of the National Food Board. Thanks, however, to the clever maneuvering of sympathetic officials, the sale was delayed long enough to allow the arrival of Allied troops in Germany to prevent the execution of this plan. Through the nucleus thus preserved, Father Hoffmann manfully undertook the second restoration of his Province when hostilities ended.

5. *The Second World War, 1939-1945*

In Europe. When Hitler's armies overran most of Europe, the Superior General stayed at the Motherhouse in Paris. Because it was almost impossible for him to exercise his functions under these conditions, he delegated most of his powers to the Superiors of the different Provinces throughout the Congregation. At the same time he tried to keep in contact with the outside world by means of a secretary who resided at Vichy in the unoccupied part of France. The darkest day for the Motherhouse itself came in 1944 when the German authorities discovered that American airmen were being sheltered in an annex of the Community. Although the airmen were warned in time and luckily escaped arrest, they left too many tell-tale signs of their passage. As a result, Father Emile Muller, the Superior of the house, along with Brothers Rufus and Gerard, suffered arrest and imprisonment. Father Muller died later that same year in the notorious concentration camp at Bergen-Belsen.

B. G. 40, 14 f. and 43 f.

Throughout Europe the war struck heavy blows at the Congregation. In France and Germany 569 members of military age were pressed into service. Seventy-five of them were killed in action. Many seminaries and other houses in Germany, the

B. G. 40, 14 ff.

Archbishop Louis Le Hunsec, sixteenth Superior General of the Congregation of the Holy Ghost (1926-1950).

Very Reverend Father Francis Griffin, seventeenth Superior General of the Congregation of the Holy Ghost (1950-   ).

The African Memorial Cathedral of Dakar, Senegal.

Netherlands, Belgium, Poland, and France were heavily damaged or destroyed. Worst of all, recruitment was drastically curtailed: the number of aspirants sank from the pre-war total of 2,572 to 1,128 in 1945. Although the repercussion of this decrease on the works of the Congregation did not make itself immediately felt, it was bound to create personnel problems between 1950 and 1960.

B. G. 40, 36 ff.   *In the Missions.* In the French colonies the work of evangelization was seriously hampered by the mobilization of many missionaries. Elsewhere Spiritans had to replace interned German and Italian priests as far away as Ethiopia. South Africa and Nigeria arrested the German Holy Ghost Fathers and Brothers stationed in their territories. While the men in South Africa received permission to stay under surveillance in their missions and carry on their work in restricted fashion, those in Nigeria were less fortunate. The English authorities shipped them off to internment camps in Jamaica. Despite the efforts of the Apostolic Delegate to the United States and of Father Collins, then Superior of the United States Province, they had to stay behind

B. G. 40, 147   barbed wire till 1947. In that year nineteen of them were permitted to enter the United States, and the other ten were sent home to Germany.

6. *Development of the Congregation and Its Missions*

Congregation. Prior to the Second World War, the Spiritans were expanding rapidly. Statistics show that the total number

D. G. C. 22   rose from 2,000 members and 1,876 aspirants in 1926 to 3,504 members and 2,572 aspirants in 1939. The war, of course, adversely affected recruitment. It caused a sudden fifty-six percent drop in the number of aspirants. However, strenuous efforts in the post war period remedied the picture to such an extent that at the end of Archbishop Le Hunsec's generalate (1950) the total figure of aspirants had again risen to well above the two thousand mark. The number of members stood at 4,289.

Little if anything was done during this generalate toward starting new provinces. Its characteristic virtue lies in consolidation rather than extension and, in this respect the period follows a pattern that can be discerned throughout the last century of the Congregation's history: expansion is always followed by consolidation. As the founding of new provinces under Father Schwinden-

D. G. C. 23 ff.

hammer was followed by their development under Father Emonet, so also the trend toward extension under Archbishop Le Roy was succeeded by a period of consolidation under Archbishop Le Hunsec. Between 1920 and 1950, most of the existing provinces in Europe and America were able to organize themselves thoroughly by founding within their borders such houses as were necessary for self-sufficiency, viz., junior and senior seminaries and novitiates. In this way they became independent of further support from the Province of France and nearly everywhere this autonomy resulted in solid and sometimes spectacular growth.

D. G. C. 29 ff.

Missions. With respect to the Congregation, the most striking feature of this period was that ecclesiastical and religious authority came to be vested in distinct persons. Hitherto it had been the established practice to combine both authorities in the person of the Vicar or Prefect Apostolic, because in this way there was no possibility of conflict between the two powers. However, the Sacred Congregation of Religious vigorously counseled their separation. From 1938 on, the new system was gradually introduced in most Spiritan missions. The Ecclesiastical Superior (Bishop, Vicar, or Prefect Apostolic) was appointed as usual by the Holy See, but the Congregation named separate Religious Superiors for the various regions. Here and there one finds evidence of some dissatisfaction on the part of the ecclesiastical superiors with respect to the new arrangement, but in general they accepted the innovation without difficulty. In reality, this division of authority is a sign that the missions are gradually approaching a level of organization that differs little from the regular dioceses of the Church in non-mission lands for, according to the accepted pattern, a resident bishop should not be both the Ordinary of a diocese and the Religious Superior of an order or congregation.

Outside Africa, most Spiritan missions are in Catholic countries which lack sufficient strength to be ecclesiastically self-sufficient. Even in these, however, as we will see more fully in Part II, significant progress has been made in training a local clergy and in forming an elite of Catholic laymen. Reports from the old French Colonies, as well as from Trinidad, Mauritius, and Haiti clearly portray the improvements that have taken place.

In Africa itself, the missionary work progressed with giant strides. The Holy Ghost missions saw their number of Catholics increase from 385,563 in 1925 to 2,624,000 in 1950. Old missions were divided and subdivided and divided again to keep up with the development. In the process, sections of these missions were passed on to other orders and congregations. Despite this, the Holy Ghost Fathers still retain a territory of about two million square miles. This is more than half the size of Europe or two thirds the size of the United States, and it contains a population of about twenty-five million.

B. G. 39, 45 ff.
One of the most significant events of this period occurred in May, 1939, when the Holy See named the first two native prelates of modern times in Negro Africa: Msgr. Joseph Faye, C.S.Sp., Prefect Apostolic of Ziguinchor in Senegal, and Bishop Joseph Kiwanuka, W.F., Vicar Apostolic of Masaka, Uganda. It was the first sign that Libermann's idea of an African Church ruled by an African clergy was approaching realization.

B. G. 39, 166
D. G. C. 32 f.
By 1941 the Church in Angola had progressed sufficiently to warrant the suppression of the old Spiritan missions in that region. The Holy See created in their stead the Archdiocese of Loanda and the Dioceses of Nova Lisboa and Silva Porto. Because of Portugal's dislike of the Propaganda, these circumscriptions were made independent of this Sacred Congregation and assigned to the Congregation for Extraordinary Ecclesiastical Affairs. Thus they were no longer missions in the strictly canonical and technical sense of the term, although in all other respects they were similar to the rest of Negro Africa. The new dioceses

B. G. 39, 169 ff.
were no longer officially entrusted to the Spiritans, although the Archbishop and one of the bishops were Holy Ghost Fathers and the Congregation still maintained its numerous personnel in these regions since hardly any other priests were available for them. At the same time the Holy See named another Spiritan Bishop of Cape Verde and asked the Congregation to extend its activities to these islands.

There is, of course, considerably more to be said about the missionary activities of the Congregation than the preceding pages would indicate. In the second part of this book we shall endeavor to present a more complete picture.

* * * * *

B. G. 41, 50
In 1949, toward the end of his second term as Superior General, Archbishop Le Hunsec notified his confreres that he would not be available for another period of twelve years and asked the Con-

B. G. 44, 56 ff. gregation to elect a successor. After the General Chapter of 1950 he remained in residence at the Motherhouse, where he died on Christmas day 1954.

GROWTH OF THE CONGREGATION OF THE HOLY GHOST SINCE 1885

Year	Frs.	Brs.	Prof.	Asps.	Total
1885	358	348	706	619	1,325
1890	463	440	903	850	1,753
1900	639	588	1,395	677	2,072
1910	781	622	1,639	824	2,463
1920	856	524	1,565	1,058	2,652
1930	1,212	744	2,567	1,874	4,414
1939	1,734	915	3,604	2,572	6,176
1949	2,496	777	4,154	1,994	6,148
1955	3,040	799	4,686	2,680	7,366

CHAPTER TWELVE

THE PRESENT SUPERIOR GENERAL:
FATHER FRANCIS GRIFFIN

1. *Election*

B. G. 41, 446   In 1950 eighty-two Provincials, District Superiors, and elected delegates attended the General Chapter. Their most important business was to conduct the election of a new Superior General. cf. p. 283   In accord with the instruction which the Holy See had given when Archbishop Le Hunsec was elected, the Chapter's choice did not fall on one of the forty bishops and prelates who belonged to the Congregation. Instead, the delegates chose a simple priest: B. G. 41, 425   Father Francis Griffin. It was the first time since 1896 that this had happened.

Father Griffin, the seventeenth Superior General since 1703, was born in 1893 in County Clare, Ireland. After studying at Rockwell College, he entered the novitiate of the Congregation at Kimmage in 1911. Five years later he was sent to the University of Fribourg, from which in 1921 he graduated *summa cum laude* in theology. On his return to Ireland he was successively appointed professor of moral theology at Kimmage and Dean of Students at Rockwell. In 1926 he went to Africa, where he became Vicar General in the Vicariate of Kilimanjaro, Tanganyika, a post he held until he was recalled to Europe in 1933 to be made a member of the General Council of the Congregation. After the Second World War he was assigned the task of officially visiting the houses and missions of the Holy Ghost Fathers in the Western Hemisphere. In 1949 he was elected Assistant to the Superior General. The next year, as we have mentioned, he was chosen to govern the Congregation for the current twelve-year period.

2. *A Program*

After the election of the new Superior General, the Chapter drew up a program of directives and recommendations, from which we select the following points of interest:

B. G. 41, 469 f.   1. With respect to the oft-debated question whether the Motherhouse should be transferred from Paris to Rome, the delegates decided to submit the question to an international committee of lawyers before making a definite recommendation. It was felt that the matter should be approached with great caution because of the intimate legal connection between the central headquarters of the Holy Ghost Fathers and their

B. G. 42, 65 ff.   legal standing in France. After a careful study of the question, French, American, and British attorneys came to the conclusion that the legal situation was too complicated to be modified without incurring serious risks. In 1934 and 1935 the Holy See itself had experienced how complex such a situation can be when it attempted to have the Motherhouse of a Sisters' Congregation transferred to Rome. After several months of negotiation, the plan had to be abandoned for fear of jeopardizing the existence of that Congregation in France. As far as the Spiritans were concerned, the Holy See declared that it saw no advantage in the contemplated transfer. In fact, it envisioned certain disadvantages. Accordingly, the authorities decided to keep the Motherhouse at the historical location which it has occupied since the beginning of the eighteenth century.

2. The Holy See was willing to offer exemption from episcopal jurisdiction *in foro externo*, but prevailing opinion among the Spiritans was against making the request for it. In past centuries such an exemption might have been desirable and useful, but it was felt that at present no one need fear undue interference on the part of the hierarchy. Exemption *in foro interno*, which the Congregation enjoyed since 1870, seemed quite adequate.

B. G. 41, 474   3. To take care of the ever-increasing demand for a more numerous personnel, it was recommended that new Provinces be inaugurated in different countries where the Congregation has not yet been established. In subsequent chapters we shall survey the efforts that are presently being made to implement this point.

B. G. 41, 479   4. The great emphasis on education in modern times both at home and in the missions makes it necessary that the greatest possible number of members be prepared to take academic and professional degrees. This matter was left to the individual

Provinces, however, so that they might determine whether university studies were to be undertaken before or after ordination to the priesthood.

B. G. 41, 480   5. To maintain contact between the various Provinces and stimulate interest in each other's problems, the interprovincial Senior Seminaries of Rome and Fribourg were to be used more extensively. Also, an exchange of students between the Provinces, either for theological studies or during vacation periods, was recommended as "normal procedure."

B. G. 41, 481   6. Regardless of its geographical location, any group of works which produces vocations and therefore may one day develop into a full-fledged Province will be encouraged by being erected into a Vice-Province. This recommendation is a clear sign of the changing times and the enormous progress made in some districts. Where formerly aspirants from the districts were few and far between, they are often quite numerous nowadays. For example, in 1952 Nigeria was able to open

B. G. 42, 383
E. P. 31, I, 109
a special junior seminary for the Congregation. It already has 82 aspirants. The District of Trinidad has given to date 31 new members to the Congregation and participates in the

B. G. 41, 487
Spiritan apostolate in Africa. Even tiny St. Pierre et Miquelon has supplied the Congregation with six priests. In Africa itself, the erection of local novitiates and provinces is a question that must be envisioned in the near future.

*   *   *   *   *   *

At this juncture, since we have reached the end of the general history of the Congregation, it will be interesting to scan the record in retrospect. Over all, the story of its two hundred and fifty-five years has been a tale of hard work and unobtrusive[1] effort in obscure and difficult positions. In many cases God has particularly blessed Spiritan labors. If one may be permitted to single out a few of the more striking examples, the recapitulation should include :

---

[1]Like many other religious orders the Spiritans have never indulged in vociferous advertizing nor in calling their achievements to the attention of the world at large. In all simplicity most of them prefer to leave the blowing of trumpets to the angels on judgment day. Even the publication of this book has been inspired not so much by a desire to attract public attention as by a wish to acquaint the Holy Ghost Fathers of the English-speaking world more fully with the record of their past.

1. The struggle of the Spiritans against the eighteenth and nineteenth century heresies of Jansenism and Gallicanism in France. Both by word and by the training given to many thousands of secular priests in the seminaries of Paris, Meaux, Verdun, and Rome, the Congregation has contributed significantly to the final victory.

2. An unblemished record of unshakable adherence to the Holy See, not only in theory but in practice.

3. The restoration of the Faith in the old French colonies and Mauritius after the French Revolution, and the solution of the recurrent religious crises by moving toward the creation of a colonial Hierarchy.

4. The pioneering labor of the Congregation in Africa. The Spiritans were the first to revive the defunct missions among the Negroes on this long-neglected continent. If Church membership has risen from practically zero in 1843 to about twenty-four million in 1957, the increase is due in large measure to the efforts of the Holy Ghost Fathers. Of course, there can be no question of minimizing the important contributions to the common task which other religious societies and missionaries have made. Of the twenty-four million African Catholics, only about four million live in territories that are still entrusted to the Congregation. Nevertheless, despite their numerous commitments throughout the world, the Spiritans have continued to maintain for more than a century a larger staff in Africa than any other congregation. It is only quite recently that another society has been able to equal the number of its missionaries.

cf. p. 162 ff.

5. The preparation of the modern apostolic doctrine of the Church by principles which Father Libermann set forth a century ago. As we have seen in Chapter VII, contemporary Church documents have given their official stamp of approval to these principles.

6. The introduction of a spirituality which is more in accord with man's nature than most of the ascetical currents hitherto in vogue. Libermann's racial descent from a people which shows great gifts of psychological insight has proved highly valuable to the Church.

Turning to the internal history of the Congregation, one is struck rather forcibly by the fact that during the last century the general policies of its Superiors General have varied greatly. One has only to compare the conditions that obtained under Schwinden-hammer with the general norms pursued by Archbishop Le Roy to arrive at this conclusion. Nevertheless, it is still more striking that despite these changes in policy, the end result has always been to bring the Spiritans closer to their historical objective. Considered as a whole, the Congregation has undertaken and brought to a high degree of vigor all the works which are in accord with the aims of its Founder and its Restorer: the planting of the Church in Africa, the spiritual care of the old civilized colonies, educational works that train priests imbued with a love for humble work and develop Catholic leadership, and social works that welcome the poor and neglected children of Christ. As Archbishop Le Roy wisely observed:

*N. D. p. VIII   Scanning the phases of our . . . history, one gets the distinct impression that men have counted in it only as the often un-witting instruments of an invisible Master who guided them and who alone saw the goal to which He led them. This fact is for us, and for everyone of us, a source of consolation and great strength.

PART TWO

THE HOLY GHOST FATHERS THROUGHOUT THE WORLD

This part constitutes a survey of the Congregation's work in the various countries where it has established itself. During the course of that survey, there will be an opportunity to trace the development of the various Provinces and works of which only the origins were recorded in preceding pages of this history.

CHAPTER THIRTEEN

EUROPE

1. FRANCE

When one takes up the Spiritan story in France after the death of Father Libermann, three distinct periods become apparent: 1852-1896, coinciding with the generalates of Fathers Schwindenhammer and Emonet; 1896-1920, extending over most of the generalate of Archbishop Le Roy; and the period since 1920 to the present. The first division was characterized by a broad expansion in educational and sociological activities; the second witnessed progressive persecution and restriction of the Congregation's endeavors in France; the third and last is marked by a widespread resumption of social work.

a. FIRST PERIOD: 1852-1896

Educational and Social Foundations. Preceding chapters have sufficiently indicated why this type of work was undertaken and how it developed. There is no need here to review questions of policy nor to enter into a detailed study of each of the various establishments. However, for the sake of the record it may be helpful to reproduce a list of Spiritan institutions that flourished in France at the end of this period.

Colleges and Seminaries	*Social Institutions*
Seminary of the Holy Ghost, Paris	St. Michael's Institute (Britanny)
Seminary-College of Langonnet	Saint-Ilan Industrial and Agricultural Schools and Orphanage
Seminary-College of Mesnières (together with its orphanage)	St. Joseph's Institute, Grand Quevilly[1]
Seminary-College of Beauvais	St. Joseph's Institute, Orgeville
College of Epinal	
Seminary-College of Merville	St. Joseph's House, Douvaine
Seminary of Seyssinet	St. Mauront's Home, Bois d'Estiaire
Seminary-College of Cellule	
College of Castelnaudary	

B. G. 3, 280 f.;
4, 211 ff.

Houses of Formation. Father Schwindenhammer was particularly anxious to have the novitiates and the senior seminary close to his residence in Paris. For that reason, in 1855 he installed the seminary in an annex of the Motherhouse and the novitiate at nearby Monsivry. The old Abbey of Notre Dame du Gard, which till then had housed these divisions, was abandoned. Six years later, when lack of space became acute, he bought an old castle and fifty acres of land in the Parisian suburb of Chevilly. In 1864 this house began its tour of service as the combined senior seminary and novitiate for clerics and Brothers. In addition, the property's large buildings sheltered one of the inevitable social works which in the second half of the nineteenth century were attached to nearly all houses of the Congregation in Europe. Father Schwindenhammer appears even to have thought of making Chevilly, if not *de jure* at least *de facto*, the Motherhouse of the Holy Ghost Fathers. Although this plan was not realized, Chevilly became the central senior house of studies for the Congregation as a whole, until the other Provinces were strong enough to establish their own

B. G. 13, 488 ff.

[1]The St. Joseph Institute for homeless boys was taken over in 1882 at the insistent and repeated request of Cardinal Bonnechose. Till then it had been operated by lay personnel who were unable to direct it properly. The boys' first reception of the Spiritans was not very encouraging: their arrival was greeted with a chorus of catcalls and a few well-aimed rocks that smashed the windows of their carriage. Despite these bad omens, the Fathers and Brothers soon gained everyone's affection and ultimately managed to bring the institute to a flourishing condition.

seminaries. Apart from temporary interruptions caused by wars and revolutions, the house has never ceased to function as one of the most important seminaries of the Congregation. In 1886, despite successive enlargements, Chevilly had become too small to accommodate all the aspirant priests and Brothers, and the Motherhouse decided to open a separate novitiate at Orly, another suburb of Paris. This new community of Orly was destined to function as the clerical novitiate till 1904 and then again from 1920 to 1939. Thousands of future Holy Ghost Fathers, both from France and from abroad, received their fundamental training in the religious life at this central novitiate.

B. G. 13, 1161 f.

Most of the junior seminaries founded and operated during this period were combined with colleges which the Congregation established in Langonnet, Cellule, Beauvais, Mesnières, Merville, and Seyssinet.

B. G. 8, 23 ff.

The Franco-Prussian War and its Aftermath. A few weeks after the beginning of this war, in July 1870, the Fathers went to Chevilly for their annual retreat. Although the war was turning out badly for France and the German armies had already begun

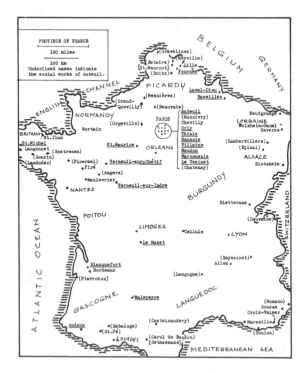

their drive on Paris, Father Schwindenhammer was not inclined to shorten the customary eight days of spiritual exercises. However, before the retreat was over, he had to call on all hands to assist in preparing for the evacuation of the institution, for Chevilly lay in a direct line between Paris and the advancing German armies. Supplies, books, archives, and the mortal remains of Father Libermann were protected from destruction by burial, while other objects were shipped to the questionable safety of Paris.

B. G. 8, 95 ff. Serious trouble arose when the French General Staff decided to make the Chevilly area a zone of defense for the Capital. Fortifications were hastily thrown up all over the seminary property and the surrounding farmland. The ensuing Battle of Chevilly, in which some 30,000 French soldiers sought to stem the German advance, took place in and around the very gardens of the seminary. The French forces fell back in retreat and the Germans occupied whatever was left standing of the buildings. They then buried their dead in the park and added new fortifications to those constructed by the French army.

The defeat of the French in the Franco-Prussian War was followed by a Revolution and a usurpation of power by the *"Commune,"* a kind of communistic regime, which controlled Paris and certain other sections of the country. Chevilly eventually found itself under the control of the *Commune* and these insurrectionists calmly "requisitioned" whatever they wanted in the Seminary while the loyal forces stood off and vigorously shelled both the village and the scholasticate. When peace was finally restored, everyone was surprised that anything at all remained standing on the property.

B. G. 8, 216 ff. During the siege of Paris, the Superior General and most of the Motherhouse staff left the city. Those who remained behind communicated with the outside world by means of carrier pigeons and balloons, but when the siege ended and the *Commune* took over, the Motherhouse had to be abandoned entirely. Only Father Besserat and a lone Brother remained behind as long as possible, staying on even after the revolutionary forces began to use the buildings. However, when the soldiers discovered that the wine cellar's location had not been revealed to them, they were so furious over this lack of cooperation of Citizen Besserat that both he and Citizen Brother had to assume a quick disguise and flee for their lives. Three days later the regular army, fighting its way through the barricades, recaptured the Motherhouse and the next day the first Spiritan re-entered. Among other things, he found that its courtyard had been used for the execution of a captured insurrectionist and for the burial of regular army soldiers.

B. G. 8, 58 ff.   The situation of the German Brothers and seminarians in France during those days of war and revolution proved to be particularly delicate because an intense popular resentment had developed against anything German. Some of them were sent to the safety of Langonnet in Britanny, but the local authorities there objected to their presence and they had to flee to Saint-Ilan, where a more lenient Provincial Commissioner permitted them to find asylum in the social institutions operated by the Congrega-

B. G. 8, 366 ff.   tion. At Toulon the situation became especially critical, for the Superior of the social institution had neglected to notify the authorities officially of the presence of two Brothers who had been born in Germany but whose national status was doubtful. As a result, local authorities closed the community and its social works, con-

B. G. 9, 378 ff.;   fiscated all its properties, and quartered fifteen hundred soldiers
648 ff.   in the buildings. It was only after repeated protests, an appeal to the Secretary of State, and a series of lawsuits, that Father Schwindenhammer succeeded in having this arbitrary confiscation rescinded and indemnities paid for the damage done to the house.

B. G. 9, 659 f.   The editor of the local leftist newspaper, who had published defamatory articles about "spies," "international monks" and "vultures preying on the goods of the town," was sentenced to a fine and twenty days in the Workhouse. Moreover, the court ordered publication of this sentence on the front page of the man's own paper as well as in the other local journals.

The Congregation suffered its greatest loss in seeing Alsace cut off from France and incorporated into the Reich. Alsace had always been a region from which the Congregation received a steady stream of vocations. Under these new political conditions,

cf. p. 208   however, this stream was in danger of dwindling to a mere trickle for, as has been related previously, the Spiritans were soon to be expelled from Germany under pretext of their alleged affiliation with the Jesuits.

Spiritan Theological Seminary at Chevilly, France. A view of the courtyard.

The medieval Abbey of Langonnet, Brittanny. Acquired by the Spiritans in 1858, it now shelters a junior seminary and a rest house for retired members.

St. Joseph's Junior Seminary, Allex, France. View of the main entrance
and of the organ loft in the chapel.

b. Second Period: 1896-1920

cf. p. 236

Restrictions and Persecution. In Chapter X it has already been indicated that many of the Congregation's educational and social works were beginning to make serious inroads into Spiritan finances. Because so many of them constituted a dangerous drain on the moderate resources of the Congregation, Archbishop Le Roy, who had become Superior General in 1896, decided to abandon or transfer to other hands those which operated at a deficit and did little to compensate for the loss by producing voca-

B. G. 18, 225;
341; 753;
20, 172
B. G. 21, 679

tions. During the next four years, even before the persecution of religious orders struck the Congregation, Le Roy suppressed the College of Castelnaudery, St. Mauront's Home, St. Joseph's Institute at Orgeville and its namesake at Douvaine. In 1902, the College of Langonnet had to be closed because everyone realized that the Government would refuse permission for its continuance. The next year crippling blows began to fall with increasing fre-

B. G. 22, 405 f.

quency. By the end of 1903 persecution had forced the Society to abandon the colleges of Epinal, Beauvais, Mesnières, Cellule, and Merville as well as the Seminary of Seyssinet. The social works of St. Ilan, St. Michel, Misserghin and Grand Quevilly shared the same fate.

With cynical benevolence, the government allowed the Holy Ghost Fathers to retain in France, in addition to the Motherhouse, one senior seminary and novitiate (Chevilly), the Abbey of Langonnet as a rest house for the aged and sick, and two tiny procures

B. G. 24, 692

in the ports of Bordeaux and Marseilles. On the strength of a verbal authorization, the Spiritans managed to retain their Algerian

cf. p. 573

foundation of Misserghin, which they had taken over in 1901, but social works there had to be closed. Junior seminarians were

B. G. 23, 454 f.

driven into exile in Italy and Belgium. Once the first confusion was over, St. Ilan, St. Michel and the St. Joseph's Institute of Grand Quevilly continued to function under the direction of "secularized" Holy Ghost Fathers and Brothers; Orly was transformed into an agricultural school; and the colleges of Beauvais, Mesnières, and Epinal were handed over to the secular clergy.

B. G. 27, 582 ff.

As one would expect, this persecution seriously affected the recruitment of vocations for the Province of France. To make matters worse, the separation of Church and State in 1905 forced three years of military service on all seminarians and young Brothers. In 1906 the Congregation, which in spite of all these harassments was in a better position than other orders, had only a hundred and fourteen aspirants left in France. Ex-seminarian Combes had done his nefarious work thoroughly and well. Nonetheless, a way was found to organize Spiritan recruitment even within the borders of France. With the approval of the Bishops of St. Brieuc, Mende, Angers, and Lourdes, the Congregation sent a number of aspirants to the private Catholic colleges of Langogne, Rostrenen, Mongazon and Saint-Pé, to study there under the direction of "secularized" Spiritans. In addition, Cellule was reopened by other "secularized" Fathers under the direction of Canon Astaix (1913). In virtue of this modified "underground," the number of aspirants began to rise again. It reached a total of three hundred just before the First World War broke out.

B. G. 29, 622 ff.   *The First World War and its Aftermath: 1914-1920.* On the eve of this conflict in July 1914, all Fathers, Brothers and aspirants of military age were mobilized and all junior seminarians were sent home. Unfortunately, the dispersal order reached the exiles in Gentinnes (Belgium) too late. Caught in enemy-occupied territory, they had to spend the whole war under the control of German occupation forces in Belgium. In France itself, once the front was stabilized after the battles of Ypres and the Marne, several seminaries of the Congregation were able to resume their function in the more remote sections of the country.

B. G. 29, 659 ff.   The buildings of Chevilly first served as a Red Cross hospital. Subsequently, in 1915 the Spiritans placed both Chevilly and Orly at the disposal of a grateful Belgian Government to serve as reception centers for hundreds of abandoned children that had been rounded up in the battle zone of Ypres. These unfortunate

B. G. 29, 729 ff.; 770 ff.; 813 ff.   youngsters were kept there until their repatriation in 1919. Meanwhile, the exile-seminary at Gentinnes in Belgium continued to function throughout the war despite manifold difficulties. During those trying years it suffered the loss of thirteen students who died from privation and disease before it was possible to return the student body to France.

B. G. 30, 415; 29, 694 ff.; 703 ff. B. G. 33, 670   When the fighting ceased in 1918, the Province had lost eighty-one members on the field of battle. It was highly gratified, however, to see Alsace once more attached to France, for this meant that its potential would be reinforced by eighty-eight members and a hundred and fifty-five aspirants who had expressed their preference for French nationality. In addition, it received the two junior seminaries of Saverne (Sabern) and Neugrange (Neuscheuren), which the German Spiritans had founded in Alsace. Moreover, the political situation had considerably improved. In the face of such popularity as was gained by mobilized monks and religious in the trenches, the government no longer dared to venture into new expulsion programs. Another period in the history of the Province had assuredly begun.

cf. p. 243

c. THIRD PERIOD: 1920 TO THE PRESENT

1. *Growth*

The first part of this period (till the beginning of the Second World War) was marked by magnificient growth and development. The exile-seminary of Suza in Italy was returned to French soil and established at Allex, the seminary of Gentinnes was handed over to the Belgian Province, and a new house of formation was added at Blotzheim in Alsace (1920). Five years later, the Province had close to a thousand clerical aspirants in its seminaries. Because the scholasticate at Chevilly could not accommodate the great number of senior seminarians, philosophy students were transferred to the White Abbey of Mortain (1923).[2] New junior seminaries were established also at Piré near Rennes, and at Ruitz, close to the Channel, and a special school for late vocations was inaugurated at Saint-Ilan. Despite the economic crisis in 1931 and the years that followed, Chevilly had to be still further enlarged to take care of the flood of theology students who passed through its gates. In 1939, on the eve of World War II, the Province had a total of 1,516 members, ten junior seminaries, and more than a thousand aspirants.

B. G. 29, 721

B. G. 29, 490

B. G. 32, 421

B. G. 31, 306

B. G. 34, 633

B. G. 36, 714

E. P. 27, 228

2. *The Second World War: 1939-1945*

This marvelous growth was brutally cut short by the armed conflict initiated by Hitler. All houses in Alsace, except part

B. G. 40, 17 f.; 150 ff.

---

[2]The Abbey was founded in 1120 by St. Vitalis for cloistered nuns, who were dressed in white—whence its name "White Abbey." Confiscated by the Revolutionary Government in 1792, the ruined buildings were purchased by a priest and restored to serve as a seminary in 1822. In 1906, when Church and State separated in France, the property was again stolen by the Government. A local society then bought it and offered it in 1923 to the Holy Ghost Fathers.

of the one in Saverne, ceased functioning for five years; many others were requisitioned, and in the offensive of 1944 Mortain, Allex, Neufgrange, Blotzheim and Saverne were rather severely damaged. Thirty-three members of the Province lost their lives in the war. Although at the end of hostilities, the senior seminaries of the Province of France still housed 318 students and the novitiate 64 candidates, only six of its junior seminaries were still functioning and they enrolled less than 300 aspirants.

3. *Post War Organization*

E. P. 31, I, 13 ff.   The post-war years made efficient recruitment more difficult than ever. Nevertheless, the job had to be undertaken if the Province was to satisfy to some extent the demands made on it by its numerous operations in the missions and at home. For this reason, a provincial reorganization took place. Under the new program, junior seminaries were founded at Bletterans in the Jura (1948) and at Maulevrier (1954), Seine et Loire. The ancient community of Saint-Ilan, which functioned already as a school for late vocations, was now exclusive reserved for clerical aspirants. Because Orly had been requisitioned successively by the French, the German, and the American Armies, and the property had been plundered and filled with reinforced concrete structures to such an extent that it was no longer adaptable to its original purpose, the clerical novitiate was transferred to Cellule. The senior scholastics still took their philosophy at Mortain and their theology at Chevilly, but a special senior seminary for university studies was now founded near the *Institut Catholique* of Lille (1951). During the war years, separate Provincial Headquarters had already been established in Paris (1942). Later, two small rest homes for recuperating missionaries at Grasse, near Nice, and Wolxheim-Canal, Alsace, were added to the larger facilities which already fulfilled that function at Misserghin in North Africa. The Brothers now have their own Postulancies at Neugrange, Alsace, and Langonnet, Britanny. Their novitiate stands at Piré, and their advanced three-year period of religious and technical training is spent at Chevilly. By the end of 1955, the Province once again had 689 aspirants and its membership reached 1,575, thereby making it the largest Province of the Holy Ghost Fathers in all the world.

E. P. 31, II, 102

4. *Works in the Homeland*

Educational Institutions. French Spiritans still staff the venerable old Seminary of the Holy Ghost which was founded by Father Poullart des Places in 1703. In 1954 this seminary was detached from the Motherhouse and transferred to Croix-Valmer in Southern France. It is the senior seminary for the overseas dioceses of the old French colonies of Guadeloupe, Martinique, Guiana and Reunion as well as of the former French island of Mauritius. Also, the Province still operates that most important of all French seminaries for the secular clergy: the Pontifical French Seminary of Rome. It has already been discussed in Chapter VIII, and a more detailed treatment of it can be found in Section Eleven of this chapter. In addition, the junior seminary of Allex is an "open" school for clerical aspirants, i.e. it trains not only those who are desirous of entering the Congregation, but accepts any qualified candidate for the priesthood as well.

cf. pp. 197 f.

Social Works. The most important social activity of the Province and the largest social institution in all France is Auteuil Institute. It may be compared to a combined multi-centered Boys' Town and Catholic Rural Settlement Office. We have learned above how the French Holy Ghost Fathers accepted this Institute and developed it into a nationwide organization. At present, under the energetic and paternal direction of Father Marc Duval and fifty-six other Spiritans, seven branches of Auteuil take care of nearly 2,000 homeless boys in the area of Paris alone. Another 2,000 are sheltered in fourteen branches of the Institute throughout France. Although some of these branches have a most interesting history, it would lead us too far afield to enter into a detailed account of each of them.[3] In addition, the Province has reopened

cf. pp. 288 ff.

---

[3]Here is the list of these branches:

1. Auteuil Institute for Homeless Boys, Paris—*Headquarters*

Branches

2. St. Theresa Branch, Paris
3. St. Bernadette Branch, Audaux, Bayonne
4. St. Remy Branch, Bazeilles, near Rheims
5. St. Joseph Branch, Blanquefort, near Bordeaux
6. St. James Branch, Fournes, near Lille
7. Don Bosco Branch, Laval Dieu, near Rheims
8. St. Louis Branch, Le Mazet, near Limoges
9. St. Charles Branch, Le Vesinet, near Versailles
10. St. Roch Branch, Malepeyre, near Montauban
11. St. Anthony Branch, Marcoussis, near Versailles
12. St. Philip Branch, Meudon, near Versailles

on a small scale the Misserghin orphanage in North Africa which was closed during the persecution of Combes. It takes care of seventy-five orphans.

Other Works. French Spiritans also minister to eight parishes in the territory surrounding Misserghin, a dozen chaplaincies in motherhouses and novitiates of nuns' congregations, the spiritual needs of colonial university students at Paris, and in addition, they direct three important centers of the Pontifical Society for the Propagation of the Faith in Paris, Marseilles, and Bordeaux.

5. *Missions*

Most of the Spiritan missions throughout the world were originally founded by French members of the Congregation. At present, the following missions are still entrusted to the Province:

1. Archdiocese of Dakar, Senegal
2. Archdiocese of Conakry, French Guinea
3. Archdiocese of Yaunde, Cameroons
4. Archdiocese of Brazzaville, French Equatorial Africa
5. Archdiocese of Bangui, French Equatorial Africa
6. Diocese of Ziguinchor, Senegal
7. Diocese of Duala, Cameroons
8. Diocese of Pointe-Noire, Gabon
9. Diocese of Libreville, Gabon
10. Diocese of Fort-Rousset, French Equatorial Africa
11. Diocese of Cayenne, French Guiana
12. Diocese of Basse-Terre and Pointe-a-Pitre, Guadeloupe
13. Diocese of St. Pierre and Fort-de-France, Martinique
14. Diocese of Saint-Denis, Reunion
15. Diocese of Majunga, Madagascar
16. Diocese of Diego-Suarez, Madagascar
17. Prefecture of Saint-Louis, Senegal
18. Prefecture of Kankan, French Guinea
19. Prefecture of St. Pierre and Miquelon

---

13. Holy Ghost Branch, Orly, Paris
14. Notre Dame Branch, St. Maurice, near Chartres
15. St. Michael Branch, St. Michael, near Vannes
16. St. John Branch, Sannois, near Versailles
17. Sacred Heart Branch, Thiais, near Paris
18. St. George Branch, Verneil-le-Chétif, near Rennes
19. St. Joan of Arc Branch, Verneuil-sur-Indre, near Tours
20. Father Brottier Center, Villaine, near Versailles
21. St. Louis Branch, Fort-de-France, Martinique

cf. pp. 364 ff.

Moreover, numerous French Fathers and Brothers labor in the missions of Angola. In Haiti, the Province operates the important College of Saint Martial and a number of other works. In many of its missions it is assisted by Fathers and Brothers belonging to the sister Provinces of Switzerland and the Netherlands.

SUPERIORS OF THE PROVINCE OF FRANCE

From 1703-1848 the Congregation was not yet organized on a provincial basis. The Superior General directly controlled all houses in France. Between 1848 and 1896 the records occasionally mention only Father Frederic Le Vavasseur as Provincial of France. In reality, the Superior General reserved the powers of the Provincial Superior to himself.

Henry Van Haecke, 1896-1898
Bernard Gerrer, 1898-1904
John Grizard, 1904-1906
Marc Voegtli, 1906-1909
Aloysius Kuentz, 1909-1910
Adolph Dunoyer, 1910-1912
Paul Benoit, 1912-1927
Henry Nique, 1927-1939
Aloysius Aman, 1939-1944
Emile Laurent, 1944-1947
Leo Cromer, 1947-1953
Lucien Rozo, 1953-

2. IRELAND

a. COLLEGES

cf. pp. 203 ff.

B. G. 30, 457

Blackrock College Annual,
1946, pp. 5 ff.

B. G. 30, 457

Chapter VIII noted that as early as 1859 the Congregation established itself in Ireland and undertook the foundation of the two great Colleges of Blackrock and Rockwell. Although in modern times there has been a sharp increase in competition through the rise of new colleges, Blackrock continues to hold first place among the leading colleges of the land. Among its most prominent living alumni are John Cardinal D'Alton, Primate of All Ireland; Prime Minister Eamon de Valera, the emancipator of the country; Archbishop John C. McQuaid, C.S.Sp., of Dublin; Frank Duff, the saintly founder of the Legion of Mary; and the Reverend Doctor Alfred O'Rahilly. Scholarly Father John D'Alton rose from a professorship at Maynooth College to the presidency of this famous institution. In a few years, he became Bishop of Meath and then Archbishop of Armagh. In 1953 the Holy See made him a Cardinal. De Valera had gone to Blackrock with the intention of becoming a Holy Ghost Father, but Father Healy advised him to enter the college division instead of the seminary. Subsequently he taught mathematics at Rockwell College before becoming the liberator of Eire. John C. McQuaid, another eminent student of the College, entered the Congregation and later functioned as the President of Blackrock until the Holy See appointed him Archbishop of Dublin and Primate of Ireland in 1940. His fellow-alumnus, Frank Duff, planned and organized the world-wide apostolate that is accomplished through the Legion of Mary. The full story of his achievements will never be known until the final record is thrown open for all to see. Dr. Alfred O'Rahilly, after a particularly brilliant career as Professor and later as President of the University of Cork, resigned to realize the ambition of his early years in Blackrock. In 1955, at the age of seventy-one, he was ordained a priest in the College Chapel by Archbishop McQuaid. Since then Father O'Rahilly has been residing in Blackrock College.

Cork University Record, 1955, pp. 14 ff.

B. G. 15, 730
B. G. 28, 355

In 1890, at the request of the Archbishop, a third college, St. Mary's, was opened at Rathmines, Dublin. During the First World War this institution was closed (1916) because it could not support itself and the Province could not adequately staff it. By 1926, however, the Archbishop began to grow so deeply concerned over the number of Catholic youths attending secular colleges that he begged the Spiritans to reopen St. Mary's. Accordingly, it resumed operation as a day-school and has functioned with notable success in this capacity ever since. Together with Blackrock and Rockwell, it brings the total number of Spiritan-directed students in Ireland to more than two thousand annually.

B. G. 32, 770

E. P. 31, I, 19 ff.

Beyond the borders of Ireland, the Province operates several other large colleges. In addition to those that are situated in the African Missions staffed by the Province, we may mention here St. Mary's College and Our Lady of Fatima College in Trinidad, Holy Ghost College in Mauritius, and St. Francis College in Pugu, Tanganyika. These four colleges take care of an additional 2,200 students.

b. OTHER WORKS

cf. p. 128

The preaching of retreats and missions, which was one of the apostolic works Father Libermann urged his priests to undertake, has always been dear to Irish Spiritans. In 1898 a special house

B. G. 18, 338

Two views of Blackrock College: the Castle and the inner courtyard.

Five of Blackrock College's most prominent living alumni.

His Eminence John Cardinal D'Alton, Archbishop of Armagh and Primate of All Ireland.

His Grace John C. McQuaid, C.S.Sp., Archbishop of Dublin and Primate of Ireland.

Frank Duff, Founder of the Legion of Mary.

Eamon de Valera, Liberator of Eire and Prime Minister.

Reverend Doctor Alfred O'Rahilly as President of the University of Cork, before his ordination to the priesthood.

for this purpose was founded near Blackrock College, first on Booterstown Avenue and then at Clareville. The Provincialate itself was attached to this house until 1912 when, through a continuous program of property acquisition, the house became an integral part of the college campus. In that same year, the Province undertook the organization of a Mission Band in the United States. For many years this group functioned as a special arm of the Irish Province in America. Its successful career was terminated only when the United States Province grew strong enough to take over the work with its own personnel.

Over and above these activities, the Province has charge of the national office of the Pontifical Association of the Holy Childhood and the chaplaincies of the Missionary Sisters of Killeshandra who were founded by Bishop Shanahan, C.S.Sp. Special mention must also be made of the fact that the Irish Fathers have contributed mightily to English spiritual and ascetical literature. The books of such Spiritans as Edward Leen, John Kearney and Bernard Kelly are read everywhere throughout the English-speaking world, and in translation they have begun to exercise their wholesome influence in other parts of the globe as well.

c. HOUSES OF FORMATION

Both Blackrock College and Rockwell College have attached to them special junior seminaries which prepare candidates for admission to the Congregation. In 1904 a novitiate for the Province was established at Prior Park, Somerset County, England, and this was later transferred to Castlehead in the Diocese of Liverpool (1907). In 1911, when Castlehead became too small to accommodate both the Irish Brothers' novitiate and the junior seminary of the nascent English Province, a new community was established in Kimmage Manor, an estate near Dublin. Two decades later, the Province's rapid growth made it necessary to transfer the novitiate to Kilshane in Tipperary (1933). Shortly after, old Kimmage Manor was flanked by several huge buildings that had to be erected for the flood of applicants to the senior seminary. For these splendid new facilities, the Province owes a great debt of gratitude to Father Daniel Murphy, then Provincial, who courageously undertook this immense construction program despite the economic depression which plagued the world at that time. Finally, in 1956, Father Patrick O'Carroll, then Provincial

B. G. 26, 856

B. G. 22, 711 ;
24, 334

B. G. 26, 255

B. G. 36, 383

B. G. 38, 459

B. G. 44, 274

Superior, decided to make a definite effort to relieve the scarcity of Irish Brothers. In former years they had been quite numerous, but recently they had begun to lag behind the rest of the Province in its rapid growth. Following the example of the Dutch Province, he opened a special house adapted to their spiritual and educational needs and established the community at Ardbraccan in County Meath.

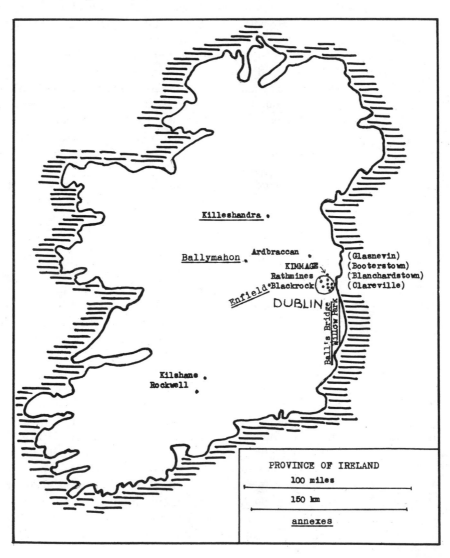

PROVINCE OF IRELAND
100 miles
150 km
annexes

Father Jules Leman, the Founder of the
Spiritan Province of Ireland.

Interior of the Chapel, Holy Ghost Senior
Seminary, Kimmage Manor, Dublin, Ireland.

An aerial view of Rockwell College.
(Courtesy *The Irish Times*—Copyright).

Kimmage Manor, the Headquarters of the Spiritan Province of Ireland.

E. P. 31, II, 102

Current statistics reveal that Ireland is the second largest province of the Congregation. It numbered 883 members and 248 aspirants as of 1955. Each year an average of more than one hundred of its members attend the National University in preparation for degrees and the strong home basis provided by its important educational works has made it possible for the Irish Province to contribute far more to the missions than would otherwise have been possible. The colleges themselves bring in many excellent vocations. They enable the aspirants of the Congregation to receive a first class education in the junior seminaries attached thereto, and they constitute effective public relations media through which the Missions are assisted in many ways. Moreover, they have the added advantage of impressing the future missionaries with the importance of higher education.

Unquestionably, the Church cannot be said to have achieved full development in any territory where its ministers have neglected to provide her with a Catholic elite that is ready to assume leadership. As experience shows, such leaders cannot be trained in missions that lack the necessary educational facilities. For this reason, the large number of fine secondary schools and colleges established by the Irish Fathers in their missions can be regarded as a guarantee that Catholic leadership will not be lacking in the territories entrusted to their care. Now that the peoples of Africa are moving swiftly toward national autonomy and political independence, events of the present demonstrate with ever-increasing clarity the wisdom of the Irish Province in clinging stubbornly to a strongly educational *modus agendi* at home. Sacrifices made to achieve academic excellence in Ireland are now proved to have been eminently worthwhile, as is easily demonstrated by the vigor of those foreign missions which have enjoyed the benefits of the Province's enlightened policies.

d. Missions

In West Africa, Irish Spiritans take care of two flourishing missionary jurisdictions in Nigeria (the Archdiocese of Onitsha and the Diocese of Owerri), as well as the Dioceses of Freetown in Sierra Leone and of Bathurst in Gambia. In East Africa, the Archdiocese of Nairobi and the Diocese of Mombasa-Zanzibar are entrusted to its care. Finally, out in the Indian Ocean, the Irish

Holy Ghost Fathers are in charge of the Diocese of Port Louis, Mauritius.

cf. p. 358
cf. p. 438

Quite recently the Province of Ireland has been engaged in laying the foundations for a new province in English-speaking Canada. This venture will be treated subsequently in the section devoted to Canadian works. By the same token, the efforts of Irish Fathers to found works in Australia will be reserved for a later discussion.

SUPERIORS OF THE PROVINCE OF IRELAND[4]

Founder: Jules Leman, 1859-1880
Peter Huvetys, 1880-1889
Jules Botrel, 1889-1900
Lawrence Healy, 1900-1907
Edward Crehan, 1907-1910
John T. Murphy, 1910-1916 (later Bishop of Port Louis)
Cornelius O'Shea, 1916-1922
Joseph Byrne, 1922-1925 (later Bishop of Moshi)
Richard Harnett, 1925-1934
Daniel Murphy, 1934-1947
Michael Finnegan, 1947
Patrick O'Carroll, 1947-1956
Timothy Driscoll, 1956-

3. GERMANY

a. THE SECOND WORLD WAR

cf. pp. 294 ff.

The last reference to the Province of Germany left it with its houses requisitioned at the beginning of the Second World War and its members of military age pressed into service with the armed B. G. 40, 400 ff. forces. Many of the older Fathers and Brothers somehow managed to stay in the requisitioned houses by acting as orderlies, cooks, and technicians who worked for the benefit of the occupants quartered there by the Government. While they were able to provide a modicum of protection for the Congregation's possessions, the final stages of the war did extensive damage to nearly every house in Germany. The Provincialate in Cologne was completely destroyed by an incendiary plane crash, the seminary at Broich and the novitiate at Heimbach suffered severe damage from air

---

[4]In all sections of this and subsequent chapters we use the term "Superiors of the Province" in a broad sense, without paying attention to the exact date on which the Province was canonically erected. The term "founder" as a rule refers to the first Superior of the first foundation in the country.

and ground artillery, and the old abbey of Knechtsteden was stripped to its very walls by the twelve hundred Polish refugees who occupied it. Previously, a Nazi official had seen to it that the ethnological collections of the Knechtsteden museum and the best works of its library were shipped to safety (!) in Berlin. Nearly a hundred members and aspirants of the Province lost their lives on the battle fields or otherwise disappeared without a trace. Some of them had been sent to the front to be killed in action for such crimes as having given a decent breakfast to a French fellow-priest among the prisoners of war. Another suffered a similar fate because a scapegoat was needed for irregularities in the Nazi administration of requisitioned houses. At the end of the hostilities in 1945, the shattered Province finally counted its losses. Only two of its junior seminaries, Menden and Donau-Eschingen, remained undamaged. The number of its aspirants had shrunk to twenty, and scores of its members were in internment camps in Russia, Jamaica and elsewhere.

b. RUINS REBUILT

There is good reason why our German confreres are respected for their energy and savoir-faire. Despite all the difficulties in-

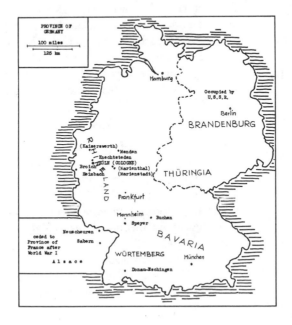

herent in the defeat of Hitler's armies and the total wreck of the German economy, they resolutely set themselves to the task of reconstruction. Such a degree of success attended their efforts that only one year later all houses were functioning again. Slowly the empty ranks began to fill. Knechtsteden was restored—for the third time in fifty years. The following year Father Hoffmann, the Provincial, succeeded in obtaining state recognition for the seminaries of Knechtsteden and Menden. This entitled them to grant official degrees—something the Province had striven in vain to achieve for more than twenty years. At the same time, permission was granted to start a recognized theological faculty in Knechtsteden. Soon after, the spiritual and technical training facilities for Brothers, completely wrecked by the war, were fully restored and a special pre-postulancy program was organized in Knechtsteden. Through it, one may venture to hope that the German Province will once again produce the substantial numbers of highly qualified and devoted Brothers for which it was so famous before the last war.

B. G. 40, 362   In 1948, after twenty-four years in office, Father Hoffmann resigned and was succeeded by Father Richard Gräf, the famous spiritual writer. His presence at the helm in these critical post-war years was ample proof that the Province had risen again not

B. G. 43, 227   only materially but spiritually as well. In 1953 he opened another junior seminary at Buchen but the next year ill health forced him

B. G. 43, 312   to resign and Father Henry Hack took over. Barring another war or similar calamities, the future looks bright for the Spiritans in

E. P. 31, II,   Germany, for the aspirants to their Province are surpassed in
102   number only by those of France.

c. Works in the Homeland

The apostolate of popular missions and retreats has always been one for which the German Fathers are very much in demand. In recent years, Father Hoffmann and Father Gräf especially have consecrated themselves to this exacting work. Father Gräf, moreover, has succeeded in extending his spiritual influence over the whole world by means of his widely-read books. One of these, *Ja Vater (Yes Father)*, has gone through forty editions and more than a dozen translations.

B. G. 40, 405 f.   In 1947 the Province opened a general college, dedicated to the Holy Ghost, for resident and non-resident students within the

Father Charles Duparquet, Founder of the
Spiritan Province of Portugal and famous
African pioneer.

Father Joseph Antunes, the Founder of the
Cunene Missions.

Theological Seminary of the Portuguese Province at Carcavelos, near Lisbon.

Father Amand Acker, the restorer of the Spiritan Province of Germany after the *Kulturkampf*.

The medieval Abbey of Knechtsteden, and its Shrine of Our Lady of Sorrows, now the Senior Seminary of the German Province.

The Spiritan Junior Seminary of Broich, near Aachen, Germany.

The Spiritan Junior Seminary of Menden, Westphalia.

ancient walls of the Abbey of Knechtsteden. In addition, the former museum buildings which had been stripped of their contents, were transformed into an asylum for homeless old people whom the war had deprived of every possession. In this way, the vast structures of the venerable abbey now accommodate a senior seminary, a college, a novitiate and technicon for Brothers, an old people's home, and a resident community of eighty-six Fathers and Brothers. In addition, the beautiful twelfth century church is a Shrine to Our Lady of Sorrows, visited each year by a hundred thousand pilgrims.

E. P. 31, I, 23

As of the last census (1955), the German Province has 350 members and 406 aspirants.

E. P. 31, II, 102

d. Missions

After the war, political conditions made it impossible for the Province to resume its activities in Benue, Nigeria. Its former Vicariate of Kroonstad, South Africa, was divided into the two Dioceses of Kroonstad and Bethlehem, with German Spiritans retaining the Diocese of Bethlehem and Dutch Dominicans taking over the more highly developed mission of Kroonstad. In the interior of Brazil the Province is charged with the Prelature of Cruzeiro do Sul, and since the war it has moved toward founding a new province in South Eastern Brazil.

cf. pp. 557 ff.

cf. p. 416

SUPERIORS OF THE PROVINCE OF GERMANY

Founder: Francis Locher, 1863
Joseph Strub, 1864-1865
John Burg, 1865-1871
Joseph Strub, 1871-1873 (the second of this name)
Amand Acker, 1895-1919
Leo Klerlein, 1919-1924 (later Vicar Apostolic of Kroonstad)
John Hoffmann, 1924-1948
Richard Gräf, 1948-1954
Henry Hack, 1954-

4. PORTUGAL

cf. pp. 208 f.;
pp. 244 ff.

Previous chapters have described the origin of the Province of Portugal, its destruction during the 1910 revolution, and the beginning of its restoration after World War I. Since then, in addition to the seminaries of Braga, Godim and Vianna do Castello, the Spiritans established themselves in Porto (1921), Guarda (1931), and

Silva (1936). After the Second World War, a special house was opened at Coimbra to provide a residence for members pursuing studies at the famous old University of Coimbra (1943). Because the existing facilities at Vianna were insufficient to take care of the swelling crowd of senior scholastics in Portugal, construction of a large new seminary was undertaken in 1953 at Carcavelos, near Lisbon.

These latter stages of the province's vigorous revival were energetically directed by Father Augustine Moura. He succeeded in enlisting support from many former students of the old Colleges of Braga and Porto who had by now risen to eminent positions. When the Holy See appointed Father Moura resident Bishop of Portalegre in 1953, the Province had already risen to a level which surpassed most of its achievements before the Revolution. Since then it has continued to grow and develop. The statistics for 1955 show a total of 357 members and 362 aspirants. Moreover, the Province is particularly blessed with a large number of Brothers.

E. P. 31, II, 102

Works. As has been mentioned above, the new Province of Portugal is almost exclusively devoted to the training of personnel

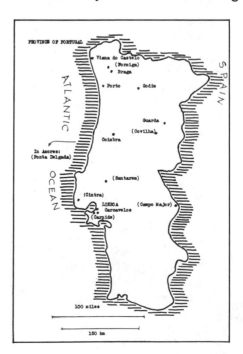

for the colonial possessions of that country. The activity of its priests and Brothers extends over the Archdiocese of Loanda, the Dioceses of Nova Lisboa, Sa de Bandeira and Silva Porto in Angola, and the island Diocese of Cape Verde. To stimulate support in the homeland, the Spiritans have organized LIAM, a missionary league with more than one hundred and twenty chapters throughout the country. Its work is supplemented by the Association of Our Lady of Africa, which has one hundred and fifty thousand members.

To further intensify this activity, the Fathers publish two excellent periodicals that go to more than fifty thousand subscribers, as well as occasional publications that sell over a million copies a year. On a more scholarly level, the Province edits a journal, *Portugal em Africa* and under the capable direction of Father Antonio Brasio, a specialist in the early history of Portuguese colonies in Africa, a splendid collection of unpublished and rare documents is being brought to light under the general title of *Monumenta Missionaria Africana.* Sponsored by the Government, seven volumes of this gigantic work have already appeared since 1952.

cf. pp. 336 f. Recently the Province has taken some steps toward the establishment of the Congregation in Spain. This venture will be discussed in Section 10 of the present Chapter.

SUPERIORS OF THE PROVINCE OF PORTUGAL

Founder: Charles Duparquet, 1867
Joseph Eigenmann, 1872-1896
Alexander Ruhle, 1896-1901
Joseph Eigenmann, 1901-1904 (second term)
Joseph Antunes, 1904-1919
Mozes Alves de Pinho, 1919-1932 (later Archbishop of Luanda)
Clement Pereira da Silva, 1932-1943
Joseph de Oliveira, 1943-1949
Augustine Moura, 1949-1953 (later Bishop of Portalegre)
Olaf Teixeira, 1953-

5. BELGIUM

cf. pp. 251 ff. In Chapter X we traced the beginnings of the Belgian Province and its early development up to the First World War. The war years from 1914 to 1918 were a time of great trial for this infant province. Its junior seminary of Lier was destroyed by artillery, and much of its personnel was called up for service with the army. Then too, because Belgium was occupied by the Germans and the Netherlands were firmly resolved to remain neutral, the Brothers' house straddling the frontier of both countries was in a particularly difficult position. The famous high tension wire that accounted for so many victims was strung right alongside the property, and armed guards constantly patrolled about the house. With wry humor, the community reported that it was protected by more than just a papal enclosure.

When peace came, the Province slowly began the long process

B. G. 34, 232   of recuperation. Since none of its houses were exceptionally large, it now had to open a special senior seminary for its philosophy students at Bon-Secours (1927) on the frontier between France and Belgium, in a residence hitherto occupied by Spiritans of the

B. G. 35, 388;   French Province. A second junior seminary for Flemish students
38, 73   followed four years later at Ingelmunster, and a clerical novitiate was begun at Hotgné in 1933.

Meanwhile the Dutch section of this combined province was progressing so rapidly that it sparked a legitimate desire to have an administrative separation into distinct entities. This desire

B. G. 35, 277   was fulfilled in 1931 when the Holy See authorized the erection of the Province of Holland. Father Sébire, the grand old man who established the Spiritans in both Belgium and Holland, stayed on as Provincial of Belgium till 1934, when he was replaced by Father George Vandenbulke.

B. G. 40, 542 ff.   In 1940, the Second World War struck new and devastating blows at unfortunate Belgium. Leaving only a few of the older Fathers and Brothers to guard the houses, everyone fled south, away from the Nazi invaders. Three members of this rear guard were slain at Gentinnes by Moroccan soldiers who were rushing northward to stop the Wehrmacht. The seminary of Gentinnes was severely damaged and plundered; the scholasticate at Louvain reeled under heavy shell-fire; and two other junior seminaries had to be closed. All the Fathers at the Novitiate in Hotgné were arrested by the Gestapo, and the Novice Master, Father Buyse, was sent to a slave labor camp in Germany. On his release from the camp after the armistice, Father Buyse was triumphantly welcomed back to his country, where no less than eleven decorations and citations, in addition to a pension, were waiting for him as tokens of gratitude for the services he had rendered his country during the war.

Father Albert Sébire, the Founder of the
Spiritan Provinces of Belgium and the
Netherlands.

Spiritan Senior Seminary, Louvain.

Four views of the Novitiate and Technical Training School constructed by Holy Ghost Brothers at Baarle-Nassau (Netherlands) and Weelde (Belgium).

B. G. 40, 545 ff. When the fighting ceased, the whole province had to be reorganized. The novitiate of Hotgné and the small seminaries of Bon-Secours and Ingelmunster were closed. Lier and Gentinnes now function as junior seminaries for Flemish and Walloon aspirants respectively. All senior seminarians were brought together at Louvain, and a special propaganda center, organized in 1946, began to function at Nijlen. According to current figures (1955), the Province has 169 members and 179 aspirants.

B. G. 41, 542
E. P. 31, II,
102

The Belgian Province of the Holy Ghost Fathers is exclusively missionary and does not possess any apostolic works in Belgium itself. The Vicariates of Kongolo and Kindu in the Belgian Congo are entrusted to its care.

SUPERIORS OF THE PROVINCE OF BELGIUM

Founder: Albert Sébire, 1900-1931
George Vandenbulke, 1931-1940
Joseph Declercq, 1940-1946
John Fryns, 1946-1955 (later Vicar Apostolic of Kindu)
Francis Proost, 1955—

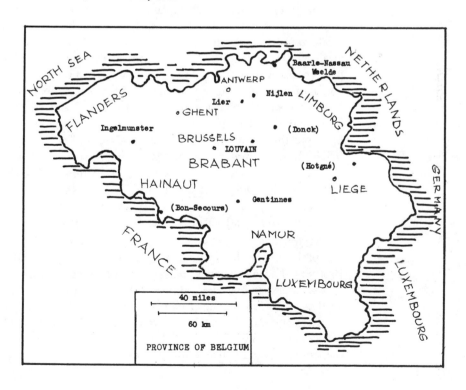

PROVINCE OF BELGIUM

6. THE NETHERLANDS

B. G. 35, 277

After the First World War, the Spiritan foundations in Holland began to develop so rapidly that in 1931 a special province was canonically erected in the Netherlands. Father Bernard Hilhorst became its first native Provincial. Three years later, when he was called to serve the Church as Vicar Apostolic of Bagamoyo in East Africa, Father Lambert Vogel succeeded him. The new Provincial, who as Superior of Weert had used the depression to give the Province a large, modern, and well-equipped junior seminary, firmly ruled the fast-growing Province until after the Second World War.

a. THE WAR YEARS

B. G. 41, 17 ff.

Unlike the first, this war did not spare Holland. Half the senior scholasticate went up in flames in 1940 when invading Nazi armies laid siege to the old Castle. Two hand-grenades were thrown into the cellars where many members of the community had sought refuge. Divine Providence was with them, however, for neither one of the missiles exploded. It must have been most uncomfortable though, to sit around those subterranean chambers awaiting the end of the battle, with all eyes gued on the deadly projectiles. When the fighting was over, it appeared that all had gotten off with nothing worse than fright, albeit it a big one. Father Luttenbacher, the Nestor of the community, seemed even to be somewhat proud of the fact that there were more bullet holes in his room than in anyone else's—a hundred and eighty to be exact. While the conflict was still raging, the house was rebuilt better than ever and it narrowly missed a second destruction during the liberation in 1945. Out of gratitude for God's protection of Spiritan lives and property, the community ever since makes an annual pilgrimage to a local shrine of the Blessed Mother of God.

At the end of the war, the novitiate at Gennep lay right in the path of the firing line and suffered heavy damages. The Brothers' house in Baarle-Nassau, requisitioned before by Dutch Nazis, was bombed and almost totally destroyed. Fortunately, all these material damages had no substantial effect on personnel, for when the war ended, the Province had no less than one hundred and twenty young Fathers ready and impatiently waiting for their chance to go and teach all nations. Only the recruitment of

Brothers was affected adversely. It ground to a temporary halt because the Dutch Nazis had ordered the dissolution of the provisional Brothers' community which had been organized at Alphen after the one at Baarle-Nassau was requisitioned.

b. Post War Development

As soon as peace was restored, provincial authorities turned their attention to the restoration of the clerical novitiate at Gennep and to the rebuilding of the Brothers' training center at Baarle-Nassau. Large workshops and living quarters were erected by the Brothers' own hands. Later they added a simple but beautiful chapel to the complex of buildings. In the technical shops, younger Brothers and postulants attain a high degree of proficiency and at the same time the product of their efforts constitutes a highly valuable source of income. Visitors who see and admire the display of superior craftsmanship by such able artisans as Brother Trudo and his associates find it difficult to leave without placing an order. From all over Europe, Superiors of religious orders and congregations come to admire the buildings and handiwork of the Brothers and to obtain first-hand information about organizing similar programs to attract vocations to the Brotherhood. Baarle-Nassau's great success is no secret: it consists in nearly five years of solid religious formation adapted to the condition of the Brothers, all of them spent in a special community wholly devoted to this work, a community where aspirants receive expert training in the particular craft for which they show special aptitude and inclination.

After the war (1946), Father Henry Strick assumed direction of the Province. He established a new community at Rhenen, and this became the administrative and public relations center of the Province. The propaganda service engaged in here is calculated not only to attract aspirants and funds necessary for running Spiritan seminaries in Holland, but aims also at the wider purpose of encouraging vocations generally among the Catholic youth of the country. Toward this objective, the Province has published a series of sixteen elementary school readers and these have been widely adopted throughout the country.

B. G. 42, 116   In 1951, a separate mission Procure was established in Halfweg, close to the centers of international air and sea transport, to serve the needs of the many Fathers and Brothers who set out for

B. G. 44, 153 Africa and other foreign countries. In 1955 another community was established at Berg-en-Dal, near the University of Nijmegen. It houses an ethnological museum and provides a residence for Fathers studying at the University. Of equal signfiance academically is the fact that the Dutch Government recently (1956) made the first move towards granting official recognition as a gymnasium[5] to the junior seminary of Weert. A special seminary for late vocations was established in 1957 at Hattem.

E. P. 31, II, 102 In 1955 the Dutch Province had 621 members and 256 aspirants. Although the Netherlands are no bigger than the State of Maryland, the Province is the third largest in the Congregation.

c. WORKS

The Spiritan Fathers do not yet have any other works in Holland except incidental ministry. Outside the Netherlands, the Province is in charge of the Diocese of Morogoro, Tanganyika;

[5]The Dutch gymnasium corresponds roughly with the American High School and Junior College.

The Spiritan Senior Seminary of Gemert, Netherlands.
(Copyright K.L.M.).

Junior Seminary of Weert, Netherlands.
(Copyright K.L.M.).

Headquarters of the Spiritan Province of the Netherlands, Rhenen, U.
(Copyright K.L.M.).

the Diocese of Doume, French Cameroons; the Prelature of Tefe in the Amazones; and the Prefecture of Bangassou in French Equatorial Africa. In addition, large numbers of Dutch Fathers and Brothers work with Spiritans of other nations in twenty-six other cf. pp. 415 f. circumscriptions of the Congregation, and in South-East Brazil they are engaged in the foundation of a future Province.

SUPERIORS OF THE PROVINCE OF THE NETHERLANDS

Founder: Albert Sébire, 1905-1931
Bernard Hilhorst, 1931-1934 (later Bishop of Morogoro)
Lambert Vogel, 1934-1946
Henry Strick, 1946-1955
Albert Blommaert, 1955-

7. GREAT BRITAIN

cf. pp. 257 ff. In Chapter X the British establishments of the Holy Ghost Fathers were left as they were in 1925 toward the end of Archbishop Le Roy's generalate. The subsequent development of these foundations must now be carried forward.

Houses of Formation. The junior seminary of the Province continues to function at Castlehead, Lancastershire, where students B. G. 41, 77 ff. are prepared for official degrees at Oxford University. In 1938 the Fathers acquired another property at Upton Hall, near Birmingham, and this they planned to use as a senior seminary. The outbreak of the war, however, postponed execution of the plan until 1945, for in war-time the senior scholasticate operated in a castle at Sandy Bridge, about ten miles from Castlehead. Quite B. G. 44, 391 recently, a special house of studies for late vocations was opened at Uddington, Lamarkshire (1956), and it is particularly worthy of note because it is the first Spiritan foundation in Scotland. cf. pp. 205 f. As has been recorded above, the Congregation's first experience with Scottish Catholic youth occurred in the former Scotch Seminary of Rockwell in Ireland. The Scots made such an excellent impression on the Fathers that their forced departure occasioned deep sadness in the community. This long-standing rapport between the Congregation and Scotland augurs well for the success of the new venture.

B. G. 40, 3 ; 172   In 1946, the Spiritan establishments in Great Britain were
at last canonically erected into an autonomous Province. The
next year, a Provincialate was erected at Bickley (Kent), not far
E. P. 31, II,   from London. At present (1955), the Province of Great Britain
102   has 106 members and 56 aspirants.

Works. In England, the Holy Ghost Fathers of the Province
have charge of the Parish of St. Joseph at Peasley Cross, near
Liverpool, a foundation originally established by the Irish Province, and another parish at New Barnet in the Archdiocese of
Westminster. Their main field of labor, however, lies in Nigeria,
where the Prefecture of Oturkpo is entrusted to their care.

SUPERIORS OF THE PROVINCE OF GREAT BRITAIN

Founder: William Carroll, 1908–1910
John Rimmer, 1910-1925
Patrick Coffey, 1925-1936
Harold Whiteside, 1936-1941
Henry Parkinson, 1941-1952
Michael Duddy, 1952-

8. POLAND

cf. p. 262

B. G. 39, 446; 557

The Spiritan Vice-Province of Poland slowly began to develop in the third decade of our century. In 1932, when the last of the World War I orphans had been brought to maturity, the orphanage at Bydgoszcz was closed. The next year, with the proceeds of the sale, a new novitiate for Brothers was opened at Puszczykowko, near Poznan. Another house for Brothers was established in 1938 at Wloki.

B. G. 40, 16 f.

When the fury of World War II began to rain its devastating blows on this unfortunate country, the hundred and twenty members and aspirants of the Congregation had to be dispersed. All houses were occupied by the Red Cross and by German troops. Some of the men died of starvation and disease in concentration camps. Then, when the Nazi troops left in 1945, the buildings were still in good condition, but wild pillaging soon left only the walls standing. By the time the Fathers and Brothers were able to reassemble, it appeared that only thirty-five of them had survived the disaster.

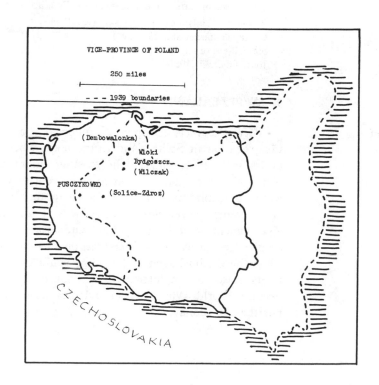

Despite these adverse conditions, they courageously set out to reopen their novitiates and restore what was left of three houses. A parish was accepted in Bydgoszcz in 1946, and exchanged two years later for another in Solice-Zdroz (Gniezno). For several years, however, all efforts to obtain permission to reopen the

B. G. 41, 10   junior seminary failed miserably. In January 1949, a mysterious fire destroyed part of the rebuilt seminary and, although reconstruction started immediately, the next month a similar fire broke

B. G. 41, 171   out. Undaunted, these brave Spiritans once again repaired the damage, and finally, in the Fall of 1949, the junior seminary at last opened its doors. A sort of senior scholasticate began to function also because it was now no longer possible to send students abroad for their philosophy and theology.

Our Province,   This revival was of brief duration. The ill-starred junior
vol. 26, no. 1,   seminary once more had to cease functioning and several Fathers
p. 3   ended up in prison. Most recent reports, however, reveal that the
B. G. 45, 115 f.   present government has released these prisoners and that there are still a few senior scholastics and aspirant Brothers.

SUPERIORS OF THE VICE PROVINCE OF POLAND

Founder: Sigismond Rydlewski, 1921-1926
Cesar Tomaszewski, 1926-1941
Stanislas Forys, 1946-1951
John Obarski, 1951-

9. SWITZERLAND

cf. pp. 261 f.   *Vice Province.* Chapter X followed the development of the Congregation in Switzerland to the point where it was hampered by its inability to enlarge the existing junior seminary at Bois-Noir. A provisional solution to this problem was found in 1929, when the aspirants were transferred to the interprovincial house of Fribourg. Seven years later it was at last possible to provide a permanent home for the junior seminarians in a beautiful newly-acquired property at Le Bouveret, on the shores of Lake Geneva. Thus the establishment at Fribourg could once again be returned to its status as an interprovincial house of studies. During the Second World War, Switzerland established its own temporary novitiate at Blonay.

St. Joseph's College, Upton Hall, England, the Senior Seminary of the Province of Great Britain.

Seminary for Late Vocations, Uddington, Scotland.

The Spiritan College of Gentinnes, Belgium.

The Junior Seminary of Bydgoszcz, Poland.

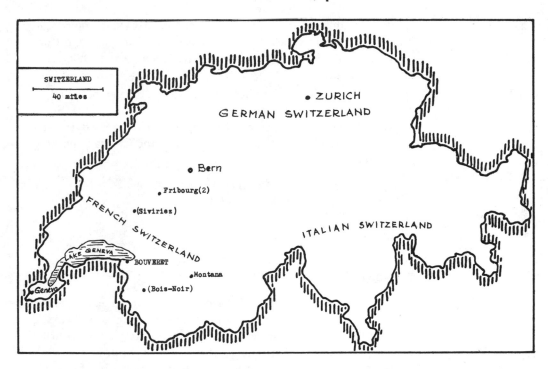

B. G. 41, 227   In 1948 a Vice-Province was erected in the country, thus giving
the Swiss that autonomy which was the object of their legitimate
B. G. 41, 228   desires. As the *Bulletin* remarked on that occasion, "Among us
any nation may aspire to its own field of missionary activity, a
field which it may claim as its mission and which it is committed
to supply with personnel and resources. If this nation receives on
its soil a missionary society that seeks its sons and its money, we
find it only right that in the public eye it should enjoy the results
produced, attributing them to itself and not to the aegis of a neighboring nation." At the moment, the Vice Province consists of only
one house (Le Bouveret)—the other three establishments of the
Congregation in Switzerland do not belong to the Vice Province—
but the Swiss ultimately aim to establish all the necessary houses
within their own territory.

B. G. 41, 231   *Works.* In Switzerland itself, the Spiritans engage only incidentally in apostolic work. Their efforts are concentrated on foreign
missions. The Vice Province has sent personnel to Madagascar,
Cameroons, Equatorial Africa, Reunion, the West Indies, and Cape

Verde. In addition, a number of its priests work in France and Canada. In recent times most of the Swiss members of the Congregation destined for the missions have gone to the Diocese of Majunga, Madagascar.

E. P. 31, II, 102 At present (1956), the Vice-Province has 109 members and 66
B. G. 41, 474 aspirants, nearly all of them French-speaking. Because of Swiss language barriers, the General Chapter of 1950 stressed the desirability of establishing the Congregation in the German-speaking part of the country as well.

SUPERIORS OF THE VICE PROVINCE OF SWITZERLAND
Founder: Joesph Villetaz, 1919-1929
John Bondallaz, 1929-1947
Anthony Clivaz, 1949
Maurice Giroud, 1949-1956
Richard Aeby, 1956-

10. SPAIN

N. D. 7, 223 As early as 1845 Father Libermann had turned his attention
N. D. 7, 256 to the problem of recruiting Spanish subjects. He was "waiting only for the right time in accord with divine providence to make a contact with some good Spanish priests and inaugurate the work in that country." The present moment, however, was not favorable because, he wrote, "Spain is not sufficiently peaceful."

cf. p. 209 In 1870, as has been said in Chapter VIII, the anticlericalism of the Portuguese Government forced the Spiritans to close their junior seminary at Santarem and to transfer the staff to Gibraltar, where the Fathers took charge of St. Bernard's College. This foundation, which lasted only a few years, was the first establishment of the Holy Ghost Fathers within the geographical limits of Spain.

B. G. 22, 503 The first foundation within its political boundaries, however,
and 679 did not come about until 1903. Under threat of expulsion from France, the Congregation opened a house at Cogullada, near Saragossa, and set about recruiting vocations in Spain. Even then, a new Spanish law in the following year made the Congregation's legal position so tenuous that Cogullada had to be abandoned.

cf. pp. 244 ff. Ten years after this first attempt, the Portuguese revolution expelled the Holy Ghost Fathers and caused them to open a junior seminary at Zamora, close to the Spanish-Portuguese frontier.

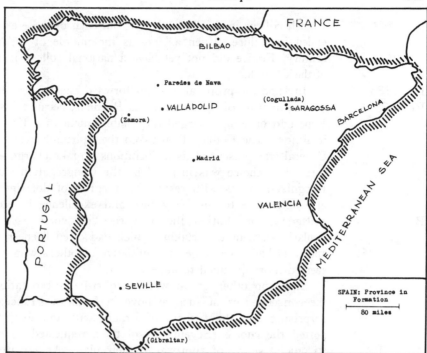

This seminary, however, was meant for Portuguese, not Spanish candidates and when things improved in Portugal after the First World War, the Spiritans closed the seminary of Zamora and returned to their native land (1920).

B. G. 41, 474

Thirty long years passed before the ever-increasing need for laborers in the vineyard caused the General Chapter of 1950 to charge the Province of Portugal with the task of making a new

B. G. 42, 228

and permanent foundation in Spain for Spaniards. That same year, a first residence and publicity center was opened in Madrid.

B. G. 44, 202;
45, 112

It was followed in 1955 by a junior seminary at Paredes de Nava in the Diocese of Palencia and two years later it reported forty students. If successful, these foundations will constitute the beginning of a new province in the Congregation.

11. ITALY

The Pontifical French Seminary. Since the sixteenth century special colleges have existed in Rome to train for the priesthood selected candidates from the various nations of the world. On several occasions, efforts had been made to establish a national

French college in the Eternal City, but each of these attempts had ended in failure. Even as late as the middle of the nineteenth century, France did not yet have a national college in the Heart of the Church.

D. C. 183
Br. 462

In 1853 the proposal was put forward anew when the Provincial Council of Bishops met at La Rochelle, because just then the Pope had once again urged the establishment of a French college in Rome. The Council then asked the Spiritans, whose Superior General was present at its deliberations, to take charge of the venture. The choice was inspired by the Congregation's universally recognized merits with respect to integrity of doctrine, unshakeable adherence to the Holy See, and excellence in ecclesiastical

B. G. 33, 663

pedagogy. In addition, the enterprise "presented itself as a particularly difficult undertaking which had often been tried in vain and thus had discouraged the initiative of others who might have seemed more qualified to undertake it."

Since no other group wanted to risk its reputation or face the consequences of such a move in Gallican France, it is not surprising that the Bishops of France with few exceptions supported the choice. Seventy-six of them requested Rome to give

Va. 220

its official stamp of approval to their plan. As a matter of fact, Pope Pius IX had already personally suggested that the Congregation undertake this work. Moreover, Father Libermann had always desired to establish a house of his congregation in Rome in order to secure the closest possible contact with the center of the Church. Thus it came about that the year after Libermann's death, Father Louis de Lannurien went off to Rome to become the founder of the French Seminary.

D. C. 184

The French Government, which at first had shown no special concern or interest in this new foundation, soon became alarmed over the decrease of Gallican tendencies in the clergy who were being trained in Rome by the Spiritans. It feared that no bishop it might nominate would be accepted by the Holy See unless he

cf. p. 216

met the approval of these priests. In fact, this fear was one of the reasons why a new effort was made in 1861 to deprive the Congregation of its legal recognition in France.

Lann. 13 ff.

After an appropriately humble start on the *Via dell' Umiltà*, the Seminary was transferred to the *Salito del Grillo*, and then in 1856 to its present location on the *Via Santa Chiara*. Three years

B. G. 1, 564

later, so much progress had been made that a grateful Pope Pius

The Interprovincial University Seminary of Fribourg, Switzerland.
—*Photo Rast, Copyright.*

The Junior Seminary of Le Bouveret, on the border of
Geneva Lake, Switzerland.

The Institute of the Holy Ghost, the interprovincial study center of the Spiritans in Rome.

The Pontifical French Seminary of Rome. A view of the cloister.

IX entrusted the Seminary to the Holy Ghost Fathers in perpetuity and in 1902, Leo XIII raised the institution to the status of a Pontifical Seminary. When it celebrated its first centennial in 1953, the staff was able to point with pride to its accomplishments: more than three thousand young men selected by their bishops for their special talents and promise had been trained at this important Spiritan institution. On their return to their homeland, many of them had found influential positions in the Church as professors and directors of seminaries, and subsequently as Bishops and Cardinals. In fact, the Seminary counted fifty-three living bishops among its alumni at the time of its centenary. Through the training it gave these leaders of the Church, the Seminary became one of the most influential factors in the destruction of Gallicanism, that pernicious trend which still plagued the Church in France during the nineteenth century.

Among the priests attached to its teaching staff, the Seminary has had several Spiritans of world-wide renown in their respective fields of learning. Limiting our catalogue to those who have passed on, we may mention Father Alphonse Eschbach in moral theology, Father Joseph Haegy in liturgy, and Father John Frey in Scripture.

The Institute of the Holy Ghost. Until 1950, the French Seminary served also as the interprovincial Roman house of studies for members of the Congregation. In this capacity, it trained one hundred and eighty of them. At the close of its first century of service, it counted no less than thirteen living Spiritan alumni who had been raised to the episcopal dignity. As early as 1938, however, the General Chapter had urged the foundation of a separate interprovincial house of studies in Rome, a seminary set aside exclusively for the members of the Congregation, where they might study and work within the proper family atmosphere of their own religious order. World War II delayed the execution of this plan till 1949, when at last the Institute of the Holy Ghost was founded on the *Corso d'Italia*. This institute also serves as the residence of the Congregation's Procurator at the Holy See.

The Russian College. In 1923, the excellent reputation of the Pontifical French Seminary inspired the Holy See to ask if the Holy Ghost Fathers would not consider founding a Russian seminary, to be established at Lille, France. Both Cardinal van Rossum, the Prefect of the Propaganda, and Pope Pius XI strongly

B. G. 21, 567

B. G. 43, 77

B. G. 43, 77

B. G. 41, 125

B. G. 31, 188 f.

urged the Spiritans to undertake this work. Its acceptance would have been wholly in accord with the tradition of the Congregation as conceived by both Father des Places and Father Libermann, but Archbishop Le Roy, who was then Superior General, thought that the Congregation had already over-extended itself. He did his utmost to escape from the proposed task. Meanwhile, Pope Pius XI decided that the Russian Seminary should be established in Rome itself and this gave Archbishop Le Roy an opportunity to repeat his objections. For the most part, they were based on lack of personnel and general unpreparedness for such an undertaking. Rome's reply was almost a formal order and it was couched in rather severe terms. Even then, at the risk of serious pontifical displeasure, Archbishop Le Roy asked once more not to have this task imposed on a congregation which was already so heavily engaged in apostolic works that the new venture might thereby be exposed to failure. Before such determined resistance, Pope Pius XI finally gave in and entrusted the seminary to the Jesuits.

B. G. 22, 474   *Junior Seminary of Suza.* During the first two decades of this century, the Spiritans had a junior seminary in the north of Italy. When Combes' inane persecution forced the seminary of Seyssinet to close its doors, Italy welcomed the exiles with open arms. The town of Suza placed a generous gift at the disposal of the Fathers so that they might restore a former Capuchin monastery. The Junior seminary remained there till 1920, averaging each year from eighty to a hundred French youths who were

B. G. 29, 721 f.   unable to follow their vocation in the fatherland. When they were granted permission to return in 1920, the seminary was transferred to Allex where it still functions as a fertile source of priests for both the Congregation and the diocese of France.

B. G. 41, 474   Although the Congregation numbers some Italians among its members, it has never had a Province in Italy. That is why the Chapter General of 1950 expressly recognized the desirability of an Italian Province and commissioned the Dutch Spiritans to investigate ways and means of establishing one.

CHAPTER FOURTEEN

NORTH AMERICA

1. UNITED STATES OF AMERICA

cf. pp. 209 ff.
In Chapter VIII we traced the origin of the Spiritan Province of the United States and the early history of its foundations in Ohio, Pennsylvania and Arkansas. In the following pages the subsequent development of the Holy Ghost Congregation in the States will be the object of our consideration.

a. Houses of Formation

B. G. 18, 733 f.; 19, 134, ff.; 22, 424 ff.
Until 1897, the Pittsburgh College of the Holy Ghost (Duquesne University) continued to function as the central community of the Congregation. In addition to the College, the community conducted a junior and senior seminary, as well as a novitiate and postulancy for the Brothers. However, in 1897 the novitiate was transferred to a newly acquired property at Cornwells Heights, just north of Philadelphia. The next year an effort was made to inaugurate a senior scholasticate there, but because of the relatively small number of students involved, the Motherhouse decided that it would be better to send them to Europe until their group would increase sufficiently to justify a special senior seminary within the Province. The departure of the senior seminarians provided an opportunity for opening a second Junior seminary at Cornwells. This work prospered so well that in 1908 a beginning was made on construction of a large building to house the growing

B. G. 23, 810 ff.
number of aspirants. Meanwhile, in 1904, a property called "Ferndale" had been acquired at Norwalk, Connecticut. When a building had been erected on the land, the clerical novitiate was transferred there and a senior scholasticate at last began to function in the same location (1906).

B. G. 30, 611; 648
After the First World War, the steady increase in candidates made it necessary to separate the novitiate from the Scholasticate. The novices were sent fourteen miles north to Ridgefield, Connecticut, where a thirty-two acre estate had been transformed into a beautiful novitiate (1922). Between 1925 and 1930 these various

341

houses all had to be enlarged to take care of the numerous aspirants who sought admission. Lest there would be too great a concentration of houses in the East, however, a new junior seminary was constructed after World War II at Ann Arbor, Michigan, in the Archdiocese of Detroit (1952). To faciliate the pursuit of academic degrees, a new collegiate seminary is presently to be constructed in Bethel Boro near Pittsburgh, Pennsylvania. Its students will reside there and follow courses at Duquesne University.

Finally, to relieve the scarcity of well-trained Brothers, whose services are so indispensable both at home and in the missions, special facilities are currently under construction at Richmond, near Detroit. This new community will comprise the Brothers' postulancy and novitiate, and the young Brothers will be kept there for an additional three-year period for advanced religious and technical training.

In 1940, the administrative headquarters of the Province, which since 1874 had been successively in Pittsburgh, Cornwells, Ferndale and New York, was at last separately housed when a special residence was acquired in Washington, D. C.

The 1955 statistics of the Province reveal a total of 365 members and 142 aspirants. Also there is a relatively large number of Fathers and Brothers from other Provinces working in the United States.

b. WORKS IN THE HOMELAND

1. *Educational Institutes*

Duquesne University. The most important of all Spiritan educational works in the Western Hemisphere is the institution known as Duquesne University. Started in 1878 as a college on Wylie Avenue, it was transferred four years later to its present location on an eminence at the top of Pittsburgh's famous Golden Triangle. A massive edifice had been constructed there by the Fathers and Brothers who had been exiled from Germany. A chapel was added to it in 1895 and then enlarged in 1904. Meanwhile, Bishop Phelan, who had succeeded Bishop Tuigg in the episcopal see of Pittsburgh, continued to support the college not only by his sympathetic encouragement but by subsidies from the diocesan treasury as well.

B. G. 42, 430

B. G. 39, 303

E. P. 31, II, 121

cf. p. 212

B. G. 17, 874; 23, 664

B. G. 34, 114

Collegiate Seminary to be built at Bethel Borough, near Pittsburgh.

St. Mary's Senior Seminary, Norwalk, Connecticut.

Holy Ghost Junior College, Cornwells Heights, near Philadelphia.

View of the Junior Seminary at Ann Arbor, near Detroit, Michigan.

B. G. 26, 477 ff.   In 1911, the State of Pennsylvania granted the College a university charter under which it was entitled to confer degrees in Arts and Sciences, Business Administration, Law, Medicine, Pharmacy and Dentistry. In subsequent years this charter was amended to include Music, Education and Nursing. At the same time, the name of the school was changed to Duquesne University of the Holy Ghost. This was done because the American practice of abbreviating names of university athletic teams to the distinctive word in their title made the Fathers fear that the sacred name of the Holy Ghost might be put to vulgar use in the course of future athletic events. For this reason they preferred to name the institute after the Marquis Duquesne, Governor General of New France, who had built a fort and established the first settlement at the river junction which later became the site of the city of Pittsburgh.

B. G. 28, 30 ff.   By obtaining its charter in 1911, Duquesne University became the first institute of higher learning under Catholic auspices in the State of Pennsylvania, but this courageous step forward was

PROVINCE OF THE UNITED STATES:
EASTERN SECTOR
200 miles

PITTSBURGH AREA
50 miles

taken only after much hesitation. The Fathers realized only too well the tremendous responsibility and the heavy financial burden that would fall on their shoulders. On the other hand, they knew that they could count on Bishop Canevin, who had succeeded Bishop Phelan. The new Bishop promised both moral support and material assistance. To show in a practical way how much he wanted to help the Spiritans in developing the University, he became its official Chancellor. Next, he recommended the University to the generosity of his priests and faithful, and then made a substantial personal contribution himself.

B. G. 28, 31 ff.   Over and above this encouraging state of affairs, prospects for State support for the new University looked very good indeed. In 1913, Duquesne applied for a grant of $210,000 for construction, maintenance and salaries. The construction grant was to be used for a large science building and when the bill proposing it came up for discussion before the Legislature at the State Capital, the House of Representatives voted 165 to 3 in favor of it. A similar bill in behalf of the University of Pittsburgh, then headed by a Presbyterian minister, was headed for defeat in the same session, but Duquesne University used its influence with Catholic members of the Legislature to help its sister institution. This assistance was effective, for the bill in favor of the University of Pittsburgh went through with three more votes than the required minimum of two thirds. Then, when the Senate gave its unanimous approval to the bill in favor of Duquesne University, all efforts seemed to have been crowned with success.

The Governor still had to append his signature, but on several occasions he had already manifested his intention to approve the grant. Everyone was much surprised, therefore, when at the last possible moment, on July 26, 1913, after approving a grant of $400,000 in favor of the University of Pittsburgh, the Governor suddenly vetoed the bill and alleged "lack of funds." Most likely, the approach of local elections in Pittsburgh constituted the real motive behind the veto of a bill against which only three members in both houses of the legislature had voted, because the November election of 1913 brought on a revival of bigotry and anti-Catholic feeling such as the city had not witnessed for several decades. These conditions may have been casting their shadow before.

B. G. 28, 562   Father Martin Hehir, then President of the University, continued his battle for equal rights to state grants for several more years. In 1917 he had a small measure of success: an allocation of $15,000 was made, the first one in the United States, he thought, which was ever granted to a university under Catholic auspices. Two years later, an allocation of $100,000 for operating expenses was passed by the Legislature, although subsequently it was reduced by fifty percent. By 1923, however, an anti-Catholic society, a forerunner of the contemporary bigoted group of "Protestants and Other Americans United for the Separation of Church and State," succeeded in having the payment of such grants to church-related universities declared illegal.

The withdrawal of State subsidies meant that the University had to look elsewhere for the funds it needed. Though the Holy Ghost Fathers work without pay and their consecrated services constitute a living endowment (its present value is close to five million dollars) the operating expenses of an institution of higher learning are extremely high and always require additional income from sources other than student fees. Fortunately, Bishop Canevin continued to stand by the beleagured Spiritans. Under his patronage a drive for a million dollar building fund was launched. The proceeds were to be used to construct a gymnasium—then the largest in the area—and a class-room building. Upon its completion, this building was called Canevin Hall and dedicated to the memory of the beloved Bishop-Chancellor who had just gone to his eternal reward. A few years later, a special library building was added to the physical plant.

The years of the Second World War brought about a new period of crisis in the history of the University. The draft of all young men of military age cut its enrollment to less than fifteen hundred, including special groups of cadets sent in by the Army Air Corps. Without the devoted aid of many friends who came to its rescue and the indefatigable efforts of Father Raymond Kirk, Duquesne would certainly have had to follow the example of many of its sister institutions and close its doors for the duration of the conflict. Contrariwise, the post war years gave rise to new problems of a difficult sort. Three large temporary buildings had to be erected to cope with the flood of veterans whose numbers in 1948 swelled the student body to beyond the 5,500 mark.

When the crest of this flood subsided after 1950, a broad expansion program was drawn up to provide permanent and adequate facilities for the 6,000 students who are expected to

B. G. 30, 58

B. G. 32, 157

B. G. 40, 503 f.

follow courses in the University during the next decade. These plans envision the extension of Duquesne over a thirty-seven acre campus in the heart of the city and the construction of a dozen new buildings. Under the leadership of the incumbent president of the University, the Very Reverend Father Vernon F. Gallagher, and with the support of alumni, industry, foundations and friends, a thirteen million dollar fund drive inaugurated the program in 1953. This program is intended to continue for the next twenty years. His Excellency, the Most Reverend John F. Dearden, Bishop of Pittsburgh and Chancellor of the University, showed his support of the plans by a contribution on behalf of the Diocese and a pledge of his personal interest. Since then, two new buildings, Trinity Hall and Assumption Hall, have been added, and a ten-story edifice to house the Schools of Law and Business Administration is presently under construction. It alone will cost two and one half million dollars.

Duquesne University, coeducational since 1911, serves not only Catholic students but non-Catholics as well. About twenty-five percent of its student body belongs to various Protestant denominations and a smaller quantity adheres to the Jewish faith. On the other hand, it counts about 500 priests and six bishops among its 20,000 living alumni. Although most of its students come from Pennsylvania and neighboring states, many other states and a dozen foreign countries are represented on the campus.

Recently, increased American interest in Africa, together with a consciousness of the role that Spiritans have played in the civilization and Christianization of that continent, led the University to found a special Institute of African Studies. Its program of courses will begin in the Fall Semester of 1958.

B. G. 40, 504 f.　　*St. Emma Academy.* In 1895, Colonel and Mrs. Edward Morrell, owners of large tracts of land in Virginia, dedicated their 2000 acre estate "Belmead" to the education of colored boys. They invited the Holy Ghost Fathers to assume the chaplaincy of this endowed institute and of a similar neighboring foundation for colored girls which had been established by the same family. Except for a brief interruption from 1899 to 1903, they continued to act in this capacity till 1928. In that year Benedictine monks took over the boys' institute, which is called St. Emma Academy, and the Spiritans withdrew their chaplains. However, in 1947, at the request of the Board of Directors, the Congregation assumed

Duquesne University, as it will look after the completion of its expansion program.

The first two new buildings erected under the Duquesne University
Development Program: Trinity Hall (top), Assumption Hall (bottom).

complete charge of the Academy which, in addition to a full high school program, has agricultural and trade school divisions as well.

Situated in a sparsely populated county (population: four per square mile) about forty-five miles west of Richmond, St. Emma is a small town in itself. Academic buildings, a Church, a gymnasium, electrical and water plants, large workshops, a store, farm buildings, and dozens of dwellings for employees make it an almost self-contained unit.

Since it is operated as a military school—the only American military academy for colored boys—both Fathers and Brothers wear regulation Army uniforms and in the exercise of their functions are regarded as Army Officers. At present, the Academy has an enrollment of about 250 students.

Notre Dame High School. The most recent educational institute operated by the Spiritans is Notre Dame High School at Riverside, California, in the Diocese of San Diego. In 1957 they acceded to Bishop Buddy's request and assumed charge of this newly-constructed facility which will accommodate 500 students.

2. *Social Works*

B. G. 15,
931 ff.

St. Joseph House, Philadelphia. In 1889, Father McElhone, a priest of the Archdiocese of Philadelphia, opened a small asylum for the homeless boys who roamed about aimlessly after they had finished working in the shops and factories of the city. The idea had possibilities but, as Archbishop Ryan realized, its success would depend on full-time direction. Upon his repeated requests, the Holy Ghost Fathers agreed to take over the venture.

B. G. 28, 24

They moved into the house on Pine Street in October 1890, and assumed responsibility for seven boys and a building that was

B. G. 16,
1014 f.

mortgaged to the tune of $5,000. Three years later, the number of youngsters had risen to eighty. Most of these were "working boys": they held jobs in the city and returned "home," as they

B. G. 17,
890 ff.

loved to call it, at night for meals, play, study, and rest. By 1894 the "Home" had been greatly enlarged and provided with many facilities. The solicitude of its directors extended not only to the more than one hundred boarders, but also to hundreds of others whom they had placed with respectable families and whose progress they followed closely.

The results obtained in five years' time surpassed all expectations, both from the religious and from the sociological point of view. The Pennsylvania State Welfare Commission declared the Home one of the best organized institutes of its kind in the whole United States. However, neither the State nor the Archdiocese gave—or give—any direct financial support to the Home. Throughout its history it has been forced to rely on the protection of its heavenly Patron who, thank God, has always proved himself an excellent provider. Thousands of benefactors have not been wanting.

B. G. 36, 152

In 1929, St. Joseph's Home, which now shelters two hundred and fifty boys, was transferred to its present location at Sixteenth Street and Allegheny Avenue, where a large set of buildings had been constructed. The Home now had its own Grade and High Schools, in addition to all other facilities which normal healthy youngsters expect. Since its inception in 1889, it has prepared more than 5,000 boys for a decent Christian life as useful members of society and about thirty of these young lads have joined the priesthood or are in the seminary—a higher percentage than obtains among Catholic boys who receive their education and training within the circle of their own family.

3. *Parishes and Missions*

Despite current interest and progress in desegregation, there are still parishes and missions which are de facto "white" or "colored" because the population groups in which they are centered are "white" and "colored." For that reason we find it convenient to maintain the distinction here.

cf. p. 228 f.

Colored Parishes and Missions. In Chapter IX we saw that the Spiritans began to undertake works for the colored in 1881, a few years after their arrival in the States. From 1910 on, the hierarchy appealed more and more frequently to the Congregation for the advancement of this aposotolate. At last, with the support of Mother Katherine Drexel, who had established the Motherhouse of her Blessed Sacrament Sisters close to Holy Ghost

Father Joseph Strub, the Founder of the
Spiritan Province of the U. S. A.

St. Mary's Church, Sharpsburg, Pa. View of the interior.

St. Emma Military Academy, Rock Castle, Va. The Chapel and one
of the dormitories on its two thousand acre campus.

St. Joseph's House, Philadelphia. View of the main building.

Seminary at Cornwells Heights, Pa., the Fathers were able to found or take over scores of colored parishes throughout the United States. It would lead us too far afield to enter into a detailed history of each of these foundations, but it may at least be pointed out that as of 1955, eighty-two Fathers[1] were stationed in forty-six colored parishes and missions with a total of 41,275 Catholics under their care and more than 8,000 children in their parochial schools. Thirty-seven of the Negro parishes are situated in the South; the remaining nine are in industrial cities of the North.[2]

---

[1]Adding the eight Fathers of St. Emma Academy, Rock Castle, Virginia, the total comes to ninety priests in colored works. This number constitutes 13% of the total of all priests (673) engaged in Negro Missions in the States.

[2]The following is a list of these colored parishes and missions:

Alabama

1. St. Mary Magdalen, Tuscaloosa (1929)

Arkansas

2. Good Shepherd Mission, Conway

3. St. John, Fort Smith (1917)

4. St. Cyprian, Helena (1928)

5. St. Gabriel, Hot Springs N. P. (1940)

Louisiana

6. Our Lady of Lourdes, Abbeville (1930)

7. St. James, Alexandria, (1911)

(Continued on succeeding page)

White Parishes. In addition to the forty-six colored parishes and missions, the Spiritans have charge of twenty-seven others throughout the United States: nine in Pennsylvania, five in Rhode Island, four in California, three in Michigan, two in Wisconsin and Arkansas, and one each in Alabama and Arizona. Many of the older ones were founded by the Congregation for the benefit of German, Polish, Portuguese and other immigrants who flocked to the States during the late nineteenth and early twentieth cen-

---

8. St. Christopher, Bunkie (1948)
9. Our Lady of the Assumption, Carenco (1925)
10. Bl. Martin de Porres, Delcambre (1948)
11. St. Augustine, Isle Brevelle (1913)
12. St. Paul, Lafayette (1914)
13. Sacred Heart, Lake Charles (1910)
14. Immaculate Heart, Lake Charles (1954)
15. Our Lady of Prompt Succor, Mansura (1944)
16. Holy Ghost, Marksville (1919)
17. Our Lady of Sorrows, Moreauville (1946)
18. St. Anthony, Natchitoches (1935)
19. St. Edward, New Iberia (1918)
20. Holy Ghost, New Orleans (1915)
21. St. Monica, New Orleans (1924)
22. Holy Ghost, Opelousas (1920)
23. St. Joseph, Opelousas (1949)
24. St. Catherine, Opelousas (1950)
25. Our Lady of the Blessed Sacrament, Shreveport (1922)
26. St. Daniel, Shreveport (1944)

Michigan

27. St. Benedict the Moor, Detroit (1932)
28. Holy Ghost, Detroit (1946)
29. Sacred Heart, Detroit (1938)

30. Holy Family Mission, Inkster (1951)

New York

31. St. Mark, New York (1912)

North Carolina

32. Our Lady of Lourdes, Sanford (1942)
33. Our Lady of Victories, Salisbury (1941)

Ohio

34. St. John the Baptist, Dayton (1928)

Oklahoma

35. St. Augustine, Muskogee (1940)
36. St. Peter Claver, Oklahoma (1926)
37. St. Monica, Tulsa (1929)
38. St. Augustine, Tulsa (1950)

Pennsylvania

39. St. Benedict, Pittsburgh (1889)
40. St. Peter Claver, Philadelphia (1889)
41. Our Lady of the Blessed Sacrament, Philadelphia (1909)

South Carolina

42. St. Peter Claver, Charleston (1917)
43. Our Lady of Mercy, Charleston (1954)
44. St. Joseph, Hartsville (1954)

Virginia

45. Queen of Peace, Arlington (1945)
46. St. Edward, Belmead-on-James (1948)

turies.[3] Many of them have developed into large parishes with beautiful churches and well-equipped schools, but one should not forget that all of them were founded by real pioneers. The Fathers had to start by renting a little hall, adding a few rooms for classes, and struggling manfully until, by dint of hard labor and the support of their loyal parishioners, they could construct the splendid parish plants of which their people are now so proud. Apart from the parishes retained by the Congregation, there are many others which owe their existence to the pioneering labor of the Spiritans, even though subsequently they were transferred to the diocesan clergy.

4. *Other Works*

B. G. 17, 885

The Pontifical Association of the Holy Childhood. In 1892 the central office of the Pontifical Association of the Holy Childhood appealed to the Holy Ghost Fathers to establish a national headquarters in the United States. Although the Association al-

---

[3]We append here a list of these parishes:

Pennsylvania
1. St. Mary, Sharpsburg (1874)
2. St. Ann, Millvale (1873)
3. St. Anthony, Millvale (1886)
4. St. Stanislaus, Pittsburgh (1886)
5. Sacred Heart, Emsworth (1891)
6. Immaculate Heart, Pittsburgh (1895)
7. Sacred Heart, Tarentum (1888)
8. Our Mother of Consolation, Mt. Carmel (1900)
9. St. Joseph, Mt. Carmel (1905)

Rhode Island
10. St. Catherine, Little Compton (1908)
11. Holy Ghost, North Tiverton (1913)
12. St. Anthony, Portsmouth (1908)
13. St. Christopher, Tiverton (1911)
14. St. Madeleine Sophie, Tiverton (1948)

California
15. Our Lady of Guadeloupe, Bakersfield (1948)
16. St. Leo, Del Mar (1945)
17. Our Lady of the Valley, Hemet (1946)
18. St. Catherine, Riverside (1945)

Michigan
19. St. Mary, Detroit (1893)
20. St. Joachim, Detroit (1885)
21. St. Joseph, Bay City (1888)

Wisconsin
22. Holy Ghost, Chippewa Falls (1901)
23. Notre Dame, Chippewa Falls (1890)

Arkansas
24. St. Joseph, Conway (1878)
25. Sacred Heart, Morrilton (1897)

Alabama
26. St. John, Tuscaloosa (1929)

Arizona
27. St. John, Tucson (1948)

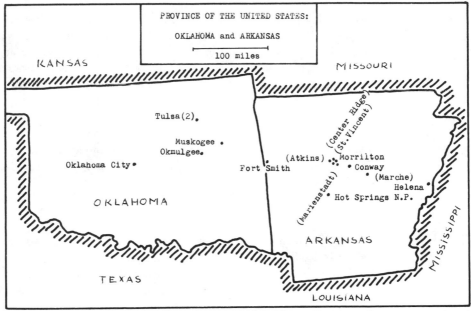

```
                    PROVINCE OF THE UNITED STATES:

                    OKLAHOMA and ARKANSAS

                           100 miles
```

KANSAS   MISSOURI

OKLAHOMA

Tulsa (2).

Muskogee .
Okmulgee.

Oklahoma City •

Fort Smith   (Atkins) .. Morrilton
                              • Conway
                                • (Marche)
                                  Helena
                    • Hot Springs N.P.

(Center Ridge)
(St. Vincent)
(Mariensladt)

ARKANSAS

MISSISSIPPI

TEXAS

LOUISIANA

ready had offices in some American dioceses, there was not yet
a national center to correlate the work of the various diocesan
directors. Because there was no over-all coordination, the work
had not progressed as well as it might have. In an endeavor to
help the Holy Childhood Association as best it could, the Congregation agreed to organize and direct the work on a nationwide level. Accordingly, Father Anthony Zielenbach, who for
some years had already been engaged in organizing local branches,
was now appointed National Director.

B. G. 19, 145;   At first, the task proved to be a formidable one. The new
21, 219 ff.   idea of centralized authority and direction met with lip-service,
apathy, and even open opposition. There were two reasons for
this: first, unlike the Protestants who, even before 1900, sent five
million dollars a year to their missions, American Catholics (except those of German descent) were not mission-minded; secondly,
the Society for the Propagation of the Faith agreed that the Bishops
of America might retain nearly half of their mission collections
for missionary work within the country. The Holy Childhood
Association was laboring under a handicap on both scores.

B. G. 25, 146   Despite these difficulties, the work began to move ahead. At
the first National Mission Congress held in Chicago in 1908,
Father Wilms, then National Director, could point out that per-

Nuestra Señora del Carmen Church of Barceloneta, Puerto Rico, one
of nine Spiritan parishes in this island.

A rural mission chapel in Puerto Rico. Ninety missions are attached to
the Spiritan parishes in this island.

Holy Ghost Church, Opelousas, Louisiana, one of the Spiritans' forty-
six colored parishes in the U. S. A.

McDonell Memorial High School, Notre Dame Parish, Chippewa Falls,
Wisconsin. Fifteen Spiritan parishes in the United States have their
own parochial High School.

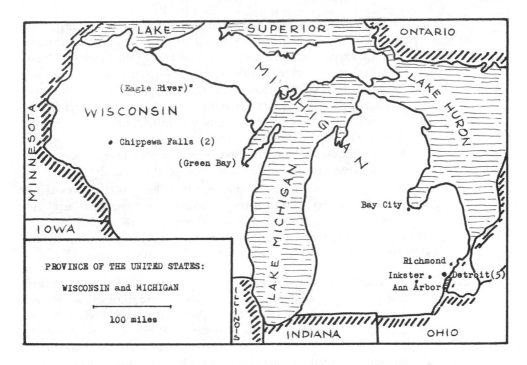

PROVINCE OF THE UNITED STATES:

WISCONSIN and MICHIGAN

100 miles

centagewise the mission contributions of Catholic children exceeded those of their parents. As a whole, however, the Catholics of the English-speaking world still stood at the bottom of the list of contributors to the missions: their gifts accounted for only one percent of the total receipts.

B. G. 28, 10 f.   The turning-point came during the First World War, when the missions lost most of their income from Europe. To relieve their distress, the Holy See sent a letter in 1915 to the Cardinals of the U. S. A. and Canada, inviting them to have the Holy Childhood
B. G. 32, 187   established in all Catholic schools throughout America. Before this letter the annual receipts did not amount to more than about $23,000 a year; after it, the figure went beyond the $100,000 mark and has kept climbing ever since.

In subsequent years local offices were set up in all dioceses. The National Office, which till 1931 had functioned in various Spiritan communities and then in a rented office in the Pittsburgh area, now needed more space and was transferred to a separate building on Pittsburgh's North Side. The continuous development of the work ultimately necessitated construction of a large new central office building in 1955. Much of the credit for this achievement as well as for the flourishing condition of the Holy Childhood Association in America must be given to its former National Director, Richard H. Ackerman, C.S.Sp., who became Auxiliary Bishop of San Diego, California, in 1956. At the end of his tenure, the Association had diocesan branches throughout the States, and 3,000,000 Catholic children were enrolled as members. The pennies they contributed during the past year amounted to a substantial bit of assistance for the missionary work of the Church.

In passing we may remark here that the United States is not the only country in which the Spiritans direct the Pontifical Association of the Holy Childhood. They are also in charge of the national offices of Ireland and Brazil. Elsewhere, as in Germany, they perform special services for the Association.

B. G. 22, 420 f.   *Mission Band and Retreats.* On various occasions, the Fathers had seriously considered forming a special group of priests to take care of the numerous requests for parochial missions which flowed into the headquarters of the Province. While it was possible to fill some of the requests, it became increasingly obvious that a specially-deputed Mission Band was the only answer to the situation. However, it was not until 1912 that such a Mission Band could be organized. At that time, the Province of Ireland sent a group of men for this specific purpose. Later, the Irishmen were replaced by Fathers of the American Province and the Band continued to function successfully till after the Second World War, when its activities were suspended temporarily because other works laid prior claim to American personnel.

B. G. 26, 856

B. G. 40, 507

cf. p. 128   The work of closed retreats, which Father Libermann had long ago envisioned for his priests, was organized in 1935 in Ferndale. Because the buildings could be used for retreats only during the summer when the scholastics were absent on vacation, a special retreat house was opened at New Canaan, Connecticut in 1948, in a magnificent estate that had been acquired for this purpose.

B. G. 40, 502

Armed Forces. Since the beginning of World War II, the American Province has contributed a number of priests to the chaplains' corps of the Army, Navy and Air Force. In addition, the Military Ordinariate of American Overseas Forces in Europe is headed by the Very Reverend Father Joseph Quinlan, the

American representative on the General Council of the Congregation.

c. MISSIONS

Outside the continental area of the United States, American Spiritans labor in Puerto Rico and the Diocese of Moshi in East Africa. Despite the recent interest of other religious groups in Africa, the American Holy Ghost Fathers in the Dark Continent are still more numerous than their compatriots from other orders and congregations.

SUPERIORS OF THE PROVINCE OF THE UNITED STATES

Founder: Joseph Strub, 1873-1890

Joseph Oster, 1890-1897 (later Prefect Apostolic of the Miquelon Islands)

Joseph Eigenmann, 1897-1898

Anthony Zielenbach, 1898-1906

John T. Murphy, 1906-1910 (later Bishop of Port Louis)

Eugene Phelan, 1910-1933

Christopher J. Plunkett, 1933-1939

George J. Collins, 1939-1949

Francis H. McGlynn, 1949-

2. CANADA

a. FRENCH CANADA

cf. pp. 259 ff.

B. G. 41, 107

In Chapter X we traced the Congregation's establishment in Canada and its slow development there prior to the Second World War. When hostilities made it impossible for Canadian aspirants to go to France for their novitiate and senior seminary years, steps had to be taken to organize adequate facilities for this purpose within Canada itself. In quick succession a novitiate for clerics and Brothers was opened at Lac-au-Saumon (1941), a senior seminary was purchased in Montreal (1943), and a publicity center was established in the same city (1946). Immediately after the war, a separate Canadian Province was canonically erected (1946). In 1955 another residence was opened at Gamelin, near Montreal, and the construction of a new senior seminary at Quebec will soon solve the housing problems of the Province.

B. G. 45, 116

B. G. 43, 324; 372; 44, 119

The College of St. Alexander continues to function as the junior seminary. Although a disastrous fire ruined most of the buildings in 1954, a generous grant of $600,000 from the Quebec Government made it possible to erect new fire-proof buildings and to generally modernize the College.

Works. In addition to the College, the Province serves the parishes of St. Edmund at Lac-au-Saumon (1942) and of St. Alexander in Limbour (1946).[4] In Africa, the Nigerian Prefecture of Kabba is entrusted to the Canadian Fathers.

E. P. 31, II, 102

As of 1955, the Province had 116 members and 117 aspirants. Its present vigor gives promise of rapid advances in the future.

SUPERIORS OF THE PROVINCE OF (FRENCH) CANADA

Founder: Amet Limbour, 1905

Joseph Oster, 1905-1908 (later Prefect Apostolic of the Miquelon Islands)

Henry Van Haecke, 1908-1909

Albert David, 1909-1911

Joseph Burgsthaler, 1911-1923

René Piacentini, 1921-1923

Gustav Le Gallois, 1923-1928

---

[4] The town of Limbour is named after the Spiritan Father Amet Limbour, the founder of St. Alexander College.

Main building of St. Alexander College, Limbour, Canada.

Father Amet Limbour, the Founder of the
Spiritan Province of Canada.

The new senior seminary of the French Canadian Province at Quebec
which will be opened in the Fall of 1958.

The new Bishop McNeil High School which will open its doors in
September 1958 at Toronto.

Paul Droesch, 1928-1938
Philip Nadon, 1938-1939
Emile Muller, 1939
Louis Taché de la Broquerie, 1939-1951
Lucien Michaud, 1951-

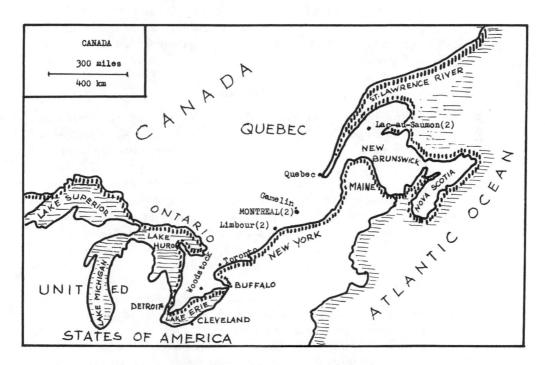

b. ENGLISH CANADA

cf. pp. 259 f.

As was mentioned in Chapter X, the Holy Ghost Fathers had been invited in 1863 and again in 1865 to establish foundations in English-speaking Canada, but the urgency of personnel needs elsewhere had prevented them from accepting these offers.

During the first quarter of the present century, it was hoped that the large number of English-speaking students at the College of St. Alexander might provide a bridge-head for expansion into the non-French part of the country. However, because of the differences in mentality and language between French and English Canadians, tensions arose, and, as we have seen, the English division of St. Alexander's had to be discontinued.

cf. p. 261

B. G. 41, 474

B. G. 43, 522;
44, 119

The General Chapter of 1950 emphasized the desirability of an English-speaking province in Canada and strongly recommended that one be started. Four years later, the Province of Ireland took the first steps to implement this recommendation by founding a community at Woodstock, Ontario. At present, the Fathers of this community serve a local parish and function as a Mission Band. In this fashion they will become thoroughly acquainted with the surrounding country by the time they open their new high school in Toronto in September, 1958.

3. St. Pierre and Miquelon

cf. pp. 28 f.

In Chapter II we learned that the Prefecture of St. Pierre and Miquelon, which is the smallest in the world (93 sq. miles), was entrusted to the Spiritans in 1765 after France had been forced to cede all its other Canadian possessions to England. Till 1874, except for the period between 1793 and 1816 when the whole population was deported by the British, the Congregation took care of these little islands off the coast of Newfoundland by means of secular priests trained in its Parisian seminary. In 1874, at the urgent invitation of the Prefect Apostolic, some members of the Congregation were sent to St. Pierre to operate a small college,

cf. pp. 227 f.

but Chapter IX recorded how, to the dismay of the population, the Fathers were forced to abandon this college and return to France under suspension by a Prefect Apostolic whom the Government had thrust on the Church.

B. G. 36, 607
ff. ; 28, 246 f. ;
29, 244

Till 1912 the Holy Ghost Fathers continued to look after the spiritual interests of the population by means of secular priests sent out under their auspices. In that year the Propaganda tried to remedy the disastrous effects of French political meddling by insisting that Spiritans become Ecclesiastical Superiors of all the old French colonies. Because the territory of St. Pierre and Miquelon was considered too small for both a secular and a regular clergy, the Motherhouse decided to serve the colony entirely by means of its own men. Father Joseph Oster, the former Provincial of the United States, was appointed the first Prefect Apostolic under the new dispensation (1916). Despite Archbishop Le Roy's protest that there was no need for purple, the Holy See made Father Oster a Prothonotary Apostolic.

B. G. 32, 242   After World War I, the Congregation reopened St. Christopher College. In so doing, they defied the local French officials who chose to ignore the fact that France had abandoned religious persecution as a policy. In its 1955 report, this college recorded a student-body of 230.

Although the tiny islands became notorious in the States during the days of Prohibition, there is little else to be said about them from the religious point of view. With the exception of a few foreign officials of the local British cable station, the whole population of five thousand is Catholic, not only in name but also in practice. In recent years this little Prefecture has given six priests to the Congregation.

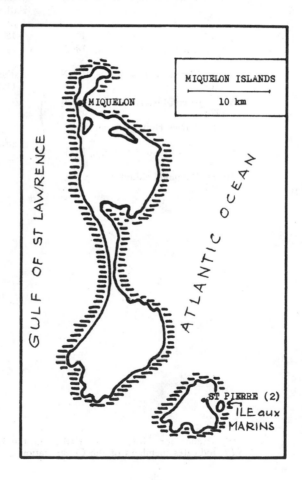

LIST OF ECCLESIASTICAL AND RELIGIOUS SUPERIORS OF ST. PIERRE AND MIQUELON

*Prefects Apostolic**	*Religious Superiors C.S.Sp.*
Father Manach, Sp., 1765 (died 1766 before reaching his post)	
Father Julien Becquet, Sp., 1767-1775	
Father Xavier Paradis, Sp., 1784-?	
Father Longueville, Sp., ?-1794	
Father Ollivier, 1816-1841	
Father Amateur Charlot, 1841-1853	
Father John Le Helleco, 1853-1866	
Father Réné Le Tournoux, 1866-1892	
(Ecclesiastical Superior till 1884)	Father Louis Payen, 1872-1877
	Father Joseph Oster, 1877-1890
	Father Joseph Frécenon, 1890-1892
Father Ange-Louis Tiberi, 1892-1899	
Msgr. Christopher Légasse, 1899-1915	Father Joseph Oster, 1912-1916 (later Prefect Apostolic)
Msgr. Joseph Oster, C.S.Sp., 1916-1922	
Msgr. Charles Heitz, C.S.Sp., 1922-1933	also Religious Superiors
Msgr. Louis Poisson, C.S.Sp., 1933-1945	
Msgr. Raymond Martin, C.S.Sp., 1945-	

Sp. stands for Holy Ghost Father in the broad sense of the term; *C.S.Sp.* indicates members of the Congregation.

CHAPTER FIFTEEN

THE WEST INDIES

1. HAITI

a. THE END OF THE SCHISM

cf. pp. 148 ff.

In Chapter VI we saw how Archbishop Rosati of St. Louis, Missouri, and Father Eugene Tisserant, Prefect Apostolic of Haiti, had been forced to abandon their efforts to heal the schism in which nearly all the priests and most of the people in Haiti were living. Subsequently, the Holy See tried to remedy the situation by working through the Archbishops of Trinidad. Successively Archbishops Smith, Spaccapietra and Etheridge were given jurisdiction over the island, but all their efforts to reconcile the schismatics failed. Their lack of success was in great part reducible to one factor: the three dozen recalcitrant priests who were living on the island. With few exceptions, they were refugees from ecclesiastical discipline in France, Italy and Spain and they justly feared that the Holy See would put an end to their disorders if it regained control over the Church in Haiti. A few of these notorious characters, such as Fathers Cessens and Moussa, were old acquaintances of the Spiritans and did their utmost to prevent a restoration of Church discipline. They and their followers succeeded in doing so as long as Emperor Soulouque (Faustin I) ruled Haiti.

B. G. 2, 592 ff.
H. R. H.
427 ff.

ibid., 358 ff.

ibid., 375 ff.,
451 ff.

ibid., 475 ff.

In 1860, however, when Haiti became a Republic, its President signed a concordat with the Holy See. At once the Propaganda asked the Congregation to lend its support to the delicate negotiations that had to be conducted. To this end, Father John Pascal[1] and several other Spiritans were assigned to help Bishop Monetti, the Apostolic Delegate. While the Bishop labored on the diplomatic level, Father Pascal and his companions performed excellent work in reconciling many of the priests with the Church. At the same time he managed to gain the abiding affection of the islanders and the entire confidence of the Government. When Bishop Mo-

B. G. 2, 236
ff.; 358 ff.;
446 ff.; 554 ff.
3, 72 ff.; 181
ff.; 321 ff.;
341* ff.; 411 ff.

B. G. 4, App., 13

[1]Father Pascal was one of the colonial priests admitted to the Congregation as novices under the reform of Father Leguay. Together with Fathers Hervé and Orinel he pronounced his vows in 1860.

netti had succeeded in reaching an agreement with General Geffrard, President of the Republic, he sailed to Europe to report to the Holy See. During his absence Father Pascal was named Ecclesiastical Superior until resident bishops could be appointed for the Archdiocese of Port-au-Prince and the four dioceses which were to be created.

B. G. 4, App. 15 f.

While Bishop Monetti was in Europe, Father Pascal stepped forward to prevent another disaster in the tormented country. Political trouble regarding boundaries had arisen between Haiti and San Domingo, the eastern half of the island, which at that time was under the protection of the Spanish Crown. The heated arguments of politicians did nothing more than add the fuel of mutual insults to the smoldering fire of hatred. Suddenly, a fleet of eight Spanish warships appeared off-shore opposite Port-au-Prince. Its commander gave the Negro Republic exactly twenty-four hours to make amends for the insults or watch their Capital being blown to bits.

Stung in their national pride, the Haitian Army officers preferred to fight, even though their pitiful lack of arms made resistance a hopeless undertaking. Orders were given for the hasty evacuation of all women and children while preparations for the siege went on apace. Father Pascal frantically appealed to reason and common sense, but the proud Haitians turned a deaf ear. Meanwhile, the deadline set by the Spaniards was rapidly approaching. In desperation, the priest finally rushed to the Governmental Palace, burst into the President's room, and with tears streaming down his cheeks besought him not to listen to his excited military advisers but to spare the city from certain destruction. His sincerity and anxious concern conquered the President. Peaceful negotiations were instituted and the Capital was saved.

Guilloux, 68 ff.

The island then returned to the work of spiritual reconstruction. General Geffrard had left the choice of episcopal candidates completely in the hands of Bishop Monetti, but Rome instructed the Apostolic Delegate not to make any move in Haitian affairs without first consulting the Holy Ghost Fathers. To facilitate compliance with this instruction, the Apostolic Delegate took up residence in the Motherhouse, while Father Schwindenhammer, the Superior General, conducted a search for episcopal candidates. Those who came to recommend themselves for the vacancies were immediately rejected, and most of those whom he approached had no desire to accept such an unenviable position. In the island itself there was talk about making Father Pascal Archbishop or at least Bishop in one of the dioceses, but the Superior General discarded the idea promptly. While the Congregation was willing to do its utmost in healing the schism by doing the spade work and selecting suitable candidates, it still maintained its firm rule not to propose any of its own members for resident bishoprics.[2]

cf. p. 218

In 1861 the choice finally fell on Father Martial Testard du Cosquer, the former Vicar General of Guadeloupe. Realizing that the situation in Haiti was still far from clear, Father du Cosquer preferred to go to his future archdiocese as a simple Monsignor and begin settling matters quietly. If he achieved success in this, he was willing to be consecrated. Accordingly, he received authorization to do so and in February 1862 he landed in Haiti. With the aid of Father Pascal, he managed to publish the pontifical bulls creating the island dioceses and to supplement the Concordat with necessary organic articles governing the status of Bishops, clergy and Church properties. Although efforts were made to defame Father Pascal and his confreres and complaints were made about "their accursed Jesuitism," the projected articles were approved by the Government. Consequently, in 1863 Monsignor du Cosquer was officially named Archbishop and consecrated in Rome. Constitution of the four other dioceses was postponed until the troubled young Republic would have a chance to settle down.

B. G. 4, 142 f.

Morality had sunk so low during the schismatic years that Voodooism had reached frightening excesses. At the very gate of the Capital, a *Papa-loi* (Voodoo sorcerer) had induced people to offer a human sacrifice to the Serpent-God and then devour the victim's still-quivering flesh. Elsewhere, hiding-places delivered up children who were being fattened for subsequent slaughter in cannibalistic ceremonies of devil worship. In fact, the tremendous inroads of savagery were one of the many reasons why the Government finally came to feel the need of the Church's moralizing influence on the island. In combatting all types of superstition and

B. G. 4, 844 f.

every kind of human perversion, Father Pascal and one of his fellow Spiritans literally worked themselves to death in 1865.

Guilloux, 286 ff.
B. G. 11, 1052 ff.

M. C. 9, 189

[2]For the same reason, in 1877 the Congregation firmly refused to allow Monsignor Ambrose Emonet, C.S.Sp., Prefect Apostolic of Guiana, to become resident Bishop of Cayes in Haiti. The same fate awaited the proposed candidacy of Father John François, C.S.Sp., Pastor of Petionville, near Port-au-Prince, and that of Father John Duret.

b. St. Martial Senior Seminary

R. H. M. 11,
530 ff.

B. G. 4, 55

One of the Archbishop's first concerns was the recruitment of a reliable and well-trained clergy. He immediately turned to the Congregation and asked it to assume charge of this work. The Spiritans had just acquired a new property at Chevilly and had transferred their own scholastics to the new campus. Consequently, it was possible to add a special Haitian division to the Parisian seminary of the Holy Ghost in 1864 and dedicate it specially as St. Martial Seminary. In 1871, however, the next Archbishop decided that his seminarians should be separated from the other colonial aspirants at Holy Ghost Seminary. Accordingly, he proposed that the Spiritans train them in their Breton community of Langonnet. When this plan did not prove feasible, he entrusted his seminary to the Society of Mary, and a house was opened for them at Pointchateau, near Nantes.[3]

Guilloux, 188

ibid. 234

c. St. Martial College-Seminary

B. G. 8, 891
ff. ; Guilloux,
187 ff.

Its Foundation. In 1865, Archbishop du Cosquer decided to open a seminary-college in Port-au-Prince in order to further stimulate vocations to the priesthood in his diocese. The Spiritans were asked to take it, and while Father Schwindenhammer at first gave his consent on the grounds that the work was "well within the purpose" of the Congregation, he later demurred because he feared that it would require too many men. In 1870 Archbishop Guilloux reiterated his predecessor's request. With some hesitation, Schwindenhammer consented to undertake the task "in a conditional and provisional way" because the seminary-college was a natural complement of the Senior Seminary of St. Martial in Paris. When the Archbishop closed the Haitian division of Holy Ghost Seminary, therefore, he removed the only reason why Schwindenhammer had accepted the seminary-college in Haiti. Fearing protests from the other missions if he maintained the college by itself, he decided to withdraw his men. Archbishop Guilloux, supported in his plea by the Spiritans already working in Haiti, managed to achieve a stay of execution until another congregation could be found for St. Martial's.

B. G. 8, 891

B. G. 8, 893

Guilloux, 574

[3]In 1893 the Society of Mary was forced to close the Seminary because of the antireligious laws. The situation was saved by Mère de Kerouartz, of the Daughters of Our Lady of the Retreat, who offered the Haitian Hierarchy part of their domain at St. Jacques, Finistère.

Guilloux, 279
ff.; B. G. 10,
886 ff.

First Attempted Withdrawal. In reality, the Archbishop was confident that the Holy Ghost Fathers would never abandon the College. For this reason he made no effort to find substitutes. One can easily imagine his emotion, therefore, when the Spiritans told him in 1875 that they would be leaving the College at the end of the year. Since it was impossible to keep this decision secret, newspapers began to write long articles bewailing the future fate of Haiti's youth. People circulated petitions and political in-

B. G. 10, 890

fluences began to inject themselves into the picture. The French Plenipotentiary Minister, for example, wrote that "the only hope for the regeneration of Haiti lay in the education provided by the Holy Ghost Fathers" and if they left, "Haiti for a long time to come would remain under the spell of evil and perhaps again of schism." Other diplomats wrote in a similar vein. Meanwhile all efforts to find substitutes for the Spiritans had failed. At this

B. G. 10, 891

juncture the Holy See added its voice to the chorus. When that happened, the Superior General admitted defeat and reversed his decision regarding the College.[4]

B. G. 10, 895 ff.

Meanwhile, St. Martial's continued to play its role ever more brilliantly in creating Catholic leaders for Haiti. An 1876 Government report on education compared St. Martial's College with the five State colleges of the land and the comparison was most flattering for the Spiritan institution. St. Martial alone had almost as many students as the other five institutions combined. For one fourth of the cost it educated three times as many students as the nearby national college of Port-au-Prince where, the report complained, students were badly housed, ill-fed, ill-instructed, and almost without any trace of discipline. St Martial's, on the other hand, had a superb physical plant, a superior staff, and strict discipline. It is hardly surprising that the Haitians looked with confidence and pride on this fine institution.

B. G. 10, 897
f.; 14, 312

The College Saves the City. In the nineteenth century nearly all the buildings in Port-au-Prince were constructed of wood and thereby constituted a serious fire hazard during the dry season. Since the municipal fire-fighting equipment left much to the desired,

---

Guilloux, 284;
B. G. 10, 903 ff.

[4]To save personnel, he returned one of the Spiritan parishes to the Archbishop. The departure of the priests from the parish (of St. Ann) had to be arranged in secret, because of the commotion the announcement had caused. Erroneously the people thought the Spiritans had been forced to withdraw under pressure from the Archbishop.

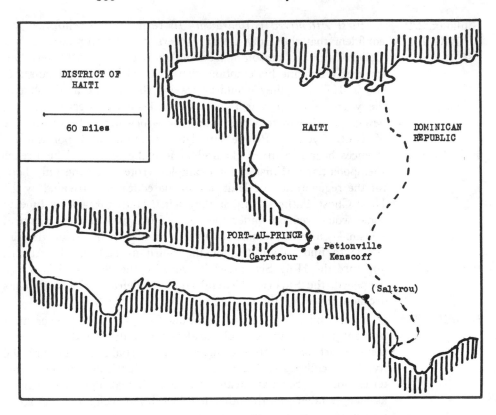

DISTRICT OF
HAITI

60 miles

HAITI

DOMINICAN
REPUBLIC

PORT-AU-PRINCE

Petionville

Carrefour   Kenscoff

(Saltrou)

any small blaze could quickly degenerate into a disastrous con-
flagration. For the protection of the College buildings, the Fathers
decided to organize their own fire brigade in 1875. Father Daniel
Weik, a former German artillery officer from the Black Forest
region, took charge of the operation. With typical German thoroughness he drilled the student brigade and placed at its service a
huge water reservoir which he constructed on the campus. By way
of equipment he added four standard pumps and one ultra-modern
steam pump capable of producing a 1,500 foot jet. Shortly after,
a tremendous fire broke out in the Capital just at a time when
none of the city pumps was functioning properly. Operating with
the precision of a Black Forest clock, Father Weik and the St.
Martial Brigade came to the rescue and succeeded in saving a large
part of the city from certain destruction. The people escorted the
tired fire-fighters home with loud "Hurrahs for the Spiritans,"

B. G. 10, 898

and a grateful government reimbursed the College for the purchase of the equipment. After the event, an article in the local paper observed that the city of Port-au-Prince had once more been saved by the work of the Holy Ghost Fathers.

During the years that followed, this fire-brigade rendered similar service in many emergencies. Before long, however, it became obvious that the excitement and the constant interruptions of frequent alarms were not exactly conducive to the tranquil atmosphere that an academic institution needs. St. Martial could not go on being half fire-house and half school. Accordingly, the brigade handed over its thrilling but distracting responsibilities to the alumni of the College and quiet returned to St. Martial's.

B. G. 11, 1051;
13, 279 ff.

Meteorological Observatory. In 1878 Father Weik, who taught physical science at the College, established a meteorological station in an abandoned fort near St. Martial. A government grant made it possible for him to build an observatory tower on top of the fort. Two years later the observatory began to function at full tilt. It soon became one of the most important institutes of its kind in that part of the world. French astronomers came to it in 1882 to watch Venus in her famous passage across the sun under conditions that would not return till 1990.

When a seismological division was established, the meteorological center became important enough to merit better quarters.

B. G. 41, 288
ff.

These had to wait, however, until after World War II when the old fort was abandoned and replaced by modern laboratories at the top of one of the new buildings on the campus. This Observatory, staffed by three capable Spiritans, provides information for the hurricane division of the U. S. Weather Bureau. Thus far fifty-seven volumes of its annual geophysical reports have been published for the information of other scientific centers throughout the world.

B. G. 29, 350 ff.

Second Attempted Withdrawal. After the First World War, the Congregation once more tried to relinquish the College. The war years had seriously diminished the potential of the Holy Ghost Fathers, and now new and insistent voices were demanding that they replace the German priests who had been expelled from the former African colonies of the Reich. Haiti was absorbing a good deal of man-power. In fact, before the war, forty-three men were attached to the district. Under these circumstances, it seemed unreasonable to maintain a college which, the reader will recall, was accepted "provisionally and temporarily" in 1871. But as a French Spiritan saying goes: "It is only the provisional that is definitive and the temporary that lasts forever." Subsequent events were to justify this adage once more.

B. G. 29, 807 ff.; 30, 308 f.

News of the impending withdrawal reached Haiti, but the island refused to believe it. However, when October 1919 arrived and the gates of the College remained closed, a veritable uproar echoed through the city. People erroneously blamed the Archdiocesan administration for the closing. Pressure mounted so high that in the beginning of November the Fathers who had their suitcases packed were practically forced to reopen St. Martial's—again "provisionally." Meanwhile the scenes of 1875 repeated themselves but this time on an even bigger scale. It was not only the entire Hierarchy and the Government of the Republic that refused to hear of the Spiritans' departure. Even the Governments of France and the United States[5] voiced their disapproval in no uncertain terms. Everyone viewed the closure as "an irreparable loss to the religious, intellectual and social interests of the Republic."

B. G. 29, 807

Finally the Holy See stepped into the picture and the Holy Ghost Fathers once more reversed their decision. It involved a great inconvenience during this period of critical personnel shortage, but they consoled themselves by recalling how close Haiti had been to the heart of Libermann. In 1846 he wrote of Father Tisserant who, the reader will remember, descended from a Haitian family:

N. D. 8, 117 f.

> Father Tisserant's love for Haiti belongs to the patrimony of the Congregation. We have gathered this love from his letters, his conversations, and from his last breath. We wish that this love may become active—like his—and we will be ready if God's providence should later offer favorable circumstances.

B. G. 29, 807 ff.

Haiti's Gratitude. The island's jubilation knew no bounds when the good news arrived. As a gesture of gratitude for several generations of service and in an effort to remove the Spiritans' "temporary and provisional" status at the College, the Republic

---

[5]In 1915, after a series of six or seven bloody revolutions in three years, the U. S. Marines had temporarily occupied the Republic to restore public order.

spontaneously passed a special law in favor of the Congregation. Although non-Haitians are ineligible to own land on the island, the Legislature made an exception in favor of the Spiritans and deeded over to them the government land on which the College stood. Next, the Archbishop presented them with the college buildings that hitherto had been owned by the Archdiocese. Where-

B. G. 32, 271

upon the Government made a grant to replace the dilapidated "temporary" chapel which had been built fifty years earlier. Not to be outdone, the people, among whom the Fathers were (and are) immensely popular, organized themselves to support the College. Haitians have been accused of many things, but no one can say that a lack of gratitude is one of their vices.

Ap. H. 28

The popularity of the College Fathers is also demonstrated in another rather unusual respect. Throughout the island's turbulent history there have been many civil wars, military coups and bloody revolutions. Yet, by an unwritten law, whatever the political upheaval may be, the vanquished are safe once they reach the sanctuary of St. Martial's College. It enjoys the right of asylum in much the same way as do the foreign embassies in South America and its record is considerably better than theirs because no violation has ever been reported. On several occasions, this privilege has saved hundreds of lives in times of stress and turmoil.

B. G. 41, 284
ff.

The College at Present. After World War II the Spiritans undertook a four-stage development program to replace a number of antiquated buildings and to expand the college's facilities. The first three of these stages, including construction of the junior division and the new observatory, have already been executed. At

E. P. 31, I, 59

present, the number of its students exceeds 1,200.

B. G. 41, 275

Although the College originally began as a seminary, the absence of vocations in the earlier days soon reduced the institute to the status of a simple college. In recent times, however, a junior seminary for secular clerics has once more been added as a special division of the boarding school. In this way, it is hoped, new vocations will come forward to fill the relatively thin ranks of the native Haitian clergy.[6]

B. G. 41, 275

The apostolic activity of the College Fathers is not limited to the religious and intellectual training of the youth entrusted to

---

[6]At present, there are about fifty priests who were born in Haiti. Nearly all of them are alumni of the Holy Ghost Fathers.

their care. It ranges far beyond the precincts of classroom and campus. Nearly all modern branches of Catholic action on the island have been started in St. Martial College. Moreover, the Fathers play a vital role in deploying the forces of press and radio against the destructive influence of Marxism and other ideological evils that have recently invaded the Republic.

d. Social Works

B. G. 17, 847 f.

St. Joseph Workshop. In 1893 the Haitian Government asked the Spiritans to take charge of a social center near the Capital. Two years later, after careful investigation, the offer was accepted. Father Amet Limbour, three other Fathers, and eight Brothers were sent to take over the work which, according to Government plans, was soon to embrace a trade school, a detention home, a lower and a higher agricultural school. By means of this complex undertaking, the Spiritans hoped to reach the poorer classes of the island which till then had been almost totally neglected.

Under the skillful direction of the Brothers, foundations were laid for the trade school. To everyone's surprise, the job was finished within five months and the mechanical shops of the school began to hum with activity. Mechanized tools seem to have been a novelty at the time, for endless files of important and unimportant visitors had to be shown around. As the tired chronicler reported:

B. G. 17, 852 f.

> Anyone in Haiti who thinks or judges, anyone who sells or steals, works or loiters, prays or drinks . . . all these and many others think that they have an obligation in conscience to pay us a visit.

B. G. 20, 186

At first the school prospered visibly. However, the financial panic of the nineties prevented the Government first from expanding the work as planned and then from even supporting the exist-

B. G. 20, 234

ing divisions in an adequate way. In 1899, it became so urgent for the Republic to marshall its faltering resources elsewhere that the shops had to be closed.

B. G. 41, 273; 291 f.

St. Theresa Re-Education Center. Fifty years were to pass before the Holy Ghost Fathers were able to resume their social role among the poor of Haiti (1949). In the slums of the capital there were thousands of abandoned children roaming about, knowing no father and at times not even a mother. In addition, there were the ubiquitous country youths who, driven by poverty or

St. Martial College, Haiti. Two views of the new buildings.

St. Martial College, Haiti. Above, the Observatory tower.

lured by dazzling dreams, flocked to the city and lived in wretched hovels without any means of subsistence. Their number was once estimated at about forty thousand.

Moved to pity by the sight of so much misery, the social-minded President of Haiti wanted to reclaim as many as possible of these abandoned youngsters. He realized that only a religious organization could adequately take care of them and therefore addressed himself to Don Bosco's Salesians who operated a small trade school within the Republic. When they appeared unable to help him, the President appealed to Rome for advice. The Holy See replied that it knew only two Congregations which operate similar works successfully on a large scale: the Salesians and the Spiritans. Since he had unsuccessfully approached the former, why not appeal to the latter?

This was a most pleasant surprise for the President. He knew the Holy Ghost Fathers as educators of the elite, but he was completely ignorant of their wide-spread activities in social service. Moreover, to his great joy, the Superior General accepted the proposition at once.

In 1949, by virtue of a new law, the Legislature entrusted this new social work to the Congregation. It was inaugurated in January 1950 under the direction of Father Louis Le Retraite, a former director of the Anteuil Institute. Mindful of the great success that has blessed the work of Auteuil in France under the patronage of St. Therese, he dedicated its Haitian counterpart also to this patroness of childhood.

Meanwhile, the Government had started to build a mamoth center capable of lodging two thousand youngsters, but the Fathers thought it wiser to limit the number of boarders to a maximum of three hundred and to open branches elsewhere later on. Otherwise, disciplinary control, religious instruction and moral training would become too cumbersome to be effective. In addition to the boarding division of three hundred, the re-education center operates an elementary school and large tradeshops for technical training. To these latter, day-students are admitted.

e. Other Works

Apart from their educational and social activities in Haiti, the Spiritans take care of 32,000 Catholics in two parishes and fourteen rural missions. The oldest of these is St. Peter at Petionville, where the Fathers arrived in 1860. The other is St. Nicolas at Kenscoff, which was separated from St. Peter in 1949. In the past, the Fathers also had charge of St. Ann in Port-au-Prince and of Saltrou in the mountains, but these have since been relinquished. For some years too, several Fathers were employed in a Mission Band, but recently, the pressure of other work has forced them to abandon this type of apostolic endeavor.

List of Religious Superiors C.S.Sp.

Eugene Tisserant, (C.S.C.M.), 1844-1845 (also Prefect Apostolic)
John Pascal, 1860-1865
John Simonet, 1866-1881
Amet Taragnat, 1881-1884
William Jaouen, 1886-1892
Marcellin Bertrand, 1892-1903
Paul Benoit, 1903-1909
Adolph Cabon, 1909-1919
John Lanore, 1919-1927
Eugene Christ, 1927-1937
Henry Goré, 1937-1947
Peter Le Bihan, 1947-1953
Etienne Grienenberger, 1953-

2. GUADELOUPE

a. INTRODUCTION

Ap. H. 32 ff.   The Carib Indians called it "Karukera," the Emerald Isle. When Columbus arrived in 1493, he renamed this island of a thousand square miles "Guadalupe" after a famous Spanish monastery. Finally, it became a French possession in 1635.

The island is reputed to be a paradise on earth. It bursts into view like a giant bouquet floating on the blue waters of the Carribbean and exuding the fragrance of vanilla, coffee and other tropical aromatics. It is a land of eternal summer, tempered by a gentle breeze, where the weary traveller may plunge into the cooling waters of palm-shaded beaches or climb its verdant mountains to enjoy breath-taking vistas of land, sea, and sky. Its gardens abound in delicious fruits and resplendent flowers, its valleys are filled with sleek cattle, its fertile fields produce an abundance of crops with a minimum of tillage.

A quarter of a million people have made their permanent residence on the island. Most of them are descendants of former slaves brought thither in past centuries from forgotten villages of Africa, a small percentage can trace their origin to pure white forbears, and a considerable number bear in their features the unmistakable signs of mixed ancestry.

Spanish Dominicans seem to have been the first missionaries on this idyllic island. They arrived in 1603, but soon met a violent death at the hands of the savage Caribs. Later, when the French occupied Guadeloupe, the Dominicans tried again and Franciscans, Carmelites, Augustinians and Jesuits then came to assist them. Though hampered by opposition from the leading citizens, who preferred to keep the slaves in total ignorance, these orders succeeded in Christianizing most of the population. Their work came to an untimely end when the French Revolution wrecked the central headquarters at home in France and severely interfered with their apostolate in Guadeloupe itself.

Holy Ghost Fathers entered upon the scene when the island was returned to France after the Napoleonic wars. At that time, it will be recalled, they took over the religious service of all the old French colonies. In the Spiritan years that followed, three periods may be distinguished in the history of Guadeloupe: from 1815 to 1851, before the creation of the colonial hierarchy; from 1851 to 1912, the time of secular bishops; and from 1912 to the present, during which the Congregation assumed full control and responsibility for the island's religious welfare.

b. THE PREFECTURE: 1815-1851

cf. p. 51 ff.

The First Prefects. As was mentioned in Chapter IV, the Congregation encountered great difficulty finding a clergy for the colonies, because in France itself the Church was still reeling under the savage blows it had been dealt during the Revolution, and the Spiritans in particular were painfully taking their first steps

Cl. C. 74 ff.

toward recovery. Nevertheless, Father Bertout, then Superior General, succeeded in finding an excellent Prefect Apostolic in the person of Father Bernard Graffe. He was a confessor of the Faith who had been exiled to Cayenne for his refusal to take the schismatic oath and later had managed to make his way to Guadeloupe. Under his direction, the first attempt was made to re-Christianize this island, which was now no longer Catholic except in name. In 1825 when a particularly violent hurricane claimed eight hundred victims on the island, the Prefect himself was one of the casualties. He died under the crumbling walls of his church.

The appointment of a successor took nearly two years, because no suitable candidate could be induced to take the unenviable position. Father Henry de Solages, who at first accepted, later declined because he felt that the territory was too small.[7] Finally, in 1828, Father Brizard, who had done excellent work in Martinique, agreed to give it a try. He lasted only a year and a half and then, when

Cl. C. 77 ff.

they accused him of a serious offense, he gave the impression of actual guilt by fleeing in panic from the island. Curiously enough, according to the general consensus of everyone who had any knowledge whatsoever of the affair, he was the innocent victim of a base calumny. Even his accusers did not dare to spell out the crime, and from the beginning to the end they remained absolutely vague in their charges. Nonetheless, he positively refused to return and justify himself. Presumably he was afraid that a hasty Governor would unceremoniously ship him back to France as a convicted offender.

Cl. C. 80;
117 f.

Two Spiritan Superiors. When the commotion over this case had died down, the Propaganda named Father Francis Lacombe as Brizard's successor. The new Prefect had studied at Holy Ghost Seminary and joined the Congregation as a director of the Seminary, but failing eyesight forced him to relinquish his teaching post and he went to Guadeloupe to work as a missionary. He was an excellent priest from every point of view. To the great satisfaction of the clergy, the people, and even of the Government, he wisely governed the Church in Guadeloupe for sixteen years. When one knows how difficult the situation could be under a government that constantly interfered in ecclesiastical affairs, this general satisfaction is eloquent commendation indeed. Although he was handicapped by a persistent shortage of priests, he made great strides toward the restoration of Catholic life on the island, without once becoming involved in any of those noisy conflicts which are so typical of the ecclesiastical history of the old French colonies during this period.

Cl. C. 120 f.

When Father Lacombe retired from active service in 1844, he was succeeded, after an interval of two years, by Father Peter

---

[7]Later he became Prefect of Reunion and annexed to his Prefecture Madagascar, New Zealand and Australia.

Guyard, a priest who had joined the Congregation under the reform of Father Leguay. Because the Government had published his nomination without waiting for official confirmation by the Holy See, the Propaganda refused to give him the title of Prefect Apostolic. Consequently, the documents refer to him simply as Ecclesiastical Superior of Guadeloupe. Although highly respected by all, Father Guyard lasted only a short time. Mr. Schoelcher, whom the 1848 Revolution had placed in charge of the old colonies, forced him to resign[8] because he wanted to appoint his own candidates to the various Prefectures.

Cl. C. 389 ff. *Father Dujougon and Father Drouelle.* The particular man Mr. Schoelcher had in mind for Guadeloupe was Father Casimir Dujougon, a member of a religious order. Much impressed by this priest's undeserved reputation for zeal in behalf of Negro slaves, Schoelcher literally forced his appointment through channels. Bypassing Father Monnet, the Spiritan Superior General, he had the nomination approved by the Papal Nuncio and then casually notified the "Citizen Superior" that Dujougon was now Prefect. To avoid sharpening the Church-State clashes of this turbulent period, the Holy See resigned itself to the appointment.

In Guadeloupe, however, a storm of protest arose among the clergy and the people. The slaves themselves had never heard of their self-appointed hero and did not want him. Subsequent events proved that these instinctive prejudices were justified. No sooner had he arrived in the colony than he exasperated the priests by his breaches of confidence and the people by his provocative arrogance. Shortly after his arrival, he found himself in a bitter conflict with the enraged Governor, who peremptorily shipped him back to France.

Before leaving the island, Father Dujougon performed the one good deed of his administration: he named as Vice-Prefect a member of his own religious Congregation—Father Victor Drouelle. This priest, who had come from the States, proved to be an extremely able man. He won the respect and veneration of everyone and in short order counteracted all the bad impressions created by his predecessor. Father Drouelle remained in charge till 1851

---

[8]Subsequently, on Libermann's suggestion, this injustice was repaired by Father Guyard's appointment to the Prefecture of Senegal.

when, thanks to Libermann's diplomacy, the hierarchy was established in Guadeloupe.

c. THE SECULAR HIERARCHY: 1851-1912

D. C. 153

Although the creation of dioceses in Guadeloupe, Martinique and Reunion gave these islands ecclesiastical autonomy, the Holy See refused to let the Spiritans disengage themselves completely from responsibility for their religious welfare. The Congregation remained in charge of training their clergy and educating a Catholic elite. Moreover, it was expected that the Holy Ghost Fathers would supervise the islands' general spiritual development without, however, transgressing in any way against episcopal authority. Because of the problems inherent in this delicate relationship, we must pause here for a note on the bishops of Guadeloupe in these troubled years.

D. C. 47 ff.

Bishop Peter Lacarrière was the first. The Minister of Ecclesiastical Affairs insisted on his nomination in 1851 despite the candidate's vile temper and utter lack of adaptability. In short order, both the Holy See and the government found him intolerable and removed him two years after he had gone to Guadeloupe. Napoleon III then intervened personally and insisted on the appointment of Gallican Bishop Theodore Forcade who, rumor had it, was a descendant of the first Napoleon.[9] He remained nine years and then went back to France. Bishop Anthony Boutonnet followed him. Guadeloupe then had another Gallican prelate who cordially detested the Spiritans for having opposed his nomination. Within six years he died and a former Navy chaplain, Bishop Joseph Reyne, succeeded him. Reyne lasted only two years and spent most of that brief period in France. Next, Bishop Francis Blanger came like a breath of fresh air bringing with him a ten-

D. C. 59 ff.

year interlude of enlightened zeal and peaceful government. After that, the see was vacant for sixteen years because a feud between the executive and legislative branches of the French government had cut off subsistence funds. During this period, Apostolic Ad-

D. C. 64 ff.

ministrators ruled the Church in Guadeloupe. At the end of this vacancy, Bishop Peter Avon came in 1899, resigned after a year, and was succeeded by the last of the series, Bishop Emmanuel Canappe, a capable and zealous prelate who died in 1907.

---

[9]The striking resemblance between the Bishop and Napoleon I, added to the unusual interest of the imperial family in his preferment, gave substance to this rumor.

This rather dreary recitation graphically demonstrates the evils attendant upon civil interference in Church affairs. The Spiritan Superior Generals knew full well the unsatisfactory character of some of these prelates, but they were powerless to prevent their nomination by capricious and irascible civil officials. Through government indiscretion, uncomplimentary Spiritan reports about the nominee sometimes came into the possession of the bishop after his appointment, and the frank appraisal of a candidate's deficiencies did not make things easier for the Holy Ghost Fathers who were to work under the prelate in question. Clearly, while the separation of Church and State in France caused something of an upheaval, one of its better by-products was evident in the elimination of Parisian officialdom from episcopal appointments.

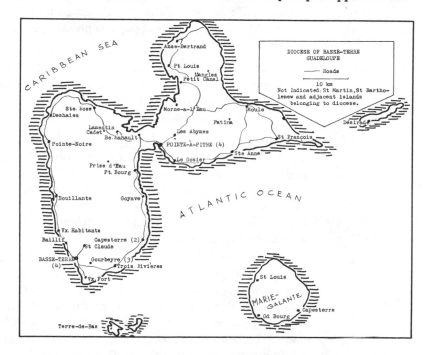

The Spiritan College of Guadeloupe. During this period, the Holy Ghost Fathers limited their activity to training the island's clerical aspirants in their central seminary at Paris and in educating Catholic leaders on Guadeloupe itself. In 1853, at the request of Bishop Forcade, they took over the seminary-college which he had just founded but was unable to staff. His arbitrary inter-

D. C. 310 f.

ference in the internal affairs of the institution, however, caused continual conflicts. By 1855 these difficulties reached such a pitch of intensity that the Spiritans had to withdraw. They were succeeded by teachers drawn from the diocesan clergy and, when the same difficulties continued under the new arrangement, Bishop Forcade transferred the college to new buildings which he had constructed practically in the back yard of his residence. However, closer supervision was hardly the answer to the problem. The College continued to decline. At last it became apparent that only a religious order could handle the situation but, since none but the Holy Ghost Fathers could be found to undertake the thankless task, Bishop Forcade faced a most uncomfortable dilemma. Matters were even more embarrassing for his successor since, prior to his nomination, this Gallican prelate had formally pledged himself to keep these defenders of papal supremacy out of his seminary-college:

D. C. 311

If I am appointed to Guadeloupe, I shall allow no one in my seminary but priests who are subject solely to the Bishop and who will follow him on the road of loyalty and submission to the laws of the State.

B. G. 6, 690 ff.

Nonetheless, shortly before Forcade's death, local pressures and the desperate condition of the College forced him to pocket his pride and ask the Spiritans to return to Guadeloupe and to take charge of educating the island's leaders once more. In 1869, the Congregation consented. From then until 1905, when the separation of Church and State forced its closure, the Fathers continued to manage this diocesan institution.

It required heroic courage to keep the College functioning during those years when yellow fever and other diseases constantly decimated an already overburdened staff.[10] If the Congregation had not been aware of its historic function to provide the island and the other old Holy Ghost Missions with a solid tradition of Catholic higher education, it would not have hesitated a single moment to withdraw its priests and send them off to more rewarding areas.

D. C. 316 ff.

The situation at Guadeloupe was especially painful because the Bishops constantly interfered in the internal affairs of the

---

[10]It was only exceptionally that a Spiritan in these colonial colleges reached the age of forty.

College. Moreover, the College was diocesan property and this usually meant that the Bishops kept control of its finances. As a result, the Spiritans had to operate it on an inadequate budget and still listen to the Bishop's everlasting complaints about the exaggerated cost of higher education. Even when the incumbent Bishop was favorable, conflicts arose over the proximity of the College to the Bishop's residence. For instance, Bishop Blanger legitimately demanded a measure of privacy, but he obtained it by boarding up the college windows that faced his house. One shudders at the thought of a hermetically sealed dormitory on a hot tropical night, yet that is exactly what eventuated. This and similar incidents occurred on an almost daily basis and they cannot be said to have contributed significantly to the peaceful pursuit of academic excellence.

The situation became completely untenable after 1882 when the government's increasingly antireligious attitude resulted in a determined attempt to secularize education. A State College was opened in the same locality and thenceforth all students of the Catholic College had to present themselves at this institution for their examinations. The result was disastrous. In 1886 and 1887 not one candidate of the Spiritan college passed the baccalaureate examination. But when these failures transferred to the State College, they took the test a few weeks later and all passed with flying colors. After several years of such manifest discrimination, and with the distraught Bishop blaming them for the sorry record, the Fathers gave up in complete discouragement and asked to leave. Nevertheless, when the Motherhouse ordered them to stay on, they remained valiantly at their post until 1905.

B. G. 23, 311 ff.   In that year, all State subsidies were withdrawn and diocesan support was withheld. With mixed emotions of regret and relief, the Spiritans left. Anticlericalism had conquered. Shortly thereafter, as if the forced closure of the College had not been enough, two mysterious attempts were made to burn down the physical plant.

B. G. 23, 756 ff.   Even after the College closed its doors, the Holy Ghost Fathers did not completely leave the island. They kept a few priests there until in 1912 when the Holy See formally charged the Spiritans with complete responsibility for the religious welfare of Guadeloupe and ordered that its bishop be a member of the Congregation.

d. SPIRITAN HIERARCHY: 1912 TO THE PRESENT

The Holy See's decision in 1912 put the Congregation in full charge of Guadeloupe, Martinique, Reunion, and, somewhat later, of Mauritius. It resulted in far greater administrative effectiveness than had ever existed before. As members of a religious society, Spiritan bishops did not look to be promoted to any metropolitan dioceses. Rather, they regarded themselves as wedded for life to the see entrusted to their care.[11] Unlike previous colonial bishops, they did not cast an anxious eye back to the finer dioceses of France, nor did they import their friends as Vicar Generals. Instead, they chose their curial officials from the local clergy who knew and understood the people and then settled down to achieve consistency and stability. As a result, conflicts between the Bishop and his clergy disappeared almost completely.

Another effect of the Pope's decision was to remedy the shortage of priests that had plagued these islands for more than thirty years. It had grown increasingly until it appeared to be approaching E. C. 43 ff. disastrous proportions when the Congregation took over. By order of the Holy See, the Spiritans had to substitute members of their own Congregation if they could not find enough other priests to fill the vacancies that existed. At first, this papal command proved extremely burdensome for an already overloaded society, but God seems to have blessed its obedience, for just at that time the number of vocations to the Congregation began to increase dramatically.

E. C. 36 ff. Moreover, now that they had complete charge, the Spiritans finally
D. C. 220 ff. had an opportunity to foster native vocations without being hampered by episcopal opposition to the recruitment of Creole seminarians. Since 1912, the results achieved by their vocation program are impressive indeed: most of the diocesan priests on these islands are now Creoles. The end result of the Holy See's decision, therefore, has been to bring these formerly helpless branches of the Church to a point of development at which their relative self-sufficiency now enables them to think ahead to a time in the future when they may even help in foreign missionary work elsewhere.

---

cf. pp. 381 f.   [11]Glancing over the list of Ecclesiastical Superiors of Guadeloupe, one is struck by the administrative stability that prevailed when Spiritans, whether Prefects or Bishops, were in charge: four Spiritan Prefects and Bishops averaged sixteen years of service, while seventeen others lasted only a mean of four years and four months. Undoubtedly, this stability is one of the reasons why the island's religious development forged ahead more vigorously under their aegis than under other regimes.

E. C. App.

As the Cardinal Prefect of the Propaganda pointed out in 1939, "this would be the most fitting reward for the apostolate of the Congregation."

B. G. 39, 588

Guadeloupe's first Spiritan bishop under the new program was Father Peter Genoud, who had been Novice Master of the French Province for sixteen years before his consecration. Although he had already reached the age of fifty-two when he assumed jurisdiction, he governed his See for thirty-three years till his death in 1945. During that time he had the consolation of seeing the Church in Guadeloupe overcome the evil effects of preceding

B. G. 41, 336

events and enter into period of strength such as it had never known before. In 1943, Father John Gay, C.S.Sp., become his Coadjutor and, when the old prelate died two years later, Bishop Gay succeeded him.

E. P. 31, I, 60 ff.

B. G. 41, 338 ff.

Spiritan Works. At present, the Holy Ghost Fathers staff about twenty-five parishes for which no diocesan clergy is as yet available. Near Basse-Terre they opened a seminary in 1939 and shortly thereafter it was transformed into a seminary-college. By a curious sort of poetic justice, then, the Spiritans resumed their historic function as educators of Catholic leaders on the island. Their tradition of social work finds expression in an institution for homeless boys where some two hunderd youngsters are given an opportunity to learn how to live and how to earn a living.

List of Ecclesiastical and Religious Superiors of Guadeloupe

Ecclesiastical Superiors	*Religious Superiors C.S.Sp.*
Prefects Apostolic	
Fr. Bernard Graffe, 1815-1825 (Vice Prefect till 1821)	
Fr. Blaise Chabert, 1825-1827 (Vice Prefect)	
Fr. Peter Brizard, 1827-1829	
Fr. Francis Lacombe, C.S.Sp., 1829-1844	
Fr. John Dupuis, 1844-1846 (Pro Prefect)	
Fr. Peter Guyard, C.S.Sp., 1846-1848 (Eccl. Superior)	
Fr. Casimir Dujougon, C.S.C., 1848-1849	
Fr. Victor Drouelle, C.S.C., 1849-1851 (Vice Prefect)	

382

1851: Creation of the Hierarchy

Bishops

Bishop Peter Lacarrière, 1851-1853

Bishop Theodore Forcade, 1853-1861

Fr. John Klein, 1853-1855

Bishop Anthony Boutonnet, 1862-1868

Fr. Francis Permot, 1869-1870

Bishop Joseph Reyne, 1870-1872

Fr. Ambrose Emonet, 1870-1871 (later Prefect Apostolic of Guiana)

Bishop Francis Blanger, 1873-1883

Fr. Victor Guilloux, 1871-1875

Fr. Jules Brunetti, 1875-1882

Fr. Emmanuel Canappe, 1883-1885 (Apostolic Administrator)

Fr. Etienne Morin, 1882-1887

Bishop Frederic Oury, 1885-1886 (never reached Guadeloupe)

Archbishop Francis Laurencin, 1885-1892 (Apostolic Administrator)

Fr. Francis Girard, 1887-1904

Archbishop Dominic Soulé, 1892-1898 (Apostolic Administrator)

Bishop Peter Avon, 1899-1901

Bishop Emmanuel Canappe, 1901-1907

Fr. Joseph Malleret, 1904-1906

Fr. Henry Van Haecke, 1906-1907

Msgr. Eugene Duval, 1907-1912 (Apostolic Administrator)

Fr. Auguste Venard, 1907-1908

Bishop Peter Genoud, C.S.Sp., 1912-1945

Fr. Joseph Malleret, 1911-1912 (later Bishop of Martinique)

Fr. Paul Lequien, 1913-1915 (later Bishop of Martinique)

Fr. Matthew Gallot, 1915-1921

Fr. Jules Levasseur, 1921-1925

Fr. Charles Manet, 1925-1926

Fr. Charles Grullot, 1926-1936

Bishop John Gay, C.S.Sp., 1945- (Coadjutor since 1943)

Fr. Louis Quentin, 1936-1947

Fr. Emile Girard, 1947-1956

Fr. John Delawarde, 1956- (district combined with Martinique)

3. MARTINIQUE

The Spiritan history of Martinique follows a basic pattern similar to that of Guadeloupe. It divides rather conveniently into the same three periods.

a. THE PREFECTURE: 1816-1851

In all the old French colonies, this period was a time of reconstruction and reorganization after the storm of the French Revolution. A succession of eight Prefects and Vice-Prefects of Martinique were presented for nomination by the Spiritan Superior General. With the help of priests supplied by Holy Ghost Seminary, they gradually prepared the island for its transformation into a diocese.

Because the Church was hampered in all its activities by excessive control on the part of civil authorities both local and Parisian, the period is rich in instances of strife between Church and State and between the Prefect and his subordinates. In fairness, however, it should be pointed out that a large proportion of the island's priests did excellent work in revitalizing the Church in Martinique.

Cl. C. 80 ff.   Its first Prefect, Father Pierron, a confessor of the Faith during the Revolution, ruled the island with zeal and moderation and avoided conflicts completely. His successor, Father Carrand, however, nullified his many good qualities by a strong conviction that understanding and conciliation were signs of weakness in a churchman. For example, when a convent sold its property to the government and both parties forgot to notify him, he placed the convent chapel under interdict and excommunicated the hapless Mother Superior.

Cl. C. 124 ff.   In 1834, the government in Paris practically forced Father Fourdinier to nominate Father Castelli to the Prefecture. It was a most unfortunate choice. Although he was an honest man, morally irreproachable, and full of good will, he totally lacked the objectivity that a good administrator needs. In a very short time everyone cordially detested him because of the animosity that beclouded most of his decisions. The government that had insisted so strongly on his appointment now groaned in embarrassment and frustration. It heaved a deep sigh of relief when the Holy See de-

Cl. C. 389 f.   posed him seven years later. After the 1848 Revolution, however, Mr. Schoelcher, the new Director of Colonies, demanded

Father Castelli's reappointment because he was sure that the Prefect's interest in the slaves had been the cause of his downfall. The second term of office was even worse than the first, because the poor man's disposition had grown all the more irascible through melancholy and nervous attacks. This time, fortunately, he lasted only one year. As a final stroke before his resignation he lashed out at his predecessor, Father Jacquier, and placed him under interdict.[12] The Venerable Francis Libermann had to intervene in Rome to get the sentence lifted.[13] Shortly thereafter, Martinique became a diocese.

b. The Secular Hierarchy: 1852-1911

D. C. 27 ff.

In general, the six prelates who occupied the See during this period were pious and zealous men who governed the diocese with prudence and wisdom. The most serious conflict of the time came about in 1860 when a divergence of views between Church and State kept the diocese vacant for more than ten years. After Bishop Porchez's death, the government pressed the candidacy of Father Mouniq, a man of doubtful character who was supported by Bishop Forcade, the Gallican prelate of Guadeloupe. When the Holy See refused to cooperate, Napoleon III personally took the matter in hand. Meanwhile, however, Pope Pius IX had done the same. After examining Father Mouniq's file the Pope's reply was: "As long as I am alive, this man will not be bishop anywhere." Nonetheless, the Emperor stubbornly persisted in considering Father Mouniq the legitimate Bishop of Martinique. He even went so far as to pay him the salary stipulated for the position by the Concordat. The issue was settled only after the Franco-Prussian War when a revolution toppled Napoleon from his throne. In the next government, a Jew became Minister of Ecclesiastical Affairs. Being totally disinterested in Gallican prerogatives in Church affairs, this gentleman very sensibly left the choice of a Martinique bishop entirely up to the Church.

---

[12]Father Castelli retired to Paris. Utterly penniless, he seems to have appealed unsuccessfully to the Ministry of Ecclesiastical Affairs. By 1864 the police had lost track of him. Most likely he had died in misery and want shortly before this time.

[13]When Martinique became a diocese, its first Bishop made further amends to Father Jacquier by naming him an honorary canon of his cathedral.

D. C. 40 ff.

In addition to this ten-year vacancy, there was a very noisy clash in 1893 when Bishop Carméné dismissed Father Cudenec as his Vicar General and replaced him with his own nephew. When the civil authorities refused to recognize the dismissal, the case degenerated into an open controversy in which eventually the entire clergy, the people, the Governor, the Ministers in Paris, the metropolitan Archbishop of Bordeaux, and finally even the Pope himself became involved. In Martinique there were rallies for and against each party, religious and secular newspapers lashed out against or vehemently defended the various protagonists, scores of wild pamphlets circulated, and even fist fights took place in the streets. After the bishop was called to Paris in 1895 to explain his action, he was forbidden to go back to his diocese. When he returned in defiance, the government cut off his salary and refused to have anything to do with him. Because of the intimate relations which still existed between Church and State, it was not long before the diocese approached a state of complete chaos. The affair came to a close only in 1897 when the Holy See called the Bishop to Rome and Leo XIII personally induced him to resign. By way of consolation, the Pope made him titular Archbishop of Hieropolis. It was a sad ending for an otherwise splendid and fruitful episcopate that lasted twenty-two years.

D. C. 305 ff.

Spiritans Works of Education. As long as the secular hierarchy governed Martinique, the Holy Ghost Fathers not only kept a watchful eye on the diocese, as they were bound to do, but they also supplied the island with priests and Catholic leaders. In addition to their central Parisian seminary for the colonial clergy, they staffed the senior seminary of Martinique which had been founded by Bishop Le Herpeur in 1851.

In 1859 the Spiritans took over the diocesan College of St. Pierre. Under the paternal direction of Father Emonet, the school soon enrolled more than three hunderd students—a very high number for that time. Although several rival colleges started in St. Pierre, none of them could compete with the Spiritan institute and all disappeared after a few years of lingering existence. When the diocesan junior seminary was founded in 1867, it too was entrusted to the Congregation's care. Moreover, since 1863 the Spiritans had operated a junior college at Fort de France.

When the suppression of government subsidies in 1880 forced the diocese to cut its budget drastically, only the College of St.

Pierre was able to survive. This institution had to be kept functioning for the foundation of a secular State college in the same city
made it imperative that a center of Catholic education be maintained there. For this reason the Spiritans valiantly stayed at their
post until the disaster of 1902.

Martin. 8 ff.   In that year, the eruption of Mont Pelée engulfed the whole city
in a sea of molten lava and devouring flame. Together with thirty
thousand others, the entire Spiritan staff of the College perished in
the horrible holocaust.[14] Only a monument remains to mark the
spot where the College once stood.[15] The next year, the Holy
Ghost Fathers regrouped their forces and opened another Seminary-
College at Fort-de-France, but perforce on a modest scale.

Martin. 15 ff.   [14]Later in the same year, another eruption destroyed the town of Morne-
Rouge with its shrine of Notre Dame de la Délivrande. Before the disaster,
the Spiritan Director of the Shrine, Father Mary, tried to persuade the people to abandon their town. When they refused, he heroically resolved to stay
with them and share their fate. Horribly burned in the catastrophe, he spent
the remaining few hours of his life in administering the last sacraments to
the dying.

[15]In 1930, signs of another eruption caused the hurried evacuation of the
rebuilt city. Fortunately, no serious tragedy ensued, although the threat of
sudden disaster still hangs over that part of Martinique.

c. Spiritan Hierarchy: 1912 till the Present

cf. pp. 266 ff.
For reasons which have been explained in Chapter X, the Holy See decided that the Congregation should henceforth nominate one of its members for the Diocese of Martinique and supplement with its own personnel whatever vacancies might exist throughout the diocese.

As in the other colonies, this inauguration of a Spiritan hierarchy was followed by great stability of administration, an efflorescence of native vocations, and the disappearance of conflicts between the Bishop and his clergy. We do not, of course, mean to suggest that the Spiritans should be credited with all these improvements. In significant measure, those anticlerical politicians who brought about the separation of Church and State contributed likewise to the peace and harmony of the time. They had acted to spite the Church, but in effect they had abdicated all control over ecclesiastical affairs. Free at last from civilian interference, the forces of religion could no longer be mobilized by political pressure to war against each other.

Bishop Malleret, the first Spiritan to occupy the See, died in 1914, two years after his appointment. Only two other prelates, Bishop Paul Lequien (+1941) and Bishop Henry de la Brunelière, have spanned by their administrations the forty-odd years between that time and the present. In accord with papal directives, the Holy Ghost Fathers have taken on a score of parishes for which a local clergy is not yet available. In addition, they have pursued their historic objective of providing the island with Catholic leadership by developing the junior college at Fort-de-France into a full-fledged Seminary-College. Their social-work tradition is given substance by an institute for homeless boys which has been affiliated with the famous Auteuil organization referred to earlier.

List of Ecclesiastical and Religious Superiors of Martinique

Ecclesiastical Superiors	*Religious Superiors C.S.Sp.*
Prefects Apostolic *	
Fr. John Pierron, 1815-1822 (Vice-Prefect)	
Fr. John Carrand, 1822-1830	
Fr. George Taillevis de Perrigny, 1830-1834 (Vice Prefect)	

Fr. Peter Castelli, 1834-1841

Fr. George Taillevis de Perrigny, 1841-1844 (Vice Prefect)

Fr. John Jacquier, Sp., 1944-1848 (Vice Prefect)

Fr. Peter Castelli, 1848-1849

Fr. Fauveau, 1849-1851 (Vice Prefect)

1851: creation of the Hierarchy

Bishops

Bishop John Le Herpeur, 1851-1858   Fr. Ambrose Emonet, 1856-1870 (later Superior General)

Bishop Louis Porchez, 1858-1860

Fr. Prudent Guesdon, 1860-1871 (Apostolic Administrator)

Fr. Francis Blanger, 1871 (Apostolic Administrator)   Fr. Anthony Grasser, 1871-1883

Bishop Amand Fava, 1871-1875

Bishop Julian Carméné, 1875-1897   Fr. Henry Van Haecke, 1883-1892

Fr. Julian Prono, 1892-1896

Fr. Philip Kieffer, 1896-1897

Bishop Etienne Tanoux, C.M., 1898-1899   Fr. Louis Veillet, 1897-1899

Bishop Mary-Charles de Cormont, 1899-1911   Fr. Joseph Malleret, 1899-1911 (later Bishop of Martinique)

Bishop Joseph Malleret, C.S.Sp., 1912-1914   Fr. Matthew Gallot, 1911-1912

Fr. Charles Guyot, 1912-1913

Bishop Paul Lequien, C.S.Sp., 1915-1941   Fr. Auguste Venard, 1913-1916

Fr. Auguste Grimault, 1916-1924 (later Vicar Apostolic of Senegambia)

Fr. Joseph Janin, 1924-1934

Fr. Emile Muller, 1934-1938

Fr. Paul Droesch, 1938-1942

Bishop Henry Varin de la Brunelière, C.S.Sp., 1941-   Fr. Bernard Arosteguy, 1942-1952

Fr. John Delewarde, 1952- (district combined with Guadeloupe in 1956)

---

*Sp. refers to Holy Ghost Father in the broad sense of the term; *C.S.Sp.* indicates members of the Congregation.

4. TRINIDAD

a. ST. MARY'S COLLEGE

B. G. 3, 6 ff.

Foundation. In 1860 Archbishop Ferdinand English asked the Holy Ghost Fathers to open a Seminary-College in the Archdiocese of Port of Spain. After some hesitation, the Congregation acceded to his repeated requests and on the feast of the Immaculate Heart of Mary, August 24, 1862, the offer was officially accepted. A few weeks later, the Archbishop died and execution of the plan

B. G. 3, 322 f.; 345* f.

was postponed. However, when government opposition unduly delayed the appointment of a successor to the See, the Propaganda insisted that the College be started at once and guaranteed that, no matter who would eventually occupy the archiepiscopal post, he

B. G. 3, 472 f.; 4, 150 ff.

would have to honor the agreement with the Spiritans. On July 7, 1863, therefore, Father Victor Guilloux and one confrere arrived on the island. Others followed later. By the first of August they had begun operations with fourteen students in a small diocesan property near the convent of the Sisters of Cluny. Six months later, this initial student body had grown to a total of eighty, the maximum number that the limited physical facilities could accommodate.

B. G. 3, 474

While the Catholics of Trinidad had welcomed the Fathers with open arms, government reaction to their arrival was not too friendly at first. British officials feared a return of French influence at a time when they were at odds with the Catholics over the appointment of a new Archbishop and promulgation of new marriage laws. As the Fathers reported it, they "cordially detested" the little band of teachers. Shortly afterwards however, when British members of the Congregation were added to the staff, this early tension gave way to such a sincere mutual regard that the French Fathers often spoke highly of the British government when they compared their position in Trinidad with that of their compatriots who had to struggle against anticlerical officialdom on the French-held islands.

B. G. 4, 445 f.; 572 f.

B. G. 8, 876 ff.

Permanent Buildings and Recognition. In 1865 the Spiritans bought a property on Pembroke Street, opposite St. Joseph's Convent, and began to build the first unit of a permanent plant. Five years later, Immaculate Conception College, as it is officially called, became affiliated with the Queen's Royal College. This affiliation entitled it to receive annual government grants and rendered its students eligible for Cambridge University diplomas. Thereafter, St. Mary's began to acquire its great reputation for academic excellence. It is a scholarly renown that has increased with the years until now the College is justly considered as one of the largest and soundest in the whole of the British Commonwealth of nations. Much of the credit for its present flourishing academic condition must be given to its venerable Dean of Studies, Father Louis Graf, who has presided over the educational endeavors of the past two generations with astonishing ability and unflagging zeal.

Attempted Withdrawals. Several times, severe personnel shortages and the pressing needs of other works induced the Holy Ghost Fathers to abandon St. Mary's College. On the occasion of each attempt, however, public reaction was much the same as that which developed when they tried to leave St. Martial's College in Haiti. In 1874 and again in 1880, when the Congregation was forced to open Colleges in Reunion and Pondicherry, the authorities decided to withdraw from St. Mary's. As soon as the impending departure was announced, alumni, parents and the whole clergy separately addressed petitions to the Holy See and to the Superior General. By their strongly-worded plea to keep the college open, they effectively prevented execution of the withdrawal. The Congregation could not abandon the work without the consent of the Holy See, and the Propaganda was not inclined to grant its permission unless the Spiritans could be suitably replaced. Despite the very flourishing condition of St. Mary's, failure attended every effort to interest the Jesuits, the Dominicans and other groups in the project. Consequently, the Holy Ghost Fathers decided to stay on, at least "provisionally."

After World War I they made a last attempt to close the college. The critical man-power shortage than plaguing the Congregation demanded a drastic redeployment of its members, but once more the plan could not be executed. The Holy See did not want the Spiritans to abandon their educational task in Trinidad, and popular reaction in the island was prompt and decisive. No one would hear of their departure. The priests of St. Mary's were regarded as one of the most important mainstays of the Archdiocese and their educational achievements were deeply appreciated by Catholics and non-Catholics alike. Local travel agencies simply refused to sell them the necessary steamship tickets. Again the

B. G. 11, 967 ff.

B. G. 11, 973 ff.

B. G. 34, 676

Main Entrance of St. Mary's College, Trinidad.

Fatima College, Trinidad.

A 1902 eruption of Mt. Pelèe, Martinique. In the May 8th explosion of this long-dormant volcano thirteen Spiritans lost their lives.

Congregation had to reverse its decision and continue its historic task.

B. G. 41, 456 ff.

Development. The steady increase of students during the thirties necessitated a huge building program. St. Mary's laid out a master-plan and entered upon a program of expansion and modernization in 1935. Large airy wings surrounded by pillared galleries gradually arose in horse-shoe pattern around four connected courtyards, and a monumental chapel came to replace the nineteenth century steel structure which hitherto had served the religious needs of the College. The cream-colored complex of

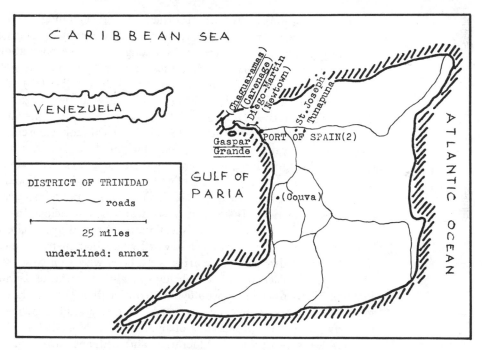

tropical-style buildings, lying in the heart of the city, unfailingly draws the admiring attention of the many Americans—service men or tourists—who visit this Capital of the British West Indian Federation. Indeed, the physical plant of the College would do credit to an academic institution in wealthier lands.

Imposing as its buildings are, they barely accommodate the twelve hundred students of all races and creeds who flock to St. Mary's in quest of higher education. One special feature of that education may be of special interest to Americans because it is currently being discussed in academic circles: for many years, the Spiritans at St. Mary's have successfully followed a program whereby students are trained in separate sections according to their intellectual abilities, so that the teaching can be adapted to the intelligence of the class without exposing the quick-witted to boredom and the plodders to despair. Students of the same year are divided into from five to seven groups according to their mental capacity. As a result, the brightest group can advance twice as fast as the slowest: they cover the curriculum in half the time.

Native Vocations. As we recorded at the beginning of this section, St. Mary's was originally started as a Seminary-College. For many years, however, vocations among the native population, whether white or colored, were almost nonexistent. It was only under the presidency of Father John English (1925-1936) and Father James Meenan (1936-1950) that this situation began to change significantly. During the last thirty years, a constantly growing number of boys began to heed the call for laborers in the Lord's vineyard. At present, the Spiritans count no less than thirty-one living Trinidadians among their confreres. Moreover, other boys have joined other religious orders and the diocesan clergy. Trinidad is no longer a burden on the personnel resources of the Congregation. Instead, it is so nearly self-sufficient that it can even take part in the Holy Ghost Fathers' world apostolate in other lands. It is particularly noteworthy too that many of these Trinidadian priests and seminaries were boys who won first, second, or third place in the Cambridge Higher Certificate Examinations. This distinction would have entitled them to substantial government scholarships for advanced university studies in medicine, law, and other professions of their choice. Nonetheless, they sacrificed the prospect of a lucrative and brilliant career in the world and preferred to follow Christ.

With justification, the Catholics of Trinidad are immensely proud of the fact that their own sons play such an important role in the Church of their native land. At the least provocation they will plunge into an enthusiastic discussion of St. Mary's three periods of development: the first stage of painful beginnings and arduous labor during which French Spiritans ploughed and sowed the seed without ever seeing the approach of harvest time; the second period in which Irish Spiritans cultivated and weeded the land; and the third stage in which the magnificent work of several generations of Holy Ghost Fathers bears fruit in a rich harvest of vocations—almost enough to man the college completely if all remained in their native land. These roots in the island itself have effectively removed any danger that the Congregation will ever abandon Trinidad.

b. College of Our Lady of Fatima

B. G. 41, 458

Since St. Mary's present location made further expansion impossible, and since the Archbishop wanted a similar institution in another part of the city, the Congregation built a new college in 1945. A site was chosen in a northern suburb of Port-of-Spain, facing the Gulf of Paria. Dedicated to our Lady of Fatima and maintaining the same high standards that made old St. Mary's famous, it merited almost immediate recognition. In fact, two additional wings had to be added only four years after its inauguration and now it has a student-body of six hundred. The combined clientele of these two colleges, though numbering some eighteen hundred boys, represents only the higher strata of Trinidad's scholarly potential. Each year, St. Mary's alone rejects three hundred applicants for admission. The two colleges are staffed by forty-six Spiritans and twenty-seven laymen.

c. Other Works

B. G. 7, 711; 8, 886 ff.

As early as 1871, the Holy Ghost Fathers began to assume the direct care of souls by accepting the parish of Diego Martin, whose pastor, Father Jouin, had been the victim of an atrocious murder the year before. In 1915, the post-war personnel crisis forced them to return the parish to the care of the Archbishop for a while, and they did not resume that charge until 1948.

B. G. 41, 458
B. G. 19, 207

For many years, the Fathers also served the adjoining parish of Carenage, near Point Cumana (of Rum and Coca Cola fame), a parish that extended all the way down to Teteron Bay. In 1894 a Spiritan had built there an auxiliary church, a school and a rectory in order to serve the local fishermen and the many vacationers who seek it as a refuge from the city heat. The region, then an ideal holiday spot, is now occupied by an American naval base and may soon become the site of the central government of the British West Indian Federation.

B. G. 15, 835

B. G. 19, 206
B. G. 41, 458

In 1890 a Holy Ghost Father took over the parish of St. Patrick in Newton, a suburb of Port of Spain. However, six years later, this parish was exchanged for the one at St. Joseph, about twelve miles from the Capital.[16] In 1943 the town of Tunapuna (population 22,000) was detached from the parish of St. Joseph and became the parish of St. Charles. Since then the Congregation has continued to serve it also.

The three parishes now served by Holy Ghost Fathers can boast of three large churches, eleven primary and three secondary schools, nearly five thousand pupils, and 14,000 parishioners.

RELIGIOUS SUPERIORS C.S.SP.

Victor Guilloux, 1863-1866 (later Prefect Apostolic of the Malgaches Islands)
Francis Corbet, 1866-1874 (later Vicar Apostolic of Diego-Suarez)
Casimir Marcot, 1874-1876
James Browne, 1876-1892 (later Pro-Vicar Apostolic of Sierra Leone)
Achilles Lemire, 1892-1894
Nicholas Brennan, 1894-1896
William Carroll, 1896-1903
John Neville, 1903-1910 (later Vicar Apostolic of Zanzibar)
Edward Crehan, 1910-1920
James Lacy, 1920-1925
John English, 1925-1936
James Meenan, 1936-1950
James Brett, 1950-

5. PUERTO RICO

B. G. 3, 25 f.

Back in 1862, the Holy Ghost Fathers were asked to extend their apostolic labors to the island of Puerto Rico but the request came at an inopportune moment: the Congregation had just accepted the immense Zanzibar mission in East Africa and St. Mary's College in Trinidad. No personnel was available for this new work. They declined regretfully because, as the chronicler reported, it could have become "the beginning of a realization of the plans which our beloved Father had envisioned with respect to the Spanish colonies."

cf. N. D. 7, 256

B. G. 35, 165
ff.; 36, 251 ff.;
Ap. H. 15 ff.

It was only about seventy years later that the Congregation actually undertook work in Puerto Rico. In January 1931, at the pressing invitation of Bishop Edwin V. Byrne of San Juan, the

B. G. 21, 295

---

[16]At the turn of the century, the parish of Couva was also served by Holy Ghost Fathers. This parish, however, was given up because it was so isolated and so far from other Spiritan residences.

Spiritans established their first residence on the island. Headed by Father Christopher J. Plunkett, four priests from the American Province assumed their duties in the town of Arecibo. This parish extended over one hundred and twenty square miles and it had fifty thousand Catholics on its books. However, only about four hundred of them really practiced their faith. The rest had been neglected for centuries and their religious illiteracy proved it. Apart from baptism, their only other demonstrations of "faith" seemed to consist in noisy processions and a number of superstitious practices that had little or nothing to do with religion. This bleak spiritual picture was complemented by the equally cheerless material situation of the parish: a church badly in need of repairs, no rectory, a few crumbling mission chapels, and a population so desperately poor that little or no financial help could be looked for in that quarter.

Undaunted by these depressing conditions, the Fathers resolutely set to work to cleanse the parish of its spiritual and material decay. The response was maddeningly slow, but after a time the picture began to improve. Redoubling their efforts, the Spiritans opened a score of mission chapels throughout the rural areas of their far-flung parish. Their tireless efforts have not been in vain, for the latest statistics show 12,000 practising Catholics in Arecibo.

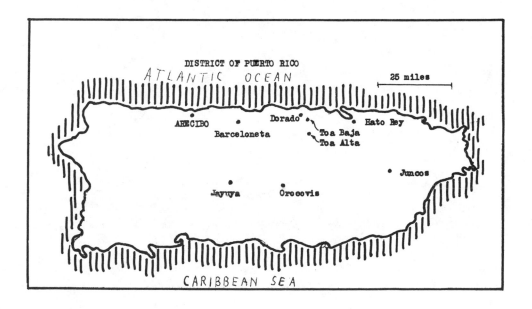

After World War II began, the Spiritans took over a number of other parishes throughout the island: Hato Rey (1941), Barceloneta (1942), Dorado, Toa Alta and Toa Baja (1943), Jayuya (1945), Juncos (1947) and Orocovis (1952). A network of ninety missions has been created around these parishes, so that even the people in the isolated hills and valleys can be now reached.

At present, about thirty American Holy Ghost Fathers care for close to 300,000 souls in Puerto Rico. Recently (1957), the Spiritan residences in the island were united into an independent district. Its first Principal Superior is the Very Reverend Robert J. Eberhardt, C.S.Sp.

6. GRENADA

B. G. 17, 817;
19, 206

At the end of the nineteenth century, the Congregation had a residence on this island to take care of the parish of St. Andrews. However, in 1896, it was decided to abandon Grenada because it was too distant from other Spiritan communities.

7. ST. MARTIN

E. P. 31, I, 62

The French half of this Franco-Dutch island is entrusted to a few Dutch Holy Ghost Fathers. Ecclesiastically, it depends on the Spiritan diocese of Guadeloupe.

CHAPTER SIXTEEN

SOUTH AMERICA

1. FRENCH GUIANA

In the Spiritan history of French Guiana, three periods may be distinguished: from 1775 to 1817, covering the time from the acceptance of the missions to the end of the Anglo-Portuguese occupation; from 1817 to 1893, spanning the years between the return of the colony to France and the expulsion of the Holy Ghost Fathers; and the period beginning in 1925 when the Spiritans returned to Guiana.

a. First Period: 1775-1817

B. G. 32, 427 ff.; Ap. H. 58 ff.; Cl. C. 35, 54 ff.

In 1768, when the suppression of the Jesuits had begun to decimate the country's clergy, the French Government asked the Spiritans to replace these priests who had labored there so successfully for more than a hundred years. At first, the Congregation declined, for it was unable to supply at once all the priests that were needed for this mission. However, the situation in Guiana grew so desperate that the Government repeated its request even more strongly in 1770. This time the Holy Ghost Fathers considered the proposal more seriously, for they were anxious to do something to relieve the religious crisis in Guiana. It had become all the more serious because death continued to strike at the diminishing ranks of the surviving ex-Jesuits in the colony.

At first, negotiations with the Government went very slowly. Guiana was the first large territory offered to the Congregation and Father Becquet, then Superior General, did not want to continue the old system of simply placing priests at the disposal of the ecclesiastical authorities. Rather, he was just then envisioning a reorganization of the Spiritans themselves. He was planning to expand the Congregation by admitting to it not only members who would engage in teaching, but also others who would join it for the specific purpose of doing missionary work. This broadening of its scope meant that new facilities had to be created in France to take care of retired missionaries. The matter of expenses inherent in this reorganization delayed his acceptance of Guiana. Originally, the Government was unwilling to make any allocation

397

of special funds for the purpose. It was not until 1775 that, thanks to the support of Father Peter de la Rue, Abbot of Isle-Dieu and Chaplain General of the Colonies, the King finally agreed to make an annual grant of ten thousand livres. The Spiritans then assumed charge of Guiana.

B. G. 32, 428 In the next seven years Father Becquet sent twenty-two priests to the colony, although not all of them were members of the Congregation. Because of the desparate situation there, Father Becquet had to send priests as quickly as possible and therefore appealed to several diocesan seminaries for help. As a result, the clergy of Guiana during this period consisted of priests who had no special relation with the Spiritans, others who were trained by them in Holy Ghost Seminary, and still others who were actual members of the Congregation. The exact number of members is difficult to ascertain, however, because extant records are regrettably incomplete. All we know is that the following Spiritans had entered the Society as candidates for the missions and were sent to Guiana: Fathers Seveno, Lanoe, Legrand, Duhamel, Moranvillé, Hérard and Hochard. To these we may add Fathers de Glicourt and Ber-
cf. pp. 29 ff. tout, although, as we related in Chapter II, they never reached their destination. Until the outbreak of the French Revolution, these Holy Ghost Fathers labored among the Indians and the slaves, in the regular parishes and as teachers in the College of Cayenne.

B. G. 32, 429 f.
R. H. C. 37,
173 ff. *The Revolution.* When the French Revolution reached Guiana in 1791, the Prefect Apostolic, Father Jacquemin,[1] openly apostatized and quickly imposed the constitutional oath on the rest of the clergy. At first, two Spiritans, Hérard and Moranvillé, conformed and followed the Prefect's orders. Hérard lived in an isolated country parish and found it impossible to consult his Superior. He acceded to the tearful pleas of his parishioners, who feared that the priest's refusal to swear would leave them without a pastor. Consequently, he took the oath but eliminated from the formula everything that was against the Catholic Church. In spite of the modification, the Government now considered him as a "constitutional" priest. When Father Legrand, his Superior, and his fellow Spiritans took him to task for the apparent capitulation, he explained the reservation he had made and they allowed

---

[1]He was a secular priest without any special relation to the Spiritans. He later became the constitutional (schismatic) bishop of Guiana. Before his death in 1819, however, he made his submission to the Church.

him to exercise his priestly functions without retracting his oath until it was necessary to take a firm stand.

P. F. E. 201 f.

Father Moranvillé's conforming is harder to excuse, for he did not live in isolation. His biographer may be correct in attributing it to an unworldly simplicity that caused him to regard the whole procedure as a mere recognition of the new revolutionary government. As a matter of fact, the objectionable part of the oath was generally regarded as inapplicable to Guiana at that time. At its inception, the Revolution was not antireligious in Guiana. It opened with a public Mass for God's blessings on the new Government (the Revolutionary Assembly had actually wanted a solemn Mass followed by procession of the Blessed Sacrament and a *Te Deum*) and elected Father Moranvillé President of the Colonial Parliament, enjoining him under the threat of penalty not to refuse his election. For these reasons it is quite possible that the priest did not see the implications of his action. Subsequently, when he realized that his loyalty to the Church was at stake, he withdrew his oath with all possible publicity. The infuriated Governor ordered him thrown into jail, but Moranvillé escaped aboard a Dutch vessel with a French man-of-war in hot pursuit. The Frenchmen caught up with him at Demerara, but it was too late. The British authorities there refused to extradite him and his would-be captors were foiled.

Ap. H. 59

In 1793, the Revolutionary Government decided that the hasty and confused oath of '91 had been invalid. It imposed a new oath, but Father Legrand and his confreres flatly refused to take it. They preferred to be banished from Guiana and take refuge in the British and Danish West Indian Islands. Shortly thereafter, Father Moranvillé followed them into exile. Three of these refugees,

cf. pp. 209 f.
B. G. 32, 185
R. H. C. 37, 185

Father Duhamel, Hérard, and Moranvillé, ultimately reached the United States (cf. Ch. III) and one of them, Father Hochard, quietly returned to Guiana with the powers of a Vice-Prefect Apostolic. There, despite the threats of a hostile Government, he managed to keep a tenuous foothold and carry on his ministry.

Meanwhile, the Paris Government had begun to deport to Cayenne priests who had refused to take the oath in France. More than three hundred of these confessors of the Faith arrived in Guiana in 1798 and 1799. Most of them died of starvation and disease within a few months of their arrival.

C1. C. 54 ff.   *Father Legrand Returns.* After Napoleon became Emperor of
France, the situation in Guiana began to improve a little—enough
to enable Father Legrand, its legitimate Ecclesiastical Superior,
to return in 1807. In Paris, meanwhile, Father Bertout was busy
with the restoration of the Holy Ghost Congregation. Legrand
got in touch with him and received a promise of reinforcements.
However, before they could be sent, the Emperor quarreled with
the Holy See and brutally suppressed the Holy Ghost Fathers
again. Communications with France were now cut off, for in 1809
A. R. 11,   Anglo-Portuguese troops occupied the colony. For ten long years,
177 ff.;   therefore, Father Legrand singlehandedly took care of the spiritual
13, 47 f.; 15,   needs of the entire colony. This sorry situation obtained until 1817
60 ff.; 16,   when Guiana was returned to the control of France. Father Bertout
41 ff.   at once sent three fine priests to the aid of the lonely survivor of
pre-revolutionary times. Consoled by this sign of better times but
broken in health by ten years of incessant labor, Father Legrand
died a few months after the new missionaries arrived.

b. Second Period: 1817-1893

Cl. C. 56 ff.   *Father Guiller.* After three years of wrangling, the government
finally recognized the canonical appointment of Father Paul Guiller,
one of the priests sent by the Holy Ghost Seminary to succeed
Father Legrand. Though somewhat inclined to be too authoritarian,
the new Prefect was a man of excellent qualities. In the twenty-
seven years he remained as spiritual leader of the Church in
Guiana he was able to repair much of the damage inflicted by the
Revolution. He reopened the Indian missions, founded new parishes, and in 1836 took charge of preparing the Negro slaves for
B. G. 32, 431 f.   their impending freedom.[2] The most conspicuous successes of his
regime were in the field of education. The Sisters of Cluny opened
a school at Cayenne and a famous settlement in Mana.[3] The

---

[2]Slavery had been abolished during the Revolution but it was reestablished in 1817.

[3]In 1828 Mother Javouhey and her intrepid Sisters took over the Mana
region when a governmental effort to colonize the area with white settlers had
failed. After another useless attempt to develop the region with white
colonists, the Sisters bought Negro slaves and began to prepare them for
life as free men. By 1838 the number of these slaves ran as high as five
hundred per year. Mother Javouhey's Sisters gave them religious instruction in addition to teaching them the rudiments of agriculture and trades.
Once they were ready for the responsibilities of freedom, the slaves received
a piece of land in the settlement and were solemnly declared free men. Full
civilian control over the Mana concession remained in the hands of the
Sisters until 1847 when the area again returned to the administrative control
of the government.

Brothers of Christian Doctrine followed suit with academic institutions for boys.

Cl. C. 261;
B. G. 32, 433 f.

N. D. 12, 68 ff.

D. C. 88

Monsignor Dossat. After the death of Father Guiller in 1847, Father John Dossat became Prefect Apostolic.[4] He was not a Spiritan in any sense of the term, but, like his predecessor, he was fully in favor of the incorporation of the colonial clergy into the Congregation. The entrance of Father Libermann and his confreres into the society did not diminish his zeal in this direction. It served only to intensify his desire. He went so far as to offer his resignation if anyone felt that such a step would facilitate negotiations. However, Father Libermann did not deem it advisable to incorporate the whole clergy. In fact, for the greater good of the mission he even had to dissuade the pious prelate from becoming a Spiritan himself. Despite this disappointment, the Prefect remained closely attached to the Holy Ghost Fathers and did everything he could to assist in the execution of their plan to have the Guiana mission reserved for members of the Congregation.[5] In 1851, one year before Libermann's death, the first of the new Spiritans arrived. In this way, after an interruption of thirty-three years,[6] the Spiritans returned to work in one of their oldest missions.

B. G. 32, 434 f.;
D. C. 88 f.

Opposition. The return of the Holy Ghost Fathers or "Libermannists," as they were now called by the secular clergy, did not by any means meet with unanimous approval. A plot was formed to have them expelled from the colony. They were accused of being too much in favor of the Negroes, of freedom, and of small property holders. The clergy argued that they were too liberal in admitting Negroes to Holy Communion and marriage. When Monsignor Dossat stepped forward to defend them, he himself became the butt of local opposition. On the pretext of his administrative ineptness, the government tried in vain to have him removed from office. During the course of the years that followed, these attacks

---

[4]In 1863 the Holy See made him a Prothonotary Apostolic.

[5]The Spiritans wanted to place the newly created colonial dioceses of Guadeloupe, Martinique and Reunion into the hands of the secular clergy and reserve for themselves the more difficult missions which had only Prefects Apostolic.

N. D. 13,
App., 57 f.

[6]We abstract here from the short sojourn of Father Hardy in Guiana during the years 1834-1835.

continued unabated but both the Prefect and the Spiritans stood their ground.

B. G. 32, 437 ff.   *Works.* Under the capable direction of saintly Father Joseph Guyodo, the Holy Ghost Fathers went to work in the Indian missions, the leprosaria, and the centers for liberated slaves. In Tonnegrande they built a church and profoundly changed the lot of the Negro population by tending to their spiritual welfare and by improving them economically through a laborer's cooperative which they organized. At Mondelice, Father Guyodo acquired a fifteen hundred acre sugar-cane plantation in 1862. He envisioned it as a giant fabric of social works: agricultural schools, orphanages, a juvenile detention home and an asylum for the aged. A large part of this plan was executed immediately and it met with prompt success. Before long, however, owners of large plantations complained about unfair labor practices (the priest offered better working conditions than they did), and all kinds of rumors began to be circulated about the social center. Although these tales had no effect on Father Guyodo, a labor shortage did result and, when political pressure pushed the institution close to the brink of insolvency, the whole project had to be abandoned.

D. C. 89 ff.   *A Spiritan Prefect Appointed.* In 1869, after the death of Monsignor Dossat, the Propaganda insisted that a Holy Ghost Father be proposed as his successor. The choice fell on Father Oliver Hervé, a priest who had rendered excellent service as Vicar General in Reunion. In 1860 he had given up that post to join the Congregation. After his profession he was appointed professor of theology at Holy Ghost Seminary, where he impressed everyone by his spirit of humility and obedience. Everything seemed to indicate that he would be the right man for Prefect and Religious Superior. Surprisingly, subsequent events did not verify this prognosis. As soon as he arrived in the colony there was confusion worse confounded. In no time at all had every religious community, including his own, up in arms against his procedures. Before very long he was in direct conflict with the Superior General, simply because Father Schwindenhammer had made some observations regarding his administration of the district. Father Hervé immediately dispatched a letter to Rome and bluntly told the Propaganda: "I want to know whether or not I depend on the Superior of the Congregation in my administration. If the answer is yes, please state it clearly; if it is no, then tell him to let me alone."

Unwilling to settle the theoretical issue of the double authority vested in Father Hervé as both Prefect and Religious Superior, the Propaganda counselled practical agreement and forbearance. Such a *modus vivendi,* however, was beyond the diplomatic abilities of the Prefect and as time went on, Rome began to regret his appointment. At this juncture, Father Hervé took steps to be raised to the episcopacy so that he might have "more elbow room." Shortly after, when he returned to Europe in 1871 to settle some affairs for his mission, he struck everyone as a man who was mentally deranged. Oddly enough, there was no difficulty in getting him to resign and come back to Paris. Then, more strangely still, his psychological disturbance vanished completely as soon as he had relinquished his position of authority. Once again he became the humble and obedient religious that he was before and he spent the remainder of his active life as professor of theology at Holy Ghost Seminary.

D. C. 92 f.   *Monsignor Ambrose Emonet.* After an interval of one year, during which Father Guyodo acted as Pro-Prefect, Father Ambrose Emonet was named Prefect Apostolic. He had gone to Guiana as official Visitor to repair the damage done by his predecessor and in a short time he became so popular that the secular clergy petitioned Rome to have him raised to the episcopal dignity. The Propaganda was quite willing to accede to this request, but political reasons prevented its execution.

B. G. 32, 440 ff.   During the nine years he spent in Guiana prior to becoming Superior General of the Congregation, Monsignor Emonet saw his mission enter into a period of bloom such as it had never experienced before. When the Jesuits had to give up serving the notorious prisons of Cayenne and the deportation centers in Guiana, he was able to replace them with his own confreres. Other priests looked after the spiritual interests of thousands of laborers in the gold mines. Mission work was undertaken among the independent Negroes and the Indians who dwelt in the almost inaccessible regions of the interior. And even though the Brazilian government objected to the missionary invasion of these politically contested areas, the Spiritans continued their widespread work among jungle tribes and ranged as far inland as Para, Brazil.

The last few years of Emonet's administration were saddened by a revival of anticlericalism in government circles. Members of religious congregations were, as usual, the first to be attacked. In 1881, just before his departure for Europe, Monsignor Emonet had to watch the secularization of his College, which had been founded originally by the Jesuits and was now operated by the Spiritans and the Brothers of Christian Doctrine.

D. C. 94 f.;
B. G. 32,
443 f.

Father Joseph Guyodo. When Monsignor Emonet resigned in 1881, the universally respected and popular Father Guyodo took over the reins of administration. However, four years were to pass before the Government would permit him to be appointed Ecclesiastical Superior of Guiana. The saintly priest, who had already spent thirty years in this mission, did not stand by idle while the authorities systematically proceeded with their program of secularizing the schools. From the standpoint of economics, their action was sheer folly, for in the secular schools the cost per student was twenty-four times as high as in the church-sponsored schools, and the educational results were notably poorer. But economics and the interest of the tax-payer never make much impression on men who are bent on driving the Church back to the sacristy.

As time went on, Father Guyodo effectively counteracted the government scheme by opening parochial schools which were so successful that the secularized schools with their costly facilities and expensive staffs remained almost empty. Obviously, this was a great setback for the anti-clerical Governor and his associates. They now began to regard the Spiritans as a dangerous political threat. In addition to their parochial work, these tireless campaigners for Christ had created a network of social and educational establishments all over the country. Their influence on the people was so great that Governor Grodet feared a political upheaval at election-time. For that reason he did his very best to make life intolerable for them, hoping thereby to force their departure from the country. But the Holy Ghost Fathers held their ground, despite the fact that their activity was hampered by all sorts of ridiculous restrictions.

cf. pp. 226 f.

The final blow fell in August, 1891. As of that month, all the pupils of the secularized Tonnegrande school were suddenly withdrawn and transferred to a parochial school. This move so infuriated the Governor that he arbitrarily dismissed the Prefect Apostolic and had him shipped back to France. Then, fearing a public protest against the exile of this beloved priest, he called out the army and the police force to maintain order when the hour of departure neared. As time went on, the other Spiritans suffered the same fate as Father Guyodo and one by one they too had to leave the country. Governor Grodet's victory did not last very long, however. One year after he had exiled the Prefect, he himself was deposed and had to leave the colony in disgrace. The armed forces were again called out, this time not to prevent demonstrations in his favor, but to protect him against the furious mobs who lined the way shouting derisively at the little cesaropapist.

D. C. 164

c. THIRD PERIOD: 1893 TO THE PRESENT

Ap. H. 62 f.

Although the Spiritans had been expelled from Guiana, they remained officially in charge of the spiritual welfare of the colony and tried to provide it *a longe* with secular priests trained in Holy Ghost Seminary. Their departure had left too many vacancies, however, and a number of parishes remained without a pastor. Even Cayenne, the capital itself, had only one priest to aid the Prefect. Moreover, as the older secular priests died or went into retirement, the progressive persecution in France affected Holy Ghost Seminary to such an extent that replacements became more and more infrequent. Churches fell into ruins, missions in the interior were abandoned, and apostolic activity had to be restricted to basic services in the larger towns.

cf. pp. 266 ff.

Alarmed by the situation, the Propaganda finally enjoined the Congregation to use its own personnel for the service of the old French colonies. As far as Guiana was concerned, this order was complied with in 1924 after Monsignor Eugene Fabre resigned as Prefect Apostolic there.[7]

B. G. 32, 445 f.; 34, 598 ff.

The Return of the Spiritans. In 1925 the Holy See named a Holy Ghost Father, Monsignor Leo Delaval, Prefect of Guiana. On his arrival he found that his entire clergy consisted of eleven

---

[7] He stayed on in the colony and worked till his death in 1935 as a simple priest.

priests, of whom six were exhausted by age or disease. Thus he had a net complement of five priests capable of aiding him in the gigantic task of reconstruction. Moreover, of all the flourishing Catholic schools that had once existed, only two were still functioning. The only encouraging feature of it all was the enthusiastic welcome with which the people greeted the return of the Spiritans. They had not forgotten the marvellous work these priests had done before they were so ignominiously expelled from the country. Father Guyodo in particular was held in reverent memory.[8]

Although handicapped by personnel shortages elsewhere, the Congregation zealously endeavored to repair in Guiana the ravages of many years of forced neglect. Little by little its priests took over most of the abandoned parishes and soon the fresh breeze of a revitalized Christianity was blowing across the land.

E. C. 20 f.

The separation of Church and State gave the Spiritans an opportunity to enforce the Church laws regarding Christian burial and baptismal sponsors. This decision gave rise to a vain attempt on the part of the local powers to expel the Congregation. The majority of politicians in the local legislative body did not fulfill the necessary conditions for acting as sponsors at baptism and those who presented themselves were promptly told so. Deeply chagrined, they voted the expulsion of the offending Spiritans. In this, they appear to have forgotten that their entire control over the clergy disappeared when Church and State had separated. Local laws now lacked the power to exile Holy Ghost Fathers. Their presence in the colony was based on a most solemn metropolitan decree of 1826, and this decree could be changed only by an equally solemn decision of the French Parliament. It would have been foolish to think that this august body would attach any weight to a colonial politician's ruffled feelings about not being able to act as Godfather at a baptism. Consequently, the Spiritans blithely stayed on.

B. G. 41, 533 ff.

Vicariate. After Monsignor Delaval died in 1931, fourteen months of negotiation finally brought about the result for which Father Libermann had striven some eighty years earlier : the Prefec-

---

[8]In 1900, seven years after the Holy Ghost Fathers had left, the inhabitants of Cayenne insisted that the mortal remains of their apostle be transferred from Africa (where he had gone to end his days) to an honorable burial-place in their city.

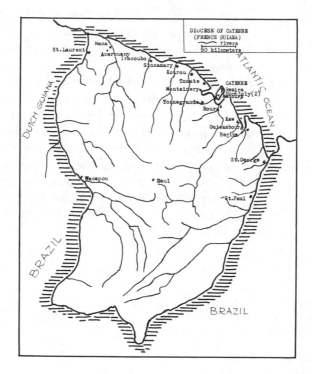

ture was raised to the rank of a Vicariate. In 1933, Father Peter Gourtay became its first Vicar Apostolic, the first "Gangster Bishop," as the newspapers called him with an obvious reference to Guiana's infamous convict prisons and detention centers. However, the days of its inhuman penal institutions were numbered, for in 1934 Father Adolph Naegel, a Spiritan who had been prison chaplain for ten years and knew all the sordid details, became a member of a government commission charged with evaluating the system. He had the great satisfaction of seeing the government concur with his blistering condemnation of a penal program that never reformed a prisoner but always poisoned the atmosphere of the colony. As a result, France's most dangerous criminals were no longer deported to Cayenne. Instead, the prisoners' ship began to repatriate those who had been incarcerated in Guiana.

Diocese. The steady development of the Vicariate was decelerated by the Second World War, but it took on an even faster pace when peace returned. In Cayenne, everything is patterned now along modern parochial lines, with a variety of youth organizations, pious associations, study circles, and other activities. On Sundays, the thirteen hundred seats of the great cathedral can no longer accommodate the crowds. Even now, however, it is still nerve-wracking work to deal with this varied population to which all the races of the earth have contributed their share. Then too, in the up-country missions, river traffic is still the major avenue of communication. In that particular area, the priestly work closely resembles the program followed in the jungle missions of Brazil's interior.

cf. pp. 410 ff.

B. G. 44, 322   In spite of the historic, ethnic, and geographic handicaps, however, Guiana's religious development progressed so satisfactorily in the last quarter-century that the Holy See created the Diocese of Cayenne in 1956. It named the incumbent Spiritan Vicar its first Resident Bishop.

LIST OF ECCLESIASTICAL AND RELIGIOUS SUPERIORS OF FRENCH GUIANA
*Ecclesiastical Superiors**   *Religious Superiors, C.S.Sp.*

Prefects Apostolic

Fr. Robillard, 1775-1777

Fr. Dominic de Glicourt, C.S. Sp., 1777 (never reached his destination)

Fr. Radel, 1778-1787

Fr. Jacquemin, 1787-1792

Fr. Legrand, C.S.Sp., 1792-1818

Fr. Matthew Hochard, C.S.Sp., 1793-1803 (Vice Prefect)

Fr. Paul Guiller, Sp. 1818-1845

Fr. Nicholas Viollot, Sp., 1845-1847 (Vice Prefect)

Msgr. John Dossat, 1847-1868   Fr. Alphonse Thoulouse, 1851

Fr. Réné John Guilmin, 1851-1853 (later Prefect Apostolic of the Malgaches Islands)

Fr. Joseph Guyodo, 1853-1868

Fr. Oliver Hervé, C.S.Sp., 1868-1872

Fr. Joseph Guyodo, C.S. Sp., 1872-1873 (Pro Prefect)

Msgr. Ambrose Emonet, C.S.Sp., 1873-1881   also Religious Superiors

Fr. Joseph Guyodo, C.S.Sp., 1881-1892 (Pro Prefect 1881-1885)

*Sp. indicates Holy Ghost Fathers in the broad sense of the term. *C.S.Sp.* denotes Holy Ghost Father in the strict sense.

Fr. Marius Pignol, 1892-1904

Fr. Michael Kraenner, 1892-1893

Msgr. Marcel Beguin, 1904-1912

Msgr. Eugent Fabre, 1914-1924

Msgr. Leo Delaval, C.S.Sp., 1925-1931

Vicars Apostolic

H. E. Peter Gourtay, C.S.Sp., Titular Bishop of Arad, 1933-1944

also Religious Superiors

H. E. Alfred Marie, C.S.Sp., Titular Bishop of Mundinizza, 1945-1946

Fr. Peter de Gulhermier, 1946-1949

1956: Diocese of Cayenne
Bishop Alfred Marie, C.S.Sp., 1956

Fr. William Robin, 1949-

2. BRAZIL

a. EARLY EFFORTS

N. D. 7, 256; 428 f.

Back in 1845, Father Libermann had considered making a foundation in Brazil. A wealthy French emigré had made him an offer of land, a house, and a chapel, in the neighborhood of Rio de Janeiro. Although nothing came of the plan, the vision of three million abandoned Negroes who were said to be living in the country haunted Libermann for a long time. He realized that

B. G. 3, 293

"a vast field could be opened there for our labors." In 1863, the same fate befell a projected mission to the State of Pernambuco, where the Congregation had been invited to undertake the evangelization of Indians and Negroes who belonged to the labor force of an immense estate.

B. G. 13, 617

Foundation of a College. The first Spiritan settlement was at last made in 1885 at Para or Belem on the north coast of Brazil. Spiritan-trained Bishop Macedo asked the Congregation to take on a Seminary-College he had just founded in his episcopal residence. Although the plea was at first turned down for lack of personnel, the Bishop succeeded in getting the support of the Pope for his cause, and the Congregation finally agreed.

B. G. 16, 954

At first, the College of Para was quite successful. But in 1890, the Brazilian government, which was then dominated by Freemasonry, withdrew all subsidies, and thereby made it difficult

B. G. 18, 813   to continue operations. The situation worsened when Bishop Macedo died and his successor imposed new and more burdensome conditions on the Holy Ghost Fathers. By then, several other colleges were functioning in the area and, since the original urgency no longer existed, the Superior General decided to withdraw his men in 1897.

b. Missions in the Interior

cf. pp. 264 f.   This decision did not mean that the Spiritans would be leaving Brazil, for, as was recorded in Chapter X, the Congregation agreed that same year to work in the vast jungle diocese of Manaos.

Ap. H. 66 ff.   The population of the prefecture of Tefe, which was separated from the diocese and entrusted to the Spiritans in 1910, amounts to about fifty-five thousand souls. Racially, many of them descend from the Portuguese and Negro settlers who inter-married with Indian tribes that had been evangelized by Jesuits and Carmelites in the eighteenth century. Their main sources of income are fishing, gathering Brazil nuts, and tapping rubber-trees. Over and above these Christians, there are uncounted numbers of uncivilized Indians deep in the jungle.

The land itself is wilder and more primitive than the imagination of any city-bred person can picture. Giant streams of yellow water, several miles wide and bedecked with floating islands of vegetation, push their way through towering forests of huge trees whose hidden mysteries of wealth or desolation are barred from man's prying eyes by forbidding walls of impenetrable undergrowth. Mud and swamps and luxurious jungles, crossed and recrossed by river upon river, are broken here and there by primitive settlements of stilted huts on little clearings along the banks. It is a world such as an imaginative artist might conjure up to recreate the face of the earth in some prehistoric period. Roads are unknown; vehicular traffic unthinkable. Rivers alone constitute the usual means of communication, although recently aeroplanes have begun to roar through the silent waterways to bring these wild fastnesses closer to the outside world.

Many of the Spiritans working in this steaming "Green Hell," as the land has been called, spend their days floating down rivers and streams to visit each tiny settlement one by one. Their arrival is the great event of the year: baptisms, confessions, marriages, Mass and sermon, everything must be squeezed into a single day, for tomorrow Father is expected down the river at another little clearing. After Mass, the missionary blesses the graves of those who died since his last visit. Then there follows a joyful *fiesta* in honor of the beloved guest and the newlyweds whose union he has sanctified. A second short exhortation follows and then the priest is conducted ceremoniously to the mission boat which will carry him down to the next settlement.

Occasionally, they will tell him about Indians hidden in a nearby jungle-clearing. Very likely, unless lack of time or his advanced age forbids it, he will then venture to approach them in company with a guide. The excursion is tiring and dangerous, for he will have to cut his way through the forest or swim across uncharted streams where electric eels may shock him, anacondas may crush him to a pulp, and schools of voracious piranhas may strip his body clean to the bone in a matter of minutes. Then, too, his reception by the Indians could be more or less unfriendly when he reaches his destination. He braves these perils nonetheless, because he knows that no one but a missionary will ever persuade these backward denisons of the wilderness to resume contact with the rest of humanity. In no other way can these scattered remnants of ancient tribes escape the threat of extinction.[9]

There are, of course, a few central stations with resident priests, Brothers and Sisters, churches, schools and workshops. Their clean white buildings and the shining spire that surmounts them greet the weary river-traveller from afar and provide a Mecca for the surrounding people who come in from all sides for festivals and Church solemnities. On these occasions, Tefe, a village of eight hundred and the capital of the region, takes on temporarily the character of a metropolis. It is in these larger stations especially that one finds technological schools, workshops, and training laboratories where Spiritan Brothers teach the mechanical trades and agricultural methods which hold the key to the future of these backward regions.

B. G. 25, 632   *Prefecture Divided.* The giant Prefecture of Tefe, which the Holy See carved out of the Diocese of Manaos in 1910, proved to

---

[9]Several Spiritans have done valuable work in studying the Indian languages and customs of these regions. The best known of these specialists is Father Constant Tastevin, the author of a dozen scientific studies on the subject, who became professor of ethnology in Paris.

be still too huge for effective coverage. It extended over the entire two thousand mile course of the Jurua River and spread back over its watershed. In 1933, the situation improved greatly when **Upper Jurua** became a separate Prelature and was confided to the **German** Province of the Holy Ghost Fathers, under the direction of Bishop Henry Ritter.

The other part of the original Prefecture continued to receive whatever personnel the hard-pressed French Province could spare from its numerous commitments in other areas. As time went on, however, its position became more and more precarious. In 1936 B. G. 42, 27   Monsignor Michael Barrat, the Prefect Apostolic,[10] had to report that his eight remaining missionaries averaged nearly seventy years of age. One by one these heroic men went to join their confreres in the cemetery of Boca de Tefe at a time when World War II

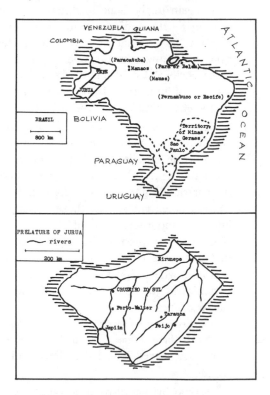

---

[10]Appointed in 1910, Msgr. Barrat kept valiantly to his task until 1946, when he resigned at the age of eighty-three.

made replacements impossible. Fortunately, the German Fathers of the Upper Jurua found it possible to release two of their own priests to come to the rescue of this hard-pressed mission.

B. G. 42, 27 ff.

When peace finally came, the Spiritans moved quickly to remedy the situation. In 1946, the Dutch Province, which then had a hundred and twenty priests available for immediate dispatch to foreign countries, took over the Prefecture. Ten priests and four Brothers were sent to Tefe at once. Father Joachim de Lange, a former missionary of Angola, became the new Prefect. Under his direction, the mission soon entered into a new period of efflorescence. Abandoned river-parishes were reopened, new ones were founded, the Seminary-College was adequately staffed, and the technical school was reopened. Motorized boats now make it possible for the Fathers to visit the remote settlements in their parishes more frequently. Moreover, the Brothers have built several new churches, enlarged others, and constructed a college for two hundred girl students at Tefe. They also run the workshops and teach at the trade school in Boca de Tefe. To insure a steady flow of supplies for the efficient operation of the missions, the Fathers opened a procure at the famous jungle city of Manaos, Capital of the State of Amazones, and took over one of the parishes there.[11]

B. G. 42,30

The Holy Ghost Seminary of Tefe, which was founded about thirty-five years ago, has begun to justify the hope that a more numerous local clergy can be formed. To date, it has already supplied the Jurua and Tefe missions with six priests, and an encouraging number of candidates are now preparing themselves for ordination in the senior seminary.

B. G. 41, 493

In 1950, the Holy See recognized the Church's great and rapid progress in this area by raising the mission to the rank of a Prelature, headed by Bishop de Lange. Comparable strides have been made in the Prelature of Jurua, which since 1947 is directed by Bishop Joseph Hascher. The two jurisdictions now care for nearly 150,000 souls, operate eighty schools and staff one college-seminary. Their Spiritan personnel has increased to forty-two.

B. G. 42, 34

[11] It is interesting to note that the Diocese of Manaos still does not have more than half a dozen diocesan priests. The rest of its clergy consists of priest-procurators of religious orders that have missionaries working in the interior.

LIST OF ECCLESIASTICAL AND RELIGIOUS SUPERIORS

Ecclesiastical Superiors	*Religious Superiors C.S.Sp.*

Tefe

Till 1910 Tefe was under the jurisdiction of the Bishop of Manaos.

Francis-Xavier Libermann, 1897-1898

Louis Friederich, 1898

Auguste Cabrolié, 1898-1909

Msgr. Michael Barrat, C.S.Sp., 1910-1946, Prefect Apostolic

H. E. Joachim de Lange, C.S.Sp., 1946-1950 Prefect Apostolic; since then Prelate *"Nullius"* with episcopal rank

also Religious Superiors till 1954

John van de Zandt, 1954- (resides in Rio de Janeiro)

Jurua

H. E. Henry Ritter, C.S.Sp., 1933-1942 Prelate *"Nullius"* with episcopal rank

H. E. Joseph Hascher, C.S.Sp., 1947-   Prelate *"Nullius"* with episcopal rank

also Religious Superior till 1939. Aloysius Engel, 1939-1943

Rudolph Lenzbach, 1943-1948 also Religious Superior, 1948-1954

Henry Pohlen, 1954- (resides in Sao Paulo)

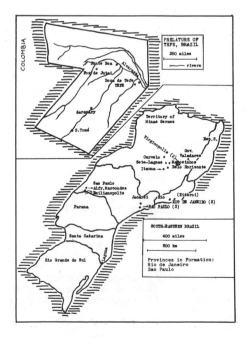

c. PROVINCES IN FORMATION

All the works described above are in the interior of Brazil, for after the closure of the College of Para, Spiritans no longer had any houses in the more populous and civilized areas nearer to the coast.

B. G. 28, 255 ;
31, 4

A semi-private effort toward establishing the Congregation in the East was made in 1916 when Father Joseph da Silva, a Spiritan missionary from Portuguese Angola, went to visit his family in Rio de Janeiro. On this occasion, he was the recipient of many invitations to bring the Holy Ghost Fathers to that part of Brazil. Father da Silva stayed on in Rio as director of an orphanage, but his efforts to obtain additional personnel were unsuccessful and in 1923 this work was abandoned.

B. G. 42, 28

B. G. 41, 474

When the Dutch and German Provinces began to send more men to Brazil after the Second World War, Bishop Hascher and Monsignor de Lange took the initiative in a new endeavor to establish a province in the South-East. In 1950, the General Chapter gave its blessing to the project. Since then, great progress has been reported by the German and Dutch Fathers. Brazil, which is larger than the United States and almost equals Europe in size, offers plenty of room for expansion. The two sponsoring Provinces can forge ahead independently.

E. P. 31, I,
77 ff.

Spiritans from Holland laid the first foundation-stone of their effort in 1948 by arousing public interest in the missions through the establishment of an ethnological museum in Teresopolis. In 1955, this interest reached a productive level when they introduced a Brazilian division of the Pontifical Association of the Holy Childhood with central offices in the capital. That same year also they opened the headquarters of the future province in Rio, where they had taken over the parish of St. George four years before. Most of their activity, however, is presently concentrated in the Territory of Minas Geraes: one parish in Governador Valadares (1955), one in Sete Lagoas (1954), one in Belo Horizonte, (1957) two in Virginopolis (1957) and the Shrine of Bom Jesus in Matozinhos (1949). In the same Territory they have assumed responsibility for the College of Curvelo since 1951, and in 1954 they opened a new Seminary-College at Itauna. At the moment, this province in formation has eleven houses in the State of Rio and the Territory of Minas Geraes, and sixty aspirants in its junior seminary.

E. P. 31, I,
82 f.

Meanwhile, the German Spiritans selected the city of Sao Paulo as the headquarters for their new province. Their activity is centered on the State of the same name. Two large city parishes of St. Boniface (1953) and St. John Climacus (1955) in Sao Paulo have been added to those of Jacarei (1952), Alfredo-Marcondes (1953), Eminianopolis (1953) and Laguna (1957) in the State of Santa Caterina. The junior seminary of this future province is situated at Eminianopolis. At present, the circumscription numbers seven houses in southeast Brazil and a procure in Rio de Janeiro.

3. PERU

B. G. 16,
959 ff.

St. Louis College. In 1891, Spiritans were called to extend their labors to the city of Lima, where there were only five parishes for 150,000 Catholics. At that time estimates revealed that Peru did not have more than ten percent of the clergy it needed for adequate spiritual service. Yet, in the face of this appalling shortage of priests, the Papal Delegate, the Redemptorist and Vincentian Superiors, and several prominent laymen of the city told the Fathers shortly after their arrival that the greatest immediate need did not lay in direct ministry, but in a first class Catholic college that would educate the country's youth. "There are many colleges and schools in Lima," they said, "but there is not a single one to which Catholic families can safely entrust their sons."

B. G. 17,
923 ff.

Within a year, the Spiritan college already had more than a hundred and fifty students—for the most part, sons of Lima's upper-class families and of the highest government officials. It was obvious that these young men, the future leaders of the nation, had to be imbued with sound Catholic principles, for informed sources did not hesitate to attribute most of the country's woes to the poor training of its youth. Even two years of civil war, which broke out shortly after the college opened, did not stop its develop-

B. G. 18, 592

ment. It had become so important in a few years' time that the President of the Republic came in person to preside at its commencement exercises in 1897.

B. G. 19, 44;
Br. 504

Strangely enough, the very success of this institution killed it. Its growth necessitated the construction of large buildings and the augmentation of its teaching staff, just at a moment when the

cf. pp. 236 f.

Congregation was passing through a grave financial crisis and had

Main building of the Seminary-College at Itauna, Minas Geraes, Brazil.

Holy Ghost Seminary-College, Tefe, Amazones. One would have to travel several weeks by water to find a building of comparable size in this Brazilian State.

Dark and forbidding, impenetrable walls of jungle rise along the innumerable rivers of Brazil's interior,

except where little patches have been cleared and a humble chapel serves as the gathering place when the mission boat stops for its visit.

to use a larger part of its man power to keep up with developments in Africa. Consequently, Archbishop Le Roy closed the College in 1898.

4. ARGENTINA

B. G. 41, 474 Although the Holy Ghost Fathers are not yet established in this South American Republic, the last General Chapter expressed itself in favor of an Argentinian foundation. It charged the Province of Portugal with the task of investigating the feasibility of a Spiritan endeavor there.

CHAPTER SEVENTEEN

INDIAN OCEAN

Under this title we will survey Spiritan activities in Reunion, Mauritius, Madagascar and adjacent islands, and then turn our attention to the French enclaves of Pondicherry and Chandernagor in India.

1. REUNION

Ap.H. 419 f.

Vincentian priests appear to have been the first Catholic missionaries to undertake regular work in the island of Reunion.[1] They arrived as early as 1665 and by 1711 their labor had produced such significant results that the Holy See created a Prefecture there and put them in charge of it.

In Reunion, as elsewhere, the French Revolution tore asunder the fabric of religious progress. As missionaries died, no one came to fill the vacancies they left behind them. By 1814 less than half a dozen old and sick priests constituted the entire remaining clergy. It was at this juncture that the Holy Ghost Fathers took charge of the mission and from then on, the pattern of its subsequent history is very similar to that of the other old French colonies. Therefore, it may be divided for convenient treatment into the usual three periods.

Cl.C. 21

a. THE PREFECTURE: 1815-1851

Ap.H. 420

This first period was one of reconstruction and restoration during which the ravages of the Revolution were diagnosed and remedied. As a matter of fact, Reunion had suffered less from persecution than did the other colonies. Throughout those years of political and social turmoil, the Church continued to function as usual. Its greatest problem lay in the fact that reinforcements could not be sent to keep the ranks of the clergy up to full strength.

During the first half of the nineteenth century, Reunion follows the routine of tension and conflict which seems to have been

---

[1] We will refer consistently to this island as Reunion, although at different periods political events gave it successively the names of Mascareigne, Bourbon, Reunion, Bonaparte, Bourbon, and Reunion once again.

418

characteristic of all French colonies at that time. Repeated reference to these altercations should not, however, lead one to think that all the priests of this period were quick to anger and slow to work. Rather, the unremitting toil of the great majority provides the historian with precious little matter for comment. Such dedication and industry is what one expects of a life consecrated to God. It is only when a man departs notably from the accepted pattern that he affects the course of history for good or ill and thereby draws attention to himself and his deeds. Moreover, it must be borne in mind that these century-old clashes took place in another era when priests were few and Canon Law was not yet codified, when contact with Paris and Rome went through primitive channels, and when the State still gripped the Church in a vice-like stranglehold of annoying interference. In the ill-defined relationships of such an atmosphere, perplexing and difficult situations were bound to arise.

Ap.H. 420

In 1817 the Spiritan Superior General managed to send a party of five priests to the rescue of the veteran missionaries who were valiantly struggling to keep the Faith alive in this distant outpost.

Cl.C. 71

The next year he found it possible to add a Prefect Apostolic in the person of Father Pasquiet, a priest who after many years of work in the United States had returned to France to spend his declining years in well-deserved retirement. Realizing the desperate condition of Reunion, this old man generously consented to dedicate his declining years to the religious welfare of the island.

Oddly enough, the tropical heat must have had a most adverse effect on the constitution of the venerable patriarch. He began almost immediately to show unmistakable signs of mental derangement and died rather tragically in 1818.

Cl. C. 72 f.

Conflict with the Governor. When illness forced his successor to return to France and thus end a quiet and fruitful regime of eight years' duration, Father Collin, a highly respected old man of more than seventy years took over as Vice Prefect (1829).

Cl. C. 182

Before long, he found himself involved in a violent quarrel with the Governor, a pitched battle which has remained famous ever since as a horrible example of the extent to which the State assumed control over the Church. On the basis of mere personal animosity, the Governor asked the Vice Prefect to transfer certain priests to other parishes. When Father Collin refused to concur for reasons of conscience, the gubernatorial office simply ordered the priests to pack their belongings and report to their new assignments. Refusing to capitulate, Father Collin withdrew their faculties and thereby made it impossible for them to function in these parishes. Whereupon the Governor suspended their salaries and shouted his now famous words: "I am the Bishop here." Ultimately, the case had to be settled through the intervention of the Spiritan Superior General and the Colonial Minister.

Cl. C. 105 f.
Goyau, II, 385 ff.

Schism. In 1829, Father Henry de Solages became the new Prefect. He was a man of great apostolic vision (or must we say dreams?) and some day he may even be canonized as a martyr. Nevertheless, he lacked that prudence without which wise government is impossible. In the less than two years he spent in Reunion prior to his departure for Madagascar (where he was to die for his Faith), he managed to become so intolerable that the Spiritan General begged the Holy See to make him resign lest

Cl. C. 106

he be sent home under military guard. The Prefect's trouble seems to have stemmed from his self-assigned role as the great reformer. In one fell swoop he set out to abolish everything that appeared even remotely irregular.

The first victim of his ill-considered zeal was Father Collin, whose rectory was shared by a sister-in-law and her daughter. These two very respectable ladies took care of the seventy-seven year old priest in most acceptable fashion. Nevertheless, soon after his arrival, de Solages peremptorily ordered Father Collin to turn his housekeepers out of the house because cohabitation was against the laws of the Church. Although the old man obeyed the heartless command, he complained bitterly about it and won everybody's sympathy. As a result, public anger mounted against the Prefect.

Shortly after, de Solages decided to settle in a truly authoritative way a minor dispute between a pastor and his curate. It seems that the pastor was right and the assistant wrong, but the Prefect did not see it that way. The pastor, however, was a stubborn old man who refused to give in. He appealed to the Governor, the Minister of the Colonies, and the Pope. When the furious Prefect interdicted him, the pastor brushed aside the sentence on the grounds that he had already appealed to higher authorities. He simply went about his duties as if nothing had happened. De Solages was so generally unpopular that the pastor soon had quite a following. The whole thing promptly developed into a schism that lasted until the Prefect left for Madagascar. Before departing, he appointed the saintly Father Dalmond as his substitute. This Vice Prefect reinstated the recalcitrant pastor and then quietly brought things back to normal.

Cl. C. 111

But only for a while. Another schism threatened. Since de Solages resented the Congregation's remote control over the colonies, he did not notify the Spiritan Motherhouse of Father Dalmond's appointment and his subsequent recognition by the Governor. As a result, the Superior General named a successor *ad interim* in the person of Father Goudot. When this priest arrived from France soon after, the island suddenly found itself with two legitimate but competing ecclesiastical superiors! Fortunately, the issue was settled before serious consequences developed, and Father Goudot returned to France.

cf. pp. 141 ff.

In 1842 under the administration of Monsignor Poncelet, Father Libermann sent his first priests to prepare the slaves for their impending liberation. Since the story of their early work has been told in Chapter VI, it need not be repeated here.

b. THE SECULAR HIERARCHY: 1851-1919

D. C. 67 ff.

After the establishment of the hierarchy in the old colonies, Reunion enjoyed a quarter-century of peace and harmony during the successive episcopates of Bishop Julian Desprez, the future Cardinal Archbishop of Toulouse; the scholarly Bishop Maupoint; and finally, Bishop Delannoy. The first two especially were very zealous and capable prelates for whom no amount of personal discomfort justified leaving good work undone. It was Bishop Maupoint, as has been noted in Chapter VIII, who gave the first impetus to the Catholic missions of Africa's east coast.

cf. p. 196

D. C. 73 ff.

In 1876, Gambetta's radical politicians espoused the nomination of Father Dominic Soulé and eventually succeeded in having their candidate become Bishop of Reunion. Nothing could have been more regrettable. Although Bishop Soulé lasted only four years before he was forced to resign, he managed to wreck the diocese quite thoroughly. The senior Vicar General was the first to feel the impact of his tornado-like wrath. After dismissing this greatly beloved old priest just before he would have qualified for a pension, Soulé appointed him in rapid succession to a number of parishes and finally forbade him to do any ministry at all. Next, he drove the Spiritans from the diocesan college which they had successfully restored after the Jesuits had been expelled some years earlier. Responsibility for this highly-respected school was then thrust on the second Vicar General and, when that startled and confused cleric failed to make an immediate go of it, he shared the fate of his senior colleague. Building up steam as he went along, Soulé next attacked his pastors, reducing them wholesale to the rank of assistants. Junior priests were quickly catapulted into pastorates and then downgraded again overnight. The Jesuits, the Christian Brothers, the various Sisters' Congregations, and a number of prominent Catholic laymen all came in for their share of his fiery blasts.

As could be expected, the victims of this tyranny—and that meant nearly everyone—did not react passively. Complaints piled up in Paris and in Rome. Finally, with the assistance of the two former Bishops of Reunion who had been transferred to metropolitan dioceses in France, and with the collaboration of all interested parties except the troublesome prelate himself, the Spiritan Superior General drew up a report which he submitted to the Holy See and the Government. Needless to say, both Church and State forced Bishop Soulé to resign at once.

D. C. 77 ; 271   During the brief vacancy after his resignation, Soulé's Vicar General (who was widely regarded as his evil genius) quickly shut down the local Jesuit chapel. Then, when Father Adam, a local Superior of the Holy Ghost Fathers in Reunion, came to the defense of the Society of Jesus, he was exiled from the diocese for his trouble.

D. C. 78 ff.   Bishop Coldefy took charge in 1880 and energetically set about restoring peace. Unfortunately, he lasted only seven years before death took him away. The regime of his successor, Bishop Fuzet, was marked by so many conflicts with priests and laity that the Papel Nuncio called him another Soulé. The Jesuits especially seem to have drawn the thunderbolts of his ire, despite the fact that he innocently protested: "I really like the Jesuits . . . but in their place!" At last, after a running battle of four years' duration his transfer to a diocese in France cleared the air once again.

D. C. 84   The next bishop of Reunion lasted twenty-seven years without getting into trouble with anyone. And for a most peculiar reason. Apparently he was so appalled at the preceding years of strife that he left the administration of his diocese completely in the hands of his Vicar Generals and timorously withdrew to his summer villa outside the capital, emerging from it only three times a year for solemn pontifical services in his Cathedral. The entire Spiritan archives of the diocese during his term of office contain only three letters signed by him—one every nine years. Such a thoroughgoing withdrawal from active government was an effective way to avoid trouble, one must admit, but it is hardly what would be hoped from a bishop whose episcopate endured from 1893 to 1919, a period that brought on an intensification of persecution, the separation of Church and State, and the devastation of World War I.

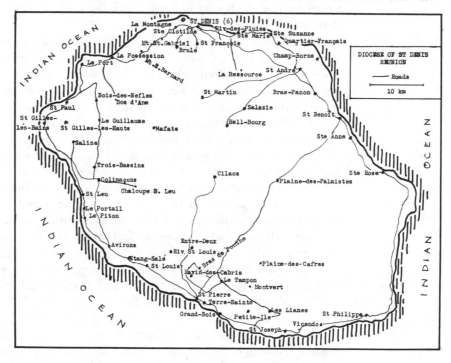

Spiritan Works. After the abolition of slavery and the Christianization of its former victims, the Holy Ghost Fathers gradually channeled their endeavors toward regular parish work, social service, and the direction of educational institutions. Little need be said regarding their parochial activity, for it follows the usual pattern. It was in the field of social work that their greatest success was scored. By 1858, the government was so impressed that it induced the Spiritans to take over Providence Institute, a giant

Ap. H. 425 ff.

enterprise that embraced, in addition to a hospital and a geriatric center, a juvenile detention home, a technical school, an agricultural school, and orphanages for boys and girls. The transformation of these tender victims of social disorganization into industrious youngsters of high moral standing caused widespread amazement. Very soon, the Institute's prosperity gave rise to that sort of admiration which ultimately degenerates into envy. The technical school in particular was soon faced with many enemies because the shoddy work of highly-paid "master-craftsmen" showed up very poorly against the superb products turned out by technical apprentices who had the benefit of careful training under expert Spiritan Brothers.

B. G. 6, 961   The Institute's tragic end came in 1868. A rioting mob, having plundered the Jesuit College, rushed to attack Providence and its more than six hundred inhabitants. Although French Marines hurried to the scene and were able to beat back the marauders, tension mounted until a state of siege was proclaimed on the island. When a shortage of troops forced the Governor to withdraw his protective guard from the Institute, the Fathers feared for the safety of their charges and under cover of darkness retreated into the mountains. Meanwhile, the cowed Governor and his council made concession after concession to the leaders of the insurrection. In the end he agreed to the expulsion of the Jesuits and the suppression and confiscation of Providence Institute, allowing it to continue only as an old-age home and an orphange with a maximum of twenty boys. In making these concessions, the Governor overlooked the fact that he was breaking the colony's solemn twenty-five year contract with the Congregation and that he had arbitrarily confiscated a property to which the Spiritans held legal title. When

B. G. 11, 454   the colony refused to honor its contract and return the stolen estate, the Congregation sued Reunion in the National Superior Court. Although the Spiritans won the case, they were unable to reopen the once-flourishing institute which in a few short years had done so much good for the poor and destitute.

Ap. H. 428   In addition to Providence Institute, the Spiritans had charge of a leper colony and, after the Jesuits' withdrawal, they also staffed the diocesan college. Soon after they took over in 1874, so many students transferred from the State College that there was bitter outcry against them in anticlerical circles. This time, however, it did not take a riot to crush the work. Bishop Soulé arrived in the colony and immediately embarked on a program of obstructionism. Less than a year later, he closed the college entirely and thus left his diocese without a single Catholic center of higher education.

c. SPIRITAN HIERARCHY: 1919 TO THE PRESENT

When the Holy See decided in 1912 that Reunion's bishops should henceforth be drawn from the Holy Ghost Congregation, Father de Beaumont was named Coadjutor to the incumbent prelate (1917). Two years later, he succeeded him as the island's bishop. At his death in 1934 his confrere, Francis de Langavant, replaced him. Once again, two Spiritans have thus far sufficed E. C. 25; 33 ff. to staff a diocesan see for a forty-year period. This remarkable stability has been followed in Reunion by the same happy results we described in Martinique and Guadeloupe: serious conflicts no longer occur; administrative policy is consistent; and native Creole vocations have increased to such an extent that now the local priests are more than twice as numerous as the secular clergy from France.

C. A. 1956 The flourishing condition of this diocese is evident to anyone who examines its latest statistics: less than eight thousand out of its population of 283,000 are non-Catholics; four hundred Creole Sisters and Brothers labor there; and nearly forty priests can point to it as their place of birth.

E. P. 31, I, 232 Aside from the Congregation's responsibility for about twenty-ff. five parishes and other works, its priests are once again engaged in educating future priests and lay-leaders in the restored Seminary-College of Cilaos.

LIST OF ECCLESIASTICAL AND RELIGIOUS SUPERIORS OF REUNION

Ecclesiastical Superiors   *Religious Superiors C.S.Sp.*
Prefects Apostolic

  Fr. Alexis Collin, 1815-1818
   (Vice Prefect)

  Fr. Pasquiet, 1818-1820

  Fr. Alexis Collin, 1820-1821
   (Vice Prefect)

  Fr. John Pastre, 1821-1828

Fr. Alexis Collin, 1828-1831
(Vice Prefect)

Fr. Henry de Solages, 1831-1832

Fr. Peter Dalmond, 1832-1835
(Vice Prefect)

[Fr. Goudot, 1832 Vice Prefect]

Msgr. Poncelet, 1835-1850

Fr. Frederic Le Vavasseur (1842-1848 C.S.C.M.) 1848-1850

Fr. John Gueret, 1850-1851
(Vice Prefect)

Fr. Marcellin Collin, 1850-1854

1851: Creation of the Hierarchy

Bishop Julian Desprez, 1851-1857

Fr. Jerome Schwindenhammer, 1854-1855

Bishop Armand Maupoint, 1857-1871

Fr. Francis Duboin, 1855-1859

Fr. Marcellin Collin, 1859-1862

Fr. Francis Duboin, 1862-1867

Fr. Bartholomew Stoffel, 1867-1870

Fr. Francis Duboin, 1870-1872
(later Vicar Apostolic of Senegal)

Bishop Victor Delannoy, 1872-1876

Fr. Bartholomew Stoffel, 1872-1874

Bishop Dominic Soulé, 1876-1880

Fr. Francis Corbet, 1874-1879
(later Vicar Apostolic of Diego Suarez)

Bishop Joseph Coldefy, 1880-1887

Fr. Bartholomew Stoffel, 1879-1889

Bishop Edmund Fuzet, 1887-1893

Fr. Casimir Colrat, 1889-1897

Bishop James Fabre, 1893-1919

Fr. Eugene Meillorat, 1898-1913

Fr. Amadeus Chardin, 1913-1919

Bishop George de la Bonnière de Beaumont, C.S.Sp., 1919-1934 (Coadjutor since 1917)

Fr. Peter Gourtay, 1919-1933
(later Vicar Apostolic of French Guiana)

Bishop Francis de Langavant, C.S.Sp., 1934-

Fr. Francis Monnier, 1932-1938

Fr. John Bolatre, 1938-1950

Fr. Peter Altmayer, 1950-1956

Fr. Louis Le Chevalier, 1956-

2. MAURITIUS

Ap. H. 431 f.

Introduction. The island derives its name from Dutch colonists who landed in the sixteenth century and decided to honor their Stadhouder Maurice of Nassau. When they abandoned their attempt at colonization in 1710, the French took over and called it Isle de France. The British captured it from them in 1810 and restored its original Dutch name.

Although Mauritius is only seven hundred and twenty square miles, it has a population of more than half a million. Its multiracial inhabitants descend from Europeans, Africans, Indians and Chinese. In their religious affiliation, about thirty-five percent are Catholic, one and one-half percent Protestant, fifteen percent Mohammedan, and the remainder belong to various Asiatic cults.

In 1818 the jurisdiction of the Ecclesiastical Superior residing in Port-Louis extended from South Africa to Australia. Subsequent divisions have reduced his territory to the islands of Mauritius, Rodriguez, and seven archipelagos as far away as the Chagos islands.

Father Laval. Libermann's priests entered upon the scene in 1841 when Bishop Collier, O.S.B., took the Holy Heart congregation under his wing and obtained Father Laval as his first mis-

cf. pp. 135 ff.

sionary. Chapter VI recorded how this saintly priest became the great apostle of Mauritius and converted sixty thousand liberated slaves. Gradually, as the new converts developed into established Christians, the Spiritans founded new parishes and took part extensively in the regular ministry of the diocese.

B. G. 6, 76 f.

St. Louis College. In 1868 the Holy Ghost Fathers finally accepted the pressing invitation of Bishop Hankinson, O.S.B., to found a college in the capital of the island. They had hesitated a long time for, although the Jesuits had tried some years earlier and failed, they did not definitely abandon the idea of making

La. 273

another attempt till 1868. One of the reasons why the Jesuits decided not to resume their efforts was the prelate's strange and persistent refusal to grant the Fathers faculties to hear even their own students' confessions.

B. G. 8, 643 ff.

The very beginning of the Spiritan College was difficult, for it had to face stiff competition from the Royal Anglican College, which was wholly financed by the British Government, and from several private schools that were run for the benefit of their commercial owners. In addition, the Holy Ghost Fathers were not free to direct the institution as they liked nor did the Bishop give any of the promised financial support to this purely diocesan college. Finally, he once again followed his old practice of refusing teaching priests faculties for hearing confessions.

La. 278

B. G. 10, 216 ff.

Although in 1872, his successor Bishop Scarisbrick made an arrangement with the Congregation in virtue of which the Spiritans became owners of the College and could operate it at their own expense and in accord with their own views, he also stubbornly withheld faculties from the teaching staff. Nevertheless, working with a free hand, they now proceeded to develop the College into a strong and reputable institution.

Gradually, the competing schools disappeared for lack of students, except of course, the government-owned Royal College. As the enrollment increased, imposing buildings arose on the campus and everything pointed to a happy and stable academic future. There was even serious question of opening an extension center in the country.

B. G. 11, 572 ff.; 12, 872

B. G. 12, 873 ff.

Oddly enough, the College came to a dramatic end soon after the new structures were finished. The government instituted a new policy whereby it became necessary to follow the British educational system. If the Spiritan College were to compete successfully with the Royal College, the Congregation would have been forced to replace a large part of its staff with English-speaking priests. Because at that time its personnel commitments for other colleges in British territories made it impossible for the Irish Province to man another academic institution, the Motherhouse regretfully notified the Bishop of its decision to close St. Louis College.

La. 273

Although the correspondence exchanged on this occasion between the prelate and the Spiritan Superior General does not mention it, the decision was at least partially influenced by the Bishop's systematic refusal to let the Fathers function as confessors even for their own students. Intransigence on this point years earlier had forced the Jesuits to close their College in disgust, and other instances of the same attitude had led the Vincentians to abandon Mauritius altogether the year before the Spiritans decided to go. The English personnel problem was, of course, the basic factor behind the decision to withdraw, for otherwise the Congregation would not have engaged in an expansion program just before closing the College entirely, but the

B. G. 12, 876

lack of jurisdiction in the confessional was certainly a contributing cause. As usual, heavy pressure was brought to bear on the Spiritans to make them stay, but the problem of man-power could not be solved. When all efforts to find a staff had failed, Bishop Scarisbrick sadly wrote: "In humble submission to Providence we will wait for the time when our Catholic College can be revived."

ibid. 878

More than forty years were to pass before the Congregation was able to provide a substitute for it by opening a Seminary-College at Quatres Bornes. After overcoming the initial difficulties inherent in such a work, the Fathers have brought this new educational unit to a flourishing condition.

Parishes. For over a century the Holy Ghost Fathers have participated in parochial work throughout the island. Their share in this ministry increased still more in 1916, when the Holy See assimilated Mauritius with the old French colonies and made the Congregation fully responsible for its religious welfare.

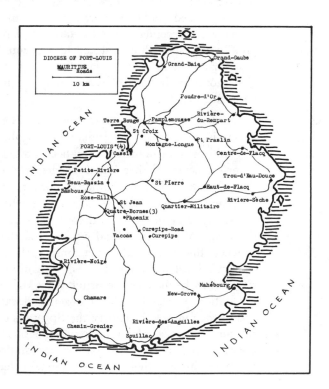

General Condition of the Diocese. Since the first Spiritan Bishop was named for Mauritius, three Holy Ghost Fathers have occupied its episcopal see. In general, the work of the clergy has been blessed with consoling results. The descendants of former slaves are strongly attached to the Church and have resisted all efforts of Protestant missionaries to proselytize them. Undoubtedly, saintly Father Laval continues to exercise his salutary influence on the island. Catholics, Mohammedans and Hindus alike visit his shrine in massive numbers. In 1957, on the anniversary date of his death, no less than 45,000 people went to pray at his grave.

B. G. 44, 467

C. A. 1954,
1955

The intensity of the island's religious life reveals itself clearly in the latest statistics of the diocese: despite the fact that there is only one priest for every three thousand Catholics, reception of the Holy Eucharist averages fifteen times a year for each practicing Catholic; confraternities, third orders and pious associations flourish; best of all, native vocations to the priesthood and the religious life have now passed the three hundred mark. A well-organized Catholic educational system numbers seventy-five primary and secondary schools staffed by Brothers, Sisters, and approximately seven hundred and fifty devoted lay teachers. On the other hand, there is still a large group of about two hundred and fifty thousand Indians of whom only a small part thus far have been converted.

La. 258

Rodrigues and the Archipelagos. The island of Rodrigues, which is situated in the Indian Ocean about three hundred and fifty miles east of Mauritius, had been visited only once by a Catholic priest before Father Laval decided to undertake its evangelization. In 1849 he sent Father Thévaux, one of the survivors of Libermann's Australian venture, to see what he could do. As one can easily imagine, the moral conditions he found were downright shocking. Moreover, a local war was on the point of breaking out between the natives. Even against such odds, the intrepid missionary's hard work was blessed with unexpected success: within six months he managed to bring about the conversion of the entire population, except for half a dozen obdurate old sinners. At the end of the nineteenth century the Spiritans established a permanent residence on the island to serve the increasing population. At present, three Holy Ghost Fathers are stationed there to take care of about thirteen thousand exceptionally fervent Catholics.

The seven archipelagoes of Chagos, Diego-Garcia, St. Brandon, Six Islands, Salomon, Aguleja and Farguhas are inhabited by some three thousand Catholics and have no resident priest. They are visited only from time to time.

ECCLESIASTICAL AND RELIGIOUS SUPERIORS OF MAURITIUS

Ecclesiastical Superiors	*Religious Superiors C.S.Sp.*
	James Laval, 1847-1859 (C.S.C.M. till 1848)
	Francis Thévaux, 1859-1872 (Marcellin Collin, 1859-1862, Official Visitor)
	Francis Duboin, 1872-1875 (later Vicar Apostolic of Senegal)
	Victor Guilloux, 1875-1878 (later Prefect Apostolic of Malgaches Islands)
	Francis Corbet, 1878-1880 (later Vicar Apostolic of Diego-Suarez)
	Francis Beaud, 1880-1885
	Anthony Garmy, 1885-1895
	Francis Ditner, 1895-1907
Bishop John T. Murphy, C.S.Sp., 1916-1926	Jerome Rochette de Lempdes, 1907-1921
(Arch)Bishop James Leen, C.S.Sp., 1926-1949 (Coadjutor since 1925)	Cesar Berthet, 1921-1927
Bishop Daniel Liston, C.S.Sp., 1949- (Coadjutor since 1947)	Charles Streicher, 1927-1950
	Gerald Bowe, 1950-

3. LITTLE MALGACHES ISLANDS

B. G. 11, 377 ff.   When France occupied the islands of Mayotte and Nossi-Bé, in 1843, the Spiritan Superior General found them added to his already heavy responsibilities. In 1850, therefore, when the Jesuits wanted to take over the evangelization of Madagascar from the Congregation and made it a condition that these tiny islands also

N. D. 12, 35 ff.; be added to their territory, Father Libermann willingly acquiesced.
310 ff.   He immediately arranged to have a Jesuit priest named Superior of the Prefecture.

Ap. H. 414   After the Jesuit Fathers had succeeded in penetrating Madagascar in 1861, they no longer regarded the Malgaches Islands as

B. G. 6, 606   necessary to their purpose and offered to return them to the Congregation. The Spiritans already had many more missions than they could conveniently staff, so they turned a deaf ear even when the offer was repeated again and again. Finally, in 1878, the Holy See itself made the request and the Congregation had no choice but to accept the islands and staff them with its own personnel.

    There has been little to report by way of missionary progress.

Ap. H. 414 ff.   Mohammedan influence is so strong in the Malgaches that apostolic efforts there do not produce anything like the results attained in other islands which are free from Islamism.

    In 1898, when the Holy Ghost Fathers took over the northern half of Madagascar, the Malgaches Prefecture was added to the domain of the Spiritan Vicar Apostolic of Diego-Suarez. Later, in 1923, it was transferred to the Vicariate of Majunga. At the same time, the Comores Islands became part of this Vicariate also. All of these islands remained under the care of the Congregation until 1932 when the Propaganda removed them from Spiritan control and entrusted them together with a small section of Northern

B. G. 35, 923 f.   Madagascar to the French Capuchins. This sudden transfer gave rise to unexpected complications which it took several years to solve.

ECCLESIASTICAL AND RELIGIOUS SUPERIORS OF THE LITTLE MALGACHES ISLANDS

Prefects Apostolic

Fr. Peter Dalmond, 1841-1847

Bishop Alexander Monnet, C.S.Sp.,
    1848-1849 (Vicar Apostolic)

Fr. Weber, C.S.Sp., 1849-1851

1851-1878: Jesuit Mission

Fr. Victor Guilloux, C.S.Sp.,
    1878-1882

Fr. Alexander Mauger, C.S.Sp.,
    1882-1886   } also Religious Superiors

Fr. John Guilmin, C.S.Sp.,
    1886-1891

Fr. Louis Walter, C.S.Sp.,
    1891-1899

1899-1923: see Diego Suarez, Madagascar

1923-1932: see Majunga, Madagascar

1933 ff.: Capuchin Mission

4. MADAGASCAR

Goyau, II, 34 ff.
B. G. 35, 811 ff.

Vincentian priests appear to have been the first to undertake the Christianization of this enormous island off the coast of East Africa. They arrived in 1648, but after twenty-three years of incessant labor and untold suffering produced no appreciable results, these valiant missionaries shook the dust from their feet.

R. H. M., 5,
414 ff.; 16,
89 ff.
B. G. 35, 815 ff.
A. R. 98, 356

A new effort was made in 1832 when Father Henry de Solages, Prefect Apostolic of Reunion, went to Madagascar. His intention was to gain admission to the Court of Queen Ranavolona and induce her to authorize the establishment of Catholic missions, but the Queen's hostile Minister intercepted the courageous apostle, imprisoned him under constant guard in a wretched hut, gave the jailors strict orders not to help him in any way, and thus left him to die a martyr's death by starvation.

N. D. Compl.,
296 ff.
N. B. 335 ff.
R. H. M., 5,
416 ff.

Eleven years later, Father Dalmond became Prefect Apostolic of Madagascar and tried to effect a permanent establishment on this island where France then had a precarious political foothold. Father Fourdinier, the Spiritan Superior General, the Jesuits, and Libermann's priests of the Holy Heart of Mary were all interested

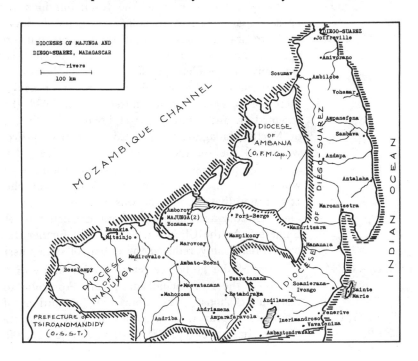

B. G. 35, 817 ff. in promoting the success of the enterprise. In 1845 Father Dalmond, accompanied by a few Jesuits and Father Monnet, then a Jesuit novice, landed at St. Augustine Bay. Although the reception was rather friendly at first, increasing hostility forced the Prefect to withdraw about four months later and concentrate his attention on the little Malgaches Islands.

cf. p. 100

N. B. 358 f.
R. H. M.,
5, 430 ff.

Shortly after, Father Monnet went to France, joined the Holy Ghost Fathers, and became their Superior General in 1848. Later that same year, when Father Libermann and his priests entered the Congregation, the Holy See named Monnet Bishop of Pella and Vicar Apostolic of Madagascar. In June 1849, a French navy vessel carried the zealous Bishop and four Jesuit priests to his dangerous mission via Rio de Janeiro and Reunion. However, he was not destined to set foot again on the land of his apostolic dreams. A pernicious fever seized him when he debarked at the off-shore island of Mayotte and in a few hours' time put an end to the eventful life of this intrepid priest. It was during the next year that Father Libermann arranged for the Jesuits to take over the Christianization of Madagascar.

B. G. 19, 305
ff.
Ap. H. 371 ff.

Forty years later, when the Jesuit missions in southern Madagascar had reached a point of splendid development, heavy pressure was brought to bear on the Spiritans to resume their apostolic activities in the northern third of the island where there was only one resident priest. It was the hottest and most humid part of the country, devoid of any roads or navigable rivers and therefore a most difficult mission. In 1898 the Congregation accepted it, and Father Corbet became the first Vicar Apostolic of North Madagascar. In 1923, after twenty-five years of hard work and the sacrifice of many young lives, the Faith showed consoling progress: over twenty-two thousand Catholics were worshipping in more than two hundred churches and chapels. It was then that the mission was divided into the two Vicariates of Diego-Suarez and Majunga, both entrusted to the Holy Ghost Fathers. As the Church advanced still further, later subdivisions have considerably reduced the extent of both missions.

B. G. 44, 244

E. P. 31, I,
224 ff.

In 1955 the Holy See set up the hierarchy of Madagascar and promoted the two incumbent Vicars Apostolic to the status of resident Bishops. The flourishing condition of these young Churches appear from a glance at their latest statistics; Diego-Suarez has over 50,000 Catholics and 17,000 catechumens;

Majunga, nearly 33,000 Catholics and 8,000 Catechumens. Both dioceses have their own junior seminaries, from which thus far a dozen native priests have been ordained. Religious vocations also are on the increase. In 1951 a special novitiate for local Spiritan Brothers was opened in Antalaha. Four years later it had seven professed members and ten aspirants. The two dioceses together operate a hundred and fifty-six grade schools in which 11,000 boys and girls receive their early training.

LIST OF ECCLESIASTICAL AND RELIGIOUS SUPERIORS

Ecclesiastical Superiors	*Religious Superiors*

All Madagascar

Fr. Peter Dalmond, 1841-1847 Prefect Apostolic (named Vicar Apostolic in 1848 after his death)

H. E. Alexander Monnet, C.S. Sp., 1848-1849 (Titular Bishop of Pella)

1851: Jesuit Mission

Vicariate of North Madagascar (Diego-Suarez)

H. E. Francis Corbet, C.S.Sp., 1898-1914 (Titular Bishop of Obba)

H. E. Augustus Fortineau, C.S.-Sp., 1914-1946 (Titular Bishop of Chytra)

also Religious Superiors till 1939

Fr. John Besnard, 1939-1951

H. E. John Wolff, C.S.Sp., 1946-1955 (Titular Bishop of Phatano)

Fr. Andrew Britschu, 1951- (District combined with that of Majunga)

Diocese of Diego-Suarez

Bishop John Wolff, C.S.Sp., 1955-

Vicariate of Majunga

H. E. Paul Pichot, C.S.Sp., 1923-1940 (Titular Bishop of Raphanea)

also Religious Superior till 1939

Fr. Maurice Huré, 1939-1942

H. E. John Wolff, C.S.Sp., 1941-1947 (Titular Bishop of Phatano)

Fr. Lucian Guelle, 1942-1951

H. E. John Batiot, C.S.Sp., 1947-1953 (Titular Bishop of Attalea)

H. E. John David, C.S.Sp., 1954-1955 (Titular Bishop of Mellopolis)

Fr. Andrew Britschu, 1951- (District combined with that of Diego-Suarez)

Diocese of Majunga

Bishop John David, C.S.Sp., 1955-

5. PONDICHERRY AND CHANDERNAGOR

Cl. C. 68 f.

Because Paris frowned on foreign priests ministering to French subjects, the Propaganda created a special prefecture in 1828 for the French-speaking inhabitants of France's enclaves in India. After two dangerous mistakes which fortunately were discovered in time, the Spiritan Superior General, Father Bertout, found the right man for the position when he presented a secular priest,

D. C. 101 ff.

Father Peter Calmels, to be the first Prefect. Father Calmels lasted more than thirty years, despite the fact that jurisdictional and governmental misunderstandings kept arising with monotonous

cf. p. 225

regularity. As the reader will recall from Chapter IX, the Prefect's jurisdiction was limited to Europeans, Creoles and people of mixed origins, while the Indians belonged to the jurisdiction of a Vicar Apostolic.

The difficulty, of course, was to draw the exact dividing line between "Indians" and "those of mixed origins." In desperation, the Propaganda decided in 1841 that a person's clothes would determine his place in the administrative scheme: Indian costume placed him in the Vicariate; European dress referred him to the Prefecture. In practice this meant that one could change jurisdictions merely by putting on a hat and coat. It necessarily resulted in confusion and interminable difficulties between the Vicar Apostolic and the Prefect.

These tiny but annoying conflicts ended only in 1880 when the Holy Ghost Fathers sent Father Francis Corbet, one of their own ment as Prefect. Very sensibly, he arranged with the Vicar that each would give the other jurisdiction in doubtful cases. At the same time he did his best to have the cause of the whole confusion removed by vigorously supporting the absorption of the Prefecture

cf. p. 226

into the Vicariate. As Chapter IX recorded, his wish was fulfilled in 1886 when the Holy See created the Archdiocese of Pondicherry to replace the two previous jurisdictions.

B. G. 2, 440
ff.; 549 ff.
B. G. 11, 513
ff.
B. G. 14, 738
ff.

The first members of the Congregation appeared on the scene in this distant Prefecture in 1861 when the Spiritans opened a technical school in Chandernagor. Later they added the College of Pondicherry and assumed responsibility for the entire service of the Prefecture. After the suppression of the Prefecture, however, they resisted all efforts to keep them in India. They withdrew entirely from Asia and thereafter concentrated their efforts on Africa.

ECCLESIASTICAL AND RELIGIOUS SUPERIORS OF PONDICHERRY

Prefects Apostolic	*Religious Superiors C.S.Sp.*
Fr. Peter Calmels, 1828-1859	
Fr. Peter Brunie, 1859-1879 (Ecclesiastical Superior)	Fr. Fritsch, 1862-1864
	Fr. Magloire Barthet, 1864-1875 (later Vicar Apostolic of Sene-gambia)
	Fr. Bartholomew Stoffel, 1875-1879
Fr. John Delassiaz, 1879-1880 (Vice Prefect)	
Fr. Francis Corbet, C.S.Sp., 1880-1886 (later Vicar Apostolic of Diego-Suarez)	also Religious Superior

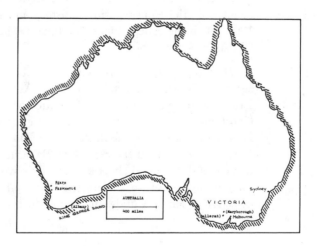

CHAPTER EIGHTEEN

AUSTRALIA

cf. pp. 93 ff.   Earlier in this book we described the Australian venture of Father Libermann's missionaries in the region of Perth and their subsequent departure for Mauritius. No further Spiritan effort

B. G. 9, 166   was directed toward evangelizing the people "down under" until 1872 when the Propaganda and the Bishops of Australia asked the Congregation to establish a college in one of the dioceses and to launch a mission among the aborigines. Lack of personnel, however, made it impossible to accede to this request immediately.

B. G. 14, 166;   Nothing happened until 1888. In that year, the Irish Province
15, 946   founded St. Patrick's College at Ballarat in South West Australia. A competent and numerous staff was sent out and was accorded an enthusiastic reception by the clergy and laity of this town of 60,000. The Archbishop of Melbourne himself went to Ballarat to welcome the Fathers and Brothers, and expressed his pleasure and delight that the famous college of Blackrock was establishing a branch in his country. Before long, the Spiritans had conquered the hearts of both students and parents, and the work seemed so well established that the next year three Spiritans travelled north to Maryborough and took over a parish. Unfortunately, administrative difficulties soon arose. When no acceptable solution could be found, the Motherhouse decided in 1891 to recall the whole group, to the great regret of the local clergy, the students and the people. This

B. G. 23, 185   chapter of the Congregation's history in Australia was closed in 1905, when the college plant was finally sold to the Brothers of the Christian Schools.

Desire for the Future. The General Chapter of 1950 went on record as favoring an establishment in Australia. It asked the Irish Province to investigate the possibilities once again. That the Holy Ghost Fathers are not yet entirely forgotten in this fifth continent is evident from an article in the *Melbourne Tribune* dated April 12, 1956, which recalled their work at Ballarat and the good will they had engendered in so short a time. This would seem to augur well for the success of any effort that the Spiritans may bend in that direction when they judge it feasible to return to Australia.

438

THE GROWTH OF THE CATHOLIC CHURCH IN THE MISSIONS OF THE HOLY GHOST FATHERS

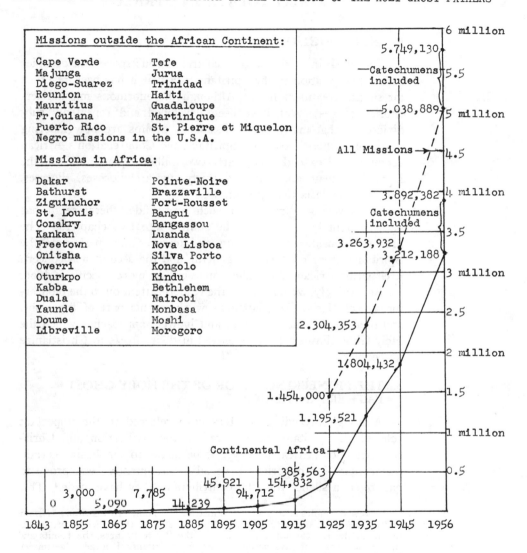

CHAPTER NINETEEN

GENERAL FEATURES OF THE SPIRITAN APOSTOLATE IN AFRICA

1. INTRODUCTION

The work in Africa is of such tremendous scope and occupies such a key position in the Spiritan story that it has been reserved for special treatment here. Although the enormous mission territories of yesteryear have been developed and repeatedly subdivided so that many other missionary groups are now laboring where once there were only Spiritans, the Congregation's African activities still extend over nearly two million square miles of the Dark Continent and embrace thirty-one archdioceses, dioceses, and other ecclesiastical jurisdictions.

In surveying a record of such magnitude, therefore, it has been thought best to divide the subject into two chapters. The first will consider certain items and features that pertain to the Spiritan history of Africa in general, and the second will concern itself with African Holy Ghost missions in more specific fashion.

Accordingly, we now invite the reader's attention to the pioneering aspect of the Congregation's work in this part of the globe, and then to the various direct and indirect approaches which the Holy Ghost Fathers have employed in their efforts to Christianize its peoples.

2. THE PIONEERING LABOR OF THE HOLY GHOST FATHERS IN AFRICA

Although preceding chapters have referred to the important role which Spiritans have played in the civilization and Christianization of Africa, it may not be amiss to emphasize certain points here, for historians have all too frequently been prone to pass over in silence the vital contributions they have made.[1] This

[1] A few examples may suffice to illustrate the point. In his *Short History of the Catholic Church* (St. Louis, 1916), p. 290, Herman Wedewer, speaking about the African missions, mentions the White Fathers, the Jesuits and the Franciscans, but says nothing about the Spiritans. Konrad Algermissen in *Christian Denominations* (St. Louis, 1946), p. 145, speaks about the vicariates in South Africa and the Sudan, but omits to name the Two Guineas and the Zanguebar missions, although these two were the starting

injustice has been righted by more recent non-Spiritan scholars and in particular by Georges Goyau, the famous French Academician who devoted a generous measure of his limitless energy to vindicating the Spiritans' historical role in Africa through the publication of several works about their apostolic endeavors there.[2]

With respect to the Holy Ghost Fathers' position as pioneers in Africa, two elements demand particular emphasis: 1) under Libermann's vivifying impulse they were the first to undertake systematically the conversion of the Negroes and 2) they had no intention whatsoever of limiting their activities to the coast. Goyau fittingly combines both points in the following statement:

C. S. Esp. 152 f.

Before the African Missions of Lyons and the Missionaries of Verona, before the White Fathers of Africa and the Priests of the Sacred Heart of St. Quentin, before the Scheut Fathers, the Jesuits, and the Benedictines, the Spiritans were the first to make an effort toward spiritual penetration through the mysterious depths of the Dark Continent. In the Equatorial West it was Bessieux, Kobès, Le Berre, Carrie, Augouard; in the South-West it was Duparquet; in the South-East, it was Horner; in the Sudan, it was Jalabert (I mention only the dead).

---

points of most missions in Negro Africa. J. de Jong in his *Handboek der Kerkgeschiedenis* (Utrecht-Brussels, 3rd ed., 1937) vol. IV, p. 301, considers Libermann as a man who like Stanley and Livingstone drew attention to the Dark Continent, but lets the actual movement of conversion be inaugurated by Cardinal Lavigerie. The *History of the Catholic Church* by Brother Gustavus, Clayton, Mo., 1915, p. 211, attributes the 1842 resumption of African missionary work to the Lyons Fathers. Reuben Parsons' *Studies in Church History*, New York, 1900, p. 299, has a White Father in charge of the Zanzibar mission. Joseph Lortz in his *History of the Church,* Milwaukee, 1939, p. 546, ignores completely the work of the Spiritans and names only the White Fathers and the Society of the Divine Word as great mission foundations. Carlton J. Hayes in "The Future of Africa," *Mission Digest,* Jan. 1954, p. 10, attributes the success of the Catholic Church in Africa to the White Fathers, the Scheutists, the Divine Word and the Mill Hill Fathers "and latterly many others," omitting entirely the Spiritans who were the pioneers and at that time still more numerous in Africa than any other society.

B. G. 35, 323

As late as 1931 the *Bulletin Général* of the Congregation pointed out the abundant errors in scientific studies about the Church's missionary work and went on to observe ruefully: "After reading the numerous publications about Africa and its evangelization which have appeared this year, we are forced to admit that our part in this great work is unknown."

[2]Georges Goyau, *La Congrégation du Saint Esprit,* Paris, 1937; *Monseigneur Augouard,* Paris, 1926; *La France missionnaire dans les cinq parties du Monde,* Paris, 1948, vol. II, pp. 139-239; and in several articles.

a. The Priority of the Spiritan Apostolate in Africa

This question of Spiritan priority must, of course, be viewed within a framework of proper qualifications. Of these there are three.

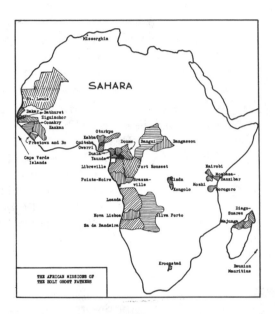

cf. pp. 75. f.

cf. p. 165

da Silva, 299

First of all, we are concerned here with the *revival* of missionary work in modern times. Anyone even superficially acquainted with Africa's religious history knows of the heroic efforts which the Jesuits, the Capuchins, and other religious orders made toward this end in former ages. But as Libermann regretfully pointed out in his famous memorandum, the work of these zealous apostles in Angola, Guinea, and elsewhere had come to nought by the nineteenth century. The old sixteenth-century Diocese of Angola still existed, but even its episcopal see had been vacant since 1826. Moreover, the subsequent resurgence of the Church there did not originate with the clergy of the diocese; it was sparked by the Holy Ghost Fathers who roamed far and wide through this ill-defined Portuguese colony.

Second, the Spiritans regard themselves as pioneers only in respect to the evangelization of Africa's *Negro* population. Before the advent of Libermann's priests in 1842, Africa above the

Sahara, i.e. Algeria, Morocco, Tunis, and Egypt, had four vicariates and one diocese. Then too, the Vicariate of the Cape of Good Hope had been staffed since 1837 by Irish secular clergy, although it must be noted that the few priests there[3] limited their attention to caring for the scattered white settlers. Before 1850 the Negro population of South Africa was accorded scarcely any attention at all.

Goyau, II, 132

Finally, one must eliminate the earlier Vincentian effort among the Copts of Abyssinia, because the dangerous mission of five priests in this country had aimed at reconciling *schismatic* Christians with the Catholic Church and was not specifically pointed toward the conversion of pagans.

The Holy Ghost Fathers' claim to priority, then, refers to modern and systematic missionary activity in Negro Africa. This Africa involves a geographical area inhabited by one hundred seventy million Negroes (about eighty-five per cent of the continent's population) and covers nearly all of the territory south of the Sahara.

Basis of the Claim. It is sometimes mistakenly assumed that the Spiritan claim to priority is based on the old Prefecture of Senegal, where the first Holy Ghost Fathers arrived in 1779, and where they re-assumed responsibility in 1816 after the French

cf. p. 508 ff.

Revolution. As we shall see, however, the work of the few priests in this Prefecture was limited for the most part to the French settlements of St. Louis and Gorée and precious little of it was

cf. pp. 80 ff.

devoted to evangelizing the native population. Rather, as the reader will have gathered from Chapter V, it is the mid-nineteenth century role played by Father Libermann and his priests in the Vicariate of the Two Guineas which entitles the Congregation to claim credit for pioneering in the revival of the African missions. Except for the two Irish-Americans, Bishop Barron and Father Kelly, who soon withdrew in despair, all the priests of the first expedition were members of Libermann's society and, after the departure of the Americans, Libermann alone had the courage to continue the perilous mission without the assistance of any priests other than those of his own congregation. The Holy Ghost Fathers have never given up the great work Libermann inaugurated and they

N. D. 5, 142;
6, 544

[3]The 1844 statistics indicate a total of ten priests for Mauritius and the Cape of Good Hope. Seven of this number worked in Mauritius, leaving only three priests in the South African Vicariate.

are not likely to do so until Africa's Church is well-established with a native hierarchy and a native clergy, capable of carrying on without the assistance of foreign priests and religious.

A. P. F. 50, 35 ff.

It may be objected that in 1846 the Propaganda created the Vicariate of Central Africa and therefore Libermann's priests began their immense task just a few years before others came to share in the enterprise. In response to this, one must observe that Spiritan priority is based not only on time but on subsequent development. Anyone who has ever studied the history of the African missions will have been struck by the fact that the Vicariate of Central Africa failed to take root. It is hardly necessary to examine here the numerous factors which doomed the painful sacrifice of so many young lives in this mission to such a failure that the Vicariate showed no significant development prior to the twentieth century.[4] Suffice it to say that no one can justly assign to it a primary role in reviving the African missions.

What about the labors of the Society of African Missions and the White Fathers of Africa—both of which are by their very nature dedicated to the conversion of Africa?[5] As has been pointed out in Chapter VIII, Bishop Brésillac founded his Society of African Missions in 1856 and only three years later the first priests of this new congregation landed in Sierra Leone. When their first attempt failed, this mission returned to the jurisdiction of the Holy Ghost Fathers. It was 1861, eighteen years after the arrival of Libermann's spiritual sons on the West Coast, that the heroic efforts of the Society of African Missions succeeded in establishing a first permanent foothold in Dahomey. By then, the Spiritans had already sent more than a hundred men into the assault on the treacherous Dark Continent.

cf. pp. 193 f.

B. G. 3, 104

As to the White Fathers of Africa, their founder, Cardinal Lavigerie, had not yet entered the senior seminary when Libermann's first expedition set foot in Africa. It was only thirty-five years later, when the Holy Ghost Fathers had already started

L. S. II, 484

---

[4]For the poignant story of the Central African Vicariate see M. B. Storme, *Evangelisatiepogingen in de binnenlanden van Afrika gedurende de XIXe eeuw,* Brussels, 1951, pp. 138 ff.

[5]Although the Holy Ghost Fathers use a large part of their available manpower for the spiritual conquest of Africa, their purpose is not connected with Africa as a matter of principle. As Libermann expressed it in one of his letters: "If fifty years hence the Negroes are all well cared for, what will prevent the missionaries from going then to the aid of another part of the Church which at that time will be the most abandoned and despised?"

their inland thrusts from the West above and below the Equator, and from the East through Zanzibar and Bagamoyo, that the first expedition of the White Fathers set out from a Spiritan mission for their daring push into the very heart of Africa.

We have insisted on the primacy of the Spiritan apostolate in Africa not from any vain motive of self-glorification, and still less to belittle the giant contributions of others, but simply to set the historical record straight. Missiological literature, especially of the cursory and popular sort, has all too often evinced a regrettable unawareness of the facts.

b. THE SPIRITAN DRIVE TOWARDS THE INTERIOR

While it may be less imperative to insist on the priority of the Holy Ghost Fathers' work in Africa than used to be the case before Georges Goyau made himself their historian, their chronicle must still be cleared of another misconception, *viz.*, that they had no desire to penetrate the interior but preferred to cling to the coastal regions. At first glance, their mission territories may seem to confirm this impression: all of them, except two twentieth-century missions in the Belgian Congo and South Africa, are connected with the coast.

Nevertheless, this first impression is far from accurate. Once again, a non-Spiritan, Dr. Storme, has presented the facts objectively in a monumental study entitled: EVANGELIZATION EFFORTS IN THE INTERIOR OF AFRICA DURING THE NINETEENTH CENTURY.[6] In the following pages we will consider the Spiritan drive to the interior and the successes or failures which it encountered on the way. At least four starting points for such drives may be distinguished: from Senegal and Upper Guinea to West Sudan, from Zanzibar to East Equatorial Africa, from Landana on the west coast below the equator to West Equatorial Africa, and from Walvis Bay in South West Africa to Bechuanaland. This last we have already discussed in Chapters VIII and X and shall not refer to it here again.

cf. pp. 194 f. ;
276 f.

The Drive from Senegal to West Sudan. The correspondence between Libermann and his first missionaries in the Two Guineas shows how all of them without exception were obsessed with the idea of plunging into the interior of Africa. The idea comes back

---

[6]M. B. Storme, *Evangelisatiepogingen in de binnenlanden van Afrika gedurende de XIXe eeuw,* Brussels, 1951.

again and again in their letters. The following are a few examples culled from such sources:

N. D. 4, 65   Once the missionaries are acclimatized, the Bishop will send them into the interior of these lands, according to the Good Lord's inspiration, as soon as he has acquired some experience of the country (Libermann, 1843).

N. D. 4, 489   The Superiors of the missions can give the missionaries permission to go into the interior to preach the word of God to the natives, on condition that they shall notify the colonial administrators . . . (Libermann's 1843 contract with the government regarding the establishment of missions).

N. D. 5, 261   If God wills, we should like very much therefore to go into the interior where, it seems, the people are more simple and easier to manage because of their isolation from foreign corruption (Fr. de Regnier, 1843).

N. D. 5, 270   If Jesus and Mary will, we shall try slowly to penetrate into the interior (Fr. Bouchet, 1844).

N. D. 5, 295   Father, speak about Gabon with the Jesuits and the Vincentians. . . . They could go to the South and the North. And we, we would follow the river and proceed to the interior (Fr. Bessieux, 1845).

N. D. 5, 311
cf. A. P. F. 19,
105   See how the Good Lord has already opened a gate to advance towards the numerous tribes which through other tribesmen have commercial relations with peoples deep in the interior (Fr. Bessieux, 1845).

N. D. 7, 166   Slowly this community will acquire experience with the country; they will try to penetrate into the interior of the territory, find suitable sites there after awhile, and establish themselves in the area. (Fr. Libermann, 1845).

N. D. 9, 215
cf. N. D.
Compl. 88   We will begin by establishing ourselves solidly on the coasts. From there we will learn the country well, and once we are well-informed about the land, we will penetrate into the lands of the interior, where the most good is to be done (Fr. Libermann, 1847).

N. D. 11, 138   The Prefect of Senegal [Fr. Vidal] has manifested his desire to establish missions in the interior of the country at a distance of from a hundred and fifty to two hundred leagues [450 to 600 miles] from the coast, and our bishops of Guinea have the same view. (1849 report to the Propagation of the Faith.)

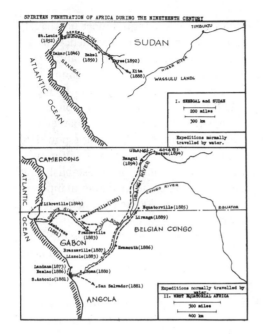

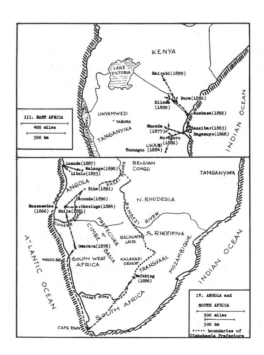

These are but a few examples chosen from an almost inexhaustible supply of comparable statements in the correspondence of the early missionaries. They were not merely pious phrases and vague plans for a distant future. With feverish impatience Bishops Bessieux and Kobès worked and travelled with their priests trying to find ways and means of going inland. As Dr. Storme points out, Libermann had to convince them that "the time was not yet ripe and that an effort to open the closed continent by a single powerful but unplanned stroke could endanger the very survival of the mission. For the future, the most important point was to establish first of all a firm bridgehead rather than waste the available manpower in a multiplicity of initiatives that were doomed to failure. . . . Not even a solid phalanx of missionaries would have been able to conquer Africa for Christianity and civilization in a single all-out assault, for as yet there was no base of operations and it would have been irresponsible to risk the lives of many missionaries and of the mission itself by such impetuousity."

Storme, 109

Experience proved that Libermann was wise in counselling restraint. Partial attempts at penetration constantly had to be given up as costly failures. By way of illustration, we will relate here a particularly daring effort—that of Father Arlabosse in 1850. After several exploratory trips in which he "pushed inland to a distance of a hundred and sixty leagues from the coast as the crow flies" (about four hundred miles up the Senegal River) this intrepid Spiritan opened a mission at Bakel so that he might be "in communication with the tribes of Boundou, Bambou, Carta, Bambara, Timbuktu, etc." When Libermann informed the Propagation, it showed its "dissatisfaction" with such daring initiative, but it was too late to halt proceedings, for the mission had already been started.

Br. 326
Storme, 112 f.
N. D. 12, 161

N. D. 12, 163

N. D. 12, 464

Soon the six Spiritan priests and Brothers there found themselves holding out against terrific odds. The impossibility of maintaining adequate supply lines to the coast, the necessity of constant sentry duty to protect life and property against hostile tribesmen, and the heavy labor of constructing a permanent mission compound soon began to exact their toll. Within a year after his arrival, Father Arlabosse had to be carried to his grave. Three years later, a flood wrought havoc with the buildings and the mission had to be closed as a failure. It never did succeed in establishing contact with the Sudan.

After this and similar experiences, these daring missionaries realized with sadness that their dream of pushing forward toward Timbuktu—the magic center of attraction for most of the early efforts at penetration—was not yet ripe for realization. They had to limit themselves to the only thing that was possible at the time: the preparation of a gradual and progressive thrust toward the interior. It was a wise decision, for when Cardinal Lavigerie's White Fathers began their drive inland to Timbuktu in 1876, their caravan had gone only a short distance before all its members were cruelly murdered. The same fate befell another expedition a few years later when it tried to reach the interior by a different route.

By then, however, the long-expected moment for a spiritual penetration had arrived. French troops had gone into the region to put an end to the degrading slave-trade and to pacify the country generally. In the wake of these forces, the first contingent of four Spiritan Fathers and two Brothers finally was able in 1888 to undertake a safari to "that mysterious Sudan which for such a long time has been the object of our longings and desires." After two months of travel, the intrepid pioneers arrived at Kita, a distance of about eight hundred miles from the coast. After a friendly reception by the native population, the missionaries set to work constructing schools, workshops, dormitories and other installations of the typical Spiritan mission center. Although death struck fearful blows—three Fathers died within three years in a single residence—and a variety of perils still surrounded them,[7] the mission steadily developed and the priests began to turn their attention another step further to the Wassulu lands beyond the Niger and to Nioro in the North. Meanwhile they started new missions at Kayes and Dinguira (1892) and made definite plans for pushing on to Timbuktu in the wake of the French forces.

However, the Spiritan drive in this direction was soon stopped short. In 1895, when this famous desert capital had fallen, Cardinal Lavigerie claimed the area as part of his jurisdiction and with the consent of the Propaganda added it to his Delegation of the Sahara and the Sudan.[8]

M. C. 8, 220 f.

M. C. 14, 25 ff.; 41 f.

B. G. 15, 109 f.; 426 ff.; cf. 14, 229

B. G. 15, 427 M. C. 21, 551 ff.

B. G. 16, 299

B. G. 17, 289 ff.; 306 ff. Br. 512

B. G. 21, 137 ff.; 428 ff.

---

[7]One day the Fathers chuckled when they read in a French newspaper that their whole mission had been wiped out and its occupants barbarously murdered.

[8]Six years later, in an amicable exchange of territory, the Holy Ghost Fathers surrendered their three missions in the Sudan to the White Fathers and in return received the Issi lands in Guinea.

It is strange to read in Glenn D. Kittler's new book *The White Fathers,*

cf. pp. 196 ff.
R. H. M. 13,
44 ff.
Storme, 381

Penetration Attempts from the East. As Chapter VIII recorded, in 1860 Bishop Maupoint of Reunion had sent Father Fava to Zanzibar to start a Catholic mission there. Fava's plan was to use this first center as the starting point from which "one day we will go to raise an altar for Christ in the heart of Africa." Two years later, the Holy Ghost Fathers went to work in the Zanguebar Prefecture which stretched along two thousand miles of coast-line from Cape Guardafui near Arabia to the Zambezi

M. C. 1, 65 ff.

River in the south, without limits to the interior. Father Horner, the Superior and the great pioneer of this mission, eagerly took

B. G. 11, 741
M. C. 2, 385 f.

over his predecessor's plans for penetration. He decided to follow the traditional Spiritan method of first founding a few central missions to educate children in the Christian way of life and then use these youngsters to establish advanced Christian villages farther inland.

M. C. 2, 3 ff.;
3, 98 f.; 277,
299 ff.; 307 f.

After the Zanzibar foundation, the first of these central missions was founded at Bagamoyo (1868). Despite famine, tornadoes, epidemics and opposition, Bagamoyo quickly developed and brought considerable fame to the humble missionaries. Nevertheless, they quickly realized that coastal missions offered little hope for the future. As they recorded in the minutes of their Chapter of 1870:

Engel, 14

"Zanzibar and Bagamoyo have importance only as preparatory works or procures to facilitate the foundation of other stations. Taken in themselves neither of these two missions has any future."

A. P. F. 44,
418

As early as 1869, therefore, Father Horner was already making plans to draw Unyamwezi into the sphere of his influence, even

---

New York, 1957, p. 216, that when Cardinal Lavigerie's priests arrived in St. Louis, Senegal, in 1894, the Holy Ghost Fathers had limited their Sudan ministry mostly to "Catholic Frenchmen" and that "no schools had been built, no hospitals, no orphanages, nothing had been done about slavery."

cf. B. G. *loc. cit.*
M. C. 37, 227

The periodic reports of the Spiritan missions in the Sudan at Kayes, Donguira and Kita constantly speak about their ransoming of slaves, their schools, their orphanage, and the agricultural education of the children.

B. G. 21, 429

When the Spiritans surrendered these missions to Bishop Bazin of the White Fathers in 1901, the prelate was very much impressed by the flourishing condition of the three stations the Congregation passed on to him. The last

B. G. 21, 381

Spiritan report of the Sudan missions (1901) noted "that for the past four or five years they were self-sufficient, the buildings were finished, the installations almost completed, and the government grants joined to the fruit of their agricultural and other works allowed them to live without any out-

A. M. C. A. pp. 138,
209 f.

side support." The most recently published record of this area (now the Prefecture of Kayes) reveals that, after the Spiritans left, no new missions were established in this territory until half a century later (1950), despite the fact that nearly four hundred thousand non-Moslem Africans still remain to be evangelized there. In view of these facts, one cannot escape the feeling that Kittler has taken unpardonable liberties with history.

Two Spiritan pioneers of the Two Guineas: Bishop John Remigius Bessieux (left) and Bishop Aloysius Kobès (right).

Three Spiritan pioneers of the Zanguebar Mission (East Africa): Father Anthony Horner (center), Father Etienne Baur (left), Father Charles Gommenginger (right).

though it took three months of trekking to get to it. The ambitious nature of his plan appears from the statement of an Arabian African explorer which Father Horner loved to repeat: "If your Zanguebar mission can maintain its present flourishing condition, your successors will go straight through Africa to join hands with their confreres in the Congo."

M. C. 3, 308

B. G. 8, 771 ff.
M. C. 4, 414 ff.; 5, 584 ff.; 596 ff.; 614 f.; 622 ff.; 6, 5 ff.; 20 f.; 33 f.; 44 f.
B. G. 8, 751 f.
A. P. F. 44, 418

Before undertaking a mission so far removed from their center, the Spiritans decided early in 1870 to start one in the Ukami region at a distance of from seven to eleven days' travel from Bagamoyo. However, when they returned from their exploratory trip to make final preparations for the new post, these French Fathers heard to their dismay how the disastrous Franco-Prussian War had ravaged their country. It meant that they could no longer count on financial support from home. Instead of being able to penetrate further, they now had to reduce their existing works and devote all their energies to maintaining the most important of their establishments.

B. G. 11, 125 ff.; 730 ff.
M. C. 9, 604; 10, 177 ff.; 189 ff.; 201 f.; 242 ff.
M. C. 10, 161

It was not until 1877 that a mission farther inland could be founded at Mhonda, a distance of about eight days' march from Bagamoyo. Lack of resources prevented Father Horner from going farther into the continent. In deep sadness he wrote: "If the Catholic missionaries are not going into the interior, to Uganda, Unyamwezi, and other places, to found new missions there, it is because they do not have the funds. It would take hundreds of thousands of francs, and they have barely enough to keep alive and maintain their modest establishments." While the Protestant Churches spent enormous sums in their efforts to penetrate Africa's interior, lack of money reduced the Catholic missions to mere planning.

Storme, 414, ff.

The Spiritans, however, were not the only ones who made ambitious plans for reaching the heart of Africa. In the Vicariate of Central Africa (Khartum), Bishop Comboni had been doing exactly the same as the Holy Ghost Fathers—biding his time until it was opportune to plunge into the inner depths of the continent. It was a dream to which he had dedicated his whole life, and by 1877 the long-awaited moment was at hand. In the same year, Father Planque, Superior General of the Society of African Missions, formulated similar plans and asked the Propaganda to entrust Equatorial Africa to his Congregation. Finally, there was the influential Cardinal Lavigerie who composed a

Ibid. 420 ff.

Ibid. 436 ff.

secret memorandum, also in 1877, asking the Propaganda to create four new vacariates in the interior and restrict all coastal missions to a maximum of five hundred kilometers (about 300 miles) in depth.   These vicariates, he pleaded, should be placed under

Lav. II, 11

the central authority of a competent person.   Although he did not mention names, his biographer Baunard observes that he would not have been loath to accept the position for himself.

As a result of the Cardinal's prestige, the Propaganda authorized him in 1878 to undertake the evangelization of Africa's

Storme, 463 ff.

inner regions around Nyanza and Tanganyika Lakes. This decision dashed the hopes of the Society of African Missions and it crushed the life-long ambition of Bishop Comboni.[9]   As for the Holy Ghost Fathers, they were suddenly cut off from the interior

M. C. 10, 337 ff.

just as they had been in West Sudan.   Although Father Horner and his confreres welcomed the White Fathers in Bagamoyo and

B. G. 11, 712 f.

aided them in preparing their caravans for the trek to the interior, their joy was mingled with sadness for, as Father Horner ex-

M. C. 10, 305

pressed it, "the evangelization of the interior had always been the dream of his life."

cf. pp. 269 ff.

The Push to Equatorial Africa from the West.   Chapter X described the early efforts of the Holy Ghost Fathers in the territory which later became the Belgian Congo.   To avoid repetition we shall not enter into this matter again beyond a brief

M. C. 18, 10 ff. ; 17 ff. ; 28 ff. ; 56 f. ; 69 ff. ; 80 ff. ; 103 ff.

indication of penetration plans and results.   By 1885 they had reached the Equator at the spot now occupied by Coquilhatville, about seven hundred miles up the Congo River.   Their intentions were even more daring for, at the foundation of Boma (1880) they had said that this would be "the gateway to the

Augouard I, 180

interior of Africa" and added: "we will stop only when we meet our confreres of Zanguebar on the Nyanza and Tanganyika

Ibid. I, 202

Lakes, [although] undoubtedly many years will pass before that happy day will come."

cf. pp. 222 ff.

We have already noted in Chapter IX how Cardinal Lavigerie tried to reserve the interior of the French Congo for his own control in 1885 and how the Holy See finally settled the issue in favor of the Spiritans by creating the Vicariate of the French Congo.   This decision gave the Holy Ghost Fathers a vicariate stretching from the West Coast of Africa to the borders of the

---

Storme, 496 ff.   [9]He died three years later in Khartum, shortly before the Madhi revolt in the Sudan annihilated his mission.

B. G. 15, 761
ff.

Br. 538 ff.

Beslier, 132
ff.

M. C. 27, 449
ff.; 514 ff.; 28,
392, ff.

B. G. 12, 632
ff.; 13, 822 ff.
M. C. 16, 130
ff.; 143 f.; 152
ff.; 165 f.; 178
ff.

Anglo-Egyptian Sudan. Three years later, Father Augouard became Vicar Apostolic of the inner part of the immense territory. His domain stretched along the Congo for about 1300 miles and was soon extended northward to the borders of Libya. Starting from Brazzaville, to which the former Spiritan station of Kuamouth had been transferred in 1887, Augouard set out to build a network of stations along the rivers. With boundless energy and speed—his native nickname was *Diata-Diata* (Quick-Quick)—he went to work. To facilitate travel, he bought a whaling boat in Europe, had it cut into pieces of about seventy pounds each, and transported it on the heads of carriers to Brazzaville. He and his confreres then laboriously reassembled the vessel and christened it the *Leo XIII* in honor of the then reigning Pontiff.[10] Rushing up and down the rivers with a floating but ever-changing community, the already legendary Bishop founded *inter alia* the missions of Liranga, Franceville, Bangui and Bessu, which were 750, 1000, 1100, and 1300 miles from Brazzaville respectively, and some were in openly cannibalistic territory.

Meanwhile, other Spiritans in Gabon went up the Ogowe River and founded a mission at Lambarene (1881). After travelling by water for forty-three days, and making an exploratory trip to the Alima River, they partially retraced their steps and established another mission at Lastourville. These explorations were made possible because passages to the interior had just been discovered by de Brazza and other famous explorers who were often accompanied in their travels by Holy Ghost Fathers.

All this sufficiently shows that the Spiritans had no intention whatsoever of limiting themselves to coastal areas. If it had not been for the fact that Cardinal Lavigerie's vicariates restricted them to the coast in East Africa, they would most likely have realized their dream of joining hands with their confreres who were penetrating from the West.

*   *   *

The following two sections of this chapter will be dedicated to a study of the means employed by the Holy Ghost Fathers in their

---

[10]In 1896 the vessel was replaced by a larger steam boat. It too was brought to Brazzaville on the heads of a caravan of six hundred carriers. Finally, in 1908, a third steamer, the *Pius X* replaced the second *Leo XIII*.

apostolic assault on Africa. While these sections bear an intimate relationship to Father Libermann's missionary doctrine as expounded in Chapter VII, it may not be amiss to point out here that Libermann imposed no rigidly determined "system" on his priests. Any idea of a fixed pattern would have been totally foreign to his method of doing things, for he considered "the system" as positively dangerous when one is dealing with concrete human situations. In 1847, he sent the following urgent plea to Father Arragon in Dakar:

cf. pp. 162 ff.

N. D. 9, 43 f.

> I am asking you only one thing and I must insist on the point: do not form any determined and fixed plans. The time has not yet come to formulate an absolute and determined method. I do not mean that we should not have a general plan, for obviously, as we are all agreed, we need one, but it would be dangerous to commit oneself irrevocably to that plan and to its details. It is good and important to have some practical ideas on those details, but we must be flexible enough to modify and change, if necessary, the way of implementing the plan and its elements. Experience will be our teacher.

Engel, 286

This openness to experience as advocated by Father Libermann is the main reason why the apostolate of the Congregation shows a "very pronounced trend of development . . ., an elaboration of firm directives after many years of experience, often after great and heroic personal and material sacrifices, diligent study and numerous bitter disappointments."

3. INDIRECT MEANS OF APOSTOLATE

As we saw in Chapter VII, Father Libermann put great stress on civilization as a preparation for the establishment of native Churches in Africa. To raise people from a state of crude savagery to a supernatural Christian life it was necessary first to teach them how to be human, for the life of grace is built on the substructure of man's natural abilities and achievements. The Spiritan Bishop Carrie expressed it thus: "We will first of all make human beings of these poor savages and only then Christians."

B. G. 14, 484

For this reason the missionaries of the Congregation have always paid great attention to everything that would be conducive to the civilization of Africa and thus indirectly serve the supreme purpose of their labors. In subsequent pages we will briefly consider these indirect means by which they laid the natural foundation for a truly African Church:

a. Economic activity;
b. Educational endeavors;
c. Charitable enterprises;
d. Scientific work;
e. Catholic press and youth organizations.[11]

a. Economic Activity

Engel, 116 ff.
K. K. A. 88 ff.

Emphasis. Dr. Joseph Schmidlin, the well-known professor of missiology and mission history, does not hesitate to say that the magnitude and steady development of the economic side of their apostolate has always been one of "the most striking characteristics of the Holy Ghost Fathers." The reason for this phenomenon must be sought in the fact that Father Libermann himself had placed so much emphasis on it, as has been sufficiently pointed out when we considered his missionary theory. The early Constitutions of the Congregation put great stress on the point:

cf. pp. 172 ff.

1878 ed.,
Constitution
96, X

> Although the missionaries' special purpose is the salvation of souls, they must take great care to do their share in promoting a well-planned civilization and the temporal interests of the peoples whose conversion is entrusted to them, by inspiring them with an esteem and love for work and by teaching them, with the aid of the Brothers, planned agriculture and the most useful arts and crafts.[12]

The Spiritan emphasis on economic development is motivated mainly by two principles: the value of work as a factor in moral training and the material and financial advantages flowing from it.

Regarding the first, we may quote just one from the innumerable observations missionaries have made in this respect:

B. G. 26, 822
cf. A.P.F. 38,
33 f.

> For us, material work is a very effective means to provide moral training for the children entrusted to us, to educate them, to form them in a Christian and Catholic way of life,

---

[11]The preparation of this and the following sections of this chapter has been greatly simplified by the outstanding study of Dr. Alois Engel, C.S.Sp., *Die Missionsmethode der Missionare v. heiligen Geist auf dem afrikanischen Festland,* Knechtsteden, 1932, pp. XII and 296.

[12]In later editions of the Constitutions much material has been omitted and incorporated in the *Spiritual Directory* and the *Missionary Directory.*

to inspire them, if not with a sincere and unselfish love of work—in his present condition the Negro is hardly capable of that—at least with a realization that it is necessary to work and to exert oneself in order to gain an honest living and to shakc off the habit of parasitism which is so widespread in the tropics and which engenders nothing but injustice, idleness and corruption.

The second principle (that of material and financial advantages) is graphically illustrated in a report from the Lambarene mission in Gabon:

B. G. 25, 416

Everyone here works as hard as possible, but we have to gain our daily bread . . . for our problem is how to feed, dress, maintain and care for, all through the three hundred sixty-five days of the year, fourteen Europeans and two hundred children and apprentices; how to feed, house, support and modestly pay our thirty-two catechists on the allocation of 6,700 francs which we annually receive from the Propagation of the Faith and the Holy Childhood.

B. G. 2, 490; 3, 130; 21, 510; 26, 84

On occasion also, there were additional reasons stemming from a desire to induce nomadic tribes to settle down, to alleviate economic distress, and to prevent neo-Christians from losing their Faith under Mohammedan masters.

Plantations and Agriculture. The development of the agricultural resources of the land has always been a typical aspect of Spiritan residences in Africa. Obviously so, for this approach most graphically illustrates the age-old Christian principle of life: *Pray and Work.* As Dr. Engel expresses it:

Engel, 127

Nearly everywhere we find the same picture: a mission begins on a small scale, its means are modest, but the missionaries' delight in work and their confidence in God are great indeed. In an astonishing way the station grows up: gardens with new vegetables and fruit trees never seen before by a tropical sky, long lines of orchards with well-kept fruit-laden trees, extensive and alluring plantations of cotton, coffee, and coconuts lie as a flowering crown around a mission which, to the surprise of the natives, has now grown into a small village with a church, schools, workshops, a hospital and similar institutions.

It would be tedious to enumerate all the missions which exemplify economic development in this way. We shall restrict ourselves therefore to a few examples: the agricultural settlement of Ngazobil, which in two years' time saw five villages arise on its lands; the tree nurseries and vegetable gardens of Thiès, Libreville's famous coconut and vanilla groves, Mayumba's banana plantations, Landana's cornfields and superb flower gardens, Catoco's golden wheat culture, Huila's flourishing vineyards, Morogoro's famous coffee plantations which for many years supplied the imperial household of Kaiser Wilhelm in Germany, Mandera's cotton fields and rubber forests, Serabu's cola plants and date palms, and Bahi's cattle farms. In most cases, this economic activity developed into sizeable agricultural enterprises. For instance, the wheat culture alone in Catoco gave work to a hundred people. Like the medieval monks who civilized Europe, the Fathers and Brothers drained swamps, cleared forests, built roads, constructed bridges and installed irrigation systems. In many instances they successfully introduced hitherto unknown species. For example, in the arid Sudan at Kayes, Spiritan Brothers managed to grow "most of the European vegetables" and at Kita their orchards abounded in such "unknown fruits" as oranges, mangoes, lemons, cinnamon, and several others.

Special mention must be made here of Father Theophilus Klaine who, during the forty-seven years he spent in Gabon, devoted all his spare time to botanical and agricultural studies. "Without any exaggeration or fear of contradiction, it used to be said that between Libreville and the Niger no one ate a cultivated mango, a choice banana, a juicy pineapple or sapodilla which was not the fruit of his unremitting labor." He also interested Europe in aukoume, a resinous kind of wood that makes an excellent veneer, and subsequently it became a major export item from forest-covered Equatorial Africa.

The vast scale on which these pioneers managed to conduct their agricultural enterprises with such primitive means caused the early African travellers—whether Catholic or not—to gaze in admiration. The mission of Bagamoyo was made world-famous by the praises bestowed on its plantations by Stanley, Baker, Serpa, Pinto, Emin Pascha, Baumann and Bartle Frere. The Sultan of Zanzibar himself told Father Horner, the Superior of the Zanguebar mission: "You are the man who has made Bagamoyo. Formerly

Margin notes:

B. G. 4, 615

B. G. 19, 267;
25, 215

B. G. 13, 781 f.

B. G. 15, 574

B. G. 11, 481

B. G. 24, 445

B. G. 17, 622

B. G. 16, 749

B. G. 20, 657

B. G. 25, 336

B. G. 31, 357

B. G. 30, 903

B. G. 18, 357

B. G. 18, 371

*Le Naturaliste
Canadien,*
1950, p. 330

ibid., 327

B. G. 11, 717

it was a poor unkempt village. Today it is an important city—thanks to the impulse you have given to the development of plantations."[13]

A complete and definitive study of the economic impact of Spiritan agricultural enterprises has yet to be made. It will amply demonstrate how simple missionaries with almost no means at their command can go a long way toward achieving goals for which modern philanthropy and Point Four Programs must spend huge sums of money.

Engel, 128 ff.

Even among the Spiritan pioneers in Africa, it is true, a few dissident voices were raised in protest at first against this emphasis on the economic approach. For instance, Father Bessieux claimed in 1846 that this sort of work might be suitable for Trappist monks but not for missionaries, and that the moralizing influence Libermann attributed to work did not find confirmation in experience. However, by 1856 his own further experience had converted him so thoroughly that Libreville—his residence—became an outstanding example of the economic approach. Meanwhile he had been named Bishop and Vicar Apostolic of the Two Guineas. Despite

Roques, 223 ff.; M. C. 23, 560; A. P. F. 49, 209 f.

his episcopal dignity, he had no misgivings about going out every day with pick-axe and shovel to work side by side with the mission boys in clearing the land and preparing it for plantations. It was an effective reply to the complaint registered by some parents that he was a slave-driver who made their children work but refused to touch a tool himself.

No doubt the reader is wondering what the Holy Ghost Fathers have done with the great wealth that undoubtedly must have resulted from all this civilizing but productive labor. The answer is very simple: not a penny of it has gone to swell their own coffers. All of it and a good deal more has been spent in maintaining in

C. A. 1955/56

Africa a field force that now amounts to about 1,500 Spiritans, 3,000 Sisters, and an army of 40,000 teachers, instructors and catechists, as well as in constructing and supporting 17,000 schools, 400 hospitals and dispensaries, 150 orphanages, innumerable churches and Christian villages, and caring in a multiplicity of ways for the sick, the poor and the outcast.

Technical Schools and Workshops. Trade-schools and workshops to teach the various arts and crafts by which people can

---

[13]In later years Bagamoyo lost most of its importance to the new harbor city of Dar es Salaam.

cf. pp. 174 ff.

raise themselves to a standard of relative well-being have, in line with Father Libermann's recommendations, always featured prominently in the Spiritan apostolate. It is in these schools and shops that the Holy Ghost Brothers have made their most marvelous contribution to the conversion of Africa.

Engel, 122 ff.

As early as 1852, a rather well-equipped technical school began to function in the Senegambia mission. It comprised divisions for woodworking, tailoring, shoemaking and printing. Following this example, most subsequent Spiritan residences in Africa undertook to introduce civilization in similar fashion by means of arts and crafts. Among the most important of these early technical schools

B. G. 12, 418; 26, 820; 24, 146; 16, 367; 14, 580; 27, 395 f.; 3, 461; 11, 717

cf. p. 197

were Ngazobil[13a] (Senegal), Boke (Sierra Leone), Onitsha (Nigeria), Libreville (Gabon), Huila (Angola), Simonsdale (Kenya), Bagamoyo, and Zanzibar. Some of these became quite famous, as for example, the establishment at Onitsha which, under the expert direction of Brother Armand, was flooded with orders from the British government; the one at Zanzibar, where the Brother-Director became the private technical advisor of his Royal Highness the Sultan; the center at Huila which, as early

B. G. 16, 651 ff.

as in 1892, had sections for woodwork, tailoring, brickmaking, tanning, shoemaking, brewing, printing, a sawmill, a water mill, and soon added weaving to its list.

The purpose of all these technical schools and workshops was clearly expressed in 1857 in a report on the new school in Gambia:

B. G. 1, 137

"This work is economically a blessing for the land, a good source of income for the support of the mission, and a powerful factor in the religious regeneration of the people."

In general, the results achieved by these schools fulfilled every

B. G. 24, 146

expectation. For instance, in 1907 Nigeria reported not only that its workshops were famous, but also that they produced the best Christians. This does not mean that everything went always per-

B. G. 30, 654

fectly and without failures. At times too many of the boys loved freedom and idleness and occasionally there were reports of strikes and revolt against the discipline involved in learning a trade, which not even the threat of expulsion could counteract. It would have

---

Africa Christo, 1957, no. 6, pp. 11 f.

[13a] It is interesting to note here that, from 1887 on, the mechanical shops of Ngazobil operated under the direction of Brother Fulgentius Defrance, a former railroad engineer of the Paris-Dieppe line. This ninety-two year old pioneer recently celebrated the seventieth anniversary of his arrival in Africa and recalled the days when the mission shops functioned as a Department of Public Works for the entire colony.

been surprising if such things had not happened. After all, they occur even in places where civilization has held sway for centuries.

In more recent times, the technical schools of many missions have been severely handicapped by the shortage of Brothers. While in some places it has been possible to replace them by trained African craftsmen, others have been forced to abandon this type of training. The latest statistics (1955-56) reveal, however, that there are two hundred and seventeen technical schools still functioning, even though eleven Spiritan dioceses in Africa no longer have a single one.

b. EDUCATIONAL ENDEAVORS

cf. pp. 172 ff.

The importance Father Libermann attached to schools in civilizing and Christianizing Africa need not be stressed here again. Chapter VII has covered his views on the subject. Those ideas found an echo in the 1878 edition of the Constitutions, which

1878 edition,
Constitution
96, VI

went on to urge the missionaries "to pay special attention to the children of chiefs and other leading personalities of the land so that later on their influence might be put to use for the benefit of the people."

Engel, 88 ff.
K. K. A. 164
ff.

These various directives emanating from the supreme authorities in the Congregation did not fall on deaf ears, for a constantly recurrent theme in the reports from the Spiritan missions in Africa was and is: "The schools are a work to which we give top priority."

cf. pp. 498 ff.

Apart from the technical schools which have been considered above and the seminaries for future priests which we will study later, the educational institutions in the African missions of the Holy Ghost Fathers may be classified as bush schools, standard grade schools, secondary schools, and colleges. In addition to these one must note the recent efforts to establish Catholic universities in Africa.

Bush Schools and Grade Schools. Generally speaking, the bush schools limit themselves to teaching the elements of religion, reading, writing and arithmetic, and all these subjects are taught in the native language. Nearly every mission residence has a large number of such one-room schools scattered throughout the more remote areas of its territory. They are visited regularly by the Fathers, but all instruction is given by catechists or lay teachers who generously sacrifice the inducements of more lucrative jobs in more attractive surroundings in order to devote their lives to the interests of the mission. Their salary is meager— barely sufficient to cover their basic needs. Although such schools are quite primitive and never aspire to high scholastic attainment, they are very efficient tools in raising the masses of backward areas to an elementary level of civilization and in spreading Christian influence.

The standard grade schools function in more heavily populated areas. Usually, their program follows the requirements laid down by the civil authorities and normally includes the study of one European language. In many places, notably in the British and Portuguese colonies, these mission schools are supported in whole or in part by the government. They are staffed for the most part by African teachers and supervised by Holy Ghost Fathers. The total number of both bush and standard grade schools in Spiritan missions throughout Africa runs very high: C. A. 1955/56   latest statistics show a total of 15,925, and this number is augmented by 946 others in insular Africa.

Secondary Schools and Colleges. As modern civilization progressed and created a need for Africans capable of staffing governmental, industrial, and commercial offices, secondary schools C. A. 1955/56   and colleges began to multiply quickly. There are now no less than two hundred sixty-seven of them in the Spiritan missions of continental Africa and an additional eighty-seven on adjacent islands. Moreover, large numbers of teacher-training colleges had to be founded so that mission schools might be staffed with competent personnel that was capable of handling the surging flood of African youngsters in quest of knowledge. The Catholic schools of the Spiritan dioceses in Onitsha and Owerri alone absorb more than eight thousand lay teachers. It is not surprising, therefore, to learn that the missions of the Holy Ghost Fathers count a hundred and five such pedagogical institutes in Africa.

The University Level. Recently this educational advance in the Spiritan missions has received additional impetus. After the B. G. 40, 373   Second World War, the Apostolic Delegate of Mombasa and the f.   Bishops of Tanganyika Territory decided that the time had come to make preparations for a Catholic University of East Africa. For this reason, they established a new educational center at

Pugu in the Archdiocese of Dar-es-Salaam and the Irish Province of the Holy Ghost Fathers agreed to staff it. St. Francis Xavier College, as it will be known until it reaches university level, opened its doors in 1950 for one hundred top level students from all over Tanganyika. Then too, across the continent in the Spiritan Archdiocese of Onitsha (Nigeria), similar steps have been taken to create a Catholic University. Because the Holy Ghost Fathers there are already burdened with a dozen colleges, they have asked American Jesuits to staff this new educational venture.

B. G. 44, 220

Religious Value. In terms of religious well-being, many missions owe their flourishing condition to the care they have lavished on their educational programs. In Southern Nigeria, for instance, Bishop Shanahan's development of an extensive school system between 1906 and 1918 "literally changed the face of the earth." The Fathers there realized that "to neglect education in Nigeria would have meant to lose all our Catholic influence and this within a few years." It is largely due to the enlightened educational policy of this bishop and his successors that the Spiritan missions of Onitsha and Owerri now rank among the very best in the world, numbering nearly 700,000 Catholics and 250,000 catechumens out of a total population of about four and a half million.

B. G. 43, 164

B. G. 32, 580

C. A. 1955/56

Generally speaking, Catholic education has developed better in English territories than in the French colonies. The reason for this is not hard to determine. In contrast to the intelligent British colonial policy of normally working hand in hand with the missions and supporting even religious schools so that the country might develop more rapidly, French authorities in the past often evinced open hostility to Catholic education and thereby forced the missions to rely on their own meager resources for the maintenance of their schools. Fortunately, this situation has improved in the last twenty-five years and has changed notably since the beginning of World War II.

Engel, 92 ff.

B. G. 42, 239
ff.; 43, 54

c. CHARITABLE ENTERPRISES

Importance. As could be expected of a Congregation which addresses itself especially to the poor and the abandoned, charitable endeavors have always figured prominently among the means that the Spiritans have used to further the establishment of God's King-

Engel 134 ff.
K. K. A. 109
ff.

School buildings in tropical style at the Spiritan missions of Kindu
(Belgian Congo), Quipeo (Angola), and Dakar (Senegal).

The beautiful church of Ankoro (Belgian Congo), built by Father Elslander in 1922.

D. C. 535   dom on earth. Libermann instructed his priests to be "the protectors, supports and defenders of the weak and the humble against all their oppressors." As a result, "in nearly all missions the Spiritans inaugurated their activity by works of charity. More than any other means, the care of orphans, the poor, the sick and the lepers made them gain the hearts of the Negroes, caused them to win their entire confidence, and thus rendered easier the salvation of the abandoned and enslaved pagan souls which at first often involved distrust and hatred."

Engel, 134 ; cf.
B. G. 16, 294

Care for the Sick. Without hesitation, the priests, the Brothers, and the valiant Sisters who assisted them in their heroic task, devoted themselves to the sick when dangerous epidemics struck. To give but one example: in Senegambia recurrent yellow fever plagues during 1866 killed nine, during 1867 fifteen, and during 1900 nine of the missionaries who ignored personal risk in caring for the dying victims of this dread disease. For the sick bereft of all attention and for helpless slaves who had managed to escape from their cannibalistic owners, the Fathers opened asylums and "freedom villages." Special care was devoted to the miseries of leprosy long before colonial governments awoke to the problem. Even now, most recent statistics show that Spiritan missions on the African continent still care for thirty-three leper colonies.

Engel, 138

C. A. 1955/56

Nearly all of the assistance given the sick is channelled through dispensaries and small hospitals attached to the various mission stations. These provide extensive service. In 1956 alone, more than four million patients had recourse to the four hundred and twenty-one dispensaries and hospitals maintained by the Spiritan missions of Africa. While the figure is certainly impressive, it should not lead one to think that the Holy Ghost Fathers in Africa devote all their time to corporal works of mercy or that they operate large hospitals in the American style. The mere fact that these four hundred and twenty-one dispensaries and hospitals accommodate only 2,380 beds should dispel any such notion. Lack of resources and qualified personnel make it impossible to build and operate hospitals as we know them. Moreover, missionaries enter the medical field only as a means to an end. They strive to alleviate the sufferings of their fellow-men insofar as their abilities permit, but they would be untrue to their calling if they concentrated on practicing the corporal works of mercy to the detriment of their prime objective, viz, the establishment of an African

C. A. 1955/56

C. A. 1955/56

Church, ruled by an African hierarchy and served by African priests. In the absence of competent medical help, the missionary frequently offers his services, but he does so to avail himself of the opportunity to dispense spiritual advice along with bodily care. A recurrent theme, therefore, in the periodic reports from Spiritan missions is that large numbers of the sick under their care have asked for baptism before death or returned subsequently for religious instruction.

Engel, 142

Engel, 156 ff.
1878 ed., Constitution 96, X

Liberation of Slaves. The 1878 edition of the Constitutions impressed on the missionaries their duty "to fight slavery and above all the shameless slave trade . . . to redeem as many as possible of these poor slaves, especially the children, so that they can be educated in a Christian way." During the first decades of their existence, most of the early Spiritan boarding-schools in the missions were filled in great part with former slave children. Since popular indignation against the ignominy of slavery had swept over Europe, the Propaganda was able to allocate large sums of money for the redemption of slaves. The Bagamoyo mission alone bought three hundred and nineteen of them between 1884 and 1888, and another three hundred in 1893 and 1894. Similar programs of redemption obtained in other missions.

B. G. 11, 707
B. G. 17, 656
A. P. F. 35,
125; 130;
39, 24
Engel, 157

Nonetheless, the purchase of these slaves did not always proceed without difficulty. In Senegambia, the local governor accused the Fathers of trafficking in slaves and forced them temporarily to reduce their purchases until the ridiculous complaint could be disposed of. Things were different on the East Coast, where the British authorities looked with favor on the Fathers' activities and frequently assigned to them entire human cargoes of captured slave-trading vessels.

M. C. 22, 378
f.; 391 f.; 400
ff.; 414 ff.
Beslier, 134 f.

It may not be superfluous to point out here that in many parts of Africa slavery was not primarily a source of cheap labor. Rather, it was calculated to provide victims for the ritual of human sacrifice and to supply cannibalistic cooking-pots with the much-prized "talking meat." Tender bodies of children were regarded as an especial delicacy. After their capture, these innocent pawns of barbarism were fattened up and then driven like cattle to a market-place that was always full of buyers. Anyone who could not afford a whole body always had a chance to combine his purchase with that of others. He simply drew a line around the portion he preferred and then waited for the chosen piece until the rest was sold.[14] As late as 1905, Spiritan missionaries in Ubangi reported that such cannibalistic slave-trading was still a common occurrence in their neighborhood.

The incredulous reader who is not acquainted with the depth of barbarism which engulfed Africa until the beginning of the present generation may be inclined to consider cannibalism as a rather exceptional occurrence. The correspondence of the missionaries, however, leaves no doubt about its common acceptance.[15] Nowadays the barbaric custom has largely disappeared, thanks to the stern repressive measures of colonial governments and the moralizing influence of the missions. Throughout their establishments, the Spiritans purchased as many slave children as possible, lodged them in orphanages in the mission compounds, gave them a careful Christian education, and taught them agriculture or a trade. Once such children had grown up, the priests settled them in special "freedom villages" and in the earlier days such villages often constituted the only Christian enclaves in otherwise fully pagan areas. In this way they made their contribution toward eradicating this vicious, demoralizing practice.

Engel, 157

---

[14]To tenderize the tough flesh of adult slaves, cannibals used to break their bones and soak the victims alive in water for several hours.

[15]The following examples may show how deeply engrained the custom was. One day a Congo mission adopted a boy whose father had been killed fighting against the French. The boy told one of the priests: "Him commander big fool. My father big fat chief, but commander make hole in ground and let him rot. Why not feast on all that fine meat?"

Goyau II, 202

Convinced by a missionary that bigamy was illicit, a chief told the priest that he had only one wife now, the best of the two. "Did you send away the other one?" he was asked. "No, I ate her," he replied. Then too, it was common practice to cook prisoners of war and even to dispatch the sick before they would be too emaciated to adorn the table.

In 1877, Father Horner, the founder of Zanguebar mission, wrote about a tribe residing in the interior:

M. C. 10, 40

Recently I met some cannibals in Bagamoyo who, at least in their own country, eat nothing but human flesh. . . . These natives are called *Maniama*, that is, flesh- or man-eaters. . . . I have been unable to ascertain the geographical position of their country.

Shanahan, 90 f.

In Nigeria, Bishop Shanahan reported similar conditions. As late as 1912 he wrote: "Every adult in this country has tasted human flesh, and . . . we live in the midst of cannibals. . . . As we go through the towns . . . we see human bones, and in particular human skulls, piled high in the courtyards before the chairs of state used by the chiefs. So traffic in human flesh still goes on. . . . Today the principal slave trade is with children of school age, and the chief traffickers in human flesh—the Arocukus—have fomented revolts at Okidja, Afikpo, and Owerri."

Ransoming of Slaves and the Purpose of the Missions. At first blush, the redemption of slaves and the religious education of ransomed captives seems to need no defense. Nevertheless, one may legitimately raise the question whether the large-scale efforts made in this direction did not constitute more of a hindrance than a help in establishing the African Catholic Church. The story of the Spiritan missions in Southern Nigeria under Bishop Joseph Shanahan provide at least a partial answer to the question.

The Antislavery Society had collected enormous sums for ransoming and educating slaves, and the Propaganda then allocated these to various missions on the basis of their needs. By way of satisfying the intention of the donors, it specified that this money was to be used for the purpose for which it had been given. Rigorous adherence to the ideas of the well-intentioned contributors, however, meant that the missionaries had to spend most of their time caring for a few thousand former slaves and leaving nearly all the free population unattended. At the same time, by African standards these slaves constituted the dregs of humanity. How could one hope, therefore, to use them in forming the nucleus of a Church which one day would pervade the masses?

To remain faithful to the supreme purpose of missionary work and to solidly establish the Church in Nigeria, Bishop Shanahan maintained, one had to concentrate on the free population and remake them into a Christian people. This method would counteract slavery all the more effectively because it would destroy the evil in its very root. For this reason, he proposed to use the antislavery funds to establish a large-scale system of schools for both free and slave children, for "those who hold the school, hold the country, hold its religion, hold its future." This view was opposed by the Propaganda, not because that august body disagreed with the Bishop, but because its hands were tied by donors of antislavery funds who had specified that the money be used for the ransom and education of slaves. After a long exchange of correspondence, the Propaganda silently tolerated the Bishop's more efficient use of these monies, especially after he declared that he would rather lose the subsidies than revert to the old system.

His own method of approach proved its effectiveness by the splendid results it achieved in a few years' time. If present-day Southern Nigeria is a country in which the Church has been solidly established, which offers great hope for the future, and in which

Shanahan, 89 ff.

Ibid. 94

Human Sacrifice, as it was formerly
practiced in Africa.
(Courtesy *Missions Catholiques*,
vol. 10, p. 475.)

Human Sacrifice to the God of War.
(Courtesy *Missions Catholiques*,
vol. 10, p. 487.)

Father William Jouga, C.S.Sp., 1841-1875, one of the first African priests of the Congregation.
(Courtesy *Missions Catholiques,* vol. 8, p. 162.)

His Excellency Thomas Mongo, First African Bishop of Duala (French Cameroons).

slavery has nearly disappeared, a great part of the credit for this happy state of affairs must be attributed to Bishop Shanahan. At the same time, events in Nigeria show how Europe's over-emotional concern with the wretched practice of slavery seriously threatened the development of the Church in Africa. Father Daigre, C.S.Sp., in his book, *Oubangui-Chari,* indicates that the situation was not confined to Nigeria: "We were quickly forced to realize that it may be humanitarian to ransom slaves, but the idea of building a society upon them and the belief that a country can be Christianized by converting them is wholly absurd."

Daigre, 175

d. Scientific Work

In evaluating the scientific work of the Holy Ghost Fathers in Africa,[16] one should keep in mind the principle by which missionaries are governed when they engage in such activities. It was very clearly stated in 1874 when the Congregation was asked to impress on its missionaries the importance of scientific contributions:

B. G. 9, 859

> Our main purpose, and therefore the one to which we should consecrate all our efforts, consists in the evangelization and the salvation of souls. Compared with this, the rest can only be something accessory and of secondary importance. Nevertheless, we must not remain indifferent to the interests of science nor is there any reason why we should not be occupied with them to a certain extent. . . . Moreover, among these endeavors there are some, such as linguistic studies, which readily fall within the scope of desirable occupations that contribute to the success of the apostolic ministry.

Within the limits of this restriction, many Spiritans have added mightily to our knowledge of the Dark Continent and its inhabitants, particularly in the fields of geography, natural history, ethnology and philology. A detailed examination of this scientific work would lie outside the intent of this book, for it would be of interest only to specialists in the field. We shall limit ourselves therefore to a few of the more significant items.

---

[16]Our consideration here will be strictly limited to scientific work in Africa. Accordingly, we will make no reference e.g. to the excellent studies published by Father Tastevin about Indian ethnology and languages, or the scholarly achievements of Holy Ghost Fathers in Europe and America.

Geography. As could be expected, geographical contributions date from those early days when large sections of Africa were still

B. G. 25, 26

unknown. Most outstanding undoubtedly are the fifty-five maps by which Bishop Augouard and other Spiritans charted large sections of the upper Congo and Ubangi Rivers for the first time. Basing themselves on fifteen years of experience in navigating

Beslier, 159
cf. Daigre,
180 f.

these rivers, and preparing their maps "in accord with the best astronomical and cartographical methods," the Fathers reached results which were so satisfactory that the geographical society of Paris granted them the Fournier Prize and the government did the printing at its own expense. Other Holy Ghost Fathers designed charts of the Stanley Pool area, West Sudan, Angola, the

M. C. 12, 454
ff.; 19, 256; 22,
157
Anthropos, I,
p. 5

interior of Ubangi and part of Zanguebar. Often, however, their geographical work consisted in the correction of maps published by hasty explorers who had not fully understood their guides. As Archbishop Le Roy pointed out: "The geographical maps of new lands so reverently received by learned societies from the hands of explorers literally crawl with errors. Generally, out of ten names there are not more than two that are correct. I could refer here to a certain map where one can see indicated as geographical names words whose literal translation is: "That is a mountain," or "Quit bothering me," or, "I don't know."

Natural History. In the course of their apostolic wanderings throughout Africa, many Spiritans showed great interest in the flora and fauna of this freshly-discovered continent. Thus Father Klaine became a botanist who not only successfully introduced many new plants into Africa, but also enriched musuems of natural

Le Naturaliste
Canadien, 1950,
pp. 96 ff.; 318
ff. B. M. 17,
820; 18, 38 f.;
280; 19, 331;
B. G. 45, 56

history with thousands of new specimens. Others, such as Fathers Sacleux, Tisserant, and Sébire, published scholarly studies of African botany. Brother Francis Ruher became a specialist in African bees with several books and articles on the subject to his credit. In grateful acknowledgment of such contributions, European taxonomists named more than two hundred genera and species after Fathers Sacleux and Klaine each, and still more after the Spiritans Duparquet, Antunes, Tisserant, Trilles, Le Roy, Raimbault and others.

Ethnology. Even more than in rivers, plants, and animals, the missionaries were interested in the primitive peoples around them. As a result, several Holy Ghost Fathers became outstanding ex-

Archbishop Prosper Augouard, of Equatorial
Africa, known as the "Cannibal Bishop."

Bishop Joseph Shanahan, the Apostle of
Southern Nigeria.

Father Charles Sacleux, one of the Spiritans' foremost African linguists.

Father Constant Tastevin, C.S.Sp., in academic gown as Professor of Ethnology at the Catholic University of Paris.

perts in ethnology and anthropology. Best known of these was Archbishop Le Roy, who became the first occupant of the newly-created chair of the History of Religions at the Catholic University of Paris and acquired a scientific reputation as well as popular renown by the publication of his studies on the pygmies and the religion of the primitives.[17] His eminence in this domain was well demonstrated by the fact that in 1906 he was invited to write the opening article of the new *International Review of Ethnology and Linguistics: Anthropos.* This he did very appropriately by means of a study entitled: "The Scientific Role of Missionaries" (*Anthropos,* vol. I, pp. 3-10). Other outstanding Spiritan ethnologists are Henry Trilles, Charles Estermann, Anthony Horner, Charles Duparquet, Albert Sébire, Joachim Correia, Maurice Briault, Charles Sacleux, Constant Tastevin and Charles Tisserant. Several of these, after returning from Africa, became Professors in their specialized subjects at various universities. Scores of others published their findings in *Anthropos* and other learned journals. In addition, they have written literally hundreds of popular-type articles on ethnological questions in magazines and journals destined for the general public.[18]

Engel, 46 ff.
L. H. 125 ff.
K. K. A. 201 ff.

Linguistics. Nothing reveals the soul of a people so much as the tongue it speaks, and nothing is more conducive to intimate contact with a people than a thorough knowledge of its language. It will hardly surprise anyone, then, that the most outstanding scientific contributions of Spiritan missionaries in Africa lie in the realm of linguistics. If any of these apostles had doubted the usefulness of such studies, he was urged on by the pressing invitations and even the strict orders of his superiors to learn thoroughly the languages of his district. Father Schwindenhammer, for instance, in indicating the purpose of an African residence always used the formula: "the conversion of the pagans and therefore the study of native languages." His successor in the generalate, Father Emonet, called this study "the first duty" of a missionary and warned that "anyone who neglects the study of languages fails in an essential point of his duty." The Vicars Apostolic of the different missions emphasized the same point and some even went so far as to make it

C. S. 3, 19; 21; 37 ff.
C. E. 3, 37 f.

Engel, 47

B. M. 18, 101; 1165

[17]*The Pygmies* appeared in French and Italian; *The Religion of the Primitives* in French (five editions), German, English, and Polish.

[18]Vol. 19 of the *Bibliotheca Missionum* uses one hundred and eighty-five pages just to list the titles of all publications of Holy Ghost Fathers about Africa between the years 1910 and 1940.

a rule that any new arrival who had not made sufficient progress after two years in learning the local language should be dismissed from the mission.

Although the missionaries generally did not fail in this respect, B. G. 32, 424 there are some isolated cases of what appears to be gross neglect in the fulfillment of linguistic duties. In 1925, for instance, the Propaganda had to remonstrate with a Spiritan Vicar Apostolic because his missionaries failed to learn the local language.

While the modern apostle usually has at his disposal grammars, dictionaries, literature, and the accumulated experience of a hundred years of his predecessors to aid him in his linguistic efforts, the same was not true for the early pioneers. Their studies were often hampered by most discouraging difficulties. To begin with, they had to face a bewildering multitude of dialectal variations in village after village. Then after eight or ten miles of travel, the language would vanish completely and be replaced by another of an apparently different kind. Interpreters were frequently unavailable or unreliable. Hardly any of the languages had ever been committed to writing, and they appeared very difficult to understand and still more formidable to speak. The only possible start seemed to lie in listening carefully and trying to catch a word here or there. How frustrating this method could be appears from an 1845 letter of Father Bessieux regarding the Pongue tongue:

N. D. 5, 297
> The language is simple and easy, but I am still far from mastering it. From the very beginning I did not have an interpreter. The first months I did nothing but try to study the language. Since none of the several persons with whom I conversed about Pongue understood French, I made up a list of words but they did not correspond with the French terms I put alongside them. Although I managed to get a large number of nouns, I could never catch a verb.

When, after many months of hard work, the Fathers finally came to know a language, they were invariably dismayed by its primitiveness. Though suitable for the simple needs of everyday life in the jungle, it wholly lacked the vocabulary that was necessary to express the more abstract concepts of Christian Faith and civilized thought. Thus the linguistic task of the missionary became more than a simple study of an existing language. He had to work toward the unification of dialects into a single language, the promotion of more universal languages (such as Swahili in the East and Lingala in the West), and above all at the enrichment of these languages by strengthening them with new words to express ideas hitherto unknown to their users.

If one considers the fact that the translation of such a simple prayer as the Our Father into the rich and cultured language of Java took ten years, he must shudder at the thought of the enormity of the task faced by the early priests in primitive Africa. One need not be surprised, therefore, if some of the solutions they worked out for linguistic difficulties are not acceptable and may still require further elaboration after more advanced study. It must be remembered that three of four centuries went by before Europe could build a Christian language and even then the task was brought to perfection only through the work of such geniuses as Tertullian, Jerome and Augustine.

It would lead us much too far afield to enter into a detailed account of the linguistic work of the Holy Ghost Fathers in Africa. The very quantity of their output is amazing. They have written approximately five hundred works in about seventy languages. Among these there are close to two hundred grammars and dictionaries, and a very large number of practical books such as catechisms, Biblical translations, prayer-books and elementary school texts. Some of them are small and badly printed pamphlets; others are monumental studies, as, for example, Father Sacleux's work on Swahili and Father Albino Alves' Bundu dictionary. A few have a very restricted use, like Father Lemblé's work in the click language of the Sandawe tribe, while others have been widely adopted for official use, e.g. Father Miranda Magelhaes' handbook of the native languages in Angola.[19]

The Spiritan linguistic works have one characteristic which distinguishes them from studies published by colonial government agencies: they pay much greater attention to dialectical variations. And for a very good reason. The first and foremost duty of these missionaries is to keep in touch with the people whom they are evangelizing. As a result, they are more concerned than others with differences, peculiarities, and modes of diction which the same

---

[19]The non-specialist usually has no idea at all about the enormous number of languages spoken in Africa. The 1930 Spiritan *Bibliographie* (p. 5) lists sixty volumes in the following languages of the Gabon mission alone: Pongue, Fan, Duma, Galoa, Eshira, Bulu, Kota, Mbete, Ivea, Ndumu and Kombe.

language displays in changing localities. For the same reason too they have written in lowly tongues that others will not even recognize as languages, such as various types of Creole French and Creole Portuguese. After all, their apostolic zeal embraces even those who understand and speak no tongue but these.[20]

e. CATHOLIC PRESS AND YOUTH ORGANIZATIONS

cf. p. 495

Bibliographie, p. 9; B. G. 1, 20; 13, 861; 16, 491; 23, 251

C. A. 1955/56

B. G. 24, 24 f.

cf. p. 513
B. G. 42, 100 f.
E. P. 31, I, 83

Catholic Press. As has already been mentioned, the first mission press began to function in Dakar as early as 1852. Three years later it undertook the publication of its first major works: a grammar and dictionary of the Wolof language. Other missions soon followed suit: for example, Landana in 1884, Loango in 1892, Caconda in 1904, etc. At present sixteen of these mission printing establishments function in Spiritan Africa.

As could be expected, for many years the output of these presses did not include any newspapers. It was limited to books and pamphlets, because the primitive level of culture did not yet create a demand for periodic literature and the mission staff was too small to engage in the editorial work that recurrent publications necessitate. The first Catholic newspaper, the *Echo de Saint Louis,* appeared in Senegal in 1906 when French anticlericalism made it mandatory to find new ways and means of maintaining the Faith. This early paper did not survive, but since then interdiocesan forces have founded the weekly *Afrique Nouvelle* in Dakar. This mission also publishes the monthly *Horizons Africains* and a few parochial church papers. Other missions have followed suit in making the press serve the cause of religion by starting Catholic weeklies and monthlies. They now number sixteen, including those of insular Africa.[21]

L. H. 129

---

[20]Practical reasons forced a Spiritan in French Guiana to write a polyglot catechism in such heterogeneous languages as Tamul, Wolof, Arabic, Annamitic and Bengali (the native languages of South-American Indians, Arabs, Senegalese, Indo Chinese and Pakistani!) As the reader knows, the population of Guiana draws its origins from all parts of the French Empire.

[21]The following papers are listed in the *État du Personnel* of 1956:

Afrique Nouvelle, Dakar, weekly, 8,200 copies
Horizons Africains, Dakar, monthly, 500 copies
The Catholic Monthly, Sierra Leone, monthly, 1,300 copies
L'Effort Camerounais, Duala, weekly, 5,000 copies
Nleb Bekristen, (The Christians' Counselor) Yaunde, weekly, 10,000 copies
Semaine de l'A. E. F., Brazzaville, weekly, 4,500 copies
La Voix de l'Oubangui, Bangui, weekly, 1,700 copies (cf. B. G. 45, 78)

B. G. 33, 32

Of this total only three appear in a native language. The oldest of these is the *Rafiki Yetu* monthly in Swahili which was founded in 1925 by Father Alphonse Loogman in Mombasa to counteract the influence of non-Catholic journals that were being published with the support of the government. One of the main reasons for the general use of European languages in these newspapers is undoubtedly the Babylonian multiplicity of tongues in Africa. In many areas the dialectal variety would make it impossible to find enough subscribers for a paper in a native language. Africans whose education has progressed to a point where they become part of the reading public often know one European language well enough to enjoy a newspaper in English, French or Portuguese. Moreover, the Catholic papers usually have at least some sections written in one of the local native tongues.

Engel, 216 f.

Youth Organizations. The first attempts to introduce Catholic youth organizations in Africa were made in Senegal in 1906. Other missions of French West Africa followed suit when the anticlerical policy of the French government secularized the schools and forced the priests to find new ways to keep the Faith intact and shield adolescents from the pernicious example of European colonists. A

B. G. 24, 23;
25, 207

Catholic Circle arose in St. Louis, Senegal. It organized its own orchestra, held musical soirees, and put on theater plays. For younger children, the Fathers created supervised playgrounds to keep them away from the corrupting influence of Mohammedan

B. G. 25, 276

companions. Conakry, French Guinea, achieved such success with its brass band, its loan library, its recreational evenings and the sports-club which it started in 1908, that antireligious elements in the colony became apprehensive and vainly tried to start a com-

B. G. 27, 157

peting group. Before World War I, in Brazzaville, the Fathers built a special youth center, equipped with athletic fields, reading-rooms, and a theater with a capacity of more than three thousand. This center was regularly visited by six to seven hundred youths

---

O Apostolado, Loanda, weekly, ? copies
Revista Mensal, Nova Lisboa, monthly, 4,784 copies
Catholic Times, Mombasa, monthly, 3,300 copies
Rafiki Yetu, (Our Friend), Mombasa, monthly, 7,000 copies
Témoignages, Diego-Suarez, monthly, 800 copies
Vavolombelona, Diego-Suarez, monthly, 800 copies
La Vie Catholique, Mauritius, ?, 5,000 copies
Légionnaires, Mauritius, ?, 2,500 copies
Recently the Owerri Diocese has undertaken the publication of a bi-weekly newspaper called *The Leader* and reports a printing of 18,000 copies.

B. G. 30, 656

and served also as a means of fostering Catholic marriages. Strangely enough, the same approach failed miserably in Rufisque (Senegal), and in Gabon only the dramatic groups were successful.

The big advance in youth work, however, dates from more recent times, especially from the period immediately preceding the Second World War, when increasing urbanization and the growth of modern materialism made this kind of social work imperative in the larger centers of population. The French-controlled terri-tories report especially great activity in such youth organizations.

B. G. 42, 106

For instance, the latest record (1951) of Sacred Heart parish in Dakar closely resembles that of a well-organized European parish: it has scout troops, sports-clubs, Catholic young workers groups,

B. G. 42, 358 f.; 43, 24

a boys' center, a young men's center, its own cinema,[22] etc. Other city missions in the French territories, e.g. Duala and Libreville follow similar patterns. In Duala (French Cameroons), after World War II, Catholic Action underwent a reorganization. One specific feature of its numerous branches was the addition of a monthly day or recollection to counteract the growing materialism of this rapidly developing Mandate of the old League of Nations. In Brazzaville, near the famous St. Ann's Cathedral built in African Gothic style, Father Lecomte constructed a sports arena that seats twenty thousand and boasts a huge swimming pool.

In the Spiritan missions outside the French sphere of influence, there seems to be considerably less concern for youth work. This particular approach does not play the same important role as appears to be the case in French territories. It may very well be that in these areas the mission school system achieves the same end.

4. THE DIRECT MEANS OF APOSTOLATE

After this brief survey of the indirect means, we must now turn our attention to the direct means which the Holy Ghost Fathers have employed in their attempts to establish the Catholic Church in Africa. Because Chapter VII has already recorded Father Libermann's general directives in this matter, our study

---

[22]The absence of anything like the American Legion of Decency has left the French movie industry with a very doubtful moral reputation. To neutralize its bad influence somewhat, the Church has organized here and there cinemas which are safe for the whole family.

will be restricted here to a consideration of his followers' application of these broad principles under the following headings:

a. The occupation of the territory.

b. The technique of convert making.

c. The building of a Christian society.

d. The native elements at work in the Church.

a. OCCUPATION OF THE TERRITORY

In the first years after their arrival in Africa, the missionaries could do very little to effectively occupy the immense territory entrusted to their care. As the reader will recall, the first Vicariate stretched along five thousand miles of coast without limits to the interior, and the complement of men was pitifully small. All the pioneers could do was gain a foothold and establish bases that would support more extensive occupation manoeuvers at a later date. Nevertheless, although death and disease continued to thin the ranks of these valiant beginners, they started very soon to work toward an effective occupation of the northern part of Guinea.

Va. 215 f.

Bishop Kobès made plans for covering the whole area with a network of missions: one in every five leagues of his vicariate. Constant misfortunes in newly-founded missions prevented him from executing his plan and at his death in 1872 only four stations survived him, but the general *modus agendi* was established.

Engel, 15 ff.

It was not until the last two decades of the nineteenth century that the Spiritan missions of Africa began systematically to divide their territory into sectors with a central residence surrounded by a large number of auxiliary stations. As a rule, such residences, occupied by from two to four priests and one or two Brothers, were constructed at strategically situated points that offered facilities for travel in all directions.

The auxiliary stations usually consisted of a humble chapel and a bush school staffed by a catechist. These were located in villages whose inhabitants showed interest in the mission and therefore offered some hope of conversion. Each string of stations along a river or jungle-track was regularly visited by one of the priests in the central residence. He and his confreres each had such a chain of stations entrusted to his personal care.

Engel, 32, f.

The system proved very successful, especially when the personnel of the central residence was sufficiently stable. Unfortunately,

in years gone by, sickness, death, and pressing needs all too often
forced the Superiors to change the men from residence to residence
with bewildering rapidity. Such exigencies prevented the missionary from becoming familiar with the peculiarities and special needs
of his charges, and from gaining their full confidence. Worse still,
it often obliged him to waste valuable time by constantly learning
new languages and dialects.

Engel, 33 ff.

The occupation of a large territory with relatively few men
makes the life of these apostles greatly different from that of a
country pastor. The priest is nearly always on the go, travelling
from village to village. In some places it has been estimated that
the missionary is absent from his residence about two hundred
days a year. The reason for this constant travel is that the numerous
bush stations and their catechists require constant supervision if
their work is to be successful. In addition, the priest has to administer the sacraments in outlying districts to those who cannot
travel great distances to the mission church. He must also visit
new areas to make the mission known and to awaken a desire for
a catechist. All this requires constant safaris which are far from
being conducted tours. Although modern means of transportation
have increasingly alleviated the burden, it still remains true that
many of the missionary's travels take place on foot or bicycle
along narrow pori and bush tracks, in a primitive boat up and
down the stream, or by ox-cart along most rudimentary roads.

Engel, 34 ff.

Originally, the creation of such networks of auxiliary stations
was an effective way to occupy a country, but supervision often
suffered from the effects of personnel shortages, especially when
many of the central missions contained a large number of educational and social works which required the constant presence
of the Fathers. It often became a question of choice between
intensive work on a relatively small number of spots or an extensive apostolate covering the largest possible territory. Usually,
however, the result was a compromise between the two until more
adequate personnel made it possible to work both intensively
and extensively.

Engel, 45 f.

More important even than occupying the land with a network of stations was the occupation of the Negroes' heart by
gaining their confidence. A sure indication of success in this
respect was the tendency even of pagans, especially in East Africa,
to select the missionary to arbitrate their disputes,—a tacit ad-

From a primitive and temporary bush shelter, the mission slowly
develops into an imposing complex of buildings, thanks to the unremitting labor and technical skill of humble Brothers.

Mohammed or Christ, who will conquer Africa? Top: Mohammedans salaaming toward Mecca. Bottom: Christians of the Cameroons leaving church after Sunday Mass.

mission that they recognized the unselfish motives of these white men. Moreover, the intimate knowledge of native languages, customs, and mentality which many of the Fathers possessed, constituted another powerful factor in their favor. The people came to look upon the priest as one of their own and on several occasions went so far as to elect him as their chief. Thus, for instance, the Nkomi tribes in Gabon solemnly inaugurated Father Bichet as the *Renima* (general king) of their land to whom henceforth the local kings deferred for all important affairs; the chiefs of the Dioba peoples in Senegambia elected Father Jouan as their leader; and in Tanganyika's mission of Tegetero the population made Father Bukkems their headman.

B. G. 19, 374

B. G. 20, 247
L. H. 50

The general respect and confidence bestowed on the missionaries made it relatively easy for them to substitute Christian practices for pagan customs. Thus, for example, they suggested that medals and rosaries be worn around the neck in place of the fetishes to which their people clung so tenaciously.[23] They went out of their way to celebrate Christian feasts with all possible splendor and they organized solemn processions of the Most Blessed Sacrament, thereby satisfying the Negro's love of pageantry and weaning him away from pagan celebrations and parades.

b. The Technique of Convert Making

Engel, 56 ff.

The Direct Approach to Pagans. The direct approach to pagan audiences has always been a feature of the Spiritan apostolate in Africa. It varies from formal sermons to an assembled populace on the village square and brief explanations for the benefit of pagan bystanders on the occasion of sick calls and funerals to simple and informal discussions in the evening before a native hut. Incidentally, this latter type of conference appeals greatly to the African's love of debate and palaver. Missionary journeys throughout the district usually offer many opportunities for such a direct approach, but it may also take place in the mission centers themselves whenever a crowd of pagans has gathered to watch the joy and splendor of Christian feastdays.

On occasion, little gifts were distributed as further incentives to attendance and friendly chiefs were sometimes asked to use

---

[23]In doing so they took great care to explain the nature of these Christian practices lest the substitution become merely a change of superstition.

their influence in making people come to the sermons.[24]   Above all, however, the Africans' love of music and singing constituted a powerful attraction.   The missionaries promptly availed themselves of it to drive their lessons home.   Dividing the audience into two choruses, the priest would put his message into a song that was chanted antiphonally until everyone knew it by heart.

As one might expect, the subject matter of such sermons was and is limited to the most fundamental Christian truths and prayers: the Creed, the Sign of the Cross, the Our Father, and the Hail Mary.   The instruction always ends with an invitation to come to the catechumenate for further lessons and ultimately for baptism in the Church.

The Catechumenate.   By this term is meant the period between a prospective convert's application to become a Christian and his actual baptism.   Because of the enormous variety of peoples and conditions in the far-flung Spiritan missions of Africa, the Congregation has never laid down very definite rules about the nature and duration of the catechumenate.   Had they existed, it would have been difficult to enforce them, for such regulations belong rather to the domain of the Vicars Apostolic appointed by the Holy See.   In general, the Motherhouse counseled against extreme measures:

B. G. 29,
692 f.

Two excesses are to be avoided: on the one hand, that of admitting people to baptism after hasty and insufficient instructions (which could result in many baptisms, but few true Christians) and on the other, that of admitting them only after such a protracted, detailed, and difficult training that it practically excludes most catechumens by discouraging them and thereby renders the work of the mission sterile.

Engel, 63 ff.

On their arrival in the Two Guineas more than one hundred years ago, the Fathers had to combat the excessive laxity of the few native priests who were stationed in the area and administered baptism after little or no instruction at all.   However, even the first Spiritan bishops of this mission did not lay down any firm and

B. G. 43, 123

[24]The early practice of giving little presents constituted a bad policy whose evil effects are still felt to this day. According to the latest report of the Sierra Leone Diocese it gave rise to distorted thinking that led the people to expect support from the Church. Consequently, in places where missions should now be self-supporting, there is need for allocations from other sources.

fixed rules but left it to the individual priests to determine how long the catechumenate would last. Only after the bitter disillusionment of numerous apostasies did these early missionaries learn the wisdom of deliberate thoroughness. After that, they not only scrutinized the candidate's knowledge of the Faith; they demanded positive guarantees that he would be able to live up to that Faith after his baptism. Thus, for instance, in Thiès they did not dare to baptize a hundred well-prepared catechumens, because "it was

B. G. 17, 249   not feasible for them to live as Christians," and in another mission they turned away a number of well-instructed girls who requested baptism, solely because they were likely to be given in marriage to

B. G. 30, 427   polygamous husbands. By 1920, in Senegambia the minimum duration of the catechumenate was two years or even more for anyone guilty of serious breaches of the Christian code during this period.

Engel, 66 ff.   French Guinea, which in 1907 was still satisfied with eighteen months, specified a minimum of two years after World War I and allowed an abbreviation of this period only in danger of death. The Nigerian missions, which at first limited the catechumenate to one year, increased the time to a year and one half in 1912, and then in 1918 to from three to four years or even longer. The results reached by this apparent severity amply justify the praxis.

Other Spiritan missions in Africa show the same trend. In Angola some missionaries at first hastily baptized after a few weeks' instruction, but bitter disappointments soon forced them to increase the catechumenate to one year and then ultimately to a minimum of two years. In East Africa, where in 1892 kind-hearted Bishop de Courmont accepted one month (to be spent in the mission), a three-year catechumenate became the rule for adults in 1912.

Nowhere are the missionaries satisfied with mere attendance at religious instruction, lusty hymn singing and a theoretical knowledge of Christian truths. No matter how perfectly a catechumen may know the tenets of the Faith, he must give positive proof of his willingness and his ability to live a Christian life and of his steadfast proposal to persevere in it. For this reason, nearly all Spiritan missions now prescribe a minimum of two years for the the catechumenate, part of which is to spent in or close to the mission.

The *General Mission Directory* of the Congregation, published in 1930, has no binding power on missionary bishops, but it condenses the experience and wisdom of a century's apostolate. In it

*Directoire
Général des
Missions,* pp.
126 ff.

we find that a probationary period of at least two years is specified and this is divided into two sections: the postulate and the
catechumenate. The first of these two is open to all, whether polygamous or not, who want to know more about Christ. Its duration
is left to the discretion of the missionaries. While in this postulate, the candidate learns the first elements of religion, the manner
of baptizing in danger of death, and the way to make an act of
perfect contrition. The catechumenate, however, is open only to
those who show a sincere desire of becoming Christians, who know
the first truths, and who are willing to repudiate idolatry and immorality (specifically polygamy).

Engel, 77 ff.

Baptismal Praxis. After his probationary period, the catechumen must successfully pass a final examination before he is
admitted to baptism. Although catechists may have prepared the
convert for this step, Spiritan practice demands that a priest give
this last examination and that it be seriously conducted. Naturally,
a candidate's ability and condition are taken into account, but he
must reveal a sound knowledge of the Faith and its practice.
Unless he does, his baptism will be deferred to a later time.[25]
Finally, to impress the neophytes with the importance of their decision, local regulations often prescribe that the ceremony take place
on a solemn holiday and that it be followed by a little feast in
honor of the new Christians.

With respect to children and adults in danger of death, the
missionaries follow the general rules of the Church—*viz.,* they
baptize all children in danger of death unless prudence forbids and
they require only the barest minimum of religious knowledge from
moribund adults who wish to receive the sacrament. It would be
difficult to estimate even roughly the total number of persons for
whom heaven has been opened in this way at the last hour of
their life, for not only the priests themselves, but the Sisters and
Brothers, Catholic laymen, catechumens, and even pagans of good
will take part in this spiritual work of mercy. In St. Louis

B. G. 12, 395

(Senegal) alone, a single Sister baptized five hundred dying children between 1877 and 1881 and her case was not exceptional.

B. G. 15, 535

[25]The strictness of this test is brought out, for instance, in a report of
the Bundi mission of Brazzaville. Usually about a third of the candidates
failed to pass and had to wait several months before being allowed to present themselves again.

C. A. 1955/56   The latest statistics of the Holy Ghost missions report a total of more than thirty thousand such baptisms in a single year.

c. The Building of a Christian Society

To build a Christian society in the midst of pagan surroundings, the Holy Ghost Fathers have relied heavily on the following means:

1. Native boarding establishments.
2. Christian family life.
3. Special Christian villages.
4. The Church's disciplinary, sacramental, and devotional practices.

1. *The Native Boarding Establishments*

Engel, 158 ff.
K. K. A. 164
ff.

Arriving in Africa when there was not yet even a hint of Christian social organization, the Spiritans in practically all their residences gathered children (usually ransomed slaves at first) into their mission compounds and separated them from their immoral environment. Then they would teach these unfortunates the rudiments of civilization, trying to inculcate in them a love of work and a practical approach to Christian living. It was a heartbreaking task, beset with many failures, but under the circumstances it appeared to be the only way to make a beginning.

Not every one of the missionaries possessed the necessary patience for this slow uphill educational work in savage surroundings under a broiling tropical sky. A few were too easily inclined to have recourse to the stick when good-will was patently lacking in their charges. However, Superiors quickly forbade the use of rods. Realizing that corporal punishment is sometimes necessary—as it is even in a well-civilized family—they permitted gentler corrective measures such as locking up recalcitrants or making them take their meals in a kneeling position. If strokes were called for—and they are still officially sanctioned in the British Commonwealth—they were preferably to be administered by lay assistants and not by the priests themselves.

In Senegambia, where the first of these native establishments began to function as early as 1844, the Fathers made the mistake of organizing them too much in the way of junior seminaries with too much emphasis on pious exercises. As Dr. Engel expresses it:

Engel, 160		"They educated the children in a European way and along monastic lines instead of preparing them for the life they would later have to lead as Christians." As a result, all too many of them refused to return to the simple life they had led before. They became idlers, beggars, thieves, and prostitutes. Fortunately, other Spiritan missions did not make the same mistake, and in Senegambia the Fathers soon adopted a different course when they realized that their first approach had been wrong. The emphasis then turned to practical training in agriculture and trades.

Despite many failures and disappointments, these boarding establishments attained the desired goal: a first generation of convinced and practising Christians that would serve as the foundation of a future Catholic society. Once this goal was reached, the boarding institutions gradually disappeared in most centers. As the Matombo mission reported in 1926:

B. G. 33, 20 f.			In the beginning . . . the Fathers were obliged to devote their time and energy to the education of young boarders in order to make them good Christians and potential founders of Christian families. Their efforts have not been in vain, as the many Christian villages prove. . . . Today there are fairly numerous weddings of children from Christian families and thus the future of our villages is secure . . . The need to gather many children in boarding schools no longer exists, at least not for the boys.

The old type boarding establishment still functions in some of the more primitive areas—where the original purpose still exists—and also in a few other places where a widely-scattered population limits the effectiveness of the mission day-schools which have been substituted for them. The boarding schools now maintained in Spiritan missions are devoted for the most part to training future teachers, catechists, and priests.

As the importance of these early boarding establishments diminished, the missionaries found it possible to engage in more active visitation of the outlying stations in their district. They could now open local day-schools and thus effectively reach a larger

B. G. 31, 95;		segment of the population. The day-school revealed itself as far
33, 157			more appealing to the freedom-loving African youngsters who hated being away from home, but flocked in great numbers to schools established in their own villages.

Engel, 170 ff.

Girls' Boarding Houses. To bring about a new generation of Christian families, the missions found it necessary to educate girls as well as boys. This task was (and still is) usually entrusted to Sisters.[26] As a rule, the early training program provided for religious instruction, basic home economics, and gardening. Sometimes a little reading was added but rarely anything more advanced,

B. G. 19, 371;
24, 217
B. G. 21, 517

because the boys did not want to marry a "lady" for fear that she would demand too great a degree of emancipation from her traditional position of inferiority. At best it would have been dangerous to teach them more, for a native girl with a little culture all too easily found a career as companion to a lonely colonist.

In the beginning, the recruitment of girls for these boarding schools met with great difficulties. Parents objected strenuously because girls were too economically valuable to be sent away from the village. At home, they could be used for cultivating the land and then they could be sold for a substantial amount to any rich old polygamist who wanted to add another wife to his collection.

B. G. 25, 213

Religion, they argued, was good for men, but not for women. Sometimes, the Fathers solved this problem by paying the dowries of a large number of girls and thereby acquiring all rights over them.

B. G. 18, 497;
21, 585

Thus, for instance, in Gabon, Father Bichet spent a large part of his personal fortune in purchasing little girls—thereby becoming their legal husband according to native law—and then trained them in the mission for eventual marriage to Christian young men. In other cases, mission-trained boys returned to their native villages, made their choice among the pagan belles, submitted the first downpayment on them, and then escorted their intended wives to the mission for Christian instruction.

B. G. 30, 632

Even after a first generation of Christian boys and girls had been formed in this way, several missions, notably those of the French Cameroons, retained a special type of girls' boarding establishment called fiancees' homes *(oeuvres des fiancées)*. Because of the widespread practice of cohabitation before marriage, the missionaries found it necessary to prepare young women for a Christian wedding by having them spend about six months in such a "fiancees' home," there to be instructed in religion, housekeeping,

---

[26]Stations without Sisters lodged the girls with Christian families or in dormitories outside the mission buildings, where during the night they would be under the guardianship of a trusted old matron or locked up securely.

and infant care.[27] Most of the girls are brought to these homes by their prospective husbands, who provide for their food and clothing during their pre-marital schooling. While the young ladies are perfectly free to leave at any time, discipline is quite strict and its enforcement is rendered easier by the fact that the boys themselves demand full compliance with the rules. A serious infraction may involve postponement of the wedding-day, and the future husbands are understandably reluctant to have their marital prospects clouded by obnoxious behavior on the part of their betrothed.

B. G. 32, 618

In general, the results obtained by this method have been thoroughly satisfactory, particularly since the first Holy Ghost Sisters came to the Cameroons and assumed charge of this work in 1924.

2. *The Promotion of Christian Family Life*

Engel, 174 ff.
K. K. A. 133
ff.

Perhaps the gravest of all problems faced by the early Spiritans in their efforts to civilize primitive tribes lay in inculcating the concept of a truly Christian family. Numerous factors offered substantial opposition to the Catholic way of life in this respect. First of all, there was the universal practice of polygamy with all its evils and all its attraction for people who were living but little above the level of the brute. A man's social and economic prestige in tribal society was determined by the number of wives he possessed. They constituted his source of income, for the more numerous his wives, the more hands there were to wield a hoe. Then too the more they produced, the more money he had for the acquisition of additional wives.[28] Moreover, the rich old polygamist was usually able to offer parents a better dowry for their marriageable daughters than could a young man of eighteen or twenty. After finishing the mission school, therefore, the boy often had to work ten to twelve years before he had saved enough to get married. In practice, these long years of waiting usually degenerated into a period of immorality and promiscuity. Then there was the cupidity of the girls' parents, who often went so far as to sell already married daughters to a new husband who might be offering a higher price. In addition, surrounded as they were by pagan examples, the boys themselves could not muster up much enthusiasm for a marriage that would

B. G. 25, 234

B. G. 20, 377

---

[27]The daily routine of these houses provides for three hours of religious instruction, six hours of work, and four hours for meals and recreation.

[28]The present French government policy of paying multiple family allowances to polygamous husbands only tends to increase this moral curse and to keep the women in a position of abject economic and moral slavery.

B. G. 26, 769

bind them to one partner for life. Consequently, many of them preferred a trial arrangement with their prospective partners for a few years before getting married officially. Others persevered in concubinage to the very end of their lives.

Reports and statistics from the early missions show how heartbreaking it was to campaign against such deeply-ingrained customs.

B. G. 12, 460

Gambia, for instance, with its two thousand Christians had not a single Catholic marriage to report in 1878 and 1879; Rufisque (one

B. G. 25,
233 f.

thousand Christians) was in the same situation in 1907, 1908, and 1909, and wistfully expressed the hope that its 1911 report might

B. G. 26, 769

be able to mention three marriages; Boke had only eight Catholic weddings between 1898 and 1912. No wonder then that the early Spiritan missionaries paid dowries for hundreds of girls, educated them in their boarding schools and, after marrying them to Christian boys, settled the newlyweds in separate villages close to the mission. After doggedly following this procedure for many years, they finally saw the dawn of a new mentality. As time went on, Christian family life at last became firmly entrenched. The 1955 statistics of the thirty-one Holy Ghost Fathers' mission territories in continental Africa show astonishing progress in this vital area:

C. A. 1954/55

they report a total of 27,508 Catholic marriages[29] out of a total of nearly three million Faithful, i.e. about nine per thousand. For the sake of comparison it may be useful to point out that the normal ratio of all marriages is eleven per thousand of population.

3. *The Foundation of Christian Settlements*

Engel, 184 ff.
K. K. A.
155 ff.

Because the neo-Christian families would have required a heroic degree of virtue to remain faithful to their obligations had they returned to fully pagan surroundings, the Spiritans founded special villages for Catholic families close to the mission compound. It was the only effective way to preserve the faith of these neophytes and at the same time create centers from which the Christian way of life could radiate over the pagan countryside. The method was officially sanctioned in the 1878 edition of the Constitutions:

1878 ed.
Const. 96,
VII

To secure the perseverance of the newly baptized [the priests] shall try to gather them in groups around the mission so as to separate them from the influence of the pagans and

---

[29] Plus an additional 488 mixed marriages.

from the bad example of Europeans. They shall then form Christian families among them and with these families establish Christian villages, so that all will be able to support and help one another in the Faith and in the observance of their religious duties.

As early as 1845 Father Briot had formulated a plan for such a village, but the initiative leading to the first real settlement came in 1852 from a group of young Christian couples in Gabon. They wanted to live near the mission and support one another in their efforts to lead a Christian life. Significant progress in founding

B. G. 9, 460

successful settlements, however, did not occur till twenty years later, when the Senegambia mission founded the villages of St. Joseph (Ngazobil) and St. Benedict (Mbodien).

B. G. 11,
305 ff.

St. Joseph is a particularly good example of the development such a settlement came to achieve. In a few years, as more and more young families came to join the first couples, they laid out a regular street-pattern, replaced the traditional one-room huts of the pagans with somewhat more pretentious quarters built on family plots, and erected a small chapel. Although fire razed the

B. G. 14, 286;
16, 261; 17,
229

village in 1877, it was quickly rebuilt. By 1885 the settlers were largely self-governing, with their own village council and their village police-force to lay down and enforce the rules of their settlement. They said morning and night prayers and the rosary in common, and went to Mass everyday. In general, the moral tone of the village was high, although contemporary reports of idleness and drunkenness indicate that these recent converts from paganism did not suddenly lose all their traditional vices.

In the following decades, the Spiritans gradually extended this system throughout most of their missions: Nigeria, the Congo, Angola, Zanguebar and, after World War I, the French Cameroons

C. A. 1928/29

as well. This mission alone in 1929 reported that each of its two thousand catechetical stations was surrounded by from three to seven such villages. Strict supervision, of course, long remained a necessity. Coming as these settlers did from a wholly pagan society, they needed the constant support of the missionaries' praise and reproach to persevere even in their secluded villages. Disappointments in the form of backsliding into paganism or flight from the settlements were numerous and severe, but the Fathers patiently continued their efforts because they were convinced that

". . . in journeyings often . . ." by any available means.

"Go, therefore, and preach to all nations, baptizing them . . . , and teaching them all that I have commanded you. . . ."

at the beginning no other system offered a better chance of success.[30]

In general, these miniature Christian societies, which recall the famous Indian reductions of Peru, achieved their purpose—*viz.,* the establishment of deep-rooted Christian family traditions and customs and centers from which the Faith could spread more easily.

B. G. 16, 362

In 1891, for example, the Nigerian chief Idigo, along with fifteen other families, founded such a village and the happiness of this settlement so profoundly impressed the pagans around it that many

B. G. 15, 715

burned their fetishes and became Christians. In 1890, pagans constructed a settlement of their own close to a Christian village

B. G. 17, 680

near Bagamoyo and begged for baptism. Five years later, the Fathers of this mission reported that so many people wanted to become Christians and live in their settlements that they no longer knew how to accommodate them. In East Africa particularly, most of the central Spiritan missions originated from settlements that became overpopulated and necessitated the removal of groups to new focal points of evangelization.

Engel, 198 ff.

Despite its great success, the system had certain disadvantages also. In 1892, a pastoral letter of Bishop de Courmont, Vicar Apostolic of Zanguebar, indicates some of these: too much economic dependence on the mission was detrimental to personal initiative and love of work;[31] there was no possibility for the families to become independent; and occasionally the priests interfered unduly in affairs that were strictly the personal concern of the family involved. Moreover, one may legitimately question whether, from a viewpoint of missionary strategy, the permanent separation of Christians from pagans would have been desirable, for it would have involved the restriction of the Christian example to those living in the immediate neighborhood of the settlements. Once the converts were strong enough in their Faith to live in little groups around a catechist anywhere throughout pagan territory, the system of isolation might well have been and usually was abandoned without great loss. Accordingly, in

B. G. 25, 469

many areas, when in the judgment of the missionaries this stage

---

[30]In cannibalistic areas these villages served also to save their inhabitants from the cooking-pots of hungry neighbors.

[31]At first, the villagers worked on properties owned by the mission. In return, it provided for their needs and left them free one day out of five to cultivate a piece of land for their own use. Later, this system was modified and the settlers worked only thirty days a year for the mission.

ff. ; 31, 99 ;   was reached, Christian families were free to settle wherever they
32, 822   wished, as long as they were not too remote for contact with
other Christians and with catechists.   At that point, more frequent association with uninstructed neighbors often resulted in
the pagans' acceptance of Christ and his Church.

4. *Promotion of the Church's Disciplinary, Sacramental, and Devotional Practices*

Engel, 201 ff.   As the periodic report of Linzolo mission pointed out in 1922:

B. G. 30, 840 f.   Evidently, the regenerating waters of baptism do not
radically change the mentality of our Negroes, but let us not
forget our own ancestors. . . . If we have few scandalous
renegades, we unfortunately have plenty of indolent, apathetic
and even temporarily estranged sheep that can find their way
back to the fold only on the shoulders of the Good Shepherd.

For this reason the Spiritan missionaries energetically availed
themselves of every means that would contribute to the perseverance of their converts.   Practically all missions organized special
catechetical instructions in which heavy emphasis was placed on
the practical application of the Church's teachings to daily life.

Church Discipline. When advice and reproach did not produce
the desired result, the priests sometimes had recourse to practices
which were common in the early history of the Church but since
B. G. 17, 420 ;   have fallen into desuetude.   For example, in Onitsha, Nigeria,
19, 339   repentant public sinners had to submit to a period of atonement
during which they were not permitted to join their fellow-Chris-
tians in the church, but had to stand near the entrance or in the
section reserved for pagans.   During this period they were not
allowed to receive any of the sacraments except that of Penance,
and even then they could not come to Confession at the times
B. G. 21, 556   reserved for Catholics in good standing.   In Gabon, on a Pentecost Sunday, a Negro woman who lived in open concubinage
with a European colonist attended the Pontifical High Mass
together with her partner.   Bishop Adam interrupted the service
and publicly excommunicated both.   As a result, the woman gave
B. G. 23, 22   up her sinful life.   During the next four years, the same prelate
proceeded four more times in the same way against people known
to be living in public adultery or concubinage.

B. G. 27, 338

B. G. 23, 22

Nor did the social position of an offender safeguard him against such measures. When the Sultan's brother in Kibosho (East Africa) apostatized for the third time and refused to listen to three public warnings, the Bishop promptly and solemnly anathematized him. Thereafter he was avoided by all Christians as if he were Judas. A similar fate befell King Felix Adande in Gabon when he refused to let his daughter return to her husband until a certain sum of money had been paid. When all admonitions appeared fruitless, the Bishop unhesitatingly leveled the Church's full weight of censure against him. The penalty was effective, for soon afterwards the king's daughter returned to her spouse and the monarch himself was reconciled to the Church.

Evidently such public penances and excommunications, which would hardly be recommended for Europe and America, must be seen in the light of local psychology and tradition. As the missionaries themselves pointed out:

B. G. 19, 339

In Europe these methods would be imprudent, but here they appear quite appropriate and our Christians themselves are the first to demand the punishment of culprits. Moreover, penances are accepted without difficulty and nothing appears more suitable to keep backsliders on the right track.

Engel, 209

The introduction of the Catholic penitentiary practice of fast and abstinence offered unusual difficulties. In the first place, ecclesiastical regulations governing the fast are based on the European routine of three meals a day. This was unknown in most parts of Africa. Since one full meal a day was more or less normal, canonically speaking most Christians (and pagans) in Africa fasted the whole year round. In addition, it was difficult to explain to them why, although they advocated fasting, most priests were unable to observe the discipline themselves without seriously jeopardizing their health through their program of intensive work in the tropical heat. Then again, abstinence laws had to make provision for such unusual items as snails, caterpillars, grasshoppers, crickets, ants, and similar local delicacies. In general, these questions were subsequently regulated in such a way that white colonists are dispensed from the fast because of the climate, but both Negroes and whites are bound by the laws of abstinence insofar as they can be applied.

Engel, 209 ff.

Liturgy and Holy Eucharist. The splendor of the Catholic liturgy unfolding around the mystical presence of God usually fills even a man of culture with deep admiration and respect. It makes a most profound impression on the African Negro for whom, even in his most degraded state, the world of the supernatural is as real as his physical surroundings. For this reason the Spiritans insisted everywhere on celebrating the great feasts of the Church with all possible splendor according to the Roman liturgy.[32] They taught their congregations to take an active part in the singing at all solemn functions. As a result, many an African church now puts European and American parishes to shame by the beauty and variety of its Gregorian chant. Whole congregations sing it with perfect ease and surprising artistry.

Frequent reception of the Holy Eucharist is particularly stressed, but at the same time emphasis is placed on careful preparation beforehand and a suitable thanksgiving afterwards. Consequently, many dioceses in Africa report a very great number of sacramental Communions. In the Spiritan dioceses of Nigeria, the French Cameroons, Morogoro (East Africa), and Bethlehem (South Africa), for example, individual reception of the Holy Eucharist averages once every two weeks, and communicants in the Diocese of Moshi are nearing an average reception of once a week. If one keeps in mind that many Christians live very far from the mission and therefore cannot go to Holy Communion as often as they would like, these figures are impressive indeed. More than anything else they indicate the strength of the Church in Africa.[33]

Devotions and Confraternities. In addition to stimulating frequent reception of the sacraments, Spiritan missionaries carefully pointed out to their neo-converts that the great devotions of the Church would provide highly efficacious means to secure their perseverance in the Faith. As early as 1849, long before the devotion became popular throughout the Christian world, they solemnly consecrated the Gabon mission to the Sacred Heart of Jesus and established an annual day of adoration specially dedicated

C. A. 1955/56

Engel, 214 ff.

B. G. 6, 540;

B. G. 45, 7
N. D. 9, 199,
348 f.

C. A. 1955/56

---

[32]Father Libermann was a great promoter of the Roman liturgy at a time when all but three dioceses of France followed the Gallican liturgy of Paris. Under his direction, Father Leo Le Vavasseur composed a liturgical handbook based on authentic Roman sources and published it in 1857. Soon many Bishops gave it official approbation for their dioceses. Successively reedited by Fathers Haegy and Stercky, this standard work on the liturgy is now being revised by Father Littner for the publication of its eighteenth edition.

[33]For all African missions of the Holy Ghost Fathers, the figures amount to about eighteen times a year per communicant.

13, 1072; 16,
488
B. G. 15, 352;
16, 294; 31,
27

thereto. Other missions, such as those of Senegambia, Bagamoyo and Loango soon followed suit. Others again, e.g. Senegal, Gambia, Sierra Leone and Cunene, promoted the same devotion by way of consecration of the family to the Sacred Heart, First Friday observances, Holy Hours of Reparation, and sodality exercises.

B. G. 2, 576

Devotion to the Blessed Virgin soon gained great popularity in the Spiritan missions. It manifested itself in the daily rosary, special prayers during the month of May, Our Lady's Sodalities, and popular pilgrimages. Before 1860, native Sisters erected the first Marian shrine in a huge baobab tree three quarters of an hour away from the Dakar mission. It became a beloved rendezvous for the neo-converts and was known as the shrine of Our Lady of the Baobab. Other devotions, such as those directed toward Our Lord's Passion, to Saint Joseph, the angels, the souls in purgatory and a variety of celestial patrons, added their salutary and srengthening influence as the years went on.

B. G. 12, 360;
171, 204; 16,
271; 32, 506;
30, 730

Sodalities and pious confraternities likewise played an important role in maintaining Christian life. They flourished in great profusion, although only a few of them can be listed here: the Apostleship of Prayer, Perpetual Adoration, the Scapular, Saint Ann's Sodality, and Saint Agnes' Union. In every instance, however, the priests took care not to promote an abundance of minor devotions to the detriment of a strong, well-balanced faith. Practically all of the supplementary religious exercises centered around Christ and His holy Mother. The remaining few were slanted toward certain aspects of Christian living. Thus, Saint Joseph and Saint Ann were proposed as examples of family life and, Saint Agnes or Saint Aloysius were held up as models of chastity.

d. Native Elements of Action in the African Church

Under this title we shall endeavor to describe the part that Africans themselves have played and are playing in the establishment of the Church in Spiritan missions. After first considering the contribution of material support, we shall proceed to discuss the lay apostolate, native religious orders of men and women, and the formation of an African clergy.

1. *The Material Support of the Church*

Engel, 218 ff.

In its first stage, any mission is entirely dependent on the resources which its priests receive from home, from the Propaganda, and from whatever enterprises they may engage in. This situation should never be considered as a permanent feature, however, for the purpose of the missionary's work—the foundation of an autonomous branch of the Church—demands that the local population ultimately supply the material resources that are needed to make it self-sufficient in its work of salvation. For this reason it has always been the policy of Spiritan missionaries to insist on local contributions for the support of the Church. To quote only one example among many, Bishop Carrie of Loango wrote in 1898:

Engel, 219

> The people themselves whom we evangelize . . . have the duty, based on divine, natural and ecclesiastical law, to maintain the laborers of the Gospel or their clergy. And we have a grave obligation to make this duty clear to them . . . and induce them to fulfill it.

Of course, not all support need be in money. Often it may take the form of labor performed on mission plantations, gifts of food, or the building and maintenance of chapels and schools. On the other hand, as soon as an area is sufficiently developed to bring currency into common usage, the Spiritans always insist on financial contributions toward the maintenance of the Church and its works. Thus, for instance, Yaunde in the French Cameroons reported an annual Church tax of one franc per adult and one half franc per child, and in 1925 this provided an income of nearly a hundred thousand francs. The latest report of this mission lists local support "in money, in kind, or in work" as its first source of income. The mission of Nigeria "began to depend less on outside revenues" as early as 1916 and by 1920 "was able to pay by itself more than fifty percent of its educational expenses. . . . Four years later, the hundreds of rural schools without government subsidy were able not only to meet the heavy burden of teachers' salaries by means of school fees and church donations but in most places even to supply the books and other materials needed by the children." The result of this local support was that "in the years following 1920, a huge network of school-chapels was extended over East Nigeria, most of which were independent of the Prefecture's treasury for the salaries of their teachers." Nearly all other missions report similar efforts to make the African Church independent of outside contributions as quickly as possible.

Left margin notes:

B. G. 30, 731 f. ; 32, 616

B. G. 42, 233
B. G. 43, 170

B. G. 43, 171

2. *The Lay Apostolate*

cf. pp. 171 ff.

Lay Catechists. As we noted in Chapter VII, Father Libermann placed great stress on the training of catechists who would help the priests in their work by giving elementary religious instruction and the first rudiments of secular learning to both children and adults.

Engel, 221 ff.
K. K. A. 283 ff.

B. G. 29, 79

In general, the Holy Ghost missionaries realized the importance of extending the range and scope of their activity by means of these lay collaborators. To quote only one among the many Vicars Apostolic who stressed the value of catechists, we may turn to Bishop Vogt of the Bagamoyo Vicariate: "We need catechists and large numbers of them if we want our mission to grow and develop. A mission without catechists is condemned to paralysis and perhaps even to death." Thus it is not surprising that most missions, notably Southern Nigeria, Angola and the Cameroons, inaugurated carefully planned training programs or special schools for lay catechists and soon had thousands of them at work throughout their territory.

B. G. 9, 184
B. G. 12, 574;
18, 460
M. C. 28, 557

On the other hand, there are a few Spiritan missions which for a long time committed the strategically serious mistake of neglecting the formation of a corps of lay co-workers. Gabon, where Libermann's spiritual sons arrived in 1842, had not yet set up a system of catechical posts as late as thirty years thereafter. Although the priests recognized their value, no worthwhile steps were taken in this direction until 1887, when the zeal of the Protestant catechists caused such serious losses that two **Fathers** finally devoted themselves to training Catholic teachers of religion. Five years later Bishop Le Roy, a convinced protagonist of catechists, became Vicar Apostolic of this mission and from then on a steadily increasing number of these valuable lay assistants began to extend the priests' sphere of influence.

Engel, 235

The most notorious failure to make use of catechists occurred in Senegambia. Despite the great and obvious need for lay help and the successful example of other missions, the vicariate neglected Libermann's advice almost entirely. As Archbishop Le Roy sadly pointed out in a hitherto unpublished study entitled *The Catechists in the Missions,*[34] "For the last fifty years, with ample means at its disposal, [the Vicariate of Senegambia] could have stemmed

---

[34]*Les catéchistes dans les missions,* Paris, n. d.

the tide of Islam with a mighty dam of catechists. We regret very much that we must admit it has failed almost completely in this respect." Instead, the Fathers concentrated their efforts on a vain and premature attempt to train a native clergy. As Dr. Engel expresses it:

Engel, 235

> It is really strange and almost inconceivable that precisely this territory whose interior was still largely untouched by Mohammedanism, whose reports clamored for laborers and constantly complained about the shortage of personnel, did not think of training a solid staff of useful catechists instead of devoting its strength exclusively to the formation of a native clergy.

B. G. 10, 110; 385

B. G. 28, 408

B. G. 32, 446

Not until 1874, thirty years after its foundation, do the periodic reports of this mission speak of catechists and the need for developing this aspect of the apostolate. Even more surprising is the fact that, even after it recognized their usefulness and necessity, another forty years had to elapse before World War I mobilized great numbers of priests and practically forced it to engage more catechists! Only after the war, when Bishop Le Hunsec, the future Superior General, became Vicar of this mission did a systematic training program finally evolve.

B. G. 26, 536 f.

Engel, 242

Usually, catechists were married laymen who received a small remuneration for their services. As a general rule, they were taught a trade so that they might have an additional source of income. Some missions, however, such as Southern Nigeria, were quite successful with young unmarried catechists. The best students of the schools of this marvellous mission often volunteered for three or four years of unpaid service prior to seeking a paying job and getting married. In Gabon, Bishop Le Roy attained great results with so-called "Married Brothers," i.e. pious laymen who dedicated themselves wholly to God's service, received their food and clothing from the mission, and followed a simple daily rule of life, but were not bound to celibacy.

Engel, 227 ff.

If ordinary neo-Christian families needed constant supervision and frequent visits from the missionary to keep them orthodox, the same was even more truly the case with these native religious teachers. Not only was there danger that they would deviate from the Faith in their teaching, but there was also the very real possibility that they might gradually slip back into pagan morals and drag the whole village down by their bad example. The old periodic missionary reports abound in complaints about unfaithful and unsatisfactory catechists. Such things should not surprise us, but they should not blind us to the great zeal and spirit of sacrifice demonstrated by these devoted men and to the very substantial contribution they made when they received careful training and were closely supervised by the priests. Even at present, the importance of their role appears from the latest statistics, where one finds a total of more than twenty-four thousand of them working in the Spiritan missions of Africa.

Legion of Mary. In more recent times, the active participation of the laity in the apostolate of the Church received great impetus by the foundation of African divisions of the Legion of Mary. In 1936 its President, Mr. Frank Duff, sent Miss Edel Quinn[35] to establish the Legion in East Africa. The members of this well-known organization of lay apostles engage in the visitation of homes, institutions and hospitals where they teach Christian doctrine, seek catechumens, induce lapsed Catholics to make their peace with God, regularize invalid marriages, and in general utilize all means open to laymen to foster the Church's work. Despite enormous difficulties, Miss Quinn succeeded so well in the Nairobi Archdiocese that it alone now has a hundred and fourteen Praesidia or local groups functioning among its people. Other Spiritan dioceses in the area report similar figures: for instance, the Moshi Diocese has a hundred and sixteen units. From Nairobi the Legion spread throughout East Africa and from there to Madagascar, Mauritius and Reunion. The extent of its salutary influence may be seen from the fact that in 1956 a single Praesidium in Nairobi was able to arrange for more than a thousand baptisms.

Two years before it began to operate in East Africa, the Legion established itself in the Onitsha Vicariate of Nigeria (1934), where it now counts a total of two hundred and seventy-one Praesidia. In the Owerri Diocese of the same country, thirty-five hundred Legionaries organized in two hundred and twenty Praesidia constitute the strong right arm of Bishop Joseph Whelan, C.S.Sp.

C. A. 1955/56

Suenens, *Edel Quinn,* 69 ff.

------

[35]She died in 1944 in Nairobi. The diocesan process, the first step towards beatification and ultimately canonization, of this zealous lay apostle was recently inaugurated by His Excellency John McCarthy, C.S.Sp., Archbishop of Nairobi.

After the Second World War, the Legion spread throughout the Spiritan missions of French Africa and the Belgian Congo. It is especially strong in the Cameroons. For instance, the Archdiocese of Yaunde has twenty-four Curiae in each of which there is a group of Praesidia. The general enthusiasm for this kind of apostolate is so great that there exists even a very unusual kind of Praesidium in Yaunde's prisons. It is composed of convicts who organize communal prayers, speak about the Faith with Moslem and Protestant inmates, and urge their fellow-Catholics to adopt the practice of frequent Confession and Communion in order to rebuild their broken lives.

The speed with which the Legion is growing in Africa is evidenced by the fact that, six months after its introduction in the Diocese of Doume in 1956, fifty Praesidia were already actively engaged in various works of the lay apostolate. The latest reports from the various missions constantly refer to the powerful way in which this zealous organization of humble laymen and laywomen aids the Church in its spiritual task. Equatorial Africa, for example, sends word that "The best and most 'productive' form of Catholic Action is undoubtedly the Legion of Mary."[36]

B. G. 42, 242;
43; 246; 44,
536; 45, 65;
etc.
B. G. 45, 78

3. *Religious Men and Women*

Native Religious Brothers. Soon after their arrival in the Two Guineas, the Holy Ghost Fathers tried to attract native vocations to the Brotherhood, but it was 1860 before two African candidates began their novitiate in Senegambia. The next year, one was allowed to take private vows and four others started their preparation for the religious life. A few years later, however, the mission had to report that this first effort had ended in failure.

A new attempt was made in 1869 when Bishop Kobès opened a novitiate of the Congregation in Ngazobil. It soon had four novices and three postulants. While two of these candidates solemnly pronounced their first vows in 1873, the Brothers' novitiate disappears from the annual reports until 1888 when Bishop Picarda reopened it with three aspirants. Nothing more is heard of it until 1925, when the mission decided to start a native religious congregation called the "Little Brothers of St. Joseph."

Engel, 251 ff.
K. K. A. 295 ff.
B. G. 2, 154;
225

B. G. 8, 510 f.

B. G. 9, 731

B. G. 15, 369

B. G. 32, 469

---

[36]Most of the information used in this section has been supplied by the Legion's headquarters in Dublin.

E. P. 31, I,
87, ff.

According to the latest statistics, this society now numbers eleven members and eight aspirants.

The meager results achieved after a century of effort graphically illustrate how difficult it is to score success in Africa with this most humble of all vocations. The requirement of celibacy seems to constitute a serious obstacle for these people who have no age-old Christian traditions to counteract the enervating and sometimes demoralizing effect of the tropics. It would lead us too far afield even to record the long list of failures other Spiritan missions have encountered in their attempts to establish a native Brotherhood. Nevertheless, the Fathers kept on trying and in recent times their efforts have produced better results.

A. M. C. 226

A. M. C. 177

E. P. 31, I, 119

B. G. 44, 177
E. P. 31, I, 214
C. A. 1955/56

In the Cameroons, they reported (June 1954) a total of twenty-nine African Brothers and fifteen postulants, all except two belonging to the native congregation of the Brothers of St. Joseph; the Spiritan missions of French Equatorial Africa at the same time recorded a total of twenty-seven professed Brothers and eleven novices; the latest report (1956) of the Owerri Diocese in Nigeria reveals twenty professed Brothers in its Congregation of St. Peter Claver :[36a] the Moshi Diocese in East Africa opened a novitiate in 1947 and already has eighteen Brothers and seventeen novices in its congregation of the Immaculate Heart of Mary, while the Angola missions reported a total of twenty-two African Brothers there. These figures do not loom very large, but they do show that progress is being made and they justify the hope that current efforts will not be attended by the same sort of failure that blasted earlier expectations.

Engel, 256 ff.

L. S. IV, 198;
N. D. 13, 247

Native Religious Sisters. Quicker and more abundant success blessed the Holy Ghost Fathers' efforts to foster religious vocations among African women. As early as 1845, Father Libermann broached the idea of Negro Sisters and shortly before his death he urged Bishop Kobès of Senegambia to make a prudent beginning. In 1858, therefore, the Bishop founded an African Congregation of the Daughters of the Holy Heart of Mary and assigned to them the care of the sick, catechetical work, and the primary education of girls. Now a century later, this society

---

[36a]Both of these congregations quite recently ceased to function as independent units. The Nigerian Brothers now constitute a Province of the Marist Brothers, and most of the Cameroonese have joined the Brothers of the Sacred Heart.

B. G. 4, 623　is the oldest of all African religious congregations.[37]　By 1865 it had its first native Mother Superior and ten years later it had already supplied thirty-eight Sisters to the mission.　Because they were at home with native languages and customs, they rendered service of inestimable value.　Despite this happy beginning, the Congregation suffered for many years from an inability to recruit A. M. C. 398　enough postulants.　Recently, thank God, the situation has considerably improved.　In 1954, it counted a total of fifty-two professed members and forty-two aspirants.

　　Other missions sooner or later followed the example of Bishop Kobès and founded special congregations of native Sisters.　A cf. pp. 581 ff.　number of them disappeared without a trace after some years of lingering existence, but ten of them have survived to the present and show promise of future vigor.　In addition, several Euro-C. A. 1955/56　pean Sisterhoods working in Africa have successfully recruited local candidates.　The latest figures on Holy Ghost missions (1956) show that the number of Sisters of African origin has now exceeded the six hundred mark.　The Diocese of Moshi, staffed for the most part by American Holy Ghost Fathers, leads the way with one hundred and twenty African Sisters, who now outnumber their white companions five to one.

4. *African Clergy*

Engel, 262 ff.　　*Priests.*　The primary goal of all apostolic activity is attained K. K. A. 305　when there is a sufficient number of native priests under the ff. R. H. M. 13,　direction of an indigenous hierarchy to carry on the work in-529 ff. A. M.　augurated by foreign missionaries.　Faithful to Father Liber-C. A., 81 ff.　mann's insistence on this point, his spiritual sons have, from the cf. p. 167　very first moment of their arrival in Africa, always dedicated A. P. F. 44,　themselves to this end.　Despite appalling difficulties and decades 106 ff., 116 f.　of bitter disappointment, they pursued it with unflagging zeal until their efforts at last began to bear substantial fruit.

N. D. 10, 78　　The first Spiritan junior seminary began to function in 1847, B. G. 45,　shortly after the Dakar mission was opened, and it had ten stu-113 f.　dents the next year.　Just a century ago, the oldest senior seminary

---

[37]We must take issue with John J. Considine who states in his interesting book *Africa, World of New Men,* New York, 1954, p. 273, that the community of African Sisters which appeared in Uganda in 1908 is "probably the first in Africa in date of foundation."　This honor belongs to the Daughters of the Holy Heart of Mary, founded fifty years earlier by Bishop Kobès.

B. G. 1, 25;
7, 197
B. G. 11, 470
B. G. 7, 265;
8, 759

in Negro Africa opened its doors in the same mission (1857). In Gabon, another junior seminary was opened in the same year. Ten years later it had fourteen aspirants. The Congo Prefecture mentioned its first efforts in the report of 1879, and on the east coast the Zanguebar mission inaugurated a seminary in 1870, seven years after the arrival of Father Horner, who was the Spiritan pioneer in that region. Two years later, there were twenty students. Most of the other Holy Ghost missions followed suit and spared no effort to prepare at least some candidates for the priesthood.[38]

C. A. 1923/24

Engel, 278

ibid., 284

For many years, the results of all these efforts were far from encouraging. Of the three hundred students, for example, who passed through Senegambia's seminary in Ngazobil during the course of sixty years, only eleven reached the priesthood. In Gabon fifty-five years went by before the first priest was ordained.[39] Between 1844 and 1924 all the Spiritan missions together succeeded in producing a total of only thirty-four priests. The immediate reasons for the very unimpressive ratio must be sought in the almost insuperable handicap of clerical celibacy, the powerful attraction of a lucrative job for ex-seminarians who were then among the very few natives with a higher education, the indolent character of primitive Africans, and the opposition of parents who objected to losing the income their sons could provide. It is only by exception that a priestly vocation will develop before the Faith has fully permeated the structure of the family and before society in general has reached a certain cultural level. Under favorable circumstances, at least one generation is needed to accomplish this,

Engel, 273 f.
cf. N. D. 9, 456 f.

ibid., 268

Engel, 285

[38] The study programs of these early seminaries varied quite widely. In Dakar, Bishop Truffet, the founder of the first seminary, set up a program which allowed only the native Wolof language, Church Latin, and an introduction to theology. As he envisioned it, the senior seminary would continue the theological training and, after tonsure, include the secular sciences as well. He feared that an earlier introduction to secular learning would tempt the students to abandon their studies and seek a well-paid job in the service of a commercial enterprise. This ill-conceived program, which would not even permit the use of a modern European language, did not survive its author's short sojourn in Africa. The opposite extreme was reached in the junior seminary of Bagamoyo. Its curriculum included French, Latin and Greek. Algebra, Plane and Solid Geometry; Physics and Chemistry; History and Geography; Vocal and Instrumental Music—altogether a program that would have done credit to many a modern seminary in Europe or America.

[39] For the sake of comparison, we reproduce here the figures of the White Fathers' Uganda mission: between 1878 and 1913 only two out of a hundred and sixty candidates reached the altar.

and where conditions are less propitious, as was the case in many Spiritan missions, two or three must pass before there can be any question of normal vocational development.

The turning point in the bleak outlook for seminaries was reached only recently in the decade preceding World War II. The statistics of 1937, for instance, indicate that although the number of African priests was still small (thirty-one for all Holy Ghost missions in Africa), there were one hundred and twenty-nine senior seminarians and six hundred and eighty junior aspirants. Since then, development has been very rapid, especially in the Cameroons, Southern Nigeria, Nova Lisboa (Angola), Morogoro and Moshi (East Africa), where African priests now constitute one third to one half of the total clergy. The latest figures show a total of 290 native priests, 302 senior seminarians and 1,448 junior aspirants are preparing for ordination in thirty-three seminaries in Spiritan missions on the African continent.

Although this demonstrates an encouraging growth, Africa still has a long way to go before its clergy will be numerically adequate. On the basis of one priest per thousand Catholics, an additional four thousand priests are needed just to take care of the present *Catholic* population in the Spiritan missions of Africa, to say nothing of the thirteen million pagans in these territories who are still waiting for the Glad Tidings of Christ.[40] No wonder, then, that the missionaries so often repeat the Savior's complaint: "The harvest indeed is great, but the laborers are few." (Luke X, 2.) Africa is still a land that is desperately short of priests. Instead of increasing, the ratio of priests to faithful is going down constantly. Because this situation obtains in the present highly decisive period of Africa's history, Pope Pius XII recently felt impelled to launch a burning appeal through his encyclical *"Fidei Donum."* He begged the Bishops, priests, and laity of the old Christian world to aid Africa's apostles in their hour of supreme distress by encouraging missionary vocations in Europe and America.

Prelates. In 1939 a significant step forward was taken in the formation of an autonomous African Church when the Holy See appointed Father Joseph Faye, C.S.Sp., a native of Senegal, as Prefect Apostolic of the newly created mission of Ziguinchor. Since then, three other African priests have become auxiliary bish-

Margin notes:

C. A. 1936/37

C. A. 1955/56

A. A. S. 49, 225 ff.

B. G. 39, 45

---

[40] In addition, these missions embrace four and one half million Mohammedans and one and one half million Protestants.

B. G. 44, 56   ops in Spiritan missions. The first of these, Most Reverend Paul Etoga, was consecrated on November 30, 1955, in an open air ceremony at Yaunde before a crowd of more than seventy thousand people, numerous public officials, and fifteen European prelates who had come to witness this solemn moment in the history of the Church. For the first time, a Negro of French Africa received the

B. G. 44, 325   fullness of the priesthood. Three months later, in a similar ceremony held on the campus of Libermann College at Duala, Cardinal Tisserant conferred the episcopal consecration on the Most Reverend Thomas Mongo before fifty thousand witnesses. In 1957 Archbishop James Knox, Apostolic Delegate, imposed his hands on Monsignor John C. Anyogu and made him auxiliary Bishop of the Onitsha Archdiocese in Nigeria. With the more rapid development of an indigenous clergy in many of the old Holy Ghost missions, one may expect similar occurrences to become commonplace in the years ahead and sections of these territories will soon be completely entrusted to an African clergy under the direction of bishops chosen

B. G. 45, 150   from among their own people. The Holy See took a significant step in this direction after the death of Bishop Bonneau in 1957, when it appointed His Excellency Thomas Mongo as his successor in the Episcopal See of Duala, French Cameroons.

5. *Political Factors and Spiritan Missionary Work*

Engel, 148 ff.   *Collaboration with Colonial Governments in the Work of Civili-*
K. K. A. 194 ff. *zation.* Because missionary activity in culturally primitive areas necessarily involves efforts to civilize the people, and because European colonial powers were keenly interested in the process, governments and missionaries often aided each other in their work: the mission by supplying personnel and the government by granting funds for building and maintenance. Everybody profited from the arrangement—the missionaries, the civil authorities, and most of all the backward people who were the object of their attention. In general, the government was unable to recruit sufficient nonmissionary personnel of the required moral caliber to undertake the giant task, because few laymen were willing to live in uncivilized areas and expose themselves and their families to an untimely death by mysterious tropical diseases. The missionaries, on the other hand, were unable to pursue their civilizing work on a large scale without government aid because they simply did not have the necessary funds. Consequently, the government and the missions usually worked—and still work—together. Such a program of col-

C. A. 1955/56

laboration prevailed in the territories controlled by Great Britain, Belgium, and Portugal, and it extended as well to the former German colonies. That is why Spiritan missions in the African countries controlled by these nations now educate close to a million children in nearly twelve thousand schools.

How seriously the work of civilization is hampered when the state refuses to collaborate with the missions is graphically illustrated by the condition of the French colonies. There Parisian anticlericalism gave little or no support to mission schools. As a result, the educational potential of Africa's youth in these areas has remained severely limited.[41] In 1950, French West Africa, with a total population of nineteen million, had only 1,125 schools attended by 137,985 pupils. This left 2,200,000 children (93%) without any education. In French Equatorial Africa, with a population of over four million, there were only 602 schools with 70,121 students, while the total number of school-age children amounted to about 600,000.[42] Such statistics contrast sharply, for instance,

C. A. 1955/56

with those of the Owerri diocese in Nigeria, where in 1956, 190,270 children attend the mission schools alone. Because of the more enlightened educational policy of England, as many children were able to receive their education in the schools of this missionary diocese as in all the governmental and private schools throughout French West and Equatorial Africa. Moreover, it must be borne in mind that the population of these French territories is eight times as large as that of the Diocese of Owerri.

Despite the more advantageous conditions in non-French colonies, some of those areas also cause the missionary to be apprehensive about the future. In the Belgian Congo, for example, the currently flourishing mission-school system is threatened by

---

cf. p. 462

[41]As was noted above, France has recently become more generous toward the private schools in its colonies. Nevertheless, even now its support of such academic institutions is still far from sufficient. The 1950

B. G. 42, 130 f.

figures for West and Equatorial Africa show a total of $866,000 allocated to 512 private schools with 66,788 pupils, i.e. about $13.00 per student.

B. G. 45, 120

The latest report (1957) shows that since 1950 the situation has considerably improved in the French Cameroons. In six years' time the number of students in elementary Catholic schools has almost doubled; that of colleges and normal schools has increased six-fold, and in the technical schools it has risen by two hundred percent.

[42]These figures include both governmental and private (mission) schools. In French West Africa about twenty-four percent of the schools are private.

B. G. 42, 130 f.

For French Equatorial Africa the figure amounts to about forty-eight percent.

repercussions from the educational policies which the present Brussels government has espoused at home. In South Africa, the mission schools are hampered by the extreme segregationist policy which this republic follows. In Nigeria, the newly-proposed educational program may severely curtail further development of Catholic schools and will, if it is adopted, interfere radically with the parents' right to send their children to a school of their own choosing.

Engel, 149 f.

Special Attention to Native Leaders. While collaborating with the colonial governments in education, Holy Ghost missionaries never forget how important a role is played in the lives of the people by their own chieftains and kings. For this reason they have always endeavored to gain the good-will of these native leaders and to have them send their children to the mission-schools. In this way, it was hoped, the succeeding generation of chiefs would be Christian, or at least favorable to the Faith. Moreover, a very salutary example would thereby be set for the subjects of these local leaders. In the Congo mission of Landana, the Fathers even opened a special school exclusively reserved for "the sons of kings, princes and the highest ranking nobility." Important gains were recorded when, as a result of this venture, the chiefs and kings themselves became Christians and personally promoted Christianity within their domains. The periodic reports abound in examples of the wholesome influence exercised by such conversions.

B. G. 13, 906;
21, 513
A. P. F. 49,
134

B. G. 11, 470

B. G. 21,
521 f.

Nigeria provides a striking example of this. In 1900, King Obi Fatou of Nsubbe received baptism. A council meeting of nine chieftains then decided that thereafter all parents should send their children to the mission school. Three of the chiefs themselves enrolled in the catechumenate. One year later, the people of Onitsha, although still largely pagan, elected Samuel Okosi Okolo King of Onitsha. He had been a catechist of the mission and his first act was to destroy the royal idol that had traditionally been used for cursing people and condemning slaves to death. He then induced the British government to impose the death penalty for the murder of new-born twins (a then current superstitious custom), and to decree heavy prison sentences for polygamy. All of these developments reached a dramatic climax in 1955, when Bishop Joseph Whelan of Owerri solemnly crowned Francis

B. G. 21, 78;
512 f.

M. C. 34,
133 ff.

B. G. 44, 18

Allagoa as Catholic King of Nembe with all the splendor of the
ancient medieval ritual for the coronation of monarchs.

Missions and Nationalism. No one saw more clearly than Father
Libermann that the activity of his French priests in uncivilized and
savage Africa would necessarily involve a measure of political
control by France. Although he had warned his priests not to
become political agents, he wrote in 1845:

cf. p. 168

> N. D. 7, 89
>
> I do not know to what extent the French government is
> interested in seizing these regions . . ., but it appears evident
> that the method by which we plan [to civilize them] is the
> most efficacious way to establish the French rule in these lands.

Yet, if any man lacked even a trace of exaggerated nationalism
in favor of France it was Libermann. We could not defend all
of his followers on the same score without doing a disservice
to historical truth or miss an opportunity to learn by the mistakes of the past. Despite Father Libermann's repeated warnings
and the Holy See's constant insistence, a few otherwise outstanding Spiritan missionaries never quite mastered a clear distinction
between God and Cesar in their work.

Of course, we cannot consider every action involving serious
political consequences as a betrayal of the missionary's primary
purpose. For instance, it would be difficult to blame Father
de Glicourt for supplying the French government with information leading to the recapture in 1779 of St. Louis, Senegal, from
the British, when we recall that this Catholic French settlement
had been forbidden to have a priest. Nor would one blame Bishop
Bessieux for refusing to be repatriated when France wanted to
abandon Gabon after the Franco-Prussian War, even though the
result of his action was to keep this colony in French hands. Then
too, the missionaries cannot be held responsible if, ten years after
they arrived at Dakar, France claimed the area as part of its sphere
of influence on the ground that French Spiritans were there.[43]
We see no reason for sharing Dr. Engel's dissatisfaction with the

cf. p. 30

Rogues,
243 f.

cf. p. 204
M. C. 1, 126;
6, 104

Engel, 151

Engel, 159

cf. p. 92

---

[43] One can hardly agree with Dr. Engel when, in his otherwise excellent study of the Spiritan missionary method, he suspects Father Briot
of undue nationalism because in 1845 he dressed the students of the mission
school in a uniform consisting of white trousers and a blue shirt with red
collar and red buttons, even though these happen to be the colors of the
French Flag. As we have seen in Chapter V, Libermann's priests in Senegal
at that time were so anxious not to appear as agents for the French government that they even broke relations with the French Navy.

B. G. 3, 319*

Holy Ghost Fathers in Ngazobil, Senegal, when they allowed the French Army commander to visit their residence with a hundred and fifty soldiers in 1863 and to "demonstrate most emphatically that he was interested in the mission and would, if necessary, support and protect it by force of arms." After all, the local chief had limited the Fathers' construction program to flimsy buildings whose walls could easily be riddled by bullets! Security such as the French commander offered was, therefore, justifiably welcome.

Beslier, 152 ff.

We should not even reproach Bishop Augouard for lending the mission steamer *Leo XIII* to a French expeditionary force when it set out to crush the power of Rabah in the Lake Chad region, for this Sudanese chief, after the fall of Khartum, had fled there with his army and for fifteen long years had terrorized the local inhabitants by a reign of plunder, slave drives, and wholesale murder. Collaboration in the defeat of this tyrannical outlaw can hardly be called reprehensible nationalism. It was exactly what one might have expected of a priest, irrespective of blood ties.

Unfortunately, even when these and similar occurrences are explained away, there still remain other less excusable facts. Augouard, for instance, constantly collaborated with Brazza in the conquest of French Equatorial Africa in such a way that, as

Mgr.
Augouard,
121
Witte, 23 f.
Storme, 570 ff.
da Silva, 301 f.

Georges Goyau expresses it, "with the crucifix in one hand and the national flag in the other, Bishop Augouard conquered a territory three times as big as the mother country for civilization and for France." He persuaded the local kings of Loango, Pointe-Noire and Cabinda to accept the French protectorate over their domains, and if it had not been for the unwillingness of Captain Cordier, Brazza's lieutenant, to confirm the treaties concluded by this Spiritan priest, nearly the whole coast from Gabon to the Congo River would have become French controlled territory.[44]

*Revue du
Foyer,* 1912,
no. 4, p. 29

In an unguarded moment during a speech he even went so far as to claim openly: "Some people have accused me of being more of a Frenchman than a missionary. They did not realize that this was the most beautiful compliment they could have paid me."

---

[44]Bishop Augouard's political activity has been the object of several special studies: F. Schwager, "Katholische Missionstaetigkeit und nationale Propaganda," *Zeitschrift fuer Missionswissenschaft,* 1916, pp. 109-134; J. Schmidlin, "Zum 'Imperialismus' der franzoesische Missionare." *op. cit.,* 1929, pp. 247-250; A. Perbal, "Le Nationalisme de Mgr. Augouard," *Revue d'histoire des Missions,* 1938, pp. 385-407 and *Les Missionaires français et le Nationalisme,* Paris, 1939, pp. 58 f.

Although we have no reason to doubt Bishop Augouard's sincere conviction that he was acting in the best interests of his mission, most people would find it hard to justify his *modus operandi*.

On the other hand, Bishop Augouard was far from being slavishly subservient to the French Government. His fearless denunciations of his country's unchristian policies caused Governor General Antonetti to remark at the Bishop's funeral that Augouard had been "an avowed enemy of the Administration." And when his good friend de Brazza favored the Islamization of the schools, the "Cannibal Bishop's" terrible thunder gave rise to the most violent and painful storm that ever raged around the ears of the disgraced Governor.

We have no desire whatsoever to imply that exaggerated nationalism was a common fault among French Spiritan missionaries. A plethora of examples might be cited to prove the opposite. For instance, when their Zanguebar missions in East Africa became the object of conflicting French, British and German interests in 1885, and the French Fathers were urged to choose sides, they promptly declared that "they abstained completely from becoming involved in political questions and restricted themselves exclusively to religious affairs." The Germans, who eventually took over the territory, acknowledged the sincerity of this contention, for their Society for the Exploration of East Africa reported:

> The French mission of the Congregation of the Holy Ghost and the Holy Heart of Mary has remained faithful to its well-known purpose, not only in theory but also in practice. As a matter of principle [the Congregation] eliminates political designs from its missions, and only rarely has it become involved in them. Without sounding the trumpet but with unflagging zeal, these missionaries devote themselves to the promotion of the Christian spirit and the benefits of our civilization among the black population.

The Angola missions, which are politically controlled by Portugal, offer another example. Although this nation was extremely jealous of its national heritage and tended to regard foreign missionaries with deep suspicion, hundreds of French Spiritans have evangelized Angola throughout the past century

Augouard, IV, p. 429

Beslier, 239 f.

B. G. 14, 609

B. G. 14, 611

without giving rise to any reasonable apprehension over the political danger of their presence.[45]

Although a few French Spiritans may have gone too far in their national preferences when the interest of their own country conflicted with that of other colonizing nations, there never was any doubt about where their sympathy lay when the welfare of their native charges was involved. In such cases they constantly gave their prudent support to the cause of the populations they had come to evangelize. This fact inspires confidence in the role they will play during the next twenty or thirty years in Africa for, as the reader undoubtedly knows, a crucial test of the purity of intention displayed by all Catholic missionaries will undoubtedly come within a few decades. Now that many regions are rapidly moving toward greater or complete political independence, it will be of extreme importance for the priests working there to avoid undue attachment to the interests of their own fatherland, and to eschew anything that might interfere with their basic function as founders of a native Church in mission lands.

*   *   *   *   *

In the preceding pages we have described the general characteristics of the Holy Ghost Fathers' apostolate in Africa. Certain features of their missionary method seem to be especially typical: their flexibility and adaptability to the situation at hand, their early efforts to train a native clergy, their emphasis on economic development by means of agriculture and technology, their wholesale establishment of Christian villages. As the primary stage is completed, they then proceed to lay greater stress on schools, colleges, and youth groups, moving with great deliberateness toward the time when the Christian society they created will reach full maturity and take the torch from their hands. Let us now turn to the actual missions in which these principles have been put into practice.

---

[45]We say "reasonable," because some Holy Ghost Fathers, such as Charles Duparquet, the founder of the modern Angola missions, were the object of violent articles and political accusations in Portuguese newspapers and other publications, despite the fact that their actions had given no justification whatsoever for these attacks. Father Duparquet in particular has been fully vindicated by Antonio Brasio, C.S.Sp., who could never be suspected of minimizing Portugal's rights. Cf. Antonio Brasio, "A 'Politica' do Padre Duparquet no Sul de Angola," *Portugal em Africa,* 1946, pp. 168 ff.; A. da Silva Rego, *Curso de Missionologia,* Lisbon, 1956, pp. 302 ff.

CHAPTER TWENTY

THE MISSIONS OF THE HOLY GHOST FATHERS
IN AFRICA

In this chapter we shall briefly consider the various African missions of the Congregation insofar as their history has not yet been covered in preceding pages. Obviously, it will be impossible to present here a detailed history of every Spiritan mission in Africa, for such an undertaking would require several volumes. We shall limit ourselves to a cursory survey of each center, dwelling somewhat longer on those that offer special points of interest.

1. SENEGAL

The Spiritan missions in Senegal comprise the old Prefecture of St. Louis, the Archdiocese of Dakar, and the Diocese of Ziguinchor.

a. THE PREFECTURE OF ST. LOUIS

cf. pp. 29 ff.

In Chapter II we related how the Congregation took charge of this ancient mission in 1779 and we traced its early history up to the French Revolution. The subsequent story may be conveniently divided into two periods: from 1816 to 1852, and from 1852 to the present. The first of these closely resembles the turbulent history of the other old French colonies.

Cl. C. 17 ff.

1816-1852. When England returned Senegal to France after the Napoleonic wars, there was not a single priest left in the Prefecture. Catholic life had all but disappeared from the two French settlements at St. Louis and Gorée, the only places effectively occupied by France.

Cl. C. 58 ff.

Though it was extremely small at that time, the Prefecture seems to have caused more conflict and turmoil than several of the other larger colonies combined. In thirty-six years the series of twelve Prefects and Vice-Prefects appears to have encountered continual and serious trouble with the government, with their fellow priests, and even with the courageous Sisters of Cluny who had established schools and hospitals in the area. Several of these stormy characters had to be deposed because they were completely unfit for their office. It would be much too tedious to follow all of them in their petty conflicts. We will limit ourselves to relating the noisiest of these affairs.

Cl. C. 60 ff.   In 1819, a Father Terrasse arrived in the colony to take over from a predecessor who had stayed only seven months and then left in disgust. Father Terrasse lasted only one month. Angered by Governor Schmaltz' authoritarian and hostile attitude, he tried to even the score by placing St. Louis under interdict before he departed for France. This heartless and irresponsible use of his power had no punitive effect whatsoever on the irreligious Governor, but it struck heavily at the innocent Sisters of Cluny and the few practising Catholics of the town. Because of Father Terrasse's persistent refusal to lift his censure and because communications with Europe were so poor, twenty months passed before the Propaganda overruled the Prefect and lifted the ban. During all this time, Mass could not be celebrated in the town nor could the sacraments be administered to anyone except the dying. Feeling somewhat responsible for the distress of the poor nuns, the Governor managed to alleviate their pitiful condition by occasionally arranging for the navy to pick up the Sisters and anyone else who wanted to avail himself of the opportunity, and transport them outside the interdicted area so that they might hear Mass and receive the sacraments from a navy chaplain.

Ap. H. 80 f.
Cl. C. 177 ff.   State interference in Church affairs reached a climax in Senegal during this period. The Governor simply regarded the Prefect and his priests as subordinate civil officials. He appointed the pastors, fixed the time for Mass, and ordered the Prefect to send the girls of the convent school to his parties because of their "educational" value. Anyone who dared oppose him ran the risk of being peremptorily shipped back to France for insubordination. Having little or no knowledge of ecclesiastical matters, the Governors

Cl. C. 202   often made ridiculous decisions. On one occasion, before leaving for France, a Prefect appointed Father Boilat confessor of the Sisters, although the nuns insisted on Father Fridoil. The petty conflict finally reached the Governor's desk. Trying to find a compromise that would satisfy both the Prefect and the Sisters, the Governor proposed this solution: Father Fridoil will hear the Sisters' confessions and then Father Boilat will give them absolution!

The untenable state of affairs ended in 1852 when, thanks to Father Libermann, a new ecclesiastical system was devised for the colonies. Under this covenant, the Congregation staffed the Prefecture, and the local government lost its death grip on Church affairs.

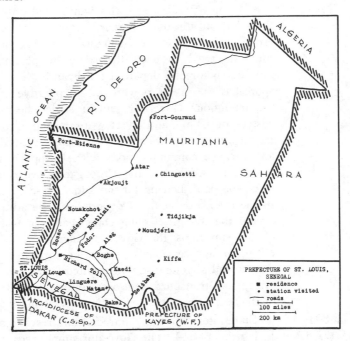

Before we consider this new period, however, we must explain why this old Spiritan-controlled Prefecture did not become the spring-board for a successful evangelization of Africa.

As has been pointed out before, the few priests sent to Senegal were State-paid and State-controlled chaplains assigned specifically to the French settlements of St. Louis and Gorée. They were not free to engage in missionary work in the proper sense of the term. Moreover, their short terms of office, their constant clashes with the government, and their ignorance of the native languages left them little if any opportunity to busy themselves with the Negroes who did not live in the immediate vicinity of their residence. Some of the Prefects, such as Father Baradère, displayed serious interest in doing something for the native population but without tangible results.

A. R. 30, 201 f.

Cl. C. 235 f.

The efforts of Father Baradère merit consideration if only because of their extravagant nature. He was convinced, and justly so, that any attempt to Christianize the Negroes would require adaptation to their temperament and customs. However, he went to such extremes in this regard that his whole plan was reduced

Piolet, V, 107

to absurdity. The priests who were to undertake this work, he decided, "must on landing leave their clothes and shoes behind, dress in loin-cloths, live on canary seed and dried fish, walk barefoot on the burning sands, sleep on mats and reeds," and identify themselves completely with the savages they hoped to convert. When no volunteers presented themselves for this utopian project, he set about starting a local native seminary. Thereafter, he systematically refused any additional European clergy lest they might try to foil his plan. When he realized in 1822 that his ideas could not be executed, he resigned his function.

Storme, 56 ff.

Although Father Baradère had failed, Mother Javouhey, Superior General of the Sisters of Cluny, saw one good point in his plan: to make use of a native clergy in the conversion of Africa. In 1824, on her own initiative, she founded a seminary in France for African candidates. Her ultimate goal was to arrive at the establishment of a male branch of her religious society, in which white and black priests would unite their efforts for the Christianization of Africa. Although this plan failed partly because of the

cf. p. 60

opposition of Father Fourdinier, the Superior General of the Holy Ghost Fathers, who feared clerical competition in the colonies, three of her Negro seminarians reached the priesthood and returned to Senegal. As has been related in Chapter VIII, it was only when Father Libermann took the lead in evangelizing Africa that the idea of a native clergy was pursued seriously and brought to a more successful conclusion.

Ap. H. 94 ff.

1852 to the Present. During most of this period, the Vicar Apostolic residing in Dakar served as Prefect Apostolic of Senegal also. Despite continuous efforts, the Catholic Church has never made much headway in this thoroughly Mohammedan country. As the reader undoubtedly knows, the same situation prevails in nearly all Islamized lands and constitutes one of the most puzzling and poignant problems faced by Christian missionaries.

B. G. 24, 20 ff.

In the last decades of the nineteenth and especially the first decade of the present century, the Prefecture was gravely afflicted by the sectarian laws of the anticlerical French government, which secularized the flourishing primary and secondary schools staffed by the Sisters of Cluny and the Brothers of Ploermel. It even drove the nuns from the hospital they had conducted for nearly a century at St. Louis. Heads high, and under the leadership of Mother Germaine whom a previous government had made an Officer of the Legion of Honor for her services to the colony, the courageous Sisters refused to leave Senegal. Settling down in makeshift quarters, they busied themselves with all kinds of charitable and apostolic works. The enraged Governor went so far as to forbid any Catholic youth meetings and even simple group outings on the ground that these disturbed the public order! The end result of all these measures was to unite the Christians still more closely with their priests and nuns. On the other hand, as far as the non-Christians were concerned, the official policy of heavily favoring Islam prevented any worthwhile expansion of the Church.

M. C. 6, 120
N. D. 9, 443

Ap. H. 101

E. P. 31, I, 93

After World War I, when this government policy was softened somewhat, the mission suffered another setback by the emigration of large numbers of native Christians to other regions: the town of St. Louis alone saw about ninety percent of its young married couples leave for other destinations. Thus it is not surprising that the Prefecture still counts only about five thousand Catholics in a population of more than one million.[1]

b. THE ARCHDIOCESE OF DAKAR

cf. pp. 75
ff.; pp. 191
ff.; pp. 445 ff.
Ap. H. 78 ff.
Br. 509 ff.
C. A. 1955/56

The earlier history of this ecclesiastical circumscription coincides with that of the Two Guineas and Senegambia. It has already been referred to on several occasions in preceding chapters.[2]

Although Dakar is one of the oldest missions of the Congregation, the number of its Catholics is still relatively small: 97,501 out of a total population of more than one and one half million

---

[1] Its territory includes nearly the whole of Mauritania in which there are about fifteen hundred Catholics.

A. M. C. 43

[2] In 1863, the Vicariate of Senegambia was separated from that of the Two Guineas. Subsequently, the Vicar of Senegambia lost jurisdiction over French Guinea (1897), West Sudan (1901), British Gambia (1931), Casamance and Upper Gambia (1939), Northern Senegal and Mauritania (1954), and Kaolack (1956). Its name was changed to the Vicariate of Dakar in 1936 and in 1955 it became the Archdiocese of Dakar. For the former

pp. 448 ff.

Spiritan missions in West Sudan, see Chapter XIX.

A. M. C. 34 ff. and even 30,000 of these are European settlers. Such unimpressive figures are due to a number of factors: the local Mohammedan chiefs whose opposition sometimes found expression in physical violence, the recurrent epidemics of yellow fever which often thinned the ranks of the missionaries, the irreligious laws of anticlerical French governments which, especially at the turn of the century, struck at Catholic schools and hospitals and courted the

cf. pp. 493 f. favor of Islamism. When one remembers that it was here also that the early missionaries made the mistake of not using catechists extensively, it is easy to see why its numerical strength is still so small. Although 300,000 pagans still inhabit the area, the bulk of the population (over 1,000,000) has embraced Mohammedanism.[3]

cf. p. 150 Misfortune seems to have pursued even the Ecclesiastical Superiors of this mission. No less than three of them have perished by drowning. Father Tisserant's shipwreck was already recounted in Chapter VI. A successor, Bishop Francis Künemann, after

B. G. 24, 500; presiding at a patronal feast in Ngazobil in 1908, disappeared from
527 the forty-ton mission schooner, the *Saint Joseph,* on the way back to Dakar. Fishermen found the little sailboat floating on its side one month later, but the bishop's sun-helmet was the only trace left of the prelate and his seven-man crew. His successor, Bishop

B. G. 29, 550 ff. Hyacinth Jalabert, went down with eighteen other Spiritans in the 1920 disaster of the *SS. Afrique.*

B. G. 42, 96 ff. Dakar, the capital of French West Africa, became the seat of an Apostolic Delegation in 1948 when its Vicar Apostolic, Bishop Marcel Lefebvre, C.S.Sp., was appointed the Holy See's official representative in all French controlled territories of continental and insular Africa. Seven years later, when the Hierarchy was established in these territories, Dakar became an Archdiocese. These administrative decisions resulted in the creation of central offices for education, social work, and the press,—an arrangement that has brought Africa's most important missionary societies into close collaboration. The White Fathers staff the press division, the Society of African Missions has the general direction of all educational works, and the Spiritans are responsible for the social program.

---

[3]These figures include the recently erected Prefecture of Kaolack.

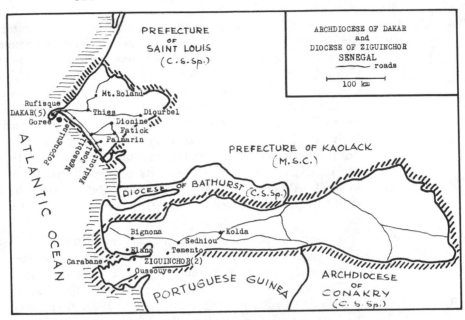

ARCHDIOCESE OF DAKAR
and
DIOCESE OF ZIGUINCHOR
SENEGAL
————— roads
100 km

PREFECTURE
OF
SAINT LOUIS
(C.S.Sp.)

Mt. Roland

Rufisque
DAKAR(5)
Goree
Thies
Diourbel
Dionine
Fatick
Palmarin

Porongine
Ngaobil
Joal
Fadiout

ATLANTIC OCEAN

PREFECTURE OF KAOLACK
(M.S.C.)

DIOCESE OF BATHURST (C.S.Sp.)

Bignona
Sedhiou
Kolda
Elana
Temento
Carabane
ZIGUINCHOR(2)
Oussouye

PORTUGUESE GUINEA

ARCHDIOCESE
OF
CONAKRY
(C.S.Sp.)

ibid.

Social works have become an important aspect of the priests' work in modern Senegal, especially in the urbanized areas. To counteract the danger of modern materialism, the missionaries have recently founded all kinds of "organizations for children, young men, and adults, not copying slavishly what is done in old Christian countries, but taking their inspiration from them and adapting these works" to local conditions.

To provide both European and native youth with an opportunity for Catholic higher education, the mission undertook the construction of a new college for seven hundred students on a twelve-acre campus near the city of Dakar and entrusted it to the Marist Fathers. Secondary education is given in thirty-seven schools and the numerous Catholic students attending the new local university are taken care of by a special organization. For the propagation of the Faith among the three hundred thousand remaining pagans, the Archdiocese now has a well-developed system of catechetical posts manned by 359 native religion-teachers.

c. THE DIOCESE OF ZIGUINCHOR

B. G. 42, 160 ff.

In 1939, the Holy See separated Southern Senegal from Dakar, constituted it an independent Prefecture, and entrusted it to Monsignor Joseph Faye, C.S.Sp., the first Negro prelate in the Spiritan missions. Though hampered by an attack of sleeping sickness and plagued by the difficulties of World War II, he did so well that when he went to Europe in 1946, everyone expected him to return with a mitre and crosier. Instead, the humble prelate resigned and withdrew shortly after to a Trappist monastery, where he was soon followed by his priest-brother Edward. His successor, Monsignor Prosper Dodds, a native of St. Louis, Senegal, modernized and developed his mission quite successfully in a few years' time by means of an admirable school system. In 1952 the Holy See raised his Prefecture to the status of a Vicariate and three years later it became a regular diocese.

C. A. 1955/56   The most recent statistics report 22,447 Catholics out of a total population of 371,563. Although Islamism is very strong in these regions, there are still 56,000 pagans among whom the work of the Church may be blessed with immediate results. Compared to the rest of Senegal, Ziguinchor (Southern Senegal) is rich in vocations. It has forty-three seminarians and twenty-four native religious Brothers and Sisters.

Protestantism has hardly any adherents in Senegal. All sects combined do not exceed 2,400 members, and most of these are immigrants living in the cities of Dakar and St. Louis.

ECCLESIASTICAL SUPERIORS OF ST. LOUIS (SENEGAL)

1. *Prefecture of St. Louis*

Fr. Dominic de Glicourt, C.S.Sp., 1779-1781
Fr. Massoulard de Maffrand, 1781-1783 (Vice Prefect)
Fr. Costes, 1783-1784
Fr. Saye, 1784 (Vice Prefect)
Fr. Le Rendu, 1784-1790
Fr. Charbonnier, 1790-1794
Fr. Giudicelli, 1816-1818
Fr. Terrasse, 1818-1819
(interdict: 1819-1820)
Fr. Henry Baradère, 1820-1822
Fr. Fournier, 1822-1824
Fr. Girardon, 1825-1832
Fr. Mohanan, 1833-1835
Fr. Mareille, 1835-1841
Fr. Maynard, 1841-1843
Fr. John Arlabosse, 1843-1848 (Vice Prefect); entered the Congregation in 1849

Fr. John Vidal, C.S.Sp., 1848-1849
Fr. David Boilat, 1849-1850 (Vice Prefect)
Fr. Peter Guyard, 1850-1852
Fr. Isaias Boulanger, C.S.Sp., 1852-1854
Fr. Emmanuel Barbier, C.S.Sp., 1854-1856
Fr. John Duret, C.S.Sp., 1856-1873 (after 1873 also Vicar Apostolic of Senegambia)
1873-1898: the Vicars Apostolic of Senegambia (Dakar)
Fr. John Pascal, C.S.Sp., 1898-1899
1899-1955: the Vicars Apostolic of Senegambia (Dakar)
Msgr. Joseph Landreau, C.S.Sp., 1955-

2. *Senegambia (Dakar)*

H. E. Aloysius Kobès, C.S.Sp., 1848-1863, Titular Bishop of Modon, (in dependence on the Vicar Apostolic of the Two Guineas)

Vicars Apostolic

H. E. Aloysius Kobès, C.S.Sp., 1863-1872
H. E. John Duret, C.S.Sp., 1873-1875, Titular Bishop of Antigone
H. E. Francis Duboin, C.S.Sp., 1876-1883, Titular Bishop of Raphanea
H. E. Francis Riehl, C.S.Sp., 1883-1886, Titular Bishop of Colophon
H. E. Mathurin Picarda, C.S.Sp., 1887-1889, Titular Bishop of Paphos
H. E. Magloire Barthet, C.S.Sp., 1889-1898, Titular Bishop of Abdera
H. E. Joachim Buleon, C.S.Sp., 1899-1900, Titular Bishop of Cariopolis
H. E. Francis Künemann, C.S.Sp., 1901-1908, Titular Bishop of Pella
H. E. Hyacinth Jalabert, C.S.Sp., 1909-1920, Titular Bishop of Telepta
H. E. Louis Le Hunsec, C.S.Sp., 1920-1926, Titular Bishop of Europus (later Superior General and Titular Archbishop of Marcianopolis)
H. E. Augustus Grimault, C.S.Sp., 1927-1946, Titular Bishop of Maximianopolis
H. E. Marcel Lefebvre, C.S.Sp., 1947-1955, Titular Bishop of Antedone; 1948 Titular Archbishop of Arcadiopolis and Apostolic Delegate of French Africa

Archbishop of Dakar

H. E. Marcel Lefebvre, C.S.Sp., 1955-
(Auxiliary Bishop H. E. George Guibert, C.S.Sp., Titular Bishop of Dices)

3. *Ziguinchor*

Prefects Apostolic

Msgr. Joseph Faye, C.S.Sp., 1939-1946
Msgr. Prosper Dodds, C.S.Sp., 1947-1952

Vicar Apostolic

Prosper Dodds, C.S.Sp., 1952-1955, Titular Bishop of Bennessa

Bishop

H. E. Prosper Dodds, C.S.Sp., 1955-

RELIGIOUS SUPERIORS, C.S.SP.

Till 1939: the Ecclesiastical Superior of Dakar
Fr. Charles Walther, 1939-1950
Fr. Alexis Quenet, 1950-1954
Fr. John Bourgoing, 1954-

2. FRENCH GUINEA

Br. 514 ff.
Ap. H. 103 ff.
B. G. 42,
196 ff.

    This country, which is situated between Portuguese Guinea and Sierra Leone and reputed to be one of Africa's most unhealthy regions, was first evangelized by the Spiritans in 1877. At the request of King Katty's sons, who had been educated at the mission school of Gorée in Senegal, the Fathers from Sierra Leone opened a residence at Boffa on the Rio Pongo.[4] The first decade of its history witnessed a tragic succession of native revolts and

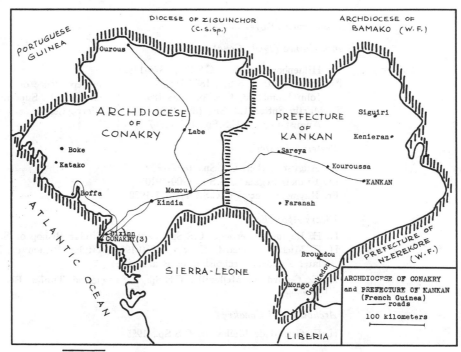

[4]In 1897, French Guinea was erected as a separate Prefecture carved out of portions of the Senegambia and Sierra Leone missions. It became a Vicariate in 1920.

military repressions in which the pioneer Fathers at Boffa often acted as mediators and arbitrators between the opposing forces and occasionally became the innocent victims of the conflict.

Poor in resources and understaffed, the mission developed very slowly and, since the immediate hinterland was fully Islamized, it clung to the coast for a long time. In 1902, however, a residence was founded beyond the Mohammedan belt at Brouadou in the eastern part of the country. Since then, thanks especially to Bishop Lerouge's energetic direction, missionary work has made more rapid progress.

In 1955, Conakry, the capital, became an archdiocese. The remainder of the colony is divided between the Spiritan Prefecture of Kankan and the White Fathers' Prefecture of Nzerekore. Latest reports list nearly 24,000 Catholics in the two circumscriptions of the Holy Ghost Fathers, with a total population of about two million of whom 350,000 are as yet untouched by Mohammedanism.

C. A. 1955/56

ECCLESIASTICAL SUPERIORS

French Guinea (1949: Conakry)

Fr. Hildephonse Muller, C.S.Sp., 1876-1881
Fr. Joseph Lutz, C.S.Sp., 1882-1885
Fr. John Raimbault, C.S.Sp., 1885-1892 } in dependence on the Ecclesiastical Superior of Sierra Leone
Fr. Martin Sutter, C.S.Sp., 1892-1894
Fr. August Lorber, C.S.Sp., 1894-1897

Prefects Apostolic

Fr. August Lorber, C.S.Sp., 1897-1899
Fr. Francis Segala, C.S.Sp., 1900-1910
Fr. Raymond Lerouge, C.S.Sp., 1911-1920

Vicars Apostolic

H. E. Raymond Lerouge, C.S.Sp., 1920-1949, Titular Bishop of Selga
H. E. Michael Bernard, C.S.Sp., 1950-1954, Titular Bishop of Eggea (later Resident Archbishop of Brazzaville)

H. E. Gerard de Melleville, C.S.Sp., 1955, elected Titular Bishop of Dalisando

Archbishop of Conakry

H. E. Gerard de Melleville, C.S.Sp., 1955-

Prefecture of Kankan

Msgr. Maurice le Mailloux, C.S.Sp., 1950-

RELIGIOUS SUPERIORS C.S.SP. OF FRENCH GUINEA

Till 1939: the Ecclesiastical Superior of French Guinea
Fr. Marius Balez, 1939-1947
Fr. George Cousart, 1947-1953
Fr. Gerard de Milleville, 1953-1955 (later Archbishop of Conakry)
Fr. Louis de Courcy, 1955-

3. CAPE VERDE ISLANDS

da Silva, 259 ff.
B. G. 42, 470 ff.

About three hundred miles off the shore of Senegal lies the archipelago of the Cape Verde Islands. It is composed of ten large and a number of smaller islands, populated by about 150,000 souls, nearly all of them Negroes or Afro-Portuguese. As early as 1533 the Holy See erected a diocese in the islands which at that time held jurisdiction over a large part of Africa.[5]

Nearly the whole population is Catholic in name, but its Faith has suffered from many years' neglect. Out of the four centuries of its existence, the diocese spent one hundred and fifty years without a resident prelate. Capuchin, Franciscan and Jesuit missionaries found it necessary to abandon the islands because of their unhealthy climate or because of political opposition. The extreme isolation of nearly all parishes made it most difficult to maintain a secular clergy worthy of the name. All this engendered an abysmal ignorance of the Faith and a moral corruption that manifested itself mostly in the form of concubinage.

The Holy Ghost Fathers arrived in these islands only in 1941. At that time, the Holy See asked them to extend their labors to this long-neglected population and it made one of them, Monsignor Faustin Moreira dos Santos, Bishop of Cape Verde.[6] At that time there were only ten priests left in the islands. Seven of these were ill and six of them had passed the age of sixty-three.

B. G. 42, 473 f.

One of the greatest obstacles the Spiritans met in their new apostolate was the scandalous way in which their predecessors tolerated moral disorder. Making a "distinction between the 'old doctrine' and the 'new doctrine,'" many people still "prefer the old pastors who demanded only baptism, marriage, and a church funeral and closed their eyes to superstitious customs and immorality. Even now they resist the new priests who insist on a serious Christian way of living . . . Concubinage seems to enjoy a

---

[5]In 1940 its jurisdiction was restricted officially to the Archipelago.
[6]The diocese is not officially entrusted to the Congregation.

kind of traditional legitimacy because, in the past, several secular priests permitted public sinners to act as baptismal sponsors and even to receive the sacraments."

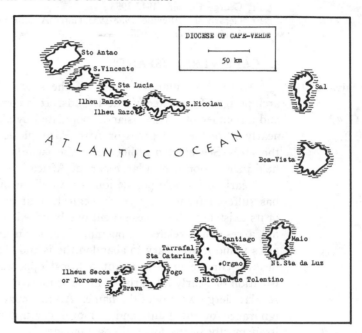

Despite these grave aberrations, which it will take a long time to abolish, the people are sincerely attached to the Church. Two Protestant sects, the Nazarenes and the Seventh Day Adventists, have been at work among them since the beginning of World War II, but they have made very little progress.

To revitalize this lapsed Christianity, the Fathers have established a chain of 238 catechists, opened two dozen schools and organized a number of pious associations. In addition, they are doing their utmost to revive the training of a local clergy which, as late as fifty years ago, was numerous enough to staff all the parishes of the diocese. Finally, a start has been made toward forming local branches of Catholic Action.

E. P. 31, I, 96

B. G. 42, 477

At present, twelve Capuchins, three Salesians, fourteen Holy Ghost Fathers, and nine Holy Ghost Sisters are working in this mission about which "one can say without fear of exaggeration that there is not a colony in the world which is as abandoned and as poor as the Cape Verde Islands."

ECCLESIASTICAL SUPERIORS OF THE DIOCESE OF CAPE VERDE

Bishop Faustino Moreïra dos Santos, C.S.Sp., 1941-1955
Bishop José-Filipe do Carmo Colaço, 1956-

RELIGIOUS SUPERIORS C.S.Sp.

Fr. Henry Alves, 1942-1946 (in dependence on the Provincial Superior of Portugal)
Fr. Francis Alves do Rego, 1946-1955
Fr. Joseph Pereira de Oliveira, 1955-

4. GAMBIA

B. G. 43, 216 ff. ; 242 ff.

Gambia is a British colony and protectorate that stretches for three hundred miles along the Gambia River and runs back seven miles deep on each bank. It has a population of about 275,000, four-fifths of whom are Mohammedans.

Although it did not become an independent mission until 1931, its Spiritan history dates back to 1849. At that time Fathers Ronac'h[7] and Warlop were the first Catholic missionaries to arrive in Bathurst and they began their apostolic labors among the Negroes of this coastal area. For a long time thereafter, all missionary efforts were confined to Bathurst and its immediate surroundings. As a result, a small community of thoroughly devout Christians grew up in this town, but the pagans of the interior

cf. pp. 493 f.

remained untouched. This tragic mistake, as we learned in Chapter XIX, gave Islam an unopposed opportunity for proselytizing. It was only in the last thirty years, under the direction of Father John Meehan, that a concerted effort was made to reach the fifty thousand natives of the protectorate who had not yet fallen under the sway of the Prophet. Father Meehan founded a string of residences and catechetical posts in the remote inland areas of Gambia and thereby began a systematic campaign of conversion.

The ordinary difficulties of every mission are intensified and compounded in Gambia by the indifference of the people, the ravages of disease and death among a constantly changing personnel, and the lack of enthusiastic government help. Fortunately, the mission was able to occupy a number of key positions before native Mohammedan officials (who, incidentally, were government sup-

N. D. 13, App., 70

[7]Father Ronac'h returned to France in 1850 and died of tuberculosis the following year. Although he has never been formally considered for beatification, he had the reputation of being a saint. The population of Brittany, where he was buried, venerates his grave.

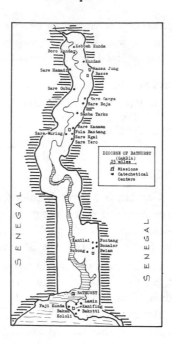

ported) could jeopardize its expansion. In 1945, when the civil authorities reorganized primary education, the mission managed to maintain its schools as an organic unit within the new system, even though the State acquired more control than it had previously enjoyed. A government effort to abolish the mission's secondary schools and replace them by a secular state-controlled institution failed before the determined resistance of a local Legislative Council that was dissatisfied with the poor record of the secular elementary schools. Nevertheless, the danger of secularization still remains. The mission's resolve never to abandon its two secondary schools may yet force it to divert much of its already meager resources to the maintenance of these establishments.

C. A. 1955/56   In 1957, the Holy See raised Gambia Prefecture to the status of a diocese. Although its latest statistics show only 4,151 Catholics, the future looks bright because there are more than 2,600 children in the forty-four schools of the mission.

ECCLESIASTICAL SUPERIORS OF GAMBIA

   Till 1931: dependent on the Ecclesiastical Superior of Dakar. then an independent mission; 1957 Diocese.

Fr. John Meehan, C.S.Sp., 1931-1946
Fr. Matthew Farrelly, C.S.Sp., 1946-1951
Msgr. Michael Moloney, C.S.Sp., Prefect Apostolic, 1951-1957
H. E. Michael Moloney, C.S.Sp., Bishop of Bathurst, 1958-

RELIGIOUS SUPERIORS C.S.SP.

Till 1931: see Senegambia (Dakar)
1931-1940: Fr. John Meehan
1940: district combined with Sierra Leone

5. SIERRA LEONE

Walker, 100

This British colony and protectorate lies between French Guinea and Liberia and has an estimated population of about two and one half million. To many people it is better known as "The White Man's Grave" because of its extremely treacherous climate. For a long time, no government official or commercial agent was allowed to remain there beyond a year. In more recent times, however, thanks to advances in hygiene and tropical medicine, conditions have much improved. The coastal population descends from former slaves out of every race and tribe in West Africa. This situation has given rise to a special kind of *lingua franca* called Pidgin English, and it is the only thing understood by uneducated natives.[8]

cf. pp. 193

Chapter VIII recorded how this country received its first Catholic missionaries in 1859 when Bishop Marion de Brésillac, the founder of the Society of African Missions, landed here with his priests in an ill-fated attempt to bring the Gospel. After the untimely death of that zealous group, the Holy See returned the mission to the Holy Ghost Fathers. In 1864, they undertook its evangelization by sending Father Blanchet and a companion over from Bathurst.

By that time Protestant pastors had been active in Sierra Leone for more than eighty years and the reception accorded the Catholic missionaries was far from friendly. Father Schwager, S.V.D., a historian of the African missions, described it as follows: "When

---

Walker, 103

[8]The following is an example of a short religious instruction in pidgin English: "You sabe God? How much God dey? Nar wan God no more dey. He big pass all ting. Three persons dey inside dat wan God—God Fader, God Son, God Holy Ghost. Now way ting God Son go do for we? He go die for we for pull sin na we soul, and after He done die for we dey done bury Him and He go Heaven for make we all sit down day inside one house wi Him, where we bin gladdie all time, palaver no dey at all, no humbug at all. Christ He make one Church no more. He wish all man for be inside one Church na Cat'lic Church."

Engel, 135　the first missionaries arrived, the bells of the numerous Protestant churches tolled, not to invite people to prepare a friendly reception, but to incite them against the Catholic priests. The move was so successful that the governor had to protect the missionaries against

B. G. 4, 97 ff.;　the fury of the angry mob." Official reports, however, do not
320, 768　mention these excesses. They merely relate that the Protestant preachers gave a series of sermons against the newcomers and stuck posters all over Freetown to denounce Rome and Popery. The excitement subsided after the arrival of an Anglican bishop who forbade such sermons and insisted that everyone be left free to live according to his convictions. Through all the uproar, the

M. C. 2, 401 f.　silent and dignified attitude of the priests and their great charity for the sick and the poor impressed the citizens of Freetown and soon gained for them much popular esteem and sympathy.

B. G. 43,　　Although Freetown, under Father Blanchet, became the start-
115 ff.　ing-point for missionary work in French Guinea, in Liberia, and
Ap. H. 111 ff.　especially in Nigeria, little progress was made in rural Sierra Leone itself. It was not until 1902 that the missionaries could report any success among the tribes of the interior. One year after that, the Irish-American Bishop John O'Gorman, C.S.Sp. came to Sierra Leone as its Vicar Apostolic. For nearly thirty years, with the assistance of other Spiritans from the American Province, he spent his energies in behalf of this stoney corner of the Lord's Vineyard. The natives' indifference to education, their lack of concern for religion, and their low economic condition made it heart-breaking work.

Since World War II, however, the situation has changed radically. There has been a sudden burst of interest in education, and the mission has profited by the new enthusiasm, particularly through a sevenfold increase of government grants for its schools. The educational system has been greatly expanded. In 1952 alone, for example, the Spiritans opened twenty new schools in the pro-tectorate—four times as many as all other public and private agen-

C. A. 1955/56　cies combined. Most recent figures show 122 Catholic primary schools, two technical, three secondary, and three teacher-training schools. The mission's splendid progress in the course of the last decade must be attributed in great part to this extensive develop-ment of teaching facilities.

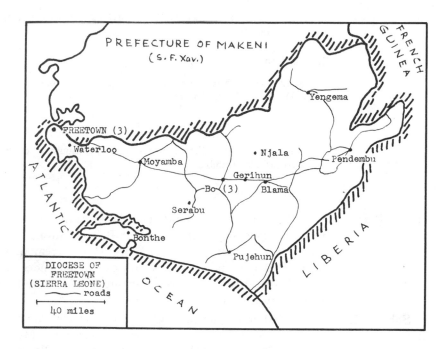

C. A. 1955/56   In 1952 the Vicariate was raised to the status of a Diocese with over 14,000 Catholics and nearly 10,000 catechumens. Protestant sects claim about 62,000 followers, and the number of Mohammedans is estimated at about 200,000. The northern province of the colony is now a Prefecture entrusted to the Xaverian priests.

Ecclesiastical Superiors

Bishop Melchior de Marion-Brézillac, S.M.A., Vicar Apostolic, 1858

Fr. John Blanchet, C.S.Sp., 1863-1869

Fr. Anthony Fritsch, C.S.Sp., 1869-1870

Fr. Joseph d'Hyevre, C.S.Sp., 1870-1874

Fr. Charles Gommenginger, C.S.Sp., 1874-1879, Vice Prefect Apostolic (in dependence on Superior General as Pro-Vicar Apostolic)

Fr. John Blanchet, C.S.Sp., 1879-1892 (second term), Pro-Vicar Apostolic

Fr. James Browne, C.S.Sp., 1892-1903, Pro-Vicar Apostolic

H. E. John O'Gorman, C.S.Sp., 1903-1932, Vicar Apostolic and Titular Bishop of Amastri

H. E. Bartholomew Wilson, C.S.Sp., 1933-1936, Vicar Apostolic and Titular Bishop of Acmonia (transferred from Bagamoyo Vicariate)

H. E. Ambrose Kelly, C.S.Sp., 1937-1952, Vicar Apostolic and Titular Bishop of Altava

H. E. Thomas Brosnahan, C.S.Sp., 1952-   , Resident Bishop of Freetown and Bo

RELIGIOUS SUPERIORS C.S.SP.

Till 1939: the Ecclesiastical Superior of Sierra Leone
Fr. David J. Lloyd, 1939-1947
Fr. Edward Kinsella, 1947-
Fr. Thomas Clarkin, 1951-1954
Fr. John Cassin, 1954-
Since 1940 the jurisdiction of the Religious Superior of Sierra Leone
also includes Gambia.

APPENDIX: LIBERIA

cf. pp. 80 ff.

In Chapter V we learned how Libermann's first missionaries, under the leadership of the American Bishop Edward Barron, inaugurated their apostolate in the Cape Palmas region of this free Negro Republic and how this first expedition ended disastrously in 1844. After that, no further attempts were made to evangelize the country for the next forty years.

C. S. L. 87 ff.
B. G. 13, 750 ff.
14, 349 ff.;
15, 439 ff.
Ap. H. 120 ff.

In 1880 and again in 1882 the Liberian government asked the Holy See to send a few missionaries to its capital, Monrovia. The Propaganda transmitted the request to Father Blanchet in Sierra Leone. He and another Spiritan went over to Liberia in 1884 and they were cordially welcomed by President Johnson[9] and his government. Local Protestant missionaries, however, disapproved thoroughly of the new arrivals. They organized a large protest meeting which sent a resolution to the government demanding the expulsion of the Catholic priests.

They seem to have protested in vain, however, because a Catholic mission, staffed by two Fathers and two Brothers, soon began to function at Monrovia, despite the fact that only two Catholics are reported to have been there at the time. After six months, the Fathers sent word that their flock had increased to twenty and that another score was scattered along the coast. This modest success incited the opposition to intensify its efforts. Children stoned the priests' residence, spies followed them and reported on their every move. Finally, the Spiritans decided to concentrate their labor on the pagans of the interior who were not yet touched by Protestantism. Before they could undertake a permanent estab-

---

[9]His family professed the Catholic Faith before it migrated to Liberia.

lishment in the hinterland, however, the extreme poverty of the mission and the unhealthy climate killed two of the confreres and incapacitated the others. By 1887 the survivors found it necessary to withdraw temporarily. Unfortunately, the urgent need of other areas kept the Holy Ghost Fathers from returning to this part of their immense mission. After another missionary failure in 1906—this time it was Grignion de Montfort's Society of Mary—the Society of African Missions succeeded in establishing itself permanently in the country.

Ecclesiastical Superiors

Bishop Edward Barron, 1842-1845, Vicar Apostolic of the Two Guineas

Fr. Auguste Lorber, C.S.Sp., 1884-1885 } in dependence on the Pro-
Fr. Nicholas Stoll, C.S.Sp., 1885-1887 } Vicar of Sierra Leone

6. NIGERIA

Thirty-one million people inhabit the 340,000 square miles of Nigeria, thereby making it one of the most densely populated countries of Africa. Politically it was the private domain of the Royal Niger Company till 1900 when the British government took over the supervision of all native kings and chieftains. At present, Nigeria is approaching independent status and will soon take its place as a member of the British Commonwealth of Nations. While predominantly Mohammedan in the North, Nigeria's South-East section constitutes one of the most abundantly blessed Spiritan missions in Africa and deserves a somewhat fuller treatment than we have been able to accord most of the other areas.[10]

R. H. M. 12, 512.ff
B. G. 14, 458 ff
Ap. H. 128 ff.
Shanahan, 8 ff.

First Beginnings. In 1884, Upper Nigeria was detached from the Vicariate of the Two Guineas and entrusted to the Society of African Missions, but Southern Nigeria remained in the hands of the Holy Ghost Fathers. After a preliminary investigation by Father Leo Lejeune, the Spiritan Superior sent Father Joseph Lutz, Father John Horné, Brother Hermas and Brother John in 1885 to open up this territory for the Church.

[10]For a more comprehensive study of its development between 1905 and 1930, see John P. Jordan, C. S. Sp., *Bishop Shanahan of Southern Nigeria,* Dublin, 1949.

All four were healthy young men in the prime of life. They had been carefully selected for the dangerous undertaking in this cannibalistic land. When they reached Akassa, the local agent of the Royal Niger Commission refused them permission to move upstream. Better luck awaited them at another little port, called Brass, where a friendly agent lent them a small boat for their expedition. Because it was too tiny to accommodate all four, only the two priests set out for the first trip. After wandering for days through creeks and mangrove swamps and open waterways, they landed finally at Onitsha. The local king received them cordially and promised them a suitable piece of land, whereupon Father Lutz left his now ailing companion behind and returned to get the Brothers. On his arrival at the coast, he found one of them dangerously ill and the other worn out by fever and nightly vigils, but they subsequently recovered sufficiently for the party to set out for Onitsha. Soon after they reached their destination, Brother John had to be carried to an early grave while Brother Hermas lay dying and Father Horné was too sick even to attend the funeral. Fortunately, Hermas recovered, but Father Horné

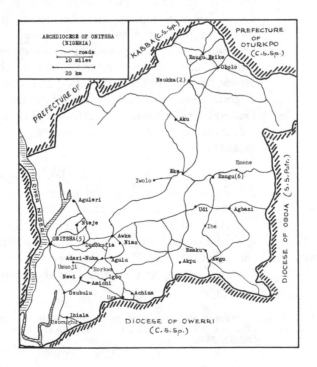

had to return to Europe to restore his shattered health. Thus it was Father Lutz and Brother Hermas who became the hardy pioneers of this mission.

On reading the detailed accounts of the untold sufferings and privations the early missionaries underwent in their apostolic wanderings both here and in other regions of Africa, one cannot suppress an intense feeling of admiration and respect for these intrepid French and Alsatian pioneers who nearly everywhere in Spiritan Africa were the laborers of the first hour. They worked and sowed in tears, all too often without seeing any sign of the golden sheaves later generations were destined to reap in happiness.

As for the pioneers of Nigeria, we may judge the barbarity of their environment from the fact that their residence faced a market-place where clothing and fruit stalls were interspersed with emporiums dealing in human flesh—a commodity that was very much in demand. According to the usual missionary procedure of the time, Father Lutz spent many an hour rescuing victims from the cooking-pots with money supplied by the Anti-slavery Society. In addition, the fearless priest travelled unescorted throughout the surrounding district to make the mission known. Although his daring trips impressed all as an open invitation to slaughter, he somehow escaped this lurid fate and soon merited the natives' deepest respect. After a while they even began to call on him as a peacemaker in their frequent local skirmishes.[11]

B. G. 17, 425 ff.   We may pause here to tell of one instance in which he
M. C. 27, 435 ff. failed to make peace in time, because it graphically illustrates the conditions that existed only a generation ago. One day, word reached him that a band of headhunting Adas tribesmen were marching on Aguleri, about twenty-five miles from Onitsha, where two Spiritans had opened a new mission. Everyone had fled and the priests were utterly defenseless. Jumping into a canoe, he rowed with all possible speed to the assistance of his confreres, only to learn on his arrival that the catechumens had rallied around the mission to defend the Fathers to the death against an enemy who outnumbered them twenty to one. Their courage had impelled the neighboring pagans to join forces with them and, when the Adas did not attack immediately, the local

Shanahan, 173   [11]He was not the only one who excelled as a peacemaker. In 1914, when the war broke out, Nigeria chieftains held a solemn assembly and gravely decided that Father Joseph Bubendorf should be sent home to Europe to settle the palaver between the big chiefs of Germany and England.

troup had gone out to intercept the enemy. A bitter fight was still raging some miles from the place where Father Lutz had just landed, so he rushed over to the battlefield to stop the slaughter or at least to take care of the wounded and baptize the dying. Alas, the intrepid priest arrived too late. The battle had just ended in victory for the village. Hundreds of headless trunks lay all over the area and jubilant preparations were underway around huge cauldrons. While the priest tried in vain to persuade the warriors to relinquish their horrible feast, another batch of prisoners came in. Before his very eyes they were summarily beheaded, dismembered and flung into the boiling water.

On reading such accounts, which were by no means exceptional, one sees why the Spiritans in Nigeria felt obliged to spend so much time ransoming children and slaves from a similar fate. Although the free population did not suffer from total neglect, these rescue operations seriously hindered real progress in the establishment of a native Christian Church and society, as is evidenced by the fact that in 1899 the number of Catholics had barely reached the two thousand mark.

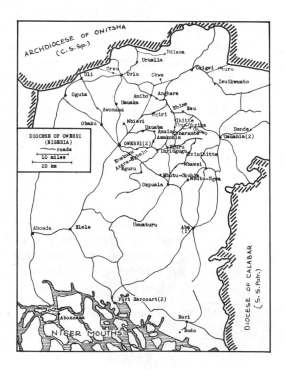

Nevertheless, despite this low figure, the Catholic Faith had already made a fairly profound impression. Signs of it showed in the universal respect for the Catholic priests who displayed such great charity toward the sick, and in the death penalty which, at the request of King Samuel Okosi, the British Government imposed in 1901 to stop the heinous practice of murdering newborn twins. If one realizes that, only fifteen years before, a young man had been killed on the spot for hiding newborn twins in a Protestant mission, one can appreciate the enormous moral advance implicit in such a request coming from a local potentate.

B. G. 21, 78;
512 f.

B. G. 14, 465

Shanahan, 29 ff.
Ap. H. 140 ff.;
Br. 520 ff.;
Walker, 81 ff.

The Successful Approach. A really significant surge forward came in 1905, when Father Joseph Shanahan, C.S.Sp., became Prefect Apostolic and made his momentous decision to concentrate on education. He arrived at an opportune moment, for the British Government had just created the first Board of Education and was seriously planning to expand the feeble school system. Realizing that sponsorship of schools within the government's educational framework would afford a unique opportunity to further the establishment of the Church, the Prefect devoted himself wholeheartedly to the task of creating a network of schools all over his territory. By 1912 he had fifty of them functioning in different towns and villages, and thereafter the mission-school system spread very rapidly. He accomplished his objective by stationing priests in a few strategic points where they would open a school and then use the best students of this school as temporary teachers for subsidiary bush-schools in the surrounding area. After a time, these apprentice teachers were replaced by other students. They would then return to finish their own training, whereupon they would go out to open new schools from which the snowballing process could continue in geometric progression. After a few years of this procedure, the original mission became the vibrant center of an enthusiastic young Christian generation.

Father Shanahan—after 1920 Bishop Shanahan—did not locate his priests merely in areas protected by British power along easy roads of communication. Without any hesitation, he sent them into the interior along narrow bush-tracks to open new schools. Although unarmed and unescorted, none of them suffered the culinary fate so commonly reserved for other travellers, both black and white, for by then the priests had acquired such a reputation for unselfish service to the people that no one dared to harm them.

B. G. 43, 174 ff.   A look at the report of 1926 shows how fully Bishop Shanahan's policy was vindicated after twenty years' implementation:
his vicariate had advanced from 2,000 to 60,000 Christians, and
90,000 catechumens were preparing for baptism.

The Present. When the prelate resigned in 1931, his successor,
Bishop Charles Heerey, C.S.Sp., continued that policy and extended it into the field of higher education by creating a network
of normal schools and colleges, thereby securing further Catholic
training for future teachers and leaders in this rapidly developing
country. When the original Vicariate was subdivided into other
ecclesiastical circumscriptions, the Holy Ghost Fathers established
C. A. 1955/56   the same pattern of operation in them. The statistics show that the
four Mission districts of the Congregation in Southern Nigeria
operate a total of 2,913 primary schools, 14 colleges, 28 normal
schools and 13 technical schools with a total of 406,914 students.[12]
Thanks especially to their splendid school system, these missions
now have 723,432 Christians and 283,472 catechumens who will
join the ranks of the Church within the next three years.

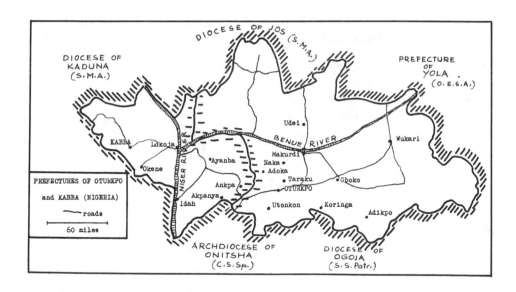

p. 461   [12]As mentioned in Chapter XIX, a Catholic university will soon be
opened in Nigeria.

Two views of the new St. Ann's Cathedral of Brazzaville, French Equatorial Africa. The tower of this huge church, built in so-called "African Gothic" style, is unfinished.

Architect's drawing of the new cathedral that is now under construction in the Diocese of Owerri, Nigeria. It will accommodate three thousand.

A partial view of the stadium built by Father Lecomte alongside St. Ann's Cathedral of Brazzaville.

In 1950, the Holy See raised the Onitsha Vicariate to the rank of an Archidocese, and Owerri became an episcopal see. Although the Nigerian clergy in these two dioceses are not yet very numerous, there are nearly four hundred seminarians preparing themselves for the priesthood. Recently the Congregation opened a seminary for local aspirants to its own ranks. There is every reason to hope that, within the foreseeable future, a self-sufficient Spiritan Province will arise in this country where cannibalism flourished only a generation ago.

B. G. 43, 204 ff.   In the Benue region north of Onitsha, the work of evangelization began only in 1930 when the German Province of the Congregation opened missions there. Nine years later, hopeful signs were already in evidence in the report of two thousand Christians and five thousand catechumens. World War II put a sudden stop to the German confreres' apostolic work, for the British authorities sent them to concentration camps in Jamaica. Since then, this mission has been taken over by English and Canadian Spiritans, for whom the Holy See has created the Prefectures of Oturpko and Kabba. Although missionary priests have been in the area only

C. A. 1955/56   since 1930, Oturpko shows great promise for the future: its latest statistics list approximately 15,000 Catholics and 33,000 catechumens. Kabba has nearly 10,000 Christians, but its future looks less brilliant because Islam is relatively strong in the area and Protestantism has already firmly entrenched itself in many sectors.

The future of the Nigerian missions is presently clouded somewhat by a disturbing tendency on the part of the new native government to arrogate to itself an intolerable measure of control over the education of all children regardless of parental wishes in the matter. Fortunately, the Christian generation that has grown up in the last fifty years is determined to defend the rights of parents to the utmost of its ability.

ECCLESIASTICAL SUPERIORS

Southern Nigeria

Fr. Joseph Lutz, C.S.Sp., 1885-1889, Superior (in dependence on the Pro-Vicar of Sierra Leone)
Fr. Joseph Lutz, C.S.Sp., 1889-1895, Prefect Apostolic
Fr. Joseph Reling, C.S.Sp., 1896-1898, Prefect Apostolic
Fr. Réné Pawlas, C.S.Sp., 1898-1900, Prefect Apostolic
Fr. Leo Lejeune, C.S.Sp., 1900-1905, Prefect Apostolic

Fr. Joseph Shanahan, C.S.Sp., 1905-1920, Prefect Apostolic

H. E. Joseph Shanahan, C.S.Sp., 1920-1931, Vicar Apostolic and Titular Bishop of Abila

H. E. Charles Heerey, C.S.Sp., 1931-1950, Vicar Apostolic and Titular Bishop of Balanea

1934: jurisdiction restricted to Onitsha-Owerri; creation of the Prefectures of Benue and Calabar; 1947: division of Onitsha-Owerri into two vicariates; 1950: creation of a resident Hierarchy.

Archdiocese of Onitsha

H. E. Charles Heerey, C.S.Sp., 1950-   (Co-adjutor Bishop H. E. John Anyogu, Nigerian secular priest, consecrated in 1957)

Vicariate of Owerri

H. E. Joseph Whelan, C.S.Sp., 1948-1950, Titular Bishop of Tiddi

Diocese of Owerri

H. E. Joseph Whelan, C.S.Sp., 1950-

Prefecture of Benue

Msgr. Philip Winterle, C.S.Sp., 1934-1937, Prefect Apostolic
Msgr. Joseph Kirsten, C.S.Sp., 1937-1947
(Bishop Charles Heerey, C.S.Sp., 1939-1948, Apostolic Administrator)
Msgr. James Hagan, C.S.Sp., 1948-1955, Prefect Apostolic
1955: jurisdiction divided into Oturkpo and Kabba.

Prefecture of Oturkpo

Msgr. James Hagan, C.S.Sp., 1955-

Prefecture of Kabba

Msgr. Auguste Delisle, C.S.Sp., 1955-

RELIGIOUS SUPERIORS C.S.SP.,

Till 1940: the Ecclesiastical Superior of Southern Nigeria (Onitsha-Owerri)
Fr. Philip O'Connor, 1940-1948
1948: district divided into Nigeria and Benue
Fr. John Jordan, 1948-1954, Principal Superior of Nigeria
Fr. Daniel Carron, 1954-
Fr. Francis Murray, 1948-1953, Principal Superior of Benue
Fr. Robert Duxbury, 1953-

7. CAMEROONS

After World War I, this former German colony, situated southeast of Nigeria, was divided between France and England as mandates of the League of Nations. The French obtained the larger part, an area of nearly 166,000 square miles, which now has a population of about three and a quarter million. The Adamawa province, where Bishop Shanahan, C.S.Sp., had been Apostolic Administrator during the World War I when the German missionaries were expelled, became a vicariate entrusted to the Fathers of the Sacred Heart. The rest of the French-controlled area was confided to the Holy Ghost Fathers' care.

We observed in Chapter X how the Spiritans returned to the Cameroons during the First World War to replace the German Pallotine Fathers, and how in 1923 the Holy See definitely placed them in charge. When the German Pallotines were forced to abandon the land in which they had worked so fruitfully, they had already accounted for thirty thousand Christians and one could see the first signs of a mass movement toward the Church. It came at a most inopportune moment, for the warring nations had mobilized hundreds of Holy Ghost Fathers and had seriously depleted their seminaries. Consequently, it was impossible to send adequate replacements for the German priests. All the Congregation could allocate was a dozen military chaplains who were obligingly assigned to the Cameroons by the French Army.

Despite the limited man-power, the destruction of many missions, and the extremely rigid baptismal examination imposed by the harassed chaplains, an ever swelling wave of catechumens clamored for admission to the Church. In 1923, when Bishop Vogt was transferred from Bagamoyo to the Cameroons as Vicar Apostolic, the number of Catholics had reached the hundred thousand mark and swarms of catechumens were under instruction for baptism. The poor bishop had only seventeen priests to help him in caring for all these people and his pleas for more men went unheeded for several more years until the ravages of the war had been sufficiently overcome to send reinforcements. By 1930, the Congregation was able to maintain a force of forty-three Fathers in the Cameroons, but at that time there were already more than two hundred thousand Catholics, and the Bishop was even more desperately short-handed than he had been seven years before.

Such phenomenal results with so small a staff can be explained only by the splendid work of the native catechists. Many neophytes returned to their villages and spontaneously set up improvised catechetical schools without even notifying the mission. It sometimes happened that a priest would suddenly find himself in an unknown village, perhaps a hundred and fifty miles away from the

Shanahan, 170 ff.

pp. 275 ff.

Ap. H. 148 ff.
B. G. 32, 606 ff.

Vogt, 117 ff.
Br. 524

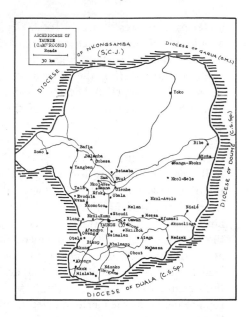

nearest mission and one that never had been visited before by a missionary, yet everyone would know the catechism and many would be making honest efforts to live according to God's law. Even old polygamists would spontaneously send away their super-numerary wives to make themselves worthy of baptism. In the face of such well-disposed sincerity, the priests could do nothing but accept them as members of the Church. Thus it was through the work of the catechists that the Faith made such admirable headway in ever-widening circles. It has been estimated that at one time about ten thousand of them were functioning in the Cameroons.

Vogt, 130 ff.
Ap. H. 151 ff.

The Sixas. A curious institution which has had extraordinary success in the Cameroons is the so-called "Sixas."[13] Before the First World War, German nuns had organized on a small scale a number of establishments in which they prepared future spouses in a kind of pre-marital novitiate. When the Sisters left because of the War, a small group of Catholic young men who wanted their fiancees to be educated in the Faith brought their betrothed to one of the Spiritan missionaries and asked him to instruct them. The hard-pressed Father knew he could not assume this additional

---

[13]This term is a native corruption of the English word "Sisters."

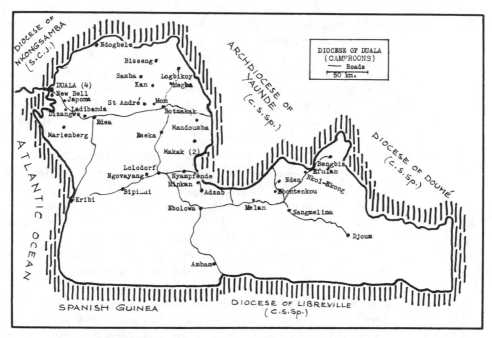

burden, but he was most reluctant to discourage such good will. Accordingly, he entrusted the girls to two African Catholic women who had previously been trained by the Sisters. The pious matrons succeeded so well that soon all other stations opened similar units. These "Sixas" remained entirely under native direction (with supervision by the priests) until the arrival of the Holy Ghost Sisters in 1924 enabled the Bishop to relinquish them gradually to the care of the nuns. The new Sixas were not run on a small scale. Since they were compulsory for all girls preparing for Christian marriage, they developed into huge institutions. The Yaunde station alone had five hundred young ladies in training at the mission itself, another hundred a few miles out, and two hundred more at a day's march away.

It would have been surprising if the success of this work had not given rise to dangerous opposition on the port of certain anti-clerical administrative circles in the Cameroons and in France. Around 1930 a movement was launched to get them abolished under the ridiculous pretext that they were camouflaged forced labor camps and interfered with the honorable native custom of polygamy. Too many girls, it was said, who had been sold to local harems as slave women, took refuge in the Sixas where the priests protected them against the polygamists to whom they had been unwillingly betrothed. When Bishop Vogt and his priests refused to be intimidated by threats and legal accusations of technical rape, slave traffic, and similar offenses, police padlocked a few Sixas, rounded up the refugee wives, and condemned them to return to their condition of slavery with their polygamous husbands. Because this method failed to produce the desired result, the governor finally asked the Minister of the Colonies to suppress the Sixas.

In 1932 meanwhile, the Spiritan Father Henry de Meaupou was killed by an infuriated polygamist to whom he refused to surrender an unwilling concubine. This tragic death made a profound impression throughout the Cameroons. A new governor arrived in the country and saw how foolish it was to ignore the fact that the colony's more than four hundred thousand Christians did not want to live according to the "honorable native custom of polygamy." There was no further move to suppress the Sixas. On the contrary, he promulgated a new marriage law two years later. It considerably improved the social position of women and recognised their natural right to a free and willing marriage. Since then, more or less regular progress has been made toward emancipating women from pagan tyranny.

B. G. 42, 230
ff.; 354 ff.
C. A. 1955/56

Progress. The mass movement toward the Church still shows no sign of abating. The latest statistics of Yaunde and Duala reveal that these two missions now have 473,477 Catholics and 53,854 catechumens. There are still 568,000 pagans, but only 60,000 of these are in Yaunde. Islam has not made much progress, for it counts less than 33,000 members in both missions together. Curiously enough, the surge toward Christianity does not extend to the Protestant churches which have had representatives in the Cameroons since 1845. In the Duala region they are fairly numerous (150,000), but their numbers have not increased in any spectacular way.

Br. 526

Strange as it may seem, the great attraction of the Catholic Faith for the Cameroonese was the sacrament of penance. Contrite confession, followed by an absolution pronounced by the priest in God's name, was the magnetic force which drew them to the Church. The intensity of their devotion to this sacrament forces the priest to spend entire days and nights in the confessional. Nor

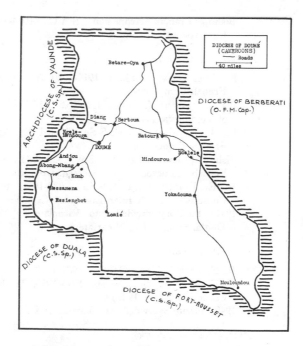

is it unusual for him to have his truck stopped along a primitive road by people who will kneel right there on the running-board to seek God's pardon for their offenses.

B. G. 42, 458 ff.

No such advance can be recorded thus far in the more primitive and less populous region of Doume, which the Dutch Holy Ghost Fathers took charge of in 1947. Nevertheless, there is great promise in its figures of 31,000 Catholics and nearly 9,000 catechumens. Moreover, among the remaining pagan population of 160,000 Islam has not made much headway. Its adherents number less than 4,000.

cf. p. 501

As was mentioned in Chapter XIX, the local clergy is rapidly increasing and two of their number have already been raised to the episcopal dignity.

In 1955, when the Holy See established the hierarchy in French Africa, Yaunde became an archdiocese, and both Duala and Doume received resident bishops.

ECCLESIASTICAL SUPERIORS OF THE CAMEROONS

Fr. Henry Vieter, S.A.C. (Pallotine Fathers), 1890-1905, Prefect Apostolic of Cameroons

Bishop Henry Vieter, S.A.C. 1905-1914, Vicar Apostolic of Cameroons

540   *The Spiritans*

Bishop Francis Henneman, S.A.C., 1914-1922, Vicar Apostolic of Cameroons[14]

French Cameroons

Fr. Jules Douvry, C.S.Sp., 1916-1920, Apostolic Administrator of French French Cameroons

Bishop Joseph Shanahan, C.S.Sp., 1917-1920?, Apostolic Administrator of Adamawa Province

Fr. Louis Malessard, C.S.Sp., 1920-1922, Apostolic Administrator of French Cameroons

Bishop Francis Vogt, C.S.Sp., 1922-1923, Apostolic Administrator of French Cameroons (transferred from the Bagamoyo Vicariate)

H. E. Francis Vogt, C.S.Sp., 1923-1931, Vicar Apostolic of French Cameroons and Titular Bishop of Celenderis

1931: territory divided into Vicariate of Yaunde and Prefecture of Duala, promoted to Vicariate in 1932.

Vicariate of Yaunde

H. E. Francis Vogt, C.S.Sp., 1931-1943

H. E. René Graffin, C.S.Sp., 1943-1955, Titular Bishop of Mosynopolis Co-adjutor since 1931)

1949: territory divided into Yaunde and Doume.

Archdiocese of Yaunde

H. E. René Graffin, C.S.Sp., 1955-
(Co-adjutor Bishop H. E. Paul Etoga, 1955)

Prefecture-Vicariate of Duala

Msgr. Mathurin Le Mailloux, C.S.Sp., 1931-1932, Prefect Apostolic

H.E. Mathurin Le Mailloux, C.S.Sp., 1932-1945, Vicar Apostolic and Titular Bishop of Turuzi

H.E. Peter Bonneau, C.S.Sp., 1946-1955, Vicar Apostolic and Titular Bishop of Themisonium

Diocese of Duala

H.E. Peter Bonneau, C.S.Sp., 1955-1957 (Co-adjutor Bishop H.E. Thomas Mongo, 1956)

H.E. Thomas Mongo, 1957-

Vicariate of Doume (1951)

H.E. James Teerenstra, C.S.Sp., 1949-1951, Titular Bishop of Bure and Auxiliary of Bishop Graffin in charge of the Vicariate of Doume

H.E. James Teerenstra, C.S.Sp., 1951-1955, Vicar Apostolic of Doume

[14]At the death of Bishop Vieter, his Co-adjutor and successor, Bishop Francis Hennemann, S. A. C., was in Germany and could not return to Cameroons. In *A. M. C.* he is listed as the Ecclesiastical Superior of Cameroons.

Diocese of Doume

H.E. James Teerenstra, C.S.Sp., 1955-

RELIGIOUS SUPERIORS C.S.SP.

Till 1940: the Ecclesiastical Superior

Duala	*Yaunde*
Fr. Albert Krummenacker, 1940-1950	Fr. Peter Bonneau, 1940-1946 (later Bishop of Duala)
Fr. Jerome Kapps, 1950-1956	Fr. Peter Richard, 1947-1956

1956: districts combined as *Yaunde-Duala*
Fr. Jerome Kapps, 1956-

Doume

Fr. James Teerenstra, 1947-1949 (later Bishop of Doume)
Fr. Theodore Valkering, 1949-

8. FRENCH EQUATORIAL AFRICA

This general title denotes the region comprised by Gabon, the Middle Congo, Ubangi-Shari and Chad. Its 950,000 square miles stretch from the South Atlantic below the Equator to the borders of Libya and the Egyptian Sudan, but its total population is only a little more than four million. The whole of this immense territory, except Chad and the Prefecture of Berberati, is still entrusted to the Congregation. With the exception of Chad, where Mohammedans constitute four fifths of the population, Islam has made relatively little progress. There are less than fifty thousand followers of the Prophet in the other areas.

a. GABON

cf. pp. 86 f.
Ap. H. 171 ff.
Br. 528 ff.

The Gabon mission, whose ecclesiastical line goes back to Bishop Edward Barron, first Vicar Apostolic of the Two Guineas, had as its pioneer Father John Remi Bessieux. In Chapter V we described the painful beginnings of this mission where many years were to pass before tangible results could be seen. In 1876, after the death of Bishop Bessieux, whom the natives referred to as "the great friend of God," the Vicariate remained limited to the single residence of St. Mary at Libreville. Every other effort at a permanent station had failed. Under his successors, however, a slow but steady development took place. Nonetheless, as late as 1912, after sixty-eight years of incessant labor, there were only twelve thousand Catholics in Gabon.

Just before World War I broke out, a significant change manifested itself. In the next ten years, Catholics increased to thirty thousand and vocations to the priesthood and the religious life began to blossom more abundantly. By 1930, the harvest, so patiently awaited by preceding generations of missionaries, began to ripen: nearly everywhere tribes and villages clamored for missionaries and catechists. Since then the movement of conversion

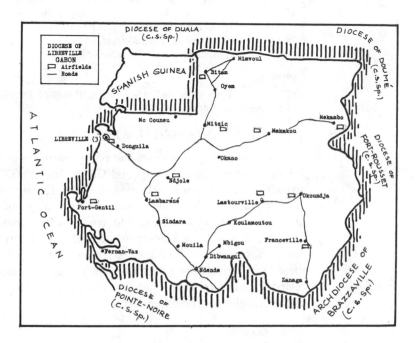

C. A. 1955/56   has gone forward steadily, and statistics now show more than 189,000 Catholics and catechumens,—nearly half the entire population. If it were possible to finance a more extensive network of catechists, the figures would be considerably higher.

The history of the region about Lastourville is particularly interesting. Its mission was founded in 1885, but twelve years

B. G. 18, 534 ff.   later the Fathers had to withdraw to Franceville because of the threatening attitude of the natives. Since the French government had not yet achieved adequate control of the area, the priests themselves were forced to act as policemen, arresting thieves and making them pay for their crimes. Moreover, the problem of supplying this distant mission proved especially difficult because most of the river-borne cargoes were stolen by the Aduma people who inhabited the area. Then too, the very lives of the priests were in constant danger. For example, Father Tristan saw his hut surrounded one night by a mob of Babamba tribesmen who were chanting menacingly to the rhythm of a tom-tom's death-beat. Then a local troubadour stepped forward and improvised a panegyric on the Mpawin braves who had just killed the white commander and eaten two of his Senegalese soldiers. These heroic deeds were now to be surpassed by the bravest men of all, the Babambas, the fearless warriors who were ready to feast on the meat of a white man. All the while, the tom-tom kept up its deadly pounding. It was only through the influence of a less bloodthirsty chief that the priest escaped with his life. Shortly before, he had been shot at by a native, while two days earlier another had drawn his dagger to kill him while he was saying Mass.

Since they had come to Africa not to be killed but to work, the Fathers decided to withdraw to the relative safety of Franceville.

Br. 533
B. G. 43, 46 f.

The Adumas watched their departure with high disdain and then sank back again into rank paganism, supremely indifferent, it seemed, to the fact that the tribes all around them were slowly becoming Christianized.

This situation continued for nearly forty years until one day an old Aduma chief came to Franceville for a big palaver with Father Adam, the Superior of the local mission. Without any introduction, he bluntly announced that the Adumas were very sorry for their past deeds and that they wanted to be Christians and to be reconciled with the priests, no matter what humiliating conditions the Fathers might impose on them. Unable to credit such a complete change of heart, the priest cautiously replied: "If you build decent chapel huts and arrange to maintain catechists at your own expense, we will see what can be done."

Oddly enough, the Adumas were sincere. They burned their fetishes in public bonfires, competed with each other in building neat little chapels, and showed themselves the most attentive audience that the catechists ever had. Soon the Fathers were overwhelmed by interviews with old pagans who wanted their matrimonial status regulated in accord with Christian law. Although the priests were very strict in their demands, within four years ten thousand Adumas entered the Church and not even the disorganization caused by World War II could stop their mass movement toward the Church.[15]

ECCLESIASTICAL SUPERIORS

Vicariate of the Two Guineas

Fr. Edward Barron, 1842, Prefect Apostolic
H. E. Edward Barron, 1842-1844, Vicar Apostolic and Titular Bishop of Constantina, later of Eucarpia
Fr. Eugene Tisserant, C.S.C.M. (C.S.Sp.), 1846-1847, Prefect Apostolic
H. E. Benedict Truffet, C.S.C.M. (C.S.Sp.), 1847, Titular Bishop of Gallipoli
H. E. John Bessieux, C.S.Sp., 1848-1863, Titular Bishop of Gallipoli
1863: name changed to *Vicariate of Gabon*
H. E. John Bessieux, C.S.Sp., 1863-1876
H. E. Peter Le Berre, C.S.Sp., 1876-1891, Titular Bishop of Archis
H. E. Alexander Le Roy, C.S.Sp., 1891-1896, Titular Bishop of Alinda (later Superior General and Titular Archbishop of Caria)
H. E. John Adam, C.S.Sp., 1897-1914, Titular Bishop of Tmui
H. E. Louis Martrou, C.S.Sp., 1914-1925, Titular Bishop of Corycea (Coadjutor since 1912)
H. E. Louis Tardy, C.S.Sp., 1925-1947, Titular Bishop of Acalia
1947: name changed to *Vicariate of Libreville*
H. E. Jerome Adam, C.S.Sp., 1947-1955, Titular Bishop of Rinocorura
1955: raised to the rank of a diocese
H. E. Jerome Adam, C.S.Sp., 1955-

RELIGIOUS SUPERIORS C.S.SP.

Till 1940: the Ecclesiastical Superior
Fr. John Fauret, 1940-1947 (later Bishop of Pointe Noire)
Fr. Henry Neyrand, 1947-1949
Fr. Augustine Berger, 1949-1951
Fr. Felix Girollet, 1951-

b. MIDDLE CONGO

The Middle Congo is divided ecclesiastically into the circumscriptions of Pointe Noire, Brazzaville, and Fort Rousset. Its 170,000 square miles are inhabited by only 700,000 people, of whom less than 5,000 are Mohammedans.

The evangelization of the Congo began in the old kingdom of Loango in 1663 when a Hungarian Capuchin, Father Bernardino, labored here briefly before death put an untimely end to his work.

pp. 279 f.

[15]For the former mission of the Holy Ghost Fathers in Spanish Guinea, see Chapter X.

A century later, French priests made another attempt, but after ten years of fruitless labor they withdrew.

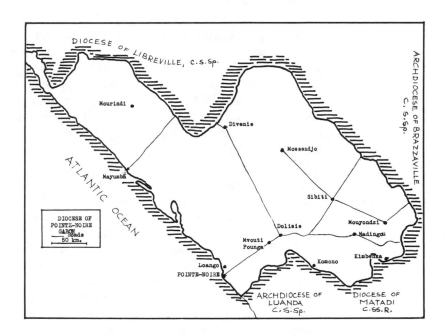

R. H. M. 14, 380 ff.; 502 ff.; 15, 504 ff.; 16 37 ff.

M. C. 27, 28 ff.

cf. pp. 452 f.

B. G. 43, 81 ff.; 44, 517 ff.

The Holy Ghost Fathers came on the scene in 1865 when the Holy See created the Congo Prefecture and Father Poussot vainly tried to establish a mission in the area. After another fruitless effort, Father Carrie managed to create a station in Landana[16] in 1873. It eventually became the starting-point of the Spiritan drive into the interior which was described in Chapter XIX.

In modern times, missionary work in the Middle Congo suffers under a number of handicaps: its rural population is now so thinly scattered that it is difficult to reach; its capital (Brazzaville) has grown at a prodigious rate with all the evils attendant on the disruption of tribal and village organization; an African Salvation Army has entered the picture since 1939 and by cleverly playing on the Negroes fear of sorcery it has managed to produce a kind of apostasy in certain areas.

___

[16]In 1885 Landana, which hitherto was a contested territory, became part of the Portuguese possessions in Africa.

Another adverse factor deserves special attention—the appearance of political and religious Messianism. The first serious manifestations of it, known as "Ngounzism," occurred shortly after World War I when Kibango, a former Protestant catechist of the Belgian Congo woke up one morning and discovered that he was a second Christ. Sending away his wife, he elected twelve apostles, began to work "miracles," and soon had a large following. He fulminated against fetishism and produced astonishing results. Encouraged by his success, he began to preach against paying taxes and working for white people. The colonial administration was disturbed by the ensuing disorders and promptly sent the prophet to jail.

Although this movement began in the Belgian Congo, it had repercussions in surrounding areas and in the Middle Congo especially, appearing repeatedly in modified forms. In the early thirties, for example, the prophet Benjamin Loamba introduced it in the Loango region under the names of "God's Spirit" and "God's Pity." His followers received the gifts of prophecy and miracles, enjoyed magic protection against all evils, taboos, and white people, and took seriously a promise of paradise on earth.

In 1929, Andrew Matsua and two other Negroes arrived in Brazzaville armed with the highest recommendations from influential but gullible Parisian authorities. With the ready permission of the Governor, they began to circulate throughout the colony, collecting money for a "mutual aid society" and preaching the expulsion of all white men. Matsua himself intended to become Governor. When the civil authorities finally realized how far the movement had spread and hesitantly took measures against it, Matsua's followers rioted and a number of people were killed and wounded. After that, hatred of white colonists continued to smolder for a long time. In 1933 Matsua directed it against the Spiritan mission of Linzolo just as it was celebrating its golden jubilee.

Since then he has originated "khakinism," a term derived from the khaki uniform he used to wear in the army. Politically, khakinism resembles the Mau Mau movement of Kenya and on a religious basis it claims that just as Christ is the Son of God and the Savior of the whites, Matsua is the Son of God and the savior of the blacks. About eighty per cent of the Catholics in Linzolo are sympathetic to Matsua's political aspirations, and about one fifth

Etudes, 184, pp. 737 ff.; 218, pp. 651 ff.
B. G. 30, 817; 861
Ap. H. 203 ff.

Ap. H. 203 ff.

B. G. 35, 137 ff.

B. G. 44, 520 f.; 545

R. H. M. 8, 80

B. G. 44, 518 ff.

have at least temporarily given up the Faith to accept him as their savior. In the Middle Congo, most of the leaders of such movements come from Protestant missions where the principle of free interpretation has been too strongly impressed on immature minds. Within the last twenty years, Brazzaville, the capital of all French Equatorial Africa, has become the center of the Church's most concentrated efforts toward saving the Faith of its converts from modern materialism. Since 1930, Brazzaville has grown up from a small town of about fifteen thousand to a city ten miles long that boasts of more than a hundred thousand people. The old central mission residence, founded in 1887, suddenly found it necessary to branch off in all directions to cover the area with a network of churches, chapels, and schools. Fortunately, Bishop Biechy foresaw this development and provided for it by acquiring suitable plots of land at strategic points well in advance of the need. Youth organizations, social groups, religious societies, and all the other apparatus of city parishes has been invoked to offer a measure of protection against the sudden exposure of bush immigrants to the glittering blandishments of a modern city. There is a large school system,

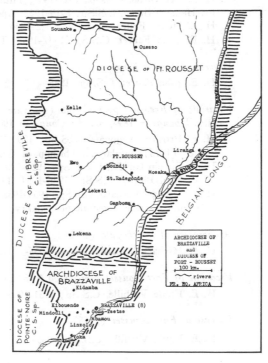

a college, and a regional Senior Seminary. A Catholic press strives to disseminate orthodox information. In 1945, work began on the huge Cathedral of St. Ann of the Congo which now dominates the skyline of Brazzaville. Although not yet completed, this structure was dedicated in 1952 in celebration of the centenary of Bishop Augouard's birth.

C. A. 1955/56   Latest statistics from the Middle Congo show a total of nearly 225,000 Catholics and 25,000 catechumens. Protestant sects have been very active in the territory. They account for more than a 100,000 followers.

ECCLESIASTICAL SUPERIORS

Prefecture of the Congo: see Portuguese Congo

Vicariate of French Congo (separated from Gabon in 1866; called *Lower Congo or Loango* in 1890: *Pointe Noire* in 1949)
   H. E. Hippolyte Carrie, C.S.Sp., 1886-1904, Titular Bishop of Dorylea
   Fr. Louis Derouet, C.S.Sp., 1904-1907, Pro-Vicar Apostolic
   H. E. Louis Derouet, C.S.Sp., 1907-1914, Titular Bishop of Camaca
   H. E. Leo Girod, C.S.Sp., 1915-1919, Titular Bishop of Obba
   Fr. Henry Friteau, C.S.Sp., 1919-1922, Apostolic Administrator
   H. E. Henry Friteau, C.S.Sp., 1922-1946, Titular Bishop of Jabruda
   H. E. John Fauret, C.S.Sp., 1947-1955, Titular Bishop of Arassa

Diocese of Pointe Noire
   H. E. John Fauret, C.S.Sp., 1955-

Vicariate of French Upper Congo (separated from French Congo in 1890; called *Ubangi* in 1894, *Middle Congo* in 1909, *Brazzaville* in 1922)
   H. E. Prosper Augouard, C.S.Sp., 1890-1921, Titular Bishop of Sinita, later (1915) Titular Archbishop of Cassiopea
   H. E. Firmin Guichard, C.S.Sp., 1922-1935, Titular Bishop of Tadama
   H. E. Paul Biechy, C.S.Sp., 1936-1954, Titular Bishop of Thelepta
   H. E. Michael Bernard, C.S.Sp., 1954-1955, Titular Bishop of Egia (formerly Vicar Apostolic of Conakry)

Archdiocese of Brazzaville (1955)
   H. E. Michael Bernard, C.S.Sp., 1955-

Vicariate of Fort Rousset (separated from Brazzaville in 1950)
   H. E. Emile Verhille, C.S.Sp., 1951-1955, Titular Bishop of Cernizza

Diocese of Fort Rousset (1955)
   H. E. Emile Verhille, C.S.Sp., 1955-

R<small>ELIGIOUS</small> S<small>UPERIORS</small> C.S.S<small>P</small>.

> *Pointe Noire* (formerly Loango, Lower Congo, French Congo)
> Till 1946: the Ecclesiastical Superior
> Fr. John Molager, 1946-1951
> Fr. John Brombeck, 1951-
> *Brazzaville* (formerly the Middle Congo, Ubangi, French Upper Congo)
> Till 1940: the Ecclesiastical Superior
> Fr. Nicholas Moysan, 1940-1950
> Fr. Paul Fourmont, 1951-

c. U<small>BANGI</small>-S<small>HARI</small>

About a million people reside within the 250,000 square miles of this country. Ecclesiastically, it has been an independent Prefecture since 1909, when it was separated from the Middle Congo Vicariate. At that time there were only two Spiritan missions in the whole area: St. Paul of the Rapids (1894), where the capital city of Bangui has since arisen, and Holy Family (1896) at Bessou. Both stations had been founded before the country was pacified and at a time when it took three months to get to these distant missions. Sentries had to be posted against nocturnal marauders; fresh graves had to be protected from cannibalistic violation.

As was customary at the time, the missionaries devoted themselves chiefly to the ransom of slaves and their eventual education through manual labor. It was not until 1907 that the focus of their attention swung to the free population. When it did, results were so promising that the Holy See made the Prefecture of Ubangi Shari an independent mission two years later, even though it still contained only the residences of St. Paul and Holy Family. The last named station was so victimized by disastrous government policies that it eventually had to be closed.

This occurred because French officials began to collect taxes in 1909, but the natives had no money and the tax was soon replaced by mandatory contribution of labor. Unhappy Negroes were herded together in labor-gangs and driven out to collect rubber. Armed militia broke up their families. They forced all able-bodied men and women to come along and leave only the children and old people at home. Agriculture ceased; famine and epidemics followed. Before long, large numbers of natives fled across the border to the Belgian Congo before the militia could stop them. Meanwhile, the missionaries had nothing to do but care for the sick and the dying,

Ap. H. 219 ff.
Daigre, 167 ff.

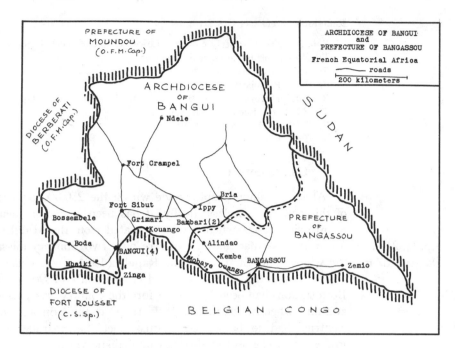

for no one dared appear for instructions lest he be arrested by the police and sent to a forced labor camp.

The Fathers' protests against this new form of slavery fell on deaf ears. Officials even tried to exclude them from the area because it was felt that they saw and heard too much. The Governor himself forbade one of the missionaries to return to a certain sector because he had been accused of engaging in political activities there. As a matter of fact, those "political activities" consisted simply in having come upon a village unexpectedly, finding there twenty-one blood-covered men and women who had just been savagely flogged by the militia. All this ended after World War I, but by then the region had been so thoroughly depopulated that the Holy Family mission had to be closed.

B. G. 41, 354 ff.   After 1928 when Monsignor Marcel Grandin became its Superior, the Ubangi Prefecture took on new momentum. The young and energetic prelate took advantage of the road system which a new colonial governor had built. New missions arose all over the immense area, each with its circle of catechists, schools, and subsidiary stations. Further impetus was given to the mission around the time of World War II, for it was then that the government changed its fifty-year-old policy of ignoring the missionaries and began at long last to support their schools.

At present, Ubangi-Shari is divided into three ecclesiastical circumscriptions: the Archdiocese of Bangui, served by the French Spiritans; the Prefecture of Bangassou, staffed by Dutch Holy Ghost Fathers; and the Diocese of Berberati, which is entrusted to the Capuchins. The two Holy Ghost missions together report a total of 71,503 Catholics and 41,403 catechumens out of a total population of 700,000. Within the same circumscription there are 42,567 Protestants and 18,200 Mohammedans.

C. A. 1955/56

ECCLESIASTICAL SUPERIORS

Prefecture of Ubangi-Shari (1909)
> Fr. Peter Cotel, C.S.Sp., 1909-1914
> Msgr. John Calloc'h, C.S.Sp., 1914-1927
> Msgr. Marcel Grandin, C.S.Sp., 1928-1937

Vicariate of Ubangi-Shari (name changed to Bangui in 1940)
> H.E. Marcel Grandin, C.S.Sp., 1937-1947, Titular Bishop of Turnos Major
> H.E. Joseph Cucherousset, C.S.Sp., 1947-1955, Titular Bishop of Stratonicea

Archdiocese of Bangui (1955)
> H.E. Joseph Cucherousset, C.S.Sp., 1955-

Prefecture of Bangassou (1954)
> Msgr. Martin Bodewes, C.S.Sp., 1955-

RELIGIOUS SUPERIORS C.S.SP.
> Before 1940: the Ecclesiastical Superior
> Fr. Albert Hemme, 1940-1947
> Fr. Aristides Morandeau, 1947-1954
> Fr. Charles Gruner, 1954-

9. KATANGA (Belgian Congo)

cf. pp. 269 ff.

In Chapter X we saw that Spiritans were the first Catholic missionaries to penetrate the Belgian Congo, that political developments forced their withdrawal at the turn of the century, and that they returned in 1907 to work in the more remote regions of the Katanga Province in a Prefecture that covers 50,000 square miles.

Ap. H. 300 ff.
B. G. 43, 349 ff.

Since then, this original Prefecture has registered a slow but steady progress that can be attributed in great part to the close collaboration between Church and State which has generally obtained in the Belgian Congo. Its chief handicap in the past was the disruptive influence of industrial and mining interests, because their extensive recruitment of African laborers made it hard to organize any mission activities in the bush country.

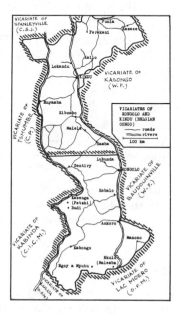

The matter of school support has tended, throughout the history of this mission, to reflect political developments in Belgium: till 1919, close collaboration; 1919-1946 at first, less cordial relations, but then a twenty-year pact that was generally favorable to the missions; 1946-1950, some measure of tension; 1950-1954 close collaboration. In recent years, the Katanga situation echoes the battle for Catholic schools which is going on in Belgium itself.

In 1956 the Holy See divided the old North Katanga Prefecture which had been raised to the status of a Vicariate in 1935. Now it constitutes the two independent Vicariates of Kongolo and Kindu,[17] both of which are staffed by Belgian Spiritans. The total population of Kongolo and Kindu approaches 335,000. Out of this number, 51,776 are Catholics and 20,025 are catechumens. Protestants claim 20,000 and Mohammedans 19,000.

C. A. 1955/56

---

[17]Part of the Vicariate of Stanleyville was added to the new circumscription.

Ecclesiastical Superiors

North Katanga

Msgr. Emile Callewaert, C.S.Sp., 1911-1922, Prefect Apostolic

Msgr. Louis Lempereur, C.S.Sp., 1922-1930, Prefect Apostolic

Msgr. Leo Louillet, C.S.Sp., 1930-1931, Prefect Apostolic

Msgr. George Haezaert, C.S.Sp., 1931-1935, Prefect Apostolic

H. E. George Haezaert, C.S.Sp., 1935-1949, Vicar Apostolic and Titular Bishop of Pertusa

1951: name changed to Vicariate of *Kongolo;* 1956: divided into Vicariates of Kongolo and Kindu

H. E. Gustave Bouve, C.S.Sp., 1950-   , Vicar Apostolic of Kongolo and Titular Bishop of Cremna

Kindu

H. E. John Fryns, C.S.Sp., 1957-   , Vicar Apostolic of Kindu and Titular Bishop of Ariasso

Religious Superiors C.S.Sp.

Fr. Emile Callewaert, 1907-1911 (later Prefect Apostolic of North Katanga)

1911-1940: the Ecclesiastical Superior

Fr. Gustave Bouve, 1940-1950 (later Vicar Apostolic of Kongolo)

Fr. Joseph de Hert, 1951-1954

Fr. Jules Op de Beeck, 1954-

10. ANGOLA AND THE PORTUGUESE CONGO

Angola and the Portuguese Congo cover an area of about 500,000 square miles on Africa's west coast, just south of the Equator. The district is inhabited by about four million people.

Ap. H. 225-299
R. H. M. 9. 53
ff; 10,42 ff.

Officially, the sixteenth century Diocese of Angola never ceased to exist, but it was so poorly manned that it had to be dismissed as a likely starting-point for the resumption of missionary activity. Nevertheless, in the eyes of the Portuguese government, the ecclesiastical jurisdiction of this tired old diocese extended over all the territories claimed by Lisbon. As a result, serious complica-

Ap. H. 262 f.
B. G. 43, 288
Correia, II,64 f.

tions arose when the Holy Ghost Fathers began evangelizing the country. A practical *modus vivendi* was maintained only by the exercise of extreme tact on the part of all concerned. Through discreet negotiation, and without too clear a reference to the jurisdictional claims of the diocese, four new ecclesiastical circumscriptions were eventually created. All of them—the Prefecture of the (Portuguese) Congo (1873); the Prefecture of Cimbebasia

(1879) ; the Mission of Cunene (1882) ; and the Mission of Lunda (1897)—were entrusted to the Holy Ghost Fathers.[18]

B. G. 18, 681

As in other parts of Africa, the Church reports consoling growth in the Angola missions. The time is past when, as in 1893, a local king might receive a missionary into his hut without being at all embarrassed over a freshly-cut human leg dangling from the kitchen ceiling. Slave traffic, for local consumption or for export, flourished at one time. Now it has all but ceased to exist.[19] There is no longer any great danger that the missionaries will be murdered in cold blood, as happened to Father Louis Delpuech and Brother Lucius Rothan in 1885,[20] and to Brother Denis Duarte in 1903.

B. G. 13. 1002 f. ; 23, 569 f.

B. G. 16, 605

pp. 276 f.

[18]Until 1886, the jurisdiction of the Congo Prefecture extended far beyond the limits of the present Portuguese territory of the same name, and up to 1892, the Prefecture of Cimbebasia held jurisdiction over a large part of South Africa, extending as far inland as the borders of the Orange Free State. Cf. Chapter X.

[19]Between 1759 and 1803 Brazil alone received 642,000 slaves from Angola and as late as 1910 it was considered the last stronghold of slavery. Cf. Carveth Wells, *Introducing Africa,* New York, 1944, p. 105.

[20]Some natives also died in the fatal skirmish that ended in death for Father Delpuech and Brother Lucius. Wild beasts immediately devoured their bodies, but the two missionaries' corpses lay untouched for five days. This phenomenon so impressed local observers that they decided to burn the persistent cadavers and bury the charred remains.

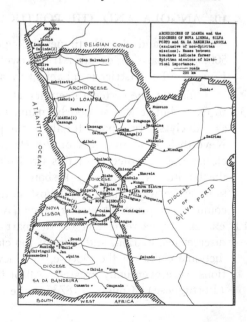

Collaboration between the civil and religious authorities has nearly always been quite close here. At first, the Portuguese looked with a deep suspicion on the French Spiritan missionaries, but little by little they learned to trust them and to realize that these priests were not the forerunners of a government that had Correia, II, 64   cast a covetous eye on their empire. Even the anticlericals came to recognize the splendid results achieved by those early pioneers, among whom we have such renowned missionaries as Father Charles Duparquet, Father Joseph Antunes, and Monsignor Alfred Keiling.

Just before World War II, progress had been so amazing that the Church just had to find a way out of the anomalous canonical situation which kept a simple Prefect Apostolic at the head of 300,000 Catholics in Cubango lest the real or imaginary rights B. G. 35, 654   of the ancient diocese would suffer infringement. To facilitate the solution, Rome had already appointed a Spiritan in 1932 to occupy the see of the old Diocese of Angola and Congo. Nevertheless a more definite arrangement had to be found. Fortunately, da Silva, 606 ff.   in 1940 the Holy See entered into a new agreement with Portugal. Thereafter, without offence to the government or detriment to the old Diocese of Angola, it could proceed with a more realistic organization of the area. All existing jurisdictions were suppressed and replaced by the Archdiocese of Loanda and the two suffragan sees of Nova Lisboa[21] and Silva Porto. These new circumscriptions were placed under the Sacred Congregation of Extraordinary Ecclesiastical Affairs—a delicate diplomatic gesture which recognized and neatly side-stepped Portugal's traditional antipathy toward the Propaganda, Rome's supreme governing body for all mission territories.[22]

None of these dioceses is officially entrusted to the Congregation, but the Holy See chose two of the first three bishops from among the Spiritans who, it should be noted, still form the large majority of the non-African clergy. The 1955 *Fides* statistics for

---

[21]A fourth diocese, that of Sa da Bandeira, was added in 1955.

[22]Technically, therefore, Angola is not regarded as a mission country and two hundred and thirty Spiritans laboring in this colony do not figure in the statistics released by the Propaganda. Apart from this technicality, they are just as much missionaries as their confreres in other parts of Africa.

these missions show a total of over 1,200,000 Catholics and 105,000 catechumens out of a total population of four million.[23]

ECCLESIASTICAL SUPERIORS

Diocese of Angola and Congo

>H. E. Moses Alves de Pinho, C.S.Sp., 1932-1941 (later Archbishop of Loanda)

Prefecture of Congo

>Fr. John Poussot, C.S.Sp., 1866-1870, Vice Prefect (later Prefect of Cimbebasia)
>
>Fr. Charles Duparquet, C.S.Sp., 1873-1878, Vice Prefect (later Prefect of Cimbebasia)
>
>Fr. Hippolyte Carrie, C.S.Sp., 1878-1886, Vice Prefect (later Vicar Apostolic of French Congo)

in dependence on Superior General as Prefect Apostolic

>1886: jurisdiction limited to Portuguese Congo
>Fr. Gustave Jauny, C.S.Sp., 1886-1887, Prefect Apostolic
>Fr. Pascal Campana, C.S.Sp., 1887-1901, Prefect Apostolic
>Fr. Joseph Magalhaes, C.S.Sp., 1902-1917, Prefect Apostolic
>Msgr. Faustin Moreira dos Santos, C.S.Sp., 1919-1941, Prefect Apostolic (later Bishop of Cape Verde)

Prefecture of Cimbebasia (1921: Cubango)

>Fr. Charles Duparquet, C.S.Sp., 1879-1887, Prefect Apostolic
>Fr. Francis Schaller, C.S.Sp., 1887-1891, Prefect Apostolic
>Fr. Ernest Lecomte, C.S.Sp., 1892-1908, Prefect Apostolic
>Fr. Lawrence André, C.S.Sp., 1909, Prefect Apostolic
>Msgr. Alfred Keiling, C.S.Sp., 1909-1937, Prefect Apostolic
>Fr. Joseph Feltin, C.S.Sp., 1937-1938, Apostolic Administrator
>Msgr. Daniel Junqueira, C.S.Sp., 1938-1941, Prefect Apostolic (later Bishop of Nova Lisboa)

Mission of Cunene

>Fr. Charles Duparquet, C.S.Sp., 1882-1883
>Fr. Gustave Costes, C.S.Sp., 1883
>Fr. Joseph Antunes, C.S.Sp., 1883-1904
>Fr. Marius Bonnefoux, C.S.Sp., 1904-1932
>Fr. Charles Estermann, C.S.Sp., 1932-1941

Mission of Lunda

>Fr. Cyril Moulin, C.S.Sp., 1897-1899
>Fr. Victor Wendling, C.S.Sp., 1899-1911
>Fr. Louis Cancella, C.S.Sp., 1911-1926

---

[23] The figures of the *Campagne Apostolique* 1955/56 do not appear trustworthy: presumably they are in error by one million. Cf. *C. A.* 1945/55.

Fr. John Cardona, C.S.Sp., 1926-1941

1941: all extant ecclesiastical jurisdictions suppressed and replaced by Archdiocese of Loanda, and the Dioceses of Nova Lisboa and Silva Porto. 1955: Diocese of Sa da Bandeira divided from Nova Lisboa.

Archdiocese of Loanda

H.E. Moses Alves de Pinho, C.S.Sp., 1941-
(also Bishop of San Tomé)

Diocese of Nova Lisboa

H.E. Daniel Junqueira, C.S.Sp., 1941-

Diocese of Silva Porto

H.E. Hildephons dos Santos, O.S.B., 1941-

Diocese of Sa da Bandeira (1955 divided from Nova Lisboa)

H.E. Altin de Santana, 1955-

RELIGIOUS SUPERIORS C.S.SP.

Till 1941: the immediate Ecclesiastical Superior (C.S.Sp.) of Congo, Cimbebasia (Cubango), Cunene, and Nova Lisboa. After ecclesiastical reorganization:

District of Loanda

Fr. Henry Gross, 1942-1950
Fr. Anthony Silva, 1950-1951
(substitute: Fr. Louis Heng)
Fr. Pompey Seabra, 1951-

District of Nova Lisboa

Fr. Charles Estermann, 1942-1951
Fr. Albin Alves Manso, 1951-1956
Fr. Celestine Belo, 1956
Fr. Joseph Felicio, 1956-

District of Silva Porto

Fr. Albin Alves Manso, 1942-1951
Fr. Pompey Seabra, 1951
1951: District suppressed and divided between Nova Lisboa and Loanda

11. KROONSTAD-BETHLEHEM (SOUTH AFRICA)

cf. pp. 276 f. The early Spiritan history of South West Africa and Bechuanaland engaged our attention in Chapter X. As was pointed out there, the Holy Ghost Fathers returned to South Africa in 1924 when their German province assumed charge of the Prefecture (and eleven years later, the Vicariate) of Kroonstad in the Orange Free State.

B. G. 44, 84 ff.   On their arrival, the priests found eight hundred white Catholics in their new mission, and in a short while they discovered an additional four hundred Negro Catholics to whom no one had been paying any attention. Working against the handicap of extreme poverty—the mission was so poor that neither the Bishop nor any of his priests could raise the money for a leave of absence in Europe—the German Fathers and Brothers built a flourishing vicariate from the ground up in a few years' time. World War II slowed their progress, for Bishop Klerlein himself was arrested for a short while,[24] and all his confreres except four were thrust behind barbed wire as enemy aliens. However, most of them were released in 1942 when they were once again permitted a somewhat restricted exercise of their ministry. Despite the limitations under which they operated, however, these stalwart missionaries increased the number of Catholics by three thousand during those dark years.

B. G. 40, 357 f.   In 1948, the Holy See divided the mission into the two Vicariates of Kroonstad and Bethlehem, the first of which it entrusted

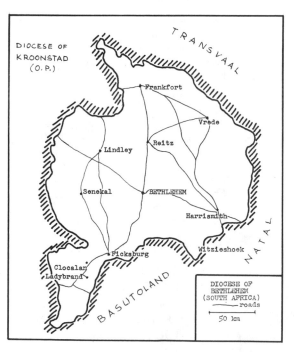

----

[24]He was released through the intercession of an Anglican minister.

to the Dominicans and the second to the Spiritans. Both of them became full dioceses in 1951.

Work in the diocese of Bethlehem differs considerably from operations in the equatorial areas of Africa. The Orange Free State is a country whose climate is similar to that of the milder regions of Europe or North America. The dread diseases of tropical Africa hold no terrors for the large number of white settlers there. On the other hand, the priests encounter numerous obstacles in their spiritual ministry. Much of the population, both black and white, shifts with the changing interests of commerce and industry; local representatives of the Dutch Reformed Church display considerable antagonism toward the Catholic Faith; a strict color bar often blocks the missionary in his work; and a policy of rigid segregation ("apartheid") has built up a socio-political way of life that systematically represses the Negroes and already bids fair to bring on a reaction that may one day set fire to the whole of South Africa.

C. A. 1955/56   The latest statistics of the Diocese of Kroonstad show a little more than 14,000 Catholics and 3,000 catechumens in a total population of 341,000, of whom 201,000 are Protestant.

ECCLESIASTICAL SUPERIORS

Kroonstad

Msgr. Leo Klerlein, C.S.Sp., 1924-1935, Prefect Apostolic

H. E. Leo Klerlein, C.S.Sp., 1935-1948, Vicar Apostolic and Titular Bishop of Voncaria

1948: Vicariate divided into the two Vicariates of Kroonstad (entrusted to Dominicans) and of Bethlehem

Bethlehem (Diocese in 1951)

Fr. Philip Winterle, C.S.Sp., 1948-1949, Apostolic Administrator

H. E. Peter Kelleter, C.S.Sp., 1949-1951, Vicar Apostolic and Titular Bishop of Sigo

H. E. Peter Kelleter, C.S.Sp., 1951-   , Resident Bishop

RELIGIOUS SUPERIORS C.S.SP.

Till 1939: the Ecclesiastical Superior
Fr. Philip Winterle, 1939-1951
Fr. Hubert Roggendorf, 1951-

12. KENYA AND TANGANYIKA

Kenya Colony's 225,000 square miles lie across the Equator on Africa's east coast and have a total population of about

5,500,000. This number includes 40,000 white settlers who have
made their homes in the healthy and fertile highlands, and
120,000 Indians who dominate the commercial world of East
Africa.

Tanganyika Territory (360,000 square miles) has a popula-
tion of 7,500,000 and lies just south of Kenya. Formerly a
German colony, it became a British Mandate of the League of
Nations after World War I.

pp. 196 ff.;
pp. 450 ff.
The early history of the Spiritan apostolate in these countries
has been dealt with in Chapters VIII and XIX when we discussed
the old Zanguebar Mission. Gradually, the Holy See detached
more and more areas from the original mission and entrusted them
to other societies, so that by World War I the Congregation retained only the three Vicariates of Zanzibar, Bagamoyo and Kile-
manjaro.

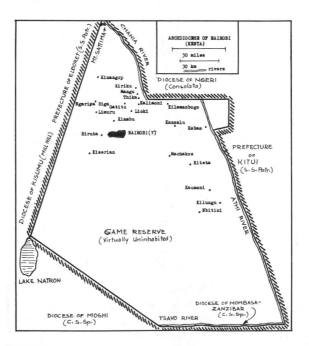

a. KENYA

The Zanzibar Vicariate originally covered the off-shore islands
of Zanzibar and Pemba, and a large sector of the mainland which
included the fast growing city of Nairobi. In 1953 it became the

Archdiocese of Nairobi and three years later the Diocese of Mombasa and Zanzibar was separated from it. Both the diocese and the archdiocese are entrusted to the Irish Province of the Holy Ghost Fathers.

B. G. 44, 128 ff.   Since 1925, when Fathers Michael Witte and Cornelius McNamara founded the Kabaa Training School for Catholic Teachers, the main emphasis of the apostolate here has been on education. These two missions have nearly 90,000 students in their schools and Colleges, and conversions proceed at a heartening rate. The 1956 statistics show nearly 100,000 Catholics and more than 65,000 catechumens.

C. A. 1955/56

C. A. 1955/56

B. G. 44,130;
144 f.

The Mau Mau Movement, which made Kenya notorious in recent years, owes its origin to the Independent Schools that were started in the thirties. At that time, a number of American- and European-trained Kikuyus decided that something should be done to smash the white man's near-monopoly of white-collar jobs and the Indians' strangle-hold on business opportunities. In an endeavor to satisfy these legitimate yearnings for greater influence, they espoused a movement to promote independent secular schools. When these schools produced inferior results and thereby thwarted their aim, the Kikuyu leaders shifted their position to a political one that was calculated to drive all foreigners from the country by inflaming the populace with anti-European and anti-missionary propaganda. In the beginning, many of the chiefs were reluctant to join a movement that demanded of its members a pledge of secrecy and loyalty unto death. They eventually capitulated, however, when extreme pressure was brought to bear on them by the leaders. Just as in French Equatorial Africa, high government officials in Kenya at first saw no great menace in the Movement until it erupted so violently all over the colony in 1952 that large numbers of troops had to be flown in to maintain public order.

cf. p.546

To date, the Spiritan missions have not suffered too seriously because of the Mau Maus. The Kiriku residence was the only one that experienced any violence, and it was attacked by a group from another district.

When the Bishop condemned the Movement and excommunicated any Catholic who took the secret oath, the Kikuyu faithful courageously expressed their loyalty to the Church, though they knew that the wrath of the Mau Mau would descend upon them with even greater ferocity than it would on the missionaries. Churches and schools are filled as they always have been, and the latest report from Kenya states that the Spiritans' "hopes in the Kikuyu region are higher than ever."

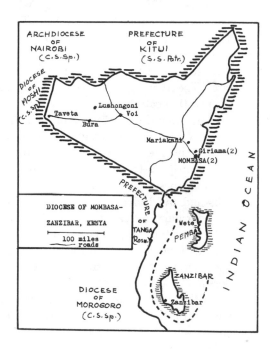

ECCLESIASTICAL SUPERIORS

Zanguebar

H. E. Armand Maupoint, 1860-1863, Bishop of Reunion, Prefect Apostolic

Fr. Anthony Horner, C.S.Sp., 1863-1872, Vice Prefect in dependence on Bishop Maupoint

Fr. Anthony Horner, C.S.Sp., 1872-1880, Vice Prefect in dependence on Superior General as Prefect

Fr. Edward Baur, C.S.Sp., 1880-1883, Vice Prefect in dependence on Superior General as Prefect

1883 : raised to the rank of Vicariate

H. E. John de Courmont, C.S.Sp., 1883-1896, Vicar Apostolic and Titular Bishop of Bodona

1887 : name changed to *North Zanguebar*

H. E. Emile Allgeyer, C.S.Sp., 1896-1913, Vicar Apostolic and Titular Bishop of Ticelia

1906: name changed to *Zanzibar*

H. E. John Neville, C.S.Sp., 1913-1930, Vicar Apostolic and Titular Bishop of Carrhae

H. E. John Heffernan, C.S.Sp., 1932-1945, Vicar Apostolic and Titular Bishop of Uzippari

H. E. John McCarthy, C.S.Sp., 1945-1953, Vicar Apostolic and Titular Bishop of Cerina

1953: Vicariate becomes *Archdiocese of Nairobi*

H. E. John McCarthy, C.S.Sp., 1953-   , Resident Archbishop of Nairobi

Diocese of Mombasa-Zanzibar (separated from Nairobi in 1955)

H. E. Eugene Butler, C.S.Sp., 1957-

Religious Superiors C.S.Sp.

Till 1939: the Ecclesiastical Superior

Fr. Michael Finnegan, 1939-1947

Fr. Daniel Murphy, 1947-1950

Fr. Peter Kelly, 1950-

b. TANGANYIKA (Bagamoyo and Kilimanjaro)

Ap. H. 355 f.
Walker, 148 ff.

At the end of World War I, the Spiritan Vicariates of Bagamoyo and Kilimanjaro were in a sad state: their German and Alsatian missionaries had been sent to internment camps in Egypt and India; several residences had been wrecked during the three-year conflict between German and Allied troops; young Catholic families had disappeared often without a trace; and financial ruin seemed almost inevitable. The two Alsatian Vicars Apostolic, Bishop Vogt and Bishop Munsch, were considered German citizens and hence *personae non gratae* to the new British rulers. They handed over the reins to two Irish Spiritans, Bishops Henry Gogarty and Bartholemew Wilson, whose prodigious labor somehow succeeded in reviving the shattered missions.

In 1932, American Holy Ghost Fathers took charge of the Kilimanjaro Vicariate, and two years later their Dutch confreres had the neighboring Vicariate of Bagamoyo entrusted to their care. Although staffed mainly by the nationals of these two countries, both missions still maintain a rather international flavor in their personnel. Americans, Dutchmen, Germans, Frenchmen, Africans and Irishmen pursue their apostolic task with fraternal good will.

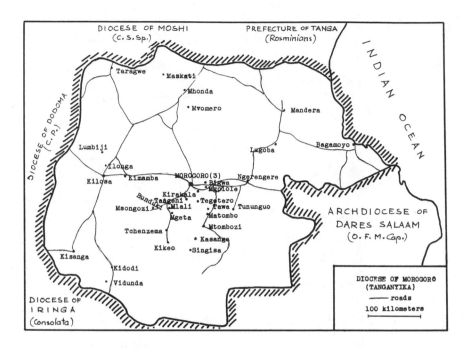

B. G. 44, 344 ff.   Famous old Bagamoyo has now lost the importance it once enjoyed. Politically and economically it has been replaced by Dar es Salaam, and the center of ecclesiastical jurisdiction has moved to Morogoro, the seat of the new diocese created in 1953. Despite its beautiful cathedral, Bagamoyo has less than five hundred Catholics surrounded by fifteen thousand Mohammedans. It would have sunk to the status of a minor station were it nor for the fact that the Bishop restored to it something of its former prestige by locating a large junior seminary there. Morogoro, on the other hand, although it dates only from 1882, now constitutes the nerve center of the Church in this area. It boasts so many Catholic institutions that people sometimes refer to it as the Vatican City of Tanganyika.

C. A. 1955/56   Under the energetic direction of Bishop Bernard Hilhorst, astonishing progress has been achieved in this mission. The latest statistics report nearly 120,000 Catholics (twenty-five percent of the population) and a well-developed school system that enrolls over 25,000 students.

B. G. 44, 176 ff.   Neighboring Moshi Diocese, as the former Kilimanjaro Vicariate is now called, operates under the direction of Bishop Joseph

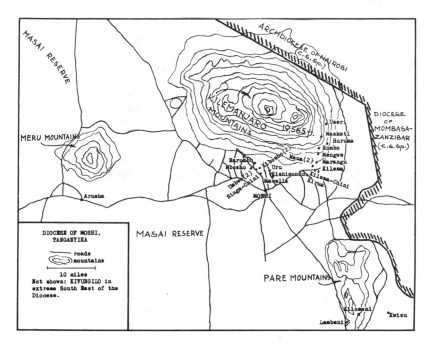

Byrne. It is one of the African missions in which the Catholic Faith has most profoundly permeated the life of the new-Christians. Frequent reception of the sacraments and the large number of vocations to the priesthood and the religious life are symptoms of its spiritual vitality. Like the other Spiritan missions in East Africa, Moshi Diocese has built up an extensive network of schools in which there are now 33,000 pupils. Its 118,000 Catholics constitute a sizeable segment of the total population of 600,000.

C. A. 1955/56

ECCLESIASTICAL SUPERIORS

Central Zanguebar (Bagamoyo)

H. E. Francis Vogt, C.S.Sp., 1906-1922, Vicar Apostolic and Titular Bishop of Celenderis (later transferred to the Cameroons)

Fr. Bartholemew Wilson, C.S.Sp., 1923-1924, Apostolic Administrator

H. E. Bartholemew Wilson, C.S.Sp., 1924-1933, Vicar Apostolic and Titular Bishop of Acmonia (later transferred to Sierra Leone)

H. E. Bernard Hilhorst, C.S.Sp., 1934-1953, Vicar Apostolic and Titular Bishop of Metellopolis

1953: erection of the *Diocese of Morogoro*

H. E. Bernard Hilhorst, C.S.Sp., 1953-1954

H. E. Herman van Elswijk, C.S.Sp., 1954-

Kilimanjaro

H. E. M. Joseph Munsch, C.S.Sp., 1910-1922, Vicar Apostolic and Titular
  Bishop of Magnesia

[Fr. Auguste Gommenginger, C.S.Sp., 1918-1920, Apostolic Adminis-
  trator]

[Fr. Joseph Soul, C.S.Sp., 1920-1922, Apostolic Administrator]

Fr. Henry Gogarty, C.S.Sp., 1922-1924, Apostolic Administrator

H. E. Henry Gogarty, C.S.Sp., 1924-1931, Vicar Apostolic and Titular
  Bishop of Themiscyra

Fr. Francis Griffin, C.S.Sp., 1931-1933, Apostolic Administrator (later
  Superior General)

H. E. Joseph Byrne, C.S.Sp., 1933-1953, Vicar Apostolic and Titular
  Bishop of Vasada

1953: erection of the *Diocese of Moshi*

H. E. Joseph Byrne, C.S.Sp., 1953-

RELIGIOUS SUPERIORS C.S.SP.

Bagamoyo District

Till 1940: the Ecclesiastical Superior
Fr. Alderic Stam, 1940-1947
Fr. Daniel Hagenaars, 1947-1956
Fr. Francis van der Poel, 1956-

Kilimanjaro District

Till 1939; the Ecclesiastical Superior
Fr. James Marron, 1939-1951
Fr. Colman Watkins, 1951-

* * * * *

We feel that it is appropriate to terminate this chapter by
reproducing the 1956 statistics of all Spiritan missions and the
latest general statistics (1955) concerning the Catholic population
of Africa, as released by the Fides press office in June, 1956. For
the sake of comparison, we have added the general population
statistics which Father John J. Considine, M. M., gives in his
work *Africa, World of New Men,* New York, 1954, pp. 352 ff.

1956 Missionary Statistics Covering Territories and Areas Entrusted to the Congregation of the Holy Ghost

	Population	Catholics			Protestants	Moslems	Others
		Baptized	Catechumens	Percentage of Population[1]			
Continental Africa							
Dakar	1,543,124	97,501	5,867	6.7%	1,804	1,125,992	311,960
Gambia	278,000	4,151	773	1.8%	3,611	215,465	56,000
Ziguinchor	371,563	22,447	1,460	6.4%	45	281,111	66,500
St. Louis	1,007,970	4,450	20	0.4%	500	1.000,000	3,000
Conakry	1,300,000	16,340	848	1.3%	732	282,000	100,000
Kankan	660,000	7,984	1,811	1.5%	403	400,000	250,000
Sierra Leone	1,250,000	14,243	9,960	1.9%	62,368	200,000	963,797
Onitsha	1,768,413	278,238	104,207	21.6%	104,000	15,000	1,272,000
Owerri[9]	2,800,000	420,293	143,647	20.1%	200,000	5,500	2,031,418
Oturkpo	1,750,000	15,258	33,218	2.8%	13,380	54,000	1,634,000
Kabba	775,000	9,643	2,400	1.6%	105,000	150,000	508,000
Duala	430,000	180,000	22,953	47.2%	150,300	18,000	60,000
Yaunde	535,841	293,477	30,901	60.5%	31,454	14,686	165,323
Doume	215,000	31,007	8,621	18.4%	16,750	3,830	154,800
Libreville	383,170	160,879	28,201	49.3%	32,432	2,143	159,415
Pointe Noire	302,246	82,961	12,402	31.6%	56,689	1,246	147,822
Brazzaville	235,000	94,839	5,845	42.8%	45,000	2,900	85,000
Fort Rousset	240,000	47,123	6,702	22.4%	2,910	527	186,900
Bangui	457,800	61,170	28,403	19.6%	28,067	15,900	323,260
Bangassou	210,000	10,333	13,000	11.1%	14,500	2,300	177,300
Loanda	1,068,067	182,669	27,186	19.6%	—	—	817,331[7]
Nova Lisboa[2]	1,676,381	684,411	57,723	44.2%	93,000	—	841,248
Silva Porto	1,000,000	98,396	30,642	12.9%	65,000	—	460,351
Kongolo	260,000	37,896	13,742	19.9%	15,966	1,097	195,170
Kindu	75,000	13,880	6,183	26.8%	3,174	8,408	43,742
Bethlehem	341,536	14,337	3,101	5.1%	201,100	—	75,000
Nairobi[3]	1,733,409	96,579	65,930	9.4%	120,000	450,000	1.000,000
Moshi	600,000	117,305	8,810	21.0%	72,358	41,221	350,000
Morogoro	492,393	119,378	5,638	25.4%	8,240	145,218	213,919
Total	23,759,913	3,217,188	680,194	16.4%	1,448,783	4,436,544	12,653,256

(Continued on succeeding page)

	Population	Catholics			Protestants	Moslems	Others
		Baptized	Catechumens	Percentage of Population[1]			
Insular Africa							
Cape Verde[4]	81,500	70,000	1,374	85.9%	35,486	—	11,500[7]
Majunga	411,294	33,278	24,409	8.4%	47,174	30,855	310,713
Diego-Suarez	624,362	57,054	30	13.0%		18,176	477,553
Reunion	283,000	282,500		99.8%	400	4,500	3,900
Mauritius	568,886	188,134	144	33.1%	8,200	81,610	263,181
TOTAL	1,969,042	630,966	25,957	33.4%	91,260	135,141	1,066,847
Total of all Africa	25,728,955	3,848,154	706,151	17.9%	1,540,043	1,571,685	13,720,103
America							
St. Pierre and Miquelon	4,974	4,974		100.0%			
U. S. A.[6]		44,817					
Puerto Rico[4]		279,757					
Haiti[4]	60,880	45,277	4,000	80.9%	4,659		6
Guadeloupe	300,000	298,163		99.4%	4,710		200
Martinique	242,000	237,090		98.0%	21,000	100	13,000
Trinidad[4]	50,000	12,000		24.0%	329	4,000	3,500
Fr. Guiana	34,521	30,469	90	88.5%	3,252	219	500
Tefe[5]	154,188	150,188		97.4%	1,480	188	500
Jurua[5]	91,605	88,000		96.1%		2,050	2,050
TOTAL	938,168	1,290,735	4,090	92.8%[8]	35,430	6,557	19,256
GRAND TOTALS	26,667,123	5,038,889	710,241	21.5%[8]	1,575,473	4,578,242	13,739,359

[1]Includes Baptized and Catechumens.
[2]The figures for the Diocese of Sa da Bandeira are not yet separately available.
[3]The figures for the Diocese of Mombasa-Zanzibar are not yet separately available.
[4]Refers only to areas served by Spiritans.
[5]Includes parishes in South East Brazil.
[6]Negro missions only.
[7]Includes all non-Catholics.
[8]Exclusive of U. S. A. and Puerto Rico.
[9]Latest unofficial figures (December, 1957) 750,000 Catholics.

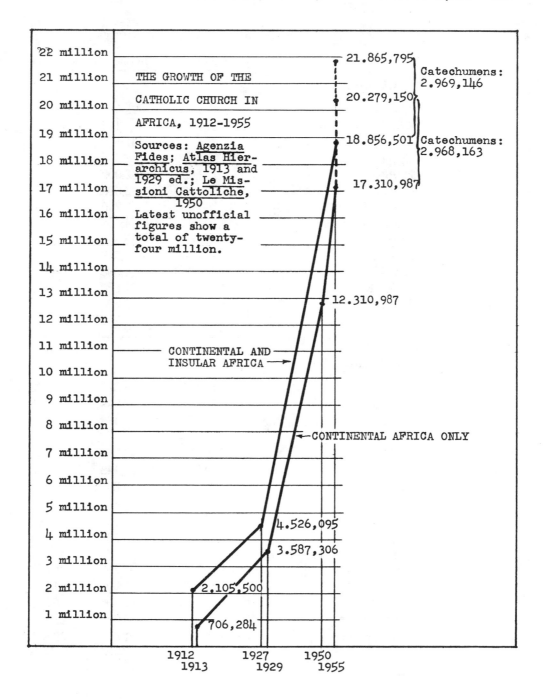

THE GROWTH OF THE
CATHOLIC CHURCH IN
AFRICA, 1912-1955

Sources: Agenzia
Fides; Atlas Hier-
archicus, 1913 and
1929 ed.; Le Mis-
sioni Cattoliche,
1950
Latest unofficial
figures show a
total of twenty-
four million.

22 million — 21.865,795
21 million
20 million — 20.279,150
19 million
18 million — 18.856,501
17 million — 17.310,987
16 million
15 million
14 million
13 million
12 million — 12.310,987
11 million
10 million
9 million
8 million
7 million
6 million
5 million
4 million — 4.526,095
3 million — 3.587,306
2 million — 2.105,500
1 million — 706,284

Catechumens:
2.969,146

Catechumens:
2.968,163

CONTINENTAL AND
INSULAR AFRICA →

←CONTINENTAL AFRICA ONLY

1912   1927   1950
1913   1929   1955

June 1955 Catholic Mission Statistics

	Population	Catholics	Catechumens
North Africa			
Algeria	8,495,000	895,566	—
British Somaliland	524,000	172	—
Ceuta Melilla	1,374,000	142,505	—
Egypt	20,874,000	188,595	—
Erytrea	1,122,000	82,000	—
Ethiopia	15,000,000	42,000	—
French Somaliland	80,000	3,790	70
Italian Somaliland	1,200,000	4,565	75
Libya	1,124,000	45,895	—
Morocco	8,495,000	498,587	—
Rio d'Oro	41,000	4,000	—
Sudan Republic	8,282,000	142,570	20,175
Tunisia	3,525,000	265,000	—
	70,136,000	2,315,245	20,320
West Africa			
Dahomey	1,549,153	184,223	29,142
Gambia	278,000	3,944	739
Ghana (Gold Coast and British Togo)	4,260,422	438,458	89,200
French Guinea	2,261,875	24,980	4,483
French Sudan	3,447,875	15,448	9,497
French Togo	1,029,946	156,842	20,348
Ivory Coast	2,309,344	181,492	44,704
Liberia	1,700,000	10,340	702
Niger	2,550,000	7,384	1,201
Nigeria (including British Cameroons)	31,000,000	1,105,234	426,238
Port. Guinea	520,000	15,000	4,800
Senegal	2,102,034	111,706	6,532
Sierra Leone	2,775,000	13,934	11,919
Upper Volta	3,200,000	91,852	37,848
	58,983,647	2,360,837	687,353

	Population	Catholics	Catechumens
Central Africa			
Angola (including San Tomé and Portuguese Congo)	4,190,200	1,209,395	105,312
Belgian Congo	12,264,000	3,693,357	671,721
French Cameroons	3,249,390	599,000	106,602
French Equatorial Africa	4,400,000	483,936	116,857
Nyassaland	2,255,978	359,415	38,935
Rhodesia (Northern)	2,115,416	349,510	70,175
Rhodesia (Southern)	2,461,000	142,042	26,875
Ruanda-Orundi	4,079,133	1,373,297	488,527
Spanish Guinea	175,000	160,382	9,500
	35,190,117	8,370,334	1,634,504
East Africa			
Kenya (including Zanzibar)	5,133,250	484,832	102,793
Tanganyika	8,305,979	1,034,845	131,778
Uganda	4,878,460	1,340,330	114,778
	18,317,689	2,860,007	349,349
South Africa			
Mozambique	5,762,000	424,879	158,374
Union of South Africa	19,744,000	979,685	50,242
	25,506,000	1,404,564	208,616
Insular Africa			
Cape Verde Islands	167,000	164,352	983
Madagascar	4,118,296	926,524	68,021
Mauritius	500,000	182,057	—
Reunion	287,000	279,055	—
Seychelles Islands	37,502	33,674	—
	5,109,798	1,585,662	69,004
Total for All Africa	213,243,251	18,896,649	2,969,146
		21,865,795*	

*Of this number 19,825,647 are in Negro Africa.

APPENDIX I

UNION WITH OTHER CONGREGATIONS

In the course of its two hundred and fifty-five years of existence, the Congregation of the Holy Ghost has on a number of occasions considered fusion or union with other religious societies. Some such unions were actually effected, while others fell short of realization. We shall indicate here in chronological order the various proposals that were made during the eighteenth and nineteenth centuries, but we find it prudent to omit the overtures toward union with the Holy Ghost Fathers which two large Congregations made since the beginning of the twentieth century.

For the sake of completeness, however, we shall mention the unions which Father Libermann and his group had contemplated prior to their entrance into the Congregation of the Holy Ghost.

A. CONGREGATIONS OF PRIESTS

1. The Society of Mary

cf. pp. 11 f.;
19 ff.

Above, in Chapters I and II, we have sifted the sparse historical data that is available concerning the union of St. Louis de Monfort's Society and the Holy Ghost Fathers.

2. Vincentian Fathers and the Foreign Missions of Paris

Fl. 473

In 1802, when Father Bertout presented Napoleon with a memorandum requesting the legal restoration of the Holy Ghost Fathers, Mr. Portalis, Secretary of Ecclesiastical Affairs, recommended that the Holy Ghost Fathers, the Foreign Missions and the Vincentian Fathers unite into a single Institute. On May 27, 1804, Napoleon actually issued a decree that ordered this fusion, but it is obvious that union by government decree would not have worked. It was never taken seriously by the three Congregations involved.

N. B. 250

A second effort in this direction was made around 1807 by Joseph Cardinal Fresch, the Chaplain General of France. He wanted the three Congregations to become a single establishment directed by the Vincentians and headquartered in Rome. Un-

doubtedly, he might have succeeded if Napoleon had not chosen
this particular time to invade the Papal States and imprison the
Pope. After his excommunication by Pius VII, the irate Emperor
simply suppressed all three Congregations.

cf. p. 52

3. CONGREGATION OF THE HOLY HEART OF MARY

pp. 130 ff.

This union was successfully accomplished in 1848. Its story is
told above in Chapter VI.

Before entering the Congregation of the Holy Ghost Fathers,
Libermann and his group had considered the possibility of uniting with:

a. *The Eudist Fathers*

In March 1839, Frederic Le Vavasseur wrote to Libermann,
who was then Novice Master of the Eudists, about the new society
which was being planned and suggested that they start in Rennes
in the novitiate of the Eudist Fathers: "We will adopt the constitutions of Father Eudes, with whatever modifications our work
demands and we will depart from France as a branch of your
community."

N. D. 1, 636

After consulting the Superior of the Eudists, Libermann replied: "He has told me that he will receive you with great pleasure
and that he would consider himself fortunate if the poor Congregation of Jesus and Mary could undertake such a great work
that is so agreeable to God." However, as we have related above,
the situation of Francis Libermann in Rennes was far from satisfactory. His departure from Rennes in 1839 definitely put an
end to all plans toward union with the Eudists.

N. D. 1, 639

cf. p. 69

b. *Congregation of Holy Cross*

In February 1842, Father Leboucher, C.S.C., paid a visit to
Libermann and proposed the fusion of the two congregations.
Just then Father Libermann was profoundly afflicted by Le
Vavasseur's constant opposition to all his ideas. In hopes that
the Superior of the Holy Cross Fathers would assume responsibility for both congregations, Libermann felt much attracted by
the proposal. The next day, however, he was ashamed of his
weakness and promised God not to falter again. Although his
willingness to consider the proposal perdured, he soon began to

N. D. 3, 25 f.

N. D. 3, 139 ff.;
143 ff.; 153 ff.

fear that Father Leboucher was indeed interested in having him and his priests join the Holy Cross Congregation, but that he had no intention of taking over the work for which their little society had been founded. After a few letters and visits that pointed up the difficulties of the affair, they dropped the plan.

B. CONGREGATIONS OF BROTHERS

1. THE LEONIST BROTHERS

pp. 146 f.　　We have related in Chapter IX how this congregation of Brothers became united with the Congregation of the Holy Ghost.

2. THE BROTHERS OF THE ANNUNCIATION

B. G. 21, 356 ff.　　The Congregation of the Brothers of Our Lady of the Annunciation had been founded at Montpellier, France, in 1840 by Father Montels. Their main objective was the care of orphans. Only three months after the foundation, the priest died. Father Louis Abram took over as his successor. Nine years later, Father Abram transferred the motherhouse of the Congregation to Misserghin in Algeria. There, the work developed and grew until by 1882 the Orphans' Institute of Misserghin possessed more than 3,000 acres under cultivation and a complex of large buildings to house the orphans and old people to whom it gave shelter. By 1885, no less than four thousand boys had been educated by the Brothers.[1] In 1887, the Propaganda definitely approved the constitutions of this flourishing congregation.

When Father Abram died in 1892, the Chapter elected Brother Liguori as his successor. Under his direction, the Institute continued its splendid work for several years. Suddenly, in 1897, disaster struck. An audit of the bursar's accounts showed that he had been an unfaithful steward. All funds were gone and an enormous debt had been accumulated—one so great, in fact, that even the sale of nearly all the land and the farms did not suffice to pay the creditors. The Institute faced bankruptcy. In an endeavor to save whatever could be saved from the fiasco, the Propaganda appointed an Apostolic Visitor—Father Xavier Libermann, a nephew of the Venerable Francis. While Father Libermann was able to correct several abuses that had crept into the Congregation since

---

[1] Five years earlier, Father Abram had founded a congregation of Sisters to function as auxiliaries.

Father Abram's death, the indebtedness of the Institute remained an insoluble problem. All the Brothers except the Superior, Brother Liguori, realized that their only salvation lay in union with another Congregation. Hence, when Brother Liguori died unexpectedly in 1900, they requested permission to join the Holy Ghost Congregation.

B. G. 21, 362 f.

Just at that time the Holy Ghost Fathers were anxious to establish a house in Algeria or Tunis, because the draft laws of France in those days exempted Brothers stationed there from military service. The Spiritans laid down certain stipulations and negoti-

B. G. 21, 106 f.; 169 ff.

ations came to a successful end in 1901. In March of that year, the Propaganda suppressed the Congregation of the Annunciation and allowed its members to enter the Congregation of the Holy Ghost. For this purpose, a special novitiate was erected in Misserghin.[2] The Institute now has an agricultural and mechanical school in addition to the orphanage.

3. The Brothers of Christian Doctrine

Goyau, II, 241 ff.

This congregation of teaching Brothers was founded early in the nineteenth century by the Venerable John de Lamennais. Soon after its establishment, the founder transferred its headquarters to Ploermel in Brittany—hence its popular name, "The Brothers of Ploermel." As early as 1837, they began to establish schools in the old French colonies and by 1852 the aging founder reported that his congregation had about nine hundred Brothers spread through more than two hundred and fifty schools in France and the colonies.

Va. 195 ff.

In an effort to secure solid spiritual training for his Brothers, Father de Lamennais appealed to Father Schwindenhammer and asked that the Holy Ghost Fathers take over the direction of the novitiate. It was for this reason that in 1853 Father Collin—one of Libermann's first novices—was sent to Ploermel. De Lamennais and Collin got along so well that the question of uniting the Brothers with the Congregation of the Holy Ghost soon came up for serious discussion. Father Schwindenhammer, along with Le Vavasseur and Briot, travelled to Brittany to open negotiations with the Venerable. However, after careful consideration, the proposed union was judged to be impractical. At that time the Holy Ghost

---

[2]In a similar way, the members of the Sisters' Congregation were allowed to join a religious society of Franciscan nuns.

Fathers were not yet numerous enough to absorb an additional nine hundred Brothers without exposing themselves to serious internal troubles. The two congregations remained on intimate terms and continued to work closely together thereafter, but the Holy Ghost Fathers gave up directing the novitiate in 1854.

C. CONGREGATIONS OF SISTERS

Obviously, there never was question of the total incorporation of nuns' congregations. In the course of the nineteenth century, however, the Spiritans seriously considered some sort of formalized association with two large groups of Sisters.

1. THE SISTERS OF THE IMMACULATE CONCEPTION

C. S. 44, 32 ff.

In 1842, Father Libermann gave some serious thought to the advisability of founding a congregation of Sisters. Several aspirants had been gathered together by Father Tisserant, and he was strongly urging the formation of a congregation that would aid

ibid., 23

the priests in their work. Although Libermann "considered it imprudent to begin such a work before [his own Congregation] had been solidly established," he saw the usefulness of such a foundation. Just then, however, Father Bessieux arrived and told him about the Congregation of the Immaculate Conception. It had been founded six years earlier by Mother Mary de Villeneuve at Castres. Because it appeared to suit very well the purpose for which his priests wanted a congregation of Sisters, Libermann was delighted to escape becoming the founder of a congregation of women and when pious ladies offered to aid him in his work, he thereafter gratefully referred them to Mother de Villeneuve.

ibid. 44

In 1850, Bishop Kobès, C.S.Sp., pressed Mother de Villeneuve for "the aggregation of her society" to the Holy Ghost Fathers "under a single Head and Superior, named by the Propaganda, just as is the case with the Vincentians and the Sisters of Charity." Father Libermann himself did nothing to promote this proposed

ibid. 45

union, but he was "quite willing to do what [the Sisters] wanted ... and to grant it ... if they asked for it." At length, Mother de Villeneuve wisely observed that as long as their Motherhouse was in Castres and Libermann was in Paris, there could be no question of any union. Moreover, she was opposed to any association as

ibid. 50

close as that of the Vincentians and the Sisters of Charity. Fearing to lose her independence, she discarded all thought of a union, hurriedly requested pontifical approbation of her group and, through the intercession of Bishop Bessieux, readily obtained it. When she died shortly after, her immediate successor kept all contacts with the Holy Ghost Fathers to the strictest minimum. After the successor's death in 1862, cordial relations between the two Congregations flourished once again. Nowadays, the Sisters work side by side with the Holy Ghost Fathers in many of their foreign missions.

2. The Sisters of Saint Joseph of Cluny

N. D. 6, 225

N. D. 6, 58

N. D. 6, 224 ff.

This congregation was founded in 1807 by Blessed Ann Mary Javouhey. By 1844 it had grown to about six hundred members, of whom some two hundred were working in the missions. It was through their labor in the colonies that Father Libermann became acquainted with the Sisters of Saint Joseph and sought contact with Mother Javouhey. He soon realized that, despite its sizeable membership and its hundred novices, the Congregation was in a precarious position. Insufficiently organized, without constitutions or pontifical approval, it was subject to the rival claims of several bishops in whose dioceses the Sisters were established. To extricate herself from the impasse, Mother Javouhey proposed to Father

N. D. 6, 226

Libermann in 1844 "that the two Congregations be united into one, making her Sisters dependent on [his] missionaries, and constituting him their Superior." She pointed out that in this way her Sisters would be certain of obtaining the unified spiritual training and guidance which was so necessary for them. Moreover, her plan had the support of the Papal Nuncio and of the Bishop of Beauvais.

Although he was frightened by the prospect of becoming entangled in difficulties with the bishops involved and apprehensive about having to take charge of six hundred Sisters, Libermann considered it would be going against God's will to oppose the plan. On the other hand, because he refused to take any positive steps

Not. 40

toward its realization, he left it up to Mother Javouhey and Bishop Gignoux of Beauvais to begin negotiations with Rome. Contrary to Mother Javouhey's expectations, Rome did not favor her plan.

After her death in 1851 and Father Libermann's in 1852, her successor again made overtures toward the desired union. Apprised of her design, Father Schwindenhammer and his Council

C. S. 44, 86

decided "to allow the Sisters to continue their efforts in Rome... reserving the right to examine later what ought to be done when

Not. 40

the Sisters present their request in a positive and official way."
In 1864 Pope Pius IX was personally consulted about the matter
by the Bishop of Autun. Although he realized the immense benefits
the Sisters were deriving from their supervision and guidance by
the Holy Ghost Fathers, the Pope recommended against any official association requiring pontifical approval. However, he willingly gave his blessing to the unofficial and moral union of the
two Congregations as it was then in force. That close but informal
association has existed ever since. Throughout the world, wherever
the Cluny Sisters are near a Spiritan residence they turn to the
Holy Ghost Fathers by preference for direction and guidance.

APPENDIX II

THE SPIRITAN HABIT

Fl. 587

The 1734 version of the Rules did not exactly determine the nature of the habit to be worn by the Holy Ghost Fathers, but merely stated that for all "the garb should be uniform, poor and simple of form." Portraits of eighteenth century Spiritans show that their dress consisted of a cassock with visible buttons, surmounted by a rabat with narrow white borders, as was customary for the clergy of France at that time. Probably they also wore the usual black sash.[3]

N. D. 13, App. p. 5
C. S. 5, 25, ff.

Father Libermann's daguerrotype and the other photograph published in *Notes et Documents* show the same dress, except that a black cord appears to have replaced the former sash.

C. S. 11, 102 ff.

The question of an official uniform for members of the Congregation was the object of a long discussion at the general meeting of 1853, because the decision had been taken to introduce the public vows of religion. As a religious society, so it was felt, the Congregation should have a distinct garb. The final choice fell on a black soutane, without visible buttons, and a black cord. Underneath the soutane members should wear the blue scapular of the Immaculate Conception, terminating at the collar in a rabat with a narrow white border. Subsequently, the scapular and the rabat have become separate items of apparel.

Some members had proposed a blue cord round the middle and another blue cord instead of a hatband, but this colorful proposal was judged to be against the simplicity proper to members of the Congregation. The camail or shoulder cape became an officially allowed optional item in 1892.

Following the persecution of 1904 in France, Holy Ghost Fathers who had been officially "secularized" but continued to work in former establishments of the Congregation dropped the use of the cord because it was too characteristic of a religious order. From these institutions the custom spread to other houses, but the

---

C. S. 11, 103

[3]In his reorganization of 1845 ff., Father Leguay abolished the rule of uniformity and poverty, but retained the requirement of simplicity. The original text was restored again in the 1885 edition of the Rules approved by the Holy See.

cord was never officially abolished. At present it is again in general use.

N. D. 7, 144
C. S. 5, 29
            Regarding the Brothers, at first they continued to wear their secular clothes unless these were unsuitable. However, as early as 1845 Father Libermann adopted for them the "soutanelle"[4] worn over a black waistcoat and black trousers, and outdoors, according to the custom of the time, a tall hat.

The General Chapter of 1875 replaced this garb by a regular soutane, reaching about eight inches above the ground, and a narrow black sash. Presumably the silk hat disappeared from the list of approved wear when it was no longer the normal dress for laymen.

As the reader undoubtedly knows, in hot climates the black soutane is usually replaced by one of white or light grey cloth.

---

[4]The "soutanelle" is a knee-length soutane or frock coat which is still worn outdoors by priests in many parts of Germany.

APPENDIX III

RELIGIOUS CONGREGATIONS FOUNDED BY HOLY GHOST FATHERS[5]

IN EUROPE

a. THE SISTERS SERVANTS OF THE HOLY HEART OF MARY

This Congregation was founded in 1860 by Father John Delaplace in Paris. Since then it has spread from France to Canada (three Provinces), the United States, Cuba and the Cameroons. Its Motherhouse is in Montgeron, France. Membership (1954): 951 professed Sisters; 107 novices. Literature: R. Piacentini, *F. J.-B. Delaplace,* Beauport-Montgeron, 1952, pp. 310. Cf. also *A. M. C.,* pp. 391 f.

b. MISSIONARY SISTERS OF THE HOLY GHOST (C.S.Sp.)

cf. p. 281

Founded in 1921 by Archbishop Alexander Le Roy, this congregation has houses in France, Portugal, the Netherlands and Canada. The Spiritan Sisters maintain missions throughout French and Portuguese Africa, in Cape Verde, Martinique and Guadeloupe. Membership (1957); 370 professed Sisters; 50 novices and postulants. Literature: *B. G.* 30, 452; 690; 799; *Roy,* 234 ff.; *Au Service de la femme noire,* Editions Suredit, (1946).

c. MISSIONARY SISTERS OF OUR LADY OF THE HOLY ROSARY

cf. pp. 281 f.

Bishop Joseph Shanahan founded this congregation in 1923. Its Motherhouse is in Killeshandra, Ireland. It also has houses in England and the United States. Its missions are in Nigeria, the Cameroons and Transvaal. Membership: 271 professed Sisters; 58 novices and postulants. Literature: John P. Jordan, *Bishop Shanahan of Southern Nigeria,* Dublin, 1949; *Silver Sheaves,* Killeshandra, 1949.

---

[5]Obviously, the Congregations of Sisters can point also to one or more pious ladies working in association with the priest as their founder or founders.

IN AMERICA

a. Missionary Sisters of Notre Dame de la Délivrande

This Congregation was founded in Martinique in 1868 by Father Anthony Dufrien. Later, it transferred its Motherhouse to Croix-Rouge near Grenoble, France. It has spread through France, Italy, Egypt, North Africa and Lebanon. Membership: 178 professed Sisters; 22 novices and postulants.

Literature: Joseph Janin, *Les Diocèses coloniaux,* Paris, 1938, pp. 282 ff.; Victor Hostachy, *Le Lis de la Martinique,* Grenoble, 1949.

b. Sisters of Our Lady of Guadeloupe

In 1945 Bishop John Gay founded this congregation at Trois Rivières, Guadeloupe. Its purpose is to aid the priests in social and parochial work. Membership (1955): 24 Sisters.

Literature: *B. G.* 41, 347; *E. P.* 31, I, 65.

IN REUNION

Daughters of Mary

cf. p. 144

This Congregation was founded in 1849 by Father Frederic Le Vavasseur. Its Motherhouse is in St. Denis, Reunion. The Sisters are established in Madagascar, Mauritius, Rodriguez, Tanganyika and France. Membership (1957): 311 professed Sisters.

Literature: Roger Dussercle, *Histoire d'une Fondation,* Port Louis, Mauritius, 1949; cf. also *C. S.* 44, pp. 92 ff.; *A. M. C. A.* 48 f.

IN AFRICA[6]

a. Daughters of the Holy Heart of Mary

Founded in 1858 by Father Emmanuel Barbier with the approval of Bishop Aloysius Kobès. Its Motherhouse is now in Dakar, Senegal. Membership (1954): 61 professed Sisters; 15 novices.

Literature: *C. S.* 44, pp. 100-106 (foundation); *B. G.* 3, 335 f.; 42, 99; 165; *A. M. C. A.* 51; *A. P. F.* 48, 133 ff., 197 ff.

---

[6]We list only congregations that have perdured to the present. Some of them are still in an experimental stage.

b. DAUGHTERS OF MARY (OF YAUNDE)

Founded in 1930 by Bishop Francis Vogt. Its Motherhouse is at Nsimalen, the Cameroons. Membership (1954) : 78 professed Sisters; 12 Novices; 8 postulants; 25 aspirants.

Literature: *Vogt,* 155 ff.; B. G. 42, 239; *A. M. C.* 397.

c. SISTERS SERVANTS OF MARY (OF DUALA)

Founded in 1939 by Bishop Mathurin Le Mailloux. Its Motherhouse is in Japoma, the Cameroons. Membership (1956) : 31 professed Sisters; 12 novices.

Literature: *B. G.* 42, 395 f.; *A. M. C. A.* 53.

d. LITTLE SISTERS OF ST. MARY (OF GABON)

Founded in 1911 by Bishop John Adam. Its Motherhouse is in Libreville, Gabon. Membership (1957) : 50 professed Sisters; 7 novices.

Literature: Marie Germaine, *Religieuses indigènes du Gabon —Les petites Soeurs de Ste Marie,* Louvain, n. d., 32 pages; *B. G.* 26, 915; 43, 24 f.; 44, 221; *A. M. C. A.* 48.

e. AFRICAN SISTERS OF THE HOLY HEART OF MARY

Founded in 1936 by Bishop Bernard Hilhorst in Tanganyika. Its Motherhouse is in Mgolole, Tanganyika. Membership (1955) : 34 professed Sisters; 6 novices; 18 postulants.

Literature: *B. G.* 44, 297 f; *E. P.* 31, I, 223.

f. SISTERS OF ST. JOSEPH OF AFRICA

Founded in 1939 by Bishop John Heffernan. Membership (1955) ; 20 professed Sisters; 5 novices. Its Motherhouse is in Bura, Kenya.

Literature: *B. G.* 44, 141; *E. P.* 31, I, 205 and 208.

g. SISTERS OF OUR LADY OF KILIMANJARO

Founded in 1931 by Bishop Henry Gogarty. Their Motherhouse is in Huruma, Tanganyika. Membership (1955) : 94 professed Sisters; 34 aspirants.

Literature: *B. G.* 44, 177; *E. P.* 31, I, 209 ff.

h. Sisters of the Most Pure Heart of Mary (Nigeria)

Founded in 1945 (?) by Bishop Charles Heerey. Their Motherhouse is in Urualla, Nigeria. Membership: 27 professed Sisters; 23 novices; 30 postulants; 71 aspirants.
Literature: *E. P.* 31, I, 112 and 119.

i. Sisters of the Holy Heart of Mary (Belgian Congo)

Founded around 1926 by Monsignor Louis Lempereur. Motherhouse: Kongolo, Belgian Congo. Membership (1955): 32 professed Sisters; 8 novices; 5 postulants.
Literature: *B. G.* 43, 384; *E. P.* 31, I, 196.

j. Sisters of the Assumption of the Blessed Virgin (Kenya)

Founded in 1957 by Archbishop Joseph McCarthy. Novitiate: Mangu (Kenya). Membership (1957): 14 postulants.
Literature: *B. G.* 45, 69.

k. Brothers of the Immaculate Heart of Mary

Founded in 1942 by Bishop Joseph Byrne. Motherhouse: Maua, Tanganyika. Membership (1955): 18 professed Brothers; 17 novices; 4 postulants.
Literature: *B. G.* 44, 177; *E. P.* 31, I, 212.

l. Little Brothers of St. Joseph (of Senegal)

Founded in 1925 by Bishop Louis Le Hunsec. Novitiate at Sebikhotane, Senegal. Membership: 11 professed Brothers; 8 novices and postulants.
Literature: *B. G.* 32, 469; *E. P.* 31, I, 88 ff.; see also above, pp. 496 f.

m. Brothers of St. Joseph[7] (of French Cameroons)

Founded in 1930 by Father Peter Richard. Motherhouse: Nlong, the Cameroons. This interdiocesan congregation absorbed the Brothers of St. Peter Claver of Middle Congo. Membership (1955): 40 professed Brothers; 18 novices; 50 postulants.

---

[7]In a recent letter, Bishop Teerenstra of Doume indicates that this Congregation has now been disbanded. Its members have joined the Brothers of the Sacred Heart (of Canada) and the Holy Ghost Congregation.

Literature: *Grands Lacs,* vol. 62, 1946 f., pp. 75-78; *Vogt,* 152 ff.; *B. G.* 42, 238 f.; 43, 83 f.; *E. P.* 31, I, 90 ff.

n. BROTHERS OF ST. PETER CLAVER (OF ANGOLA)

Founded in 1947 by Bishop Daniel Junqueira. Motherhouse: Nova Lisboa, Angola. This congregation succeeded another one of the same name founded by Monsignor Alfred Keiling. Membership (1955): 18 professed Brothers; 4 novices; 12 postulants; 66 aspirants.

Literature: *B. G. 27,* 149; *43,* 448 f.; *E. P. 21,* I, 176; 183; 184; 187.

o. BROTHERS OF ST. PETER CLAVER (OF KENYA)

Recently started by Archbishop Joseph McCarthy at Kaumoni, Kenya, with five postulants. Cf. *E. P.* 31, I, 201.

p. BROTHERS OF ?

Recently started by Bishop Gustave Bouve at Malela, Belgian Congo, with sixteen postulants. Cf. *E. P.* 31, I, 195.

APPENDIX IV

ECCLESIASTICAL CIRCUMSCRIPTIONS ENTRUSTED
TO THE SPIRITANS

A. AMERICA

1. Prefecture of the St. Pierre and Miquelon Islands.
2. Diocese of Basse-Terre and Pointe-à-Pitre, Guadeloupe.
3. Diocese of Saint-Pierre and Fort-de-France, Martinique.
4. Diocese of Cayenne, French Guiana.
5. Prelature *"nullius"* of Tefe, Brazil.
6. Prelature *"nullius"* of Jurua, Brazil.

B. AFRICA

7. Archdiocese of Dakar, Senegal.
8. Diocese of Ziguinchor, Senegal.
9. Prefecture of St. Louis, Senegal.
10. Archdiocese of Conakry, French Guinea.
11. Prefecture of Kankan, French Guinea.
12. Diocese of Freetown and Bo, Sierra Leone.
13. Diocese of Bathurst, Gambia.
14. Archdiocese of Onitsha, Nigeria.
15. Diocese of Owerri, Nigeria.
16. Prefecture of Oturkpo, Nigeria.
17. Prefecture of Kabba, Nigeria.
18. Diocese of Duala, French Cameroons.
19. Archdiocese of Yaunde, French Cameroons.
20. Diocese of Doume, French Cameroons.
21. Diocese of Libreville, Gabon.
22. Diocese of Pointe-Noire, French Equatorial Africa.
23. Archdiocese of Brazzaville, French Equatorial Africa.
24. Diocese of Fort-Rousset, French Equatorial Africa.
25. Archdiocese of Bangui, French Equatorial Africa.
26. Prefecture of Bangassou, French Equatorial Africa.
27. Vicariate of Kongolo, Belgian Congo.
28. Vicariate of Kindu, Belgian Congo.
29. Diocese of Bethlehem, Orange Free State, South Africa.
30. Archdiocese of Nairobi, Kenya.

31. Diocese of Mombasa-Zanzibar, Kenya.
32. Diocese of Moshi, Tanganyika.
33. Diocese of Morogoro, Tanganyika.

p. 555   As Chapter XX indicated, since 1941 the **overseas territories** of Portugal are no longer formally entrusted to **any congregation.** However, in the following areas the Holy Ghost **Fathers still** constitute the majority of the non-native clergy:
34. Archdiocese of Loanda, Angola.
35. Diocese of Nova Lisboa, Angola.
36. Diocese of Silva Porto, Angola.
37. Diocese of Sa da Bandeira, Angola.
38. Diocese of Cape Verde, Cape Verde Islands.

C. ISLANDS OF THE INDIAN OCEAN

39. Diocese of Diego-Suarez, Madagascar.
40. Diocese of Majunga, Madagascar.
41. Diocese of Saint-Denis, Reunion.
42. Diocese of Port Louis, Mauritius.

APPENDIX V

EDUCATIONAL INSTITUTIONS OPERATED BY THE HOLY GHOST FATHERS

A. INSTITUTES OPEN TO ALL QUALIFIED STUDENTS

AMERICA

1. Duquesne University, Pittsburgh, Pa., U. S. A., (1878).
2. St. Emma Military Academy, Rock Castle, Virginia, U. S. A., (1947).
3. Notre Dame High School, Riverside, California, U. S. A., (1957).
4. St. Alexander College, Limbour, Canada, (1905).
5. Bishop MacNeil High School, Toronto, Canada, (1958).
6. St. Christopher College, Saint Pierre and Miquelon Islands, (1920).
7. St. Martial College, Port au Prince, Haiti, (1871).
8. Seminary-College, Gourbeyre, Guadeloupe, (1939).
9. Seminary-College, Fort-de-France, Martinique, (1865).
10. St. Mary's College, Port of Spain, Trinidad, (1863).
11. College of Our Lady of Fatima, Port of Spain, Trinidad, (1948).
12. College "Sant Ana," Itauna, Brazil, (1954).
13. College "Padre Curvelo," Curvelo, Brazil, (1951).
14. Seminary-College of the Holy Ghost, Tefe, Brazil, (1912).

EUROPE

15. Holy Ghost Seminary, Croix-Valmer, France, (1703).[8]
16. St. Joseph Junior Seminary, Allex, France, (1875).
17. The Pontifical French Seminary, Rome, Italy, (1853).
18. Blackrock College, Dublin, Ireland, (1860).
19. Rockwell College, Cashel, Ireland, (1864).
20. St. Mary's College, Dublin, Ireland, (1890).
21. Holy Ghost College, Knechtsteden, Germany, (1947).

---

[8]Transferred from Paris in 1954.

AFRICA

22. Libermann Seminary (interdiocesan), Sebikhotane, **Senegal**.
23. St. Louis Seminary-College, Ziguinchor, **Senegal**.
24. Seminary-College, Dixinn, French Guinea.
25. Catholic Training College, Bo, Sierra Leone.
26. Christ the King College, Bo, Sierra Leone.
27. St. Edward's Secondary School, Brookfields, **Sierra Leone**.
28. St. Augustine's Secondary School, Bathurst, **Gambia**.
29. St. Peter's Training College, Achina, Nigeria.
30. St. Anthony's Training College, Agulu, Nigeria.
31. Bigard Memorial Seminary, Enugu, Nigeria.
32. St. Theresa's College, Nsukka, Nigeria.
33. Christ the King College, Onitsha, Nigeria.
34. Mount St. Mary's Training College, Azaraegbulu, **Nigeria**.
35. St. Peter Claver Seminary, Okpala, Nigeria.
36. Holy Ghost College, Owerri, Nigeria.
37. Stella Maris College, Port-Harcourt, Nigeria.
38. Holy Ghost Training College, Umuahia, Nigeria.
39. St. Michael's College, Aliade, Nigeria.
40. Our Lady of Fatima Training College, Nsu, **Nigeria**.
41. Sacred Heart College, Eziukwu-Aba, Nigeria.
42. Catholic Training College, Umaturu-Etehe, **Nigeria**.
43. Our Lady of Fatima Training College, Bori, **Nigeria**.
44. St. Joseph's Seminary, Akono, French Cameroons.
45. Bessieux Seminary-College, Libreville, Gabon.
46. Libermann Seminary (interdiocesan), **Brazzaville**, **French** Equatorial Africa.
47. Junior Seminary, Mbamou, French Equatorial Africa.
48. Junior Seminary, Makoua, French Equatorial Africa.
49. Junior Seminary, Fort Sibut, French Equatorial Africa.
50. St. Joseph Seminary, Malange, Angola.
51. Junior Seminary, Caala, Angola.
52. Teofilo Duarte College, Cuima, Angola.
53. Alexander Herculano College, Nova Lisboa, **Angola**.
54. Christ the King Seminary, Nova Lisboa, Angola.
55. Sacred Heart Seminary, Vila Junqeira, Angola.
56. Junior Seminary, Jau, Angola.
57. St. John Berchmans Seminary, Kongolo, Belgian Congo.
58. Holy Ghost College, Kindu, Belgian Congo.
59. Queen of the Apostles' Seminary, Ngong, Kenya.

60. Holy Ghost College, Mangu, Kenya.
61. St. Mary's College, Nairobi, Kenya.
62. St. Francis College, Pugu, Tanganyika.
63. Our Lady of the Angels Seminary, Kibosho, **Tanganyika**.
64. St. James' Seminary, Kilema-Chini, Tanganyika.
65. St. Patrick's Training College, Singa-Chini, **Tanganyika**.
66. Junior Seminary, Bagamoyo, Tanganyika.
67. Catholic Teacher Training School, Morogoro, **Tanganyika**.
68. St. Thomas' Seminary, Morogoro, Tanganyika.
69. Bishop Shanahan Training College, Orlu, **Nigeria**.
70. St. Pius X College, Bodo, Nigeria.

ISLANDS OF THE INDIAN OCEAN

71. St. John's Seminary, Diego-Suarez, Madagascar.
72. St. Paul's Seminary, Majunga, Madagascar.
73. St. John Vianney Seminary-College, Cilaos, Reunion.
74. Holy Ghost College, Quatre Bornes, Mauritius.

B. INSTITUTES RESERVED EXCLUSIVELY FOR MEMBERS AND ASPIRANTS OF THE CONGREGATION

AMERICA

1. St. Mary's Seminary, Ferndale, Norwalk, Conn., U. S. A., (1906).
2. Holy Ghost College, Cornwells Heights, Pa., U. S. A., (1897).
3. Holy Ghost Fathers Junior Seminary, Ann Arbor, Mich., U. S. A., (1949).
4. Immaculate Heart of Mary Collegiate Seminary, Bethel Borough, Pa., U. S. A.[9]
5. Junior Seminary (attached to St. Alexander College), Limbour, Quebec, Canada, (1905).
6. Holy Ghost Senior Seminary, Montreal, Canada, (1943). To be transferred to Quebec in 1958.
7. Junior Seminary attached to Sant-Ana College, Itauna, Brazil, (1953).
8. Institute of the Holy Ghost, Emilianopolis, Brazil, (1953).

---

[9]Construction of this new seminary is scheduled to start in 1958.

EUROPE

9. Interprovincial Scholasticate, Fribourg, Switzerland, (1904).
10. Institute of the Holy Ghost, Rome, Italy, (1949).
11. Junior Seminary, Bletterans, France, (1948).
12. Junior Seminary, Blotzheim, France, 1920).
13. Theological Seminary, Chevilly, France, (1864).
14. Junior Seminary, Langonnet, France, (1858).
15. University Seminary of the Holy Ghost, Lille, France, (1951).
16. Junior Seminary, Maulevrier, France, (1954).
17. Philosophical Seminary, Mortain, France, (1923).
18. St. Joseph Junior Seminary, Neugrange, France, (1904).
19. Junior Seminary, Saint-Ilan, France, (1855).
20. St. Florent Junior Seminary, Saverne, France, (1900).
21. Junior Seminary attached to Blackrock College, Dublin, Ireland, (1860).
22. Holy Ghost Missionary College, Kimmage, Dublin, Ireland, (1911).
23. Junior Seminary attached to Rockwell College, Ireland, (1864).
24. Junior Seminary, Broich, Germany, (1905).
25. Junior Seminary, Buchen, Germany, (1953).
26. Junior Seminary, Donaueschingen, Germany, (1921).
27. Senior Seminary Knechtsteden, Germany, (1895).
28. Junior Seminary, Menden, Germany, (1927).
29. Junior Seminary, Speyer, Germany, (1922).
30. Junior Seminary, Braga, Portugal, (1919).
31. Theological Seminary, Carcavelos, Portugal, (1952).
32. University Seminary, Coimbra, Portugal, (1943).
33. Junior Seminary, Godim, Portugal, (1921).
34. Philosophical Seminary, Viana do Castelo, Portugal, (1922).
35. Junior Seminary, Paredes de Nava, Spain, (1955).
36. Spiritan College, Gentinnes, Belgium, (1908).
37. Junior Seminary, Lier, Belgium, (1900).
38. Senior Seminary, Louvain, Belgium, (1911).
39. Junior Seminary, Weert, Netherlands, (1904).
40. Senior Seminary, Gemert, Netherlands, (1914).
41. Seminary for Late Vocations, Hattem, Netherlands, (1957).
42. St. Mary's College, Castlehead, England, (1907).
43. St. Joseph's College, Upton Hall, England, (1945).
44. Seminary for Late Vocations, Uddington, Scotland, (1956).

45. Junior Seminary, Bouveret, Switzerland, (1920).
46. Junior Seminary, Bydgoszcz, Poland, (1924).

AFRICA

47. Junior Seminary, Ihiala, Nigeria, (1952).

APPENDIX VI

PROVINCES AND DISTRICTS OF THE CONGREGATION[10]

PROVINCES

1. France
2. Ireland
3. Germany
4. Portugal
5. United States of America
6. Belgium
7. Netherlands
8. Great Britain
9. (French) Canada
10. Poland (Vice Province)
11. Switzerland (Vice Province)

In preparation:

1. Spain (dependent on Portugal)
2. English Canada (dependent on Ireland)
3. Nigeria (dependent on Nigeria District)
4. South East Brazil   a. Rio de Janeiro division (dependent on Tefe district)

                 b. Sao Paulo division (dependent on Jurua district)

DISTRICTS

AMERICA

1. St. Pierre and Miquelon
2. Haiti
3. Guadeloupe and Martinique
4. Trinidad
5. Puerto Rico
6. French Guiana
7. Tefe, Brazil
8. Jurua, Brazil

AFRICA

9. Senegal
10. Cape Verde Islands
11. French Guinea
12. Sierra Leone and Gambia
13. Nigeria (Onitsha and Owerri)
14. Benue, Nigeria (Oturkpo and Kabba)

---

[10]Concerning the difference between Province and District, see p. 237.

593

15. Yaunde-Duala, Cameroons
16. Doume, Cameroons
17. Gabon
18. Brazzaville
19. Ubangui
20. Loanda, Angola

21. Nova Lisboa, Angola
22. Kongolo-Kindu, Belgian Congo
23. Bethlehem, South Africa
24. Kenya
25. Kilimanjaro
26. Bagamoyo

INDIAN OCEAN

27. Madagascar
28. Reunion

29. Mauritius

EUROPE

30. Auteuil, France

GENEALOGY OF SPIRITAN PROVINCES[11]

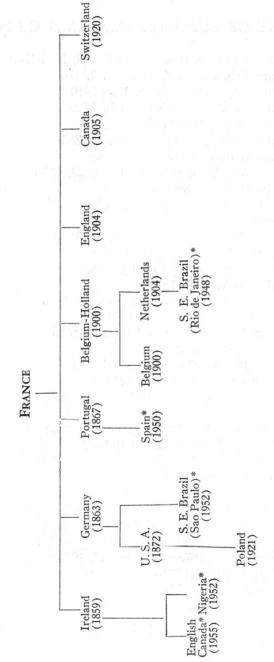

FRANCE

Ireland (1859)
Germany (1863)
U.S.A. (1872)
S. E. Brazil (Sao Paulo)* (1952)
Poland (1921)
English Canada* (1955)
Nigeria* (1952)
Portugal (1867)
Spain* (1950)
Belgium–Holland (1900)
Belgium (1900)
Netherlands (1904)
S. E. Brazil (Rio de Janeiro)* (1948)
England (1904)
Canada (1905)
Switzerland (1920)

[11]The number indicates the year of the first foundation. An asterisk denotes provinces in formation.

APPENDIX VII

LIST OF SUPERIOR GENERALS C.S.Sp.

1. Fr. Claude Francis Poullart des Places, 1703-1709
   born Feb. 26, 1679; died Oct. 2, 1709
2. Fr. James Hyacinth Garnier, 1709-1710
   born about 1687; died March, 1710
3. Fr. Louis Bouic, 1710-1763
   born Aug. 5, 1864; died Jan. 2, 1763
4. Fr. Francis Becquet, 1763-1788
   born March 14, 1705; died Oct. 28, 1788
5. Fr. John Duflos, 1788-1805
   born July 10, 1726; died Feb. 28, 1805
6. Fr. James Bertout, 1805-1832
   born May 4, 1753; died Dec. 10, 1832
7. Fr. Amable Fourdinier, 1832-1845
   born Aug. 31, 1788; died Jan. 5, 1845
8. Fr. Nicholas Warnet, 1845
   born May 30, 1795; died Aug. 30, 1863
9. Fr. Alexander Leguay, 1845-1848
   born April 7, 1794; died Feb. 27, 1865
10. Fr. Alexander Monnet, 1848
    born Jan. 4, 1812; died Dec. 1, 1849
11. Fr. Francis Libermann, 1848-1852
    born April 12, 1802; died Feb. 2, 1852
12. Fr. Ignatius Schwindenhammer, 1852-1881
    born Feb. 15, 1818; died March 6, 1881
13. Fr. Frederic Le Vavasseur, 1881-1882
    born Feb. 25, 1811; died Jan. 16, 1882
14. Fr. Ambrose Emonet, 1883-1895
    born March 26, 1828; died June 28, 1898
15. H. E. Archbishop Alexander Le Roy, 1896-1926
    born Jan. 19, 1854; died April 21, 1938
16. H. E. Archbishop Louis Le Hunsec, 1926-1950
    born Jan. 6, 1878; died Dec. 25, 1954
17. Fr. Francis Griffin, 1950-
    born Sept. 16, 1893;

APPENDIX VIII

THE EVOLUTION OF THE VICARIATE OF THE TWO GUINEAS AND OF THE MISSIONS WHICH GRADUALLY RESTRICTED ITS TERRITORY

PREFATORY REMARKS

Heavy print indicates circumscriptions served by the Holy Ghost Fathers.

Names in italics refer to actually existing dioceses and other ecclesiastical divisions.

Dotted rectangles mark areas which originated outside the limits of the territories comprised in these schemata.

The heavy black line indicates which present diocese or archdiocese is the direct successor of the original mission.

Symbols used for the different religious orders having missions in the territories listed in the schemata:

A. A.	Assumptionists
C. I. C. M.	Scheutists
C. M.	Vincentians
C. P.	Passionists
C. S. C. M.	Priests of the Holy Heart of Mary (later united with the Congregation of the Holy Ghost)
C. S. Sp.	Spiritans
C. SS. CC.	Picpus Priests
C. SS. R.	Redemptorists
I. C.	Rosminians
I. M. C.	Consolata Missionaries
M. S. C.	Missionaries of the Sacred Heart
O. E. S. A.	Augustinians
O. F. M.	Franciscans
O. F. M. Cap.	Capuchins
O. M. I.	Oblates of Mary Immaculate
O. P.	Dominicans
O. S. B.	Benedictines
O. S. C.	Order of the Holy Cross
S. A. C.	Pallotines
S. C. J.	Priests of the Sacred Heart
S. J.	Jesuits
S. M. A.	Society of African Missions
S. M. M.	Monfortists
S. M. S. J. M.	Mill Hill Fathers
S. S. Patr.	Priests of St. Patrick
S. V. D.	Society of the Divine Word
S. X.	Xaverians
W. F.	White Fathers

Symbols used for the different kinds of ecclesiastical circum-scriptions:

A.   Archdiocese

Ab.   Abbacy

D.   Diocese

M.   Mission

P.   Prefecture

PV.   Pro-Vicariate

V.   Vicariate

MAIN SOURCES

Acta apostolicae Sedis
Le Missioni Cattoliche, Rome, 1950
Bulletin général (de la Congrégation du St.-Esprit)
A Catholic Directory of East Africa, Mombasa, 1950
Annuaire des Missions Catholiques en Afrique Française, Dakar,
    1955
Releases of the *Agenzia Fides*

For information regarding the evolution of the Vicariate of the Independent Congo State a debt of gratitude is owed to the Very Reverend Father Proost, Superior of the Spiritan Province of Belgium.

APPENDIX IX

THE EVOLUTION OF THE PREFECTURE OF ZANGUEBAR AND OF THE MISSIONS WHICH GRADUALLY RESTRICTED ITS TERRITORY

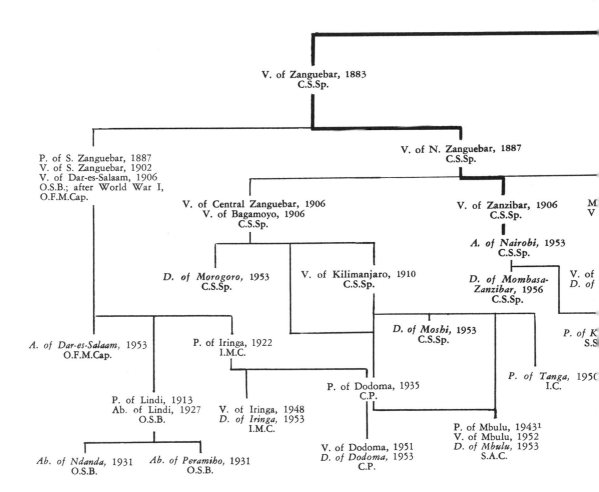

V. of Zanguebar, 1883
C.S.Sp.

P. of S. Zanguebar, 1887
V. of S. Zanguebar, 1902
V. of Dar-es-Salaam, 1906
O.S.B.; after World War I,
O.F.M.Cap.

V. of N. Zanguebar, 1887
C.S.Sp.

V. of Central Zanguebar, 1906
V. of Bagamoyo, 1906
C.S.Sp.

V. of Zanzibar, 1906
C.S.Sp.

M
V

A. of Nairobi, 1953
C.S.Sp.

D. of Morogoro, 1953
C.S.Sp.

V. of Kilimanjaro, 1910
C.S.Sp.

D. of Mombasa-
Zanzibar, 1956
C.S.Sp.

V. of
D. of

A. of Dar-es-Salaam, 1953
O.F.M.Cap.

P. of Iringa, 1922
I.M.C.

D. of Moshi, 1953
C.S.Sp.

P. of K
S.S

P. of Lindi, 1913
Ab. of Lindi, 1927
O.S.B.

V. of Iringa, 1948
D. of Iringa, 1953
I.M.C.

P. of Dodoma, 1935
C.P.

P. of Tanga, 195(
I.C.

P. of Mbulu, 1943[1]
V. of Mbulu, 1952
D. of Mbulu, 1953
S.A.C.

Ab. of Ndanda, 1931
O.S.B.

Ab. of Peramiho, 1931
O.S.B.

V. of Dodoma, 1951
D. of Dodoma, 1953
C.P.

PREFECTURE OF ZANGUEBAR, 1860[2]
C.S.Sp.

PV. of Victoria Nyanza, 1880
V. of Victoria Nyanza, 1883
W.F.

of Kenya, 1905   P. of Benadir, 1904
of Kenya, 1909   *V. of Mogadiscio, 1927*
   I.M.C.   O.F.M.

V. of N. Victoria Nyanza, 1894
V. of Uganda, 1915
W.F.

V. of S.

Nyeri, 1926   P. of· Meru, 1926
Nyeri, 1953   *D. of Meru, 1953*
.M.C.   I.M.C.

V. of Upper Nile, 1894   *A. of Rubaga, 1953*   V. of Masaka, 1939   V. of Bukob
S.M.S.J.M.   W.F.   *D. of Masaka, 1953*   W.F
                                                              African Clergy

ui, 1957
Patr.

P. of Kavirondo, 1925   V. of Kampala, 1948   V. of Rwenzori, 1934   V. of Kagera, 195
V. of Kisumu, 1932   *D. of Kampala, 1953*   *D. Mbarara, 1953*   *D. of Rutabo, 195*
D. of Kisumu, 1953   S.M.S.J.M.   W.F.   African Clergy
S.M.S.J.M.

P. of Eldoret, 1953   *D. of Tororo, 1953*
   S.S.Patr.   S.M.S.J.M.

D.

P. of M
D. of M
I

BIBLIOGRAPHY

Acta Apostolicae Sedis, Rome, 1909 ff. Contains all official documents, appointments, etc. emanating from the Holy See.

L' Ami de la Religion (et du Roi), Paris, 1814-1862. Ecclesiastical news bulletins.

Annales de la Propagation de la Foi, Lyon, 1822 ff. General index 1822-1853. Important source of information especially for the earlier period in the nineteenth century revival of the Catholic missions.

Annuaire des Missions Catholiques d'Afrique, D. A. de Dakar, edition 1957, Paris, 1956. 592 pages.

Annuaire des Missions Catholiques en Afrique Française (1955), Paris, 1955, 493 pages.

Atlas missionnaire des Pères du St. Esprit, Paris, 1936. Antiquated but still useful.

"Au Cameroun Spiritain," *Grand Lacs,* vol. 62, 1946-47, pp. 206-336. A series of articles about the various aspects of missionary labor in the Cameroons.

Chanoine Augouard (ed.), *Mgr. Augouard. "28 années au Congo, Lettres de Mgr. Augouard.* Vols. I and II, Poitiers, 1905; vol. III (subtitle *"36 années au Congo"*), *ibid.,* 1914; vol. IV (subtitle *"44 années au Congo"*), Evreux, 1934.

Martin J. Bane, S.M.A., *The Catholic Story of Liberia,* New York, 1950, 163 pages.

Jean Barassin, C.S.Sp., *Bourbon des origines jusqu'en 1714,* Paris, 1953. 448 pages. First volume of a new series of studies regarding the religious history of Reunion.

Mgr. Baunard, *Le Cardinal Lavigerie,* Paris, 1922. 2 vols.

E. Baur and A. Le Roy, C.S.Sp., *Voyage dans l'Oudoé, l'Ouzigoua et l'Ousogara,* 4th ed., Tours, 1899. 367 pages. Early East African mission history.

Johannes Beckmann, *Die Katholische Kirche im neuen Afrika,* Einsiedeln, 1947. 372 pages. Comprehensive study.

G. Beslier, *L'Apôtre du Congo, Mgr. Augouard,* Paris, 1926. 262 pages.

Biographies, 1703-1803. Paris, 1909. 105 pages. Short biographies of some eighteenth century Holy Ghost Fathers.

Ernest Bismarck, C.S.Sp., *Pater Amand Acker (1848-1923),* Knechtsteden, 1925. 60 pages.

Pierre Blanchard, "L'Abnégation chez le Vénérable Père Libermann," *Le renoncement dans la vie chrétienne selon St. Jean Eudes et ses disciples,* Paris, 1956, pp. 93-110.

Antonio Brasio, C.S.Sp., *Monumenta Missionaria Africana,* Lisbon, 1952 ff. Thus far 7 vols. have been published. Important collection of documents about the ancient African missions.

Maurice Briault, C.S.Sp., *Le Vénérable Père F. M. P. Libermann,* Paris, 1946. 580 pages.

Sur les pistes de l'A. E. F., 2nd ed., Paris, 1948. 285 pages.

Dans la forêt du Gabon, Paris, n. d., 195 pages.

Sous le Zéro Équatorial, 2nd ed., Paris, 1928. 247 pages.

"La Mission du Bas-Niger apres cinquante ans d'existence," *Revue d'Histoire des Missions,* vol. 12, 1935, pp. 512-563.

"Le Congo-Océan et les Missions catholiques," *Revue d'Histoire des Missions,* vol. 12, 1935, pp. 71-76.

"Cinquante années de missions au royaume de Loango," *Revue d'Histoire des Missions,* vol. 14, 1937, pp. 380-388; pp. 502-513.

"Le cinquantenaire de la Mission du Congo français," *Revue d'Histoire des Missions,* vol. 15, 1938, pp. 504-522; vol. 16, 1939, pp. 37-54.

A. Brou, S.J., "Les Missions dans les colonies françaises," *Revue d'Histoire des Missions,* 1931, pp. 162-181. Contains many errors regarding the Spiritan missions.

"Le prophétisme protestant," *Études,* 1925, vol. 184, pp. 730-747.

"Le Prophétisme dans les églises protestantes indigènes d'Afrique," *Revue d'Histoire des Missions,* vol. 8, 1931, pp. 71-84.

"L'expansion missionnaire en Afrique depuis cent ans," *Revue d'Histoire des Missions,* vol. 14, 1937, pp. 108-128.

Walbert Buhlmann, "P. Charles Sacleux, C.S.Sp., Missionar und Wissenschaftler," *Zeitschrift fuer Missionswissenschaft,* vol. 4 (1948), pp. 17-32.

Bulletin Général (de la Congrégation du St. Esprit), Paris, 1857 ff. 45 volumes. Periodic reports about all works of the Holy Ghost Fathers and their Congregation in general. A very rich source of information about a century of apostolic labor. General index 1857-1950.

Adolphe Cabon, C.S.Sp., *Notes et Documents relatifs à la Vie et l'Oeuvre du Vénérable Francois-Marie-Paul Libermann,* Paris, 1929-1956. 13 volumes, 2 appendices and 1 vol. of complements. Outstanding collection of documents and letters.

Mgr. Alexis-Jean-Marie Guilloux, Port-au-Prince, 1929. 626 pages. Religious history of Haiti.

La première expédition des Missionnaires du St. Coeur de Marie en Guinée (Paris, 1930), 51 pages.

"La spiritualité du Vénérable Libermann," *La Vie Spirituelle,* vol. 50, 1937, pp. 42-60.

Bibliographie, Paris, 1930. 44 pages.

"Le Séminaire des Colonies," *Revue d'Histoire des Missions,* vol. 13, 1936, pp. 563-572; vol. 14, 1937, pp. 74-90.

Notes sur l'Histoire religieuse d'Haiti. De la Révolution au Concordat (1789-1860), Port-au-Prince, 1933. 515 pages.

"Le clergé de la Guyane sous le Révolution," *Revue d'Histoire des Colonies,* 1950, pp. 173-202.

"Le Séminaire St. Jacques d'Haiti," *Revue d'Histoire des Missions,* vol. 11, 1934, pp. 530-550.

Campagne Apostolique. Missionary statistics published regularly since 1925 by the Holy Ghost Fathers. Usually inserted in the *Bulletin Général.*

Bernard U. Campbell, "Memoir of Rev. J. F. Moranvillé," *United States Catholic Magazine,* vol. 1, 1843, pp. 433 ff.

A Catholic Directory of East Africa (1950), Mombasa, 1950. 187 pages.

Chroniques des Missions confiées à la Congrégation du St. Esprit, Aperçu Historique et Exercice 1930-1931, Paris, 1932; *Années 1931-1933,* Paris, 1935; *Années 1934-1936;* Paris, 1936.

John J. Considine, M. M., *Africa. World of New Men,* New York, 1954, 398 pages.

Joaquim Alves Correia, C.S.Sp., *A Dilatação da Fé no Imperio Portuguẽs,* Lisbon, 1936, 2 vols.

Civilizando Angola e Congo, Braga, 1922, 101 pages.

Evangelizadores do Trabalho, Braga, 1923, 78 pages. The role of Brothers in missionary work.

J. Daigre, C.S.Sp., *Oubangui-Chari,* Issoudun, 3rd ed., 1950. 200 pages.

A. da Silva Rego, *Curso de Missionologia,* Lisbon, 1956. 700 pages. Contains the history of missionary work in Portuguese overseas territories.

Albert David, C.S.Sp., *Les Missionnaires du Séminaire du St. Esprit à Quebec et en Acadie au XVIIIe siècle,* Paris, 1926. 58 pages.

"Le Séminaire du St. Esprit et les Missions de la Nouvelle France au XVIIIe siècle," *Bulletin des Recherches Historiques,* 1929, pp. 278-283.

"Les Spiritains dans l'Amérique Septentrionale au XVIIIe siecle," *ibid.,* pp. 314-319.

"Messire Pierre Maillard, Apôtre des Micmacs," *ibid.,* pp. 365-375.

"Les deux premiers Prêtres Acadiens," *ibid.,* pp. 444-446.

"Les Spiritains en Acadie," *ibid.,* pp. 460-463.

"L'Abbé Le Loutre," *Revue de l'Université d'Ottawa,* vol. I, pp. 474-485; vol. II, pp. 65-75.

"Le Judas de l'Acadie," *ibid.,* vol. III, pp. 492-513; vol. IV, pp. 22-35.

"L'Apôtre des Micmacs," ibid., vol. V, pp. 425-452.

"A propos du Testament de l'Abbé Maillard," *Nova Francia,* 1927, pp. 99-109; 149-163.

Decrees of the General Chapter (C.S.Sp.), 1950, Washington, 1950. 40 pages.

F. Delaplace and J. M. Pivault, C.S.Sp., *Le Père Jacques-Désiré Laval,* 2nd ed., Paris, n.d. 396 pages.

J. Dellicour, "Mgr. Augouard et le Congo Belge," *Institut Royal Colonial Belge, Bulletin des Séances,* vol. XV, 1944, pp. 10-31.

H. de Maupeou, C.S.Sp., "Le R. P. Horner et la fondation de la mission de Zanguebar," *Revue d'Histoire des Missions,* vol. 9, 1932, pp. 506-533.

A. de Winter, C.S.Sp., "De Nederlandse Provincie van de Congregatie van de H. Geest," *Libermann Herdenking,* Gemert, 1952, pp. 99-110.

J. de Wit, "Un appel oublié au missionnaires belges," *Le Mouvement des Missions Catholiques au Congo,* Brussels, 1911, pp. 101 ff.; 149 ff. Concerning Libermann's memorandum for the Belgian Hierarchy.

J. de Witte, *Monseigneur Augouard,* Paris, 1924. 372 pages.

L. Dohmen, C.S.Sp., *Der Ehrwürdige P. Libermann. Ein Apostel der Neger in 19. Jahrhundert.* Speyer, 1947. 180 pages.

H. Döring, C.S.Sp., *Vom Juden zum Ordenstifter,* Knechtsteden, 1920. 352 pages.

Droit religieux de la Congrégation du St. Esprit et du St. Coeur de Marie. 2e Partie: *Historique de la Congrégation.* (Lithographed), n.d. pp. 16-46.

P. Dubois, S.J., *Répertoire Africain,* Rome, 1932. 400 pages.

Charles Duparquet, C.S.Sp., *Voyage en Cimbebasie,* Lyon, 1881. 79 pages. Also in *M. C.* 12, 367 ff., 379 ff., 404 ff., 416 ff., 432 ff.; 13, 476 f., 484 ff., 500 f., 514 f., 524 f., 538 f., 559 ff., 568 ff., 580 f., 597 ff., 606 ff.

Documents relatifs à la Préfecture Apostolique du Congo, Paris, 1881. 38 pages.

"Les Spiritains à St. Pierre et Miquelon," *ibid.,* pp. 437-441.

Abbé Durand, *Voyages du P. Duparquet dans l'Afrique australe d'après ses lettres,* Paris (1879). 36 pages.

Roger Dussercle, C.S.Sp., *Du Kilema-Ndaro au Cameroun. Mgr. F. X. Vogt,* Paris, 1954. 206 pages.

Archipel de Chagos. En Mission, 10 Nov., 1933-11 Jan., 1934. Port Louis, 1934. 191 pages.

Archipel de Chagos. En Mission. Diego-Six Îles-Peros. Sept.-Nov., 1934, Port Louis, 1935. 217 pages.

L'île de l'Aigle, Port Louis, 1936. 304 pages. These 3 vols. concern the archipelagoes depending on Mauritius.

Histoire d'une Fondation, Port Louis, 1949. 392 pages. Concerning the "Daughters of Mary" founded by Father Le Vavasseur.

Ambrose Emonet, C.S.Sp., *Circulaires du T. R. Père Emonet,* Paris, 1882 ff. One vol.

Alois Engel, C.S.Sp., *Die Missionsmethode der Missionare vom heiligen Geist auf dem Afrikanischen Festland,* Knechtsteden, 1932. 296 pages. Outstanding study about the missionary methods of the Holy Ghost Fathers in Africa.

A. Eschbach, C.S.Sp., *La vie et l'oeuvre de Claude-François Poullart des Places,* Rome, 1916. 128 pages.

Vita del Ven. Servo di Dio F. M. P. Libermann, 2nd ed., Rome, n.d. 131 pages.

État du Personnel et des Oeuvres de la Congrégation du St. Esprit, Paris, 1883 ff. 31 volumes. Directory of the Holy Ghost Fathers which contains much information about the condition of their works.

Pierre Eyckeler, S.M.M., *Le Testament d'un Saint,* Maastricht, 1953. 212 pages. Concerning St. Louis de Montfort. Contains much information about his relationship with the Spiritans.

M. Fava, "Lettre de M. l'Abbé Fava, Vicaire Général de St. Denis et Vice Préfet Apostolique de Zanguebar (25 juillet, 1861, à Mgr. de Maupoint)," *Revue d'Histoire des Missions,* vol. 10, 1933, pp. 107-121.

Salvatore J. Federici, C.S.Sp., "Collaboration of Venerable Libermann and Bishop Barron," *Records of the American Catholic Historical Society of Philadelphia,* vol 43, 1942, pp. 65-85.

Henry P. Fisher, C.S.Sp., "The Catholic Church in Liberia," *Records of the American Catholic Historical Society of Philadelphia,* vol. 40, 1929, pp. 249-310. Partially out of date.

J. Galinand, S.J., *Le R. P. Allaire, Missionnaire au Congo,* Paris, (1899). 155 pages.

J. Galopeau, C.S.Sp., "Étude sur le Vénérable le Libermann et l'érection des Diocèses coloniaux au XIX siècle," *Revue d'Histoire des Missions,* 1928, pp. 225-271.

Mgr. Gaume, *Voyage du P. Horner à la Côte orientale d'Afrique,* Paris, 1872, 267 pages. Partly published also in *M. C.* vols. 5 and 6.

Mgr. J. Gay, C.S.Sp., *La Doctrine missionnaire du Vénérable Père Libermann,* Paris, 1943. 173 pages.
Libermann, Paris, 1955. 154 pages.

P. Goepfert, C.S.Sp., *The Life of the Venerable Francis Mary Paul Libermann,* Dublin, 1880. 580 pages.

H. A. Gogarty, C.S.Sp., *In the Land of the Kikuyus,* Dublin, 1920. 129 pages.
Kilema-njaro. An East African Vicariate, New York, 1927. 137 pages.

Henry Goré, C.S.Sp., *Mgr. Alexandre Le Roy,* Paris n.d. 268 pages.

Georges Goyau, *La France missionnaire dans les cinq parties du monde,* Paris, 1946, 2 vols.
La Congrégation du Saint-Esprit, Paris, 7th ed., n.d. 284 pages.
Mgr. Augouard, Paris, (1926).
"La doctrine missionnaire du Père Libermann," *Études Missionnaires,* avril 1937, pp. 1-20.
"Les débuts de l'Apostolat au Congo et dans l'Angola (1482-1590)," *Revue d'Histoire des Missions,* vol. 8, 1931, pp. 481-514.
"Le Père des Acadiens: Jean Louis Le Loutre," *Revue d'Histoire des Missions,* vol. 13, 1936, pp. 481-513.

J. M. Grizard, C.S.Sp., *Réflexions sur l'ouvrage du P. Lithard,* (lithographed), Paris, 1924. Concerning Lithard's *"Mémorial des Bontés du Coeur de Marie."* About the fusion of Libermann's congregation and the Holy Ghost Fathers.

Jules Groell, C.S.Sp., *Le Révérend Père Amet Limbour,* Grenoble, 1926. 145 pages.

C. P. Groves, *The Planting of Christianity in Africa,* London, 1948 ff. Thus far 3 vols. published, going up to 1914. Covers all Christian denominations.

Guida delle Missioni Cattoliche, Rome, 1935. 970 pages.

Abbé Guilbaud, *Les étapes de la Guadeloupe religieuse,* Basse Terre, 1935. 228 pages.

Léonide Guiot, *La Mission du Su-Tchuen au XVIIIe siècle. Vie et apostolat de Mgr. Pottier,* Paris, 1892. 521 pages.

Marian Habig, O.F.M., "First American Foreign Missioners," *Illinois Catholic Historical Review,* vol. 11, 1929, pp. 239-250. About Bishop Barron and Father Kelly, pp. 241-243.

Historique de la Fusion, n.d. MS. 21 pages. Supports Archbishop Le Roy and Father Le Floch.

Th. Hück, *P. Ludwig Karl Gommenginger. Erlebnisse und Arbeiten eines afrikanischen Missionar,* Rixheim, 1900. 454 pages.

Côme Jaffré, C.S.Sp., "L'Afrique aux Africains, ou le "Ngounzisme au Congo." *Etudes* (Paris), vol. 218, 1934, pp. 651-664.

Joseph Janin, C.S.Sp., *La Religion Aux Colonies Françaises sous l'Ancien Regime* (1626-1815), Paris, 1942. 234 pages.

Le Clergé Colonial de 1815 à 1850, Toulouse, 1936. 421 pages.

Les Diocèses Coloniaux (1851-1912), Paris, 1938. 363 pages.

Les Églises Créoles Françaises (1912-1938), Paris, 1939. 93 pages.

L'Evangélisation des Antilles françaises," *Revue d'Histoire des Missions,* Vol. 13, 1936, pp. 376-396.

Ouvriers Missionnaires, Paris, 1944. 296 pages. The Brothers in the missions.

Rosalie Javouhey, *Notice sur les rapports de la Congrégation de St. Joseph de Cluny avec celle du St. Esprit et de l'Immaculé Coeur de Marie,* Paris, 1867. 288 pages.

John P. Jordan, *Bishop Shanahan of Southern Nigeria,* Dublin, 1949. 264 pages.

Bernard J. Kelly, C.S.Sp., *The Spiritual Teaching of Venerable Francis Libermann,* Dublin, 1955. 201 pages.

Glenn D. Kittler, *The White Fathers,* New York, 1956. 299 pages.

La Congrégation du St. Esprit, Paris, 1925. 79 pages.

La Congrégation du St. Esprit. Ses Supérieurs Généraux. Les Supérieurs de ses Missions, Paris, 1930. 28 pages.

Louis de Lannurien, C.S.Sp., Unpublished MS. about the "Fusion."

A. Lalouse, C.S.Sp., *Missionnaires d'avant-garde sur la côte de Guinée,* Ngazobil, n.d. 31 pages. The first expedition to the Two Guineas.

Mgr. Auguste Laveille, *Le Bienheureux Louis Marie Grignion de Montfort et ses Familles Religieuses,* Tours, 1916. 441 pages.

G. Le Faucheur, C.S.Sp., "Madagascar et les Spiritains," *Revue d'Histoire des Missions,* Vol. 5, 1928, pp. 407-437.

Henri Le Floch, C.S.Sp., *Claude François Poullart des Places,* 2nd ed., Paris, 1915. 683 pages.

Louis-Marie Barazar de Lannurien et la Mission du Vénérable Libermann, Rome, 1910. 28 pages.

L'Acte d'Union du V. Libermann et de ses disciples à la Congrégation du St. Esprit d'après les actes et les documents de la Propagande, Rome, 1915. 52 pages.

Note pour la nouvelle édition de la Vie de Claude François Poullart des Places, Rome, 1915. 30 pages.

Supplément à l'Acte d'Union. Note sur le Mémoire "La Fusion," (Rome, 1916). 18 pages.

C. Le Gallo, "Le R.P. Charles Sacleux, C.S.Sp.," *Le Naturaliste Canadien,* vol. 77, 1950, pp. 96-111.

"Le Père Theophile Klaine," *ibid.,* pp. 318-333.

Le Missioni Cattoliche, Rome, 1950. 548 pages.

Alexander Le Roy, C.S.Sp., *Le T.R.P. Fréderic Le Vavasseur,* Paris, n.d. 264 pages.

vol. V of J. Piolet (editor), *Les Missions Catholiques Françaises au XIX siècle.* With the exception of a few chapters this whole volume about Africa was written by Archbishop Le Roy.

Circulaires de Mgr. Le Roy, Paris, 1896 ff. One volume.

Directoire Général des Missions, Paris, 1930. 248 pages.

"Le rôle scientifique des missionnaires," *Anthropos,* I, 1906, pp. 3-10.

À travers le Zanguebar, Lyon, 1884. 202 pages. Also published in *Les Missions Catholiques,* vol. XVI (1884); *Le Missioni Cattoliche,* vol. XII (1884); *Die Katholische Missionen,* vol. XIV (1886).

Au Kilema-Ndjaro, 4th ed., Paris (1928). 379 pages. First published in *Les Missions Catholiques,* vol. XXIV f. (1892 f.).

"Le cinquantenaire du Vicariat du Zanguebar," *Revue d' Histoire des Missions,* 1934, vol. 11, pp. 1-4.

See also E. Baur.

A. L. Letacq, "Notice sur les travaux scientifiques du P. Duparquet," *Bulletin mensuel de la Societé scientifique Flammarion,* 1890, pp. 49-57.

Lettre à M. Berquet (sic) *professeur en théologie au séminaire de Verdun, au sujet de la thèse, qu'il a fait soutenir au mois d'avril 1740,* Cologne, 1741. 92 pages.

Lettre (Seconde) à M. Becquet au sujet de la seconde thèse, qu'il a fait soutenir au mois d'avril. The Jansenist controversy.

L. Liagre, C.S.Sp., *Le Vénérable Père Libermann. L'Homme, la Doctrine,* Paris, 1948. 238 pages.

"Sainte Thérèse de l'Enfant Jesus et le Vénérable Libermann," *Annales de S. Thérèse de Lisieux. Études et Documents Thérésiens,* Oct. 1936, pp. 121-128; janvier 1937, pp. 22-32.

G. Lee, C.S.Sp., *The Life of the Venerable Francis Libermann,* London, 2nd ed., 1937. 321 pages.

Léon Leloir, W. F., *Libermann,* Namur, 1939; Gentinnes, 1952. 62 pages.

Les Missions Catholiques, Lyon, 1868 ff. A very rich source of first hand information about missionary affairs.

Francis Libermann, C.S.Sp., *Lettres Spirituelles du Vénérable Libermann,* 2nd ed., Paris, n.d. 4 volumes.
  Écrits spirituels du Vénérable Libermann, Paris, 1891. 696 pages. *Supplement,* Paris, 1891. 238 pages.
  Commentaire du S. Évangile selon St. Jean, Ngazobil, 1872 (2nd ed., Paris, n.d.) 739 pages.
  See also (Adolphe Cabon) *Notes et Documents* etc. and (J. B. Pascal), *Directoire Spirituel.*

Victor Lithard, C.S.Sp., *Mémorial des Bontés du Coeur de Marie,* Paris, 1923. 193 pages.
  "Le Vénérable Libermann, auteur spirituel," *Revue d'Ascetique et Mystique,* vol. 19, 1939, pp. 141-170.
  Spiritualité Spiritaine. Paris, 1939. 272 pages.

Edward Loffeld, C.S.Sp., "Een Missie-Generaal en een Missieplan," *Het Missiewerk,* vol. 22, 1941, pp. 65-79; 131-141; 184-196. Father Libermann's plans for Africa.

Robert F. McNamara, "Father Maurice of Greece, N. Y.: a Footnote to the Liberian Mission," *Records of the American Catholic Historical Society of Philadelphia,* vol. 61, 1950, pp. 155-183.

Mgr. Amand-René Maupoint, *Madagascar et ses deux premiers évêques.* Vol. I: *Mgr. Pierre Dalmond,* Paris, 2nd ed., 1870. 284 pages. Vol. II: *Mgr. Alexandre Monnet,* Paris, 2nd ed., 1870, 336 pages.

Patrick Francis Cardinal Moran, *History of the Catholic Church in Australasia,* Sydney, n.d. 2 volumes.

M. C. Moreau, *Les Prêtres français émigrés aux Etats Unis,* Paris, 1856. 520 pages.

Dr. Alphons Mulders, *Missiegeschiedenis, Antwerp,* 1957. 565 pages. Competent general history of Catholic missions.

Nécrologe de la Congrégation du St. Esprit, 1709-1930, Paris, 1930. *Supplement,* 1930-1948, Paris, 1949. 394 and 64 pages.

Nos Oeuvres et nos Victimes de la Martinique, Paris, 1903. 43 pages. Concerning the 1902 disaster caused by the eruption of Montagne Pelée.

Notes et Documents relatifs à l'histoire de la Congrégation du St. Esprit, 1703-1914, Paris, 1917. 128 pages. Records the most important documents regarding the history of the Congregation.

Notices Biographiques, Paris, 1908 ff. 4 volumes. Another volume bears the title *Biographies.* Short biographies of deceased Spiritans.

Nouvelles Ecclesiastiques ou Mémoires pour servir à l'histoire de la Constitution "Unigenitus," Paris, 1728-1803; also Utrecht, 1730-1794. The Jansenist controversy.

(J. B. Pascal, C.S.Sp.), *La Fusion,* 1916, (lithographed). 19 pages. Opposed to Archbishop Le Roy's view of the "Fusion."

Directoire Spirituel ou Instructions du Vénérable F. M. P. Libermann aux membres de la Congrégation. 2nd ed., Paris, n.d. 620 pages.

F. Pellegrin, "Rapport sur les travaux botaniques du R. P. Charles Sacleux, C.S.Sp.," *Bulletin de la Societé Botanique de France,* 1930, vol. 77, pp. 450-452.

A. Perbal, O.M.I., "Le Nationalisme de Mgr. Augouard," *Revue d'Histoire des Missions,* 1938, pp. 385-407.

R. Piacentini, C.S.Sp., *F. J. B. Delaplace,* Beauport-Montgeron, 1952. 310 pages.

Yves Pichon, C.S.Sp., *Le Père Brottier,* Paris, 7th ed., 1938. 455 pages.

Card. J. B. Pitra, O.S.B., *Vie du Vénérable Serviteur de Dieu François-Marie-Paul Libermann,* 5th ed., Paris, 1913. 575 pages.

F. Proost, C.S.Sp., "Libermann en Belgie," *Africa Christo,* 1952, no. 4, pp. 9 ff.

Joseph Quérard, *Vie du Bienheureux Louis Marie Grignion de Montfort,* 1887. 4 volumes.

Joseph Theodor Rath, C.S.Sp., "Hundert Jahre Missionare vom Heiligen Geist," *Missionswissenschaft und Religionswissenschaft,* 1949, no. 1, pp. 1 ff.
Unfinished manuscript about the early history of the Holy Ghost Fathers. 70 pages in folio.

J. Remy, C.S.Sp., "La Congrégation du St. Esprit et le Clergé indigène," *Revue d'Histoire des Missions,* vol. 13, 1936, pp. 529-562.

Abbé Renard, *Essai bibliographique sur l'histoire religieuse des Antilles françaises,* Paris, (1932). 95 pages.

Père Rétif, S.J., *Pauvreté Spirituelle et Mission d'après le Père Libermann,* Paris, 1955. 206 pages.

L. A. Ricklin, *Travaux et voyages du R. P. Horner,* Paris, 1880. 340 pages. Early East African missionary history. Also published in *M. C.* 9, 506 ff., 609 ff.; 10, 177 ff., 189 ff., 201 ff.

Auguste Roeykens, O.M.Cap., "Les Pères du St. Esprit et l'acceptation de la Mission du Congo au XIXe siècle, *Aequatoria,* 1950, pp. 67 ff.; 93 ff.; 1951, pp. 41 ff.

Norman Mc.L. Rogers, "The Abbé Le Loutre," *The Canadian Historical Review,* 1930, pp. 105-128.

L. Roques, C.S.Sp., *Le Pionnier du Gabon, J. R. Bessieux,* Paris (1956). 250 pages.

Paul Roussier, "L'ancien clergé colonial français," *Revue d'Histoire des Missions,* 1928, pp. 572-595; 1929, pp. 77-103, 260-282, 407-429, 548-569; 1930, pp. 74-113. About eighteenth century clergy.

Joseph Schmidlin, *Catholic Mission History,* Techny, Illinois, 1933, 862 pages.

"Zum' Imperialismus' der franzoesische Missionare," *Zeitschrift fuer Missionswissenschaft,* 1916, pp. 109-134.

F. Schwager, "Katholische Missionstaetigkeit und nationale Propaganda," *Zeitschrift fuer Missionswissenschaft,* 1916, pp. 109-134.

Ignace Schwindenhammer, C.S.Sp., *Circulaires du T. R. P. Ignace Schwindenhammer,* Paris, 1852 ff. 2 volumes.

Antoine Soucy, C.S.Sp., "L'Érection des évêchés aux Antilles Françaises," *Revue d'Histoire de l'Amérique Française,* 1952, pp. 505-520.

J. Soul, C.S.Sp., "Mgr. Maupoint et la Fondation des missions d'Afrique orientale," *Revue d'Histoire des Missions,* vol. 13, 1936, pp. 44-52.

Charles L. Souvay, "The Catholic Church in Contemporary France," *Catholic Historical Review,* 1932-33, vol. 18, pp. 205-228. The question of the "Action Française."

Msgr. William F. Stadelman, C.S.Sp., *The Association of the Holy Childhood—History of the American Branch,* Pittsburgh, 1922. 26 pages.

M. B. Storme, C.I.C.M., *Evangelisatiepogingen in de binnenlanden van Afrika gedurende de XIXe eeuw,* Brussels, 1951. 712 pages. Very competent study of nineteenth century missionary efforts to penetrate central Africa.

Robert Streit, O.M.I. and Johannes Dindinger, O.M.I., *Bibliotheca Missionum,* vols. XVI-XX *(Afrikanische Missionsliteratur),* Freiburg, 1951 ff. Indispensable tool for missionary studies about Africa. Supplements are published each year to keep the collection up to date.

Msgr. Leon-Joseph Suenens, *Edel Quinn, Envoy of the Legion of Mary to Africa,* Dublin, 1955. 272 pages.

Constant Tastevin, C.S.Sp., "La région du Moyen-Amazone ou Solimoes," *Géographie,* vol. 48 (1927), pp. 259-282.

"Le premier cinquantenaire de la Mission de Huila ou du Cunène," *Revue d'Histoire des Missions,* 1932, pp. 53-84.

"Le cinquantenaire de la Préfecture du Coubango," *Revue d'Histoire des Missions,* 1933, pp. 42-69.

Pierre Thomas, C.S. Sp., Unpublished MS about life of Father Poullart des Places.

J. van der Kooy, S.M.A., "Wapenbroeders," *Libermann Herdenking,* Gemert, 1952, pp. 85. ff. Holy Ghost Fathers and the Society of African Missions.

A. L. van Kaam, C.S.Sp., *De Eerbiedwaardige Frans Libermann, Een poging tot Synthese,* Rhenen, (1954). 643 pages. Excellent as a psychological study of Libermann.

Lambert Vogel, C.S.Sp., *Claude François Poullart des Places,* Gemert, 1941. 257 pages.

"De spiritualiteit van de Eerbiedwaardige Pater F. M. P. Libermann," *Ons Geestelyk Leven,* vol. 28, 1952, pp. 279-290.

Dienaar Der Slaven, Rhenen, 1952. 286 pages.

J. Vulquin, C.S.Sp., *L'Esprit du Vénérable Libermann,* Paris, 1893. 158 pages.

La Direction spirituelle d'après les écrits et les exemples du Vénérable Libermann, 3rd ed., Paris, 1940. 176 pages.

Reginald F. Walker, C.S.Sp., *The Holy Ghost Fathers in Africa. Centenary of Missionary Effort,* Dublin, 1933. 196 pages. Mostly concerned with the missions entrusted to the Irish Province of the Congregation. Largely out of date, but still useful.

Dr. J. Wils, "Het taalkundig werk der Paters van de Heilige Geest," *Libermann Herdenking,* Gemert, 1952, pp. 125-133.

Ralph Wiltgen, S.V.D., *Gold Coast Mission History, 1471-1880,* Techny, Illinois, 1956. 181 pages.

INDEX OF NAMES*

---

*Sp. refers to Spiritans in the broad sense of the term; C.S.Sp. indicates members of the Congregation.

The index does not include marginal references.

Names composed of two or more words are listed under the first letter *of the first* word; for instance, *Op de Beeck* under *O*.

613

INDEX OF SUBJECT MATTER*

---

*Abbreviations: *Eccl. Sup.* Ecclesiastical Superiors; *Rel. Sup.* Religious Superiors; *Fr. Eq. Afr.* French Equatorial Africa.